THE IDEA OF HISTORY

The late **R. G. Collingwood** was Waynflete Professor of Metaphysical Philosophy in the University of Oxford from 1935 to 1941. Four of his books are available in paperback from Oxford University Press: *The Principles of Art*, *The Idea of History*, *The Idea of Nature*, and *An Autobiography*. In 1989 the Press published his *Essays in Political Philosophy*, and in 1992 a revised edition of the last work published in his lifetime, *The New Leviathan*, accompanied by new material from his manuscripts; both of these books are edited and introduced by David Boucher.

Jan van der Dussen is Professor of History and Philosophy in the Department of Humanities at the Open University of the Netherlands. His previous publications include *History as a Science: The Philosophy of R. G. Collingwood* (Martinus Nijhoff, 1981).

THE
IDEA OF HISTORY

R. G. COLLINGWOOD

Revised Edition

WITH

Lectures 1926–1928

EDITED WITH AN INTRODUCTION BY

JAN VAN DER DUSSEN

Oxford   New York

OXFORD UNIVERSITY PRESS

Oxford University Press, Great Clarendon Street, Oxford OX2 6DP

Oxford New York

Athens Auckland Bangkok Bogota Bombay
Buenos Aires Calcutta Cape Town Dar es Salaam
Delhi Florence Hong Kong Istanbul Karachi
Kuala Lumpur Madras Madrid Melbourne
Mexico City Nairobi Paris Singapore
Taipei Tokyo Toronto Warsaw

and associated companies in
Berlin Ibadan

Oxford is a registered trade mark of Oxford University Press

First published by Clarendon Press 1993
First issued as an Oxford University paperback 1994

British Library Cataloguing in Publication Data

Data available

Library of Congress Cataloging in Publication Data
Collingwood, R. G. (Robin George), 1889–1943.
The idea of history / R. G. Collingwood;
edited with an introduction by Jan van der Dussen.—Rev. ed.,
with lectures 1926–1928.
p. cm.
Includes bibliogaphical references.
1. History—Philosophy. I. Dussen, Jan van der. II. Title.
D16.8C592 1993 901–dc20 92-40412

ISBN 0-19-285306-6

9 10 8

Printed in Great Britain by
Cox & Wyman Ltd,
Reading, Berkshire

PREFACE

The Idea of History is undoubtedly Collingwood's best-known book. From its appearance in 1946 it has aroused much attention, and in the subsequent discussions on the philosophy of history, as they have developed since the Second World War, it has in fact never failed to play a crucial role. One could even say that its appearance has been a major factor in the revival of the interest in the philosophy of history, a subject formerly usually associated with German philosophers around the turn of the century like Dilthey, Windelband, and Rickert. The many reprints and translations of *The Idea of History* are another indication of its permanent influence.

In this revised edition of *The Idea of History* the original text remains intact. To this has been added, however, new material from Collingwood's unpublished manuscripts, which have only recently become available. In this way it will be possible to study Collingwood's views on the philosophy of history within the context of his main work on the subject.

The original edition of *The Idea of History* had been edited posthumously by his pupil T. M. Knox. The latter added to it a preface in which Collingwood's philosophy of history was put into the wider context of his philosophical views and their development. Subsequent research on Collingwood's philosophy, however, has brought out some important inadequacies of the interpretations given by Knox in his preface. A new introduction was therefore needed, taking into account the research on Collingwood's philosophy of history as it has developed during the subsequent decades.

In this new introduction I explain how the publication of *The Idea of History* has taken shape and also assess the way the book was edited by Knox. This is followed by a short exposition of the reception of *The Idea of History*. Since for a proper assessment of Collingwood's philosophy of history it is necessary to put it into an appropriate context, the development of his ideas on the subject must be considered. In this connection I have also made an attempt to assess the nature of the newly added manuscripts of 1926, 1927, and 1928.

The new and somewhat lengthy introduction to this revised

edition of *The Idea of History* is especially needed with a view to the rather complicated way this book has come about. It should in this connection in particular be noted that it is in fact a composition of contributions by Collingwood to the philosophy of history ranging from 1926 to 1939. In order to make this clear the dates of the various parts of the original edition of *The Idea of History* have been added to its table of contents.

I am sure that I am speaking for everyone when I express my gratitude to Mrs Teresa Smith, daughter of Collingwood, for allowing the publication of his previously unpublished lectures on the philosophy of history in this revised edition of *The Idea of History*. I am confident that it will be welcomed not only by the growing group of scholars and students interested in Collingwood's thought, but also by philosophers and historians in general. *The Idea of History* has been widely read since its publication, and I am confident that this revised edition has much to offer both the new generation of Collingwood's readers, and those familiar with the first edition.

Special appreciation should also be expressed to Oxford University Press for publishing *The Idea of History* in its present form, and especially to Mrs Angela Blackburn and Mrs Frances Morphy, who, in co-operation with Mrs Teresa Smith, have done so much to make it possible.

I would also like to use this opportunity to express my special appreciation to Martijn Bakker, Marjet Derks, Leo ten Hag, Anita Hendricx, Rik Peters, and Herman Simissen, all members of a group of Collingwoodian friends and students, with whom I have not only discussed for some years the many aspects of Collingwood's philosophy, but who have also assisted with editing the manuscripts.

Finally I would like to thank David Boucher and Professor Dray both for their invaluable help in making my English more or less tolerable and for their critical comments.

W.J.v.d.D.

Heerlen
July 1992

CONTENTS

EDITOR'S INTRODUCTION

1. INTRODUCTION

THE origin and subsequent reception of Collingwood's posthumously published *The Idea of History* is an interesting story in its own right. Although Collingwood intended to write a book about the development of the concept of history and entitle it *The Idea of History*, had he been able to complete it, it would not have taken the form of the book which T. M. Knox compiled. Collingwood's early death in January 1943 prevented him from finishing the large-scale project of which *The Idea of History* would have been part. What he had planned was to relate some of his previously published books to a number of projected volumes. The series was to have been divided into three categories: 'Philosophical Essays', 'Philosophical Principles', and 'Studies in the History of Ideas'. Oxford University Press had agreed to the proposal and the arrangement had been made to have them published.[1] The 'Philosophical Essays' were to include *An Essay on Philosophical Method* (published in 1933), and *An Essay on Metaphysics*, which was later published in 1940. *The Principles of Art* (published in 1938) and *The Principles of History* were to comprise the second category in the series. Only one-third of the latter volume had been written by 1939 and it was subsequently never finished. The last category was to consist of *The Idea of Nature* and *The Idea of History*, both of which were edited by T. M. Knox and published after Collingwood's death.

Of the last three books only *The Idea of Nature* was close to being fully complete in draft form. The reason for Collingwood's failure to complete his project was twofold: the worsening condition of his health and the outbreak of war. As an uncompromising opponent of fascism and nazism he considered it his duty to give a fundamental analysis of what was at stake in the war. In his opinion it was nothing less than a fundamental conflict of ideals: fascism and nazism constituted a

---

[1] The arrangement was made in an exchange of letters between Oxford University Press and Collingwood of 18 and 19 October 1939. In a letter to the Press of 3 June 1939 Collingwood already referred to the first two categories.

revolt against civilization which had to be resisted at all costs. He worked out his ideas in *The New Leviathan*. The latter, however, was not a complete departure from his work on history. For the book tries, among other things, to develop a theory of duty which is related to civilization and the gradual elimination of force from the relations between people. Barbarism, exemplified by fascism and nazism, constituted a threat to this ideal. History and duty were, for Collingwood, the highest levels of theoretical and practical reason, both being concerned with the concrete individual. *The New Leviathan* was Collingwood's last book and was completed under the most severe conditions of ill health. In view of the series of strokes which became increasingly incapacitating during Collingwood's later years, it is remarkable that this book was ever completed.

At his death Collingwood left behind a large number of manuscripts, around 4,000 pages in total, on the most diverse subjects: religion, literary criticism, ethics, epistemology, metaphysics, cosmology, folklore and magic, politics, philosophy of history, Roman Britain, and archaeology. In his will he forbade their publication except on the initiative of his heirs in consultation with Oxford University Press. Since 1978 the manuscripts have been deposited in the Bodleian Library at Oxford and have been available for consultation, before that time having been generally unknown to scholars. Shortly after Collingwood's death, however, T. M. Knox, a former pupil of Collingwood and one of his most devoted students, was asked to make a selection from the manuscripts which might be fit for publication. What Knox saw, however, was mainly the manuscripts of Collingwood's later years and of these he limited himself to ones that the latter intended eventually to work up into a publication. These consisted of the aforementioned *The Idea of Nature*, *The Idea of History*, and *The Principles of History*.

Collingwood gave lectures on the history of theories of cosmology in 1934, 1935, and 1937. These lectures, which he titled 'Nature and Mind', were based on his extensive study of the subject conducted in 1933–4. He began to revise them in 1939 with a view to their publication. They were eventually published as *The Idea of Nature* in 1945, with—in his own words— 'little editing' by T. M. Knox.

2. *THE IDEA OF HISTORY*: EPILEGOMENA (PART V)

The two remaining manuscripts which Knox considered for publication were on the philosophy of history. The first was a set of lectures called 'Lectures on the Philosophy of History', which Collingwood had written and delivered during the first two terms of 1936. They were repeated in a revised form in 1940 under the title 'The Idea of History', and Collingwood intended to work them into a book with the same title.

The second manuscript, *The Principles of History*, was of a different nature: it was Collingwood's intention to have it published as a separate book and he mainly worked at it in February 1939 on the island of Java in the Dutch East Indies, during a trip he made to recuperate after suffering a major stroke. Among the manuscripts are the notes made in preparation for the book and one of them reads:

Scheme for a book. 9–2–39. '*The Principles of History*'. *Main* topics will include (1) A simple account of the most obvious characteristics of history *as a special science*. (2) Relations between this and others. (3) Relation of history as thought to practical life. These could be Books I, II, III.[2]

Of these books only the first was finished. This consisted of four chapters, dealing respectively with the concepts of evidence, action, re-enactment, and history as the self-knowledge of mind. It is not certain whether Collingwood really finished the last chapter of the first book, for the last time he refers to it in his diary is on 27 March: 'Tried to begin ch. IV of *Principles of History* in morning—stuff wouldn't flow.' What is certain is that Collingwood placed immense value on the project. After his return to England he wrote a letter to the archaeologist F. G. Simpson saying that *The Principles of History* is 'the book which my whole life has been spent in preparing to write. If I can finish that, I shall have nothing to grumble at.' Although, for the reasons given above, the book was never finished, Collingwood still intended to complete it, as is evidenced in the letter of 19 October 1939 to Oxford University Press.

[2] Bodleian Library Collingwood Papers, dep. 13, 'Historiography, xi–1938–1939', p. 20.

The manuscript of *The Principles of History* had a note on it by Collingwood authorizing his wife, in case he was prevented from finishing it, 'to publish it with the above title, with a preface by yourself explaining that it is a fragment of what I had, for 25 years at least, looked forward to writing as my chief work'. This note is quoted by Knox in a letter to Oxford University Press of 31 March 1945. After this he continues:

In spite of the authority given for publication, I think it would be a mistake to publish *The Principles of History* as it stands. It is divided into three chapters. A good deal of the second and third chapters is contained already in the *Autobiography* and the *Essay on Metaphysics*, and I am not satisfied that we ought to press the wording of a note written in all probability when R.G.C. was unusually ill.

Knox was mistaken in saying that the first part of *The Principles of History* was divided into three chapters, for there were in fact four, the last of which he had himself partly edited.

The manuscript of *The Principles of History* contained about ninety pages. The first chapter (on evidence) and the fourth (on history as the self-knowledge of mind) were included by Knox in *The Idea of History* under the title 'Historical Evidence' (pp. 249–82; pp. 4–31 of the *Principles*) and 'History and Freedom' (pp. 315–20; pp. 76–8, with an added 77a & b, of the *Principles*). In his original preface to *The Idea of History* Knox reports that he has also included Part III, §8 (pp. 122–6, on Hegel and Marx) from the manuscript of *The Principles of History*. This seems plausible, since this part begins more or less where 'History and Freedom' ends (p. 320): in the latter the argument is developed that the idea of human freedom is necessarily bound up with the one of an autonomous science of history, while in 'Hegel and Marx' it is argued that both philosophers had as yet failed to achieve an autonomous historical science and still employed non-historical methods.[3]

The reliability of Knox's treatment of parts of the text of *The Principles of History* remains a matter of contention. It should be noted, however, that in his scheme for *The Principles of History* Collingwood identifies the subject of the fourth chapter: 'History as the self-knowledge of mind. Exclusion of

[3] In his letter to Oxford University Press of 31 March 1945 Knox mentions that this part is from pp. 81–3 of the manuscript of *The Principles of History*.

other sciences of mind', while Knox has printed parts of it under the title 'History and Freedom'. The section begins with the statement: 'We study history, I have maintained, in order to attain self-knowledge.' Collingwood continues by suggesting that the thesis will be illustrated by showing 'how our knowledge that human activity is free has been attained only through our discovery of history' (p. 315). This means that Knox has probably omitted the beginning of the fourth chapter of *The Principles of History* dealing with the proper subject of history as the self-knowledge of mind and has confined himself to Collingwood's own illustration of the thesis. What is certain is that the sentence 'In my historical sketch of the idea of history' (p. 315) has been added by Knox: the sketch was not intended by Collingwood to be the subject of *The Principles of History*.

This brings us to the question of how Knox edited *The Idea of History* and in particular which changes were made by him. What can be determined without doubt is Collingwood's original intention to publish two books separately, *The Idea of History* and *The Principles of History*. Knox's disregard of Collingwood's authorization to publish *The Principles of History* resulted in the subject-matter of both books being incorporated into the one volume of *The Idea of History* in which parts of *The Principles of History* were included, but also two essays published earlier by Collingwood ('Human Nature and Human History', pp. 205–31, and 'The Historical Imagination', pp. 231–49).[4] The parts from *The Principles of History* and the published essays were put together by Knox under the heading 'Epilegomena' as Part V of *The Idea of History*. In this he also included the three chapters of the second part of Collingwood's lectures on the philosophy of history to which the latter had given the title 'Metaphysical Epilegomena': 'History as Re-enactment of Past Experience' (pp. 282–302), 'The Subject-matter of History' (pp. 302–15), and 'Progress as created by Historical Thinking' (pp. 321–34). It should be noted, however, that in his 'Metaphysical Epilegomena'

---

[4] 'Human Nature and Human History' was published separately (London, 1936) and reprinted in *Proceedings of the British Academy* 22 (1937), pp. 97–127. 'The Historical Imagination' was Collingwood's inaugural lecture as Waynflete Professor of Metaphysical Philosophy on 28 October 1935.

Collingwood had given different titles to the first and third of these chapters, 'Re-enactment of Past Experience the Essence of History' and 'Progress', respectively.

It is also certain that Knox omitted chapters two and three of *The Principles of History*. In his scheme for this book the second chapter was described by Collingwood as follows: 'State and expound the conception of *Action* (*res gestae*). Contrast this with the conception of *Process* or *Change* and the pseudo-history which that implies', and the third chapter as: 'Conception of *Re-enactment* and contrast the *Dead Past* and *Completeness*'. With hindsight it is of course unfortunate that these chapters were not published. What is even more unfortunate is that this portion of the manuscript of *The Principles of History* was lost, as well as almost all original manuscripts on which *The Idea of History* is based. Most probably it was destroyed by Oxford University Press, following common practice with regard to published manuscripts, in ignorance of the fact that in this case only a part had been used.

We have seen that the reason given by Knox for not including the second and third chapters of *The Principles of History* was that in his opinion a 'good deal' was already contained in the *Autobiography* and *An Essay on Metaphysics*.[5] Especially with regard to the latter book this argument is hardly convincing, since the conceptions of action and re-enactment are not discussed in it. And quite apart from this, it would have been preferable, of course, to have had access to the more than forty pages Collingwood wrote on these topics besides the few pages discussing them in the *Autobiography*.

Summing up what has been said so far on the way *The Idea of History* was compiled by Knox, the first thing to be noted is that the second part of Collingwood's lectures on the philosophy of history of 1936 (the 'Metaphysical Epilegomena') has

---

[5] On p. vi of his preface to *The Idea of History* Knox refers to another reason, however. In spite of Collingwood's authority to have the manuscript of *The Principles of History* published, he says, 'I have not felt justified in printing more than the three excerpts which appear below as Part III, §8 and Part V, §§3 and 6. And even these I have included with some misgivings. They are written in Collingwood's later manner, and their style and temper is sometimes rather out of key with the rest of the book; but their inclusion serves to round off his view of history and to expound in more detail some points only briefly indicated elsewhere.'

been considerably expanded by Knox into a separate Epilegomena (pp. 205–334). What is even more important to note,
however, is that these Epilegomena contain elements which
are quite different, both with regard to their date of composition (running from 1935 to 1939) and their character. The different nature and background of the various essays should be
especially emphasized: they consist of lectures, published
essays, and the first draft of a book that was never finished.
The composition of the Epilegomena may be summarized as
follows:

§1 Human Nature and Human History: published in 1936
§2 The Historical Imagination: published in 1935
§3 Historical Evidence: first chapter of *The Principles of
   History*, written in 1939
§4 History as Re-enactment of Past Experience: lectures of
   1936
§5 The Subject-matter of History: lectures of 1936
§6 History and Freedom: part of chapter four of *The Principles of History*, written in 1939
§7 Progress as created by Historical Thinking: lectures of
   1936.

3. *THE IDEA OF HISTORY*: INTRODUCTION AND PARTS I–IV

As its name already indicates the Epilegomena are not the
main part of *The Idea of History*. Its major component consists of the lectures on the philosophy of history given by
Collingwood in 1936, which deal with a history of the idea of
history from the Greeks to the present. This part of the lectures originally contained 153 pages, while the 'Metaphysical
Epilegomena' took 41 pages.

As has already been indicated the manuscript itself has been
lost. What has remained is a table of contents of the second
term's course and 24 more or less occasional pages. Attached
to them is a rather mysterious note by Knox saying: 'Passages
from the Ms. of the Idea of History, either not used or used in
a different form in the published work.'[6] This leads us to the

---

[6] Bodleian Library Collingwood Papers, dep. 15.

delicate question of the way *The Idea of History* was edited, and in particular the liberties taken in doing this. Since this question has not been raised before it is justifiable to deal with it in some detail.

Before Knox began working on the manuscripts he gave an indication of how he conceived the project in his letter to Oxford University Press of 31 March 1945. 'A fair amount of editing will be required', he writes, 'in order to avoid repetitions, to reduce the material to chapters etc., to excise tones of the lecture form and so on. More editing will be needed than was the case with the *Idea of Nature*.' Having finished the job he writes on 31 October 1945:

Even now I have the feeling that if I kept it by me for another six months, I would still find things to revise, but, on the whole, I have come to the conclusion that the book is now ready for the printer and that further improvement, short of making a fair copy of the whole, is hardly practicable.

In a similar vein Knox reports in his preface to the first edition of *The Idea of History* that 'since the greater part of the available material was little more than a first draft, much more editing has been necessary here than in *The Idea of Nature*' (p. v).

The main body of the manuscript was written in 1936 for a course that was repeated in 1937. When Collingwood lectured again on the subject during one term in 1940 under the title 'The Idea of History', the 'Metaphysical Epilegomena' were probably left out, since with *The Principles of History* a fresh start had been made on the same subject.[7] In the lectures of 1940 revisions were made within the text of 1936. Since only a few occasional pages of the manuscript are left, it is difficult to assess the nature of them. In his preface Knox declares that Collingwood revised part of the 1936 manuscript in 1940, 'especially the section on Greece and Rome'.[8] What he does not

---

[7] In particular in the third chapter of the first part of *The Principles of History* the conception of re-enactment was discussed anew. In 1940 the title of the lectures also changed into 'The Idea of History' in contrast to 'Lectures on the Philosophy of History' of 1936.

[8] Among the manuscripts is a notebook entitled 'Historiography', with six pages of notes. On p. 2 is written: '8–iii–40. The *Idea of History* (Notes for lectures, on discovering that the Ms. which contains the results of my last 15 years' work on the subject has disappeared)' (Bodleian Library Collingwood

mention is that the introduction has also been altered considerably. For not only the first two pages, but some subsequent pages of the introduction of 1936 have survived (pp. 8–12) and they differ substantially from the introduction of *The Idea of History*, which is therefore apparently based on alterations made in 1940: Collingwood's opening passage on the three senses of the name 'philosophy of history' is more elaborate, and the nature of historical knowledge is discussed in a way differing from *The Idea of History*. Most likely this part had been changed by Collingwood, since the subject was dealt with anew by him in *The Principles of History*. One may conclude, therefore, that he wrote a revised introduction in 1940.

There is evidence that *The Idea of History* contains passages from various parts collected together to form sections. For instance the surviving page 8 of the manuscript begins with 'the philosophy of science was no longer a particular branch of philosophical investigation'. The same passage is found at the end of p. 6 of *The Idea of History*; the passage concerned is reproduced until 'Of these two stages, we must be content if this book represents the first' on p. 7. After this, three pages of the manuscript are skipped—in which among other things the difference between a historical and natural process is discussed. Knox then adds 'What I am attempting here is', while the words 'a philosophical inquiry into the nature of history' until the end of the sentence (p. 7) are again reproduced from p. 11 of the manuscript.[9]

In other cases the hand of Knox is even more apparent. There is for instance one page of the manuscript (p. 19d) which is clearly written in 1940 (Collingwood's handwriting was at that time markedly different), the text of which is to be found starting from the lower half of p. 31 and running to the first half of p. 33 of *The Idea of History*. In the text of this

Papers, dep. 13). After this remark we find a rough sketch which resembles the framework of Part I of *The Idea of History*, which deals with Greco-Roman historiography. It is probable, therefore, that the manuscript Collingwood refers to is the section on Greece and Rome of the 1936 lectures.

[9] It is possible, of course, that this new composition is due to Collingwood's revision of 1940. However, the passages referred to are taken over from pp. 8 and 11 of the manuscripts of 1936. Moreover, on p. 8 'these lectures' is changed into 'this book' in Collingwood's later handwriting of 1940.

book there are some clear alterations, however, which must have been made by Knox. His interference with the text can be ascertained with an even greater degree of confidence with regard to the end of p. 41 and the beginning of p. 42 of *The Idea of History*, which comes from the manuscript of 1936, but which has at the end of p. 41 a few sentences taken from an addition made by Collingwood in 1940 ('Beginning of lecture 9'). Two sentences from the same addition are then also to be found at the beginning of p. 46 of *The Idea of History*.

An obvious example of Knox's manipulation of the text is to be found on p. 73. The text from the middle of that page is from p. 68 of the manuscript of 1936. In the latter, however, there is a long passage between the sentence beginning with 'The English school, then, is reorientating philosophy in the direction of history' and the one beginning with 'There must be some significance, in the case of so determined and profound a thinker'. In this passage Collingwood criticizes Locke's and Hume's static and permanent conception of human nature. 'A thoroughgoing reorientation of philosophy in the direction of history', Collingwood says among other things, 'would eliminate these conceptions as relics of metaphysical dogmatism, and would insist that our condition can only mean the condition of human beings here and now, and that human nature means human nature as we find it.' This passage has not only been left out by Knox, but in order to have the text run smoothly he has also made certain changes and additions: 'The English school, then, is reorientating philosophy in the direction of history; but it is not aware that it is doing so', becomes 'The English school, then, is reorientating philosophy in the direction of history, *though as a whole* it is not *clearly* aware that it is doing so' (italics added). After this sentence Knox added: 'Nevertheless, Hume is less blind to the situation than his predecessors were.' There seems to be little connection between this and the passage which he omitted.[10]

---

[10] The possibility should be taken into account that Collingwood had omitted the passage concerned himself in his revision of 1940. However, p. 68 of the manuscript of 1936 begins with 'clouds of doubt, but that Nature herself', and this passage is taken over by Knox on p. 73 of *The Idea of History* until the end of the paragraph. Page 68 of the manuscript contains, moreover, a word that has been added by Collingwood in 1940 ('substantialistically').

There is one page among the manuscripts where the two versions of 1936 and 1940 are available. It deals with the relation between Hegel and Kant and is reproduced on p. 121 of *The Idea of History*. Over the second half of the text of 1936 Collingwood stuck a new version in 1940. In this case we are in the position, therefore, to assess what Knox has done with the text. It is surprising then to see that the second half of p. 121 of *The Idea of History* is in fact Knox's own restatement of the version of 1940. It is also curious to note that a few pages further on (p. 123) Knox has reproduced—with some minor changes—a part from a subsequent page from the manuscript of 1936. For p. 123 is part of the paragraph on Hegel and Marx (Part III, §8) and we have seen that this paragraph is taken from the fourth chapter of *The Principles of History*. This means that one has in this case a patchwork from manuscripts from 1936 and 1939.

It should also be noted that Knox's suggestion, made in his preface (p. vii), that in Part IV, §1 (iv) (on Bury) he has made use of a book review contributed by Collingwood to the *English Historical Review* is hardly credible, since it in fact does not correspond at all to the original text of the review. Taking into account considerations like these there seems indeed reason to doubt whether Knox has always been as scrupulous in editing *The Idea of History* as one should have wished.

4. *THE IDEA OF HISTORY*: KNOX'S PREFACE

Collingwood once reviewed a book that had appeared posthumously and had been edited by someone else. He says: 'It was a task involving much labour, and requiring, as is evident, tact and judgment . . . the polishing of an unfinished manuscript by another hand is a task which no one would undertake except as a labour of love.'[11] Exactly the same could be said of the posthumous publication of his own book *The Idea of History*. As a devoted pupil and friend of Collingwood, Knox considered it his duty to edit this book together with *The Idea of Nature*. It was as it were a last tribute to someone he highly

---

[11] R. G. Collingwood, review of S. Dill, *Roman Society in Gaul in the Merovingian Age* (London, 1926), in *Antiquity*, 1 (1927), p. 117.

appreciated as a person and teacher. His preface to the first edition of *The Idea of History* not only gives expression to this, but should also be seen as an attempt to save Collingwood from possible oblivion. Since at the time of its appearance the various aspects of Collingwood's ideas and their development were not widely known, Knox's description of them became very influential and functioned as the starting-point for most of the subsequent interpretations. Taking into account the literature that has appeared on Collingwood during the last decades and the evidence now available in Collingwood's manuscripts, there is reason to believe that the picture given by Knox in his preface is of a rather idiosyncratic nature and certain questions need to be asked of it.

The most influential of Knox's opinions concerns Collingwood's philosophical development. In his view Collingwood's works could be divided into three groups:

The first consists of what he came to regard as juvenilia, *Religion and Philosophy* (1916) and *Speculum Mentis* (1924). The second begins with the *Essay on Philosophical Method* (1933) and continues with *The Idea of Nature* (which dates, except for its Conclusion, from 1934) and much (1936) of *The Idea of History*. The last comprises the *Autobiography* (1939), the *Essay on Metaphysics* (1940), and *The New Leviathan* (1942). *The Principles of Art* (1938) is akin in part to the second group, in part to the third (p. vii).

Knox is full of admiration for what Collingwood wrote during his 'second period' (1933–6): in his opinion Collingwood was then at the zenith of his powers, exemplified in particular by *An Essay on Philosophical Method*. Between 1936 and 1938, however, a radical change took place in Collingwood's development, according to Knox, which was definitely not for the better. What was especially unfortunate, in Knox's view, was the fact that Collingwood came to espouse a dogmatic form of scepticism and historicism. This was especially the case with his *Autobiography* and *An Essay on Metaphysics*. Knox was particularly offended by the fact that in these works all knowledge was reduced to history and, quoting from the preparatory notes for *The Principles of History*, that even 'philosophy as a separate discipline is liquidated by being converted into history'. Knox asserts that he has 'documentary evidence' that in contrast with this position Collingwood in 1936 'still believed in the possibility of metaphysics as a separate study, distinct altogether from history' (p. x) (it is to be found in a letter from Collingwood to Knox).

Though many later interpreters have endorsed Knox's notion of a 'radical conversion' in Collingwood's development, others, like L. Rubinoff and L. O. Mink, have emphasized the basic unity of Collingwood's thought and development. I will not dwell on this discussion here, but only refer to the factor which in Knox's view was decisive in the alleged change in Collingwood's ideas: his ill health, which had been a problem from 1932 and led from 1938 to a series of strokes. Knox suggests that Collingwood's illness marred his judgement, this manifesting itself in an extreme and dogmatic form of historicism and a sometimes excessively passionate and even rather hectoring style.

With Collingwood's manuscripts at our disposal I do not think Knox's position can be sustained any longer. With regard to the possible influence of Collingwood's ill health it should first of all be observed that his illness started at an earlier date than Knox asserts. For it all started with the complications of chicken-pox which Collingwood contracted in April 1931. For a whole year he was seriously ill and in the first term of 1932 he took leave of absence.[12] Secondly, *An Essay on Philosophical Method* was not finished, as Knox contends, in the spring of 1932, but more than a year later. So the book was written after a period of serious illness and not, as Knox suggests, before it. Since Knox values highly *An Essay on Philosophical Method* and even considers it Collingwood's most important book, this fact seriously weakens his suggestion that Collingwood's judgement was marred by his illness. This suggestion is most clearly disproved, however, by the fact that Collingwood's last book *The New Leviathan*, though written when he was in a worse condition than ever before, shows no sign (with the exception of the last part) of a diminishing grasp on the subject: reviewing this book the political philosopher E. Barker even observes that 'there could not be

---

[12] Referring to this Knox says in his preface to *The Idea of History*: 'It was not then realized that this was the beginning of the ill health against which the rest of his life was to be an heroic struggle' (p. xxi).

better thinking than there is in the first two parts of the *New Leviathan*'.[13]

Knox's suggestion that Collingwood's thought has been marred by his ill health can also be challenged, of course, by observing that it is far from clear why this should have expressed itself in the form of an extreme historicist and sceptical viewpoint. With regard to this aspect it should also be noted that the manuscripts give evidence that on the one hand Collingwood was in his last years well aware of the dangers of an extreme form of scepticism[14] and that on the other hand he had in fact prior to 1936 developed ideas on metaphysics which were a clear prefiguration of the ones expounded later in *An Essay on Metaphysics*.

Finally an observation needs to be made on a passage that has been quoted often by various interpreters of Collingwood and accordingly has been quite influential in the interpretation of his ideas. Knox maintains that 'in a manuscript written in 1936' Collingwood says the following:

St. Augustine looked at Roman history from the point of view of an early Christian; Tillemont, from that of a seventeenth-century Frenchman; Gibbon, from that of an eighteenth-century Englishman; Mommsen, from that of a nineteenth-century German. There is no point in asking which was the right point of view. Each was the only one possible for the man who adopted it (p. xii).

The question of the status of this passage is of some significance because of its frequent use in sustaining the claim that Collingwood was both a historicist and relativist.[15] The passage is not found in the manuscripts. When asked about this Knox informed me that the passage was part of a letter written by Collingwood to him. The passage concerned does not appear,

---

[13] *Oxford Magazine*, 4 Feb. 1943, p. 163.

[14] Indeed, when Collingwood was gravely ill, that is, while writing *The New Leviathan*, he did not express historicist and sceptical views.

[15] It is interesting to note that in the essay 'The Philosophy of History' of 1930 the same issue is discussed by Collingwood, saying: 'Everyone brings his own mind to the study of history, and approaches it from the point of view which is characteristic of himself and his generation.' He comments on it, however, that 'this does not reduce history to something arbitrary or capricious. It remains genuine knowledge' (W. Debbins (ed.), *R. G. Collingwood: Essays in the Philosophy of History* (Austin, Tex., 1965), pp. 138–9).

however, among the letters from Collingwood to Knox in the latter's papers deposited in St Andrews University Library.

5. THE RECEPTION OF *THE IDEA OF HISTORY*

There is at present a great interest in the various aspects of Collingwood's thought, but this has not always been the case. On the contrary, while Collingwood failed to receive the recognition he deserved as a philosopher during his life, usually being labelled as an unfashionable 'idealist', after his death there was every indication that his work would fade into oblivion. It has largely been the publication of *The Idea of History* that has prevented this fate. For almost immediately after its appearance in 1946 this book attracted much attention, this only increasing with the passage of time. It is a strange irony that Collingwood, who had published such an enormous quantity of work during his life, attained most of his fame after his death as the result of the publication of a book which is in fact a patchwork put together from lectures, printed work, and parts of the first draft for *The Principles of History*.

A whole volume could be devoted to the history of the reception of *The Idea of History* and the discussion of the views expressed in it. Such a history would not only be intrinsically valuable, but would also form one of the essential elements in a history of the philosophy of history in general after the Second World War. For it is no exaggeration to say that during this period there has hardly been a study in this field—at least in the English-speaking world—in which Collingwood's contribution has not come up for discussion in one way or another.

It is not easy to give a reason for the attention *The Idea of History* attracted so promptly after its publication. One that might be mentioned perhaps is the fact that its appearance coincided with a more general interest in the philosophy of history in the years following the Second World War, an interest aroused by works like A. Toynbee's *Study of History* and K. Popper's *Open Society and its Enemies*.

Immediately after its appearance the importance of *The Idea of History* was recognized, both by historians and philosophers. Though the more detailed comments subsequently came almost exclusively from philosophers, the first reviews were written, interestingly enough, by historians. M. Beloff, for instance, in a review titled 'The Historians' Philosopher', says about *The Idea of History* that not 'a better introduction to historical studies [could] be imagined than a combination of the *Autobiography* and this latest work'.[16] Though A. L. Rowse did not endorse all aspects of Collingwood's views, he calls it 'in spite of its defects . . . one of the most important works ever devoted to the subject'.[17]

It is understandable that historians were most interested in the first four parts of *The Idea of History*, because of the historical survey of the idea of history given in it. Philosophers, on the other hand, have focused their attention almost exclusively on the Epilegomena. The first occasion when some aspects of Collingwood's views were discussed was at a joint session of the Aristotelian Society and the Mind Association in July 1947.[18] From that date till the present day there has been a ceaseless flow of publications on Collingwood's philosophy of history. In the 1950s, especially with contributions by W. H. Dray and A. Donagan, the philosophical discussion became increasingly detailed and sophisticated. Though this has greatly advanced the understanding of Collingwood's ideas, it also had the effect that few historians have been able to contribute to the debates which were conducted at higher levels of philosophical discussion.

One of the main theses of Collingwood's philosophy of history is the close relation between history *a parte objecti*, the historical process, and history *a parte subjecti*, the thought of the historian. With regard to both aspects Collingwood has put forward definite positions—not only in *The Idea of History*, but in his *Autobiography* as well—which have attracted much attention. The first states that all history should be seen as the history of thought and the second that history is essentially the re-enactment of past thought.

At first the reactions to these doctrines were mainly critical.

---

[16] *Time and Tide*, 28 September 1946.
[17] *Sunday Times*, 29 September 1946.
[18] 'Explanation in History and Philosophy', *Aristotelian Society*, Supp. Vol. 21 (1947), pp. 33–77.

From the side of the historians the main reason was that the position of all history being the history of thought was taken as a directive for historical research and as such considered ill-suited to their practice: it is usually rejected as an unacceptable limitation on the historian's activities and at best considered the product of an apparently extravagant philosophical theory. The alleged defect of the theory is more specifically concentrated on the points that it is too overtly intellectualistic, that it fails to take into account the less rational aspects of human actions, and that it also cannot account for social and economic history which tends to be concerned with aggregates or groups and mass behaviour, rather than individual actions.

The fate of the re-enactment doctrine was initially similar in that the comments were mainly critical, and it was also first interpreted in a methodological way, in this case as a directive for attaining knowledge of the past. Collingwood's position implied, it was thought, that historical knowledge was unique in establishing a direct contact with the past, which many critics interpreted as a form of intuition. They generally argued that it implied a subjectivist theory of truth. The theory was non-inferential and unscientific, and, as far as they were concerned, it did not take into account general knowledge.

The doctrines of all history being the history of thought, and of re-enactment are, one could say, the core of Collingwood's philosophy of history. The comments on these doctrines obviously had much wider implications. One could refer, for instance, to the nature of thought, the relation between thought and action, or the role of objective conditions in history, and, more generally and related to these, the relevance of re-enactment to historical explanation. An extensive literature has emerged on these subjects which shows no sign of diminishing.

Reviewing the interpretations given of Collingwood's views one is indeed struck not only by their occasionally bewildering diversity, but especially by their sometimes remarkable discrepancy. On the question of the possibility of objective historical knowledge, for instance, all the major positions that can be distinguished on this theme have in fact been imputed to Collingwood. He is said to have had 'a pathetic belief in the possibility of indisputable knowledge',[19] to have flirted at times 'with a complete relativism',[20] and to have held that 'reconstructions of past thoughts are corrigible and, in a sense, hypothetical'.[21] Similarly one interpreter maintains that the re-enactment doctrine 'must . . . inevitably lead to scepticism',[22] while another contends that Collingwood's theory of history 'is intended to answer scepticism about the possibility of historical knowledge',[23] and a third that 'Collingwood's analysis was not designed to show that a particular explanatory re-enactment could ever be beyond doubt or conclusive in any final sense'.[24] One is also confronted with most curious contradictions. For example, one interpreter sees Collingwood as a dualist and blames him for 'his adherence to a metaphysics of the type which G. Ryle has attacked as "the dogma of the ghost in the machine"',[25] while another speaks of 'Collingwood's monism', adding that it is 'like Ryle's, though perhaps even more radically'.[26]

What could be the reason for this striking and sometimes astonishing variety in interpretations of Collingwood's ideas, which is certainly unusual, at least to this degree, in the history of philosophy and which W. H. Walsh has, with understatement, called 'a curious episode in the history of ideas'?

I think various reasons may be given for it. It should in the first place be remembered that it was only at the end of his life that Collingwood tried to settle finally his accounts of his ideas on the philosophy of history. Though he had worked on the subject for many years, about which more will be said in due

[19] G. J. Renier, *History: Its Purpose and Methods* (London, 1950), p. 215.

[20] D. M. Mackinnon, review of *The Idea of History*, in *Journal of Theological Studies*, 48 (1947), p. 252.

[21] A. Donagan, 'The Verification of Historical Theses', *Philosophical Quarterly*, 6 (1956), p. 200.

[22] M. Mandelbaum, review of *The Idea of History*, in *Journal of Philosophy*, 44 (1947), p. 187.

[23] J. W. Meiland, *Scepticism and Historical Knowledge* (New York, 1965), p. 63.

[24] R. Martin, *Historical Explanation: Re-enactment and Practical Inference* (Ithaca, NY, 1977), p. 57.

[25] J. Cohen, 'A Survey of Work in the Philosophy of History, 1946–1950', *Philosophical Quarterly*, 2 (1952), p. 173.

[26] P. Skagestad, *Making Sense of History: The Philosophies of Popper and Collingwood* (Oslo, 1975), p. 66.

course, his publications in the subject were too scanty and scattered to have attracted much attention. We have seen how his plans to have his thoughts on the philosophy of history published in the two volumes *The Idea of History* and *The Principles of History* failed to be realized. Secondly, the ignorance of Collingwood's unpublished manuscripts, some of the most important of these being on the philosophy of history, was a major impediment to the interpretation of his ideas. Collingwood's interpreters cannot of course be blamed for negative factors relating to the lack of accessibility, but they must bear some responsibility for the fact that his publications, both the relatively rare ones on the philosophy of history and others which are relevant to it, have been insufficiently taken into account. With regard to the latter, one could refer for instance to *The Principles of Art*, in which Collingwood explains his philosophy of mind. It was L. O. Mink's *Mind, History, and Dialectic* (1969) which explicitly discussed for the first time the relevance of Collingwood's philosophy of mind for a better understanding of his philosophy of history.

There is also a positive side to the reception of Collingwood's philosophy of history. In reviewing this reception it is evident that it is not all confusion, but there is also a rational progression to be discerned in the way the arguments of commentators have developed. This is especially the case with the re-enactment doctrine, by far the most widely discussed aspect of Collingwood's philosophy of history.

We have seen that initially this doctrine was interpreted and thus criticized as a methodology involving an intuitive capacity in the historian. In 1956 this 'received interpretation' was criticized in a fundamental way by A. Donagan.[27] The re-enactment doctrine should not be seen as a methodological prescription for acquiring historical knowledge, he maintained, but as the answer to the philosophical question of how historical knowledge is possible. This position was shortly afterwards endorsed by W. H. Dray.[28] But the latter also

[27] A. Donagan, 'The Verification of Historical Theses', *Philosophical Quarterly*, 6 (1956), pp. 193–208.

[28] W. H. Dray, *Laws and Explanation in History* (Oxford, 1957), p. 128; id., 'R. G. Collingwood and the Acquaintance Theory of Knowledge', *Revue*

developed from this basic assumption an interpretation of his own: understanding by rethinking should be seen as following a practical argument in which a rational necessity is discerned. This view was worked out in depth by Dray in his well-known *Laws and Explanation in History* (1957), in which a 'rational explanation model' is put against the positivist 'covering law model'. One could say, therefore, that through this study the ideas of Collingwood for the first time became influential in a major discussion in the philosophy of history.

After the contributions by Donagan and Dray the method-ological interpretation of the re-enactment doctrine, especially in its intuitive version, has constantly lost ground. At present all serious studies on Collingwood reject this interpretation and take the philosophical one as their starting-point. What was once the 'alternative' view has therefore become the 'received' one. With hindsight this may indeed be seen as an advance, for Collingwood's manuscripts, published in this volume, establish conclusively that his re-enactment doctrine should actually be seen as the answer to a philosophical question and not to a methodological one. They also show that in addition Collingwood developed definite ideas on the method-ology of history similar to those found in *The Idea of History*, especially in the essays 'The Historical Imagination' and 'His-torical Evidence'.

Discussions of Collingwood's philosophy of history have been impaired by the methodological interpretation of the re-enactment doctrine. With the diminishing influence of the lat-ter the former could be dealt with in a more fruitful way. Recent developments show that this is what has happened and that Collingwood's views on the logic of question and answer and on evidence, but also the more implicit views of his prac-tice as an archaeologist and historian, have increasingly got the attention they deserve.

internationale de philosophie, 11 (1957), pp. 420–32; id., 'Historical Under-standing as Re-thinking', *University of Toronto Quarterly*, 27 (1958), pp. 200–15.

6. THE DEVELOPMENT OF COLLINGWOOD'S PHILOSOPHY OF HISTORY: INTRODUCTION

When Knox begins his preface to *The Idea of History* with the words 'during the first six months of 1936 Collingwood wrote thirty-two lectures on *The Philosophy of History*', this information is correct, but nevertheless misleading. Knox does not mention that Collingwood had in fact previously lectured annually on the philosophy of history from 1926 to 1931. This means that the lectures of 1936 are not the beginning of Collingwood's thought on history, but that it already had a history of its own spanning at least ten years. Among the manuscripts the lectures of 1926 and 1928 are complete. They are of great interest, since in two versions Collingwood develops his philosophy of history explicitly for the first time. In response to a question from the present editor, Knox claimed that he did not use these lectures in his edition of *The Idea of History* because he was unaware of their existence. This is plausible, since the manuscripts do not appear on the list of titles which Oxford University Press sent to Knox for his scrutiny.

The lectures of 1926 and 1928 are reproduced for the first time in this revised edition of *The Idea of History*. Before dealing with them, however, it is necessary to put them in a proper context, which entails saying something about the development of Collingwood's ideas on history. With regard to his development in general, attention has usually been focused on Knox's 'radical conversion' thesis, presented in the preface to *The Idea of History*. Something has already been said about this above; we will here concentrate on the development of Collingwood's thought on history. This subject should be considered apart from the question of Collingwood's alleged 1936 'conversion'.

In his *Autobiography*, written in 1938, Collingwood gave a most vivid picture of the evolution of his thought. Though some commentators, partly influenced by Knox's interpretation, have questioned its reliability, I think Collingwood's own account is on the whole trustworthy. There is in particular no reason to doubt that his often quoted saying that 'my life's work hitherto, as seen from my fiftieth year, has been in the main an attempt to bring about a *rapprochement* between philosophy and history' (p. 77) is basically correct. Both the description given of his controversy with the realist position and the lessons learnt from his practice as an archaeologist can be seen as an illustration of this *rapprochement*. Collingwood's publications and the manuscripts that have survived exemplify as well the close relation in his thought between philosophy and history.

In discussing the relation between philosophy and history in Collingwood's thought one should of course take both subjects seriously. Many commentators have given insufficient attention to this dual aspect of Collingwood's philosophy of history, with the result that one of the main theses of the *Autobiography* cannot be grasped. In this connection it should also be noted that Collingwood was active in the field of both archaeology and history. His special field was Roman Britain, and it is obvious that in such a field historical and archaeological work cannot be sharply divided. The subjects are not, however, the same and if one mentions only one of them in connection with Collingwood's activities, as is sometimes done, it can produce distortion. This is especially the case if one takes academic practice into account as it has developed since Collingwood's death, archaeology and history having developed into separate academic disciplines. Though Collingwood speaks intermittently of history and archaeology, he worked in fact on three tracks: philosophy, history, and archaeology, the *rapprochement* between them therefore being of an even more complex nature.

Though Collingwood is at present primarily known as a philosopher, this was not the case in his own lifetime. For in the philosophical climate at Oxford between the wars he was a more or less isolated figure. 'In part, the trouble was', S. Toulmin remarks in his introduction to the *Autobiography*, 'that Collingwood needed a bigger pond than the Oxford of his time provided.' It was not only his resistance to prevailing realism, one could say, but also his interest in the historical dimension of philosophy and in Continental philosophers like Vico, Hegel, Croce, and de Ruggiero, which made this desirable.

The appreciation of Collingwood's work as a historian and archaeologist has been quite different. For during his life his reputation as the main expert on Roman Britain and the intricate problems related to Hadrian's Wall remained unchallenged. Besides many articles and reviews on these subjects Collingwood published *Roman Britain* (1923, revised in 1932), the handbook *The Archaeology of Roman Britain* (1930), and the first part of *Roman Britain and the English Settlements* (1936). Mention should also be made of the posthumous *Roman Inscriptions of Britain*, i. *Inscriptions on Stone* (1965), on which he worked for many years. Though he eventually occupied the prestigious chair of Waynflete Professor of Metaphysical Philosophy at the University of Oxford from 1935, prior to that Collingwood was well aware of the divergent appreciations of his work. For on 4 October 1927 he wrote to his friend the Italian philosopher de Ruggiero:

I find myself writing gloomily. For four months I have been deep in historical studies, and there I find myself among friends and willing collaborators; the return to philosophy means a return to a work in which I become more and more conscious of being an outlaw.[29]

It is clear from this that besides his work as a philosopher Collingwood's lifelong involvement in history and archaeology should be taken seriously. This is well illustrated by the way in which in the *Autobiography* the realists are heavily criticized for their lack of historical consciousness and accordingly their defective epistemology. Collingwood reports how he used his archaeological practice as a 'flank attack' on the realist position and as a 'laboratory' of how the history of philosophy should be conceived. He refers here to his principle not to lapse into 'blind digging', the usual practice of the old days, when digs were made for reasons of curiosity, nostalgia, or even for treasure. Against this Collingwood used to emphasize the importance of 'scientific' excavation, which entailed the methodological principle always to approach a site with a specific question in mind. It was this principle that was generalized by Collingwood into his logic of question and answer, the 'Baconian' approach, which he pre-eminently considered the hallmark of science, including the science of history.

[29] Bodleian Library Collingwood Papers, dep. 27.

6.1. THE DEVELOPMENT OF COLLINGWOOD'S PHILOSOPHY OF HISTORY: 1925–1930

The relation between philosophy and history in Collingwood's thought can also be seen from a different viewpoint. Its main characteristics are to be found in his publications from *Speculum Mentis* (1924) to the essay 'The Philosophy of History' (1930). In *Speculum Mentis* Collingwood makes a distinction between art, religion, science, history, and philosophy as 'forms of experience'. They are discussed in their mutual relations, expressing a dialectical development from what is implied at one level to what becomes explicit at the next, with philosophy as the highest stage. However, each form of experience also has a development of its own, and in the case of history Collingwood points out that it ultimately leads to the science of history as it came into being in the eighteenth century and further developed in the nineteenth, this being called by him history 'in the special sense of the word', history in the 'highest' sense, or 'historians' history' (pp. 203, 211, 216).

Within each form of experience in *Speculum Mentis* a distinction is made between its own view of itself, each thinking itself the only valid one, and a philosophical view. The first leads to dogmatism and with history this takes the form of a realism which considers facts as independently existing. Since the infinite world of facts can never be known this inevitably leads to scepticism, which, Collingwood argues, can only be overcome by philosophy, that is, the stage of 'absolute' or 'concrete' knowledge.

After *Speculum Mentis* one sees an important and remarkable switch in Collingwood's thought about the relation between philosophy and history. For from 1925 he concentrates on a philosophical study of history from the inside, that is, on the nature of historical thought. Following Kant he states in 'The Nature and Aims of a Philosophy of History' (1925)[30] explicitly for the first time that a philosophy of history ought to take up a 'critical attitude' towards history, which inquires into its 'nature and value, the presuppositions and implications'. Collingwood explores this subject further in

---

[30] Reprinted in Debbins (ed.), *Essays*, pp. 34–56.

'The Limits of Historical Knowledge', published in 1928 but written in 1927.[31] Here he discusses historical 'facts' not as independently existing entities, but in the sense of evidence or sources on which a historical study has to be based. He considers this the essential distinguishing feature of history as compared with science, which can make use of experiments. The evidence on which the historian is dependent, Collingwood argues, is also the limit of his knowledge: a historian can never go further than the evidence allows him to go. Coupled with this view he rejects the illusion that it is the 'real' past the historian is aiming at: 'what really happened' cannot be anything else than 'what the evidence indicates'. In this viewpoint one finds already an important element of Collingwood's mature philosophy of history as expressed in *The Idea of History*, with its emphasis on the autonomy of the historian and his dependence on evidence.

In 1930 Collingwood published 'The Philosophy of History',[32] which may not only be considered the provisional conclusion of his thought on history, but also as an outline of future work he intended to do in this field. Though this essay has hardly been noticed by those commenting on Collingwood's philosophy of history it is nevertheless of some importance. It is also of special interest because of the way history as 'a universal and necessary human interest' is related to history as a science. The first cannot only be seen as the equivalent of what in *Speculum Mentis* is called a 'form of experience', but also of what in *An Essay on Philosophical Method* is explained as a philosophical concept. Seen from the distinction made in the latter book between philosophical and empirical concepts, history as a science should therefore be taken as the empirical concept of history. The transition from the philosophical to the empirical concept of history is described smoothly by Collingwood. For history is said to be a universal and necessary human interest, though an interest of a special nature: it is an intellectual interest and consequently a form of knowledge. From this it is concluded that 'the business of the philosophy of history is to discover the essential characteristics of this form of knowledge'.[33]

[31] Reprinted ibid., pp. 90–103.   [32] Reprinted ibid., pp. 121–39.
[33] Ibid., p. 124.

What is missing in this short sketch of the development of Collingwood's philosophy of history are his lectures on the subject. The lectures of 1926 and 1928 are published in this edition of *The Idea of History* and will be discussed hereafter separately. For a better understanding of the context within which these lectures were seen by Collingwood himself, it is interesting to refer to a report Collingwood wrote in January 1932 to the Faculty of Literae Humaniores in his capacity as University Lecturer.[34] It reads:

By appointing me Lecturer in Philosophy and Roman History, I understand the University to mean, not only that I am to study and teach these two subjects, but also that I am to study and teach them in their mutual connexions: i.e. in philosophy, to investigate the philosophy of history, and, in history, not to neglect the methods and logic of historical work, and to emphasize the relation between history and its sources.

As one of his projects he further mentions:

A study of the philosophical problems arising out of history: especially a) logical and epistemological problems connected with the question 'how is historical knowledge possible?', b) metaphysical problems concerned with the nature and reality of the objects of historical thought.

(It is striking how almost the same wording is used as on p. 77 of the *Autobiography*, when Collingwood explains his conception of the *rapprochement* between philosophy and history.) On this project Collingwood remarks:

This I regard as my chief work, involving the whole of my philosophical and historical studies in their mutual connexions. I am of opinion that there is important work to be done here, and that it cannot be done except by a trained and practising historian who is also in constant work as a philosopher.

The importance Collingwood apparently attached to his essay 'The Philosophy of History' may be gauged from his observation that it 'is in effect the synopsis of a complete treatise, but I do not intend to begin writing such a treatise until I have done several years' work on various aspects of the subject'.

[34] Reprinted in W. J. van der Dussen, *History as a Science: The Philosophy of R. G. Collingwood* (The Hague, 1981), pp. 435–8.

Collingwood's thought on the philosophy of history came to a provisional conclusion around 1930. This is not only documented in the report of 1932,[35] but also confirmed by his *Autobiography*, where he says that his 'train of thought' on the philosophy of history 'was not complete until about 1930' (p. 115).

6.2 THE DEVELOPMENT OF COLLINGWOOD'S PHILOSOPHY OF HISTORY: FROM 1935

In the years following 1930 Collingwood concentrated on other subjects. In philosophy he returned to the work which was to result in *An Essay on Philosophical Method*, which in a later report to the Faculty is described as 'intended to serve as preface to a series of philosophical works based on the conception of method there expounded'. This was first done in his 'Notes towards a Metaphysic' of 1933–4, which contain a few hundred pages in manuscript. Starting from the problem of the relation between matter, life, and mind, various cosmological and related theories are discussed in them, among others those of Alexander and Whitehead. Besides this, Collingwood concentrated on his work in archaeology and history. This resulted in various publications, both on the economic aspects of Roman Britain and the pre-Roman 'pre-history' of this area, while in 1935 he completed his contribution to *Roman Britain and the English Settlements*.

Although Collingwood developed no cosmological theory of his own, two important by-products came out of his work in this field. In his 'Notes towards a Metaphysic' he developed a historical review of theories on nature, on which he lectured in 1934, 1935, and 1937. These lectures were revised in 1939–40 and resulted, as we have seen, in the publication of *The Idea of Nature*. Secondly, his discussion of the relation between nature and mind resulted in Collingwood's position on the difference between natural and historical processes: he developed in particular the view that their difference is in essence based on the fact that in nature the past should be seen as being separated from

[35] He mentions that his 'philosophical and historical studies in their mutual connexions' had gradually reached in the last four years 'a provisional solution of most of the chief problems'.

the present, while in mental processes, which are typical for human history, the past is retained in the present.

In the manuscript 'Reality as History', written in December 1935 and being described by Collingwood as 'an experimental essay designed to test how far the thesis can be maintained that all reality is history and all knowledge historical knowledge', this thesis is further explored. It also deals with its repercussions for historical knowledge, which is put against natural science. The principle of historical understanding, Collingwood argues, is that the flux of reality is made intelligible and not reduced to fixed entities as in Greek thought or to fixed laws as in modern science. In the same essay the consequences of this position for the idea of human nature are discussed, man being characterized as a 'rebellious child' of nature.

With 'Reality as History' we have come to the 'second phase' in the development of Collingwood's philosophy of history, the first one being from 1925 to 1930. We have seen that in 1930 he had come to a provisional conclusion of his ideas on the subject and that in the following years he worked on other subjects. In 1935, however, Collingwood returned to the philosophy of history with 'The Historical Imagination', an essay now well known because of its publication in *The Idea of History*. That he delivered it on the occasion of his inaugural on 28 October 1935 is an indication of his intention in his new chair to pursue further the discussion of the connexion between philosophy and history which he had started ten years before. It was followed by the manuscript 'Reality as History', and in January 1936 he read a paper on 'Can Historians be Impartial?'. In March of the same year the first draft of 'Human Nature and Human History' was written, the final version of which was reprinted in *The Idea of History*.

Besides these essays, not only the manuscript 'Notes on History of Historiography and Philosophy of History' of 1936, but, in particular, the lectures on the philosophy of history of the same year, give clear evidence of the revival of Collingwood's interest in the subject of the philosophy of history. The lectures have a completely different plan from the ones of 1926 and 1928; the background to their publication in *The Idea of History* has been discussed above. It is interesting to note that in his 'Notes on History of Historiography and Philosophy of History', which were apparently written in preparation for the lectures, Collingwood returns to the subject of the re-enactment of past thought.[36] 'The formula needs a good deal of clearing-up,' he remarks, and then gives an exposition of the equivocality of the word 'thought', which can both mean *noēsis* (act of thinking) and *noēma* (the object of thought). His conclusion is that history should be seen as *noēseōs noēsis* (an act of thinking about an act of thinking). The act of thinking by the historian, Collingwood argues, is of a peculiar kind, since not only the object of his thought, but also the relation to it is peculiar: 'for the act in this special case absorbs the object into itself, makes it a factor in itself', implying the transcendence of it. What Collingwood refers to in this passage is the concept of 'incapsulation' of past thought in the present thought of the historian, as explained in the *Autobiography* (p. 114). However, in the chapter on the re-enactment doctrine in *The Idea of History*—being part of the 'Metaphysical Epilegomena' of the lectures of 1936—this concept is not yet explicitly worked out by Collingwood.

After his lectures on the philosophy of history in 1936 Collingwood turned again to other subjects (though the lectures were repeated in 1937), this time mainly folklore and metaphysics. But beginning with his *Autobiography*, written in September 1938, Collingwood returned again—for the third time—to the philosophy of history, this time with a plan to write *The Principles of History*. Though he began working on it in February 1939, during his stay in the Dutch East Indies, it was, as we have seen, never realized. (It should be mentioned, in passing, that *An Essay on Metaphysics* was written in the interim period by Collingwood on board the ship to the East.)

Since it was Collingwood's intention in writing *The Principles of History* to develop a completely new book on the subject, it is interesting to speculate on the new approach he might have taken. Speculation of this type is rather hazardous because in addition to the few extracts published in *The Idea of History* only the scheme for the book remains.[37] There are

---

[36] Bodleian Library Collingwood Papers, Dep. 13, pp. 19–22.
[37] Reprinted in Van der Dussen, *History as a Science*, pp. 431–2.

some indicators, however, which are interesting to note. In the first place it is striking that after the lectures of 1928 and 1936 Collingwood's third chapter of *The Principles of History* (which, as was noted above, is lost) contained a third discussion of re-enactment. It is curious that Collingwood now contrasts re-enactment with 'the dead past and completeness' and does not discuss it, as he had previously done, within the context of the question of how historical knowledge is possible and how history should be studied.

It is indeed probable that in *The Principles of History* Collingwood wanted to emphasize some wider repercussions of the re-enactment doctrine. An indication of their context is given in the manuscripts with the preparatory notes on historiography, where he says that the past being re-enactable 'it is not something that has finished happening' and that the past being in this way actual 'is the same thing as its being historically known'.[38] One may assume, therefore, that in the lost part of *The Principles of History* the discussion of the re-enactment doctrine was reopened by Collingwood within the context of the idea of the actuality of the past in the present, which was contrasted with the notion of a dead and complete past.

The scheme for *The Principles of History* not only indicates that the re-enactment doctrine was discussed within a new and wider context, but that it was Collingwood's intention to do this with his general concept of history as well. An indication of this may be found for instance in the fourth chapter of the first part of *The Principles of History*, called by Collingwood 'History as the self-knowledge of mind' and edited by Knox under the title 'History and Freedom'. In this short essay Collingwood develops a remarkable argument with regard to the idea of the close connection between history *a parte subjecti* and history *a parte objecti*. The idea of history as an autonomous science and free from the domination of natural science, it is argued, is not only closely connected with, but is in fact inseparable from the notion 'that rational action is free from the domination of nature and builds its own world of human affairs, *Res Gestae*, at its own bidding and in its own way' (p. 318). Collingwood is even of the opinion that the idea

---

[38] Bodleian Library Collingwood Papers, dep. 13, p. 19.

of human freedom could only be fully grasped when the idea of history as an autonomous science had been developed. This argument may be considered an example of what in the introductory chapter of *The Idea of History* is called 'the second stage' of the philosophy of history. This stage is contrasted by Collingwood with one in which the philosophy of history is conceived as the analysis of history as a specific form of knowledge and is described by him as 'a general overhauling of all philosophical questions in the light of the results reached by the philosophy of history in the narrower sense' (pp. 6–7).

From the scheme for *The Principles of History* it may be inferred that Collingwood indeed planned to develop in this book a philosophy of history 'in the wide sense', that is, to elaborate the implications of his ideas on history for certain general philosophical questions. This is made clear when he says in the final part of his scheme for *The Principles of History* that 'history is the negation of the traditional distinction between theory and practice', that distinction being dependent on taking 'the contemplation of nature, where the object is presupposed', as 'our typical case of knowledge', whereas in history 'the object is enacted and is therefore not an *object* at all'. 'If this is worked out carefully,' he adds, 'then should follow without difficulty a characterization of an historical morality and an historical civilization, contrasting with our "scientific" one.'

This part of *The Principles of History* was never worked out by Collingwood, the main reason being, as we have seen, that at the outbreak of the war he decided to work on *The New Leviathan*. Certain aspects of its argument, however, were developed in this book and more specifically in his lectures on 'Goodness, Rightness, Utility', delivered in 1940.[39] In these lectures Collingwood confronts the conception of duty with that of utility and of right. While the latter contain degrees of capriciousness and irrationality, duty is the expression of real freedom and rationality, since an action based on it is strictly individual and springs from the consciousness of an individual situation. The fact of an agent's awareness of his action and

---

[39] Extracts of these are reprinted in David Boucher (ed.), *R. G. Collingwood: Essays in Political Philosophy* (Oxford, 1989), pp. 150–9. The complete text of the lectures is published in Boucher's revised edition of *The New Leviathan* (Oxford, 1992), pp. 391–479.

situation as unique is equated by Collingwood with history. For history too deals with 'individual actions done by human beings in individual situations'. Besides this, Collingwood argues, in his activity as an historian he is aware 'of his own situation as an historian' with certain evidence of the past and 'of his acting in that situation, namely his activity as interpreting this evidence'.[40] So, as in his essay 'History and Freedom', we see Collingwood here equating the historian's enterprise with a certain vision on a wider philosophical question, this time with regard to ethics, notably his view on the concept of duty. This may indeed be seen as a part of the elaboration of a historical morality as mentioned in the scheme for *The Principles of History*, while a historical civilization would be elaborated in *The New Leviathan*.

From the foregoing it may be concluded that at the end of his life Collingwood was mainly interested in developing a philosophy of history in the wide sense, that is 'a complete philosophy conceived from an historical point of view' (p. 7). He did not limit himself, however, to this aspect, since the first chapter of *The Principles of History* deals with the conception of evidence. It is illustrative that in his final book on history Collingwood again started by dealing with this issue, for it was exactly this which had exemplified his major shift in philosophy of history in the 1920s: we have seen that it is a central topic of 'The Limits of Historical Knowledge', while it was also the starting-point for the lectures of 1926. Since in 'The Historical Imagination' too the relation to evidence is called the 'most important' rule of method for the historian (p. 246), we see therefore Collingwood paying special attention to the conception of evidence at the beginning of the three 'phases' in the development of his philosophy of history. This conception should be seen, of course, within the wider context of Collingwood's epistemology.

The fact that 'The Historical Imagination' and 'Historical Evidence' are placed together in *The Idea of History* may suggest that they form a single argument. This is not correct, for not only are they written with an interval of four years separating them—the one in 1935 and the other in 1939—but on

---

[40] David Boucher (ed.), *R. G. Collingwood: Essays in Political Philosophy* (Oxford, 1989), p. 155.

further consideration they can be seen to contain different arguments and even to be contradictory in certain essential respects.

In 'The Historical Imagination' Collingwood makes a distinction between three views on history, called by him the 'common-sense' theory, historical criticism, and constructive history. In 'Historical Evidence' a similar distinction is made. This time Collingwood distinguishes scissors-and-paste history, critical history, and scientific history. While scissors-and-paste history is the equivalent of the 'common-sense' theory of the earlier essay, it is curious that critical history is valued differently. For in 'The Historical Imagination' it is appreciated as part of a 'Copernican revolution' and connected with the Baconian approach (pp. 236–7), while in 'Historical Evidence' it is criticized as a phase in scissors-and-paste history, though 'on the eve of its dissolution' (p. 260). The sharp distinction made in the latter essay between critical and scientific history is certainly not in conformity with Collingwood's usual position. For he used not only to emphasize that evidence should always be seen in relation to the asking of certain questions, but also to certain principles of interpretation.

That the argument developed in 'Historical Evidence' is not in line with more considered viewpoints developed elsewhere by Collingwood may also be illustrated by the way the inferential nature of history is discussed. In this first chapter of *The Principles of History* historical inferences are compared with inferences of a deductive and inductive nature. The character of a historical inference is not worked out by Collingwood, however. The only thing he says about it is that, like exact science, it yields compulsion. He even maintains that a historical argument may be proved 'as conclusively as a demonstration in mathematics' (p. 262). The only qualification made is that this is true for scientific history and not for scissors-and-paste history. Collingwood gives no argument for this thesis and limits himself to the practice of the science of history, even to the point of saying 'I'm not arguing, I'm telling you' (p. 263).

Collingwood's failure to argue for the thesis that a conclusion in history can be as conclusive as a demonstration in mathematics is of course a source of weakness and has properly been criticized. It is evident that in 'Historical Evidence'

the nature of the relation between evidence and historical
knowledge is not dealt with in a satisfactory way. In 'The Historical Imagination', however, although the nature of a historical inference is not explicitly discussed, the subject is more
adequately treated. For in this essay the imaginative and constructive nature of historical thought is emphasized and one
could say that it is exactly this aspect that plays the major role
in historical inferences. In contrast to what is said in 'Historical Evidence' it is also maintained that 'in history, as in all
serious matters, no achievement is final' (p. 248).

The upshot of the preceding argument is that the chapter on
'Historical Evidence' cannot plausibly be considered as
Collingwood's final, let alone his most considered, opinion on
the subject. In this connection one should especially take into
account the fact that it is only a first draft of the first chapter of
The Principles of History. For a more satisfactory discussion of
the same subject one has to return to the lectures on the philosophy of history, given by Collingwood in 1926 and 1928.

7. THE LECTURES ON THE PHILOSOPHY OF HISTORY OF 1926 AND 1928

Collingwood used to write out his lectures in full. Of those he
wrote on the philosophy of history only the manuscripts of
1926 and 1928 remain in their entirety. In fact, in the absence
of the original manuscript of the lectures of 1936, those of 1926
and 1928, along with parts of *The Idea of History*, the *Autobiography*, and some articles, are the only major texts of
Collingwood's philosophy of history that can with certainty be
considered authentic. This is a rather odd observation if one
takes into account not only the quantity of Collingwood's
publications, but also the fact that he considered the philosophy of history to be his main interest and the fact that his
fame after his death has mainly been based on his contribution
to it. The concurrence of circumstances out of which this
could have arisen has already been explained above.

The lectures of 1926 and 1928 are especially important in
that they contain Collingwood's first comprehensive statements of his ideas on the philosophy of history. Thus through
them the first phase of his philosophy of history is well docu-

mented. Many well-known aspects of his later philosophy of history are developed here for the first time, thus offering a most valuable opportunity for a better understanding of his views. Sometimes, however, the lectures show a different argument or emphasis than those highlighted by previous discussions on Collingwood's philosophy of history. They may therefore also contribute to a possible reconsideration of certain aspects of his thought.

In interpreting the lectures it is particularly relevant to notice the importance of putting them in their proper perspective and context. Though they certainly illuminate various aspects of Collingwood's philosophy of history, they should not be taken as the expression of his final view on the subject. Collingwood himself at least would have strongly opposed such an interpretation. For in his view, mind is by its very nature always in development and his own thought not only well exemplifies this claim, but he viewed it in these terms himself. His lectures on ethics, for instance, were constantly rewritten and the two versions of 1926 and 1928 of his lectures on the philosophy of history provide another illustration of his meticulousness in this respect. In *An Essay on Philosophical Method* philosophy is described as 'a form of human thought, subject to change, liable to error, capable of progress'. 'The philosopher therefore', Collingwood continues, 'like every student, must sum up his progress from time to time, and express his conclusions in a systematic form, if progress is to continue' (p. 180). In the preface to the lectures of 1928 Collingwood warns, however, that 'no system is more than a temporary resting-place for thought'. He speaks in the same lectures and in those of 1926 of each historical study being an 'interim report' in the advance made in research. With regard to philosophy Collingwood liked to refer in this connexion to the phrase by Hegel 'bis hierher is das Bewusstsein gekommen' ('consciousness has reached this point').

Another quotation of which Collingwood was fond and often used was Plato's description of thinking as a 'dialogue of the soul with itself'. He preferred to put this into practice himself by writing and many of the manuscripts give evidence of this approach: in his 'Notes towards a Metaphysic' Collingwood even explicitly speaks of an attempt to 'think on paper'.

His lectures should be seen as the products of the same attempts, this probably being the reason that they were completely written down.

After these preliminary observations the lectures of 1926 and 1928 should speak for themselves. So we will limit ourselves to some comments on their background in order to facilitate their better understanding.

In December 1925, two weeks before he began on his lectures on the philosophy of history, Collingwood wrote a paper called 'Some Perplexities about Time: With an Attempted Solution',[41] which he was to read for the Aristotelian Society in February 1926. It is of special interest, because it served, one could say, as the starting-point for his lectures. In discussing the concept of time Collingwood makes a distinction within being between the actual and the ideal. The only real is the present, he maintains, but it is composed of two ideal elements, the past (necessity) and the future (possibility). Though past and future as such are ideal they are respectively as 'living in the present' and as 'germinating in the present', according to Collingwood, 'wholly real and indeed are just the present itself'.[42] Though the paper deals with the conception of time and not with the question of how knowledge of the past is possible, Collingwood makes some observations on the latter in passing. 'What we know must, I suppose, really exist', he says, and continues: 'And if that is so we cannot really know either the past or the future . . . Of the past as past and the future as future we can have only conjecture, better or worse grounded.' He must admit, of course, that the conjectures of both are of a different nature, concluding that 'the past and the future, therefore, both baffle our endeavours to know them, but in different ways and for different reasons'.[43]

This frankly acknowledged bafflement on the nature of historical knowledge is a clear indication that on the one hand Collingwood's ideas on the philosophy of history were not yet developed and on the other that his lectures on the subject which were written immediately after the paper on time should indeed be taken as an attempt 'to settle accounts' with himself, as it is put in the introduction to the lectures.

[41] *Proceedings of the Aristotelian Society*, NS 26 (1925–6), pp. 135–50.
[42] Ibid., p. 149. [43] Ibid., pp. 146–7.

It is apparent from the beginning of the 1926 lectures that they are to be understood as a sequel to the earlier paper, because in the lectures he discusses the concept of time and the difference between historical knowledge and memory. After this the nature of historical knowledge is extensively dealt with, concentrating on the sources of history and the principles of their interpretation. At the end Collingwood returns to the conclusion of his paper on time, saying that the past should be seen as an ideal element in the present and in this sense actually existing as the present. Collingwood still adheres to the idea that only the actual can be known and this implies a serious problem concerning the status of knowledge of the past. The only thing that is said about it is that being an ideal element in the present the past 'can therefore be studied in the same general way and to the same extent to which any abstraction may be studied'.

This is hardly a satisfying answer to the fundamental philosophical question of how historical knowledge is possible. Collingwood himself seems to have been aware of this and apparently did not consider his lectures of 1926 his last word on the subject. For on 18 August 1926 he writes to de Ruggiero: 'For myself, I am trying to clear up my conception of History—helped greatly, but not wholly satisfied, by both Croce and Gentile, and developing further the view expressed in *Speculum Mentis*. And always pursuing the study of history itself.'[44]

In his *Autobiography* Collingwood reports that 'another step forward' in his conception of history was registered in 1928, when on vacation at the country-house Le Martouret near Die (France) (p. 107), and it is because of the importance of this episode in the development of his thought that it is included in this revised edition of *The Idea of History*.

The 'Die manuscript' is a newly written series of lectures on the philosophy of history under the title 'Outlines of a Philosophy of History'. This time Collingwood begins where he had ended his lectures in 1926: with the unsolved problem of the relation between the ideal past and the actual present, to be dealt with from the perspective of how the question of the

---

[44] Reprinted in A. G. Olivetti, *Due saggi su R. G. Collingwood: Con un' appendice di lettere inedite di Collingwood a G. de Ruggiero* (Padova, 1977), p. 99.

possibility and legitimacy of historical knowledge can be solved in a philosophically satisfactory way. It is within this context that the notorious conception of the re-enactment of past thought and the doctrine of all history being the history of thought are developed for the first time.

In this first chapter of the lectures many aspects of both doctrines, that have caused such a great deal of controversy, are discussed. Though the terms are not yet always explicitly used, the idea of encapsulation of past thought in the present, the distinction between thought in its mediacy and immediacy, the nature of thought, and the question of the identity of thoughts past and present are to be found. It is curious to note, however, that when Collingwood refers in his *Autobiography* to the Die manuscript he mentions in the first instance the distinction made between history proper and pseudo-history, which is implied by the doctrine that all history is the history of thought.

The views developed by Collingwood in the first chapter of the Die manuscript are the most conspicuous new element as compared with the lectures of 1926. Sometimes, however, they put some of the subjects which are also dealt with in the first lectures in different perspective. This is especially the case where problems are discussed within the context of the close relation, as emphasized by Collingwood, between history *a parte subjecti* and *a parte objecti*, which is an implication of the newly developed doctrines of the first chapter.

The lectures of both 1926 and 1928 give a unique insight into the origins of Collingwood's philosophy of history. Some of the subjects discussed and even the terms used will appear familiar to readers of *The Idea of History* and the *Autobiography*, like the notions of authorities, scissors-and-paste history, the history of history, the Baconian approach, or the logic of question and answer and the nature of evidence. In some cases, however, it is clear that Collingwood has subsequently changed his opinion. In the lectures of 1928, for instance, the notion of causality in history is rejected, although Collingwood was later to develop a specific notion of cause in the historical sense; likewise in the same lectures the idea is rejected that gaps between fragments of knowledge are to be filled by imagination, while in 'The Historical Imagination' such

filling-in is considered a fundamental characteristic of historical thinking. In cases like these the exhortation to see Collingwood's philosophy of history itself as having a history is
particularly important.

The lectures also show certain characteristics which are not
in line with the way Collingwood's philosophy of history is
usually discussed. It is striking, for instance, how much attention is paid in them to the interpretive aspects of the study of
history and to how interpretation actually proceeds in diverse
ways and at all levels, from the examination of sources to various kinds of narrative construction. This contrasts rather con-
spicuously with, for instance, the emphasis on the subject of
explanation which has prevailed for some time within the philosophy of history, Collingwood's views having played a role
in this connection as well. I would maintain that the views
expounded by Collingwood in the lectures of 1926 and 1928 are
not without interest for current debates. This is certainly the
case with regard to the now much debated topic of the narrative aspect of history, but the lectures are also relevant, for
instance, to the much less debated subject of the interpretation
of evidence.

What will probably impress the reader most is the degree to
which the lectures demonstrate the broad experience of their
author in the practice of both archaeology and history and the
way this gives substance and authenticity to philosophical
arguments. The lectures are furthermore written in an elegant
style and offer a concise argumentation, notwithstanding the
fact that aspects of them will doubtless become the subject of
debate. That the lectures of 1926 were written in five days and
the ones of 1928 during a vacation spent in France is of course
amazing and illustrates the unprecedented energy with which
Collingwood at the height of his powers could throw himself
into his work.

The lectures of 1926 are preceded by a 'Preliminary Discussion', which was added by Collingwood in 1927 as a new introduction when he repeated his lectures on the philosophy of
history of the preceding year. The 'Preliminary Discussion'
was written during a trip to Italy in April 1927, while staying
in the house of de Ruggiero at Rome. It was given the subtitle
'The Idea of a Philosophy of Something, and, in particular, a

Philosophy of History'. Collingwood later added a remark at Die saying: 'Written in Rome, by fits and starts, April 1927. I haven't read it since, but from my recollection of the frame or frames of mind in which it was composed I suspect it of being chaotic and practically valueless.' It does, however, have a value for us in giving an insight into what Collingwood was thinking about the philosophy of history at the time. It is interesting more specifically because of the clarification it provides of his conception of the relation, on the one hand between philosophy of history and philosophy in general and on the other between philosophy of history and the study of history itself. It is also valuable as an 'interim report' on his position with regard to this subject after writing *Speculum Mentis* and before he wrote the later essay 'The Philosophy of History' and *An Essay on Philosophical Method*.

The 'Preliminary Discussion' has a strong Kantian flavour. Philosophy should deal, Collingwood argues, with the universal and necessary, that is, with transcendental concepts. Like concepts such as thought, action, art, and science, Collingwood considers history in its philosophical sense as a transcendental concept. This sense should be distinguished, Collingwood maintains, from our empirical concept of it, the concept of history as practised by historians. The empirical concept of history, however, has its own transcendentals, to be understood as the universal and necessary characteristics of the study of history.

Collingwood's career as a philosopher, archaeologist, and historian admirably expresses his lifelong conviction that the study of history is of the first importance, both individually for the human mind and collectively for the process of history. Because of this he stressed equally the need to have an adequate understanding of the nature of history and of the principles of its study. This required a close examination of history's universal and necessary aspects. It is these that are explored in a unique way in the lectures of 1926 and 1928, which are therefore a most valuable complement to Collingwood's philosophy of history as we have come to know it from *The Idea of History*.

SELECT BIBLIOGRAPHY ON
COLLINGWOOD'S PHILOSOPHY

BOUCHER, D. (ed.), *R. G. Collingwood: Essays in Political Philosophy* (Oxford, 1989).

—— *The Social and Political Thought of R. G. Collingwood* (Cambridge, 1989).

DEBBINS, W. (ed.), *R. G. Collingwood: Essays in the Philosophy of History* (Austin, Tex., 1965) (an edition of Collingwood's articles on philosophy of history from 1921 to 1930).

DONAGAN, A., *The Later Philosophy of R. G. Collingwood* (Oxford, 1962; repr. Chicago, 1985).

JOHNSTON, W. M., *The Formative Years of R. G. Collingwood* (The Hague, 1967).

KRAUSZ, M. (ed.), *Critical Essays on the Philosophy of R. G. Collingwood* (Oxford, 1972).

MINK, L. O., *Mind, History, and Dialectic: The Philosophy of R. G. Collingwood* (Bloomington, Ind., 1969; repr. Middletown, Conn., 1987).

PATRICK, J., *The Magdalen Metaphysicals: Idealism and Orthodoxy at Oxford, 1901–1945* (Macon, Ga., 1985).

RUBINOFF, L., *Collingwood and the Reform of Metaphysics: A Study in the Philosophy of Mind* (Toronto, 1970).

RUSSELL, A. F., *Logic, Philosophy and History: A Study in the Philosophy of History Based on the Work of R. G. Collingwood* (Lanham, Md., 1984).

SAARI, H., *Re-enactment: A Study in R. G. Collingwood's Philosophy of History* (Åbo, 1984).

SHALOM, A., *R. G. Collingwood, philosophe et historien* (Paris, 1967).

SKAGESTAD, P., *Making Sense of History: The Philosophies of Popper and Collingwood* (Oslo, 1975).

TAYLOR, D. S., *R. G. Collingwood: A Bibliography. The Complete Manuscripts and Publications, Selected Secondary Writings, with Selective Annotation* (New York, 1988).

VAN DER DUSSEN, W. J., *History as a Science: The Philosophy of R. G. Collingwood* (The Hague, 1981).

THE
IDEA OF HISTORY

CONTENTS

[Introduction and Parts I–IV are from 1936/1940.]

Part V. EPILEGOMENA

INTRODUCTION

§ 1. *The philosophy of history*

THIS book is an essay in the philosophy of history. The name 'philosophy of history' was invented in the eighteenth century by Voltaire, who meant by it no more than critical or scientific history, a type of historical thinking in which the historian made up his mind for himself instead of repeating whatever stories he found in old books. The same name was used by Hegel and other writers at the end of the eighteenth century; but they gave it a different sense and regarded it as meaning simply universal or world history. A third use of the phrase is found in several nineteenth-century positivists for whom the philosophy of history was the discovery of general laws governing the course of the events which it was history's business to recount.

The tasks imposed on the 'philosophy' of history by Voltaire and Hegel could be discharged only by history itself, while the positivists were attempting to make out of history, not a philosophy, but an empirical science, like meteorology. In each of these instances, it was a conception of philosophy which governed the conception of the philosophy of history: for Voltaire, philosophy meant independent and critical thinking; for Hegel, it meant thinking about the world as a whole; for nineteenth-century positivism, it meant the discovery of uniform laws.

My use of the term 'philosophy of history' differs from all of these, and in order to explain what I understand by it I will first say something of my conception of philosophy.

Philosophy is reflective. The philosophizing mind never simply thinks about an object, it always, while thinking about any object, thinks also about its own thought about that object. Philosophy may thus be called thought of the second degree, thought about thought. For example, to discover the distance of the earth from the sun is a task for thought of the first degree, in this case for astronomy; to discover what it is exactly that we are doing when we discover the distance of the earth from the sun is a task for thought of the second degree, in this instance for logic or the theory of science.

This is not to say that philosophy is the science of mind, or psychology. Psychology is thought of the first degree; it treats mind in just the same way in which biology treats life. It does not deal with the relation between thought and its object, it deals directly with thought as something quite separate from its object, something that simply happens in the world, as a special kind of phenomenon, one that can be discussed by itself. Philosophy is never concerned with thought by itself; it is always concerned with its relation to its object, and is therefore concerned with the object just as much as with the thought.

This distinction between philosophy and psychology may be illustrated in the different attitudes adopted by these disciplines to historical thinking, which is a special kind of thinking concerned with a special kind of object, which we will provisionally define as the past. The psychologist may interest himself in historical thinking; he may analyse the peculiar kinds of mental event that go on in historians; he might for example argue that historians are people who build up a fantasy-world, like artists, because they are too neurotic to live effectively in the actual world, but, unlike artists, project this fantasy-world into the past because they connect the origin of their neuroses with past events in their own childhood and always go back and back to the past in a vain attempt to disentangle these neuroses. This analysis might go into further detail, and show how the historian's interest in a commanding figure such as Julius Caesar expresses his childish attitude to his father, and so on. I do not suggest that such analysis is a waste of time. I only describe a typical case of it in order to point out that it concentrates its attention exclusively on the subjective term in the original subject-object relation. It attends to the historian's thought, not to its object the past. The whole psychological analysis of historical thought would be exactly the same if there were no such thing as the past at all, if Julius Caesar were an imaginary character, and if history were not knowledge but pure fancy.

For the philosopher, the fact demanding attention is neither the past by itself, as it is for the historian, nor the historian's thought about it by itself, as it is for the psychologist, but the two things in their mutual relation. Thought in its relation to its object is not mere thought but knowledge; thus, what is for psychology the theory of mere thought, of mental events in abstraction from any object, is for philosophy the theory of knowledge. Where the psychologist asks himself: How do historians think? the philosopher asks himself: How do historians know? How do they come to apprehend the past? Conversely, it is the historian's business, not the philosopher's, to apprehend the past as a thing in itself, to say for example that so many years ago such-and-such events actually happened. The philosopher is concerned with these events not as things in themselves but as things known to the historian, and to ask, not what kind of events they were and when and where they took place, but what it is about them that makes it possible for historians to know them.

Thus the philosopher has to think about the historian's mind, but in doing so he is not duplicating the work of the psychologist, for to him the historian's thought is not a complex of mental phenomena but a system of knowledge. He also thinks about the past, but not in such a way as to duplicate the work of the historian: for the past, to him, is not a series of events but a system of things known. One might put this by saying that the philosopher, in so far as he thinks about the subjective side of history, is an epistemologist, and so far as he thinks about the objective side a metaphysician; but that way of putting it would be dangerous as conveying a suggestion that the epistemological and metaphysical parts of his work can be treated separately, and this would be a mistake. Philosophy cannot separate the study of knowing from the study of what is known. This impossibility follows directly from the idea of philosophy as thought of the second degree.

If this is the general character of philosophical thinking, what do I mean when I qualify the term 'philosophy' by adding, 'of history'? In what sense is there a special philosophy of history different from philosophy in general and from the philosophy of anything else?

It is generally, though somewhat precariously, agreed that there are distinctions within the body of philosophy. Most people distinguish logic or the theory of knowledge from ethics or the theory of action; although most of those who make the distinction would also agree that knowing is in some sense a kind of action, and that action as it is studied by ethics is (or at least involves) certain kinds of knowing. The thought which the logician studies is a thought which aims at the discovery of truth, and is thus an example of activity directed towards an end, and these are ethical conceptions. The action which the moral philosopher studies is an action based on knowledge or belief as to what is right or wrong, and knowledge or belief is an epistemological conception. Thus logic and ethics are connected and indeed inseparable, although they are distinct. If there is a philosophy of history, it will be no less intimately connected with the other special philosophical sciences than these two are connected with each other.

We have then to ask why the philosophy of history should be a subject of special study, instead of being merged in a general theory of knowledge. Throughout the course of European civilization people have in some degree thought historically; but we seldom reflect on the activities which we perform quite easily. It is only the difficulties which we encounter that force upon us a consciousness of our own efforts to overcome them. Thus the subject-matter of philosophy, as the organized and scientific development of self-consciousness, depends from time to time on the special problems in which, at any given time, men find special difficulties. To look at the topics specially prominent in the philosophy of any given people at any given period of their history is to find an indication of the special problems which they feel to be calling forth the whole energies of their minds. The peripheral or subsidiary topics will reveal the things about which they feel no special difficulty.

Now, our philosophical tradition goes back in a continuous line to sixth-century Greece, and at that time the special problem of thought was the task of laying the foundations of mathematics. Greek philosophy therefore placed mathematics in the centre of its picture, and when it discussed the theory of knowledge it understood by it first and foremost the theory of mathematical knowledge.

Since then there have been, down to a century ago, two great constructive ages of European history. In the Middle Ages the central problems of thought were concerned with theology, and the problems of philosophy therefore arose out of reflection on theology and were concerned with the relations of God and man. From the sixteenth to the nineteenth centuries the main effort of thought was concerned with laying the foundations of natural science, and philosophy took as its main theme the relation of the human mind as subject to the natural world of things around it in space as object. All this time, of course, people were also thinking historically, but their historical thought was always of a comparatively simple or even rudimentary kind; it raised no problems which it did not find easy to solve, and was never forced to reflect upon itself. But in the eighteenth century people began thinking critically about history, as they had already learnt to think critically about the external world, because history began to be regarded as a special form of thought, not quite like mathematics or theology or science.

The result of this reflection was that a theory of knowledge proceeding on the assumption that mathematics or theology or science, or all three together, could exhaust the problems of knowledge in general, was no longer satisfactory. Historical thought has an object with peculiarities of its own. The past, consisting of particular events in space and time which are no longer happening, cannot be apprehended by mathematical thinking, because mathematical thinking apprehends objects that have no special location in space and time, and it is just that lack of peculiar spatio-temporal location that makes them knowable. Nor can the past be apprehended by theological thinking, because the object of that kind of thinking is a single infinite object, and historical events are finite and plural. Nor by scientific thinking, because the truths which science discovers are known to be true by being found through observation and experiment exemplified in what we actually perceive, whereas the past has vanished and our ideas about it can never be verified as we verify our scientific hypotheses. Theories of knowledge designed to account for mathematical and theological and scientific knowledge thus do not touch on the special problems of historical knowledge; and if they offer themselves as complete accounts of knowledge they actually imply that historical knowledge is impossible.

This did not matter so long as historical knowledge had not yet obtruded itself on the consciousness of philosophers by encountering special difficulties and devising a special technique to meet them. But when that happened, as it did, roughly speaking, in the nineteenth century, the situation was that current theories of knowledge were directed towards the special problems of science, and inherited a tradition based on the study of mathematics and theology, whereas this new historical technique, growing up on all sides, was unaccounted for. A special inquiry was therefore needed whose task should be the study of this new problem or group of problems, the philosophical problems created by the existence of organized and systomatized historical research. This new inquiry might justly claim the title philosophy of history, and it is to this inquiry that this book is a contribution.

Two stages are to be expected as the inquiry proceeds. First, the philosophy of history will have to be worked out, not, indeed, in a watertight compartment, for there are none in philosophy, but in a relatively isolated condition, regarded as a special study of a special problem. The problem requires special treatment just because the traditional philosophies do not deal with it, and it requires to be isolated because it is a general rule that what a philosophy does not assert it denies, so that the traditional philosophies carry with them the implication that historical knowledge is impossible. The philosophy of history has therefore to leave them alone until it can build up an independent demonstration of how history is possible.

The second stage will be to work out the connexions between this new branch of philosophy and the old traditional doctrines. Any addition to the body of philosophical ideas alters to some extent everything that was there already, and the establishment of a new philosophical science necessitates a revision of all the old ones. For example, the establishment of modern natural science, and of the philosophical theory produced by reflection upon it, reacted upon the established logic by producing widespread discontent with the syllogistic logic and substituting for it the new methodologies of Descartes and Bacon; the same thing reacted upon the theological metaphysics which the seventeenth century had inherited from the Middle Ages and produced the new conceptions of God which we find for example in Descartes and Spinoza. Spinoza's God is the God of medieval theology as revised in the light of seventeenth-century science. Thus, by the time of Spinoza, the philosophy of science was no longer a particular branch of philosophical investigation separate from the rest: it had permeated all the rest and produced a complete philosophy all conceived in a scientific spirit. In the present case this will mean a general overhauling of all philosophical questions in the light of the results reached by the philosophy of history in the narrower sense, and this will produce a new philosophy which will be a philosophy of history in the wide sense, i.e., a complete philosophy conceived from an historical point of view.

Of these two stages, we must be content if this book represents the first. What I am attempting here is a philosophical inquiry into the nature of history regarded as a special type or form of knowledge with a special type of object, leaving aside, for the present, the further question how that inquiry will affect other departments of philosophical study.

§ 2. *History's nature, object, method, and value*

What history is, what it is about, how it proceeds, and what it is for, are questions which to some extent different people would answer in different ways. But in spite of differences there is a large measure of agreement between the answers. And this agreement becomes closer if the answers are subjected to scrutiny with a view to discarding those which proceed from unqualified witnesses. History, like theology or natural science, is a special form of thought. If that is so, questions about the nature, object, method, and value of this form of thought must be answered by persons having two qualifications.

First, they must have experience of that form of thought. They must be historians. In a sense we are all historians nowadays. All educated persons have gone through a process of education which has included a certain amount of historical thinking. But this does not qualify them to give an opinion about the nature, object, method, and value of historical thinking. For in the first place, the experience of historical thinking which they have thus acquired is probably very superficial; and the opinions based on it are therefore no better grounded than a man's opinion of the French people based on a single week-end visit to Paris. In the second place, experience of anything whatever gained through the ordinary educational channels, as well as being superficial, is invariably out of date. Experience of historical thinking, so gained, is modelled on text-books, and text-books always describe not what is now being thought by real live historians, but what was thought by real live historians at some time in the past when the raw material was being created out of which the text-book has been put together. And it is not only the results of historical thought which are out of date by the time they get into the text-book. It is also the principles of historical thought: that is, the ideas as to the nature, object, method, and value of historical thinking. In the third place, and connected with this, there is a peculiar illusion incidental to all knowledge acquired in the way of education: the illusion of finality. When a student is *in statu pupillari* with respect to any subject whatever, he has to believe that things are settled because the text-books and his teachers regard them as settled. When he emerges from that state and goes on studying the subject for himself he finds that nothing is settled. The dogmatism which is an invariable mark of immaturity drops away from him. He looks at so-called facts with a new eye. He says to himself: 'My teacher and text-books told me that such and such was true; but is it true? What reasons had they for thinking it true, and were these reasons adequate?' On the other hand, if he emerges from the status of pupil without continuing to pursue the subject he never rids himself of this dogmatic attitude. And this makes him a person peculiarly unfitted to answer the questions I have mentioned. No one, for example, is likely to answer them worse than an Oxford philosopher who, having read Greats in his youth, was once a student of history and thinks that this youthful experience of historical thinking entitles him to say what history is, what it is about, how it proceeds, and what it is for.

The second qualification for answering these questions is that a man should not only have experience of historical thinking but should also have reflected upon that experience. He must be not only an historian but a philosopher; and in particular his philosophical thought must have included special attention to the problems of historical thought. Now it is possible to be a quite good historian (though not an historian of the highest order) without thus reflecting upon one's own historical thinking. It is even easier to be a quite good teacher of history (though not the very best kind of teacher) without such reflection. At the same time, it is important to remember that experience comes first, and reflection on that experience second. Even the least reflective historian has the first qualification. He possesses the experience on which to reflect; and when he is asked to reflect on it his reflections have a good chance of being to the point. An historian who has never worked much at philosophy will probably answer our four questions in a more intelligent and valuable way than a philosopher who has never worked much at history.

I shall therefore propound answers to my four questions such as I think any present-day historian would accept. Here they will be rough and ready answers, but they will serve for a provisional definition of our subject-matter and they will be defended and elaborated as the argument proceeds.

(a) *The definition of history.* Every historian would agree, I think, that history is a kind of research or inquiry. What kind of inquiry it is I do not yet ask. The point is that generically it belongs to what we call the sciences: that is, the forms of thought whereby we ask questions and try to answer them. Science in general, it is important to realize, does not consist in collecting what we already know and arranging it in this or that kind of pattern. It consists in fastening upon something we do not know, and trying to discover it. Playing patience with things we already know may be a useful means towards this end, but it is not the end itself. It is at best only the means. It is scientifically valuable only in so far as the new arrangement gives us the answer to a question we have already decided to ask. That is why all science begins from the knowledge of our own ignorance: not our ignorance of everything, but our ignorance of some definite thing—the origin of parliament, the cause of cancer, the chemical composition of the sun, the way to make a pump work without muscular exertion on the part of a man or a horse or some other docile animal. Science is finding things out: and in that sense history is a science.

(b) *The object of history.* One science differs from another in that it finds out things of a different kind. What kind of things does history find out? I answer, *res gestae*: actions of human beings that have been done in the past. Although this answer raises all kinds of further questions many of which are controversial, still, however they may be answered, the answers do not discredit the proposition that history is the science of *res gestae*, the attempt to answer questions about human actions done in the past.

(c) *How does history proceed?* History proceeds by the interpretation of evidence: where evidence is a collective name for things which singly are called documents, and a document is a thing existing here and now, of such a kind that the historian, by thinking about it, can get answers to the questions he asks about past events. Here again there are plenty of difficult questions to ask as to what the characteristics of evidence are and how it is interpreted. But there is no need for us to raise them at this stage. However they are answered, historians will agree that historical procedure, or method, consists essentially of interpreting evidence.

(d) Lastly, *what is history for?* This is perhaps a harder question than the others; a man who answers it will have to reflect rather more widely than a man who answers the three we have answered already. He must reflect not only on historical thinking but on other things as well, because to say that something is 'for' something implies a distinction between A and B, where A is good for something and B is that for which something is good. But I will suggest an answer, and express the opinion that no historian would reject it, although the further questions to which it gives rise are numerous and difficult.

My answer is that history is 'for' human self-knowledge. It is generally thought to be of importance to man that he should know himself: where knowing himself means knowing not his merely personal peculiarities, the things that distinguish him from other men, but his nature as man. Knowing yourself means knowing, first, what it is to be a man; secondly, knowing what it is to be the kind of man you are; and thirdly, knowing what it is to be the man *you* are and nobody else is. Knowing yourself means knowing what you can do; and since nobody knows what he can do until he tries, the only clue to what man can do is what man has done. The value of history, then, is that it teaches us what man has done and thus what man is.

§ 3. *The problem of Parts I–IV*

The idea of history which I have just briefly summarized belongs to modern times, and before I proceed in Part V to expound and elaborate this idea in more detail I propose to cast light upon it by investigating its history. Historians nowadays think that history should be (a) a science, or an answering of questions; (b) concerned with human actions in the past;

(*c*) pursued by interpretation of evidence; and (*d*) for the sake of human self-knowledge. But this is not the way in which people have always thought of history. For example, a recent author[1] writes of the Sumerians in the third millennium before Christ:

'Historiography is represented by official inscriptions commemorating the building of palaces and of temples. The theocratic style of the scribes attributes everything to the action of the divinity, as can be seen from the following passage, one of many examples.

'"A dispute arises between the kings of Lagash and of Umma about the boundaries of their respective territories. The dispute is submitted to the arbitration of Mesilim, king of Kish, and is settled by the gods, of whom the kings of Kish, Lagash, and Umma are merely the agents or ministers:

'"Upon the truthful word of the god Enlil, king of the territories, the god Ningirsu and the god Shara deliberated. Mesilim, king of Kish, at the behest of his god, Gu-Silim, . . . erected in [this] place a stela. Ush, *isag* of Umma, acted in accordance with his ambitious designs. He removed Mesilim's stela and came to the plain of Lagash. At the righteous word of the god Ningirsu, warrior of the god Enlil, a combat with Umma took place. At the word of the god Enlil, the great divine net laid low the enemies, and funerary *tells* were placed in their stead in the plain."'

Monsieur Jean, it will be noticed, says not that Sumerian historiography *was* this kind of thing, but that in Sumerian literature historiography *is represented by* this kind of thing. I take him to mean that this kind of thing is not really history, but is something in certain ways resembling history. My comment on this would be as follows. An inscription like this expresses a form of thought which no modern historian would call history, because, in the first place, it lacks the character of science: it is not an attempt to answer a question of whose answer the writer begins by being ignorant; it is merely a record of something the writer knows for a fact; and in the second place the fact recorded is not certain actions on the part of human beings, it is certain actions on the part of gods. No doubt these divine actions resulted in actions done by human beings; but they are conceived in the first instance not as

---

[1] Monsieur Charles F. Jean, in Edward Eyre, *European Civilization* (London, 1935), vol. i, p. 259.

human actions but as divine actions; and to that extent the thought expressed is not historical in respect of its object, and consequently is not historical in respect of its method, for there is no interpretation of evidence, nor in respect of its value, for there is no suggestion that its aim is to further human self-knowledge. The knowledge furthered by such a record is not, or at any rate is not primarily, man's knowledge of man, but man's knowledge of the gods.

From the writer's point of view, therefore, this is not what we call an historical text. The writer was not writing history, he was writing religion. From our point of view it can be used as historical evidence, since a modern historian with his eye fixed on human *res gestae* can interpret it as evidence concerning actions done by Mesilim and Ush and their subjects. But it only acquires its character as historical evidence posthumously, as it were, in virtue of our own historical attitude towards it; in the same way in which prehistoric flints or Roman pottery acquire the posthumous character of historical evidence, not because the men who made them thought of them as historical evidence, but because *we* think of them as historical evidence.

The ancient Sumerians left behind them nothing at all that we should call history. If they had any such thing as an historical consciousness, they have left no record of it. We may say that they must have had such a thing; to us, the historical consciousness is so real and so all-pervasive a feature of life that we cannot see how anyone can have lacked it; but whether we are right so to argue is very doubtful. If we stick to facts as revealed to us by the documents, I think we must say that the historical consciousness of the ancient Sumerians is what scientists call an occult entity, something which the rules of scientific method forbid us to assert on the principle of Occam's Razor that *entia non sunt multiplicanda praeter necessitatem*.

Four thousand years ago, then, our forerunners in civilization did not possess what we call the idea of history. This, so far as we can see, was not because they had the thing itself but had not reflected upon it. It was because they did not possess the thing itself. History did not exist. There existed, instead, something which in certain ways resembled what we call history, but this differed from what we call history in respect of every one of the four characteristics which we have identified in history as it exists to-day.

History as it exists to-day, therefore, has come into existence in the last four thousand years in western Asia and Europe. How did this happen? By what stages has the thing called history come into existence? That is the question to which a somewhat bald and summary answer is offered in Parts I–IV.

PART I

GRECO-ROMAN HISTORIOGRAPHY

§ 1. *Theocratic history and myth*

By what steps and stages did the modern European idea of history come into existence? Since I do not think that any of these stages occurred outside the Mediterranean region, that is, Europe, the Near East from the Mediterranean to Mesopotamia, and the northern African coastlands, I am precluded from saying anything about historical thought in China or in any other part of the world except the region I have mentioned.

I have quoted one example of early Mesopotamian history from a document of about 2500 B.C. I say history, but I ought rather to say quasi-history, because, as I have pointed out, the thought expressed in this document resembles what we call history in making statements about the past, but differs from it, first, in that these statements are not answers to questions, not the fruits of research, but mere assertions of what the writer already knows; and secondly, that the deeds recorded are not human actions but, in the first instance at any rate, divine actions. The gods are conceived on the analogy of human sovereigns, directing the actions of kings and chiefs as these direct the actions of their human subordinates; the hierarchical system of government is carried upwards by a kind of extrapolation. Instead of the series: subject, lower official, higher official, king, we have the series: subject, lower official, higher official, king, god. Whether the king and the god are sharply distinguished so that the god is conceived as the real head of the community and the king as his servant, or whether the king and the god are somehow identified, the king being conceived as an incarnation of the god or at any rate as in some way or other divine, not merely human, is a question into which we need not enter, because, however we answer it, the result will be that government is conceived theocratically.

History of this kind I propose to call *theocratic history*; in which phrase 'history' means not history proper, that is scientific history, but a statement of known facts for the information of persons to whom they are not known, but who, as worshippers of the god in question, ought to know the deeds whereby he has made himself manifest.

There is another kind of quasi-history, of which we also find examples in Mesopotamian literature, namely the *myth*. Theocratic history, although it is not primarily the history of human actions, is nevertheless concerned with them in the sense that the divine characters in the story are the superhuman rulers of human societies, whose actions, therefore, are actions done partly to those societies and partly through them. In theocratic history humanity is not an agent, but partly an instrument and partly a patient, of the actions recorded. Moreover, these actions are thought of as having definite places in a time-series, as occurring at dates in the past. Myth, on the contrary, is not concerned with human actions at all. The human element has been completely purged away and the characters of the story are simply gods. And the divine actions that are recorded are not dated events in the past: they are conceived as having occurred in the past, indeed, but in a dateless past which is so remote that nobody knows when it was. It is outside all our time-reckonings and called 'the beginning of things'. Hence, when a myth is couched in what seems a temporal shape, because it relates events one of which follows another in a definite order, the shape is not strictly speaking temporal, it is quasi-temporal: the narrator is using the language of time-succession as a metaphor in which to express relations which he does not conceive as really temporal. The subject-matter which is thus mythically expressed in the language of temporal succession is, in myth proper, the relations between various gods or various elements of the divine nature. Hence myth proper has always the character of *theogony*.

For an example, let us consider the main outline of the Babylonian *Poem on the Creation*. We have it in a text of the seventh century B.C., but this professes to be, and doubtless is, a copy of very much older texts, probably going back to the same period as the document I have already quoted:

'The poem begins at the origin of all things. Nothing exists as yet, not even the gods. Out of this nothingness appear the cosmic principles *Apsu*, fresh water, and *Tiamat*, salt water.' The first step in the theogony is the birth of *Mummu*, the first-born son of Apsu and Tiamat. 'The gods increase and multiply.

Then they become rebellious against [this original] divine triad.
Apsu decides to destroy them. . . . But the wise *Ea* triumphs by
the use of magic. He casts a powerful spell upon the waters,
Apsu's element, puts his ancestor to sleep', and makes Mummu
captive. Tiamat now 'plans to avenge the conquered. She
marries Qingu, makes him head of her army, and confides to his
care the tablets of fate.' Ea, divining her plans, reveals them to
the ancient god Anshar. At first Tiamat triumphs over this
coalition, but now arises Marduk, who challenges Tiamat to
single combat, kills her, cuts her body in two 'like a fish', and
makes out of one half the heavens, in which he places the stars,
and out of the other the earth. Out of Marduk's blood, man is
made.[1]

These two forms of quasi-history, theocratic history and myth,
dominated the whole of the Near East until the rise of Greece.
For example, the Moabite Stone (ninth century B.C.) is a perfect
document of theocratic history, showing that little change has
taken place in that form of thought for between one and two
millennia:

'I am Mesha, the son of Kemosh, king of Moab. My father was
king over Moab thirty years and I became king after my father.
And I made this high-place for Kemosh, for he saved me from my
downfall and made me triumph over my enemies.

'Omri, king of Israel, was the oppressor of Moab for many long
days because Kemosh was angered against his country. His son succeeded him, and he also said "I will oppress Moab". It was in my
day that he said it. And I triumphed over him and his house. And
Israel perished for ever.

'And Omri took possession of the land of Mehedeba and lived there
during his life and half his sons' lives, forty years; but Kemosh
restored it to us in my lifetime.'

Or again, here is a quotation from the account, put into the
mouth of Esar-Haddon, king of Nineveh early in the seventh
century B.C., of his campaign against the enemies who had killed
his father Sennacherib:

'The fear of the great gods, my lords, overthrew them. When
they beheld the rush of my terrible battle, they were beside themselves. The goddess Ishtar, goddess of battle and of fighting, she

---

[1] Jean, in Eyre, op. cit., pp. 271 ff.

who loves my priesthood, remained at my side and broke their line. She broke their battle-line, and in their assembly they said "It is our king!" "[1]

The Hebrew scriptures contain a great deal of both theocratic history and myth. From the point of view from which I am now considering these ancient literatures, the quasi-historical elements in the Old Testament do not greatly differ from the corresponding elements in Mesopotamian and Egyptian literature. The main difference is that whereas the theocratic element in these other literatures is on the whole particularistic, in the Hebrew scriptures it tends to be universalistic. I mean, the gods whose deeds are recorded in these other literatures are on the whole regarded as the divine heads of particular societies. The God of the Hebrews is certainly regarded as in a special sense the divine head of the Hebrew community; but under the influence of the 'prophetic' movement, that is, from about the middle of the eighth century onwards, they came to conceive Him more and more as the divine head of all mankind; and therefore expected Him no longer to protect their interests as against those of other particular societies, but to deal with them according to their deserts; and to deal with other particular societies in the same way. And this tendency away from particularism in the direction of universalism affects not only the theocratic history of the Hebrews but also their mythology. Unlike the Babylonian creation-legend, the Hebrew creation-legend contains an attempt, not indeed a very well-thought-out attempt (for every child, I suppose, has asked its elders the unanswerable question, 'Who was Cain's wife?'), but still an attempt, to account not only for the origin of man in general but for the origin of the various peoples into which mankind, as known to the authors of the legend, was divided. Indeed one might almost say that the peculiarity of the Hebrew legend as compared with the Babylonian is that it replaces theogony by ethnogony.

§ 2. *The creation of scientific history by Herodotus*

As compared with all this, the work of the Greek historians as we possess it in detail in the fifth-century historians, Herodotus and Thucydides, takes us into a new world. The Greeks quite

[1] Ibid., p. 364.

clearly and consciously recognized both that history is, or can be, a science, and that it has to do with human actions. Greek history is not legend, it is research; it is an attempt to get answers to definite questions about matters of which one recognizes oneself as ignorant. It is not theocratic, it is humanistic; the matters inquired into are not τὰ θεῖα, they are τὰ ἀνθρώπινα. Moreover, it is not mythical. The events inquired into are not events in a dateless past, at the beginning of things: they are events in a dated past, a certain number of years ago.

This is not to say that legend, either in the form of theocratic history or in the form of myth, was a thing foreign to the Greek mind. The work of Homer is not research, it is legend; and to a great extent it is theocratic legend. The gods appear in Homer as intervening in human affairs in a way not very different from the way in which they appear in the theocratic histories of the Near East. Similarly, Hesiod has given us an example of myth. Nor is it to say that these legendary elements, theocratic or mythical as the case may be, are entirely absent even from the classical works of the fifth-century historians. F. M. Cornford in his *Thucydides Mythistoricus* (London, 1907) drew attention to the existence of such elements even in the hard-headed and scientific Thucydides. He was of course perfectly right; and similar legendary elements are notoriously frequent in Herodotus. But what is remarkable about the Greeks was not the fact that their historical thought contained a certain residue of elements which we should call non-historical, but the fact that, side by side with these, it contained elements of what we call history.

The four characteristics of history which I enumerated in the Introduction were (a) that it is scientific, or begins by asking questions, whereas the writer of legends begins by knowing something and tells what he knows; (b) that it is humanistic, or asks questions about things done by men at determinate times in the past; (c) that it is rational, or bases the answers which it gives to its questions on grounds, namely appeal to evidence; (d) that it is self-revelatory, or exists in order to tell man what man is by telling him what man has done. Now the first, second, and fourth of these characteristics clearly appear in Herodotus: (i) The fact that history as a science was a Greek invention is recorded to this day by its very name. History is a Greek word, meaning simply an investigation or inquiry. Herodotus, who uses it in the title of his work, thereby 'marks a literary revolution' (as Croiset, an historian of Greek literature, says[1]). Previous writers had been λογογράφοι, writers-down of current stories: 'the historian', say How and Wells, 'sets out to "find" the truth.' It is the use of this word, and its implications, that make Herodotus the father of history. The conversion of legend-writing into the science of history was not native to the Greek mind, it was a fifth-century invention, and Herodotus was the man who invented it. (ii) It is equally clear that history for Herodotus is humanistic as distinct from either mythical or theocratic. As he says in his preface, his purpose is to describe the deeds of men. (iii) His end, as he describes it himself, is that these deeds shall not be forgotten by posterity. Here we have my fourth characteristic of history, namely that it ministers to man's knowledge of man. In particular, Herodotus points out, it reveals man as a rational agent: that is, its function is partly to discover what men have done and partly to discover why they have done it (δι᾽ ἣν αἰτίην ἐπολέμησαν). Herodotus does not confine his attention to bare events; he considers these events in a thoroughly humanistic manner as actions of human beings who had reasons for acting as they did: and the historian is concerned with these reasons.

These three points reappear in the preface of Thucydides, which was obviously written with an eye on that of Herodotus. Thucydides, writing Attic and not Ionic, does not of course use the word ἱστορίη, but he refers to it in other terms: to make it clear that he is no logographer but a scientific student, asking questions instead of repeating legends, he defends his choice of subject by saying that events earlier than those of the Peloponnesian War cannot be accurately ascertained—σαφῶς μὲν εὑρεῖν ἀδύνατα ἦν. He emphasizes the humanistic purpose and the self-revelatory function of history, in words modelled on those of his predecessor. And in one way he improves on Herodotus, for Herodotus makes no mention of evidence (the third of the characteristics mentioned above), and one is left to gather from the body of his work what his idea of evidence was; but Thucydides does say explicitly that historical inquiry rests on

---

[1] *Histoire de la littérature grecque*, vol. ii, p. 589, *apud* How and Wells, *Commentary on Herodotus* (Oxford, 1912), vol. i, p. 53.

evidence, ἐκ τεκμηρίων σκοποῦντί μοι, 'when I consider in the light of the evidence'. What they thought about the nature of evidence, and the way in which an historian interprets it, is a subject to which I shall return in § 5.

§ 3. *Anti-historical tendency of Greek thought*

In the meantime, I should like to point out how remarkable a thing is this creation of scientific history by Herodotus, for he was an ancient Greek, and ancient Greek thought as a whole has a very definite prevailing tendency not only uncongenial to the growth of historical thought but actually based, one might say, on a rigorously anti-historical metaphysics. History is a science of human action: what the historian puts before himself is things that men have done in the past, and these belong to a world of change, a world where things come to be and cease to be. Such things, according to the prevalent Greek metaphysical view, ought not to be knowable, and therefore history ought to be impossible.

For the Greeks, the same difficulty arose with the world of nature since it too was a world of this kind. If everything in the world changes, they asked, what is there in such a world for the mind to grasp? They were quite sure that anything which can be an object of genuine knowledge must be permanent; for it must have some definite character of its own, and therefore cannot contain in itself the seeds of its own destruction. If it is to be knowable it must be determinate; if it is determinate, it must be so completely and exclusively what it is that no internal change and no external force can ever set about making it into something else. Greek thought achieved its first triumph when it discovered in the objects of mathematical knowledge something that satisfied these conditions. A straight bar of iron may be bent into a curve, a flat surface of water may be broken into waves, but the straight line and the plane surface, as the mathematician thinks of them, are eternal objects that cannot change their characteristics.

Following the line of argument thus opened up, Greek thought worked out a distinction between two types of thought, knowledge proper (ἐπιστήμη) and what we translate by 'opinion', δόξα. Opinion is the empirical semi-knowledge we have of matters of fact, which are always changing. It is our fleeting acquaintance with the fleeting actualities of the world; it thus only holds good for its own proper duration, for the here and now; and it is immediate, ungrounded in reasons, incapable of demonstration. True knowledge, on the contrary, holds good not only here and now but everywhere and always, and it is based on demonstrative reasoning and thus capable of meeting and overthrowing error by the weapon of dialectical criticism.

Thus, for the Greeks, process could be known only so far as it was perceived, and the knowledge of it could never be demonstrative. An exaggerated statement of this view, as we get it in the Eleatics, would misuse the weapon of dialectic, which is really valid only against error in the sphere of knowledge strictly so called, to prove that change does not exist and that the 'opinions' we have about the changing are really not even opinions but sheer illusions. Plato rejects that doctrine and sees in the world of change something not indeed intelligible but real to the extent of being perceptible, something intermediate between the nullity with which the Eleatics had identified it and the complete reality and intelligibility of the eternal. On such a theory, history ought to be impossible. For history must have these two characteristics: first it must be about what is transitory, and secondly it must be scientific or demonstrative. But on this theory what is transitory cannot be demonstratively known; it cannot be the object of science; it can only be a matter of αἴσθησις, perception, whereby human sensibility catches the fleeting moment as it flies. And it is essential to the Greek point of view that this momentary sensuous perception of momentary changing things cannot be a science or the basis of a science.

§ 4. *Greek conception of history's nature and value*

The ardour with which the Greeks pursued the ideal of an unchanging and eternal object of knowledge might easily mislead us as to their historical interests. It might, if we read them carelessly, make us think them uninterested in history, somewhat as Plato's attack on the poets might make an unintelligent reader fancy that Plato cared little for poetry. In order to interpret such things correctly we must remember that no competent thinker or writer wastes his time attacking a man of straw. An intense polemic against a certain doctrine is an infallible sign that the doctrine in question figures largely in the writer's environment and even has a strong attraction for himself. The Greek pursuit of the eternal was as eager as it was, precisely because the Greeks themselves had an unusually vivid sense of the temporal. They lived in a time when history was moving with extraordinary rapidity, and in a country where earthquake and erosion change the face of the land with a violence hardly to be seen elsewhere. They saw all nature as a spectacle of incessant change, and human life as changing more violently than anything else. Unlike the Chinese, or the medieval civilization of Europe, whose conception of human society was anchored in the hope of retaining the chief features of its structure unchanged, they made it their first aim to face and reconcile themselves to the fact that such permanence is impossible. This recognition of the necessity of change in human affairs gave to the Greeks a peculiar sensitiveness to history.

Knowing that nothing in life can persist unchanged, they came habitually to ask themselves what exactly the changes had been which, they knew, must have come about in order to bring the present into existence. Their historical consciousness was thus not a consciousness of agelong tradition moulding the life of one generation after another into a uniform pattern; it was a consciousness of violent περιπέτειαι, catastrophic changes from one state of things to its opposite, from smallness to greatness, from pride to abasement, from happiness to misery. This was how they interpreted the general character of human life in their dramas, and this was how they narrated the particular parts of it in their history. The only thing that a shrewd and critical Greek like Herodotus would say about the divine power that ordains the course of history is that it is φθονερὸν καὶ ταραχῶδες: it rejoices in upsetting and disturbing things. He was only repeating (i. 32) what every Greek knew: that the power of Zeus is manifested in the thunderbolt, that of Poseidon in the earthquake, that of Apollo in the pestilence, and that of Aphrodite in the passion that destroyed at once the pride of Phaedra and the chastity of Hippolytus.

It is true that these catastrophic changes in the condition of human life, which to the Greeks were the proper theme of history, were unintelligible. There could be no ἐπιστήμη of them, no demonstrative scientific knowledge. But all the same history had for the Greeks a definite value. Plato himself laid it down[1] that right opinion (which is the sort of pseudo-knowledge that perception gives us of what changes) was no less useful for the conduct of life than scientific knowledge, and the poets maintained their traditional place in Greek life as the teachers of sound principles by showing that in the general pattern of these changes certain antecedents normally led to certain consequents. Notably, an excess in any one direction led to a violent change into its own opposite. Why this was so they could not tell; but they thought it a matter of observation that it was so; that people who became extremely rich or extremely powerful were thereby brought into special danger of being reduced to a condition of extreme poverty or weakness. There is here no theory of causation; the thought does not resemble that of seventeenth-century inductive science with its metaphysical basis in the axiom of cause and effect; the riches of Croesus are not the cause of his downfall, they are merely a symptom, to the intelligent observer, that something is happening in the rhythm of his life which is likely to lead to a downfall. Still less is the downfall a punishment for anything that, in an intelligible moral sense, could be called wrongdoing. When Amasis in Herodotus (iii. 43) broke off his alliance with Polycrates, he did it simply on the ground that Polycrates was too prosperous: the pendulum had swung too far one way and was likely to swing as far in the other. Such examples have their value to the person who can make use of them; for he can use his own will to arrest these rhythms in his life before they reach the danger-point, and check the thirst for power and wealth instead of allowing it to drive him to excess. Thus history has a value; its teachings are useful for human life; simply because the rhythm of its changes is likely to repeat itself, similar antecedents leading to similar consequents; the history of notable events is worth remembering in order to serve as a basis for prognostic judgements, not demonstrable but probable, laying down not what will happen but what is likely to happen, indicating the points of danger in rhythms now going on.

This conception of history was the very opposite of deterministic, because the Greeks regarded the course of history as flexible and open to salutary modification by the well-instructed

[1] *Meno*, 97 a–b.

human will. Nothing that happens is inevitable. The person who is about to be involved in a tragedy is actually over-whelmed by it only because he is too blind to see his danger. If he saw it, he could guard against it. Thus the Greeks had a lively and indeed a naïve sense of the power of man to control his own destiny, and thought of this power as limited only by the limitations of his knowledge. The fate that broods over human life is, from this Greek point of view, a destructive power only because man is blind to its workings. Granted that he cannot understand these workings, he can yet have right opinions about them, and in so far as he acquires such opinions he becomes able to put himself in a position where the blows of fate will miss him.

On the other hand, valuable as the teachings of history are, their value is limited by the unintelligibility of its subject-matter; and that is why Aristotle said[1] that poetry is more scientific than history, for history is a mere collection of empi-rical facts, whereas poetry extracts from such facts a universal judgement. History tells us that Croesus fell and that Polycrates fell; poetry, according to Aristotle's idea of it, makes not these singular judgements but the universal judgement that very rich men, as such, fall. Even this is, in Aristotle's view, only a partially scientific judgement, for no one can see why rich men should fall; the universal cannot be syllogistically demonstrated; but it approaches the status of a true universal because we can use it as the major premiss for a new syllogism applying this generaliza-tion to fresh cases. Thus poetry is for Aristotle the distilled essence of the teaching of history. In poetry the lessons of history do not become any more intelligible and they remain undemonstrated and therefore merely probable, but they be-come more compendious and therefore more useful.

Such was the way in which the Greeks conceived the nature and value of history. They could not, consistently with their general philosophical attitude, regard it as scientific. They had to consider it as, at bottom, not a science but a mere aggregate of perceptions. What, then, was their conception of historical evidence? The answer is that, conformably with this view, they identified historical evidence with the reports of facts given by eyewitnesses of those facts. Evidence consists of

---

[1] *Poetics*, 1451[b]5 ff.

eyewitnesses' narratives, and historical method consists of eliciting these.

§ 5. *Greek historical method and its limitations*

Quite clearly, it was in this way that Herodotus conceived of evidence and method. This does not mean that he uncritically believed whatever eyewitnesses told him. On the contrary, he is in practice highly critical of their narratives. And here again he is typically Greek. The Greeks as a whole were skilled in the practice of the law courts, and a Greek would find no difficulty ✓ in applying to historical testimony the same kind of criticism which he was accustomed to direct upon witnesses in court. The work of Herodotus or Thucydides depends in the main on the testimony of eyewitnesses with whom the historian had personal contact. And his skill as a researcher consisted in the fact that he must have cross-questioned an eyewitness of past events until he had called up in the informant's own mind an historical picture of those events far fuller and more coherent than any he could have volunteered for himself. The result of this process was to create in the informant's mind for the first time a genuine knowledge of the past events which he had perceived but of which up till then he had δόξα only, not ἐπιστήμη.

This conception of the way in which a Greek historian collected his material makes it a very different thing from the way in which a modern historian may use printed memoirs. Instead of the easy-going belief on the informant's part that his prima facie recollection was adequate to the facts, there could grow up in his mind a chastened and criticized recollection which had stood the fire of such questions as 'Are you quite sure that you remember it just like that? Have you not now contradicted what you were saying yesterday? How do you reconcile your account of that event with the very different account given by so-and-so?' This method of using the testimony of eyewitnesses is undoubtedly the method which underlies the extraordinary solidity and consistency of the narratives which Herodotus and Thucydides finally wrote about fifth-century Greece.

No other method deserving the name scientific was available to the fifth-century historians, but it had three limitations:

First, it inevitably imposed on its users a shortness of historical perspective. The modern historian knows that if only he had the capacity he could become the interpreter of the whole past of mankind; but whatever Greek historians might have thought of Plato's description of the philosopher as the spectator of all time, they would never have ventured to claim Plato's words as a description of themselves. Their method tied them on a tether whose length was the length of living memory: the only source they could criticize was an eyewitness with whom they could converse face to face. It is true that they relate events from a remoter past, but as soon as Greek historical writing tries to go beyond its tether, it becomes a far weaker and more precarious thing. For instance, we must not deceive ourselves into thinking that any scientific value attaches to what Herodotus tells us about the sixth century or to what Thucydides tells us about events before the Pentecontaetia. From our twentieth-century point of view, these early stories in Herodotus and Thucydides are very interesting, but they are mere logography and not scientific. They are traditions which the author who hands them down to us has not been able to raise to the level of history because he has not been able to pass them through the crucible of the only critical method he knew. Nevertheless, this contrast in Herodotus and Thucydides between the unreliability of everything farther back than living memory and the critical precision of what comes within living memory is a mark not of the failure of fifth-century historiography but of its success. The point about Herodotus and Thucydides is not that the remote past is for them still outside the scope of scientific history but that the recent past is within that scope. Scientific history has been invented. Its field is still narrow; but within that field it is secure. Moreover, this narrowness of field did not matter much to the Greeks, because the extreme rapidity with which their own civilization was developing and changing afforded plenty of first-class historical material within the confines set by their method, and for the same reason they could produce first-rate historical work without developing what in fact they never did develop, any lively curiosity concerning the remote past.

Secondly, the Greek historian's method precludes him from choosing his subject. He cannot, like Gibbon, begin by wishing to write a great historical work and go on to ask himself what he shall write about. The only thing he can write about is the events which have happened within living memory to people with whom he can have personal contact. Instead of the historian choosing the subject, the subject chooses the historian; I mean that history is written only because memorable things have happened which call for a chronicler among the contemporaries of the people who have seen them. One might almost say that in ancient Greece there were no historians in the sense in which there were artists and philosophers; there were no people who devoted their lives to the study of history; the historian was only the autobiographer of his generation and autobiography is not a profession.

Thirdly, Greek historical method made it impossible for the various particular histories to be gathered up into one all-embracing history. Nowadays we think of monographs on various subjects as ideally forming parts of a universal history, so that if their subjects are carefully chosen and their scale and treatment carefully controlled they might serve as chapters in a single historical work; and this is the way in which a writer like Grote actually treated Herodotus' account of the Persian War and Thucydides' of the Peloponnesian. But if any given history is the autobiography of a generation, it cannot be re-written when that generation has passed away, because the evidence on which it was based will have perished. The work that a contemporary based on that evidence can thus never be improved upon or criticized, and it can never be absorbed into a larger whole, because it is like a work of art, something having the uniqueness and individuality of a statue or a poem. Thucydides' work is a κτῆμα ἐς αἰεί, that of Herodotus was written to rescue glorious deeds from the oblivion of time, precisely because when their generation was dead and gone the work could never be done again. The rewriting of their histories, or their incorporation into the history of a longer period, would have seemed to them an absurdity. To the Greek historians, therefore, there could never be any such thing as a history of Greece. There could be a history of a fairly extensive complex of events, like the Persian War or the Peloponnesian War; but only on two conditions. First, this complex of events must be complete in itself: it must have a beginning, a middle, and an end, like the plot of an Aristotelian tragedy. Secondly, it must be εὐσύνοπτος, like an Aristotelian city-state. As Aristotle thought[1] that no community of civilized men under a single government could exceed in size the number of citizens that could be within earshot of a single herald, the dimensions of the political organism being thus limited by a purely physical fact, so the Greek theory of history implies that no historical narrative could exceed in length the years of a man's lifetime, within which alone the critical methods at its disposal could be applied.

§ 6. *Herodotus and Thucydides*

The greatness of Herodotus stands out in the sharpest relief when, as the father of history, he is set against a background consisting of the general tendencies of Greek thought. The most dominant of these was anti-historical, as I have argued, because it involved the position that only what is unchanging can be known. Therefore history is a forlorn hope, an attempt to know what, being transitory, is unknowable. But we have already seen that, by skilful questioning, Herodotus was able to elicit ἐπιστήμη from his informant's δόξα and thus to attain knowledge in a field where Greeks had thought it impossible.

His success must remind us of one of his contemporaries, a man who was not afraid, either in war or in philosophy, to embark on forlorn hopes. Socrates brought philosophy down from heaven to earth by insisting that he himself knew nothing, and inventing a technique whereby, through skilful questioning, knowledge could be generated in the minds of others as ignorant as himself. Knowledge of what? Knowledge of human affairs: in particular, of the moral ideas that guide human conduct.

The parallel between the work of the two men is so striking that I put Herodotus side by side with Socrates as one of the great innovating geniuses of the fifth century. But his achievement ran so strongly counter to the current of Greek thought that it did not long survive its creator. Socrates was after all in the direct line of the Greek intellectual tradition, and that is why his work was taken up and developed by Plato and many other disciples. Not so Herodotus. Herodotus had no successors.

Even if I conceded to an objector that Thucydides worthily carried on the Herodotean tradition, the question would still remain: Who carried it on when Thucydides had finished with it? And the only answer is: Nobody carried it on. These fifth-

---

[1] *Politics*, 1326ᵇ2–26.

century giants had no fourth-century successors anything like equal in stature to themselves. The decay of Greek art from the late fifth century onwards is undeniable; but it did not entail a decay of Greek science. Greek philosophy still had Plato and Aristotle to come. The natural sciences were still to have a long and brilliant life. If history is a science, why did history share the fate of the arts and not the fate of the other sciences? Why does Plato write as if Herodotus had never lived?

The answer is that the Greek mind tended to harden and narrow itself in its anti-historical tendency. The genius of Herodotus triumphed over that tendency, but after him the search for unchangeable and eternal objects of knowledge gradually stifled the historical consciousness, and forced men to abandon the Herodotean hope of achieving a scientific knowledge of past human actions.

This is not a mere conjecture. We can see the thing happening. The man in whom it happened was Thucydides.

The difference between the scientific outlook of Herodotus and that of Thucydides is hardly less remarkable than the difference between their literary styles. The style of Herodotus is easy, spontaneous, convincing. That of Thucydides is harsh, artificial, repellent. In reading Thucydides I ask myself, What is the matter with the man, that he writes like that? I answer: he has a bad conscience. He is trying to justify himself for writing history at all by turning it into something that is not history. Mr. C. N. Cochrane, in his *Thucydides and the Science of History* (London, 1929), has argued, I think rightly, that the dominant influence on Thucydides is the influence of Hippocratic medicine. Hippocrates was not only the father of medicine, he was also the father of psychology, and his influence is evident not only in such things as the Thucydidean description of the plague, but in such studies in morbid psychology as the description of war-neurosis in general and the special instances of it in the Corcyrean revolution and the Melian dialogue. Herodotus may be the father of history, but Thucydides is the father of psychological history.

Now what is psychological history? It is not history at all, but natural science of a special kind. It does not narrate facts for the sake of narrating facts. Its chief purpose is to affirm laws, psychological laws. A psychological law is not an event nor yet a complex of events: it is an unchanging rule which governs the relations between events. I think that every one who knows both authors will agree with me when I say that what chiefly interests Herodotus is the events themselves; what chiefly interests Thucydides is the laws according to which they happen. But these laws are precisely such eternal and unchanging forms as, according to the main trend of Greek thought, are the only knowable things.

Thucydides is not the successor of Herodotus in historical thought but the man in whom the historical thought of Herodotus was overlaid and smothered beneath anti-historical motives. This is a thesis which may be illustrated by mentioning one familiar feature of Thucydides' method. Consider his speeches. Custom has dulled our susceptibilities; but let us ask ourselves for a moment: could a just man who had a really historical mind have permitted himself the use of such a convention? Think first of their style. Is it not, historically speaking, an outrage to make all these very different characters talk in one and the same fashion, and that a fashion in which no one can ever have spoken when addressing troops before a battle or when pleading for the lives of the conquered? Is it not clear that the style betrays a lack of interest in the question what such and such a man really said on such and such an occasion? Secondly, think of their contents. Can we say that, however unhistorical their style may be, their substance is historical? The question has been variously answered. Thucydides does say (i. 22) that he kept 'as closely as possible' to the general sense of what was actually said; but how close was this? He does not claim that it was very close, because he adds that he has given the speeches roughly as he thought the speakers would have said what was appropriate to the occasion; and when we consider the speeches themselves in their context, it is difficult to resist the conclusion that the judge of 'what was appropriate' was Thucydides himself. Grote argued long ago[1] that the Melian dialogue contains more imagination than history, and I have seen no convincing refutation of his argument. The speeches seem to me to be in substance not history but Thucydidean comments upon the acts of the speakers, Thucydidean reconstructions of their motives and intentions. Even if this be denied, the very controversy on

[1] *History of Greece* (London, 1862), vol. v, p. 95.

this question may be regarded as evidence that the Thucydidean speech is both in style and in content a convention characteristic of an author whose mind cannot be fully concentrated on the events themselves, but is constantly being drawn away from the events to some lesson that lurks behind them, some unchanging and eternal truth of which the events are, Platonically speaking, παραδείγματα or μιμήματα.

§ 7. *The Hellenistic period*

After the fifth century B.C. the historian's outlook underwent an enlargement in time. When Greek thought, having attained a consciousness of itself and its own worth, set out to conquer the world, it embarked on an adventure whose development was too vast to fall within the view of a single generation, and yet its consciousness of its own mission gave it a conviction of the essential unity of that development. This helped the Greeks to overcome the particularism which had coloured all their historiography before the time of Alexander the Great. In their eyes history had been essentially the history of one particular social unit at one particular time:

(i) They were conscious that this particular social unit was only one among many; and, in so far as it came into contact, friendly or hostile, with others during the given space of time, these others put in an appearance on the stage of history. But although for this reason Herodotus has to say something about the Persians, he is interested in them not for their own sake but only as enemies of the Greeks: worthy and honourable enemies, but still enemies and no more. (ii) They were conscious in the fifth century, and even earlier, that there was such a thing as the human world, the totality of all particular social units; they called it ἡ οἰκουμένη, as distinct from ὁ κόσμος, the natural world. But the unity of this human world was for them only a geographical, not an historical, unity. The consciousness of that unity was not an historical consciousness. The idea of oecumenical history, world-history, was still non-existent. (iii) They were conscious that the history of the particular society in which they were interested had been going on for a long time. But they did not try to trace it back very far. The reason for this I have already explained. The only genuinely historical method hitherto invented depended on cross-questioning eyewitnesses;

at once curiously and beneficially

consequently the backward limit of any historian's field was dictated by the limits of human memory.

These three limitations were all overcome in what is called the Hellenistic period.

(i) The symbol of the parochial outlook of the fifth-century Greeks is the linguistic distinction between Greeks and Barbarians. The fourth century did not obliterate this distinction, but it abolished its rigidity. This was not a matter of theory, it was a matter of practice. It became a familiar fact about the contemporary world that Barbarians could become Greeks. This graecizing of Barbarians is called in Greek Hellenism (ἑλληνίζειν means to talk Greek, and, in a wider sense, to adopt Greek manners and customs) ; and the Hellenistic period is the period when Greek manners and customs were adopted by Barbarians. Thus the Greek historical consciousness, which for Herodotus had been primarily the consciousness of hostility between Greeks and Barbarians (the Persian Wars), becomes the consciousness of co-operation between Greeks and Barbarians, a co-operation in which Greeks take the lead, and Barbarians, by following that lead, become Greeks, heirs to Greek culture, and thus heirs to the Greek historical consciousness.

(ii) Through the conquests of Alexander the Great, whereby the οἰκουμένη or at least a very large part of it (and a part which included all the non-Greek peoples in whom the Greeks were specially interested) became a single political unit, the 'world' became something more than a geographical expression. It became an historical expression. The whole empire of Alexander now shared a single history of the Greek world. Potentially, the whole οἰκουμένη shared it. Any ordinarily well-informed person knew as a fact that Greek history was a single history that held good from the Adriatic to the Indus and from the Danube to the Sahara. For a philosopher, reflecting on this fact, it was possible to extend the same idea over the whole οἰκουμένη: 'The poet says, Dear city of Cecrops: wilt thou not say, Dear city of Zeus?' That is, of course, from Marcus Aurelius[1] in the second century A.D.; but the idea, the idea of the whole world as a single historical unit, is a typically Stoic idea, and Stoicism is a typical product of the Hellenistic period. It was Hellenism that created the idea of oecumenical history.

[1] *Meditations*, iv. 23.

(iii) But a world-history could not be written on the strength of testimony from living eyewitnesses, and therefore a new method was required, namely compilation. It was necessary to construct a patchwork history whose materials were drawn from 'authorities', that is, from the works of previous historians who had already written the histories of particular societies at particular times. This is what I call the 'scissors-and-paste' historical method. It consists in excerpting the required material from writers whose work cannot be checked on Herodotean principles, because the eyewitnesses who co-operated in that work are no longer alive. As a method, this is far inferior to the Socratic method of the fifth century. It is not a wholly uncritical method, because judgement can and must be exercised as to whether this or that statement, made by this or that authority, is true. But it cannot be used at all without the assurance that this or that authority is on the whole a good historian. Consequently, the oecumenical history of the Hellenistic age (which includes the Roman age) is based on a high estimate of the work done by the particularistic historians of the Hellenic age.

It was especially the vividness and excellence of the work done by Herodotus and Thucydides that re-created a lively idea of the fifth century in the minds of later generations and increased the backward scope of historical thought. Just as the past achievements of great artists gave people a sense that artistic styles other than that of their own day were valuable, so that a generation of literary and artistic scholars and dilettanti arose for whom the preservation and enjoyment of classical art was an end in itself, so there arose historians of a new type who could feel themselves imaginatively as contemporaries of Herodotus and Thucydides while yet remaining men of their own time and able to compare their own times with the past. This past the Hellenistic historians could feel as their own past, and thus it became possible to write a new kind of history with a dramatic unity of any size, so long as the historian could collect materials for it and could weld them into a single story.

§ 8. *Polybius*

The idea of this new kind of history is full-grown in the work of Polybius. Like all real historians, Polybius has a definite theme; he has a story to tell, a story of notable and memorable

things, namely the conquest of the world by Rome; but he
begins that story at a point more than 150 years before the time
of writing, so that the extent of his field is five generations
instead of one. His ability to do this is connected with the fact
that he is working in Rome, whose people had a kind of historical
consciousness quite different from that of the Greeks. History
for them meant continuity: the inheritance from the past of
institutions scrupulously preserved in the form in which they
were received; the moulding of life according to the pattern of
✓ ancestral custom. The Romans, acutely conscious of their own
continuity with their past, were careful to preserve memorials
of that past; they not only kept their ancestral portraits in the
house, as a visible symbol of the continuing and watchful
presence of their forefathers directing their own life, but they
preserved ancient traditions of their own corporate history to
an extent unknown to the Greeks. These traditions were no
doubt affected by the inevitable tendency to project the
characteristics of late Republican Rome into the history of her
earliest days; but Polybius, with his critical and philosophical
mind, guarded against the historical dangers of that distortion
by only beginning his narrative where his authorities became,
in his own opinion, trustworthy: and in using these sources he
never allowed his critical faculty to go to sleep. It is to the
Romans, acting as always under the tuition of the Hellenistic
mind, that we owe the conception of a history both oecumenical
and national, a history in which the hero of the story is the con-
✓ tinuing and corporate spirit of a people and in which the plot
of the story is the unification of the world under that people's
leadership. Even here, we have not arrived at the conception
of national history as we understand it: national history as the
complete biography, so to speak, of a people from its very beginnings. For Polybius, the history of Rome begins with Rome
already fully formed, adult, ready to go forth on her mission of
conquest. The difficult problem of how a national spirit comes
into existence is not yet tackled. For Polybius, the given,
ready-made national spirit is the ὑποκείμενον of history, the
unchanging substance that underlies all change. Just as the
Greeks could not even contemplate the possibility of raising
the problem which we should call the problem of the origin of
the Hellenic people, so even for Polybius there is no problem of

the origin of the Roman people; if he knew the traditions about the foundation of Rome, as he doubtless did, he silently cut them out of his field of vision as lying behind the point at which historical science, as he conceived it, could begin.

With this larger conception of the field of history comes a more precise conception of history itself. Polybius uses the word ἱστορία not in its original and quite general sense as meaning any kind of inquiry, but in its modern sense of history: the thing is now conceived as a special type of research needing a special name of its own. He is an advocate of the claims of this science to universal study for its own sake, and points out in the first sentence of his work that this is a thing not hitherto done; he thinks of himself as the first person to conceive of history as such as a form of thought having a universal value. But he expresses this value in a way which shows that he has come to terms with the anti-historical or substantialistic tendency which, as I said before, dominated the Greek mind. History, according to this tendency, cannot be a science, for there can be no science of transitory things. Its value is not a theoretical or scientific value, it can only be a practical value— the kind of value which Plato had ascribed to δόξα, the quasi-knowledge of what is not eternal and intelligible but temporal and perceptible. Polybius accepts and emphasizes this notion. History, for him, is worth studying not because it is scientifically true or demonstrative, but because it is a school and training-ground for political life.

But a person who had accepted this notion in the fifth century (as no one did, because Herodotus still thought of history as a science and Thucydides, so far as I can see, did not raise the question of the value of history at all) would have inferred that the value of history lies in its power of training individual statesmen, a Pericles or the like, to conduct the affairs of their own community with skill and success. This view was held by Isocrates in the fourth century, but it had become impossible by the time of Polybius. The naïve self-confidence of the Hellenic age has disappeared with the disappearance of the city-state. Polybius does not think that the study of history will enable men to avoid the mistakes of their predecessors and surpass them in worldly success; the success to which the study of history can lead is for him an inner success, a victory not over circumstance but over self. What we learn from the tragedies of its heroes is not to avoid such tragedies in our own lives, but to bear them bravely when fortune brings them. The idea of fortune, τύχη, bulks largely in this conception of history, and imports into it a new element of determinism. As the canvas on which the historian paints his picture grows larger, the power attributed to the individual will grows less. Man finds himself no longer master of his fate in the sense that what he tries to do succeeds or fails in proportion to his own intelligence or lack of it ; his fate is master of him, and the freedom of his will is shown not in controlling the outward events of his life but in controlling the inward temper in which he faces these events. Here Polybius is applying to history the same Hellenistic conceptions which the Stoics and Epicureans applied to ethics. Both these schools agreed in thinking that the problem of moral life was not how to control events in the world around us, as the classical Greek moralists had thought, but how to preserve a purely inward integrity and balance of mind when the attempt to control outward events had been abandoned. For Hellenistic thought, self-consciousness is no longer, as it was for Hellenic thought, a power to conquer the world; it is a citadel providing a safe retreat from a world both hostile and intractable.

§ 9. *Livy and Tacitus*

With Polybius the Hellenistic tradition of historical thought passes into the hands of Rome. The only original development it received there was from Livy, who conceived the magnificent idea of a complete history of Rome from her very beginning. A great part of Polybius' work had been done on the fifth-century method, in collaboration with his friends of the Scipionic circle who had achieved the culminating stages in the construction of the new Roman world. It was only the introductory phases of Polybius' narrative that had to depend by scissors-and-paste means on the work of earlier authorities. In Livy the centre of gravity is changed. It is no mere introduction, it is the whole body of his work, that is constructed by scissors and paste. Livy's whole task is to assemble the traditional records of early Roman history and weld them together into a single continuous narrative, the history of Rome. It was the first time anything of the sort had been done. The Romans, serenely

confident in their own superiority to all other peoples and their
monopoly of the only virtues deserving the name, thought their
own history the only one worth narrating ; and hence the history
of Rome as narrated by Livy was to the Roman mind not one
out of a number of possible particular histories but universal
history, the history of the only genuinely historical reality:
oecumenical history, because Rome had now, like Alexander's
Empire, become the world.

Livy was a philosophical historian ; less philosophical no
doubt than Polybius, but far more philosophical than any later
Roman historian. His preface therefore deserves the closest study.
I shall comment briefly on a few points in it. First, he pitches
the scientific claims of his work very low. He makes no claim to
original research or original method. He writes as if his chance of
standing out from the ruck of historical writers depended chiefly
on his literary qualities ; and certainly these qualities are, as all
his readers have agreed, outstanding. I need not quote the praise
of such qualified critics as Quintilian.[1] Secondly, he emphasizes
his moral purpose. He says that his readers will doubtless prefer
to be told about the recent past ; but he wants them to read
about the remote past, because he wishes to hold up before them
the moral example of the early days when Roman society was
simple and uncorrupted, and to show them how the foundations
of Roman greatness were laid in this primitive morality.
Thirdly, he is clear that history is humanistic. It flatters our
conceit, he says, to think of our origins as divine ; but the
historian's business is not to flatter his reader's conceit but to
paint the doings and manners of men.

Livy's attitude towards his authorities is sometimes misrepresented. Like Herodotus, he is often charged with the
grossest credulity ; but, like Herodotus, wrongly. He does his
best to be critical ; but the methodical criticism practised by
every modern historian was still not invented. Here was a mass
of legends ; all he could do with them was to decide, as best he
could, whether or not they were trustworthy. Three courses
were open to him: to repeat them, accepting their substantial
accuracy ; to reject them ; or to repeat them with the caution that
he was not sure of their truth. Thus, at the outset of his history,
Livy says that the traditions referring to events before the

[1] *Inst. or.* x. i. 101.

foundation of Rome, or rather to events before those immediately leading up to that foundation, are fables rather than sound traditions and can neither be affirmed nor criticized. He therefore repeats them with a caution, merely remarking that they show a tendency to magnify the origins of the city by mingling divine agencies with human; but once he comes to the foundation of Rome he accepts the tradition pretty much as he finds it. There is here only the very crudest attempt at historical criticism. Presented with a great wealth of traditional material, the historian takes it all at its face value; he makes no attempt to discover how the tradition has grown up and through what various distorting media it has reached him; he therefore cannot reinterpret a tradition, that is, explain it as meaning something other than it explicitly says. He has to take it or leave it, and, on the whole, Livy's tendency is to accept his tradition and repeat it in good faith.

The Roman Empire was not an age of vigorous and progressive thought. It did singularly little to advance knowledge on any of the paths that the Greeks had opened up. It kept alive for a time the Stoic and Epicurean philosophies without developing them; only in Neoplatonism did it show any philosophical originality. In natural science it did nothing to surpass the achievements of the Hellenistic Age. Even in applied natural science it was extemely weak. It used Hellenistic fortification, Hellenistic artillery, and arts and crafts partly Hellenistic and partly Celtic. In history its interest survived but its vigour failed. No one ever took up Livy's task again and tried to do it better. After him, historians either copied him or drew in their horns and confined themselves to a narrative of the recent past. So far as method goes, Tacitus already represents a decline.

As a contributor to historical literature, Tacitus is a gigantic figure; but it is permissible to wonder whether he was an historian at all. He imitates the parochial outlook of the fifth-century Greeks without imitating their virtues. He is obsessed with the history of affairs at Rome, neglecting the Empire, or seeing it only as refracted through the spectacles of a home-keeping Roman; and his outlook on these purely Roman affairs is narrow in the extreme. He is flagrantly biased in favour of the senatorial opposition; he couples a contempt for peaceful administration with an admiration for conquest and military glory, an admiration blinded by his remarkable ignorance of the actualities of warfare. All these defects make him curiously unfitted to be the historian of the early Principate, but at bottom they are only symptoms of a graver and more general defect. What is really wrong with Tacitus is that he has never thought out the fundamental problems of his enterprise. His attitude towards the philosophical groundwork of history is frivolous, and he takes over the current pragmatic view of its purpose in the spirit of a rhetorician rather than that of a serious thinker.

'His professed purpose in writing is to hold up signal examples of political vice and virtue for posterity to execrate or to admire, and to teach his readers, even through a narrative which he fears may weary them by its monotonous horrors, that good citizens may live under bad rulers; and that it is not mere destiny or the chapter of accidents, but personal character and discretion, dignified moderation and reserve, that best guard a senator of rank unharmed through time of peril, in which not only the defiant on one side, but almost as often the sycophant on the other, are struck down as the course of events or even the changing humours of the prince may prompt.'[1]

This attitude leads Tacitus to distort history systematically by representing it as essentially a clash of characters, exaggeratedly good with exaggeratedly bad. History cannot be scientifically written unless the historian can re-enact in his own mind the experience of the people whose actions he is narrating. Tacitus never tried to do this: his characters are seen not from inside, with understanding and sympathy, but from outside, as mere spectacles of virtue or vice. One can hardly read his descriptions of an Agricola or a Domitian without being reminded of Socrates' laugh at Glaucon's imaginary portraits of the perfectly good and the perfectly bad man: 'My word, Glaucon, how energetically you are polishing them up like statues for a prize competition!'[2]

Tacitus has been praised for his character-drawing; but the principles on which he draws character are fundamentally vicious and make his character-drawing an outrage on historical truth. He found warrant for it, no doubt, in the Stoic and Epicurean philosophies of his age, to which I have already referred:

---

[1] Furneaux in *Cornelii Taciti Annalium Libri I–IV*, edited . . . for the use of schools (Oxford, 1886), pp. 3–4.   [2] Plato, *Republic*, 361 d.

the defeatist philosophies which, starting from the assumption that the good man cannot conquer or control a wicked world, taught him how to preserve himself unspotted from its wickedness. This false antithesis between the individual man's character and his social environment justifies, in a sense, Tacitus' method of exhibiting the actions of an historical figure as flowing simply from his own personal character, and making no allowance either for the way in which a man's actions may be determined partly by his environment and only in part by his character, or for the way in which character itself may be moulded by the forces to which a man is subjected by his environment. Actually, as Socrates urged against Glaucon, the individual character considered in isolation from its environment is an abstraction, not a really existing thing. What a man does depends only to a limited extent on what kind of man he is. No one can resist the forces of his environment. Either he conquers the world or the world will conquer him.

Thus Livy and Tacitus stand side by side as the two great monuments to the barrenness of Roman historical thought. Livy has attempted a really great task, but he has failed in it because his method is too simple to cope with the complexity of his material, and his story of the ancient history of Rome is too deeply permeated with fabulous elements to be ranked with the greatest works of historical thought. Tacitus has attempted a new approach, the psychological-didactic; but instead of being an enrichment of historical method this is really an impoverishment, and indicates a declining standard of historical honesty. Subsequent historians under the Roman Empire, instead of overcoming the obstacles by which Livy and Tacitus were baffled, never even equalled their achievement. As the Empire went on, historians began more and more to content themselves with the wretched business of compilation, amassing in an uncritical spirit what they found in earlier works and arranging it with no end in view except, at best, edification or some other kind of propaganda.

§ 10. *Character of Greco-Roman historiography:* (i) *Humanism*

Greco-Roman historiography as a whole has firmly grasped one at least of the four characteristics enumerated in the Introduction (§ ii): it is humanistic. It is a narrative of human history, the history of man's deeds, man's purposes, man's successes and failures. It admits, no doubt, a divine agency; but the function of this agency is strictly limited. The will of the gods as manifested in history only appears rarely; in the best historians hardly at all and then only as a will supporting and seconding the will of man and enabling him to succeed where otherwise he would have failed. The gods have no plan of their own for the development of human affairs; they only grant success or decree failure for the plans of men. This is why a more searching analysis of human actions themselves, discovering in them alone the grounds for their success or failure, tends to eliminate the gods altogether, and to substitute for them mere personifications of human activity, like the genius of the Emperor, the goddess Rome, or the virtues represented on Roman Imperial coins. The ultimate development of this tendency is to find the cause of all historical events in the personality, whether individual or corporate, of human agents. The philosophical idea underlying it is the idea of the human will as freely choosing its own ends and limited in the success it achieves in their pursuit only by its own force and by the power of the intellect which apprehends them and works out means to their achievement. This implies that whatever happens in history happens as a direct result of human will; that some one is directly responsible for it, to be praised or blamed according as it is a good thing or a bad.

Greco-Roman humanism, however, had a special weakness of its own because of its inadequate moral or psychological insight. It was based on the idea of man as essentially a rational animal, by which I mean the doctrine that every individual human being is an animal capable of reason. So far as any given man develops that capacity and becomes actually, and not potentially, reasonable, he makes a success of his life: according to the Hellenic idea, he becomes a force in political life and a maker of history; according to the Hellenistic-Roman idea, he becomes capable of living wisely, sheltered behind his own rationality, in a wild and wicked world. Now the idea that every agent is wholly and directly responsible for everything that he does is a naïve idea which takes no account of certain important regions in moral experience. On the one hand, there is no getting away from the fact that men's characters are formed by their actions and experiences: the man himself undergoes change as his activities develop. On the other hand, there is the fact that to a very great extent people do not know what they are doing until they have done it, if then. The extent to which people act with a clear idea of their ends, knowing what effects they are aiming at, is easily exaggerated. Most human action is tentative, experimental, directed not by a knowledge of what it will lead to but rather by a desire to know what will come of it. Looking back over our actions, or over any stretch of past history, we see that something has taken shape as the actions went on which certainly was not present to our minds, or to the mind of any one, when the actions which brought it into existence began. The ethical thought of the Greco-Roman world attributed far too much to the deliberate plan or policy of the agent, far too little to the force of a blind activity embarking on a course of action without foreseeing its end and being led to that end only through the necessary development of that course itself

§ 11. *Character of Greco-Roman historiography:* (*ii*) *Substantialism*

If its humanism, however weak, is the chief merit of Greco-Roman historiography, its chief defect is substantialism. By this I mean that it is constructed on the basis of a metaphysical system whose chief category is the category of substance. Substance does not mean matter or physical substance; indeed many Greek metaphysicians thought that no substance could be material. For Plato, it would seem, substances are immaterial though not mental; they are objective forms. For Aristotle, in the last resort, the only ultimately real substance is mind. Now a substantialistic metaphysics implies a theory of knowledge according to which only what is unchanging is knowable. But what is unchanging is not historical. What is historical is the transitory event. The substance to which an event happens, or from whose nature it proceeds, is nothing to the historian. Hence the attempt to think historically and the attempt to think in terms of substance were incompatible.

In Herodotus we have an attempt at a really historical point of view. For him events are important in themselves and knowable by themselves. But already in Thucydides the historical point of view is being dimmed by substantialism. For Thucydides the events are important chiefly for the light they throw on eternal and substantial entities of which they are mere accidents. The stream of historical thought which flowed so freely in Herodotus is beginning to freeze up.

As time goes on this freezing process continues, and by the time of Livy history is frozen solid. A distinction is now taken for granted between act and agent, regarded as a special case of substance and accident. It is taken for granted that the historian's proper business is with acts, which come into being in time, develop in time through their phases, and terminate in time. The agent from which they flow, being a substance, is eternal and unchanging and consequently stands outside history. In order that acts may flow from it, the agent itself must exist unchanged throughout the series of its acts: for it has to exist before this series begins and nothing that happens as the series goes on can add anything to it or take away anything from it. History cannot explain how any agent came into being or underwent any change of nature; for it is metaphysically axiomatic that an agent, being a substance, can never have come into being and can never undergo any change of nature. We have already seen how these ideas affected the work of Polybius.

We have sometimes been taught to contrast the unphilosophical Romans with the philosophical Greeks, and we may thus have been led to think that if the Romans were as unphilosophical as all that they would not allow metaphysical considerations to affect their historical work. Nevertheless it was so. And the completeness with which the practical and hard-headed Romans adopted the substantialistic metaphysics of the Greeks does not appear in the Roman historians alone. It appears with equal clarity in the Roman lawyers. Roman law, from beginning to end, is constructed on a framework of substantialistic metaphysical principles which influence its every detail.

I will give two examples of how this influence appears in the two greatest Roman historians.

First, in Livy. Livy set himself the task of writing a history of Rome. Now, a modern historian would have interpreted this as meaning a history of how Rome came to be what it is, a history of the process which brought into existence the characteristic Roman institutions and moulded the typical Roman character. It never occurs to Livy to adopt any such interpretation.

Rome is the heroine of his narrative. Rome is the agent whose actions he is describing. Therefore Rome is a substance, changeless and eternal. From the beginning of the narrative Rome is ready-made and complete. To the end of the narrative she has undergone no spiritual change. The traditions on which Livy relied projected such institutions as augury, the legion, the Senate, and so forth, into the very first years of the city, with the assumption that they remained thereafter unchanged; hence the origin of Rome, as he describes it, was a kind of miraculous leap into existence of the complete city as it existed at a later date. For a parallel, we should have to imagine an historian of England assuming that Hengist created a parliament of Lords and Commons. Rome is described as 'the eternal city'. Why is Rome so called? Because people still think of Rome, as Livy thought of her: substantialistically, non-historically.

Secondly, in Tacitus. Furneaux pointed out long ago[1] that when Tacitus describes the way in which the character of a man like Tiberius broke down beneath the strain of empire, he represents the process not as a change in the structure or conformation of a personality but as the revelation of features in it which had hitherto been hypocritically concealed. Why does Tacitus so misrepresent facts? Is it simply out of spite, in order to blacken the characters of the men whom he has cast for the part of villains? Is it in pursuance of a rhetorical purpose, to hold up awful examples to point his moral and adorn his tale? Not at all. It is because the idea of development in a character, an idea so familiar to ourselves, is to him a metaphysical impossibility. A 'character' is an agent, not an action; actions come and go, but the 'characters' (as we call them), the agents from whom they proceed, are substances, and therefore eternal and unchanging. Features in the character of a Tiberius or a Nero which only appeared comparatively late in life must have been there all the time. A good man cannot become bad. A man who shows himself bad when old must have been equally bad when young, and his vices concealed by hypocrisy. As the Greeks put it, ἀρχὴ ἄνδρα δείξει.[2] Power does not alter a man's character; it only shows what kind of man he already was.

Greco-Roman historiography can therefore never show how

---

[1] *The Annals of Tacitus* (Oxford, 1896), vol. i, p. 158.
[2] Quoted from Bias in Aristotle, *Nic. Eth.* 1130ª1.

anything comes into existence; all the agencies that appear on the stage of history have to be assumed ready-made before history begins, and they are related to historical events exactly as a machine is related to its own movements. The scope of history is limited to describing what people and things do, the nature of these people and things remaining outside its field of vision. The nemesis of this substantialistic attitude was historical scepticism: events, as mere transitory accidents, were regarded as unknowable; the agent, as a substance, was knowable indeed, but not to the historian. But what, then, was the use of history? For Platonism history could have a pragmatic value, and the idea of this as the sole value of history intensifies from Isocrates to Tacitus. And as this process goes on it produces a kind of defeatism about historical accuracy and an unconscientiousness in the historical mind as such.

PART II

THE INFLUENCE OF CHRISTIANITY

§ 1. *The leaven of Christian ideas*

THREE great crises have occurred in the history of European historiography. The first was the crisis of the fifth century B.C. when the idea of history as a science, a form of research, an ἱστορίη, came into being. The second was the crisis of the fourth and fifth centuries A.D. when the idea of history was remodelled by the revolutionary effect of Christian thought. I have now to describe this process and to show how Christianity jettisoned two of the leading ideas in Greco-Roman historiography, namely (i) the optimistic idea of human nature and (ii) the substantialistic idea of eternal entities underlying the process of historical change.

(i) The moral experience which Christianity expressed contained as one of its most important elements a sense of human blindness in action: not a fortuitous blindness due to individual failure of insight, but a necessary blindness inherent in action itself. According to Christian doctrine, it is inevitable that man should act in the dark without knowing what will come of his action. That inability to achieve ends clearly conceived in advance, which in Greek is called ἁμαρτία, missing one's mark, is no longer regarded as accidental but as a permanent element in human nature, arising out of the condition of man as man. This is the original sin upon which St. Augustine laid such stress, and which he connected psychologically with the force of natural desire. Human action, on this view, is not designed in view of preconceived ends by the intellect; it is actuated *a tergo* by immediate and blind desire. It is not only the uninstructed vulgar, it is man as such, that does what he wants to do instead of thinking out a reasonable course of action. Desire is not the tamed horse of Plato's metaphor, it is a runaway horse, and the 'sin' (to use the technical term of theology) into which it leads us is not a sin which we deliberately choose to commit, it is an inherent and original sin proper to our nature. From this it follows that the achievements of man are due not to his own proper forces of will and intellect, but to something other than himself, causing him to desire ends that are worth pursuing. He therefore behaves, from the point of view of the historian, as if he were the wise architect of his own fortunes; but the wisdom displayed in his action is not his, it is the wisdom of God, by whose grace man's desires are directed to worthy ends. Thus the plans which are realized by human action (such plans, I mean, as the conquest of the world by Rome) come about not because men have conceived them, decided on their goodness, and devised means to execute them, but because men, doing from time to time what at the moment they wanted to do, have executed the purposes of God. This conception of grace is the correlative of the conception of original sin.

(ii) The metaphysical doctrine of substance in Greco-Roman philosophy was challenged by the Christian doctrine of creation. According to this doctrine nothing is eternal except God, and all else has been created by God. The human soul is no longer regarded as a past existence *ab aeterno*, and its immortality in that sense is denied; each soul is believed to be a fresh creation. Similarly, peoples and nations considered collectively are not eternal substances but have been created by God. And what God has created He can modify by a reorientation of its nature towards fresh ends: thus by the operation of His grace He can bring about development in the character of a person or a people already created. Even the substances, so called, which were still tolerated by early Christian thought were not really substances as substances had been conceived by the thinkers of antiquity. The human soul is still called a substance, but it is now conceived as a substance created by God at a certain time and depending on God for its continued existence. The natural world is still called a substance, but with the same qualification. God Himself is still called a substance, but His character as substance is now regarded as unknowable: not only undiscoverable by unaided human reason, but not even capable of being revealed. All we can know about God is His activities. By degrees, as the leaven of Christianity worked, even these quasi-substances disappeared. It was in the thirteenth century that St. Thomas Aquinas threw overboard the conception of divine substance and defined God in terms of activity, as *actus purus*. In the eighteenth, Berkeley jettisoned the conception of material substance, and Hume the conception of spiritual substance. The stage was then set for the third crisis in the history of European historiography and for the long-delayed entrance of history as, at last, a science.

The introduction of Christian ideas had a threefold effect on the way in which history was conceived:

(*a*) A new attitude towards history grew up, according to which the historical process is the working out not of man's purposes but of God's; God's purpose being a purpose for man, a purpose to be embodied in human life and through the activity of human wills, God's part in this working-out being limited to predetermining the end and to determining from time to time the objects which human beings desire. Thus each human agent knows what he wants and pursues it, but he does not know why he wants it: the reason why he wants it is that God has caused him to want it in order to advance the process of realizing His purpose. In one sense man is the agent throughout history, for everything that happens in history happens by his will; in another sense God is the sole agent, for it is only by the working of God's providence that the operation of man's will at any given moment leads to *this* result, and not to a different one. In one sense, again, man is the end for whose sake historical events happen, for God's purpose is man's well-being; in another sense man exists merely as a means to the accomplishment of God's ends, for God has created him only in order to work out His purpose in terms of human life. By this new attitude to human action history gained enormously, because the recognition that what happens in history need not happen through anyone's deliberately wishing it to happen is an indispensable precondition of understanding any historical process.

(*b*) This new view of history makes it possible to see not only the actions of historical agents, but the existence and nature of those agents themselves, as vehicles of God's purposes and therefore as historically important. Just as the individual soul is a thing created in the fullness of time to have just those characteristics which the time requires if God's purpose is to be fulfilled, so a thing like Rome is not an eternal entity but a transient thing that has come into existence at the appropriate time in history to fulfil a certain definite function and to pass away when that function has been fulfilled. This was a profound revolution in historical thinking; it meant that the process of historical change was no longer conceived as flowing, so to speak, over the surface of things, and affecting their accidents only, but as involving their very substance and thus entailing a real creation and a real destruction. It is the application to history of the Christian conception of God as no mere workman fashioning the world out of a pre-existing matter but as a creator, calling it into existence out of nothing. Here, too, the gain to history is immense, because the recognition that the historical process creates its own vehicles, so that entities like Rome or England are not the presuppositions but the products of that process, is the first step towards grasping the peculiar characteristics of history.

(c) These two modifications in the conception of history were derived, as we have seen, from the Christian doctrines of original sin, grace, and creation. A third was based on the universalism of the Christian attitude. For the Christian, all men are equal in the sight of God: there is no chosen people, no privileged race or class, no one community whose fortunes are more important than those of another. All persons and all peoples are involved in the working out of God's purpose, and therefore the historical process is everywhere and always of the same kind, and every part of it is a part of the same whole. The Christian cannot be content with Roman history or Jewish history or any other partial and particularistic history: he demands a history of the world, a universal history whose theme shall be the general development of God's purposes for human life. The infusion of Christian ideas overcomes not only the characteristic humanism and the substantialism of Greco-Roman history, but also its particularism.

§ 2. *Characteristics of Christian historiography*

Any history written on Christian principles will be of necessity universal, providential, apocalyptic, and periodized.

(i) It will be a *universal* history, or history of the world, going back to the origin of man. It will describe how the various races of men came into existence and peopled the various habitable parts of the earth. It will describe the rise and fall of civilizations and powers. Greco-Roman oecumenical history is not universal in this sense, because it has a particularistic centre of gravity. Greece or Rome is the centre round which it revolves. Christian universal history has undergone a Copernican revolution, whereby the very idea of such a centre of gravity is destroyed.

(ii) It will ascribe events not to the wisdom of their human agents but to the workings of *Providence* preordaining their course. The theocratic history of the Near East is not providential in this sense, because it is not universal but particularistic. The theocratic historian is interested in the doings of a particular society, and the God who presides over these doings is a God for whom that particular society is a chosen people. Providential history, on the other hand, treats history indeed as a play written by God, but a play wherein no character is the author's favourite character.

(iii) It will set itself to detect an intelligible pattern in this general course of events, and in particular it will attach a central importance in this pattern to the historical life of Christ, which is clearly one of the chief preordained features of the pattern. It will make its narrative crystallize itself round that event, and treat earlier events as leading up to it or preparing for it, and subsequent events as developing its consequences. It will therefore divide history at the birth of Christ into two parts, each having a peculiar and unique character of its own: the first, a forward-looking character, consisting in blind preparation for an event not yet revealed; the second a backward-looking character depending on the fact that the revelation has now been made. A history thus divided into two periods, a period of darkness and a period of light, I shall call *apocalyptic* history.

(iv) Having divided the past into two, it will then naturally tend to subdivide it again: and thus to distinguish other events, not so important as the birth of Christ but important in their way, which make everything after them different in quality from what went before. Thus history is divided into epochs or *periods*, each with peculiar characteristics of its own, and each marked off from the one before it by an event which in the technical language of this kind of historiography is called epoch-making.

All these four elements were in fact consciously imported into historical thought by the early Christians. We may take Eusebius of Caesarea, in the third and early fourth century, as an example. In his *Chronicle* he set himself to compose a universal history where all events were brought within a single chronological framework instead of having events in Greece dated by Olympiads, events in Rome dated by consuls, and so on. This was compilation; but it was a very different thing from the compilations of pagan scholars under the late Empire, because it was inspired by a new purpose, the purpose of showing that the events thus chronicled formed a pattern with the birth of Christ in its centre. It was with this end in view that Eusebius composed another work, the so-called *Praeparatio Evangelica*, in which he showed that the history of the pre-Christian world could be regarded as a process designed to culminate in the Incarnation. Jewish religion, Greek philosophy, Roman law, combined to build up a matrix in which it was possible for the Christian revelation to take root and grow to maturity; if Christ had been born into the world at any other time, the world would not have been able to receive Him.

Eusebius was only one of a large number of men who were struggling to work out in detail the consequences of the Christian conception of man; and when we find many of the Fathers like Jerome, Ambrose, and even Augustine speaking of pagan learning and literature with contempt and hostility it is necessary to remind ourselves that this contempt arises not from lack of education or a barbarous indifference towards knowledge as such, but from the vigour with which these men were pursuing a new ideal of knowledge, working in the teeth of opposition for a reorientation of the entire structure of human thought. In the case of history, the only thing with which we are here concerned, the reorientation not only succeeded at the time, but left its heritage as a permanent enrichment of historical thought.

The conception of history as in principle the history of the world, where struggles like that between Greece and Persia or between Rome and Carthage are looked at impartially with an eye not to the success of one combatant but to the upshot of the struggle from the standpoint of posterity, became a commonplace. The symbol of this universalism is the adoption of a single chronological framework for all historical events. The single universal chronology, invented by Isidore of Seville in the seventh century and popularized by the Venerable Bede in the eighth, dating everything forward and backward from the birth of Christ, still shows where the idea came from.

The providential idea became a commonplace. We are taught

in our school text-books, for example, that in the eighteenth
century the English conquered an empire in a fit of absence of
mind: that is, they carried out what to us looking back on it
appears as a plan, though no such plan was present in their
minds at the time.

The apocalyptic idea became a commonplace, although
historians have placed their apocalyptic moment at all sorts of
times: the Renaissance, the invention of printing, the scientific
movement of the seventeenth century, the Enlightenment of the
eighteenth, the French Revolution, the Liberal movement of
the nineteenth century, or even, as with Marxist historians, in
the future.

And the idea of epoch-making events has become a commonplace, and with it the division of history into periods each with
its own peculiar character.

All these elements, so familiar in modern historical thought,
are totally absent from Greco-Roman historiography and were
consciously and laboriously worked out by the early Christians.

§ 3. *Medieval historiography*

The medieval historiography which devoted itself to the
working out of these conceptions is in one way a continuation
of Hellenistic and Roman historiography. The method remains
unchanged. The medieval historian still depends for his facts
on tradition, and has no effective weapons for criticizing that
tradition. Here he is on a par with Livy, and retains both the
weakness of Livy and his strength. He has no means of studying
the growth of the traditions that have come down to him or
analysing them into their various components. His only criticism is a personal, unscientific, unsystematic criticism, which
often betrays him into what, to us, seems foolish credulity. And
on the other side of the account he often displays remarkable
stylistic merit and imaginative power. For example, the humble
monk of St. Albans who has left us the *Flores Historiarum*
ascribed to Matthew of Westminster has told stories about King
Alfred and the cakes, Lady Godiva, King Canute on the shore
at Bosham, and so on, which may be fabulous but are imperish-
able gems of literature and deserve no less than the history of
Thucydides to be cherished as κτήματα ἐς αἰεί.

But unlike Livy the medieval historian treats this material

from a universalistic point of view. Even in the Middle Ages nationalism was a real thing; but an historian who flattered national rivalries and national pride knew that he was doing wrong. His business was not to praise England or France but to narrate the *gesta Dei*. He saw history not as a mere play of human purposes, in which he took the side of his own friends, but as a process, having an objective necessity of its own, wherein even the most intelligent and powerful human agent finds himself involved, not because God is destructive and mischievous, as in Herodotus, but because God is provident and constructive, has a plan of his own with which he will allow no man to interfere; so the human agent finds himself caught up in the stream of the divine purpose, and carried along in it with or without his consent. History, as the will of God, orders itself, and does not depend for its orderliness on the human agent's will to order it. Plans emerge, and get themselves carried into effect, which no human being has planned; and even men who think they are working against the emergence of these plans are in fact contributing to them. They may assassinate Caesar but they cannot arrest the downfall of the Republic; the very assassination adds a new feature to that downfall. Hence the total course of historical events is a criterion which serves to judge the individuals taking part in it.[1] The duty of the individual is to become a willing instrument for furthering its objective purposes. If he sets himself against it, he cannot arrest or alter it, all he can do is to secure his own condemnation by it, frustrating himself and reducing his own life to futility. This is a Patristic doctrine: the Devil is defined by the early Christian writer Hippolytus as ὁ ἀντιτάττων τοῖς κοσμικοῖς.

The great task of medieval historiography was the task of discovering and expounding this objective or divine plan. It was a plan developed in time and therefore through a definite series of stages, and it was reflection on this fact which produced the conception of historical ages each initiated by an epoch-making event. Now, the attempt to distinguish periods in history is a mark of advanced and mature historical thought, not afraid to interpret facts instead of merely ascertaining them;

[1] Schiller's famous aphorism *Die Weltgeschichte ist das Weltgericht* is a familiar medieval maxim revived in the late eighteenth century and typical of the medievalism which in many ways characterized the Romantics.

but here as elsewhere medieval thought, though never deficient
in boldness and originality, showed itself unable to make good
its promises. To illustrate this, I will take a single example of
medieval periodizing. In the twelfth century Joachim of Floris
divided history into three periods: the reign of the Father or
unincarnate God, that is, the pre-Christian age; the reign of the
Son or the Christian age; and the reign of the Holy Ghost which
was to begin in the future. This reference to a future age betrays
an important characteristic of medieval historiography. If
challenged to explain how he knew that there was in history
any objective plan at all, the medieval historian would have
replied that he knew it by revelation; it was part of what Christ
had revealed to man concerning God. And this revelation not
only gave the key to what God had done in the past, it showed
us what God was going to do in the future. The Christian
revelation thus gave us a view of the entire history of the world,
from its creation in the past to its end in the future, as seen in
the timeless and eternal vision of God. Thus medieval historiography looked forward to the end of history as something fore-
ordained by God and through revelation foreknown to man:
it thus contained in itself an eschatology.

Eschatology is always an intrusive element in history. The
historian's business is to know the past, not to know the future;
and whenever historians claim to be able to determine the future
in advance of its happening, we may know with certainty that
something has gone wrong with their fundamental conception
of history. Further, we may know exactly what it is that has
gone wrong. What has happened is that they have split up the
single reality of the historical process into two separate things,
one which determines and one which is determined: the abstract
law and the mere fact, the universal and the particular. They
have hypostatized the universal into a false particular supposed
to exist by itself and for itself, and yet in that isolation they
still conceive it as determining the course of particular events.
The universal, being thus isolated from the temporal process,
does not work in that process, it only works upon it. The
temporal process is something passive, shaped by a timeless
force working upon it from without. Hence, because the force
works in exactly the same way at all times, the knowledge of
how it works now is also a knowledge of how it will work in the

future, and if we know how it has determined the flow of events at any one time, we thereby know how it would determine it at any other, and therefore we can foretell the future. Thus, in medieval thought, the complete opposition between the objective purpose of God and the subjective purpose of man, so conceived that God's purpose appears as the imposition of a certain objective plan upon history quite irrespective of man's subjective purposes, leads inevitably to the idea that man's purposes make no difference to the course of history and that the only force which determines it is the divine nature. Hence, the divine nature being revealed, those to whom it is revealed by faith can see by faith what the future must be. This may seem to have affinities with substantialism, but it is something quite different, namely transcendence. God in medieval theology is not substance but pure act; and transcendence means that the divine activity is conceived not as working in and through human activity but as working outside it and overruling it, not immanent in the world of human action but transcending that world.

What has happened here is that the pendulum of thought has swung from an abstract and one-sided humanism in Greco-Roman historiography to an equally abstract and one-sided theocentric view in medieval. The work of providence in history is recognized, but recognized in a way which leaves nothing for man to do. One result of this is that historians, as we have seen, fell into the error of thinking that they could forecast the future. Another result is that in their anxiety to detect the general plan of history, and their belief that this plan was God's and not man's, they tended to look for the essence of history outside history itself, by looking away from man's actions in order to detect the plan of God; and consequently the actual detail of human actions became for them relatively unimportant, and they neglected that prime duty of the historian, a willingness to bestow infinite pains on discovering what actually happened. This is why medieval historiography is so weak in critical method. That weakness was not an accident. It did not depend on the limitation of the sources and materials at the disposal of scholars. It depended on a limitation not of what they could do but of what they wanted to do. They did not want an accurate and scientific study of the actual facts of history; what they wanted was an accurate and scientific study of the divine attributes, a theology based securely on the double foundation of faith and reason, which should enable them to determine *a priori* what must have happened and what must be going to happen in the historical process.

The consequence of this is that when medieval historiography is looked at from the point of view of a merely scholarly historian, the kind of historian who cares for nothing except accuracy in facts, it seems not only unsatisfactory but deliberately and repulsively wrong-headed; and the nineteenth-century historians, who did in general take a merely scholarly view of the nature of history, regarded it with extreme lack of sympathy. Nowadays, when we are less obsessed by the demand for critical accuracy and more interested in interpreting facts, we can look at it with a more friendly eye. We have so far gone back to the medieval view of history that we think of nations and civilizations as rising and falling in obedience to a law that has little to do with the purposes of the human beings that compose them, and we are perhaps not altogether ill-disposed to theories which teach that large-scale historical changes are due to some kind of dialectic working objectively and shaping the historical process by a necessity that does not depend on the human will. This brings us into somewhat close contact with the medieval historians, and if we are to avoid the errors to which ideas of their kind are liable, it is useful for us to study medieval historiography and to see how that antithesis between objective necessity and subjective will led to neglect of historical accuracy, and betrayed historians into an unscholarly credulity and a blind acceptance of tradition. The medieval historian had every excuse for being in that sense unscholarly; no one had yet discovered how to criticize sources and to ascertain facts in a scholarly manner, for this was the work of historical thought in the centuries that followed the close of the Middle Ages; but for us, now that that work has been done, there is no excuse; and if we went back to the medieval conception of history with all its errors, we should be exemplifying and hastening that downfall of civilization which some historians are, perhaps prematurely, proclaiming.

§ 4. *The Renaissance historians*

At the close of the Middle Ages one of the main tasks of
European thought was to bring about a fresh reorientation
of historical studies. The great theological and philosophical
systems which had provided a basis for determining the general
plan of history *a priori* had ceased to command assent, and
with the Renaissance a return was made to a humanistic view
of history based on that of the ancients. Accurate scholarship
became important, because human actions were no longer felt
to be dwarfed into insignificance in comparison with a divine
plan. Historical thought once more placed man in the centre
of its picture. But in spite of the new interest in Greco-Roman
thought, the Renaissance conception of man was profoundly
different from the Greco-Roman; and when a writer like
Machiavelli, in the early sixteenth century, expressed his ideas
about history in the shape of a commentary on the first ten
books of Livy he was not reinstating Livy's own view of history.
Man, for the Renaissance historian, was not man as depicted
by ancient philosophy, controlling his actions and creating his
destiny by the work of his intellect, but man as depicted by
Christian thought, a creature of passion and impulse. History
thus became the history of human passions, regarded as necessary manifestations of human nature.

The positive fruits of this new movement were found first of
all in a great clearing away of what had been fanciful and ill-
founded medieval historiography. It was shown, for example,
by Jean Bodin[1] in the mid-sixteenth century that the accepted
scheme of periods, the Four Empires, was based not on accurate
interpretation of the facts but on an arbitrary scheme borrowed
from the Book of Daniel;[2] and numerous scholars, mostly of

[1] *Methodus ad facilem historiarum cognitionem* (1566), Cap. vii: 'Confutatio
eorum qui quatuor monarchias . . . statuunt.'

[2] It is significant of the medievalist tendencies of late-eighteenth-century
romanticism, to which I have already called attention in the case of Schiller,
that Hegel reaffirms the long-exploded scheme of the Four Empires in his
passage about world history at the end of the *Philosophie des Rechts*. Readers
of Hegel, accustomed to his inveterate habit of dividing every subject, according to the pattern of his dialectic, into triads, are startled to find that his outline
of world history in the concluding pages of that book is divided into four
sections headed: 'The Oriental Empire, the Greek Empire, the Roman Empire,
the Germanic Empire.' Such readers are apt to think that, for once, facts

Italian origin, set themselves to overthrow the legends in which various countries had concealed their ignorance of their own origins; Polydore Virgil, for example, in the early sixteenth century, destroyed the old story about the foundation of Britain by Brutus the Trojan and laid the foundations of a critical history of England.

By the beginning of the seventeenth century Bacon was able to sum up the situation by dividing his map of knowledge into the three great realms of poetry, history, and philosophy, ruled over by the three faculties of imagination, memory, and understanding. To say that memory presides over history is to say that the essential work of history is to recall and record the past in its actual facts as they actually happened. What Bacon is doing here is to insist that history should be, above all, an interest in the past for its own sake. This is a negation of the claim that historians can foreknow the future, and at the same time it negates the idea that the historian's main function is to detect a divine plan running through the facts. His interest is in the facts themselves.

But the position of history as thus defined was precarious. It had freed itself from the errors of medieval thought, but it had still to find its own proper function. It had a definite programme, the rediscovery of the past, but it had no methods or principles by which this programme could be carried out. Actually, Bacon's definition of history as the realm of memory was wrong, because the past only requires historical investigation so far as it is not and cannot be remembered. If it could be remembered, there would be no need of historians. Bacon's own contemporary Camden was already at work in the best Renaissance tradition on the topography and archaeology of Britain, showing how unremembered history could be reconstructed from data somewhat as, at the same time, natural scientists were using data as the basis of scientific theories. The question how the historian's understanding works to supplement the deficiencies of his memory was a question that Bacon never asked.

have been too strong for the Hegelian dialectic. But it is not facts that have broken through the dialectical scheme; it is a recrudescence of medieval periodizing.

§ 5. *Descartes*

The constructive movement of seventeenth-century thought concentrated itself on the problems of natural science and left those of history on one side. Descartes, like Bacon, distinguished poetry, history, and philosophy, and added a fourth term, divinity; but of these four things he applied his new method to philosophy alone, with its three main divisions of mathematics, physics, and metaphysics, for it was only here that he hoped to attain secure and certain knowledge. Poetry, he said, was more a gift of nature than a discipline; divinity depended on faith in revelation; history, however interesting and instructive, however valuable towards the formation of a practical attitude in life, could not claim truth, for the events which it described never happened exactly as it described them. Thus the reformation of knowledge which Descartes envisaged, and actually did bring about, was designed to contribute nothing to historical thought, because he did not believe history to be, strictly speaking, a branch of knowledge at all.

It is worth while to look more closely at the paragraph on history in the first part of the *Discourse on Method*:

'I thought by now that I had spent enough labour on the study of ancient languages, on the reading of ancient authors, and on their histories and narratives. To live with men of an earlier age is like travelling in foreign lands. It is useful to know something of the manners of other peoples in order to judge more impartially of our own, and not despise and ridicule whatever differs from them, like men who have never been outside their native country. But those who travel too long end by being strangers in their own homes, and those who study too curiously the actions of antiquity are ignorant of what is done among ourselves to-day. Moreover these narratives tell of things which cannot have happened as if they had really taken place, and thus invite us to attempt what is beyond our powers or to hope for what is beyond our fate. And even histories, true though they be, and neither exaggerating nor altering the value of things, omit circumstances of a meaner and less dignified kind in order to become more worthy of a reader's attention; hence the things which they describe never happened exactly as they describe them, and men who try to model their own acts upon them are prone to the madness of romantic paladins and meditate hyperbolical deeds.'

Descartes here makes four points which it is well to distinguish: (1) Historical escapism: the historian is a traveller who
by living away from home becomes a stranger to his own age.
(2) Historical pyrrhonism: historical narratives are not trustworthy accounts of the past. (3) Anti-utilitarian idea of history:
untrustworthy narratives cannot really assist us to understand
what is possible and thus to act effectively in the present.
(4) History as fantasy-building: the way in which historians,
even at best, distort the past is by making it appear more
splendid than it really was.

(1) One answer to the 'escapist' view of history would be to
show that the historian can genuinely see into the past only so
far as he stands firmly rooted in the present; that is, his business
is not to leap clean out of his own period of history but to be
in every respect a man of his age and to see the past as it appears
from the standpoint of that age. This is actually the true
answer; but in order that it should be given it was necessary
for the theory of knowledge to advance farther than Descartes
took it. It was not until the time of Kant that philosphers conceived the idea of knowledge as directed to an object relative
to the knower's own point of view. The Kantian 'Copernican
revolution' contained implicitly, though Kant himself did not
work it out, a theory of how historical knowledge is possible not
only without the historian's abandoning the standpoint of his own
age, but precisely because he does not abandon that standpoint.

(2) To say that historical narratives relate events that cannot
have happened is to say that we have some criterion, other than
the narratives which reach us, by which to judge what could
have happened. Descartes is here adumbrating a genuinely
critical attitude in history which if fully developed would be
the answer to his own objection.

(3) The Renaissance scholars, in reviving many elements of
the Greco-Roman conception of history, had revived the idea
that its value was a practical value, instructing men in the art
of politics and practical life. This idea was inevitable so long
as people could find no theoretical basis for the alternative belief
that its value was theoretical and consisted in truth. Descartes
was quite right to reject it; he was in fact anticipating Hegel's
remark, in the introduction to his *Philosophy of History*, that
the practical lesson of history is that no one ever learns anything

from history; but he did not see that the historical work of his own day, in the hands of men like Buchanan and Grotius, and still more of others in the generation then beginning, like Tillemont and the Bollandist scholars, was actuated by a sheer desire for truth, and that the pragmatic conception which he was criticizing was dead by the time he wrote.

(4) In saying that historical narratives exaggerate the grandeur and splendour of the past, Descartes was actually propounding a criterion by which they could be criticized and by which the truth they concealed or distorted could be rediscovered. If he had continued in that vein, he might have laid down a method or code of rules for historical criticism; actually this is one of the rules laid down at the beginning of the next century by Vico. But Descartes did not realize this, because his intellectual interests were so definitely orientated towards mathematics and physics that when writing about history he could mistake a fertile suggestion towards the improvement of historical method for a demonstration that no such improvement was possible.

Thus the attitude of Descartes towards history was curiously ambiguous. So far as his intention went, his work tended to throw doubt on its value, however that value was conceived, because he meant to direct people away from it and towards exact science. In the nineteenth century science went on its own way independently of philosophy, because the post-Kantian idealists had taken up an increasingly sceptical attitude towards it; and the breach has only begun to be healed in our own time. This estrangement was exactly paralleled by that between history and philosophy in the seventeenth century, which was due to a parallel cause, the historical scepticism of Descartes.

§ 6. Cartesian historiography

In point of fact, Descartes's scepticism by no means discouraged the historians. Rather they behaved as if they had taken it as a challenge, an invitation to go away and work out their own methods for themselves, satisfying themselves that critical history was possible, and then come back to the philosophers with a new world of knowledge in their hands. During the latter half of the seventeenth century a new school of historical thought arose which, in spite of the paradox contained in the phrase, might be called Cartesian historiography, somewhat as the classical French drama of the same period has been called a school of Cartesian poetry. I call it Cartesian historiography because it was based, like the Cartesian philosophy, on systematic scepticism and thoroughgoing recognition of critical principles. The main idea of this new school was that the testimony of written authorities must not be accepted without submitting it to a process of criticism based on at least three rules of method: (1) Descartes's own implicit rule, that no authority must induce us to believe what we know cannot have happened; (2) the rule that different authorities must be confronted with each other and harmonized; (3) the rule that written authorities must be checked by the use of non-literary evidence. History thus conceived was still based on written authorities, or what Bacon would have called memory; but historians were now learning to treat their authorities in a thoroughly critical spirit.

As examples of this school I have already mentioned Tillemont and the Bollandists. Tillemont's *History of the Roman Emperors* was the first attempt to write Roman history with systematic attention to reconciling the statements of different authorities; the Bollandists, a school of Benedictine scholars, set themselves to rewrite the lives of the saints on a critical basis, purging away all exaggeratedly miraculous elements and going more deeply than any one had hitherto done into the problem of sources and the way in which traditions had grown up. It is to this period and especially to the Bollandists that we owe the idea of dissecting a tradition, allowing for the distortion of the medium through which it has reached us, and thus getting rid once for all of the old dilemma between either accepting it *en bloc* as true or rejecting it as false. At the same time, detailed studies were being made of the possibilities of coins, inscriptions, charters, and other non-literary documents, used to check and illustrate the narratives and descriptions of literary historians. It was during this period, for example, that John Horsley of Morpeth in Northumberland made the first systematic collection of Roman inscriptions in Britain, following the lead of Italian, French, and German scholars.

This movement was very little noticed by philosophers. The only one of leading rank who was much affected by it was Leibniz, who applied the new methods of historical scholarship to the history of philosophy with momentous results. We can even call him the modern founder of that study. He never wrote on it at length, but his work is everywhere permeated with knowledge of ancient and medieval philosophical thought, and we owe to him the conception of philosophy as a continuous historical tradition in which new progress comes about not by propounding completely new and revolutionary ideas but by preserving and developing what he calls the *philosophia perennis*, the permanent and unchanging truths which have always been known. This conception, of course, lays too much stress on the idea of permanence and too little on that of change; philosophical truth is conceived too much as an unchanging deposit of external and eternally known verities and too little as something always needing to be re-created by an effort of thought that transcends the past; but that is only a way of saying that Leibniz's conception of history characteristically belonged to a period when the relations between the permanent and the changing, between truths of reason and truths of fact, had not yet been clearly thought out. Leibniz marks a *rapprochement* between the alienated spheres of philosophy and history, not yet an effective contact between them.

In spite of this strongly historical bent in Leibniz, and in spite of the brilliant work which made Spinoza the founder of Biblical criticism, the general tendency of the Cartesian school was sharply anti-historical. And it was precisely this fact that led to the general downfall and discredit of Cartesianism. The powerful new movement of historical thought, growing up as it were under the ban of Cartesian philosophy, constituted by its very existence a refutation of that philosophy; and when the time came for a definite attack upon its principles, the persons who led that attack were quite naturally persons whose main constructive interest was in history. I shall give some account of two such attacks.

§ 7. *Anti-Cartesianism:* (i) *Vico*

The first is that of Vico, who was working in Naples in the early eighteenth century. The interest of Vico's work lies in the fact that he was in the first place a trained and brilliant historian, who set himself the task of formulating the principles of historical method as Bacon had formulated those of scientific;

and in the course of this constructive work he found himself confronted by the Cartesian philosophy as something against which a polemic had to be undertaken. He did not impugn the validity of mathematical knowledge, but he did impugn the Cartesian theory of knowledge with its implication that no other kind of knowledge was possible. Hence he attacked the Cartesian principle that the criterion of truth is the clear and distinct idea. He pointed out that in effect this was only a subjective or psychological criterion. The fact that I think my ideas clear and distinct only proves that I believe them, not that they are true. In saying this, Vico is substantially agreeing with Hume, that belief is nothing but the vivacity of our perceptions. Any idea, says Vico, however false, may convince us by its seeming self-evidence, and nothing is easier than to think our beliefs self-evident when in fact they are baseless fictions reached by sophistical argument: once more, a Humian point. What we need, Vico contends, is a principle by which to distinguish what can be known from what cannot; a doctrine of the necessary limits of human knowledge. This, of course, brings Vico into line with Locke, whose critical empiricism was to supply a starting-point for the other main attack on Cartesianism.

Vico finds this principle in the doctrine that *verum et factum convertuntur*: that is, the condition of being able to know anything truly, to understand it as opposed to merely perceiving it, is that the knower himself should have made it. On this principle nature is intelligible only to God, but mathematics is intelligible to man, because the objects of mathematical thought are fictions or hypotheses which the mathematician has constructed. Any piece of mathematical thinking begins with a *fiat: let* ABC be a triangle and *let* AB = AC. It is because by this act of will the mathematician makes the triangle, because it is his *factum*, that he can have true knowledge of it. This is not, in the ordinary sense of the word, 'idealism'. The existence of the triangle does not depend on its being known : to know things is not to create them; on the contrary, nothing can be known unless it has already been created, and whether a given mind can know it depends on how it has been created.

It follows from the *verum-factum* principle that history, which is emphatically something made by the human mind, is especially adapted to be an object of human knowledge. Vico regards the historical process as a process whereby human beings build up systems of language, custom, law, government, &c.: i.e. he thinks of history as the history of the genesis and development of human societies and their institutions. Here we reach for the first time a completely modern idea of what the subject-matter of history is. There is no antithesis between the isolated actions of men and the divine plan that holds them together, as there was for the Middle Ages; and, on the other hand, there is no suggestion that primitive man (in whom Vico was peculiarly interested) foresaw what was going to come of the developments he was initiating; the plan of history is a wholly human plan, but it does not pre-exist in the shape of an unrealized intention to its own gradual realization. Man is no mere demiurge, fashioning human society as Plato's God fashions the world on an ideal model; like God Himself, he is a real creator, bringing into existence both form and matter together in the corporate work of his own historical development. The fabric of human society is created by man out of nothing, and every detail of this fabric is therefore a human *factum*, eminently knowable to the human mind as such.

Vico is here giving us the results of his long and fruitful researches into the history of such things as law and language. He has found these researches capable of yielding knowledge just as certain as the knowledge Descartes had ascribed to the results of mathematical and physical research; and he expresses the way in which this knowledge has arisen by saying in effect that the historian can reconstruct in his own mind the process by which these things have been created by men in the past. There is a kind of pre-established harmony between the historian's mind and the object which he sets out to study; but this pre-established harmony, unlike that of Leibniz, is not based on a miracle—it is based on the common human nature uniting the historian with the men whose work he is studying.

This new attitude towards history is profoundly anti-Cartesian because the whole structure of the Cartesian system was conditioned by a problem which in the world of history does not arise: the problem of scepticism, the problem of the relation between ideas and things. Descartes, starting his researches into the method of natural science from the sceptical point of view which then prevailed in France, had to begin by assuring himself that there really was such a thing as the material world. For history as conceived by Vico no such problem could exist. The sceptical point of view is impossible. History, for Vico, is not concerned with the past as past. It is concerned, in the first instance, with the actual structure of the society in which we live ; the manners and customs which we share with the people around us. In order to study these we need not ask whether they really exist. The question has no meaning. Descartes, looking at the fire, asked himself whether in addition to his own idea of a fire there was also a real fire. For Vico, looking at such a thing as the Italian language of his own day, no parallel question could arise. The distinction between the idea of such an historical reality and the reality itself would be meaningless. The Italian language is exactly what the people who use it think it is. For the historian, the human point of view is final. What God thinks about the Italian language is a question which he need not ask, and which he knows he could not answer. Search for the thing in itself is for him as pointless as it is futile. And Descartes himself half recognized this when he said[1] that in matters of morality his rule was to accept the laws and institutions of the country in which he lived, and to govern his conduct according to the best opinions which he found commonly received around him : thus admitting that the individual could not construct these things for himself *a priori* but must recognize them as historical facts pertaining to the society in which he lives. It is true that Descartes only adopted these rules provisionally, hoping that the time would come when he would be able to construct his own system of conduct on a metaphysical basis ; but the time never did come, and in the nature of the case never could ; Descartes's hope was only one example of the exaggerated views he held about the possibilities of *a priori* speculation. History is a kind of knowledge in which questions about ideas and questions about facts are not distinguishable ; and the whole point of Descartes's philosophy consists in distinguishing those two types of question.

With Vico's conception of history as a philosophically justi-fiable form of knowledge went a conception of historical know-ledge as capable of far wider development. Once the historian

[1] *Discourse on Method*, part iii.

answers the question how historical knowledge in general is possible, he can proceed to the solution of historical problems hitherto insoluble. This is done by forming a clear conception of historical method and working out the rules which it obeys. Vico was peculiarly interested in what he called the history of remote and obscure periods, that is, in the extension of historical knowledge; and in this connexion he laid down certain rules of method.

First, he held that certain periods of history had a general character, colouring every detail, which reappeared in other periods, so that two different periods might have the same general character, and it was possible to argue analogically from one to the other. He instanced the general resemblance between the Homeric period of Greek history and the European Middle Ages, both of which he called by the generic name of heroic periods. Their common features were such things as government by a warrior-aristocracy, an agricultural economy, a ballad-literature, a morality based on the idea of personal prowess and loyalty, and so forth. To learn more than Homer can tell us about the Homeric age, therefore, we should study the Middle Ages and then see how far we can apply what we have learnt there to early Greece.

Secondly, he showed that these similar periods tended to recur in the same order. Every heroic period is followed by a classical period, where thought prevails over imagination, prose over poetry, industry over agriculture, and a morality based on peace over one based on war. This in turn is followed by a decline into a new barbarism, but a barbarism quite different from the heroic barbarism of the imagination; it is what he calls a barbarism of reflection, where thought still rules, but a thought which has exhausted its creative power and only constructs meaningless networks of artificial and pedantic distinctions. Vico sometimes puts his cycle in the following way: first, the guiding principle of history is brute strength; then valiant or heroic strength; then valiant justice; then brilliant originality; then constructive reflection; and lastly a kind of spendthrift and wasteful opulence which destroys what has been constructed. But he is quite aware that any such scheme is too rigid not to admit of countless exceptions.

Thirdly, this cyclical movement is not a mere rotation of

history through a cycle of fixed phases; it is not a circle but a spiral; for history never repeats itself but comes round to each new phase in a form differentiated by what has gone before. Thus the Christian barbarism of the Middle Ages is differentiated from the pagan barbarism of the Homeric age by everything that makes it distinctively an expression of the Christian mind. For this reason, because history is always creating novelties, the cyclical law does not permit us to forecast the future, and this distinguishes Vico's use of it from the old Greco-Roman idea of a strictly circular movement in history (found for example in Plato, Polybius, and Renaissance historians like Machiavelli and Campanella) and brings it into line with the principle, to whose fundamental importance I have already referred, that the true historian never prophesies.

Vico then goes on to enumerate certain prejudices against which historians have always to be on their guard, like the 'idols' in Bacon's *Novum Organum*. He distinguishes five of these sources of error:

1. Magnificent opinions concerning antiquity, i.e. the prejudice in favour of exaggerating the wealth, power, grandeur, &c., of the period which the historian is studying. The principle which Vico is here expressing negatively is the principle that what makes a past period of history worth studying is not the intrinsic worth of its achievements taken by themselves but its relation to the general course of history. The prejudice is a very real one; e.g. I find that people who are interested in Roman provincial civilization have a strong reluctance to believe (as I have proved from archaeological evidence) that Roman London had only about 10,000–15,000 inhabitants. They would rather it had 50,000–100,000, because they have magnificent opinions concerning antiquity.

2. The conceit of nations. Every nation in dealing with its own past history has a prejudice in favour of painting it in the most favourable colours. Histories of England written by and for English people do not enlarge on military failures, and so forth.

3. The conceit of the learned. This, as Vico interprets it, takes the special form of a prejudice on the part of the historian which makes him suppose that the people about whom he is thinking were like himself in being scholars and students and

in general people of reflective intellect. The academic mind fancies that the persons in whom it is interested must have been academic persons themselves. Actually, Vico held, the·most effective men in history have been the least academically minded. Historical greatness and reflective intellect are very rarely combined. The scale of values which governs the historian's own life is very different from that which governed the lives of his chief characters.

4. The fallacy of sources, or what Vico calls the scholastic succession of nations. This error consists in thinking that when two nations have a similar idea or institution one must have learnt it from the other, and Vico shows that it depends on denying the original creative power of the human mind, which can rediscover ideas for itself without learning them from another. He is quite right to warn historians against this fallacy. In point of fact, even where it is certain that one nation has taught another, as China has taught Japan, Greece Rome, Rome Gaul, and so on, the learner invariably learns not what the other has to teach but only the lessons for which its previous historical development has prepared it.

5. Lastly, there is the prejudice of thinking the ancients better informed than ourselves about the times that lay nearer to them. Actually, to take an example that is not one of Vico's, the scholars of King Alfred's time knew much less about Anglo-Saxon origins than we do. Vico's warning against this prejudice is of great importance because, when developed on its positive side, it becomes the principle that the historian does not depend on an unbroken tradition for his knowledge but can reconstruct by scientific methods a picture of a past age which he has not derived from any tradition whatever. This is the explicit denial that history depends on what Bacon called memory, or in other words the statements of authorities.

Vico is not content with negative warnings; he goes on positively to indicate certain methods by which the historian can transcend mere reliance on the statements of authorities. His observations here are commonplaces to the historian of to-day, but in his own time they were revolutionary.

1. He shows how linguistic study can throw light on history. Etymology can show what kind of life a people was leading while its language was coming into existence. The historian is aiming

at a reconstruction of the mental life, the ideas, of the people he is studying; their stock of words shows what their stock of ideas was; and the way in which they use an old word metaphorically in a new sense, when they want to express a new idea, shows what their stock of ideas was before that new one came into existence. Thus, Latin words like *intellegere* and *disserere* show how, when Romans needed words for understanding and discussing, they borrowed from an agricultural vocabulary the words for gleaning and sowing.

2. He makes a similar use of mythology. The gods of primitive religion represent a semi-poetical way of expressing the social structure of the people who invented them. Thus, in Greco-Roman mythology, Vico saw a representation of the domestic, economic, and political life of the ancients. These myths were the way in which a primitive and imaginative mind expressed to itself what a more reflective mind would have stated in codes of law and morality.

3. He propounds a new method (strange as its novelty may appear to us) of using tradition: by taking it not as literally true but as a confused memory of facts distorted through a medium whose refractive index we can to a certain extent define. All traditions are true, but none of them mean what they say; in order to discover what they mean, we must know what kind of people invented them and what such a kind of people would mean by saying that kind of thing.

4. In order to find the key to this reinterpretation we must remember that minds at a given stage of development will tend to create the same kind of products. Savages, at all times and in all places, are savages in mind; by studying modern savages we can learn what ancient savages were like, and thus find out how to interpret the savage myths and legends that conceal the facts of remotest ancient history. Children are savages of a kind, and children's fairy-tales may help in the same direction. Modern peasants are unreflective and imaginative persons, and their ideas throw light on the ideas of primitive society; and so forth.

To sum up: Vico has done two things. First, he has used to the full the advance in critical method which had been achieved by historians of the late seventeenth century and carried this process a stage farther by showing how historical thought can be constructive as well as critical, cutting it loose from its dependence on written authorities and making it genuinely original or self-dependent, able to recover by scientific analysis of data truths which have been completely forgotten. Secondly, he has developed the philosophical principles implicit in his historical work up to a point where he can deliver a counter-attack on the scientific and metaphysical philosophy of Cartesianism, demanding a broader basis for the theory of knowledge and criticizing the narrowness and abstractness of the prevailing philosophical creed. Actually he was too far ahead of his time to have very much immediate influence. The extraordinary merit of his work was not recognized until, two generations later, German thought had reached on its own account a point much akin to his own, through the great blossoming of historical studies which took place in Germany in the late eighteenth century. When that happened, German scholars rediscovered Vico and attached a great value to him, thus exemplifying his own doctrine that ideas are propagated not by 'diffusion', like articles of commerce, but by the independent discovery by each nation of what it needs at any given stage in its own development.

§ 8. *Anti-Cartesianism*: (ii) *Locke, Berkeley, and Hume*

The second and, so far as its historical consequences went, by far the more effective attack on Cartesianism was that delivered by the Lockian school culminating in Hume. At first, the empiricism of this school, though already in conscious opposition to Descartes, had no conscious relation to the problems of historical thought. But as the school developed it gradually became clear that the point of view which it was working out could be used in the interests of history, if only in a negative sense, that is, in order to destroy the Cartesianism which had banished history from a place on the map of knowledge. Locke and Berkeley show in their philosophical writings no special preoccupation with the problems of historical thought (though Locke's description of his own method as the 'historical plain method' shows that he was not unaware of the relation between his own anti-Cartesianism and the study of history. In his *Essay*, Introduction, § 2, he says that by this he means that he aims at giving an 'account of the ways whereby our understandings come to attain those notions of things we have'.

Our 'notions of things' are thus treated by Locke exactly as manners and customs are treated by Vico; the Cartesian problem of the relation between ideas and things being in each case ruled out as a problem that does not arise). But in France the eagerness with which a Lockian philosophy was adopted by the men of the Enlightenment, Voltaire and the Encyclopaedists, whose interests were definitely orientated towards history, shows that this philosophy was in some way peculiarly adapted to serve as a weapon for historical thought first in its defence and then in its counter-attack against the tradition of Descartes. The revolt against Cartesianism is in fact the chief negative feature of French thought in the eighteenth century: its chief positive features are, first, its increasingly historical tone and, secondly, its adoption of a Lockian type of philosophy; and it is obvious that these three features were mutually interdependent.

The main points of the Lockian philosophy are easily enumerated. In each case I think it will be clear that the point is, negatively, anti-Cartesian and, positively, a contribution towards a reorientation of philosophy in the direction of history.

1. The denial of innate ideas and the insistence that knowledge comes through experience.—The conception of innate ideas is an anti-historical conception. If all knowledge consists in making explicit our innate ideas, and if all such ideas are present as potentialities in every human mind, all possible knowledge can theoretically be produced afresh by every human being for himself by his own unaided efforts, and there is no need for that corporate building-up of the body of knowledge which is the special work of history. If all knowledge is based on experience, it is an historical product; truth, as Bacon had already reasserted,[1] is the daughter of time; the best knowledge is a fruit of the ripest and richest experience. Thus an historical view of knowledge is already implicit in the first book of Locke's *Essay*.

2. The denial of any argument intended to bridge an alleged gulf between ideas and things, the denial being grounded on the doctrine that knowledge is concerned not with a reality distinct from our ideas but with the agreement and disagreement of our ideas themselves.—As applied to physical science this doctrine is obviously paradoxical, for in physical science we seem

[1] *Novum Organum*, bk. i, § lxxxiv, quoting Aulus Gellius, *Noctes Atticae*, xii. II.

to aim at knowledge of something incapable of being reduced to ideas; but as applied to our historical knowledge of human institutions like morality, language, law, and politics it is not only devoid of paradox, it is the most natural way of looking at these things, as we have already seen.

3. The denial of abstract ideas and the insistence that all ideas are concrete.—This, which Berkeley showed to be implicit in Locke, is paradoxical as applied to mathematics and physics, but once more is obviously the natural way of thinking about history, where knowledge consists not of abstract generalizations but of concrete ideas.

4. The conception of human knowledge as falling necessarily short of absolute truth and certainty, but capable of attaining (in Locke's words) such certainty as our condition needs; or (as Hume puts it) that reason is incapable of dispelling the clouds of doubt, but that Nature herself (our human nature) suffices for that purpose and lays upon us in our practical life an absolute necessity to live and talk and act like other people.—This is cold comfort for a Cartesian intent upon the problems of mathematics and physics, but it is a solid basis for historical knowledge, that being precisely concerned with what Locke calls our condition, the actual state of human affairs, or the way in which men live and talk and act.

The English school, then, is reorientating philosophy in the direction of history, though as a whole it is not clearly aware that it is doing so. Nevertheless, Hume is less blind to the situation than his predecessors were. There must be some significance, in the case of so determined and profound a thinker, in the fact that he deserted philosophical studies in favour of historical at about the age of thirty-five. If in the light of his later interests we look through his philosophical works in search of references to history, we find a few such references; not very many, but quite enough to show that history already interested him, that he was thinking about it philosophically, and that he was curiously confident in the power of his own philosophical theories to explain the problems to which they gave rise.

Of these references I shall consider two. In the first we find Hume applying the principles of his philosophy to the case of historical knowledge conceived in the spirit of the methods worked out by the scholars of the late seventeenth century.

'We believe that Caesar was killed in the senate-house on the Ides of March; and that because this fact is established on the unanimous testimony of historians, who agree to assign this precise time and place to that event. Here are certain characters and letters present either to our memory or senses; which characters we likewise remember to have been used as the signs of certain ideas; and these ideas were either in the minds of such as were immediately present at that action, and received the ideas directly from its existence; or they were derived from the testimony of others, and that again from another testimony, by a visible gradation, till we arrive at those who were eye-witnesses and spectators of the event. 'Tis obvious all this chain of argument or connexion of causes and effects, is at first founded on those characters or letters, which are seen or remembered, and that without the authority either of the memory or senses our whole reasoning would be chimerical and without foundation.'[1]

Here the historian's data are given him by direct perception, they are what Hume calls impressions; he actually sees certain documents in front of him. The question is, Why do those impressions cause him to believe that Caesar was killed at a certain time and place? Hume's answer is easy: the association of these visible signs with certain ideas is a matter of fact, attested by our memory; the association being constant, we believe that the people who originally committed those words to paper meant by them what we should ourselves mean; and thus we believe, assuming their veracity, that they believed what they said, viz. that they actually saw Caesar die at that time and place. This is a quite satisfactory solution for the problem of history as it appeared to an historian of the early eighteenth century who could be content if he had shown historical knowledge to be a system of reasonable beliefs based on testimony. And if the philosopher could go on to show, as Hume did, that no other kind of knowledge was more than a system of reasonable beliefs, the claim of history to a place on the map of knowledge was vindicated.

Secondly, Hume was quite aware that contemporary philosophical thought had cast doubt on the validity of historical knowledge, and he goes out of his way to rebut the stock argument, especially because that argument might claim (unjustly, as he thinks) to be supported by his own principles:

[1] *Treatise of Human Nature*, bk. i, pt. iii, § 4.

' 'Tis evident there is no point of ancient history, of which we can have any assurance, but by passing through many millions of causes and effects, and through a chain of arguments of almost an immeasurable length. Before the knowledge of the fact could come to the first historian, it must be conveyed through many mouths; and after it is committed to writing, each new copy is a new object, of which the connexion with the foregoing is known only by experience and observation. Perhaps therefore it may be concluded, from the precedent reasoning, that the evidence of all ancient history must now be lost, as the chain of causes increases and runs on to a greater length.'

Hume goes on to argue that this is contrary to common sense: the evidence of ancient history does not thus decay with mere length. The solution is that

'though the links are innumerable . . . yet they are all of the same kind, and depend on the fidelity of printers and copists. . . . There is no variation in the steps. After we know one, we know all of them; and after we have made one, we can have no scruple as to the rest.'[1]

Thus we see that already in his twenties, when he wrote the *Treatise*, Hume had reflected on the problems of historical thought, had decided that the Cartesian objections to it were invalid, and had arrived at a philosophical system which in his own opinion rebutted those objections and placed history on a footing at least as sound as that of any other science. I would not go so far as to call his entire philosophy a reasoned defence of historical thought, but that was undoubtedly one of the things which it implicitly undertook; and it seems to me that when he had finished his philosophical work and asked himself what he had accomplished in it, he could have said with justice that one thing at any rate was the demonstration that history was a legitimate and valid type of knowledge, more legitimate in fact than most others because not promising more than it could perform and not depending on any questionable metaphysical hypotheses. In the general scepticism to which he was led, the sciences which suffered most were those whose claims were most dogmatic and absolute; the whirlwind of his philosophical criticism, levelling all thought to the position of natural and reasonable belief, left undamaged the fabric of history, as a type of thought which alone could be satisfied with that condition. Nevertheless, Hume remained unconscious of the full impact of his philosophy upon history, and as a writer of history he ranks with the men of the Enlightenment, barred like them from scientific history by a substantialistic view of human nature which was really quite inconsistent with his philosophical principles.

§ 9. *The Enlightenment*

Hume, in his historical work, and his slightly older contemporary Voltaire stand at the head of a new school of historical thought. Their work and that of their followers may be defined as the historiography of the Enlightenment. By the Enlightenment, *Aufklärung*, is meant that endeavour, so characteristic of the early eighteenth century, to secularize every department of human life and thought. It was a revolt not only against the power of institutional religion but against religion as such. Voltaire regarded himself as the leader of a crusade against Christianity, fighting under the motto *Écrasez l'infâme*, where *l'infâme* meant superstition, religion considered as a function of what was backward and barbarous in human life. The philosophical theory underlying this movement was that certain forms of mental activity are primitive forms, destined to perish when mind arrives at maturity. According to Vico, poetry is the natural mode in which the savage or childish mind expresses itself; the sublimest poetry, he maintains, is the poetry of barbarous or heroic ages, the poetry of Homer or Dante; as man develops, reason prevails over imagination and passion, and poetry is displaced by prose. Intermediately between the poetic or purely imaginative way of presenting its experience to itself, and the prosaic or purely rational, Vico placed a third, the mythical or semi-imaginative. This is the stage of development which puts upon the whole of experience a religious interpretation. Thus Vico thinks of art, religion, and philosophy as three different ways in which the human mind expresses or formulates to itself its whole experience. They cannot live peaceably side by side; their relation to each other is one of dialectical succession in a definite order. It follows that a religious attitude towards life is destined to be superseded by a rational or philo-sophical one.

No such theory was consciously formulated either by Voltaire or by Hume. But had such a theory been brought to their notice, they might have accepted it, and identified themselves and their colleagues with the agency which was actually bring-ing the religious era of human history to an end and inaugurating a non-religious rational era. Actually, however, their polemical attitude towards religion was too violent and one-sided to have received support from any such theory of its place in human history. For them it was a thing devoid of all positive value whatever, it was just sheer error, due to the unscrupulous and calculating hypocrisy of a class of beings called priests, who, they seem to have thought, invented it to serve as an instrument of domination over the mass of men. Terms like religion, priest, Middle Ages, barbarism, were for such persons not historical or philosophical or sociological terms with a definite scientific meaning, as they were for Vico, but simply terms of abuse: they had an emotional, not a conceptual, signi-ficance. As soon as a term like 'religion' or 'barbarism' has a conceptual significance, the thing that goes by such a name has to be regarded as something with a positive function in human history, and therefore not a mere evil or error but a thing with its own proper value in its own proper place. A truly historical view of human history sees everything in that history as having its own *raison d'être* and coming into existence in order to serve the needs of the men whose minds have corporately created it. To think of any phase in history as altogether irrational is to look at it not as an historian but as a publicist, a polemical writer of tracts for the times. Thus the historical outlook of the Enlightenment was not genuinely historical; in its main motive it was polemical and anti-historical.

For this reason writers like Voltaire and Hume did very little to improve the methods of historical research. They took over the methods devised in the preceding generation by men like Mabillon and Tillemont and the Bollandists, and even these methods they did not use in a really scholarly spirit. They were not sufficiently interested in history for its own sake to per-severe in the task of reconstructing the history of obscure and remote periods. Voltaire openly proclaimed that no securely based historical knowledge was attainable for events earlier than the close of the fifteenth century; Hume's *History of England* is a very slight and sketchy piece of work until he comes to the same period, the age of the Tudors. The real cause of this restriction of interest to the modern period was that with their narrow conception of reason they had no sympathy for, and therefore no insight into, what from their point of view were non-rational periods of human history; they only began to be interested in history at the point where it began to be the history of a modern spirit akin to their own, a scientific spirit. In economic terms this meant the spirit of modern industry and commerce. In political terms it meant the spirit of enlightened despotism. They had no conception of institutions as created by the spirit of a people in its historical development; they conceived them as inventions, artifices devised by ingenious thinkers, and imposed by them on the mass of the people. Their idea of religion as due to priestcraft was merely an application of this same principle, the only one they understood, to a phase of history where it did not apply.

The Enlightenment in its narrower sense, as an essentially polemical and negative movement, a crusade against religion, never rose higher than its source, and Voltaire remained its best and most characteristic expression. But it developed in various directions without losing its original character. Based as it was on the idea that human life is and has always been in the main a blind, irrational business, but is capable of being converted into something rational, it contained in itself the germs of two immediate developments: a backward-looking or more strictly historical development which should exhibit past history as the play of irrational forces, and a forward-looking or more practical or political development, forecasting and endeavouring to bring about a millennium in which the rule of reason shall have been established.

(*a*) As examples of the first tendency we may quote Montesquieu and Gibbon. Montesquieu had the merit of seizing upon the differences between different nations and different cultures, but he misunderstood the essential character of these differences. Instead of explaining their history by reference to human reason, he thought of it as due to differences in climate and geography. Man, in other words, is regarded as a part of nature, and the explanation of historical events is sought in the facts of the natural world. History so conceived would become a kind of natural history of man, or anthropology, where institutions appear not as free inventions of human reason in the course of its development, but as the necessary effects of natural causes. Montesquieu in fact conceived human life as a reflection of geographical and climatic conditions, not otherwise than the life of plants, and this implies that historical changes are simply different ways in which one single and unchangeable thing, human nature, reacts to different stimuli. This misconception of human nature and human action is the real flaw in any theory which, like Montesquieu's, attempts to explain the features of a civilization by reference to geographical facts. To be sure, there is an intimate relation between any culture and its natural environment; but what determines its character is not the facts of that environment, in themselves, but what man is able to get out of them; and that depends on what kind of man he is. As an historian, Montesquieu was uncritical in the extreme; but his insistence on the relation of man to his environment (even though he misconceived the character of that relation) and on the economic factors which in his view underlay political institutions was important not only in itself but for the future development of historical thought.

Gibbon, a typical Enlightenment historian, agreed with all this to the extent of conceiving history as anything but an exhibition of human wisdom; but instead of finding its positive principle in the laws of nature which, as it were, replace for Montesquieu the wisdom of man and create for him social organizations which he could not create for himself, Gibbon finds the motive force of history in human irrationality itself, and his narrative displays what he calls the triumph of barbarism and religion. But in order that there may be such a triumph there must first be something for this irrationality to triumph over; and thus Gibbon places the beginning of his narrative in a golden age when human reason ruled over a happy world, the Antonine period. This conception of a golden age in the past gives Gibbon a rather special place among Enlightenment historians and assimilates him on the one hand to his predecessors, the humanists of the Renaissance, and on the other to his successors, the Romantics at the close of the eighteenth century.

(b) In its forward-looking aspect, where the golden age is conceived as lying in the near future, this movement may be represented by Condorcet, whose *Esquisse d'un tableau des progrès de l'esprit humain*, written during the French Revolution when he was in prison awaiting execution, looks forward to a Utopian future where tyrants and their slaves, priests and their dupes, will have disappeared, and people will behave rationally in the enjoyment of life, liberty, and the pursuit of happiness.

It will be plain from the examples that have been given that the historiography of the Enlightenment is apocalyptic to an extreme degree, as indeed the very word 'enlightenment' suggests. The central point of history, for these writers, is the sunrise of the modern scientific spirit. Before that, everything was superstition and darkness, error and imposture. And of these things there can be no history, not only because they are unworthy of historical study, but because there is in them no rational or necessary development: the story of them is a tale told by an idiot, full of sound and fury, signifying nothing.

Thus in the crucial case, namely the origin of the modern scientific spirit, these writers could have no conception of historical origins or processes. Pure reason cannot come into existence out of pure unreason. There can be no development leading from the one to the other. The sunrise of the scientific spirit was, from the point of view of the Enlightenment, a sheer miracle, unprepared in the previous course of events and uncaused by any cause that could be adequate to such an effect. This inability to explain or expound historically what they regarded as the most important event in history was of course symptomatic; it meant that in a general way they had no satisfactory theory of historical causation and could not seriously believe in the origin or genesis of anything whatever. Consequently, throughout their historical work, their account of causes is superficial to absurdity. It was these historians, for example, who invented the grotesque idea that the Renaissance in Europe was due to the fall of Constantinople and the consequent expulsion of scholars in search of new homes; and a typical expression of this attitude is the remark of Pascal that if Cleopatra's nose had been longer the whole history of the world would have been different—typical, that is, of a bankruptcy of historical method which in despair of genuine explanation acquiesces in the most trivial causes for the vastest effects. Such inability to discover genuine historical causes is, no doubt, connected with the Humian theory of causation according to which we can never perceive any connexion between any two events.

Perhaps the best short way of describing the historiography of the Enlightenment is to say that it took over the conception of historical research which had been devised by the Church historians of the late seventeenth century, and turned it against its authors, using it in a deliberately anti-clerical spirit instead of a deliberately clerical one. No attempt was made to lift history above the level of propaganda; on the contrary, that aspect of it was intensified, for the crusade in favour of reason was still a holy war; and Montesquieu hit the nail on the head when he remarked[1] that in spirit Voltaire was a monastic historian writing for monks. At the same time, the historians of this period did achieve certain definite advances. Intolerant and unreasonable though they were, they were fighting for tolerance. Unable though they were to appreciate the creative power of a popular spirit, they were writing from the point of view of the subject, not the government, and were therefore bringing into an altogether new prominence the history of the arts and sciences, industry, trade, and culture in general. Superficial though they were in their search for causes, they did at least search for them, and thus implicitly conceived history as (in spite of Hume) a process in which one event led necessarily to the next. There was thus a leaven at work in their own thought which was tending to disrupt their own dogmas and transcend their own limitations. Deep down beneath the surface of their work lay a conception of the historical process as a process developing neither by the will of enlightened despots nor by the rigid plans of a transcendent God, but by a necessity of its own, an immanent necessity in which unreason itself is only a disguised form of reason.

§ 10. *The science of human nature*

In § 1 of this Part, I pointed out that Hume's attack on spiritual substance was the philosophical forerunner of scientific history because it destroyed the last vestiges of the substan-

[1] 'Voltaire . . . est comme les moines, qui n'écrivent pas pour le sujet qu'ils traitent, mais pour la gloire de leur ordre. Voltaire écrit pour son couvent' (*Pensées diverses* in *Œuvres*, Paris, 1866, vol. ii, p. 427).

tialism in Greco-Roman thought. In § 8 I showed how Locke and his followers were reorientating philosophy in the direction of history, although of this they were not fully conscious. What prevented eighteenth-century history from becoming scientific by reaping the full fruits of the philosophical revolution was an unnoticed relic of substantialism implicit in the Enlightenment's quest for a science of human nature. Just as the ancient historians conceived the Roman character, for example, as a thing that had never really come into existence but had always existed and had always been the same, so the eighteenth-century historians, who recognized that all true history is the history of mankind, assumed that human nature had existed ever since the creation of the world exactly as it existed among themselves. Human nature was conceived substantialistically as something static and permanent, an unvarying substratum underlying the course of historical changes and all human activities. History never repeated itself but human nature remained eternally unaltered.

This assumption is present, as we have seen, in Montesquieu, but it also lies at the back of all the philosophical work of the eighteenth century, not to mention earlier periods. The Cartesian innate ideas are the ways of thinking which are natural to the human mind as such, everywhere and always. The Lockian human understanding is something assumed to be everywhere the same, though imperfectly developed in children, idiots, and savages. The Kantian mind which as intuition is the source of space and time, as understanding the source of the categories, and as reason the source of the Ideas of God, freedom, and immortality, is a purely human mind, but Kant unquestioningly assumes it to be the only kind of human mind that exists or ever has existed. Even so sceptical a thinker as Hume accepts this assumption, as I have already hinted. In the Introduction to his *Treatise of Human Nature* he explains the project of his work by saying that 'all the sciences have a relation, greater or less, to human nature, and however wide any of them may seem to run from it, they still return back by one passage or another. Even *Mathematics*, *Natural Philosophy*, and *Natural Religion*' (i.e. the three Cartesian sciences, mathematics, physics, and metaphysics) 'are in some measure dependent on the science of MAN : since they lie under the cognizance of men, and are judged of by their powers and faculties'. Consequently the 'science of man', that is, the science which investigates the 'principles and operations of our reasoning faculty', 'our tastes and sentiments', and 'men as united in society', is 'the only solid foundation for all the other sciences'.

In all this, Hume never shows the slightest suspicion that the human nature he is analysing in his philosophical work is the nature of a western European in the early eighteenth century, and that the very same enterprise if undertaken at a widely different time or place might have yielded widely different results. He always assumes that *our* reasoning faculty, *our* tastes and sentiments, and so forth, are something perfectly uniform and invariable, underlying and conditioning all historical changes. As I have already suggested, his attack on the idea of spiritual substance should, if successful, have demolished this conception of human nature as something solid and permanent and uniform; but it did nothing of the kind, because Hume substituted for the idea of spiritual substance the idea of constant tendencies to associate ideas in particular ways, and these laws of association were just as uniform and unchanging as any substance.

Hume's abolition of spiritual substance amounted to laying down the principle that we must never separate what a mind is from what it does, and that therefore a mind's nature is nothing but the ways in which it thinks and acts. The concept of mental substance was thus resolved into the concept of mental process. But this did not in itself necessitate an historical conception of mind, because all process is not historical process. A process is historical only when it creates its own laws; and according to Hume's theory of mind the laws of mental process are ready-made and unchanging from their beginning. He did not think of mind as learning to think and act in new ways as the process of its activity developed. He certainly thought that his new science of human nature, if successfully achieved, would lead to further progress in the arts and sciences; but not by altering human nature itself—that, he never suggests to be possible—only by improving our understanding of it.

Philosophically, this conception was self-contradictory. If that which we come to understand better is something other than ourselves, for example the chemical properties of matter our improved understanding of it in no way improves the thing itself. If, on the other hand, that which we understand better is our own understanding, an improvement in *that* science is an improvement not only in its subject but in its object also. By coming to think more truly about the human understanding we are coming to improve our own understanding. Hence the historical development of the science of human nature entails an historical development in human nature itself.

This was concealed from eighteenth-century philosophers, because they based their programme for a science of mind on the analogy of the established sciences of nature and failed to notice the lack of complete parallelism between the two cases. Men like Bacon had pointed out that improved knowledge of nature would give us improved power over nature, and this was quite true. Coal tar, for example, once its chemistry is understood, ceases to be refuse and becomes the raw material of dyes, resins, and other products, but the fact that these chemical discoveries have been made in no way alters the nature of coal tar or its by-products. Nature stays put, and is the same whether we understand it or not. To put this in Berkeleian language, it is God's thought, not our thought, that makes nature what it is; in coming to know nature we are not creating anything new, we are only rethinking God's thoughts for ourselves. The eighteenth-century philosophers assumed that exactly the same principles applied to the knowledge of our own mind, which they called human nature in order to express their conception of its resemblance to nature properly so called. They thought of human nature as something which stayed put, however much or however little one knew about it, exactly as nature stays put. They assumed without question a fallacious principle which may be put in the form of a rule-of-three sum: knowledge of nature: nature : : knowledge of mind : mind. This assumption fatally distorted their conception of history in two ways:

(1) Assuming human nature to be constant, they made it impossible for themselves to arrive at the conception of a history of human nature itself; for such a conception implies that human nature is not a constant but a variable. The eighteenth century wished for a universal history, a history of man: but a genuine history of man would have to be a history of how man came to be what he is, and this would imply thinking of

human nature, the human nature actually existing in eighteenth-century Europe, as the product of an historical process, whereas it was regarded as the unchanging presupposition of any such process.

(2) The same error gave them a false view not only of the past but of the future, because it made them look forward to a Utopia in which all the problems of human life should have been solved. For if human nature itself undergoes no change when we come to understand it better, every new discovery we make about it will solve the problems which now perplex us because of our ignorance, and no new problems will be created. Our advancing knowledge of human nature will therefore gradually relieve us of the various difficulties under which we now labour, and human life will consequently become better and better, happier and happier. And if the advance in the science of human nature extends to the discovery of the fundamental laws governing its manifestations, which thinkers of that age thought quite possible on the analogy of the way in which the seventeenth-century scientists had discovered the fundamental laws of physics, the millennium will be achieved. Thus the eighteenth-century conception of progress was based on the same false analogy between knowledge of nature and knowledge of mind. The truth is that if the human mind comes to understand itself better, it thereby comes to operate in new and different ways. A race of men that has acquired the kind of self-knowledge at which the eighteenth-century thinkers were aiming would act in ways not hitherto known, and these new ways of acting would give rise to new moral and social and political problems, and the millennium would be as far away as ever.

PART III

THE THRESHOLD OF SCIENTIFIC HISTORY

§ 1. *Romanticism*

BEFORE any further progress could be made in historical thought, two things were necessary: first, the horizon of history had to be widened through a more sympathetic investigation of those past ages which the Enlightenment had treated as unenlightened or barbaric and left in obscurity; and secondly, the conception of human nature as something uniform and unchanging had to be attacked. It was Herder who first made substantial advances in both of these directions, but he was assisted, so far as the first of them is concerned, by the work of Rousseau.

Rousseau was a child of the Enlightenment, but through his reinterpretation of its principles he became the father of the Romantic movement. He realized that rulers could give their people nothing except what the people themselves were ready to accept, and consequently he argued that the enlightened despot of Voltaire's conception was powerless unless there were an enlightened people. For the idea of a despotic will, imposing on a passive people what the despot knew to be good for it, Rousseau substituted the idea of a general will on the part of the people itself, a will on the part of the people as a whole to pursue its interest as a whole.

In the sphere of practical politics this involved an optimism or Utopianism not greatly different from that of people like Condorcet, though it was differently based: where the Enlightenment based its Utopian expectations on the hope of obtaining enlightened rulers, the Romanticists based theirs on the hope of obtaining an enlightened people by means of popular education. But in the sphere of history the results were very different and indeed revolutionary. The general will as Rousseau conceived it, although it might be more or less enlightened, had always existed and had always been operative. Unlike reason in the Enlightenment theory, it had not come into the world at a comparatively recent date. The principle on which Rousseau explained history, therefore, was a principle which could be applied not only to the recent history of the civilized world but to the history of all races and all times. Ages of barbarism and superstition became at least in principle intelligible and it was possible to see the whole of human history, if not as the history of human reason, at least as the history of human will.

Further, Rousseau's conception of education depends on the doctrine that the child, undeveloped though he may be, has a life of his own, with his own ideals and conceptions, and that the teacher must understand and sympathize with this life, treat it with respect, and help it to develop in a way proper and natural to itself. This conception, applied to history, means that the historian must never do what the Enlightenment historians were always doing, that is, regard past ages with contempt and disgust, but must look at them sympathetically and find in them the expression of genuine and valuable human achievements. Rousseau was so much carried away by this idea as to assert (in his *Discourse on the Arts and Sciences*) that primitive savagery is superior to civilized life; but that exaggeration he later withdrew,[1] and the only part of it that survived as a permanent possession of the Romantic school was the habit of looking back to primitive times as representing a form of society with a value of its own, a value which the development of civilization had lost. When one compares, for example, the complete lack of any sympathy for the Middle Ages shown by Hume with the intense sympathy for the same thing which is found in Sir Walter Scott, one can see how this tendency of Romanticism had enriched its historical outlook.

On this side of its thought Romanticism represents a new tendency to see a positive value and interest in civilizations very different from its own. This, by itself, might develop into a futile nostalgia for the past, a desire, for example, to bring back the Middle Ages; but actually that development was checked by the presence in Romanticism of another conception, viz., the conception of history as a progress, a development of human reason or the education of mankind. According to this conception, past stages in history led necessarily to the present; a given form of civilization can exist only when the time is ripe for it, and has its value just because those are the conditions of its existing; if therefore we could bring back the Middle Ages we should only be going back to a stage in the process which has led

[1] e.g. by implication in *Contrat Social*, I. viii.

to the present, and the process would go on as before. Thus the Romanticists conceived the value of a past stage of history like the Middle Ages in a double way: partly as something of permanent value in itself, as a unique achievement of the human mind, and partly as taking its place in a course of development leading on to things of still greater value.

Thus the Romanticists tended to look upon the past as such with an admiration and sympathy resembling that felt by the humanists for Greco-Roman antiquity; but in spite of the resemblance the difference was very great.[1] The difference in principle is that the humanists despised the past as such, but regarded certain past facts as lifted, so to speak, clean out of the time-process by their own intrinsic excellence, thus becoming classics or permanent models for imitation; whereas the Romantics admired and sympathized with these or other past achievements because in them they recognized the spirit of their own past, valuable to them because it was their own.

This Romantic sympathy with the past, instanced for example in Bishop Percy with his collection of medieval English ballad literature, did not disguise the gulf separating it from the present but actually presupposed that gulf, consciously insisting on the vast dissimilarity between present-day life and that of the past. Thus the tendency of the Enlightenment to care only for the present and the most recent past was counteracted, and people were led to think of the past as all worthy of study and all of a piece. The scope of historical thought was vastly widened, and historians began to think of the entire history of man as a single process of development from a beginning in savagery to an end in a perfectly rational and civilized society.

§ 2. Herder

The first and in some ways the most important expression of

---

[1] For this reason it was a blunder on the part of Walter Pater to include a chapter on Winckelmann in his work on the Renaissance. Winckelmann's study of Greek art was not at all like that of Renaissance scholars. He conceived a profoundly original idea, the idea that there is a history of art, not to be confused with the biographies of artists: a history of art itself, developing through the work of successive artists, without their conscious awareness of any such development. The artist, for this conception, is merely the unconscious vehicle of a particular stage in the development of art. Similar ideas were applied afterwards by Hegel and others to the history of politics, philosophy, and other achievements of the human mind.

this new attitude to the past was Herder's *Ideen zur Philosophie der Menschengeschichte*, written in four volumes published between 1784 and 1791. Herder sees human life as closely related to its setting in the natural world. The general character of this world as he conceived it is that of an organism so designed as to develop within itself higher organisms. The physical universe is a kind of matrix within which, at a specially favoured region which from this point of view may be regarded as its centre, there crystallizes out a peculiar structure, the solar system. This again is a matrix within which its own special conditions give rise to the earth, which is, so far as we know, peculiar among the planets in being a fit theatre for life and in that sense, as the seat of the next stage in evolution, the centre of the solar system. Within the material fabric of the earth there arise special mineral formations, special geographical organisms (the continents), and so forth. Life, in its primitive form as vegetable life, is a further elaboration or crystallization of a highly complex kind. Animal life is a further specialization of vegetable life, human life a further specialization of animal. In each case the new specialization exists in an environment consisting of the unspecialized matrix from which it has emerged, and is itself nothing but a focal point at which the inner nature of this matrix emerges into complete realization. Thus man is the perfect or typical animal; animals are perfect plants, and so on. And in the same way, at two removes, human nature is the perfection of plant nature: thus, Herder explains, sexual love in man is really the same thing as the flowering and fruiting of plants, raised to a higher power.

Herder's general view of nature is frankly teleological. He thinks of each stage in evolution as designed by nature to prepare for the next. None is an end in itself. But with man the process reaches a culmination, because man *is* an end in himself: for man, in his rational and moral life, justifies his own existence. Since the purpose of nature in creating man is to create a rational being, human nature develops itself as a system of spiritual powers whose full development still lies in the future. Man is thus a link between two worlds, the natural world out of which he has grown and the spiritual world which through him is not indeed coming into existence, for it exists eternally in the shape of spiritual laws, but is realizing itself on the earth.

As a natural being, man is divided into the various races of mankind, each closely related to its geographical environment and having its original physical and mental characteristics moulded by that environment; but each race, once formed, is a specific type of humanity which has permanent characteristics of its own depending not on its immediate relation to its environment but on its own inbred peculiarities (as a plant formed in one environment remains the same when transplanted into another). The sensuous and imaginative faculties of different races are thus genuinely differentiated; each race has its own conception of happiness and its own ideal of life. But this racially differentiated humanity is, once more, a matrix in which there arises a higher type of human organism, namely the historical organism, that is, a race whose life instead of remaining static develops in time into higher and higher forms. The favoured centre in which this historical life arises is Europe, owing to its geographical and climatic peculiarities; so that in Europe alone human life is genuinely historical, whereas in China or India or among the natives of America there is no true historical progress but only a static unchanging civilization or a series of changes in which old forms of life are replaced by new forms without that steady cumulative development which is the peculiarity of historical progress. Europe is thus a privileged region of human life, as man is privileged among the animals, the animals among living organisms, and organisms among earthly existents.

Herder's book contains a marvellous quantity of fertile and valuable thoughts. It is one of the richest and most stimulating books on its subject in existence. But the development of thought in it is often loose and hasty. Herder was not a cautious thinker; he jumped to conclusions by analogical methods without testing them, and he was not critical of his own ideas. For instance, it is not really true that Europe is the only country that has a history, though doubtless it was the only country about which in Herder's time Europeans had much historical knowledge. And his doctrine of the differentiation of races, a crucial step in his whole argument, should not be accepted without scrutiny.

Herder, so far as I know, was the first thinker to recognize in a systematic way that there are differences between different kinds of men, and that human nature is not uniform but diversi-fied. He pointed out that what makes Chinese civilization, for example, what it is cannot be the geography and climate of China but only the peculiar nature of the Chinese. If different kinds of men are placed in the same environment, they will exploit the resources of that environment in different ways and thus create different kinds of civilization. The determining fact in history, therefore, is the special peculiarities not of man in general but of this or that kind of man. These special peculiari-ties Herder regarded as racial peculiarities: that is, the inherited psychological characteristics of the varieties of the human species. Herder is thus the father of anthropology, meaning by that the science which (a) distinguishes various physical types of human beings, and (b) studies the manners and customs of these various types as expressions of psychological peculiarities going with physical ones.

This was an important new step in the conception of human nature, because it recognized that human nature was not a datum but a problem: not something everywhere uniform, whose fundamental characteristics could be discovered once for all, but something variable, whose special characteristics called for separate investigation in special cases. But even so, the con-ception was not a genuinely historical one. The psychological characteristics of each race were regarded as fixed and uniform, so that instead of the Enlightenment's conception of a single fixed human nature we now have the conception of several fixed human natures. Each of these is regarded not as an historical product but as a presupposition of history. There is still no conception of a people's character as having been made what it is by that people's historical experience; on the contrary, its historical experience is regarded as a mere result of its fixed character.

At the present time, we have seen enough of the evil conse-quences of this theory to be on our guard against it. The racial theory of civilization has ceased to be scientifically respectable. To-day we only know it as a sophistical excuse for national pride and national hatred. The idea that there is a European race whose peculiar virtues render it fit to dominate the rest of the world, or an English race whose innate qualities make imperial-ism a duty, or a Nordic race whose predominance in America is the necessary condition of American greatness, and whose purity in Germany is indispensable to the purity of German culture, we know to be scientifically baseless and politically disastrous. We know that physical anthropology and cultural anthropology are different studies, and we find it difficult to see how any one can have confused them. Consequently we are not inclined to be grateful to Herder for having started so pernicious a doctrine.

It would be possible to defend him by arguing that his theory of racial differences does not in itself give any ground for believing in the superiority of one race over another. One might argue that it only implies each type of man to have its own form of life, its own conception of happiness, and its own rhythm of historical development. On this showing, the social institutions and political forms of different peoples can differ without being intrinsically better or worse than one another, and the goodness of a certain political form is never an absolute goodness but only a goodness relative to the people that has created it.

But this would not be a legitimate interpretation of Herder's thought. It is essential to his whole point of view that the differences between the social and political institutions of different races are derived not from the historical experience of each race but from its innate psychological peculiarities, and this is fatal to a true understanding of history. The differentiations between different cultures which can be explained on these lines are not historical differentiations, like that between, say. medieval and Renaissance culture, but non-historical differentiations like that between a community of bees and a community of ants. Human nature has been divided up, but it is still human nature, still nature and not mind; and in terms of practical politics this means that the task of creating or improving a culture is assimilated to that of creating or improving a breed of domestic animals. Once Herder's theory of race is accepted, there is no escaping the Nazi marriage laws.

The problem which Herder bequeathed to his successors, therefore, was the problem of thinking out clearly the distinction between nature and man: nature as a process or sum of processes governed by laws which are blindly obeyed, man as a process or sum of processes governed (as Kant was to put it) not by law simply but by consciousness of law. It had to be shown that history is a process of this second type: that is to say, that the life of man is an historical life because it is a mental or spiritual life.

§ 3. *Kant*

Herder's first volume was published in the spring of 1784 when he was forty. Kant, whose pupil he had been, evidently read the book as soon as it appeared, and although he dissented from many of its doctrines, as his somewhat acid review was to show a year later, it did stimulate him to think for himself about the problems it raised and to write an essay of his own which constitutes his chief work on the philosophy of history. Influenced by his pupil though he was, Kant was already sixty when he read the first part of the *Ideen*, and his mind had been formed by the Enlightenment as it took root in Germany under the aegis of Frederick the Great and of Voltaire, whom Frederick brought to the Prussian court. Hence Kant represents, as compared with Herder, a certain astringent tendency towards anti-Romanticism. In the true style of the Enlightenment, he regards past history as a spectacle of human irrationality and looks forward to a Utopia of rational life. What is really remarkable in him is the way in which he combines the Enlightenment point of view with the Romanticist, very much as in his theory of knowledge he combines rationalism and empiricism.

The essay to which I have referred was published in November 1784, and is called *An Idea for a Universal History from the Cosmopolitan Point of View* (*Idee zu einer allgemeinen Geschichte in weltbürgerlicher Absicht*). Historical study was not one of Kant's main interests, but his exceptional power of picking up the threads of a philosophical discussion even on a subject of which he knew comparatively little enabled him to develop lines of thought which he had found in writers like Voltaire, Rousseau, and Herder and produce something new and valuable, just as his study of Baumgarten enabled him to write a most important work on aesthetics although his artistic culture was of the slightest.

Kant begins his essay by saying that although as noumena, or things in themselves, human acts are determined by moral laws, yet as phenomena, from the point of view of a spectator, they are determined according to natural laws as the effects of causes. History, narrating the course of human actions, deals with them as phenomena, and therefore sees them as subject to natural laws. To detect these laws is certainly difficult, if not impossible; but it is at any rate worth considering whether the general course of history may not show a development in mankind similar to that which biography reveals in a single individual. Here Kant is using the Romanticist idea of the education of mankind not as a dogma or accepted principle but as what he calls in his own technical language an Idea, that is, a guiding principle of interpretation in the light of which we look at facts in order to see whether it improves our understanding of them. As an example of what he means, he points out that every marriage in itself, as it actually happens, is a perfectly free moral act on the part of certain persons; but marriage statistics actually show a surprising uniformity, and from the historian's point of view therefore the statistics can be looked at as if there were some cause determining, under a law of nature, how many marriages there shall be in each year. Just as the statistician deals with these free acts as if they were thus determined, so the historian may look at human history as if it were a process determined in the same way according to a law. If so, what kind of law would this be? It would certainly not be due to human wisdom: for if we review history we find it on the whole not a record of human wisdom but far more a record of human folly, vanity, and wickedness. Even philosophers, Kant observes, wise though they are believed to be, are not wise enough to plan out their own lives and live according to the rules they have made for themselves. Thus, if there is a general progress in the life of mankind, that progress is certainly not due to a plan made for his own guidance by man. But none the less there might be such a plan, namely a plan of nature, which man fulfils without understanding it. To detect such a plan in human history would be a proper task for a new Kepler, and to explain its necessity would require another Newton.

Kant does not say what he means by a plan of nature. In order to interpret the phrase we must turn to the second half of the *Critique of Judgement*, in which the conception of teleology in nature is expounded. Here we find that, according to Kant, the idea that nature has purposes is an idea which we cannot indeed prove or disprove by scientific inquiry, but it is an idea without which we cannot understand nature at all. We do not actually believe it in the way in which we believe a scientific law, but we adopt it as a point of view, admittedly a subjective point of view, from which it is not only possible but profitable, and not only profitable but necessary, to look at the facts of nature. A species of plants or animals looks to us as if it had been ingeniously designed to maintain itself individually by nutrition and self-defence and collectively by reproduction. For example, we see a hedgehog when frightened roll itself into a prickly ball. We do not think this is due to the individual cleverness of this particular hedgehog; all hedgehogs do it, and do it by nature; it is as if nature had endowed the hedgehog with that particular defensive mechanism in order to protect it against carnivorous enemies. In calling it a defensive mechanism we are using the language of metaphor; for a mechanism means a device, and a device implies an inventor; but Kant's point is that without using metaphors of this type we cannot talk or think about nature at all. Likewise, he maintains, we cannot think about history without using similarly teleological metaphors. We use phrases like the conquest of the Mediterranean world by Rome; but actually what we mean by Rome is only this and that individual Roman, and what we mean by the conquest of the Mediterranean world is only the sum of this and that individual piece of warfare or administration which these men carried out. None of them actually said 'I am playing my part in a great movement, the conquest of the Mediterranean world by Rome', but they acted as if they did say that, and we, in looking at the history of their actions, find that these actions can only be envisaged as if they were controlled by a purpose to achieve that conquest, which, as it certainly was not the purpose of this or that individual Roman, we metaphorically describe as a purpose of nature.

It may further be observed that from Kant's point of view it was just as legitimate to talk about a plan of nature revealed in the phenomena studied by the historian as to talk about laws of nature revealed in those studied by the scientist. What laws of nature are to the scientist, plans of nature are to the historian. When the scientist describes himself as discovering laws of nature, he does not mean that there is a legislator called nature; what he means is that phenomena show a regularity and orderliness which not only can be but must be described in some such metaphor. Similarly when the historian speaks of a plan of nature developing itself in history he does not mean that there is an actual mind called nature which consciously makes a plan to be carried out in history, he means that history proceeds as if there were such a mind. Nevertheless this parallelism between plan of nature and law of nature has implications which betray a serious weakness in Kant's philosophy of history.

We have seen that the eighteenth-century philosophers in general misrepresented mind by assimilating it to nature. In particular they talked about human nature as if it were merely one special kind of nature; when what they were really talking about was mind, or something radically different from nature. Kant attempted to avoid this error by his distinction, based on Leibniz, between phenomena and things in themselves. He thought that what makes nature nature, what gives it the peculiarities by which we recognize it as nature, is the fact of its being phenomenon, that is, the fact of its being looked at from outside, from the point of view of a spectator. If we could get inside the phenomena, and relive their inner life in our own minds, their natural characteristics would, he thought, disappear: we should now be apprehending them as things in themselves, and in doing so we should discover that their inner reality is mind. Everything is really and in itself mind; everything is phenomenally, or seen from a spectator's point of view, nature. Thus human action, as we experience it in our own inner life, is mind, that is to say, free self-determining moral activity; but human action as seen from outside, as the historian sees it, is just as much nature as anything is, and for the same reason, namely, because it is being looked at, and thus converted into phenomenon.

Granted this principle, Kant is certainly justified in calling the plan of history a plan of nature, for the parallelism between laws of nature in science and plans of nature in history is complete. But the principle itself is open to grave doubts because it distorts both science and history. (a) It distorts science because it implies that behind the phenomena of nature as studied by the scientist there is a reality, nature as it is in itself, which is nothing else than mind; and this is the foundation of that mystical view of nature, so prevalent in the late eighteenth and early nineteenth centuries, which instead of treating natural phenomena as things deserving of study for their own sake treated them as a kind of veil concealing a spiritual reality somehow akin to ourselves. (*b*) It distorts history because it implies that the historian is a mere spectator of the events he describes. This implication is explicitly avowed by Hume in his essay on *The Study of History*: 'To see all the human race, from the beginning of time, pass, as it were, in review before us, . . . what spectacle can be imagined so magnificent, so various, so interesting?'[1] This view of history Kant took for granted, and for him it could have only one meaning. If history is a spectacle, it is a phenomenon; if a phenomenon, it is nature, because nature, for Kant, is an epistemological term and means things seen as a spectacle. No doubt Kant was only adopting a commonplace of his age; nevertheless, he was wrong, because history is not a spectacle. The events of history do not pass in review' before the historian. They have finished happening before he begins thinking about them. He has to re-create them inside his own mind, re-enacting for himself so much of the experience of the men who took part in them as he wishes to understand. It is because the eighteenth century did not know this, but falsely regarded history as a spectacle, that it reduced history to nature, subordinating historical processes to laws of geography and climatology, as in Montesquieu, or to laws of human biology, as in Herder.

Kant's parallel between the laws of nature and the plan of nature thus has its roots in the erroneous view of history characteristic of his age. And yet, by his special conception of what the plan of nature was, he took an important step towards overcoming the error. His own ethical work was avowedly (in his own sense of this word) 'metaphysical' in character, that is, it was an attempt to discuss mind not in its phenomenal aspect as a kind of nature, but as a thing in itself; and here he identified the essence of mind as freedom, that is, in his own sense of the word 'freedom', not as mere liberty of choice but as autonomy, the power to make laws for oneself. This enabled him to put forward a new interpretation of the idea of history as the education of the human race. For him, it meant the development of humanity into the state of being fully mind, that is, fully free. The plan of nature in history was therefore understood by Kant

[1] *Philosophical Works* (Edinburgh, 1826), iv. 531.

as a plan for the development of human freedom. In the first section of his *Fundamental Principles of the Metaphysic of Morals* he asks, What is the purpose of nature in endowing man with reason? and he answers, It cannot be to make man happy; it can only be to give him the power of becoming a moral agent. The purpose of nature in creating man is therefore the development of moral freedom; and the course of human history can therefore be conceived as the working-out of this development. It is thus Kant's analysis of human nature as essentially moral nature or freedom that gives him the final key to his conception of history.

We can now return to the summary of Kant's argument. Nature's purpose in creating any of her creatures is, of course, the existence of that creature, the realization of its essence. The teleology of nature is an internal teleology, not an external: she does not make grass to feed cows, and cows to feed men; she makes grass in order that there should be grass, and so on. Man's essence is his reason; therefore she makes men in order that they should be rational. Now it is a peculiarity of reason that it cannot be completely developed in the lifetime of a single individual. No one, for example, can invent the whole of mathematics out of his own head. He has to profit by the work already done by others. Man is an animal that has the peculiar faculty of profiting by the experience of others; and he has this faculty because he is rational, for reason is a kind of experience in which this is possible. If what you want is food, the fact that another cow has eaten a certain blade of grass only prevents you from eating that blade; but if what you want is knowledge, the fact that Pythagoras has discovered the theorem about the square on the hypotenuse gives that piece of knowledge to you more easily than you could have got it for yourself. Consequently the purpose of nature for the development of man's reason is a purpose that can be fully realized only in the history of the human race and not in an individual life.

Kant has here achieved the remarkable feat of showing why there should be such a thing as history; it is, he shows, because man is a rational being, and the full development of his potentialities therefore requires an historical process. It is an argument parallel to that by which Plato shows in the second book of the *Republic* why there must be a community. As against the Sophists, who held that the State is artificial, Plato showed that it was natural because it was based on the fact that the individual man is not self-dependent; he needs the economic services of others in order to satisfy his own desires. As an economic being, he must have a state to live in; similarly, Kant shows that, as a rational being, he must have an historical process to live in.

History, then, is a progress towards rationality, which is at the same time an advance in rationality. This, of course, was by Kant's time a commonplace both of Enlightenment and Romantic thought. We must be careful not to confuse it with the apparently similar but really very different late-nineteenth-century identification of history with progress. The evolutionary metaphysics of the late nineteenth century held that all time-processes were, as such, progressive in character, and that history is a progress merely because it is a sequence of events in time: thus the progressiveness of history was by these thinkers merely one case of evolution or the progressiveness of nature. But the eighteenth century regarded nature as unprogressive, and thought of the progressiveness of history as something differentiating history from nature. There might even, it was thought, be a human society in which there was no progress in rationality; this would be a society without a history, like the non-historical or merely natural societies of bees or ants. Outside the state of nature, however, Kant thought that there was progress, and he therefore asks, Why does human society progress instead of stagnating, and how does this progress come about?

The question is an urgent one because he thinks that a non-historical or stagnant society would be the happiest kind; one in which people lived peaceably in a friendly and easy style, as in the state of nature depicted by Locke, where men 'order their actions and dispose of their possessions and persons as they think fit, within the bounds of the Law of Nature', 'a state also of equality, wherein the power and jurisdiction is reciprocal, no one having more than another', because every man has an equal right to punish transgressions of the law of nature, 'thereby to preserve the innocent and restrain offenders'.[1] As Locke freely admits, there are inconveniences in a state of nature arising

[1] *Of Civil Government*, bk. ii, chap. 2.

from the fact that, there, every man is judge in his own cause;
or, as Kant puts it,[1] such a state, in which all men allow their
talents to rust unused, is not one that can be regarded as morally
desirable, possible though it is, and in many ways attractive.
Indeed, neither Locke nor Kant, nor I think any one else of
their age, regarded the state of nature as only an abstract possibility, still less as a downright fiction. Hobbes, when this point
was raised, replied,[2] first, that 'the savage people in many places
of America, except the government of small families the concord
whereof dependeth on naturall lust, have no government at
all', and secondly that 'in all times kings and persons of sove-
raigne authority' are in a state of nature with regard to one
another. Locke[3] replies similarly that all sovereign states are
mutually in a state of nature. And a perfect example of the
state of nature as understood by these philosophers is afforded
by the life of the early Norwegian colonists of Iceland, as
described in the sagas.

Kant's question, therefore, is this: Since such a state of
nature is possible, and is in the main a happy state, though from
the point of view of moral and intellectual development a low
one, what is the force which drives men to leave it behind and
embark on the difficult voyage of progress? To this question
there had hitherto been a choice of two answers. According to
the Greco-Roman view, which was revised by the Renaissance
and reaffirmed by the Enlightenment, the force making for progress in human history was human wisdom, human virtue,
human merit in general. According to the Christian view, which
prevailed from the late Roman Empire to the close of the Middle
Ages, it was the providential wisdom and care of God, working
in despite of human folly and wickedness. Kant has left both
these views so far behind that he never even mentions either of
them.

His own answer is: this force is nothing else than the evil in
human nature; the irrational and immoral elements of pride,
ambition, and greed. These evil elements in human nature make
the continuance of a stagnant and peaceful society impossible.
They give rise to an antagonism between man and man, and a

[1] *Kant's Theory of Ethics*, tr. T. K. Abbott (London, 1923), pp. 40–1.
[2] *Leviathan*, part I, chap. 13.
[3] Loc. cit.

conflict between two motives that sway each man's conduct: one a social motive, desire for a peaceful and friendly life, the other an anti-social motive, a desire to domineer over and exploit his neighbours. The resulting discontent with his own position in life, whatever that position may be, is the spring which drives man to overthrow the social system in which he lives, and this restlessness is the means which nature uses to bring about the advancement of human life. This discontent is not a divine discontent which refuses to acquiesce in the existing state of things because it cannot satisfy the moral demands of a good will; it is not the discontent of the philanthropist or reformer of society; it is a purely selfish discontent which, in view of the happiness of a stagnant life, is not even based on an enlightened view of the individual's own advantage. To quote Kant:[1] 'Man desires concord; but nature knows better what is good for his species' (not, observe, for man as an individual; nor even for man corporately as a society or historical totality; but for man corporately as a species or biological abstraction); 'she desires discord. Man wants to live easy and content; but nature compels him to leave ease and inactive contentment behind, and throw himself into toils and labours in order that these may drive him to use his wits in the discovery of means to rise above them.' Nature, that is to say, does not care for human happiness; she has implanted in man propensities to sacrifice his own happiness and destroy that of others, and in following these propensities blindly he is making himself the tool of nature in her plan, which is certainly not his, for the moral and intellectual advancement of his species.

Kant is here whole-heartedly adopting the view, a pessimistic view if you like so to call it, that the spectacle of human history is in the main a spectacle of human folly, ambition, greed, and wickedness, and that any one who goes to it for examples of wisdom and virtue will be disappointed. This is the point of view of Voltaire's *Candide* as against the Leibnitian confidence that all is for the best in the best of all possible worlds. But he has raised this view to the level of a philosophical doctrine by arguing that if history is the process in which man *becomes* rational, he cannot *be* rational at the beginning of it; therefore the force which serves as mainspring of the process cannot be

---

[1] *Idee zu einer a. Gesch.*, vierter Satz.

human reason but must be the opposite of reason, that is, passion: intellectual ignorance and moral baseness. Here again the Kantian theory of history is an application of the Kantian ethics, according to which inclination, desire, passion is the opposite of reason or the good will and is therefore in itself evil, the force against which the good will has to fight.

This doctrine is not unworthy of its great author. It is inspiring and stimulating, like Herder's, and far more clearly thought out. Yet it is not well founded. It is based on a rhetorical pessimism about the folly, wickedness, and misery that have characterized the past history of man. This is not a just or sane view of the facts. At all times in the past about which anything is known, there have been occasions when men were wise enough to think successfully what they had to think, good enough to do efficiently what they had to do, and happy enough to find life not only tolerable but attractive. And if anybody objects: 'Occasions, yes, but how few!' the answer is: 'More numerous, at any rate, than those of the opposite kind; for otherwise all human life would long ago have disappeared.'

And the consequences of this exaggerated gloom about the past are seen in Kant's exaggerated hopes for the future. In the last section of his essay he looks forward to a time when man shall have become rational, when the blind forces of evil which have hitherto driven him along the path of progress shall have been conquered. There will then be a reign of peace, when the problem of working out a sound and reasonable political system shall have been solved and a political millennium achieved through the creation of a rational system both of national life and international relations. He half realizes that in human affairs a millennium like this is a contradiction in terms; but yet the prediction is no mere excrescence on his doctrine; it is a logical consequence of it, an exaggerated optimism on one side balancing, and due to, an exaggerated pessimism on the other. This exaggerated division of history into a wholly irrational past and a wholly rational future is the legacy which Kant inherits from the Enlightenment. A profounder knowledge of history would have taught him that what has brought progress about has not been the sheer ignorance or the sheer badness but the concrete actuality of human effort itself, with all its good and bad elements commingled.

In spite of his exaggerations, Kant has made a great contribution to historical thought. At the end of his essay he outlines a programme for a kind of historical inquiry which, he says, has not yet been undertaken, and, he modestly adds, could not be undertaken by one so little learned in history as himself: a universal history which shall show how the human race has gradually become more and more rational, and therefore more and more free: a history of the self-development of the spirit of man. Such a task, he says, will need two qualifications: historical learning and a philosophical head. Mere scholarship will not do it, and mere philosophy will not do it; the two must be combined into a new form of thought owing something to both of them. Similarly, Vico, at the beginning of the century, demanded what he described as a union of philology and philosophy, a scholarly attention to detail and a philosophical attention to principles. I think we may say that in the next hundred years a serious and sustained attempt was made, certainly not always successful, to carry out Kant's programme, and to consider history as the process by which the spirit of man has come to the fuller and fuller development of its original potentialities.

Kant's 'idea', as he calls it, may be summarized in four points: (i) *Universal history* is a feasible ideal, but demands a union of historical and philosophical thought: the facts must be understood as well as narrated, seen from within and not only from outside. (ii) It presupposes a *plan*, i.e. it exhibits a *progress*, or shows something as coming progressively into being. (iii) That which is thus coming into existence is *human rationality*, i.e. intelligence, moral freedom. (iv) The means by which it is being brought into existence is *human irrationality*, i.e. passion, ignorance, selfishness.

I will summarize my criticisms of Kant in a few brief comments on these points. The essence of these comments is that throughout, as in other parts of his philosophical work, he has drawn his antitheses too rigidly.

i (*a*) Universal history and particular history. The antithesis is too rigid. If universal history means a history of everything that has happened, it is impossible. If particular history means a particular study which does not involve a definite conception of the nature and significance of history as a whole, that too is impossible. Particular history is only a name for history itself in its detail; universal history is only a name for the historian's conception of history as such.

i (b) Historical thought and philosophical thought. Again the antithesis is too rigid. The union of the two which Kant desiderates is just historical thought itself, seeing the events it describes not as mere observed phenomena but from within.

ii (a) All history certainly shows progress, i.e. it is the development of something; but to call this progress a plan of nature as Kant does is to use mythological language.

ii (b) The goal of this progress is not, as Kant thought, in the future. History terminates not in the future but in the present. The historian's task is to show how the present has come into existence; he cannot show how the future will have come into existence, for he does not know what the future will be.

iii. That which is coming into existence is certainly human rationality, but this does not mean the disappearance of human irrationality. Once more, the antithesis is too rigid.

iv. Passion and ignorance have certainly done their work, and an important work, in past history, but they have never been mere passion and mere ignorance; they have been rather a blind and blundering will for good and a dim and deluded wisdom.

§ 4. *Schiller*

The most direct follower of Kant, in the theory of history as in the theory of art, was the poet Schiller. He was a keen and gifted thinker, in philosophy a brilliant amateur rather than a persevering worker like Kant; but he had the advantage of Kant in being himself a poet of distinction and for some time, when he occupied the chair of history at Jena, a professional historian. Consequently, just as he reinterprets Kant's philosophy of art by bringing to it the experience of a working poet, so he reinterprets Kant's philosophy of history by bringing to it the experience of a working historian. It is very interesting to see, in his inaugural lecture given at Jena in 1789, how this experience enables him to overcome certain errors in Kant's theory.

The lecture is entitled *The Nature and Value of Universal History* (*Was heißt und zu welchem Ende studiert man Universal-*

geschichte?). Schiller follows Kant in advocating the study of universal history and in recognizing that it requires a philosophical mind as well as historical scholarship. He paints a lively picture of the contrast between the *Brotgelehrte* or daily-bread scholar (the professional researcher with his dry-as-dust attitude towards the bare facts which are the dry bones of history, a man whose ambition is to become as narrow a specialist as possible and go on knowing more and more about less and less) and the philosophical historian who takes all history for his province and makes it his business to see the connexions between the facts and detect the large-scale rhythms of the historical process. The philosophical historian achieves these results by entering sympathetically into the actions which he describes; unlike the scientist who studies nature, he does not stand over against the facts as mere objects for cognition; on the contrary, he throws himself into them and feels them imaginatively as experiences of his own. This is really the historical method of the Romantic school; and what Schiller is doing, in effect, is to agree with Kant as to the need for a philosophical as opposed to a merely scholarly attitude towards history and to maintain that this philosophical attitude is nothing else than the Romanticist attitude, for which sympathy becomes an integral element in historical knowledge, the element which enables the historian to get inside the facts he is studying.

Universal history, so conceived, is the history of progress from savage beginnings to modern civilization. So far Schiller agrees with Kant, but with two important differences. (i) Whereas Kant places the goal of progress in a future millennium, Schiller places it in the present, and asserts that the ultimate aim of universal history is to show how the present, with such things as modern language, modern law, modern social institutions, modern clothing, and so forth, came to be what it is. Here Schiller definitely improves on Kant, owing no doubt to his actual experience of historical work, which has shown him that history throws no light on the future and that the historical series cannot be extrapolated beyond the present. (ii) Whereas Kant restricts the task of history to the study of political evolution, Schiller includes in it the history of art, of religion, of economics and so forth, and here again he improves on his predecessor.

§ 5. *Fichte*

Another pupil of Kant who developed his ideas on history in a fertile manner was Fichte, who published his Berlin lectures on *The Characteristics of the Present Age* (*Grundzüge des gegenwärtigen Zeitalters*) in 1806. Fichte agrees with Schiller and disagrees with Kant in conceiving the present as the focal point in which the lines of historical development converge: consequently, for him, the fundamental task of the historian is to understand the period of history in which he lives. Every period of history has a peculiar character of its own, penetrating into every detail of its life; and the task Fichte sets himself in these lectures is to analyse the peculiar character of his own age, to show what its central features are and how the others are derived from them. He puts this by saying that every age is the concrete embodiment of a single idea or concept; and accepting as he does the Kantian doctrine that history as a whole is the unfolding of a plan, the development of something akin to the plot of a drama, he holds that the fundamental ideas or concepts of various successive ages form a sequence which, because it is a sequence of concepts, is a logical sequence, one concept leading necessarily to the next. Thus Fichte's theory of the logical structure of the concept serves him as a clue to the periodizing of history.

Every concept, he thinks, has a logical structure involving three phases: thesis, antithesis, synthesis. The concept is first embodied in a pure or abstract form; then it generates its own opposite and realizes itself in the shape of an antithesis between itself and this opposite; then the antithesis is overcome by the negation of the opposite. Now the fundamental concept of history (here Fichte again follows Kant) is rational freedom, and freedom, like any concept, must develop through these necessary stages. Hence the beginning of history is an age in which rational freedom is exemplified in an absolutely simple or immediate shape without any opposition: here freedom exists in the form of blind instinct, freedom to do as one likes, and the society which is the concrete embodiment of this concept is the state of nature, primitive society where there is no government, no authority, but only people doing, so far as conditions permit, what seems good to them. According to the general principles of Fichte's philosophy, however, a freedom of this crude or immediate kind can only develop into a more genuine freedom by generating its own opposite: so, by a logical necessity, there arises a second stage in which the freedom of the individual freely limits itself by the creation of an authority over against itself, the authority of a ruler imposing upon him laws not of his own making. This is the period of authoritarian government, where freedom itself seems to have disappeared, but it has not really disappeared, it has developed into a new stage in which it has created its own opposite (the ruler, as Hobbes showed, is freely created by the common act of the people who thus voluntarily become his subjects) in order to become freedom of a new and better type, i.e. to become what Rousseau called civil freedom as distinct from natural freedom. But Hobbes was wrong in thinking that the process of the growth of freedom ends here. The opposition must be cancelled by a third stage, a revolutionary stage in which authority is rejected and destroyed not because it is a misused authority but simply because it is authority; the subject has come to feel that he can do without authority and take the work of government into his own hands, so as to be both subject and sovereign at once. It is therefore not authority that is destroyed; what is destroyed is the merely external relation between authority and that over which authority is exercised. Revolution is not anarchy, it is the seizure of government by the subjects. Henceforth the distinction between governing and being governed still exists as a real distinction, but it is a distinction without a difference: the same persons govern and are governed.

But Fichte does not stop here. He does not identify his own age with the age of revolution. He thinks that his contemporaries have got beyond that. The conception of the individual as possessing within himself an authority over himself is, in its first and crudest form, the revolutionary idea. But this concept too must generate its own opposite, namely, the idea of an objective reality, a self-existing body of truth which is the criterion of thought and the guide of conduct. This stage of development is science, where the objective truth is that which stands over against thought and where acting rightly means acting in conformity with scientific knowledge. The scientific frame of mind is (as it were) counter-revolutionary: we can destroy human tyrants, but we cannot destroy the facts; things are what they are and their consequences will be what they will be, and if we flout the laws of man we cannot flout the laws of nature. But, once more, the antagonism between mind and nature can be and must be overcome, and its overcoming is the rise of a new kind of rational freedom, the freedom of art, where mind and nature are reunited, mind recognizing in nature its own counterpart and related to it not by way of obedience but by way of sympathy and love. The agent identifies himself with that for whose sake he acts, and thus achieves the highest degree of freedom. This Fichte regards as the characteristic feature of his own age: the free self-devotion of the individual to an end which, though objective, he regards as his own end.

The chief difficulty which a reader finds in dealing with Fichte's view of history is the difficulty of being patient with what appears so silly. In particular, there seem to be two specially flagrant errors at work in his mind: (1) the idea that the present state of the world is perfect, a complete and final achievement of all that history has been working to bring about, and (2) the idea that the historical succession of ages can be determined *a priori* by reference to abstract logical considerations. I think it can be shown that in spite of their apparent silliness there is some truth in both these ideas.

(1) The historian (and for that matter the philosopher) is not God, looking at the world from above and outside. He is a man, and a man of his own time and place. He looks at the past from the point of view of the present: he looks at other countries and civilizations from the point of view of his own. This point of view is valid only for him and people situated like him, but for him it *is* valid. He must stand firm in it, because it is the only one accessible to him, and unless he *has* a point of view he can see nothing at all. For example, the judgement passed on the achievements of the Middle Ages will necessarily differ according as the historian is a man of the eighteenth, nineteenth, or twentieth century. We, in the twentieth century, know how the eighteenth and nineteenth centuries looked at these things, and we know that their views are not views that we can share. We call them historical errors, and we can show reasons for rejecting them. We can easily conceive the work of medieval history as being done better than it was done in the eighteenth century; but we cannot conceive it as being done better than it is in our own times, because if we had a clear idea of how it could be done

better we should be in a position to do it better, and this better way of doing it would be an accomplished fact. The present is our own activities; we are carrying out these activities as well as we know how; and consequently, from the point of view of the present, there must always be a coincidence between what is and what ought to be, the actual and the ideal. The Greeks were trying to be Greeks; the Middle Ages were trying to be medieval; the aim of every age is to be itself; and thus the present is always perfect in the sense that it always succeeds in being what it is trying to be. This does not imply that the historical process has nothing more to do; it only implies that, so far, it has done what it meant to do, and that we cannot tell what it is going to do next.

(2) The idea of constructing history *a priori* seems very foolish; but Fichte was here following up Kant's discovery that in all knowledge, of whatever kind, there are *a priori* elements. In every field of knowledge there are certain fundamental concepts or categories, and corresponding to them certain fundamental principles or axioms, which belong to the form or structure of that type of knowledge and are derived (according to the Kantian philosophy) not from the empirical subject-matter but from the point of view of the knower. Now in history the general conditions of knowledge are derived from the fundamental principle that the knower is placed in the present, and from the point of view of the present is looking at the past. The first axiom of intuition for history (to adopt Kant's terminology) is that every historical event is situated somewhere in past time. This is not a generalization empirically discovered by the historian in the course of his inquiry, it is an *a priori* condition of historical knowledge. But according to the Kantian doctrine of the schematism of the categories, time-relations are schemata or factual representations of conceptual relations: thus the time-relation of before and after is a schema of the conceptual relation of logical antecedent and logical consequent. The whole world of events in time is thus a schematized representation of the world of logical or conceptual relations. Fichte's attempt to detect a conceptual scheme underlying the temporal succession of historical periods is thus a perfectly legitimate application to history of the Kantian doctrine of the schematism of the categories.

This is, no doubt, a somewhat weak defence of Fichte. It comes to saying that if he made a silly mistake about history he was only following a silly mistake of a more general kind made by Kant. But anybody who calls these notions silly mistakes is claiming to understand better than Kant or Fichte the relation between logical sequence and temporal sequence. Ever since Plato in the *Timaeus* said that time is the moving image of eternity, philosophers have for the most part agreed that there was some relation between these two things and that the necessary sequence by which one event leads to another in time was in some way identical in character with the necessary sequence by which one thing leads to another in a non-temporal logical series. If this is denied, and if it is maintained that temporal sequence and logical implication have nothing to do with each other, historical knowledge becomes impossible, for it follows that we can never say about any event 'this *must* have happened'; the past can never appear as the conclusion of a logical inference. If the temporal series is a mere aggregate of disconnected events, we can never argue back from the present to the past. But historical thinking consists precisely of arguing back in this way; and it is therefore based on the assumption (or, as Kant and Fichte would have said, on the *a priori* principle) that there is an internal or necessary connexion between the events of a time-series such that one event leads necessarily to another and we can argue back from the second to the first. On this principle there is only one way in which the present state of things can have come into existence, and history is the analysis of the present in order to see what this process must have been. I am not defending the particular way in which Fichte reconstructed the past history of his own age; I think it was very faulty, and its faults (so far as they are faults of principle) were due to his following Kant in separating too sharply the *a priori* elements in knowledge from the empirical. This made him think that history can be reconstructed on a purely *a priori* basis without reliance on the empirical evidence of documents; but in so far as he insisted that all historical knowledge contains *a priori* concepts and principles he was right, and understood the nature of history better than the people ule him because they think that history is purely

In one way, Fichte's philosophy of history makes an important advance on Kant's. In Kant's there are two conceptions presupposed by history itself: (1) a plan of nature, conceived as something formed in advance of its own execution ; (2) human nature, with its passions, conceived as the matter in which this form is to be carried out. History itself is the result of imposing this pre-existing form on this pre-existing matter. Thus, the historical process is not conceived as really creative: it is merely a putting together of two abstractions, and there is no attempt to show why the two should ever come together, or indeed why either, let alone both, should exist. Kant's theory, in fact, rests on a number of disconnected assumptions, none of which it attempts to justify. Fichte's theory is logically much simpler and much less exposed to the charge of multiplying entities unnecessarily. The only thing which it presupposes as required before history begins is the concept itself, with its own proper logical structure, and the dynamic relation between the elements in that structure. The driving force in history is just this dynamic movement of the concept, so that instead of two things, a plan and a driving force, in Fichte there is only one, the plan being a dynamic plan (the logical structure of the concept) which supplies its own motive force. The fruits of this Fichtean discovery ripened in Hegel.

§ 6. *Schelling*

Schelling was Hegel's junior, and it may be open to dispute whether the doctrines which Hegel shared with Schelling were reached by independent thinking or under Schelling's influence. But since Schelling published a system of philosophy (perhaps more than one) including his views on history long before Hegel wrote the first sketch of his philosophy of history in the Heidelberg *Encyclopaedia*, it will be convenient to say something of Schelling's views first.

Schelling gave a more systematic development to the ideas of Kant and Fichte, and his thought turned on two principles: first, the idea that whatever exists is knowable, i.e. an embodiment of rationality or, in his own language, a manifestation of the Absolute ; secondly, the idea of a relation between two terms which though opposites are both in this way embodiments of the Absolute: the Absolute itself being an identity in which their differences disappear. This two-term pattern reappears all through his philosophy.

There are, according to Schelling,[1] two great realms of the knowable: Nature and History. Each, as intelligible, is a manifestation of the Absolute, but they embody it in opposite ways. Nature consists of things distributed in space, whose intelligibility consists merely in the way in which they are distributed, or in the regular and determinate relations between them. History consists of the thoughts and actions of minds, which are not only intelligible but intelligent, intelligible to themselves, not merely to something other than themselves: hence they are a more adequate embodiment of the Absolute because they contain in themselves both sides of the knowledge-relation, they are subject as well as object. As objectively intelligible, the activity of mind in history is necessary: as subjectively intelligent, it is free. The course of historical development is thus the complete genesis of mind's self-awareness as at once free and under law, that is, morally and politically autonomous (here Schelling follows Kant). The stages through which this development passes are determined by the logical structure of the concept itself (here he follows Fichte): it is therefore in its largest features divisible into two: first a phase where man conceives the Absolute as nature, where reality is conceived as broken up and dispersed into separate realities (polytheism), and where political forms come into existence and perish like natural organisms leaving nothing behind them; and secondly a phase where the Absolute is conceived as history, that is, as a continuous development where man freely works out the purposes of the Absolute, co-operating with providence in its plan for the development of human rationality. This is the modern age, where human life is controlled by scientific, historical, and philosophical thought.

The most important of the conceptions which Schelling is here trying to work out is the conception that in history the Absolute itself is coming into full and complete existence. Even Fichte thought that the logical structure of the concept was complete before history began and served as a presupposition of the process; in Schelling the dynamic structure of the Absolute is not

[1] *System of Transcendental Idealism*, 1800. *Werke* (Stuttgart and Augsburg, 1858), part I, vol. iii, pp. 587–604.

the ground of the dynamic element in history, it is that element itself. The material universe has always been intelligible in so far as it has always been a manifestation of the Absolute ; but the Absolute cannot be identical with the barely intelligible, for mere intelligibility is a mere potentiality, which must be actual-ized by becoming actually understood. Nature *qua* intelligible demands a knower to understand it, and exhibits its full essence only when there is a mind that knows it. Then for the first time is there an actual knower and an actual known, and rationality, which is the Absolute, has advanced to a higher and more com-plete manifestation of itself. But there now arises a new kind of intelligibility: mind itself is not only a knower but a knowable, and consequently the Absolute cannot be satisfied with a situation in which mind knows nature, there must be a further stage in which mind knows itself. As the process of self-knowledge advances, new stages in self-knowledge enrich the knowing mind and thus create new things for it to know. History is a temporal process in which both knowledge and the knowable are progressively coming into existence, and this is expressed by calling history the self-realization of the Absolute, where the Absolute means both reason as the knowable and reason as the knower.

§ 7. *Hegel*

The culmination of the historical movement which began in 1784 with Herder came with Hegel, whose lectures on the philo-sophy of history were first delivered in 1822–3. Any one who reads his *Philosophy of History* by itself cannot but think it a profoundly original and revolutionary work, wherein history for the first time steps out full-grown on the stage of philo-sophical thought. But when consideration is given to the work of his predecessors, his book becomes far less startling and far less original.

He proposes a new kind of history, to be called the philosophy of history (the proposal and the terminology being as old as Voltaire) ; but the philosophy of history is for him not a philo-sophical reflection on history but history itself raised to a higher power and become philosophical as distinct from merely empiri-cal, that is, history not merely *ascertained* as so much fact but *understood* by apprehending the reasons why the facts happened as they did. This philosophical history will be a universal history of mankind (here Hegel follows Herder) and will exhibit a progress from primitive times to the civilization of to-day. The plot of this story is the development of freedom, which is identical with the moral reason of man as exhibited in an external system of social relations, so that the question which philosophical history has to answer is the question how the State came into existence (all this is taken from Kant). But the historian knows nothing of the future; history culminates not in a future Utopia but in the actual present (this is Schiller). Man's freedom is the same thing as his consciousness of his freedom, so the development of freedom is a development of consciousness, a process of thought or logical development, in which the various necessary phases or moments of the concept are successively achieved (this is Fichte). Lastly, philosophical history exhibits no merely human process but a cosmic process, a process in which the world comes to realize itself in self-consciousness as spirit (this is Schelling). Thus, every one of the characteristic features of Hegel's philosophy of history is drawn by him from his predecessors, but he has combined their views with extraordinary skill into a theory so coherent and so unified that it deserves independent consideration as a whole, and I propose, therefore, to draw attention to some of its distinctive features.

First, Hegel refuses to approach history by way of nature. He insists that nature and history are different things. Each is a process or congeries of processes; but the processes of nature are not historical: nature has no history. The processes of nature are cyclical; nature goes round and round, and nothing is constructed or built up by the repetition of such revolutions. Each sunrise, each spring, each high tide, is like the last; the law governing the cycle does not change as the cycle repeats itself. Nature is a system of higher and lower organisms, the higher depending on the lower; logically, the higher organisms are posterior to the lower, but not temporally; Hegel flatly denies the evolutionary theory which makes the higher develop in time out of the lower, asserting that people who believe this are mistaking a logical succession for a temporal one. History, on the contrary, never repeats itself; its movements travel not in circles but in spirals, and apparent repetitions are always differentiated by having acquired something new. Thus wars reappear from time to time in history, but every new war is in some ways a new kind of war, owing to the lessons learnt by human beings in the last one.

Hegel must be given credit for having stated an important distinction; but he has stated it wrongly. He is right to distinguish the non-historical processes of nature from the historical processes of human life, but wrong to reinforce this distinction by denying the doctrine of evolution. Since Darwin we have found ourselves obliged to accept that doctrine and to conceive the process of nature as resembling the process of history in a way in which Hegel thought it did not resemble it, namely, by producing increments of itself as it goes on. But it remains true that the process of nature is different from the process of history —that, for example, the succession of geological periods is not a truly historical succession—because it is peculiar to history that the historian re-enacts in his own mind the thoughts and motives of the agents whose actions he is narrating, and no succession of events is an historical succession unless it consists of acts whose motives can, in principle at least, be thus re-enacted. Geology presents us with a series of *events*, but history is not history unless it presents us with a series of *acts*. Thus Hegel's conclusion is right, that there is no history except the history of human life, and that, not merely as life, but as rational life, the life of thinking beings.

Secondly, and following immediately from this, all history is the history of thought. In so far as human actions are mere events, the historian cannot understand them; strictly, he cannot even ascertain that they have happened. They are only knowable to him as the outward expression of thoughts. For example, to reconstruct the history of a political struggle like that between the Roman emperors of the first century and the senatorial opposition, what the historian has to do is to see how the two parties conceived the political situation as it stood, and how they proposed to develop that situation: he must grasp their political ideas both concerning their actual present and concerning their possible future. Here again Hegel was certainly right; it is not knowing what people did but understanding what they thought that is the proper definition of the historian's task.

Thirdly, the force which is the mainspring of the historical process (to use Kant's phrase) is reason. This is a very important and difficult doctrine. What Hegel means by it is that everything which happens in history happens by the will of man, for the historical process consists of human actions; and the will of man is nothing but man's thought expressing itself outwardly in action. If it is said that human thought is often or generally far from reasonable, Hegel will reply that this is an error which comes of failing to apprehend the historical situation in which a given piece of thinking is done. Thinking is never done *in vacuo*; it is always done by a determinate person in a determinate situation; and every historical character in every historical situation thinks and acts as rationally as that person in that situation *can* think and act, and nobody can do more. This is a very fertile and valuable principle, which Hegel worked out with important consequences. He held that the abstractly rational man conceived by the Enlightenment is nothing real; the reality is always a man who is both rational and passionate, never purely one or the other, his passions being those of a rational being and his thoughts those of a passionate being; and, further, without passion there is no reason and no action. To prove, therefore, that someone acted in a certain way from passion—e.g. a judge sentencing a criminal in a fit of anger or a statesman overriding opposition from motives of ambition—is not to prove that he did not act rationally; for the judge's sentence or the statesman's policy may be a just or a wise one notwithstanding this passionate element in its execution. Hence, Hegel maintains, the admitted fact that human history exhibits itself as a display of passions does not prove that it is not controlled by reason. He thinks of passion as the stuff, so to speak, out of which history is made: it is, from one point of view, a display of passions and nothing else; but all the same it is a display of reason, for reason uses passion itself as its tool in bringing about its ends.

This conception of the *cunning of reason*, the conception of reason as tricking the passions into the position of its agents, is a famous difficulty of Hegel's theory. He seems to personify reason into something outside human life, which brings about through the agency of blind and passionate men purposes which are its purposes and not theirs. Sometimes, perhaps, Hegel falls into a view like the theological view of the Middle Ages, where the plans that are executed in history are the plans of God and in no sense the plans of man; or (if it is possible to distinguish the two) the crypto-theological view of the Enlightenment historians and Kant, where the plans that are executed in history are the plans not of man but of nature. On the whole, however, it is clear that what Hegel wanted to do was to get away from this view. The reason whose plans are executed in history is, for Hegel, neither an abstract natural reason nor a transcendent divine reason, but human reason, the reason of finite persons. And the relation which he asserts between reason and passion is not a relation between God or nature as rational and man as passionate, but a relation between human reason and human passion. This must be remembered when it is said that Hegel's view of history is a rationalistic view; his rationalism is of a very curious kind because it conceives irrational elements as essential to reason itself. This conception of the intimate relation between reason and unreason in human life and in mind as such really heralds a new conception of man, a dynamic instead of a static conception, and signifies that Hegel is working away from the abstract and static theory of human nature which prevailed in the eighteenth century.

Fourthly, since all history is the history of thought and exhibits the self-development of reason, the historical process is at bottom a logical process. Historical transitions are, so to speak, logical transitions set out on a time-scale. History is nothing but a kind of logic where the relation of logical priority and posteriority is not so much replaced as enriched or consolidated by becoming a relation of temporal priority and posteriority. Hence the developments that take place in history are never accidental, they are necessary; and our knowledge of an historical process is not merely empirical, it is *a priori*, we can *see* the necessity of it.

Nothing in Hegel's philosophy has aroused more protest and hostility than this idea of history as a logical process developed in time and of our knowledge of it as *a priori*, but I have already argued in connexion with Fichte that this idea is not so absurd as at first sight it may seem; and indeed most of the objections to it are mere misunderstandings. Fichte's error, as I pointed out in § 5, was to think that history could be reconstructed on a purely *a priori* basis without reliance on empirical evidence.

Hegel's critics, on the other hand, commonly fall into the opposite error of believing that historical knowledge is purely empirical; that this is an error I also argued in § 5. Hegel himself avoided both those errors. Like Kant he distinguished pure *a priori* knowledge from knowledge containing *a priori* elements, and he regarded history as an instance not of the former but of the latter. History in his view consisted of empirical events which were the outward expressions of thought, and the thoughts behind the events—not the events themselves—formed a chain of logically connected concepts. When you only look at the events and not at the thoughts behind them you see no necessary connexion at all, and the people who blame Hegel for thinking that there are necessary connexions in history are looking at history empirically, as mere outward facts, and assure us quite rightly that when they look at it in that way they see no logical connexions. Quite right, Hegel would have answered; between the mere events, there *are* none. But history consists of actions, and actions have an inside and an outside; on the outside they are mere events, related in space and time but not otherwise; on the inside they are thoughts, bound to each other by logical connexions. What Hegel is doing is to insist that the historian must first work empirically by studying documents and other evidence; it is only in this way that he can establish what the facts are. But he must then look at the facts from the inside, and tell us what they look like from that point of view. It is no reply to him to say that they look different from the outside.

This retort, I think, applies even to the most serious and systematic of all Hegel's critics, namely Croce. He maintains that Hegel's whole philosophy of history is a gigantic blunder, produced by confusing two quite different things: namely opposition and distinction. Concepts, Croce says, are related by opposition: good and bad, true and false, freedom and necessity, and so forth; and the theory of their relation, he admits, has been well expounded by Hegel in his theory of dialectic, which describes the way in which any concept stands in a necessary relation to its own opposite, generating it at first and then negating it, so that the way in which the concept lives is by creating and overcoming oppositions. But the individual things which are the instances of concepts are never related to each other by way of opposition, only by way of distinction: consequently the relations between them are not dialectical, and in history, which is the history of individual actions and persons and civilizations, there is consequently no dialectic, whereas Hegel's whole philosophy of history turns on the principle that every historical process is a dialectical process in which one form of life, for example Greece, generates its own opposite, in this case Rome, and out of this thesis and antithesis there arises a synthesis, in this case the Christian world.

Plausible though Croce's view is, it does not really get to the heart of the problem. It implies that in talking of history we should never use words like opposition or antagonism, and synthesis or reconciliation: we ought not for example to say that despotism and liberalism are opposite political doctrines, we ought only to say that they are different: we ought not to speak of an opposition, but only of a difference, between Whigs and Tories, or Catholics and Protestants. Now, it is true that we do not need to use terms like opposition (let me call them *dialectical* terms) when we are talking only of the outward events of history; but when we are talking of the inward thoughts which underlie these events it seems to me that we cannot avoid them. For example, we can describe the mere outward events of the colonization of New England without using any dialectical language; but when we try to see these events as a deliberate attempt on the part of the Pilgrim Fathers to carry out in terms of practice a Protestant idea of life, we are talking about thoughts and we must describe them in dialectical terms; we must for example speak of the opposition between the congregational idea of religious institutions and the episcopal idea, and admit that the relation between the idea of a priesthood based on apostolic succession and the idea of one not so based is a dialectical relation. From this point of view Greek civilization is the realizing of the Greek idea of life, that is, the Greek conception of man; Roman civilization is the realizing of the Roman conception of man; and between these two conceptions the relation, on Croce's own showing, is a dialectical relation. But this is all that Hegel ever maintained.

A fifth point, and another on which Hegel has been bitterly criticized, is his doctrine that history ends not in the future but in the present. For example, the very able and sympathetic

Swiss writer Eduard Fueter says[1] that a philosophy of history which traces the course of human life from its beginning to the end of the world and the last judgement, as medieval thinkers did, is a respectable and dignified thing: but Hegel's philosophy of history, which makes history end not with the last judgement but with the present day, only ends in glorifying and idealizing the present, denying that any further progress is possible, and providing a pseudo-philosophical justification for a policy of rigid and unintelligent conservatism.

But here again Hegel, like Fichte, is surely in the right. The philosophy of history is, according to his idea of it, history itself philosophically considered, that is, seen from the inside. But the historian has no knowledge of the future; what documents, what evidence, has he from which to ascertain facts that have not yet happened? And the more philosophically he looks at history the more clearly he recognizes that the future is and always must be a closed book to him. History *must* end with the present, because nothing else has happened. But this does not mean glorifying the present or thinking that future progress is impossible. It only means recognizing the present as a fact and realizing that we do not know what future progress will be. As Hegel put it, the future is an object not of knowledge but of hopes and fears; and hopes and fears are not history. If Hegel in the practical politics of his later life was an unintelligent conservative, that was the fault of Hegel as a man; there is no reason to regard it as the fault of his philosophy of history.

But although on these points Hegel seems to be in the right as against his critics, it is impossible to read his *Philosophy of History* without feeling that, magnificent work though it is, it has great faults. I do not refer merely to Hegel's ignorance of the many historical facts that have been discovered since his time; I refer to something deeper in the very method and fabric of his work. It is a striking fact, and one which many readers have noticed, that as an historian Hegel was at his best in his lectures on the history of philosophy, which are a genuine triumph of historical method and have been the model for all subsequent histories of thought. This means that his method, based as it was on the principle that all history is the history of thought, was not only legitimate but brilliantly successful when

[1] *Geschichte der neueren Historiographie* (Munich and Berlin, 1911), p. 433.

the subject-matter with which he was dealing was thought at its purest, i.e. philosophical thought; but this is not the subject-matter of his *Philosophy of History*.

Hegel himself held that there are many kinds of thought, and that they differ in degree as more or less perfect examples of rationality. At the bottom comes what he calls subjective mind, the kind of thought that psychology deals with, where thought is hardly more than the living organism's consciousness of its own sensations. Then, next higher in the scale, comes what he calls objective mind, where thought expresses itself by creating outward manifestations of itself in social and political systems. Then, at the top, comes absolute mind, in its three forms of art, religion, and philosophy. These all transcend the sphere of social and political life and overcome the opposition between subject and object, the thinker and the institution or law which he finds in existence and has to obey: a work of art, a religious belief, or a philosophical system is a perfectly free and at the same time a perfectly objective expression of the mind that conceives it.

Now in the *Philosophy of History*, Hegel is restricting the field of his study to political history. Here he is following Kant; but Kant had a good reason for doing this and Hegel had not. On the strength of his distinction between phenomena and things in themselves Kant, as we have seen, regarded historical events as phenomena, events in a time series of which the historian is a spectator. Human actions as things in themselves are in his view moral actions; and he thought that the same actions which, as things in themselves, were moral actions were, as phenomena, political actions. Hence history must and can only be the history of politics. When Hegel repudiated the Kantian distinction between phenomena and things in themselves, he repudiated by implication the Kantian doctrines that all history is political history and that history is a spectacle. Hence the central position of the State in his *Philosophy of History* is an anachronism, and to be consistent with himself he ought to have held that the historian's business is to study not so much the process of objective mind as the history of absolute mind, i.e. art, religion, and philosophy. And in fact nearly half of Hegel's collected works is devoted to the study of these three things. The *Philosophy of History* is an illogical excrescence on the corpus of Hegel's works. The legitimate fruit of his revolution in historical method, so far as that fruit is to be found in his own writings, is the eight volumes entitled *Aesthetics*, *Philosophy of Religion*, and *History of Philosophy*.

The ordinary criticism of Hegel is therefore mistaken. Beginning with the recognition that his philosophy of history is somehow unsatisfactory, which every one must admit, it argues: 'This is what comes of treating history as rational. The moral is that history is not human thought developing itself, it is just brute fact.' The right criticism would run: 'This is what comes of treating political history by itself as if it were the whole of history. The moral is that political developments should be conceived by the historian as integrated with economic, artistic, religious, and philosophical developments and that the historian should not be content with anything short of a history of man in his concrete actuality.' In point of fact, this second criticism was the one which would seem consciously or unconsciously to have influenced certain nineteenth-century historians.

§ 8. *Hegel and Marx*

Nineteenth-century historiography did not abandon Hegel's belief that history is rational—to do that would have been to abandon history itself—but rather aimed at achieving a history of concrete mind by insisting on the elements which in his formal *Philosophy of History* Hegel had neglected, and working them into a solid whole. Of his more immediate disciples, Baur specialized in the history of Christian doctrine, and Marx in the history of economic activity, while Ranke was later to apply systematically his conception of historical movements or periods as the realization of a conception or idea such as Protestantism. Capitalism in Marx or Protestantism in Ranke is an 'idea' in the true Hegelian sense: a thought, a conception of man's life held by man himself, and thus akin to a Kantian category, but a category historically conditioned: a way in which people come to think at a certain time, and in accordance with which they organize their whole life, only to find that the idea changes by a dialectic of its own into a different idea and that the manner of life which expressed it will not hold together, but breaks up and transforms itself into the expression of a second idea which replaces the first.

Marx's view of history has both the strength and the weakness of Hegel's: its strength, in penetrating behind the facts to the logical nexus of underlying concepts; its weakness, in selecting one aspect of human life (in Hegel the political, in Marx the economic) as in this sense fully rational by itself. Marx, like Hegel, insisted that human history is not a number of different parallel histories, economic, political, artistic, religious, and so on, but one single history. But like Hegel, again, he conceived this unity not as an organic unity in which every thread of the developing process preserved its own continuity as well as its intimate connexion with the others, but as a unity in which there was only one continuous thread (in Hegel the thread of political history, in Marx that of economic history), the other factors having no continuity of their own but being, for Marx, at every point in their development mere reflections of the basic economic fact. This committed Marx to the paradox that if certain people held, for example, certain philosophical views, they had no philosophical reasons for holding them, but only economic reasons. Historical studies of politics, of art, of religion, of philosophy, constructed on this principle, can have no real historical value; they are mere exercises in ingenuity where, for example, the real and important problem of discovering the connexion between Quakerism and banking is burked by saying in effect that Quakerism is only the way in which bankers think about banking. The Marxian paradox, however, is only symptomatic of an anti-historical naturalism which infects much of his thought and which can best be illustrated by reference to his attitude to Hegel's dialectic.

Marx made a famous boast that he had taken Hegel's dialectic and 'stood it on its head'; but he did not mean quite what he said. Hegel's dialectic begins with thought, goes on to nature, and ends with mind. Marx did not invert this order. He referred to the first and second terms only, not the third, and he meant that whereas Hegel's dialectic began with thought and went on to nature, his own dialectic began with nature and went on to thought.

Marx was not a philosophical ignoramus, and he did not for a moment suppose that the priority of thought over nature in Hegel meant that Hegel regarded nature as a product of mind. He knew that Hegel, like himself, regarded mind as a product (a dialectical product) of nature. He knew that the word 'thought', in the sense in which Hegel called logic the 'science of thought', meant not that which thinks but that which it thinks. Logic, for Hegel, is not a science of 'how we think', it is a science of Platonic forms, abstract entities, 'ideas'—if we remember to take seriously Hegel's own warning that we must not suppose ideas to exist only in people's heads. That would be 'subjective idealism', a thing that Hegel abominated. They only got into people's heads, according to him, because people were able to think; and if the 'ideas' had not been independent of people's thinking them, there would not have been any people or, indeed, any world of nature either; because these 'ideas' were the logical framework within which alone a world of nature and men, of unthinking beings and thinking beings, was possible.

These 'ideas' not only made a framework for nature, they also made a framework for history. History, as the actions in which man expressed his thoughts, had the general outlines of its structure laid down for it in advance by the conditions under which the thinking activity, mind, alone can exist. Among these conditions are the two following: first, that mind should arise within and continue to inhabit a world of nature; secondly, that it should work by apprehending those necessities which lie behind nature. Accordingly, the historical activities of man, as activities that take place or go on, take place or go on in a natural environment, and could not go on otherwise; but their 'content', i.e. what in particular people think and what in particular people do by way of expressing this thought, is determined not by nature but by the 'ideas', the necessities studied by logic. Thus logic is the key to history, in the sense that men's thoughts and actions, as studied by history, follow a pattern which is the coloured version of the pattern logic has already drawn in black and white.

This is what Marx was thinking of when he said he had turned Hegel's dialectic upside down. When he made that statement, what he had in mind was history, perhaps the only thing in which Marx was much interested. And the point of his remark was that whereas for Hegel, because logic came before nature, it was for logic to determine the pattern on which history worked, and for nature only to determine the environment in which it worked, for Marx himself nature was more than the environment of history, it was the source from which its pattern was derived. It was no use, he thought, to draw patterns for history out of logic, like the famous Hegelian pattern for the three stages of freedom: 'For the Oriental world, one is free; for the Greco-Roman world, some are free; for the modern world, all are free.' It was better to draw patterns out of the world of nature as Marx did with his no less famous one of 'primitive communism, capitalism, socialism', where the meaning of the terms is professedly derived not from 'ideas' but from natural facts.

What Marx was doing was to reassert the fundamental principle of eighteenth-century historical naturalism, the principle that historical events have natural causes. He reasserted this principle, no doubt, with a difference. The Hegelian side in the pedigree of his thought gave it the right to bear in its arms the term 'dialectical'. The materialism on which he so strongly insisted was not ordinary eighteenth-century materialism, it was 'dialectical materialism'. The difference is not unimportant; but it must not be exaggerated. Dialectical materialism was still materialism. And the whole point of Marx's conjuring-trick with the Hegelian dialectic was accordingly this: that whereas Hegel had broken away from the historical naturalism of the eighteenth century, and had not indeed achieved, except in a partial way, but had at any rate demanded an autonomous history (for a history that recognized no authority except that of logical necessity might not undeservedly claim the title of autonomous), Marx went back on this demand and subjected history once more to that dominion by natural science from which Hegel had proclaimed it free.

The step which Marx took was a retrograde one; but, like so many other retrograde steps, it was more retrograde in appearance than it was in reality; for the territory he was evacuating was territory that had never been effectively occupied. Hegel had demanded an autonomous history, but he had not in fact achieved it. He had seen, as it were prophetically, that history ought on principle to be liberated from its pupilage to natural science; but in his own actual historical thinking that liberation had not been fully achieved. It had not been achieved, that is to say, with regard to what he ordinarily called history, i.e. political and economic history; a field in which Hegel was not a master and in which he mainly contented himself with scissors-

and-paste methods. In his history of philosophy, however, and here alone, he did enter into effective occupation of an historical field, and it was here that he must have convinced himself, as he has convinced many a reader, that his claim of autonomy for historical thought was in principle justified. That is one reason why dialectical materialism has always had its greatest successes with political and economic history, and its greatest failures in the history of philosophy.

If Marx's reversal of the Hegelian dialectic was a backward step, it was also a preliminary to an advance. It was based on the realities of the situation which Hegel bequeathed to his pupils, and, in particular, it led to a great advance in the handling of that particular kind of history, economic history, in which Hegel was weak and in which Marx was exceptionally strong. If all modern treatment of the history of philosophy goes back to Hegel as the great modern master of the subject, all modern treatment of economic history goes back in the same sense to Marx. Nevertheless, the practice of research can no more be left to-day where Hegel left it for the history of philosophy, or where Marx left it for economic history, than the theory of history can be left where Hegel left it with his 'philosophy of history' or where Marx left it with his 'dialectical materialism'. These were expedients whereby a type of history which had not passed beyond the scissors-and-paste stage attempted to conceal the defects inherent in that stage by the adoption of non-historical methods. They belong to the embryology of historical thought. The conditions which justified, and indeed necessitated, them no longer exist.

§ 9. *Positivism*

The historical materialism of Marx and his colleagues exercised little immediate influence on historical practice, which in the nineteenth century came more and more to suspect all philosophies of history as baseless speculations. This was connected with a general tendency in the same century towards positivism. Positivism may be defined as philosophy acting in the service of natural science, as in the Middle Ages philosophy acted in the service of theology. But the positivists had their own notion (rather a superficial notion) of what natural science was. They thought it consisted of two things: first, ascertaining facts;

secondly, framing laws. The facts were immediately ascertained
by sensuous perception. The laws were framed through generalizing from these facts by induction. Under this influence a new
kind of historiography arose, which may be called positivistic
historiography.

Throwing themselves with enthusiasm into the first part of
the positivist programme, historians set to work to ascertain all
the facts they could. The result was a vast increase of detailed
historical knowledge, based to an unprecedented degree on
accurate and critical examination of evidence. This was the age
which enriched history by the compilation of vast masses of
carefully sifted material, like the calendars of close and patent
rolls, the corpus of Latin inscriptions, new editions of historical
texts and sources of every kind, and the whole apparatus of
archaeological research. The best historian, like Mommsen or
Maitland, became the greatest master of detail. The historical
conscience identified itself with an infinite scrupulosity about
any and every isolated matter of fact. The ideal of universal
history was swept aside as a vain dream, and the ideal of
historical literature became the monograph.

But all through this period there was a certain uneasiness
about the ultimate purpose of this detailed research. It had
been undertaken in obedience to the spirit of positivism according to which the ascertaining of facts was only the first stage of a
process whose second stage was the discovery of laws. The
historians themselves for the most part were quite happy going
on ascertaining new facts; the field for discovery was inexhaustible, and they asked nothing better than to explore it.
But philosophers who understood the positivist programme
looked on at this enthusiasm with misgiving. When, they asked,
were the historians going to embark on the second stage? And
at the same time ordinary people who were not specialists in
history became bored; they did not see that it mattered whether
this or that fact were discovered or not; and a gulf gradually
widened between the historian and the ordinary intelligent man.
Positivist philosophers complained that so long as it stuck to
mere facts history was not scientific; ordinary men complained
that the facts which it was bringing to light were not interesting.
These two complaints came to much the same thing. Each
implied that the mere ascertaining of facts for their own sake

was unsatisfactory, and that its justification lay beyond itself in something further that could or should be done with the facts thus ascertained.

It was in this situation that Auguste Comte demanded that historical facts should be used as the raw material of something more important and more genuinely interesting than themselves. Every natural science, said the positivists, began by ascertaining facts and then went on to discover their causal connexions; accepting this assertion, Comte proposed that there should be a new science called sociology, which was to begin by discovering the facts about human life (this being the work of the historians) and then go on to discover the causal connexions between these facts. The sociologist would thus be a kind of super-historian, raising history to the rank of a science by thinking scientifically about the same facts about which the historian thought only empirically.

This programme was very like the Kantian and post-Kantian programme for reinterpreting hoards of facts into a grandiose philosophy of history. The only difference was that for the idealists this projected super-history was to be based on the conception of mind as something peculiar and different from nature: whereas for the positivists it was based on the conception of mind as in no way fundamentally different from nature. Historical process, for the positivists, was in kind identical with natural process, and that was why the methods of natural science were applicable to the interpretation of history.

This programme appears at first sight to throw away with one single careless gesture all the advances which the eighteenth century had so laboriously made in the understanding of history. But this was not actually the case. The new positivistic denial of a fundamental distinction between nature and history really implied not so much a rejection of the eighteenth-century conception of history as a criticism of the eighteenth-century conception of nature. One indication of this is that nineteenth-century thought in general, hostile though it was to much of Hegel's philosophy of history, was far more fundamentally hostile to his philosophy of nature. Hegel, as we have seen, regarded differences between higher and lower organisms as logical, not as temporal, and he thus rejected the idea of evolution. But in the generation after his death, the life of nature began to be thought of as a progressive life, and to that extent a life resembling the life of history. In 1859, when Darwin published *The Origin of Species*, this conception was not new. In scientific circles the conception of nature as a static system, where all species were (in the old phrase) special creations, had long been superseded by the conception of species as coming into existence in a time-process. The novelty of Darwin's idea was not that he believed in evolution, but that he held it to be brought about by what he called natural selection, a process akin to the artificial selection by which man improves the breeds of domestic animals. But in the popular mind this was not clearly recognized, and Darwin came to stand as the champion and indeed the inventor of the very idea of evolution. In its general effect on thought, *The Origin of Species* thus figures as the book which first informed everybody that the old idea of nature as a static system had been abandoned.

The effect of this discovery was vastly to increase the prestige of historical thought. Hitherto the relation between historical and scientific thought, i.e. thought about history and thought about nature, had been antagonistic. History demanded for itself a subject-matter essentially progressive; science, one essentially static. With Darwin, the scientific point of view capitulated to the historical, and both now agreed in conceiving their subject-matter as progressive. Evolution could now be used as a generic term covering both historical progress and natural progress. The victory of evolution in scientific circles meant that the positivistic reduction of history to nature was qualified by a partial reduction of nature to history.

This *rapprochement* had its dangers. It tended to injure natural science by leading to the assumption that natural evolution was automatically progressive, creative by its own law of better and better forms of life; and it might have injured history through the assumption that historical progress depended on the same so-called law of nature and that the methods of natural science, in its new evolutionary form, were adequate to the study of historical processes. What prevented this injury to history was the fact that historical method had now found itself and become a far more definite, systematic, and self-conscious thing than it had been half a century earlier.

The historians of the early and middle nineteenth century

had worked out a new method of handling sources, the method of
philological criticism. This essentially consisted of two operations: first, the analysis of sources (which still meant literary or
narrative sources) into their component parts, distinguishing
earlier and later elements in them and thus enabling the
historian to discriminate between the more and the less trustworthy portions; and secondly, the internal criticism of even
the more trustworthy parts, showing how the author's point of
view affected his statement of the facts, and so enabling the
historian to make allowance for the distortions thus produced.
The classical example of this method is Niebuhr's treatment of
Livy, where he argues that a great part of what was usually
taken for early Roman history is patriotic fiction of a much later
period; and that even the earliest stratum is not sober historical
fact but something analogous to ballad-literature, a national
epic (as he calls it) of the ancient Roman people. Behind that
epic, Niebuhr detected the historical reality of early Rome as a
society of peasant-farmers. I need not here trace the history of
this method back through Herder to Vico; the important point
to notice is that by the middle of the nineteenth century it had
become the secure possession of all competent historians, at least
in Germany.

Now, the result of possessing this method was that historians
knew how to do their own work in their own way, and no longer
ran much risk of being misled by the attempted assimilation of
historical method to scientific. From Germany the new method
spread by degrees to France and England, and wherever it
spread it taught historians that they had a task of a quite
special kind to carry out, a task concerning which positivism
had nothing useful to teach them. Their business, they saw,
was to ascertain facts by the use of this critical method, and to
reject the invitation given them by the positivists to hurry on
to a supposed second stage, the discovery of general laws.
Consequently the claims of Comtian sociology were quietly set
aside by the abler and more conscientious historians, who came
to regard it as sufficient for them to discover and state the facts
themselves: in the famous words of Ranke, *wie es eigentlich
gewesen*.[1] History as the knowledge of individual facts was

---

[1] *Geschichten der romanischen und germanischen Völker*, preface to the 1st
edition (*Werke*, Leipzig, 1874, vol. xxxiii–xxxiv, p. vii).

gradually detaching itself as an autonomous study from science as the knowledge of general laws.

But although this growing autonomy of historical thought enabled it to resist to some extent the extremer forms of the positivist spirit, it was nevertheless deeply influenced by that spirit. As I have already explained, nineteenth-century historiography accepted the first part of the positivist programme, the collection of facts, even if it declined the second, the discovery of laws. But it still conceived its facts in a positivistic manner, i.e. as separate or atomic. This led historians to adopt two rules of method in their treatment of facts: (i) Each fact was to be regarded as a thing capable of being ascertained by a separate act of cognition or process of research, and thus the total field of the historically knowable was cut up into an infinity of minute facts each to be separately considered. (ii) Each fact was to be thought of not only as independent of all the rest but as independent of the knower, so that all subjective elements (as they were called) in the historian's point of view had to be eliminated. The historian must pass no judgement on the facts: he must only say what they were.

Both these rules of method had a certain value: the first trained historians to attend accurately to matters of detail, the second trained them to avoid colouring their subject-matter with their own emotional reactions. But both were in principle vicious. The first led to the corollary that nothing was a legitimate problem for history unless it was either a microscopic problem, or else capable of being treated as a group of microscopic problems. Thus Mommsen, by far the greatest historian of the positivistic age, was able to compile a corpus of inscriptions or a handbook of Roman constitutional law with almost incredible accuracy, and was able to show how to use the corpus by, for example, treating military epitaphs statistically and thus finding out where the legions were recruited at different times; but his attempt to write a history of Rome broke down exactly at the point where his own contributions to Roman history began to be important. He devoted his life to the study of the Roman Empire, and his *History of Rome* ends at the battle of Actium. The legacy of positivism to modern historiography on this side of its work, therefore, is a combination of unprecedented mastery over small-scale problems with unprecedented weakness in dealing with large-scale problems.

The second rule, against passing judgements on the facts, had effects no less crippling. Not only did it prevent historians from discussing in a proper and methodical way such questions as: Was this or that policy a wise one? Was this or that economic system sound? Was this or that movement in science or art or religion an advance, and if so why?; it also prevented them from either sharing or criticizing the judgements made by people in the past about events or institutions contemporary with themselves: for example, they could recount all the facts about Emperor-worship in the Roman world, but because they did not allow themselves to form judgements about its value and significance as a religious and spiritual force they could not understand what the people who practised it really felt about it. What did the ancients think about slavery? What was the attitude of ordinary people in the Middle Ages towards the Church and its system of creed and doctrine? In a movement like the rise of nationalism, how much was due to popular emotion, how much to economic forces, how much to deliberate policy? Questions like these, which for Romantic historians had been objects of methodical investigation, were ruled out by the positivist methods as illegitimate. The refusal to judge the facts came to mean that history could only be the history of external events, not the history of the thought out of which these events grew. This was why positivistic historiography bogged itself in the old error of identifying history with political history (e.g. in Ranke and still more in Freeman), and ignored the history of art, religion, science, &c., because these were subjects with which it was incapable of dealing. For example, the history of philosophy was never during that period studied with such success as it had been by Hegel, and a theory actually grew up (which to a Romantic historian, or to us to-day, would seem merely comic) that philosophy or art has properly speaking no history at all.

All these consequences flowed from a certain error in historical theory. The conception of history as dealing with facts and nothing but facts may seem harmless enough, but what is a fact? According to the positivistic theory of knowledge, a fact is something immediately given in perception. When it is said that science consists first in ascertaining facts and then in discovering laws, the facts, here, are facts directly observed by the scientist: for example, the fact that this guinea-pig, after receiving an injection of this culture, develops tetanus. If any one doubts the fact he can repeat the experiment with another guinea-pig, which will do just as well; and consequently, for the scientist, the question whether the facts really are what they are said to be is never a vital question, because he can always reproduce the facts under his own eyes. In science, then, the facts are empirical facts, facts perceived as they occur.

In history, the word 'fact' bears a very different meaning. The fact that in the second century the legions began to be recruited wholly outside Italy is not immediately given. It is arrived at inferentially by a process of interpreting data according to a complicated system of rules and assumptions. A theory of historical knowledge would discover what these rules and assumptions are, and would ask how far they are necessary and legitimate. All this was entirely neglected by the positivistic historians, who thus never asked themselves the difficult question: How is historical knowledge possible? How and under what conditions can the historian know facts which, being now gone beyond recall or repetition, cannot be for him objects of perception? They were precluded from asking this question by their false analogy between scientific facts and historical facts. Owing to this false analogy, they thought such a question could need no answer. But, owing to the same false analogy, they were all the time misconceiving the nature of historical facts, and consequently distorting the actual work of historical research in the ways I have described.

PART IV

SCIENTIFIC HISTORY

§ 1. *England*

(i) *Bradley*

IN European philosophy towards the end of the nineteenth century there was a kind of springtime of new growth after the winter that had set in at Hegel's death. On its negative side this new movement of thought showed itself mainly as a revolt against positivism. But positivism, though it actually was a philosophical system, refused to claim that title. It claimed only to be scientific. It was in fact nothing but the methodology of natural science raised to the level of a universal methodology: natural science identifying itself with knowledge. Consequently an attack on positivism was bound to appear in addition as a revolt against science and also as a revolt against intellect as such. Properly understood it was neither of these things. It was not a revolt against science, it was a revolt against the philosophy which claimed that science was the only kind of knowledge that existed or ever could exist. It was not a revolt against the intellect, it was a revolt against the theory which limited the intellect to the kind of thinking characteristic of natural science. But every revolt against one thing is a revolt in the interests of something else, and on its positive side this new movement of thought was an attempt (becoming clearer and clearer as the movement progressed towards maturity) to vindicate history as a form of knowledge distinct from natural science and yet valid in its own right.

Nevertheless, the early sponsors of these new ideas did their work under the shadow of positivism, and they had great difficulty in disentangling themselves from the positivist point of view. If they succeeded in overcoming this difficulty at certain points of their thought, they relapsed into positivism at others. Consequently when we now look back on the movement we see it as a confused mixture of positivism and various anti-positivist motives; and when we try to criticize its results and reduce them to order we soon realize that the easiest way of doing this would be by eliminating the anti-positivistic elements and regarding it as an incoherent statement of positivism. This, of course, would be a false interpretation; it would imply mistaking the ferment of new growth for the vacillations of a feeble and inconsistent thought, and developing the ideas of these new philosophers in exactly the wrong direction, by backing out of the difficulties they raise instead of facing and overcoming them. In analysing the thought of a philosopher, just as in analysing, say, a political situation, one will always find incoherences and contradictions; these contradictions are always between retrograde and progressive elements; and it is of the utmost importance, if we are to make anything of our analysis, to distinguish correctly which are the progressive elements and which the retrograde. The great merit of studying our subject historically is that it enables us to make this distinction with certainty.

In England the leader of the new movement to which I have referred was F. H. Bradley, and his first published work was specifically concerned with the problems of history. This was *The Presuppositions of Critical History*, written in 1874. The situation out of which this essay grew was the condition of Biblical criticism as developed by the Tübingen school, notably F. C. Baur and David Strauss. These German theologians had applied the new methods of historical criticism to the narratives of the New Testament, and the result was very destructive to belief in the credibility of those narratives. The destructiveness of this result, however, was due not simply to the use of critical methods, but to the positivistic spirit in which those methods were used. The critical historian is one who is no longer content to say 'the authorities say that such and such an event happened, and therefore I believe that it did'. He says 'the authorities say that it happened, and it is for me to decide whether they are telling the truth or not'. Thus, critical historians were bound to ask whether the New Testament narratives, in this or that particular, were reporting historical fact or fictions that grew up as part of the legendary tradition of a new religious sect. Either alternative was theoretically possible. Take for example the story of the Resurrection of Jesus. Thomas Arnold, who was once professor of history at Oxford as well as headmaster of Rugby, described that as the best-attested fact in history. But, replied the critics, its being well attested only proves that a lot of people believed it, not that it happened. So far their argument was soundly based, but their positivistic assumptions began to be evident when they claimed to be able to show: (*a*) that it cannot have happened, (*b*) that the people who believed it had good cause for believing it even though it did not happen. (*a*) It cannot have happened, so they argued, because it was a miracle, and a miracle is a breach of the laws of nature; the laws of nature are discovered by science, and therefore the whole prestige and authority of science is thrown into the scales on the side of denying that the Resurrection really took place. (*b*) But the members of the early Church were not scientifically minded people; they lived in an atmosphere where the distinction between what could and what could not happen meant nothing; everyone in those days believed in miracles; and therefore it is only natural that their imaginations should invent miracles like this, so creditable to their own Church and reflecting such glory on its founder.

The result was that the critics, without the smallest anti-religious or anti-Christian bias but on the contrary wishing to base their own Christian beliefs only on the solid rock of critically ascertained historical fact, set to work to rewrite the New Testament narratives leaving out the miraculous elements. At first they did not realize how far this committed them to scepticism about Christian origins, but very soon the problem arose: If the miracles are omitted together with everything else that is tarred with the same brush, what is left? According to the critical theory, the early Christians only put the miracles in because they were unscientific, imaginative, credulous people; but that fact vitiates not only their testimony to the miracles but all their other testimony as well. Why then should we believe that Jesus ever lived at all? Surely, argued the more extreme critics, all the New Testament can really tell us is that the people who wrote it lived and were the kind of people they show themselves to be in their writings: a sect of Jews with strange beliefs, whom a combination of circumstances raised by degrees to the religious mastery of the Roman world. A radical historical scepticism resulted not from the use of critical methods but from a combination of those methods with uncriticized and unnoticed positivistic assumptions.

This is the background of Bradley's essay. Instead of taking sides with or against the critics in the controversy that raged round their conclusions, he sets himself the task of investigating philosophically their methods and the principles on which they depend. He starts with the fact that critical history exists, and that all history is to some extent critical, since no historian copies out the statements of his authorities just as he finds them. 'Critical history', then, 'must have a criterion'; and it is clear that the criterion can only be the historian himself. The way in which he handles his authorities will and must depend on what he brings to the study of them. Now the historian is a man with an experience of his own; he experiences the world in which he lives; and it is this experience which he brings with him to the interpretation of historical evidence. He cannot be simply a tranquil mirror reflecting what that evidence tells him; until he has exerted himself and laboured to interpret it, it tells him nothing, for in itself it is only 'a host of jarring witnesses, a chaos of disjointed and discrepant narrations'. What he makes out of this welter of material depends on what he is: that is to say, upon the body of experience which he brings with him to the work. But the evidence on which he has to work is itself already composed of testimony, that is, of statements made by various people; and because these are meant to be statements of objective fact, and not mere records of subjective feeling, they contain judgement and inference and are liable to error. What the critical historian has to do is to decide whether the persons whose testimony he is using were, on this or that occasion, judging correctly or erroneously. This decision must be made on the basis of his own experience. This experience tells him what kind of things can happen; and this is the canon by which he criticizes testimony.

The crux arises when our witness alleges a fact wholly without analogy in our own experience. Can we believe him or must we reject that part of his testimony? Bradley's answer is that if in our own experience we encountered a fact unlike anything we had encountered before, we should think ourselves entitled to believe in its reality only when we had verified it by 'the most careful examination often repeated'. These then are the only terms on which I can believe such a fact or testimony: I must be assured that the witness is as conscientious an observer as myself, and that he, too, has verified his observation in the same way: in that case 'his judgement is to me precisely the same as my own'. In other words, he must not be such a man as to allow his beliefs about what has happened to be influenced by a religious or other view of the world in which I do not share; for if so, his judgement cannot be to me the same as my own; and he must have taken the same amount of trouble to ascertain the fact which I should myself take. But in history these conditions cannot possibly be fulfilled; for the witness is always a son of his time, and the mere progress of human knowledge makes it impossible that his point of view and standard of accuracy should be identical with my own. Consequently, no historical testimony can establish the reality of facts that have no analogy in our present experience. All we can do in cases where it tries and fails to do this is to conclude that the witness has made a mistake, and to treat this mistake itself as an historical fact that has to be explained. Sometimes we can infer what the fact was which he thus mistakenly reported; sometimes this cannot be done, and we can only say that the testimony exists but that we have not the data for reconstructing the fact.

Such is Bradley's argument in outline. It is so rich and goes so deep into its subject that no brief commentary can do it justice. But I will try to disentangle the points in it which seem satisfactory from those which are less so.

On the positive side of the account, Bradley is absolutely right in holding that historical knowledge is no mere passive acceptance of testimony, but a critical interpretation of it; that this criticism implies a criterion; and that the criterion is something the historian brings with him to the work of interpretation, that is to say, the criterion is the historian himself. He is right in holding that to accept testimony means making the thought of the witness one's own thought: re-enacting that thought in one's own mind. For example, if a witness says that Caesar was murdered, and I accept his statement, my own statement 'this man was right to say that Caesar was murdered', implies a statement of my own, 'Caesar was murdered', and this is the original statement of the witness. Bradley stops short, however, of taking the next step and realizing that the historian re-enacts in his own mind not only the thought of the witness but the thought of the agent whose action the witness reports.

Where he goes wrong, I think, is in his conception of the

relation between the historian's criterion and that to which he applies it. His view is that the historian brings to his work a ready-made body of experience by which he judges the statements contained in his authorities. Because this body of experience is conceived as ready-made, it cannot be modified by the historian's own work *as* an historian: it has to be there, complete, before he begins his historical work. Consequently this experience is regarded not as consisting of historical knowledge but as knowledge of some other kind, and Bradley in fact conceives it as scientific knowledge, knowledge of the laws of nature. This is where the positivism of his age begins to infect his thought. He regards the historian's scientific knowledge as giving him the means of distinguishing between what can and what cannot happen; and this scientific knowledge he conceives in the positivistic manner, as based on induction from observed facts on the principle that the future will resemble the past and the unknown the known.

The inductive logic of John Stuart Mill is the shadow which broods over all this part of Bradley's essay. But there is an inner inconsistency in this logic itself. On the one side, it claims that scientific thought reveals to us laws of nature to which there cannot be exceptions; on the other, it holds that this revelation is based on induction from experience, and therefore can never give us universal knowledge that is more than probable. Hence in the last resort the attempt to base history on science breaks down; for although there might be facts which are inconsistent with the laws of nature as we conceive them (that is, miracles might happen), the occurrence of these facts is so improbable that no possible testimony would convince us of it. This impasse really wrecks the whole theory; for what is true in the extreme case of miracle is true in principle of any event whatever. And it was Bradley's consciousness of this, no doubt, that led him after composing this essay to devote himself to the searching examination of Mill's *Logic* whose results he published in his *Principles of Logic* nine years later.

Bradley rightly saw that the historian's criterion is something which he brings with him to the study of the evidence, and that this something is simply himself; but it is himself not *qua* scientist, as Bradley thought, but *qua* historian. It is only by practising historical thought that he learns to think historically.

His criterion is therefore never ready-made; the experience from which it is derived is his experience of historical thinking, and it grows with every growth in his historical knowledge. History is its own criterion; it does not depend for its validity on something outside itself, it is an autonomous form of thought with its own principles and its own methods. Its principles are the laws of the historical spirit and no others; and the historical spirit creates itself in the work of historical inquiry. This was too bold a claim on behalf of history for any one to make in an age when natural science was absolute sovereign of the intellectual world; but it is the claim which Bradley's thought logically implies, and in time it was seen to be a necessary and just one.

Although this claim was not explicitly made by Bradley himself, and although in his later philosophical career he did not explicitly return to the problem of history, he did actually proceed to construct, first, a logic orientated (though readers seldom recognize this) towards the epistemology of history, and then a metaphysic in which reality was conceived from a radically historical point of view. I cannot here demonstrate this in detail, but I will briefly illustrate it. In the *Principles of Logic*, Bradley's sustained polemic against positivistic logic has a constructive aspect in its sustained appeal to and analysis of historical knowledge. For example, in dealing with the quantity of judgements he maintains[1] that the abstract universal and the abstract particular do not exist: 'the *concrete* particular and the *concrete* universal both have reality, and they are different names for the individual. What is real is the individual; and this individual, though one and the same, has internal differences. You may hence regard it in two opposite ways. So far as it is one against other individuals, it is particular. So far as it is the same throughout its diversity, it is universal.' Here Bradley is stating the identity of the universal and individual judgement, which, as Croce was to explain twenty years later, is the definition of historical knowledge. And in order to show that history is what he is thinking of, Bradley goes on to illustrate his thesis by saying: 'Thus a man is particular by virtue of his limiting and exclusive relations to all other phenomena. He is universal because he is one throughout all his different

[1] Op. cit., second edition, Oxford 1922, vol. i, p. 188.

attributes. You may call him particular, or again universal, because, being individual, he actually is both. . . . The individual is both a concrete particular and a concrete universal.'

Nothing could be a clearer statement of the doctrine that reality consists neither of isolated particulars nor of abstract universals but of individual facts whose being is historical. And this doctrine is the fundamental thesis of Bradley's *Logic*. When we turn to *Appearance and Reality*, we find the same thought pushed a stage farther. The fundamental thesis there is that reality is not something other than its appearances, hidden behind them, but is these appearances themselves, forming a whole of which we can say that it forms a single system consisting of experience and that all our experiences form part of it. A reality so defined can only be the life of mind itself, that is, history. Even the ultimate problem which Bradley left unsolved betrays at once the fact that history was the thing which he was trying to understand and the precise way in which he stopped short of understanding it. The terms of this problem are as follows. Reality is not only experience it is immediate experience, it has the immediacy of feeling. But thought divides, distinguishes, mediates ; therefore, just so far as we think about reality, we deform it by destroying its immediacy, and thus thought can never grasp reality. We enjoy reality in the immediate flow of our mental life, but when we think, we cease to enjoy it, because it ceases to be immediate : we break it up into discrete parts, and this break-up destroys its immediacy and therefore destroys itself. Bradley has thus bequeathed to his successors a dilemma. Either reality is the immediate flow of subjective life, in which case it is subjective but not objective, it is enjoyed but cannot be known, or else it is that which we know, in which case it is objective and not subjective, it is a world of real things outside the subjective life of our mind and outside each other. Bradley himself accepted the first horn of the dilemma ; but to accept either horn is to be committed to the fundamental error of conceiving the life of mind as a mere immediate flow of feelings and sensations, devoid of all reflection and self-knowledge. So conceived, mind is itself, but it does not know itself ; the being of mind is such as to make self-knowledge impossible.

(ii) *Bradley's successors*

The effect of Bradley's work on subsequent English philosophy was to induce it, in general, to accept this error as an axiomatic truth, and to adopt the second horn of the resulting dilemma. In Oxford, the result was Cook Wilson and Oxford realism; in Cambridge, it was Bertrand Russell and Cambridge realism. Realism in both cases meant the doctrine that what mind knows is something other than itself, and that mind in itself, the activity of knowing, is immediate experience and therefore unknowable. Alexander has expressed the Bradleian dilemma with admirable clearness when he lays it down[1] that knowledge is a relation between two things, a mind and its object, and that the mind therefore does not know itself, it only enjoys itself. Everything that we know is thus placed outside the mind, and constitutes a body of things whose proper collective name is nature; history, which is the mind's knowledge of itself, is ruled out as impossible. This argument is doubtless in fact derived from the empiricist tradition of English thought, but not directly. It is not based on Locke and Hume, for their primary aim was to enrich and develop the mind's knowledge of itself; it is based on the naturalistic empiricism of the nineteenth century, where (true to the principles of positivism) knowledge meant natural science. The reaction against Bradley, due in the last resort to Bradley's own faults, has reinforced and hardened this tradition, so that the English philosophy of the last generation has deliberately orientated itself towards natural science and has turned away from the problem of history with a kind of instinctive repugnance. Its central problem has always been our knowledge of the external world as given in perception and conceived by scientific thought. When one searches its literature for any discussion, however slight, of the problems of history, the result is astonishing in its meagreness. On that topic there seems to be in the main a conspiracy of silence.

A serious attempt to cope with the philosophy of history was made by Robert Flint in a number of volumes between 1874 and 1893, but these were limited to a collection and discussion of views put forward by other writers, and although they are learned and painstaking works they throw little light on the subject, for Flint never properly thought out his own point of

[1] *Space, Time, and Deity* (London, 1920), vol. i, pp. 11–13.

view, and consequently his criticism of others is superficial and unsympathetic.

The few other English philosophers who have dealt with the problem of history since Bradley have contributed nothing of value until the last few years. Bosanquet, who was closely associated with Bradley himself, treated history with open contempt as a false form of thought, 'the doubtful story of successive events'.[1] That is to say, he assumed as correct the positivistic view of its subject-matter as consisting of isolated facts separated from one another in time, and he saw that if this was their nature historical knowledge was impossible. In his *Logic*, where great attention is bestowed on the methods of scientific research, nothing is said about those of history. Elsewhere he describes history as 'a hybrid form of experience, incapable of any considerable degree of "being or trueness"',[2] in which reality is misconceived by being treated as contingent.

This complete misunderstanding of history has been restated and emphasized in later times by Dr. Inge,[3] who follows Bosanquet in conceiving the proper object of knowledge Platonically as a timeless world of pure universality. It is reflected, too, in treatises on logic like those of Cook Wilson and Joseph, where the special problems of historical thinking are passed over in silence. More recently still, the kind of logic which professes to be most up to date has inspired a text-book by Miss L. Susan Stebbing (*A Modern Introduction to Logic*, edn. 2, London, 1933). This contains one chapter on historical method (chapter xix, esp. pp. 382–8). Its substance is derived entirely from a well-known French manual written by Langlois and Seignobos (*Introduction aux études historiques*, Paris, 1898) to expound the pre-scientific form of history which I call 'scissors-and-paste history'; it is therefore about as useful to the modern reader as would be a discussion of physics in which no mention was made of relativity.

(iii) *Late nineteenth-century historiography*

Those who pursued historical research in the late nineteenth century were very little interested in the theory of what they

---

[1] *The Principle of Individuality and Value* (London, 1912), p. 79.
[2] Ibid., pp. 78–9.
[3] *God and the Astronomers* (London, 1933), chaps. iii and iv.

were doing. Characteristically of a positivistic age, the historians of that period were more or less openly contemptuous, as a matter of professional convention, of philosophy in general and the philosophy of history in particular. In their contempt for philosophy they were in part echoing the ordinary parrot-cry of positivism that natural science had now finally dethroned philosophical thought; but in part they were reacting against positivism too, for positivism itself was a philosophy, maintaining the doctrine that natural science was the perfect type of knowledge; and even the least reflective historian could see that a blind worship of natural science must be hostile to historical research. Their contempt for the philosophy of history had no reference to Hegel's or any other genuine philosophy of history, of which they knew nothing; it was directed against positivistic fabrications like Buckle's attempt to discover historical laws or Herbert Spencer's identification of history with natural evolution. In the main, English historians of the late nineteenth century thus went on their own way without often pausing to utter general reflections on their work; on the rare occasions when they did so, as for example in Freeman's book on *The Methods of Historical Study* (London, 1886), or here and there in inaugural lectures, nothing worthy of notice came of it.

In spite of this general detachment of English historians from philosophical thought, however, they were influenced very definitely by their intellectual environment. In the later nineteenth century the idea of progress became almost an article of faith. This conception was a piece of sheer metaphysics derived from evolutionary naturalism and foisted upon history by the temper of the age. It had its roots no doubt in the eighteenth-century conception of history as the progress of the human race in and towards rationality; but in the nineteenth, theoretical reason had come to mean the mastery of nature (knowledge being equated with natural science, and natural science, in the popular view, with technology) and practical reason had come to mean the pursuit of pleasure (morality being equated with promoting the greatest happiness of the greatest number, and happiness with quantity of pleasure). The progress of humanity, from the nineteenth-century point of view, meant getting richer and richer and having a better and better time. And the evolutionary philosophy of Spencer seemed to prove that such a process must of necessity go on, and go on indefinitely; while the then economic condition of England appeared to corroborate that doctrine in at least the one most interesting case.

In order to realize the lengths to which this dogma of progress was pushed, it is necessary to go slumming among the most unsavoury relics of third-rate historical work. A certain Robert Mackenzie published in 1880 a book called *The Nineteenth Century—A History*, depicting that century as a time of progress from a state of barbarism, ignorance, and bestiality which can hardly be exaggerated, to a reign of science, enlightenment, and democracy. France before the Revolution was a country in which liberty was wholly extinct, the king one of the meanest and basest of human creatures, the nobility omnipotent to oppress and merciless in using their power. Britain (not England, for the author was a Scot) presents a picture drawn in the same colours except that savage criminal laws and brutalizing industrial conditions play a larger part. A beam of sunshine steals over the scene with the advent of the Reform Bill, the most beneficent event in British history, ushering in a new era when legislation instead of being uniformly selfish in aim was uniformly directed at overthrowing iniquitous preferences. A brilliant period follows when all wrongs were being righted as fast as possible; everybody was rapidly getting happier and happier until a culmination of joy was reached in the dazzling victories of the Crimea. But the victories of peace were no less dazzling; they include the splendours of the cotton trade, the magnificent conception of steam locomotion, which awakened the dormant love of travel and taught people in distant parts of the earth to love one another instead of hating one another as before; the bold conception of stretching an electric pathway in the depths of the Atlantic, which gave every village the inestimable privilege of instantaneous communication with every part of the inhabited globe; newspapers, by which every morning the same topics are presented to all minds, generally with intelligence and moderation, often with consummate skill; breech-loading rifles, ironclads, heavy artillery, and torpedoes (these, too, among the blessings of peace); a vastly increased consumption of tea, sugar, and spirits; lucifer matches, and so forth. I spare the reader any account of the chapters on France, Prussia, Austria, Italy, Russia, Turkey, the United

States, and the Papacy, and pass straight to the author's conclusion:

'Human history is a record of progress—a record of accumulating knowledge and increasing wisdom, of continual advancement from a lower to a higher platform of intelligence and well-being. Each generation passes on to the next the treasures which it inherited, beneficially modified by its own experience, enlarged by the fruits of all the victories which itself has gained. The rate of this progress . . . is irregular and even fitful . . . but the stagnation is only apparent. . . . The nineteenth century has witnessed progress rapid beyond all precedent, for it has witnessed the overthrow of the barriers which prevented progress. . . . Despotism thwarts and frustrates the forces by which providence has provided for the progress of man; liberty secures for these forces their natural scope and exercise. . . . The growth of man's well-being, rescued from the mischievous tampering of self-willed princes, is left now to the beneficent regulation of great providential laws.'

These rhapsodies, if not out of date on their first publication, were certainly outmoded a decade later, when they were still being reprinted. Spencerian evolutionism, with its belief in the inheritance of acquired characteristics and the beneficent kindliness of natural law, had by that time been succeeded by a new naturalism of gloomier cast. Huxley in 1893 delivered his Romanes lecture on *Evolution and Ethics*, in which he maintained that social progress was possible only by flying in the face of natural law: by 'checking the cosmic process at every step and substituting for it another which may be called the ethical process'. The life of man, in so far as it follows the laws of nature, is the life of a brute, differing from other brutes only in being more intelligent. The theory of evolution, he concluded, offered no basis for the hope of a millennium. The result of such reflections was that historians studied the past in a new spirit of detachment. They began to think of it as the proper field for a dispassionate and therefore truly scientific study, from which partisan spirit, praise and blame, should be banished. They began to criticize Gibbon not for having taken sides against Christianity in particular but for having taken sides at all; Macaulay not for being a Whig historian but for being a party historian. This was the period of Stubbs and Maitland, the period when English historians first mastered the objectively scientific critical methods of the great Germans, and learnt to study facts in all their detail with a proper apparatus of scholarship.

(iv) *Bury*

One historian of that period stands out from the rest in having an altogether unusual equipment of philosophical training. J. B. Bury was not a powerful philosophical intellect, but he read a certain amount of philosophy, and realized that there were philosophical problems connected with historical research. His work therefore took on a certain air of self-consciousness. In the preface to his *History of Greece* he makes the unusual admission that the book is written from his own point of view; in the introduction to his edition of Gibbon he explains the principles on which he has edited him, and in a number of scattered essays he discusses points of historical theory. He also undertook such semi-philosophical works as an historical book on *The Idea of Progress* and a shorter one called *A History of Freedom of Thought*.

These writings reveal Bury as a positivist in historical theory, but a perplexed and inconsistent one. History for him, in the true positivistic manner, consists of an assemblage of isolated facts, each capable of being ascertained or investigated without reference to the others. Thus he was able to accomplish the very strange feat of bringing Gibbon up to date by means of footnotes, adding to the aggregate of knowledge already contained in his pages the numerous facts that had been ascertained in the meantime, without suspecting that the very discovery of these facts resulted from an historical mentality so different from Gibbon's own that the result was not unlike adding a saxophone obbligato to an Elizabethan madrigal. He never saw that one new fact added to a mass of old ones involved the complete transformation of the old. This view of history as consisting of detached parts achieved its classical expression, for the English public, in the Cambridge histories, modern, medieval, and ancient, vast compilations where the chapters, sometimes even the subdivisions of a chapter, are written by different hands, the editor being given the task of assembling the fruit of this mass-production into a single whole. Bury was one of the editors, though the original scheme was due to Lord Acton, a generation earlier.

If we follow the development of Bury's thought[1] on the principles and methods of history, we find him in 1900 still content to deal with the survival of the Eastern Empire according to the strict formulae of positivism: the treatment of an event not as unique but as an instance of a certain type, and the explanation of it by discovering a cause applicable not to it alone but to every event of the same general kind. Here the method is exactly that of the empirical sciences of nature as analysed by positivistic logic. By 1903, when he delivered his Cambridge inaugural lecture, Bury had begun to revolt against this method. In that lecture he proclaimed that historical thought as we now understand it is a new thing in the world, barely a century old: not at all the same thing as natural science, but having a special character of its own, offering to mankind a new view of the world and a new armoury of intellectual weapons. What, he asks, might we not make of the human world in which we live, when we realize the possibilities of this new intellectual attitude towards it? Here the uniqueness of historical thought is clearly seen and impressively stated; but when Bury goes on to ask what this new thing is, he replies: 'History is simply a science, no less and no more'. The lecture exhibits a mind torn between two conceptions: one, obscure but powerful, of the difference between history and science, the other, clear and paralysing, of their indistinguishable identity. Bury has made a violent effort to free himself from this latter conception, and failed.

Next year, conscious of his failure, he returned to the attack in a lecture on *The Place of Modern History in the Perspective of Knowledge*. Is history, he asks, a mere reservoir of facts accumulated for the use of sociologists and anthropologists, or is it an independent discipline to be studied for its own sake? He cannot answer this question, for he sees that it is a philosophical one and realizes that it lies, therefore, outside his competence. But he will go so far as to answer it hypothetically. If we adopt a naturalistic philosophy,

'then I think we must conclude that the place of history, within the frame of such a system, is subordinate to sociology or anthropology.

[1] I am here drawing on my review of his posthumous *Selected Essays*, edited by H. W. V. Temperley (Cambridge, 1930) in the *English Historical Review*, 1931, p. 461.

. . . But on an idealistic interpretation of knowledge it is otherwise. . . . If thought is not the result, but the presupposition, of the processes of nature, it follows that history, of which thought is the characteristic and guiding force, belongs to a different order of ideas from the kingdom of nature, and demands a different interpretation.'

There he leaves it. The moment was a dramatic one in the development of his mind. His conviction of the dignity and worth of historical thought had come into open conflict with his own positivistic training and principles. Committed as he was to the service of history, he accepted the consequences.

In 1909 he published an essay on *Darwinism and History*, deliberately attacking the idea that historical events can be explained by reference to general laws. Uniformities, yes; laws, no. What really determines them is 'chance coincidence'. Examples are 'the sudden death of a leader, a marriage without issue', and in general the decisive function of individuality, which sociology falsely eliminates in order to facilitate its task of assimilating history to the uniformity of science. The 'chapter of accidents' everywhere enters as a disturbing element into historical processes. In an essay called *Cleopatra's Nose* (1916) he repeats the same idea. History is determined not by causal sequences such as form the subject-matter of science, but by the fortuitous 'collision of two or more independent chains of causes'. Here the very words of Bury's argument seem to echo those of Cournot in his *Considérations sur la marche des idées et des événements dans les temps modernes* (Paris, 1872), where he expounded a conception of chance, based on the distinction between 'general causes' and 'special causes': chance being defined as 'l'*indépendance* mutuelle de plusieurs séries de causes et d'effets qui concourent *accidentellement*' (his italics; op. cit. i. 1). A note in Bury's *Idea of Progress*,[1] read together with a footnote to *Darwinism and History*,[2] suggests that he may have derived his own doctrine from Cournot, who, however; develops it by pointing out that in so far as anything is merely fortuitous there can be no history of it. The true function of history, he holds, is to distinguish the necessary from the merely accidental. Bury is developing, or rather disintegrating, this theory by adding to it the doctrine that, in so far as history is individual, everything in it is accidental and nothing necessary, but after

[1] London, 1920, p. 368.   [2] *Selected Essays*, p. 37.

illustrating what he means he concludes his essay by suggesting 'that as time goes on contingencies will become less important in human evolution and chance have less power over the course of events'.

The impression made on a reader by the last paragraph of this essay is a painful one. With great toil, Bury had in the preceding dozen years reached a conception of history as knowledge of the individual. He realized, early in that process, that this conception was essential to the dignity and worth of historical thought. But by 1916 he is so dissatisfied with what he has discovered that he is prepared to give it up; to see in this very individuality an irrational, because accidental, element in the world and to hope that, with the march of science, it may one day be eliminated. If he had grasped his own idea firmly, he would have realized both that this hope was vain (for he had really proved, in the preceding pages, that accidents in his sense of the word must necessarily happen) and also that by entertaining it he was turning traitor to his own historical vocation.

This disastrous conclusion, from which he never afterwards deviated, was due to the fact that instead of conceiving individuality as the very substance of the historical process, he had never thought of it as more than a partial and occasional interference with sequences which in their general structure are causal sequences. Individuality for him only meant the unusual, the exceptional, an interruption in the ordinary course of events: where the ordinary course of events means a course of events causally determined and scientifically comprehensible. But Bury himself knew, or had known in 1904, that history does not consist of events causally determined and scientifically comprehensible; these are ideas appropriate to the interpretation of nature, and history, as he then rightly said, 'demands a different interpretation'. If he had logically developed the ideas of his earlier essay he would have concluded that individuality, instead of appearing in history only now and then in the shape of the accidental or contingent, is just that out of which history is made; what prevented him from advancing to this conclusion was his positivistic prejudice that individuality as such is unintelligible, and that in consequence the generalizations of science are the only possible form of knowledge.

Thus, after realizing that an 'idealistic' philosophy was the only one which could account for the possibility of historical knowledge, Bury fell back into the 'naturalistic' one which he had tried to repudiate. The phrase 'contingency of history' expresses this final collapse of his thought. Contingency means unintelligibility; and the contingency of history is simply a name for 'the role of the individual' seen through the spectacles of a positivism for which nothing is intelligible except what is general. Professor Norman H. Baynes, Bury's successor as our leading master of late Roman and Byzantine history, has spoken bitterly of 'the devastating doctrine of contingency in history' which dimmed Bury's historical insight towards the end of his life. The criticism is just. Bury had done his best work under the inspiration of a belief in the autonomy and dignity of historical thought; but the atmosphere of positivism in which his mind had formed itself undermined this belief, and reduced the proper object of historical knowledge to the level of something which, precisely because it was not an object of scientific thought, was unintelligible.

(v) *Oakeshott*

Bury, however, did set historians an example of attempting to think out the philosophical implications of their own work, and this example was not thrown away. In Cambridge, it was followed by at least one historian of the next generation, by an historian armed with a preparation vastly superior to Bury's in philosophical studies. I refer to Mr. Michael J. Oakeshott of Caius College who published a book called *Experience and its Modes* (Cambridge, 1933), in which he dealt at length and in a masterly way with the philosophical problem of history. The general thesis of the book is that experience is a 'concrete whole which analysis divides into experiencing and what is experienced'; and experience is not (as it is for Bradley) immediate consciousness, the mere flow of sensations and feelings, it is also and always thought, judgement, assertion of reality. There is no sensation which is not also thought, no intuition which is not also judgement, no volition which is not also cognition. These distinctions, like that between subject and object, are in no sense arbitrary or unreal; they represent no false dissection of experience itself, they are integral elements in it; but they are distinctions, not divisions, and above all they are distinctions within experience, not distinctions between elements in experience and something foreign to it. Hence thought as such is not, as in Bradley, a falsification of experience involving the break-up of its immediacy; thought is experience itself; and thought, as 'experience without reservation or arrest, without presupposition or postulate, without limit or category', is philosophy.

Here Bradley's dilemma is transcended. Because experience is no longer conceived as immediate, but as containing mediation or thought within itself, the real is no longer divided into that which 'knows' but cannot be known ('knows', because a knowledge where the knower can never say 'I know' is not knowledge at all) and that which is 'known' but cannot know. Mind's right to know itself is re-established.

The question now arises: What is the difference between such forms of thought as history and science? Each is an attempt to envisage reality (that is, experience) from a particular point of view, in terms of a particular category. History is the way in which we conceive the world *sub specie praeteritorum*: its differentia is the attempt to organize the whole world of experience in the shape of past events. Science is the way in which we conceive the world *sub specie quantitatis*: its differentia is the attempt to organize the world of experience as a system of measurements. Such attempts differ radically from that of philosophy, for in philosophy there is no such primary and inviolable postulate. If we ask for a parallel formula applying to philosophy and inquire: 'In terms of what, then, does philosophy seek to conceive the world of experience?', there is no answer to the question. Philosophy is the attempt to conceive reality not in any particular way, but just to conceive it.

Oakeshott states this idea by saying that whereas philosophy is experience itself, history and science and so forth are 'modes' of experience. Experience is 'modified' (the conception, of course, comes from Descartes and Spinoza) by arresting it at a certain point, and there, using the point of arrest as a fixed postulate or category, constructing a 'world of ideas' in terms of that postulate. Such a world of ideas is not a constituent element in experience itself, not, as it were, a reach of its river, but a backwater, a digression from its unreserved flow. It is not, however, a 'world of mere ideas'. It is not only coherent in itself, it is a way of representing experience as a whole. It is not *a* world, a separate sphere of experience in which things of a special kind are known in a special way, but *the* world, as seen from that fixed point in experience, and therefore, subject to that qualification, rightly seen.

History, then, is experience as a whole, conceived as a system of past events. From this point of view Oakeshott develops a brilliant and penetrating account of the aims of historical thought and the character of its object. He begins by showing that history is a whole or a world. It does not consist of isolated events. This involves him in a vigorous and triumphant attack on the positivistic theory of history as a series of events external to one another, each to be apprehended (if indeed anything can be thus apprehended) in isolation from the rest. 'The historical series', he concludes (op. cit., p. 92), 'is a bogy.' History is not a series but a world: which means that its various parts bear upon one another, criticize one another, make one another intelligible. Next, he shows that it is not only a world but a world of ideas. It is not a world of objective events which the historian somehow exhumes from the past and makes the object of a present cognition. It is the historian's world of ideas. 'The distinction between history as it happened (the course of events) and history as it is thought, the distinction between history itself and merely experienced history, must go; it is not merely false, it is meaningless' (p. 93). What the historian is doing, when he fancies he is merely cognizing past events as they actually happened, is in reality organizing his present consciousness; as can be seen when we reflect on the impossibility of separating 'what has come to us' from 'our interpretation of it' (p. 94). This does not mean that it is a world of mere ideas; mere ideas are abstractions and are nowhere found in experience; like all real ideas the historian's ideas are critical ideas, true ideas, thoughts.

Further, history is like every form of experience in that it starts with a given world of ideas and ends by making that world coherent. The data or materials with which the historian starts are not independent of his experience, they are his historical experience itself in its initial form: they are ideas already conceived in the light of his own historical postulates, and the criticism of historical knowledge turns primarily not on the discovery of hitherto unknown materials but on the revision of these initial postulates. The growth of historical knowledge, consequently, comes about not by adding new facts to those already known, but by transforming the old ideas in the light of the new. ' The process in historical thinking is never a process of incorporation; it is always a process by which a given world of ideas is transformed into a world that is more than a world' (p. 99).

So much for generalities. But what in particular are the postulates in virtue of which historical experience is history, and not experience at large or in some other special form ? The first postulate is the idea of the past. But history is not the past as such. The historical past is a special past: not the merely remembered past, nor the merely fancied past; not a past that merely might have been or merely must have been; not the whole past, for although the distinction between an historical and a non-historical past has often been wrongly and arbitrarily drawn, the distinction is a real one; not the practical past, the past to which we are personally attached, as in the patriotic love of our country's past achievements or the religious value which we attach to the circumstances in which our own creed was born. The historical past is 'the past for its own sake' (p. 106), the past just in so far as it is past, different from the present and independent of it: a fixed and finished past, a dead past. Or rather, this is how the historian thinks of it. But so to think of it is to forget that history is experience. A fixed and finished past is a past divorced from present experience; and therefore divorced from evidence (since evidence is always present) and therefore unknowable. 'What really happened' is only 'what the evidence obliges us to believe' (p. 107). Thus the facts of history are present facts. The historical past is the world of ideas which the present evidence creates in the present. In historical inference we do not move from our present world to a past world; the movement in experience is always a movement within a present world of ideas.

The paradoxical result is that the historical past is not past at all; it is present. It is not a past surviving into the present; it must *be* the present. But it is not the present as such, the merely contemporary. It is present, because all experience whatever is present; but not merely present. It is also past, and this pastness involves a modification of its character as experience. The historical past does not stand over against the present world of experience as something different from it; it is a special organization of that world *sub specie praeteritorum*. 'History, because it is experience, is present . . .; but because it is history, the formulation of experience as a whole *sub specie praeteritorum*, it is the continuous assertion of a past which is not past and of a present which is not present' (p. 111). This means, I think, that the historian's thought is a perfectly genuine experience, but what he is experiencing is what is going on in his mind now; in so far as he places it, as it were, at arm's length from him in the past, he is misconceiving it; he is arranging in imaginary pigeon-holes of past time what is actually all present and not past at all. And this does not imply that he is making historical mistakes about the past. There *is* no past, except for a person involved in the historical mode of experience; and for him the past is what he carefully and critically thinks it to be. He makes no mistake *qua* historian: the only mistake he makes is the philosophical mistake of arranging in the past what is actually all present experience.

I shall not analyse the whole of Oakeshott's argument. I have said enough to indicate its general direction and character. The first thing to be said about it is that it entirely vindicates the autonomy of historical thought. The historian is master in his own house; he owes nothing to the scientist or to anyone else. And this house is not built and furnished out of mere ideas of his own, which may or may not correspond with the ideas of other historians or with the real past which they are all alike trying to know; it is a house inhabited by all historians, and it consists not of ideas about history but of history itself. From this double point of view—the autonomy and objectivity of historical thought, which are only two names for its rationality, its character as a genuine form of experience—Oakeshott is able without difficulty to criticize every form of historical positivism, whether as taught by Bury, to whom he makes frequent and penetrating reference, or as practised by the naturalistic anthropologists and their chief, Sir James Frazer. Moreover, though he does not actually do this, he is in a position to make short work of philosophical objections to the idea of history itself, such as are lodged by writers like Bosanquet and Dr. Inge.

This constitutes a new and valuable achievement for English

thought. But there is a further problem which, as I understand him, Oakeshott has failed to solve. History for him is not a necessary phase or element in experience as such; on the contrary, it is a backwater of thought due to an arrest of experience at a certain point. If we ask why there should be such an arrest, there is no answer. If we ask whether such an arrest is justified, that is, whether experience itself is enriched by it, the answer is in the negative. Genuine experience, undistorted by any such arrest, can only be philosophy. The historian is a philosopher who has turned aside from the path of philosophical thought to play a game which is none the less arbitrary for being only one of a potentially infinite number of such games, others being those of science and practical life. The problem which Oakeshott has failed to solve is the question why there is or should be such a thing as history at all. No doubt, he would state this differently: what I call failing to answer this question he would describe as discovering that the question has no answer. For him it is a mere fact that experience is arrested at that point. But I think this belief is inconsistent with his own philosophical principles. A mere fact, divorced from other facts, is for him (as for myself) a monstrosity; in his own words, nothing real, but an abstraction. If philosophy is concrete experience it cannot tolerate such things; it cannot separate the *what* from the *why*. The double question is therefore a legitimate and inevitable one: first, What exactly is the point in experience at which it arrests itself to become history, and how is this point arrived at in the development of experience itself? Secondly, How and why does it happen that when this point is reached an arrest sometimes occurs there? These questions Oakeshott has not answered; and he could only answer them by doing what he has not done, namely giving such an account of experience itself, such a map of the river of experience, as would show the position of this and other points at which arrests may take place.

The reason why he has not done this, I am compelled to think, is because, in spite of his insistence on the conception of experience as no mere immediacy but as containing within itself thought, judgement, assertion of reality, he has not worked out the implications of this conception. It implies that experience is no mere featureless flow of ideas, but understands itself, that is, has features and grasps them. It implies that the modes of

experience arise out of these features and are therefore, in some
sort, not accidental but necessary, not backwaters off the stream
but reaches or currents or eddies in the stream itself, integral
parts of its flow. It implies that such special forms of experience
as history must be somehow conceived as integrated within the
whole of experience.

This failure to explain how and why history arises within
experience as a necessary mode of it results, unless I am mistaken, in a failure to clear up one feature of history itself. We
have seen that Oakeshott states a dilemma: the object of
historical thought is either present or past: the historian thinks
of it as past, but that is where he is wrong; that is in fact the
philosophical error which makes him an historian; it is really
present. And this is connected with another dilemma which he
states at the beginning of his whole argument: either we must
think of historical experience from inside, as it appears to the
historian, or from outside, as it appears to the philosopher; but
obviously our inquiry is a philosophical one, therefore we must
reject the historian's point of view altogether. Now, in the sequel
it appears to me that instead of abiding by this programme he
escapes between the horns of this second dilemma by expounding the nature of historical experience as it appears to one who
is simultaneously historian and philosopher. I say this because
his exposition of the nature of history, as it proceeds, clears up
points of principle where confusion and error would hamper,
and actually have hampered, the historian's own work. Unless
I am mistaken, Oakeshott himself is a more powerful historian
for having cleared up these points. His philosophy has got inside
his history; and instead of resulting in a situation where historical experience, remaining simply what it always was, has
been studied successfully by something quite different, namely,
philosophical thought, historical experience itself has been
revivified and illuminated by that thought.

Now let us return to the first dilemma: either past or present,
but not both. According to Oakeshott, the historian is an historian just because he makes the philosophical mistake of thinking that the present is past. But he himself has exploded that
error. An exploded error, if its refutation is really grasped, has
no more power over the intellect. The explosion of this error,
therefore, should result in the simple disappearance of history

as a mode of experience. But it does not ; for Oakeshott, history remains a genuine and legitimate activity of thought. Why is this ? I can only suppose it to be because the so-called error was not an error at all. Once more, there is an escape between the horns of the dilemma. The historian, if he thinks his past is a dead past, is certainly making a mistake ; but Oakeshott supposes that there is no third alternative to the disjunction that the past is either a dead past or not past at all but simply present. The third alternative is that it should be a living past, a past which, because it was thought and not mere natural event, can be re-enacted in the present and in that re-enactment known as past. If this third alternative could be accepted, we should get the result that history is not based on a philosophical error and is therefore not in his sense a mode of experience, but an integral part of experience itself.

The reason why Oakeshott rules out this third alternative (which he does without any discussion or even mention of it) is, I think, connected with his failure to grasp the consequences of admitting that experience contains in itself an element of mediation, thought, or assertion of reality. Of a merely immediate experience, like that of sheer feeling (if there is such a thing), it is true that what is inside it cannot be also outside it. The subjective is merely subjective and cannot be also objective. But in an experience which is mediation or thought, that which is experienced is real, and is experienced as real. So far as historical experience is thought, therefore, what it experiences or thinks as past really is past. The fact that it is also present does not prevent it from being past, any more than, when I perceive a distant object, where perceiving means not only sensation but thought, the fact that I perceive it here prevents it from being there. If I look at the sun and am dazzled, my being dazzled is here only, in me and not in the sun ; but in so far as I perceive the sun, by thinking 'what dazzles me is there in the sky', I perceive it as there, away from me. Similarly the historian thinks of his object as there, or rather then, away from him in time ; and, because history is knowledge and not mere immediate experience, he can experience it both as then and as now: now in the immediacy of historical experience, but then in its mediacy.

In spite of this limitation, Oakeshott's work not only represents the high-water mark of English thought upon history, but shows a complete transcendence of the positivism in which that thought has been involved, and from which it has tried in vain to free itself, for at least half a century. It is therefore full of hope for the future of English historiography. True, it has failed to show that history is a necessary form of experience; it has only demonstrated that men are at liberty to be historians, not that they are under any obligation to be so; but, granted they choose to be, it has demonstrated their indefeasible right, and their peremptory duty, to play their game according to its own rules; to tolerate no interference, and listen to no analogies, from any outside quarter.

(vi) *Toynbee*

As a contrast with Oakeshott's work, which represents the transformation of historical thought from a positivistic stage to a new stage which I may perhaps call idealistic, by philosophical criticism of its principles from within, I may here mention Professor Arnold Toynbee's great *Study of History*,[1] which represents a restatement of the positivistic view itself. Toynbee has given us the first three volumes of a much larger projected work; and whatever may appear in the later volumes, these three have no doubt given a sufficient sample of his method and indication of his aims. In its details his work is enormously impressive by virtue of the almost incredible mass of erudition contained in it; but here I am concerned not with details but with principles. The main principle seems to be that the subject-matter of history is the lives of certain unitary divisions of the human species which Toynbee calls societies. One of these is our own, which he calls Western Christendom. Another is Eastern or Byzantine Christendom. A third is Islamic society: a fourth, Hindu society: a fifth, Far Eastern society. All these exist as civilizations at the present day, but we can also detect what appear to be fossilized relics of societies now extinct; one set of such relics including Monophysite and Nestorian Christians in the East, together with the Jews and Parsees, and another including the various branches of Buddhism and the Jains of

[1] Vols. i–iii, London 1934. [Collingwood wrote this passage in 1936 and it was not subsequently revised. Vols. iv–vi of *A Study of History* were published in 1939.]

India. Differences and relations between these societies he calls oecumenical; differences and relations within a single society, such as those between Athens and Sparta, or France and Germany, he regards as quite different in kind, and these he calls parochial. The field of the historian's study offers him an infinite variety of tasks, but among these the most important are concerned with discerning and distinguishing these entities called societies and studying the relations between them.

This study is pursued by means of certain general concepts or categories. One of these categories is *affiliation* and its correlative *apparentation*, exemplified for instance in the relation between our own society and the Hellenic society from which it is historically derived. Some societies are, so to speak, Melchizedek societies, not affiliated to any other; some have no others affiliated to them: some are interrelated through affiliation to the same parent society and so on: thus it is possible to arrange societies according to the concept of affiliation into various classes, exhibiting the concept in these various ways. Another category is that of *civilization*, as distinct from *primitive society*. Every society is either primitive or civilized; the vast majority are primitive, and these are in general relatively small in geographical extent and in population, relatively short-lived, and commonly meeting their end through violence, either at the hands of a civilized society or through destruction by another uncivilized one. Civilizations are rarer in number and individually larger in scale; but the important thing to bear in mind about them is that the unity which they form is the unity not of an individual but of a class. There is no one thing, civilization, except in the sense of the common character 'civilizedness' belonging to the many different civilizations. The unity of civilization is an illusion fostered by the peculiar way in which our own civilization has entangled all others in the meshes of its own economic system, and is at once dispelled if instead of attending to the economic map of the world we look at its cultural map. Another category is that of *interregnum* or *time of troubles*, the chaotic period between the decay of one society and the rise of one affiliated to it, like the European Dark Ages between the death of Hellenism and the rise of Western Christendom. Another is that of the *internal proletariat*, the body of persons within a society which owes nothing to that society except its physical life, although it may very well become the dominant element in the society affiliated to it, e.g. the Christians towards the close of the Hellenic society. Another is that of the *external proletariat*, or barbarian world surrounding a given society, which joins hands with the internal proletariat to break it up when its creative power is exhausted. Others are the *universal State* and *universal Church*, organizations concentrating in themselves the entire political and religious life respectively of the society in which they arise. By studying historical records in the light of these categories we can detect many societies now extinct which have been civilized in their time: a Syriac, a Minoan, a Sumeric, a Hittite, a Babylonic, an Andean, a Yucatec, a Mexic, a Mayan, and an Egyptiac, this last the longest-lived of all, for it lasted from the 4th millennium B.C. to the first century A.D.

With these prolegomena, Toynbee gets to work on his main task, which is the comparative study of civilizations. His first chief question is how and why civilizations arise: his second, how and why they grow; his third, how and why they break down. He then goes on, according to the general plan prefixed to his first volume, to study the nature of universal states and universal churches, heroic ages, and contacts between civilizations in space and time; the whole work is to close with sections on the prospects of Western civilization and on 'the inspirations of historians'.

I began discussing Toynbee's work by saying that it represented a restatement of historical positivism. What I meant was that the principles which constitute its individuality are principles derived from the methodology of natural science. These principles are based on the conception of external relations. The natural scientist finds himself confronted by separate, discrete facts which can be counted: or alternatively he cuts up the phenomena that confront him into such countable discrete facts. He then proceeds to determine the relations between them, these relations being always links connecting one fact with another external to it. A collection of facts thus linked together forms, again, a single fact whose relations to others of the same order are of the same external kind. If the scientist's methods are to work at all, the first thing necessary is that a clear line should be drawn between one fact and another. There must be no overlapping.

These are the principles on which Toynbee deals with history. The first thing he does is to cut up the field of historical study into a specifiable number of distinct sections, each called a society. Each society is wholly self-contained. It is for Toynbee a very important question whether Western Christendom is a continuation of Hellenic society or a different society related to it by way of affiliation. The right answer, according to him, is the second. Anyone who gives the first, or who blurs the absolute distinction between the two answers, has committed an unpardonable offence against the first canon of historical method as he conceives it. We are not allowed to say that Hellenic civilization has turned into Western Christendom by a process of development involving the accentuation of some of its elements, the fading away of others, and the emergence of certain new elements within itself and the borrowing of others from external sources. The philosophical principle involved in saying that would be the principle that a civilization may develop into new forms while yet remaining itself, whereas Toynbee's principle is that if a civilization changes it ceases to be itself and a new civilization comes into being. And this dilemma as regards development in time holds good equally with regard to contacts in space. Such contacts are external contacts between one society and another; they therefore presuppose a clean cut between one society and its neighbours. We must be able to say exactly where one society leaves off and another begins. We are not allowed to say that one shades off into the next.

This is the positivistic conception of individuality, the conception according to which the individual is constituted as such by being cut off from everything else by a sharp boundary distinguishing clearly what is within it from what is outside. The inner and the outer are mutually exclusive. This is the kind of individuality which is possessed by a stone or any other material body. It is the primary characteristic of the world of nature, and distinguishes that world from the world of mind, where individuality consists not of separateness from environment but of the power to absorb environment into itself. It is therefore not what individuality means in history, so far as the world of history is a world of mind. The historian who studies a civilization other than his own can apprehend the mental life of that civilization only by re-enacting its experience for himself. If the Western European of to-day studies Hellenic civilization historically, he enters into possession of the mental wealth of that civilization and makes it an integral part of his own. As a matter of fact, Western civilization has formed itself by doing exactly this, by reconstructing within its own mind the mind of the Hellenic world and developing the wealth of that mind in new directions. Thus Western civilization is not related to Hellenic in any merely external way. The relation is an internal one. Western civilization expresses, and indeed achieves, its individuality not by distinguishing itself from Hellenic civilization but by identifying itself therewith.

Toynbee has failed to see this because his general conception of history is ultimately naturalistic; he regards the life of a society as a natural and not a mental life, something at bottom merely biological and best understood on biological analogies. And this is connected with the fact that he never reaches the conception of historical knowledge as the re-enactment of the past in the historian's mind. He regards history as a mere spectacle, something consisting of facts observed and recorded by the historian, phenomena presented externally to his gaze, not experiences into which he must enter and which he must make his own. This is merely a way of saying that he has not undertaken any philosophical analysis of the way in which his historical knowledge has been attained. He possesses enormous quantities of it, but he treats it as if it were something he finds ready-made in books, and the problem that interests him is only the problem of arranging it when collected. His whole scheme is really a scheme of pigeon-holes elaborately arranged and labelled, into which ready-made historical facts can be put. Such schemes are not in themselves vicious; but they always entail certain dangers: notably the danger of forgetting that the facts thus pigeon-holed have to be separated from their context by an act of dissection. This act, become habitual, leads to an obsession: one forgets that the historical fact, as it actually exists and as the historian actually knows it, is always a process in which something is changing into something else. This element of process is the life of history. In order to pigeon-hole historical facts, the living body of history must first be killed (that is, its essential character as process must be denied) so that it may be dissected.

The criticism which must be passed on Toynbee's principles is thus twofold. First, he regards history itself, the historical process, as cut up by sharp lines into mutually exclusive parts, and denies the continuity of the process in virtue of which every part overlaps and interpenetrates others. His distinction between societies or civilizations is really a distinction between focal points in the process: he has misunderstood it as a distinction between chunks or lumps of fact into which the process is divided. Secondly, he misconceives the relation between the historical process and the historian who knows it. He regards the historian as the intelligent spectator of history, in the same way in which the scientist is the intelligent spectator of nature: he fails to see that the historian is an integral element in the process of history itself, reviving in himself the experiences of which he achieves historical knowledge. Just as the various parts of the process are misconceived as placed outside one another, so the process as a whole and the historian are placed outside one another. And these two criticisms come in the last resort to the same thing: namely that history is converted into nature, and the past, instead of living in the present, as it does in history, is conceived as a dead past, as it is in nature. But at the same time I must add that this criticism only affects fundamental principles. In the detail of his work, Toynbee shows a very fine historical sense and only rarely allows his actual historical judgements to be falsified by the errors in his principles. One place where this does happen is in his judgement of the Roman Empire, which he regards as a mere phase in the decline of Hellenism. That is to say, because its relation to Greece is too close to permit of its being regarded as a distinct civilization, and because that is the only condition on which he could allow it a genuine achievement of its own, his dilemma forces him to ignore all that it did achieve and to treat it as a mere phenomenon of decay. But in history as it actually happens there are no mere phenomena of decay: every decline is also a rise, and it is only the historian's personal failures of knowledge or sympathy—partly due to mere ignorance, partly to the preoccupations of his own practical life—that prevent him from seeing this double character, at once creative and destructive, of any historical process whatever.

§ 2. Germany

(i) Windelband

In Germany, the home of historical criticism, a great deal of interest was taken towards the end of the nineteenth century, and increasingly after it, in the theory of history and, in particular, the nature of the distinction between it and science. Among the heirlooms which Germany inherited from her great philosophical period, the age of Kant and Hegel, was the idea that Nature and History were in some sense two distinct worlds each with a character of its own. Philosophers of the nineteenth century used to repeat the distinction as a commonplace, which passed from hand to mouth so often that its significance was worn quite flat in the process. Lotze, for example, in his *Microcosmus*, published in 1856, asserted that Nature is the realm of necessity and History the realm of freedom: an echo of post-Kantian idealism which, in Lotze, means nothing definite, as the vague and empty chapters on history in that work prove all too clearly. Lotze inherited from the German idealists, and in particular from Kant, the idea that man has a dual nature; a physiologist by early training, he insisted that man's body is nothing but a bundle of mechanisms, but at the same time he held that man's mind is free: thus man as body inhabits the world of nature but as mind he inhabits the world of history. But instead of working out the relation between these two things, as the great idealists had done, Lotze left the whole question in the air and never attempted to think it out at all. His work is characteristic of the woolly and emotional nebulosities which in Germany followed the collapse of the idealist school.

Other German writers used other formulae for characterizing the terms of the same familiar antithesis. In his *Grundriss der Historik* (Jena, 1858) the distinguished historian Droysen defined nature as the coexistence of being (*das Nebeneinander des Seienden*) and history as the succession of becoming (*das Nacheinander des Gewordenen*); a merely rhetorical antithesis which owed any plausibility it might possess to overlooking the fact that in the world of nature too there are events and processes which follow one another in a determinate order, and that in history there are things which coexist, like liberalism and capitalism, and whose coexistence is a problem for historical thought. The triviality of such formulae showed that people were merely presupposing the distinction between nature and history, not trying to understand it.

The first genuine attempt to understand it came with the advent of the neo-Kantian school late in the century. It followed from the general principles of this school that, to understand the difference between nature and history, one must approach the distinction from the subjective side: that is, one must distinguish the ways in which the scientist and the historian do their thinking. It was from this point of view that Windelband, the eminent historian of philosophy, approached the subject in a Rectorial Address,[1] delivered at Strassburg in 1894, which at once became famous.

Here he laid it down that history and science were two different things each with a method of its own. Science, he explained, had as its purpose the formulation of general laws: history, the description of individual facts. This distinction he pompously baptized by saying that there were two kinds of science (*Wissenschaft*): *nomothetic* science, which is science in the common sense of the word, and *idiographic* science, which is history. This distinction between science as knowledge of the universal and history as knowledge of the individual was in itself of very small value. It was not even accurate as a statement of the prima facie difference: for the judgement 'this is a case of typhoid fever' is not history but science, although it is a description of individual fact, and the statement 'all Roman silver of the third century is debased' is not science but history although it is a generalization. Of course, there is a sense in which Windelband's distinction can be defended against this criticism: the generalization about third-century coinage is really a statement about an individual fact, namely the monetary policy of the late Roman Empire; and the diagnosis of this disease as typhoid is not so much an individual judgement as the subsumption of a certain fact under a general formula, namely, the definition of typhoid. The business of the scientist as such is not to diagnose

---

[1] *Geschichte und Naturwissenschaft.* Reprinted in *Präludien*, vol. ii (5th edn., Tübingen, 1915), pp. 136–60.

typhoid in a particular case (though in a subsidiary way that is his business too) but to define it in its general nature; and the business of the historian as such is to explore the individual features of individual historical events, not to construct generalizations, though that too is a thing that enters into his work as a secondary feature. But when this is said, it is admitted that the formulation of laws and the description of individuals are not two mutually exclusive forms of thought, between which the whole field of reality can be divided by an amicable agreement, as Windelband thinks.

All that Windelband is really doing in his discussion of the relation between science and history is to put forward a claim on the part of historians to do their own work in their own way and be let alone; it represents a kind of secessionist movement of historians from the general body of a civilization in thrall to natural science. But what this work is, and what is the way in which it can or should be done, Windelband cannot tell us. Nor is he conscious of this inability. When he speaks of an 'idiographic science' he is implying that there can be scientific, i.e. rational or non-empirical, knowledge of the individual; but, strange as it may seem in so learned an historian of thought, he does not realize that the whole tradition of European philosophy from the early Greeks to his own day had declared with one voice that this knowledge is an impossibility: the individual, as a fleeting and transient existence, can only be perceived or experienced as it occurs and can never be the object of that stable and logically constructed thing which is called scientific knowledge. The point had been very clearly made by Schopenhauer:[1]

'History lacks the fundamental characteristic of science, namely the subordination of the objects of consciousness; all it can do is to present a simple co-ordination of the facts it has registered. Hence there is no system in history as there is in the other sciences . . . . The sciences, being systems of cognitions, speak always of kinds; history always of individuals. History, therefore, would be a science of individuals, which implies a self-contradiction.'

To this self-contradiction Windelband shows himself strangely blind, especially in such passages as that in which he congratu-

[1] *Die Welt als Wille und Vorstellung* (3rd edn., 1859), vol. ii, pp. 499–509, *Über Geschichte.*

lates his modern countrymen on replacing the old-fashioned word 'history', *Geschichte*, by the new and better one *Kulturwissenschaft*, science of culture. The only change really introduced by this word lies in the fact of its verbal similarity to the name of a natural science; that is to say, the sole reason for adopting it is that it enables people to forget how deep is the difference between history and natural science and to slur over the distinction in the positivistic manner, by assimilating history to the general pattern of science.

So far as Windelband dealt at all with the question how there can be a science of the individual, he answered it by saying that the historian's knowledge of historical events consists of judgements of value, that is, pronouncements on the spiritual worth of the actions which he is investigating. Thus the historian's thought is ethical thought, and history is a branch of morals. But this is to answer the question how history can be a science by saying that it is not a science. In his *Introduction to Philosophy*,[1] Windelband divides the whole subject-matter into two parts: the theory of knowledge and the theory of value, and history falls in the second part. Thus history ends by being extruded from the sphere of knowledge altogether, and we are left with the conclusion that what the historian does with the individual is not to know or think it, but somehow to intuit its value; an activity on the whole akin to that of the artist. But, once more, the relation between history and art is not systematically thought out.

(ii) *Rickert*

Closely connected with Windelband's thought, but much more systematic, is that of Rickert, whose first work on the subject was published at Freiburg in 1896. Rickert maintains in effect that Windelband was really stating two distinctions between science and history instead of one. The first is the distinction between generalizing and individualizing thought: the second, the distinction between valuing and non-valuing thought. Combining these two, he gets four types of sciences: (1) non-valuing and generalizing, or pure natural science; (2) non-valuing and individualizing, or the quasi-historical sciences of nature like geology, evolutionary biology, &c.; (3) valuing

[1] Eng. tr. London [1921].

and generalizing, or the quasi-scientific sciences of history like sociology, economics, theoretical jurisprudence, and so forth; (4) valuing and individualizing, or history proper. Further, he sees that Windelband's attempt to divide reality into two mutually exclusive spheres of nature and history cannot be defended. Nature as it really exists does not consist of laws; it consists of individual facts, just like history. Consequently Rickert arrives at the formula that reality as a whole is really history. Natural science is a network of generalizations and formulae built up by the human intellect: in the last resort an arbitrary intellectual construction, not corresponding to any reality. This is the idea expressed in the title of his book, *Die Grenzen der naturwissenschaftlichen Begriffsbildung*, the limits of the formation of scientific concepts. Thus, his four kinds of sciences together form a scale having at one end the extreme case of arbitrary and abstract thought, a mere manipulation of artificial concepts: at the other, the extreme case of concrete and genuine knowledge, the knowledge of reality in its individual existence.

At first sight this seems a conclusive counter-attack on positivism. Natural science, from being held up as the one and only type of genuine knowledge, has been degraded to the position of an arbitrary play of abstractions, constructed in the air and achieving its perfection just so far as it leaves out the actual truth of concrete fact: history is regarded not only as a possible and legitimate form of knowledge but as the only genuine knowledge that exists or can exist. But this *revanche* not only fails in doing justice to natural science, it also misunderstands history. Rickert regards nature, after the positivistic manner, as cut up into separate facts and he goes on to deform history by regarding it in a similar way as an assemblage of individual facts supposed to differ from the facts of nature only in being vehicles of value. But the essence of history lies not in its consisting of individual facts, however valuable these facts may be, but in the process or development leading from one to another. Rickert fails to see that the peculiarity of historical thought is the way in which the historian's mind, as the mind of the present day, apprehends the process by which this mind itself has come into existence through the mental development of the past. He fails to see that what gives value to past facts is the fact that they are not mere past facts, they are not a dead past but a living past, a heritage of past thoughts which by the work of his historical consciousness the historian makes his own. The past cut off from the present, converted into a mere spectacle, can have no value at all; it is history converted into nature. Thus, in the long run, positivism has its revenge on Rickert; historical facts become mere disjointed occurrences, and as such can stand to each other only in the same kind of external relations of time and space, contiguity, resemblance, and causation, as the facts of nature.

(iii) *Simmel*

A third attempt at a philosophy of history, taking shape during the same period, was that of Simmel, whose first essay[1] on the subject dates from 1892. Simmel's was a lively and versatile mind, gifted with a good deal of originality and penetration, but defective in solid thought; and his work on history is full of good observations but of little value as a systematic study of the problem. He realized vividly that for the historian there can be no question of knowing facts in an empirical sense of the word 'know': the historian can never be acquainted with his object, precisely because that object is the past: it consists of events that have finished happening and are no longer there to be observed. Consequently the problem of distinguishing history from science as Windelband and Rickert stated it does not arise. The facts of nature and the facts of history are not facts in the same sense of the word. The facts of nature are what the scientist can perceive or produce in the laboratory under his own eyes; the facts of history are not 'there' at all: all that the historian has before him are documents and relics from which he has somehow to reconstruct the facts. Further, he sees that history is an affair of spirit, of human personalities, and that the only thing that enables the historian to reconstruct it is the fact that he himself is a spirit and a personality. All this is excellent. But now comes Simmel's problem. The historian, beginning from his documents, constructs in his own mind what professes to be a picture of the past. This picture is in his mind and nowhere else; it is a subjective mental construction. But he claims that this subjective construction possesses objective

---

[1] *Die Probleme der Geschichtsphilosophie* (Leipzig).

truth. How can this be? How can the merely subjective picture constructed in the historian's mind be projected into the past and described as something that actually happened?

Once more, it is greatly to Simmel's credit that he sees this problem. But he cannot solve it. He can only say that the historian feels convinced of the objective reality of his subjective constructions: he regards them as something real, irrespectively of his thinking them at this moment. But obviously, this is no solution. The question is not whether the historian feels this conviction, but by what right he feels it. Is it an illusion, or is it based on some solid ground? Simmel cannot answer that question. And the reason seems to be that he has not gone far enough in his criticism of the notion of historical fact. He has rightly seen that past facts, as past, are not present to the historian's perception; but because he has not sufficiently grasped the nature of the historical process he does not realize that the historian's own mind is heir to the past and has come to be what it is through the development of the past into the present, so that in him the past is living in the present. He thinks of the historical past as a dead past, and when he asks how the historian can revive it in his own mind he naturally can give no answer. He has confused the historical process, in which the past lives on in the present, with a natural process, in which the past dies when the present is born. This reduction of the historical process to a natural process is part of the legacy of positivism, so that here once more Simmel's failure to construct a philosophy of history is due to his incomplete escape from a positivistic point of view.

(iv) *Dilthey*

The best work done on the subject during this period was that of the lonely and neglected genius Dilthey, whose first and only book upon it was published as early as 1883 and was called *Introduction to the Sciences of Mind* (*Einleitung in die Geisteswissenschaften*). But he continued until 1910 to publish scattered essays, always interesting and important, partly on the history of thought, notably a series of very able studies on the formation of the modern mind since the Renaissance and Reformation, and partly on the theory of history. It was his intention to write a great *Critique of Historical Reason* on the model of the Kantian critiques, but this intention was never carried out.

In the *Introduction to the Sciences of Mind* he took up the position, eleven years before Windelband, that history deals with concrete individuals and natural science with abstract generalizations. But this never led him to a satisfactory philosophy of history, because the individuals of which he was thinking were conceived as isolated past facts and were not integrated into a genuine process of historical development. We have already seen (Pt. III, § 9) that this way of conceiving history was the characteristic weakness of historical thought itself during that period, and also that the same conception in Windelband and Rickert blocked the way to a true understanding of the philosophical problem of history.

But Dilthey was not satisfied with this position. In later essays[1] he raises the question how the historian actually performs the work of coming to know the past, starting as he does simply from documents and data which do not by themselves reveal it. These data, he replies, offer him only the occasion for reliving in his own mind the spiritual activity which originally produced them. It is in virtue of his own spiritual life, and in proportion to the intrinsic richness of that life, that he can thus infuse life into the dead materials with which he finds himself confronted. Thus genuine historical knowledge is an inward experience (*Erlebnis*) of its own object, whereas scientific knowledge is the attempt to understand (*begreifen*) phenomena presented to him as outward spectacles. This conception of the historian as living in his object, or rather making his object live in him, is a great advance on anything achieved by any of Dilthey's German contemporaries. But a problem still remains, because life for Dilthey means immediate experience, as distinct from reflection or knowledge; and it is not enough for the historian to *be* Julius Caesar or Napoleon, since that does not constitute a knowledge of Julius Caesar or Napoleon any more than the obvious fact that he *is* himself constitutes a knowledge of himself.

This problem Dilthey tries to solve by recourse to psychology. By existing at all, I am myself; but it is only by means of psychological analysis that I come to know myself, that is, to understand the structure of my own personality. Similarly, the

[1] *Gesammelte Schriften*, vol. vii.

historian who relives the past in his own mind must, if he is to be an historian, understand the past which he is reliving. By simply reliving it, he is developing and enlarging his own personality, incorporating in his own experience the experience of others in the past; but whatever is so incorporated becomes part of the structure of his personality, and the rule still holds good that this structure can be understood only in terms of psychology. What this means in practice may be seen from one of Dilthey's last works, in which he deals with the history of philosophy according to his own formula, reducing it to a study in the psychology of philosophers, on the principle that there are certain fundamental types of mental structure, and that each type has a certain necessary attitude to, and conception of, the world.[1] The differences between different philosophies are thus reduced to mere resultants of differences in psychological structure or disposition. But this way of treating the subject makes nonsense of it. The only question that matters about a philosophy is whether it is right or wrong. If a given philosopher thinks as he does because, being that kind of man, he cannot help thinking like that, this question does not arise. Philosophy handled from this psychological point of view ceases to be philosophy at all.

This shows that something has gone wrong with Dilthey's argument, and it is not difficult to see what it is. Psychology is not history but science, a science constructed on naturalistic principles. To say that history becomes intelligible only when conceived in terms of psychology is to say that historical knowledge is impossible and that the only kind of knowledge is scientific knowledge: history by itself is mere life, immediate experience, and therefore the historian as such merely experiences a life which the psychologist as such and he alone understands. Dilthey has come up against the question which Windelband and the rest had not the penetration to recognize: the question how there can be a knowledge, as distinct from an immediate experience, of the individual. He has answered that question by admitting that there cannot be such a knowledge, and falling back on the positivistic view that the only way in which the universal (the proper object of knowledge) can be known is by means of natural science or a science constructed

[1] *Das Wesen der Philosophie* (*Gesammelte Schriften*. vol. v).

on naturalistic principles. Thus in the end he, like the rest of his generation, surrenders to positivism.

The point at which his argument goes wrong is no less easy to identify. Dilthey, as I have explained, argues that to be myself is one thing, namely. immediate experience: to understand myself is another, namely psychological science. He assumes that the self-knowledge of mind is identical with psychology. But on his own showing history has a good claim to share that title. I may now be experiencing an immediate feeling of discomfort, and I may ask myself why I have this feeling. I may answer that question by reflecting that this morning I received a letter criticizing my conduct in what seems to me a valid and unanswerable manner. Here I am not making psychological generalizations; I am recognizing in its detail a certain individual event or series of events, which are already present to my consciousness as a feeling of discomfort or dissatisfaction with myself. To understand that feeling is to recognize it as the outcome of a certain historical process. Here the self-understanding of my mind is nothing else than historical knowledge. Push the case a step farther. When, as an historian, I relive in my own mind a certain experience of Julius Caesar, I am not simply being Julius Caesar; on the contrary, I am myself, and know that I am myself; the way in which I incorporate Julius Caesar's experience in my own personality is not by confusing myself with him, but by distinguishing myself from him and at the same time making his experience my own. The living past of history lives in the present; but it lives not in the immediate experience of the present, but only in the self-knowledge of the present. This Dilthey has overlooked; he thinks it lives in the present's immediate experience of itself; but that immediate experience is not historical thought.

Dilthey and Simmel have in fact chosen opposite horns of the same false dilemma. Each realizes that the historical past, that is, the experience and thought of the agents whose acts the historian studies, must become part of the historian's own personal experience. Each then argues that this experience, because his own, is merely private and personal, an immediate experience within his own mind and nothing objective. Each sees that it must be something objective if it is to be an object of historical knowledge. But how can it be objective when it is purely subjective? How can it be something knowable if it is merely a state of his own mind? Simmel says, by projecting it into the past: with the result that history becomes merely the illusory projection of our own states of mind upon the blank screen of the unknowable past. Dilthey says, by becoming the object of psychological analysis: with the result that history disappears altogether and is replaced by psychology. The answer to both doctrines is that since the past is not a dead past but lives on in the present, the historian's knowledge is not exposed to the dilemma at all: it is not either knowledge of the past and therefore not knowledge of the present, or else knowledge of the present and therefore not knowledge of the past; it is knowledge of the past in the present, the self-knowledge of the historian's own mind as the present revival and reliving of past experiences.

These four men between them started a vigorous movement in Germany for the study of the philosophy of history. Wilhelm Bauer, in his *Introduction to the Study of History*,[1] went so far as to say that in his own time the philosophy of history was being much more actively pursued than history itself. But although books and pamphlets on the subject have poured from the press, genuinely new ideas have been rare. The general problem bequeathed to posterity by the writers I have analysed may be stated by saying that it concerns the distinction between history and natural science, or historical process and natural process. It starts from the positivistic principle that natural science is the only true form of knowledge, which implies that all processes are natural processes; the problem is how to get away from that principle. Over and over again, as we have seen, the principle has been denied, but those who denied it have never completely freed their minds from its influence. However strongly they have insisted that history is a development and a spiritual development, they have failed to make good the implications of these phrases and have uniformly, in the last resort, fallen back on thinking of history as if it were nature. The peculiarity of an historical or spiritual process is that since the mind is that which knows itself, the historical process which is the life of the mind is a self-knowing process: a process which understands itself, criticizes itself, values itself, and so forth. The German

[1] *Einführung in das Studium der Geschichte* (Tübingen, 1921).

school of *Geschichtsphilosophie* has never grasped this. It has always regarded history as an object confronting the historian in the same way in which nature confronts the scientist: the task of understanding, valuing, or criticizing it is not done by itself for itself, it is done to it by the historian standing outside it. The result of this is that the spirituality or subjectivity which properly belongs to the historical life of mind itself is taken away from it and given to the historian. This converts the historical process into a natural process, a process intelligible to an intelligent spectator but not to itself. The life of mind thus conceived remains a life but ceases to be a mental life; it becomes a merely physiological life or at best a life of irrational instinct: a life which, however emphatically it is called a spiritual life, is being conceived as a natural life. The German movement of which I am speaking thus never succeeds in escaping from naturalism, that is, from the conversion of mind into nature.

(v) *Meyer*

At the close of the nineteenth century the extreme form of this naturalism may be seen in the positivistic historians like K. Lamprecht, P. Barth, E. Bernheim, the author of a well-known handbook of historical method,[1] K. Breysig, and other writers, who have conceived the true or highest task of history as the discovery of causal laws connecting certain constant types of historical phenomena. Perversions of history on these lines all share one characteristic in common, namely a distinction between two kinds of history: empirical history, which merely discharges the humble office of ascertaining the facts, and philosophical or scientific history, which has the nobler task of discovering the laws connecting the facts. Wherever this distinction is detected, the cloven hoof of naturalism has betrayed itself. There is no such thing as empirical history, for the facts are not empirically present to the historian's mind: they are past events, to be apprehended not empirically but by a process of inference according to rational principles from data given or rather discovered in the light of these principles; and there is no such thing as the supposed further stage of philosophical or scientific history which discovers their causes or laws or in general explains them, because an historical fact once

[1] *Lehrbuch der historischen Methode* (Leipzig, 1889), 6th edn., 1908.

genuinely ascertained, grasped by the historian's re-enactment of the agent's thought in his own mind, is already explained. For the historian there is no difference between discovering what happened and discovering why it happened.

The best historians everywhere are conscious of this in their own actual work, and in Germany many of them, partly through their experience of actual research and partly through the influence of the philosophers already discussed, have now come to realize enough of it to resist the claims of positivism at least in its extremer forms. But their realization of it down to the present has generally been at best partial, and consequently even the strongest opponents of positivism have been a good deal influenced by it and have taken up a somewhat confused position on questions of theory and method.

A good example of this is afforded by Eduard Meyer, one of the most distinguished of recent German historians, whose essay on *The Theory and Methodology of History* (*Zur Theorie und Methodik der Geschichte*), published at Halle in 1902 and later reissued in a revised form,[1] shows how a first-rate historian of long experience thought about the principles of his own work at the beginning of the present century. Here, as in Bury but far more clearly thought out, we find an attempt to disentangle history from errors and fallacies due to the influence of natural science: an anti-positivistic view of its task, which in the long run fails to rise decisively above the atmosphere of positivism.

Meyer begins by a detailed and penetrating criticism of the positivistic tendency, which was prevalent in the nineties and to which I have just referred. If the task of history is supposed to consist in ascertaining general laws governing the course of historical events, it is expurgated of three factors which are in reality of high importance: chance or accident, free will, and ideas or the demands and conceptions of men. The historically significant is identified with the typical or recurring: thus history becomes the history of groups or societies, and the individual disappears from it except in the guise of a mere instance of general laws. The task of history, so conceived, is to establish certain social and psychological types of life, following one another in a determinate order. Meyer quotes Lamprecht[2] as

---

[1] *Kleine Schriften* (Halle, 1910), pp. 3–67.
[2] In *Zukunft*, 2 Jan. 1897.

the leading exponent of this idea. Lamprecht distinguished[1] six phases of this kind in the life of the German nation, and generalized this result for application to every national history. But by such analysis, says Meyer, the living figures of history are destroyed and their place is taken by vague generalities and unreal phantoms. The result is a reign of empty catchwords. As against all this, Meyer contends that the proper object of historical thought is historical fact in its individuality, and that chance and free will are determining causes that cannot be banished from history without destroying its very essence. Not only is the historian as such uninterested in the so-called laws of this pseudo-science, but there are no historical laws. Breysig[2] has attempted to state twenty-four of them, but every one is either false or so vague that history can find no value in them. They may serve as clues for investigating historical facts, but they lack all necessity. The historian's failure to establish them results not from poverty of material or weakness of intellect, but from the nature of historical knowledge itself, whose business is the discovery and exposition of events in their individuality.

When Meyer leaves polemics and goes on to expound the positive principles of historical thought, he begins by laying down the first principle that its object is past events or rather changes as such. Theoretically, therefore, it deals with any and every change, but by custom it deals only with those in human affairs. This limitation, however, he does not explain or defend. Yet it is of crucial importance, and his failure to explain it is a serious weakness in his theory. The real reason for it is that the historian is not concerned with events as such but with actions, i.e. events brought about by the will and expressing the thought of a free and intelligent agent, and discovers this thought by rethinking it in his own mind: but this Meyer fails to see, and he never gets farther towards answering the question 'What is an historical fact?' than to say: 'An historical fact is a past event.'

The first consequence of this failure is an embarrassment over the distinction between the infinite multiplicity of events that have actually happened and the much smaller number of events which the historian is able or anxious to investigate. Meyer

---

[1] *Deutsche Geschichte* (Berlin, 1892).

[2] *Der Stufenbau und die Gesetze der Weltgeschichte* (Berlin, 1905).

bases this distinction on the fact that the historian can know only those events for which he has evidence: but even then, the number of knowable events far exceeds the number of those that are historically interesting. Many events are knowable and known, but no historian thinks of them as historical events. What then constitutes the historicity of an event? For Meyer, those events are historical which have been efficacious (*wirksam*), i.e. have produced consequences. For example, the philosophy of Spinoza was for a long time quite without influence, but later people became interested in it and it began to influence their thought. Hence from being a non-historical fact it became an historical one: it is non-historical for the historian of the seventeenth century but becomes historical for the historian of the eighteenth. This is surely a quite arbitrary and perverse distinction. For the historian of the seventeenth century Spinoza is a highly interesting phenomenon, whether or not he was read and accepted as a leader of thought; because the formation of his philosophy was in itself a noteworthy achievement of the seventeenth-century mind. What makes that philosophy an object of our historical study is not the fact that Novalis or Hegel studied it but the fact that *we* can study it, reconstruct it in our own minds, and thus appreciate its philosophical value.

Meyer's false position here is due to a relic in his own thought of the positivistic spirit against which he was protesting. He sees that a mere past event taken in isolation cannot be an object of historical knowledge, but he thinks that it becomes one in virtue of its connexions with other events, these connexions being conceived by him in the positivistic manner as external causal connexions. This, however, begs the question. If the historical importance of an event is defined as its efficacy in producing further events, what constitutes the historical importance of those others? For he would hardly hold that an event becomes historically important through producing consequences themselves devoid of historical importance. If, however, the historical importance of Spinoza consists in his influencing the German Romantics, wherein consists the historical importance of the German Romantics? Pursuing this line of inquiry we shall ultimately reach the present day, and conclude that the historical importance of Spinoza is his importance to us here and now. Further we cannot go; for, as Meyer observes, it is impossible to judge the historical importance of anything in the present, since we cannot yet tell what is going to come of it.

This reflection deprives of its value a great deal of Meyer's positive theory concerning historical method. The whole conception of the historical past as consisting of events linked together in causal series is fundamental for that theory. On it depends Meyer's conception of historical research, as the search for causes; of historical necessity, as the determination of an event by such causes; of historical contingency or chance, as the intersection of two or more causal series; of historical importance, as the productiveness of further events in series: and so forth. All these conceptions are tainted by positivism and consequently fallacious.

The valuable side of his theory consists in his doctrine of historical interest. Here alone he shows real grasp on a truth of principle. Having realized that even when we confine ourselves to important events in the sense above defined, we are still confronted with an embarrassingly large number of them, he goes on to reduce this number by appeal to a new principle of selection based on the interest of the historian and of the present-day life of which the historian is a representative. It is the historian as a living agent who brings out of himself the problems whose solution he desires to find and thus constructs the clues with which he is to approach his material. This subjective element is an essential factor in all historical knowledge. Yet even here Meyer does not grasp the full import of his own doctrine. He is still worried by the fact that however much information we have concerning a given period we still might obtain more, and this more might modify the results already thought secure. Hence, he argues, all historical knowledge is uncertain. He fails to see that the historian's problem is a present problem, not a future one: it is to interpret the material now available, not to anticipate future discoveries. To quote Oakeshott again, the word 'truth' has no meaning for the historian unless it means 'what the evidence obliges us to believe'.

Meyer's great merit lies in his effective criticism of the openly positivistic sociological pseudo-history fashionable in his time. In details, too, his essay constantly reveals a lively sense of historical reality. But where his theory breaks down is in his failure to press his attack on positivism to its logical conclusion.

He is content to acquiesce in a naïve realism which treats historical fact as one thing and the historian's knowledge of it as another. He thus conceives history in the last resort as a mere spectacle seen from outside, not as a process to which the historian himself is integral as at once part of it and the self-consciousness of it. All intimacy in the relation between the historian and his subject-matter disappears, the conception of historical importance becomes meaningless, and consequently Meyer's principles of historical method, depending as they do on the selection of the important, vanish into thin air.

(vi) *Spengler*

In sharp contrast to Meyer's work, and to the work of the better twentieth-century German historians, is Oswald Spengler's relapse into positivistic naturalism. *Der Untergang des Abendlandes*[1] has had such a vogue in this country and in America, as well as in Germany, that it may be worth while to indicate here again my reasons for regarding it as radically unsound.

According to Spengler, history is a succession of self-contained individual units which he calls cultures. Each culture has a special character of its own; each exists in order to express this character in every detail of its life and development. But each resembles all the others in having an identical life-cycle, resembling that of an organism. It begins with the barbarism of a primitive society; it goes on to develop a political organization, arts and sciences, and so forth, at first in a stiff and archaic manner, then blossoming into its classical period, then congealing into decadence, and finally sinking into a new type of barbarism where everything is commercialized and vulgarized, and here its life ends. Out of this decadent condition nothing new emerges; that culture is dead and its creative power is spent. Further, not only is the cycle of phases fixed, but the time which it takes is fixed; so that if we nowadays, for example, can detect the point at which we stand in the cycle of our own culture, we can accurately foretell what the future phases of it will be.

This conception is openly positivistic. For history itself is substituted a morphology of history, a naturalistic science whose

[1] Eng. tr.: *The Decline of the West*, 2 vols., London, 1926-8. For a fuller consideration of the book see my article in *Antiquity*, vol. i, 1927, pp. 311-25.

value consists in external analysis, the establishment of general laws, and (conclusive mark of non-historical thought) the claim to foretell the future on scientific principles. The facts are positivistically conceived as isolated from each other instead of growing organically out of each other; but the facts are now huge chunks of fact—bigger and better facts, each with a fixed internal structure, but each related to the others non-historically. Their only interrelations are (a) temporal and spatial, (b) morphological, i.e. relations consisting in similarity of structure. This anti-historical and merely naturalistic view of history infects even Spengler's conception of the inner detail of each culture taken by itself; for the succession of phases within a culture, as he conceives it, is no more historical than the succession of the various phases in the life of an insect as egg, larva, pupa, and imago. Thus at every point the idea of historical process as a mental process, where the past is conserved in the present, is elaborately denied. Every phase in a culture turns automatically into the next when its time is ripe, irrespectively of what the individual persons living in it may do. Further, the unique characteristic which marks off any one culture from any other and pervades all its details (the Greekness of Greek culture, the Western-Europeanness of Western European culture, and so on) is conceived not as an ideal of life worked out and achieved by the men of that culture through a spiritual effort, whether conscious or unconscious; it belongs to them as a natural possession, in exactly the same way in which dark skin-pigment belongs to negroes or blue eyes to Scandinavians. The whole groundwork of the theory is thus based on a deliberate and painstaking attempt to extrude from history everything that makes it historical, and to substitute at every point a naturalistic conception of principle for the corresponding historical one.

Spengler's book is loaded with a mass of historical learning, but even this is constantly deformed and perverted to fit his thesis. To take one example out of many, he maintains that as part of its fundamental character the classical or Graeco-Roman culture lacked all sense of time, cared nothing for the past or the future, and therefore (unlike the Egyptian, which had a keen time-sense) did not build tombs for its dead. He seems to have forgotten that in Rome orchestral concerts are held every week in the mausoleum of Augustus; that the tomb

of Hadrian was for centuries the fortress of the Popes; and that
for miles and miles outside the city the ancient roads are lined
with the vastest collection of tombs in the whole world. Even
the positivistic thinkers of the nineteenth century, in their misguided attempts to reduce history to a science, went no farther
in the reckless and unscrupulous falsification of facts.

There are obvious similarities between Spengler and Toynbee. The main difference is that with Spengler the isolation of
the various cultures is as complete as that of the Leibnitian
monads. The relations of time, place, and similarity between
them are only perceptible from the detached point of view of
the historian. For Toynbee, these relations, though external,
form part of the experience of the civilizations themselves. It is
essential to Toynbee's view that some societies should be
affiliated to others; the continuity of history is thus safeguarded,
though only in a form which robs it of its full meaning: in
Spengler's nothing like affiliation is possible. There is no
positive relation whatever between one culture and another.
Thus the triumph of naturalism, which in Toynbee only affects
general principles, in Spengler penetrates into every detail.

§ 3. *France*

(i) *Ravaisson's spiritualism*

It is only right that France, the native land of positivism,
should also be the country in which positivism has been most
tenaciously and brilliantly criticized. And the attack on
positivism to which French thought has devoted its best
energies in the late nineteenth and early twentieth century, like
so many other critical and revolutionary movements in the
same country, has in fact only been another proof of the in-
domitable consistency of the French mind. The Enlightenment
which in the eighteenth century attacked the fortress of established religion was in essence a self-assertion of human reason
and human liberty against dogma and superstition as such.
Positivism converted natural science into a new system of
dogma and superstition; and the reawakening of French philosophy to attack that new fortress might once more have
inscribed on its banners the old motto *Écrasez l'infâme*.

This new movement of French thought, unlike that of German, was not consciously and explicitly orientated towards history. But a close inspection of its main characteristics shows that the idea of history was one of its leading conceptions. If we identify the idea of history with the idea of spiritual life or process, the closeness of the connexion becomes obvious, for notoriously the idea of spiritual process is the guiding idea of modern French philosophy. In one way, paradoxical though it may seem, this movement of French thought has a firmer hold on the problem of history than the parallel movement in Germany. For the German movement, however much it talks about history, is always thinking of it in terms of epistemology: its real interest is in the historian's subjective mental processes; and with its general prejudice against metaphysics (a prejudice partly neo-Kantian and partly positivistic) it evades the task of inquiring into the objective nature of the historical process itself, with the result that, as we have seen, it conceives that process as a mere spectacle for the historian's mind and thus converts it into a natural process. But the French mind, resolutely metaphysical in its tradition of thought, concentrates on grasping the character of spiritual process itself, with the result that it has gone far to solve the problem of the philosophy of history without ever mentioning the word history at all.

All I shall do here is to pick out a few points in this singularly rich and varied movement, and show how they bear on our main question. Two themes are constantly recurring throughout its texture: one negative, a criticism of natural science, the other positive, an exposition of the conception of spiritual life or process. They are the negative and positive sides of one single idea. Natural science, raised by positivism to the rank of metaphysics, conceives reality as a system of processes governed everywhere by the law of causality. Everything is what it is because it is determined by something else. Spiritual life is a world whose reality is its freedom or spontaneity: not a lawless or chaotic world, but a world whose laws are freely made by that same spirit which freely obeys them. If such a world exists at all, the metaphysics of positivism must be fallacious. Consequently it must be shown that this metaphysics is unsound; it must be attacked on its own ground and refuted there. In other words, it must be shown that however much the methods of natural science may be justified in their own sphere, this sphere is something short of reality as a whole; it is a limited and dependent reality, dependent for its very existence on the freedom or spontaneity which positivism denies.

Ravaisson[1] in the sixties took the first step towards such an argument by contending that the conception of reality as mechanical, or governed by efficient causes, cannot stand as a metaphysical doctrine because it fails to give any account of the whole within which these causes operate. In order that this whole should exist and maintain itself there must be in it not only a principle of efficient causation, linking part to part, but also a principle of teleology or final causation, which organizes the parts into a whole. This is Leibniz's conception of a synthesis of efficient and final causes, together with the further doctrine, also derived from Leibniz, that our knowledge of the teleological principle is derived from our consciousness of it as the working principle of our own minds. Our knowledge of ourselves as spirit, as a self-creative and self-organizing life, thus enables us to detect a similar life in nature; and (although positivism fails to see this) it is only because nature is a teleologically living organism that there are causal relations between its parts. Here we see an attempt to establish the reality of spirit by resolving the reality of nature itself into spirit; but we already know, from our analysis of later German thought, that such a resolution not only fails to do justice to natural science, by denying that there is anything genuinely natural, but endangers the conception of spirit by identifying it with something that is to be found in nature. The danger is that a third term, neither mere nature nor genuine spirit, tends to be substituted for both. This third term is life, conceived not as spiritual life or the process of mind, but as biological or physiological life, a fundamental conception in the work of Bergson.

(ii) *Lachelier's idealism*

In order to escape this danger it was necessary to insist that the life of the spirit is not mere life but rationality, that is, the activity of thinking. The man who saw this was Lachelier, one of the greatest of modern French philosophers. During his long life as a teacher, to whom in that capacity French thought owes

[1] *Rapport sur la philosophie en France au XIXme siècle* (Paris, 1867).

an incalculable debt, Lachelier published little, but what he did publish is a model of profound thought and clear expression. His brief essay on *Psychology and Metaphysics*[1] is a masterly exposition of the thesis that psychology, as a naturalistic science, cannot grasp mind as it actually is; it can only study the immediate data of consciousness, our sensations and feelings; but the essence of mind is that it knows, that is, has as its objects not mere states of itself but a real world. What enables it to know is the fact that it thinks; and the activity of thought is a free or self-creative process, which depends on nothing else except itself in order to exist. If then we ask why thought exists, the only possible answer is that existence itself, whatever else it may be, is the activity of thinking. The centre of Lachelier's argument here is the idea that knowledge itself is a function of freedom; it is only because the activity of spirit is absolutely spontaneous that knowledge is possible. Hence natural science, instead of casting doubt on the reality of spirit by failing to discover it in nature, or vindicating it by discovering it there (which it can never do), vindicates it in a quite different way, by being itself a product of spiritual activity in the scientist. This clear conception of the life of spirit as a life that is both freedom and knowledge and also knowledge of its own freedom, a life which no scientific thought can detect or analyse in psychological terms, is just what we found lacking in the German school. It is not yet a theory of history, but it is the basis of such a theory.

If other French thinkers had grasped Lachelier's conception, they would not have needed to pursue the criticisms of natural science which occupied so large a place in the French philosophy of the late nineteenth and early twentieth centuries. Lachelier's argument had in fact cut away the foundations of the structure whose upper works they were attacking: not science itself, but the philosophy which attempted to show that science was the only possible form of knowledge and therefore by implication reduced mind to nature. I need not, therefore, describe the work done by Boutroux and his school, who attempted to vindicate the reality of the spiritual life by throwing doubt on the solidity of scientific knowledge. But in order to show what became of these criticisms when pushed home and erected into a con-

[1] *Œuvres* (Paris, 1933), vol. i, pp. 169–219.

structive philosophy, I must say something of the work of Bergson.

(iii) *Bergson's evolutionism*

The essentially constructive character of Bergson's mind is revealed by the fact that his first book emphasizes the positive side of the double theme which I have described as characteristic of modern French thought. The *Essai sur les Données immé-diates de la Conscience* (translated into English in 1913 under the title *Time and Free Will*) is an exposition of the characteristics of our own mental life as present in actual experience. This life is a succession of mental states, but it is a succession in a very special sense of the word. One state does not follow another, for one does not cease to exist when the next begins; they inter-penetrate one another, the past living on in the present, fused with it, and present in the sense that it confers upon it a peculiar quality derived from the fact of the fusion. For example, in listening to a tune we do not experience the different notes separately: the way in which we hear each note, the state of mind which is the hearing of that note, is affected by the way in which we heard the last and, indeed, all the previous ones. The total experience of hearing the tune is thus a progressive and irreversible series of experiences which telescope into one another; it is therefore not many experiences, but one expe-rience, organized in a peculiar way. The way in which it is organized is time, and this in fact is just what time is: it is a manifold of parts which, unlike those of space, interpenetrate one another, the present including the past. This temporal organization is peculiar to consciousness, and is the foundation of freedom: for, because the present contains the past in itself the present is not determined by the past as something external to it, a cause of which it is the effect: the present is a free and living activity which embraces and sustains its own past by its own act.

So far Bergson's analysis of consciousness affords a valuable contribution to the theory of history, although he does not use it in that way. We have already seen that an essential element in any such theory must be the conception of mental life as a process in which the past is not a mere spectacle to the present, but actually lives in the present. But the process which Bergson is describing, although it is a mental process, is not a rational process. It is not a succession of thoughts, it is a mere succession of immediate feelings and sensations. These feelings and sensations are not knowledge; our awareness of them is purely subjective, not objective; in experiencing them we are not knowing anything that is independent of the experience. To obtain knowledge, we must look outside ourselves; and when we do this we find ourselves looking at a world of things separated from one another in space, not interpenetrating one another even in their time-aspect, for the time in which they change is quite different from the interpenetrating time of inner consciousness; it is the clock-time of the external world, a spatialized time in which different times exclude one another just like parts of space. Thus the science which is our knowledge of this external world, the work of the intellect, affords a complete contrast with our inner experience: the intellect is a faculty which cuts things up into separate and self-contained parcels. Why should we have a faculty that does anything so strange? The answer Bergson gives is that we need it for the purpose of acting. Thus natural science is not a way of knowing the real world; its value lies not in its truth but in its utility; by scientific thought we do not know nature, we dismember it in order to master it.

In all his later works Bergson never gets beyond this original dualism, though it constantly assumes fresh forms. The life of consciousness always remains for him a life of immediate experience, devoid of all thought, all reflection, all rationality. Its consciousness is only the intuition of its own states. Consequently its process, although it resembles an historical process in the way in which it preserves its past in its present, falls short of being a genuinely historical process because the past which is preserved in the present is not a known past; it is only a past whose reverberations in the present are immediately experienced as the present itself is immediately experienced. These reverberations at last die away; and when they have done so, just because they are no longer immediately experienced and cannot be experienced otherwise, there can be no reviving of them. Consequently there can be no history; for history is not immediate self-enjoyment, it is reflection, mediation, thought. It is an intellectual labour whose purpose is to think the life of the mind instead of merely enjoying it. But according to Bergson's philosophy this is impossible: what is inward can only be enjoyed, not thought; what is thought is always the outward, and the outward is the unreal, that which has been fabricated for the purposes of action.

(iv) *Modern French historiography*

Modern French thought, working along these lines (for Bergson has enjoyed and still enjoys a popularity which reveals the essential correctness of his analysis of the mind of his nation), possesses a peculiarly vivid consciousness of itself as a living and active process, and has a wonderful ability to vivify whatever it can absorb into that process. Whatever is not so absorbed the French mind conceives as something of a totally different kind, a mere mechanism, to be reckoned with in action according as it is a tractable and useful mechanism or an intractable and hostile one, but never to be entered into or sympathized with as a spiritual life akin to itself. This is how the French attitude in international politics develops itself in a manner quite Bergsonian. And the spirit of modern French historiography works in the same way. The French historian seeks, following Bergson's well-known rule, *s'installer dans le mouvement*, to work himself into the movement of the history he is studying, and to feel that movement as something that goes on within himself. Recapturing the rhythm of this movement by an act of imaginative sympathy, he can express it with extraordinary brilliance and fidelity. For examples I need only refer to one or two masterpieces of recent French historical literature, such as Camille Jullian's *Histoire de la Gaule* or Monsieur Élie Halévy's works on *Philosophical Radicalism* or the *History of the English People*. When once this sympathetic insight has been achieved, it is easy to state the essential lines of the process in a few pages; and this is why French historians excel all others in writing brief and pregnant works, popular in the best sense of the word, conveying to the general public a vivid feeling of the character of a period or movement: exactly what German historians, muscle-bound in their struggle with the facts, cannot do. But what the French cannot do is what the Germans do so well: to treat isolated facts with scientific accuracy and detachment. The great scandal of recent French scholarship, the widespread acceptance of the Glozel forgeries, showed both the weakness of modern French scholars in scientific technique and the way in which a question which ought to have been a purely technical one became in their minds a question of national honour. The Glozel controversy, grotesquely enough, gave rise to the formation of an international commission to settle it ; and of course the findings of that commission were not accepted.

Thus in the last resort the modern French movement finds itself entangled in the same error as the German. Each of them ultimately confuses mind with nature and fails to distinguish the historical process from the natural process. But whereas the German movement tries to find the historical process objectively existing outside the thinker's mind, and fails to find it there just because it is not outside, the French movement tries to find it existing subjectively inside the thinker's mind, and fails to find it because, being thus enclosed within the subjectivity of the thinker, it ceases to be a process of knowledge and becomes a process of immediate experience: it becomes a merely psychological process, a process of sensations, feelings, and sentiments. The root of the error in both cases is the same. The subjective and the objective are regarded as two different things, heterogeneous in their essence, however intimately related. This conception is right in the case of natural science, where the process of scientific thought is a spiritual or historical process having as its object a natural process ; but it is wrong in the case of history, where the process of historical thought is homogeneous with the process of history itself, both being processes of thought. The only philosophical movement which has grasped this peculiarity of historical thought firmly and has used it as a systematic principle is that which was initiated by Croce in Italy.

§ 4. *Italy*

(i) *Croce's essay of 1893*

Modern Italian philosophy is far less rich in competent writers and in varied points of view than either French or German ; and, in particular, its literature on the theory of history as such, though more considerable than the French, bulks very small as compared with the German. But as compared with French philosophy it is more important for the subject of history, because it approaches the subject directly and places it in the centre of its problems; and it starts with an advantage over the German in the fact that the tradition of historical work, which in Germany hardly goes back beyond the eighteenth century, in Italy goes back to Machiavelli and even to Petrarch. Ever since the nineteenth century the leaders of Italian thought have been building up a tradition of serious and sustained historical research; and the length, variety, and richness of this tradition give a peculiar weight to the pronouncements of modern Italians on the subject, as one that has worked itself into the very bones of their civilization.

In 1893, when Benedetto Croce wrote his first essay on the theory of history at the age of twenty-seven, not only was he personally an historian of some distinction, but he had behind him a certain amount of recent Italian philosophical thought on the same subject. This, however, he absorbed into his own work so completely that for our purposes it may be passed over.

This essay was entitled *History subsumed under the Concept of Art.*[1] The question whether history was a science or an art had been lately discussed, especially in Germany, and for the most part the answer had been given that it was a science. One remembers that Windelband's attack on this answer was not made until 1894. Croce's essay may therefore be profitably compared with Windelband's; in many ways they are alike, but even at this early stage of his career it was obvious that Croce was superior to Windelband as a philosophic intelligence, and saw further into the real question at issue.

He began by clearing up the conception of art. He pointed out that art is neither a means of giving and receiving sensuous pleasure, nor a representation of natural fact, nor the construction and enjoyment of systems of formal relations (the three theories of it then most in favour), but the intuitive vision of individuality. The artist sees and represents this individuality: his public sees it as he has represented it. Art is thus not an activity of the emotions, but a cognitive activity: it is knowledge of the individual. Science, on the contrary, is knowledge of the general: its work is to construct general concepts and to work out the relations between them. Now history is altogether concerned with concrete individual facts. 'History', says Croce,

---

[1] *La Storia ridotta sotto il concetto generale dell' Arte.* Reprinted in *Primi Saggi* (Bari, 1919).

'has only one duty: to narrate facts.' What is called seeking for the causes of these facts is only looking closer at the facts themselves and apprehending the individual relations between them. It is useless, because meaningless, to call history 'descriptive science', for the fact that it is descriptive makes it no longer a science. Here Croce gives in advance the right answer to Windelband. The term 'description' may, no doubt, be used as a name for the analytic and generalizing account which empirical science gives of its object; but if it means what it means in history, the phrase 'descriptive science' is a *contradictio in adjecto*. The aim of the scientist is to understand facts in the sense of recognizing them as instances of general laws; but in this sense history does not understand its object; it contemplates it, and that is all. This is exactly what the artist does; so that the comparison between history and art, already made by Dilthey in 1883 and by Simmel in 1892, both of whom Croce quotes, is wholly just. But for him the relation goes farther than a mere comparison: it is an identity. Each is precisely the same thing: the intuition and representation of the individual.

Obviously, the matter could not be left here. If history is art, it is at least a very peculiar kind of art. All the artist does is to state what he sees; the historian has both to do this and also to assure himself that what he sees is the truth. Croce puts this by saying that art in general, in the wide sense, represents or narrates the possible; history represents or narrates that which has really happened. That which has happened is, of course, not impossible; if it were, it would not have happened; the real thus falls inside the sphere of the possible, not outside it, and thus history as narration of the real falls inside art as the narration of the possible.

Such is the argument of Croce's essay. It attracted a good deal of attention and was criticized in many quarters, but in re-reading the criticisms to-day one sees that Croce's answers were on the whole justified; he had penetrated farther into the subject than any of his critics. The real weakness of his argument is the one to which he himself called attention in his preface to a reprint of it twenty-six years later.

'I did not detect', he writes, 'the new problem raised by the conception of history as artistic representation of the real. I did not see that a representation in which the real is dialectically distinguished from the possible is something more than a merely artistic representation or intuition ; it comes about by virtue of the concept ; not indeed the empirical or abstract concept of science, but the concept which is philosophy and, as such, is both representation and judgement, universal and individual in one.'

In other words: art as such is pure intuition and does not contain thought ; but in order to distinguish the real from the merely possible, one must think ; consequently, to define history as the intuition of the real is to say in one breath that it is art and also that it is more than art. If the phrase 'descriptive science' is a *contradictio in adjecto*, so is the phrase 'intuition of the real': for intuition, just because it is intuition and not thought, knows nothing of any distinction between the real and the imaginary.

Even with this weakness, Croce's early theory already marks an advance on the German view which it so much resembles. Each seizes upon the distinction between the individual and the universal as the key to the distinction between history and science. Each leaves itself with unsolved problems on its hands. But the difference is that the Germans were content to go on calling history a science, without answering the question how a science of the individual is possible ; and the result was that they conceived historical science and natural science as two kinds of science, a conception which left the door open to naturalism, re-insinuating itself into the idea of history along the traditional associations of the word 'science'. Croce, by denying that history was a science at all, cut himself at one blow loose from naturalism, and set his face towards an idea of history as something radically different from nature. We have seen that the problem of philosophy everywhere in the late nineteenth century was the problem of liberating itself from the tyranny of natural science ; the boldness of Croce's move was therefore exactly what the situation demanded. It was the clean cut which he made in 1893 between the idea of history and the idea of science that enabled him to develop the conception of history so much farther than any philosopher of his generation.

It took him some time to see wherein his early theory was defective. In his first large-scale philosophical work, the *Aesthetic* of 1902, he still repeats his original view of history: it does not search for laws, he says,[1] nor frame concepts, it does not use induction or deduction, it does not demonstrate, it narrates. Inasmuch as its task is to present the spectacle of a completely determined individual, it is identical with art. And when he goes on to raise the question how history differs from the pure imagination of art, he answers it in the old way, by saying that it distinguishes as art does not between the real and the unreal.

(ii) *Croce's second position: the 'Logic'*

It was only in his *Logic*, published in 1909, that he faced the question how this distinction was possible. Logic is the theory of thought, and only thought can make the distinction between truth and falsehood which marks history off from art in the strict (and, as Croce would now admit, the only true) sense. To think is to make judgements, and logic traditionally distinguishes two kinds of judgement, the universal and the individual. The universal judgement defines the content of a conception, as when we say that the three angles of any triangle are equal to two right angles. The individual judgement states an individual matter of fact, as when we say that this triangle encloses the property of so-and-so. These are the two kinds of cognition which have been called *a priori* and empirical (Kant), *vérités de raison* and *vérités de fait* (Leibniz), relations between ideas and matters of fact (Hume), and so forth.

Now, Croce argues,[2] the traditional division of truths into these two classes is false. To distinguish the existence of the individual as a mere matter of fact, a *vérité de fait*, from *vérités de raison*, implies that the existence of the individual is irrational. But that is absurd. An individual fact would not be what it is had there not been reasons for it. And on the other hand to distinguish a universal truth as a *vérité de raison* from *vérités de fait* implies that universal truths are not realized in matters of fact. But what is a universal truth, unless it is true universally of the facts to which it applies?

He concludes that necessary or universal truth and contingent or individual truth are not two different kinds of cognition but inseparable elements in every real cognition. A universal

[1] Eng. tr., 2nd edn. (London, 1922), pp. 26–8
[2] Eng. tr. (London, 1917), pp. 198 ff.

truth is true only as realized in a particular instance: the universal must, as he puts it, be incarnate in the individual. And he goes on to show that even in judgements which at first sight appear to be utterly and abstractly universal, pure definitions, there is really what he calls an historical element, an element of *this*, *here*, and *now*, inasmuch as the definition has been framed by an individual historical thinker to meet a problem that has arisen in a particular way at a particular time in the history of thought. On the other hand, the individual or historical judgement is no mere intuition of a given fact or apprehension of a sense-datum; it is a judgement with a predicate; this predicate is a concept; and this concept is present to the mind of the person who makes the judgement as a universal idea of which, if he understands his own thought, he must be able to give a definition. Thus, there is only one kind of judgement, and it is both individual and universal: individual in so far as it describes an individual state of things, and universal in so far as it describes it by thinking it under universal concepts.

To illustrate this double argument. First, that the universal judgement is really individual. John Stuart Mill defined a right act as one which procures the greatest happiness of the greatest number. This looks at first sight an utterly non-historical judgement, true of all times and places if indeed it is true at all. But what Mill was doing when he made it was describing what we mean when we call an action 'right'; and here the word *we* means not all human beings everywhere and always, but nineteenth-century Englishmen with the moral and political ideas of their time. Mill is describing, whether well or ill, a particular phase in the history of human morality. He may not know that he is doing this, but this is what he is doing.

Secondly, that the individual judgement of history is universal in the sense that its predicate is a concept of which a definition could and should be forthcoming. I open a history book at random and read the following sentence: 'It must not be forgotten that monarchs such as Louis XI and Ferdinand the Catholic, notwithstanding their crimes, completed the national work of making France and Spain two great and powerful nations.' This sentence implies that the writer and reader understand the terms 'crime', 'nation', 'powerful', and so forth, and understand them in the same sense: it implies that the writer and reader possess in common a certain system of ethical and political ideas. The sentence, as an historical judgement, assumes that these ideas are coherent and logically defensible ; that is, it presupposes an ethical and political philosophy. It is through the medium of this ethical and political philosophy that we grasp the historical reality of Louis XI ; and conversely, it is because we find the concepts of this philosophy realized in Louis XI that we grasp what those concepts are.

This is Croce's doctrine of the mutual implication of the universal or definitive judgement and the individual or historical judgement, and his solution of the problem how philosophy (i.e. the universal judgement) is related to history. Instead of trying to place philosophy and history outside one another in two mutually exclusive spheres, and thus making an adequate theory of history impossible, he brings them together into a single whole, a judgement whose subject is the individual while its predicate is the universal. History is thus no longer conceived as mere intuition of the individual ; it does not simply apprehend the individual, in which case it would be art ; it judges the individual ; and hence the universality, the *a priori* character, which belongs indefeasibly to all thought, is present in history in the form of the predicate of the historical judgement. What makes the historian a thinker is the fact that he thinks out the meanings of these predicates, and finds these meanings embodied in the individuals he contemplates. But this thinking-out of the meaning of a concept is philosophy ; hence philosophy is an integral part of historical thinking itself ; the individual judgement of history is a judgement only because it contains in itself, as one of its elements, philosophical thinking.

(iii) *History and philosophy*

This involves a very remarkable and original view of the relation between philosophy and history. Hitherto it had generally been assumed that philosophy was the queen of the sciences, and that history occupied a humble place somewhere among her subjects, or on the outskirts of her realm. But for Croce, in this culminating phase of his thought, the task of philosophy is limited to thinking out the meaning of concepts which as actual functions of thought exist only as predicates of historical judgements. There is only one kind of judgement, the individual judgement of history. In other words, all reality is history and all knowledge is historical knowledge. Philosophy is only a constituent element within history; it is the universal element in a thought whose concrete being is individual.

This may be compared with the German view, found for example in Rickert, that all reality is historical. But Rickert has arrived at his doctrine by way of the nominalistic principle that all concepts are mere fictions of the intellect, which implies that the judgement 'Louis XI committed crimes' is a merely verbal proposition and means 'the word crime is a word which I apply to the actions of Louis XI'. For Croce, 'crime' is not a word but a concept, and the statement that Louis XI committed crimes is therefore a statement not about the historian's arbitrary use of words but about the actions of Louis XI. Rickert and Croce might agree that historical fact is the only reality; but the meanings they would attach to these words are wholly different. Rickert would mean that reality consists of isolated unique events, bare particulars conceived as particulars are conceived, for example, by the logic of Mill; particulars having in them no element of universality: the universal, on such a view, being added to the particular by an arbitrary act of the mind. Croce would mean that reality consists of concepts or universals embodied in particular facts, the particular being nothing but the incarnation of the universal.

(iv) *History and nature*

But what, all this time, has become of natural science, and how is the natural process related on Croce's view to the historical? The answer is that, for him, natural science is not knowledge at all, but action. He draws a sharp distinction between the concepts of science and the concepts of philosophy. The concepts of philosophy are functions of thought, universal and necessary: to affirm them is simply for thought to think itself. It is impossible, for example, to think without thinking that our thought is true: thus the act of thought in affirming itself affirms the distinction between truth and falsehood. The concepts of science, on the contrary, are arbitrary constructions; there is not one of them that need be thought. They are of two kinds, empirical, like the concepts of cat or rose, and abstract, like the concepts of triangle or uniform movement. In the former case the concept is only a way in which we choose to group certain facts which we might with equal truth group otherwise. In the latter, the concept has no instances at all; it cannot be true, because it is true of nothing; all we can do is to posit it and work out its implications hypothetically. These arbitrary constructions are in reality not concepts, therefore, but (we may call them) conceptual fictions; Croce also calls them pseudo-concepts. And the whole of natural science consists of thought about pseudo-concepts. But what is the point of constructing pseudo-concepts? What are they? They are not errors, he insists, any more than they are truths. Their value is a practical value. By making them we are manipulating in ways useful to us realities which we do not thereby understand better, but which thereby become more tractable to our purposes. Here we find Croce adopting the pragmatist theory of natural science which we have already found in Bergson. But there is this important difference: that whereas, for Bergson, the reality which we thus manipulate is in itself nothing but immediate inward experience, which makes it unintelligible how any action of ours or any one else's can turn it into objective spatial facts, for Croce the reality which we convert into nature by applying pseudo-concepts to it is in itself history, sequences of facts that really happen and are knowable to our historical thought as they really are. It is an historical fact that we observe a cat killing a bird; like all historical facts, this is the incarnation of a concept at a particular place and time; and the true and only possible way of knowing it is to know it as an historical fact. As so known, it takes its place in the body of historical knowledge. But we may, instead of knowing it as it really is, fabricate for our own purposes the pseudo-concepts cat and bird, and thus arrive at the general rule not to leave a cat alone with a canary.

Thus nature, for Croce, is in one sense real and in one sense unreal. It is real, if nature means individual events as they happen and are observed to happen; but in that sense nature is only a part of history. It is unreal, if nature means a system of abstract general laws; for these laws are only the pseudo-concepts under which we arrange the historical facts that we observe and remember and expect.

On this view the distinction which I have sometimes drawn

in the preceding chapters between natural processes and historical processes disappears. History is no longer in any special sense knowledge of the human as opposed to the natural world. It is simply the knowledge of facts or events as they actually happen, in their concrete individuality. A distinction remains, but it is not a distinction between man or spirit and nature. It is the distinction between apprehending the individuality of a thing by thinking oneself into it, making its life one's own, and analysing or classifying it from an external point of view. To do the first is to grasp it as an historical fact; to do the second is to make it a subject-matter for science. It is easy to see that either of these two attitudes may be taken up towards human beings and their activities. For example, to study a past philosopher's thought in such a way as to make it one's own, relive it as he lived it, as a thought arising out of certain determinate problems and situations and pursued so far and no farther, is to treat it historically. If a thinker cannot do this, and can only analyse its parts and classify it as belonging to this or that type (as Dilthey handled the history of philosophy in the last stage of his thought) he is treating it as subject-matter for science and making it into mere nature. To quote Croce himself:[1]

'Do you wish to understand the true history of a neolithic Ligurian or Sicilian? Try, if you can, to become a neolithic Ligurian or Sicilian in your mind. If you cannot do that, or do not care to, content yourself with describing and arranging in series the skulls, implements, and drawings which have been found belonging to these neolithic peoples. Do you wish to understand the true history of a blade of grass? Try to become a blade of grass; and, if you cannot do it, satisfy yourself with analysing its parts, and even arranging them in a sort of ideal or fanciful history.'

As concerns neolithic man, the advice is obviously good. If you can enter into his mind and make his thoughts your own, you can write his history, and not otherwise; if you cannot, all you can do is to arrange his relics in some kind of tidy order, and the result is ethnology or archaeology but it is not history. Yet the reality of neolithic man was an historical reality. When he made a certain implement, he had a purpose in mind;

[1] *Teoria e Storia della Storiografia* (Bari, 1917), p. 119; Eng. tr., *Theory and History of Historiography* (London, 1921), pp. 134–5.

the implement came into being as an expression of his spirit, and if you treat it as non-spiritual that is only because of the failure of your historical insight. But is this true of a blade of grass? Is its articulation and growth an expression of its own spiritual life? I am not so sure. And when we come to a crystal, or a stalactite, my scepticism reaches the point of rebellion. The process by which these things form themselves appears to me to be a process in which, through no lack of our own historical sympathy, we look in vain for any expression of thought. It is an event; it has individuality; but it seems to lack that inwardness which, according to this passage of Croce, is made (and, I think, rightly made) the criterion of historicity. The resolution of nature into spirit seems to me incomplete, and not at all proved by the converse fact that spirit, by being handled scientifically instead of historically, can be resolved into nature.

But this raises a problem which is outside my present subject. I shall therefore not pursue it, unless and except so far as the attempted resolution of nature into spirit affects the conception of spirit, that is, of history, itself. And I do not find that in Croce's work there is any such affection. This is because, whether or no there is such a thing as nature, as distinct from spirit, at least it cannot enter as a factor into the world of spirit. When people think that it can, and speak (as we saw that Montesquieu, for example, did) of the influence of geography or climate on history, they are mistaking the effect of a certain person's or people's conception of nature on their actions for an effect of nature itself. The fact that certain people live, for example, on an island has in itself no effect on their history; what has an effect is the way they conceive that insular position; whether for example they regard the sea as a barrier or as a highway to traffic. Had it been otherwise, their insular position, being a constant fact, would have produced a constant effect on their historical life; whereas it will produce one effect if they have not mastered the art of navigation, a different effect if they have mastered it better than their neighbours, a third if they have mastered it worse than their neighbours, and a fourth if every one uses aeroplanes. In itself, it is merely a raw material for historical activity, and the character of historical life depends on how this raw material is used.

(v) *Croce's final view: the autonomy of history*

Croce has thus vindicated the autonomy of history, its right to conduct its own business in its own way, both against philosophy and against science. Philosophy cannot interfere with history according to the Hegelian formula of superimposing a philosophical history on the top of ordinary history, because that distinction is meaningless. Ordinary history is already philosophical history: it contains philosophy inside itself in the shape of predicates to its judgements. Philosophical history is a term synonymous with history. And within the concrete whole which is historical knowledge, philosophical knowledge is a component part: it is the thinking out of predicate-concepts. Croce put this by defining philosophy as the methodology of history.

As against science, the vindication proceeds on opposite lines. History is secured against the encroachments of science not because it already contains science as an element within itself, but because it must be complete before science begins. Science is a cutting-up and rearranging of materials which must be given to it at the start; and these materials are historical facts. When the scientist tells us that his theories are based on facts—observations and experiments—he means that they are based on history, for the idea of fact and the idea of history are synonymous. That a certain guinea-pig has been inoculated in a certain way and has then developed certain symptoms is a matter of history. The pathologist is a person who takes this and certain similar facts and arranges them in a certain way. Consequently history must be kept free from any interference on the part of science, for unless it first established facts by its own independent work there would be no material for the scientist to handle.

It was in Croce's work of 1912 and 1913[1] that these ideas were fully worked out. In that work we find not only a complete expression of the autonomy of history, but also a double demonstration of its necessity: its necessity relatively to philosophy as the concrete thought of which philosophy is only the methodological moment, and its necessity relatively to science

[1] These being the dates of the essays which in 1915 formed the book *Zur Theorie und Geschichte der Historiographie* (Tübingen) published in 1917 at Bari as *Teoria e Storia della Storiografia*.

as the source of all 'scientific facts'—a phrase which only means those historical facts which the scientist arranges into classes.

Let us look in some detail at the conception of history which emerges from this point of view.[1] All history is contemporary history: not in the ordinary sense of the word, where contemporary history means the history of the comparatively recent past, but in the strict sense: the consciousness of one's own activity as one actually performs it. History is thus the self-knowledge of the living mind. For even when the events which the historian studies are events that happened in the distant past, the condition of their being historically known is that they should 'vibrate in the historian's mind', that is to say, that the evidence for them should be here and now before him and intelligible to him. For history is not contained in books or documents; it lives only, as a present interest and pursuit, in the mind of the historian when he criticizes and interprets those documents, and by so doing relives for himself the states of mind into which he inquires.

It follows that the subject-matter of history is not the past as such, but the past for which we possess historical evidence. Much of the past has perished, in the sense that we have no documents for reconstructing it. We believe, for example, on the strength of mere testimony, that there were great painters among the ancient Greeks; but this belief is not historical knowledge, because, their works having perished, we have no means of reliving in our own minds their artistic experience. There were also great sculptors; but this we do not merely believe, we know it; for we possess their works and can make them part of our own present aesthetic life. Our history of Greek sculpture is our present aesthetic experience of these works.

This distinction serves to distinguish two very different things: history and chronicle. The names of the great Greek painters, as handed down to us by tradition, do not form a history of Greek painting: they form a chronicle of Greek painting. Chronicle, then, is the past as merely believed upon testimony but not historically known. And this belief is a mere act of will: the will to preserve certain statements which we do not under-

---

[1] [The section on Croce was written in 1936 and not subsequently amplified to take account of his *La Storia come Pensiero e come Azione* (Bari, 1938), Eng. tr., *History as the Story of Liberty* (London, 1941).]

stand. If we did understand them, they would be history. Every history becomes chronicle when related by a person who cannot relive the experiences of its characters: the history of philosophy, for example, as written or read by people who do not understand the thoughts of the philosophers in question. In order that there should be chronicle, there must first be history: for chronicle is the body of history from which the spirit has gone; the corpse of history.

History, so far from depending on testimony, has therefore no relation with testimony at all. Testimony is merely chronicle. So far as any one speaks of authorities or of accepting statements or the like, he is talking of chronicle and not of history. History is based on a synthesis of two things which only exist in that synthesis: evidence and criticism. Evidence is only evidence so far as it is used as evidence, that is to say, interpreted on critical principles; and principles are only principles so far as they are put into practice in the work of interpreting evidence.

But the past leaves relics of itself, even when these relics are not used by any one as materials for its history; and these relics are of many kinds, and include the relics of historical thought itself, that is, chronicles. We preserve these relics, hoping that in the future they may become what now they are not, namely historical evidence. What particular parts and aspects of the past we now recall by historical thought depends on our present interests and attitude towards life; but we are always aware that there are other parts and other aspects which there is no need for us to recall at present, and in so far as we recognize that these too will one day interest us we make it our business not to lose or destroy their records. This task of keeping relics against the time when they will become material for history is the task of pure scholars, archivists, and antiquaries. Just as the antiquary keeps implements and pots in his museum without necessarily reconstructing history from them, and as the archivist in the same way keeps public documents, so the pure scholar edits and emends and reprints texts of, for example, ancient philosophy without necessarily understanding the philosophical ideas they express, and therefore without being able to reconstruct the history of philosophy.

This work of scholarship is often taken for history itself; and as so taken it becomes a special type of pseudo-history, which

Croce calls philological history. As thus misconceived, history consists in accepting and preserving testimony, and the writing of history consists in transcribing, translating, and compiling. Such work is useful, but it is not history; there is no criticism, no interpretation, no reliving of past experience in one's own mind. It is mere learning or scholarship. But it is possible, in exaggerated reaction against the claims of learning to be regarded as identical with history, to run to the other extreme. What the mere scholar lacks is living experience. By itself, this living experience is mere feeling or passion; and a one-sided insistence on feeling or passion produces a second type of pseudo-history, romantic or poetical history, whose true purpose is not to discover the truth about the past but to express the author's feelings towards it: patriotic history, partisan history, history inspired by liberal or humanitarian or socialist ideals; in general, all history whose function is to express either the historian's love and admiration for his subject, or else his hatred and contempt for it: 'writing it up' or 'debunking' it. And in this context Croce points out that whenever historians indulge in conjecture or permit themselves to assert mere possibilities they are in fact giving way to the temptation of poeticizing or romanticizing history: they are going beyond what the evidence proves and expressing their own personal feelings by permitting themselves to believe what they would like to believe. Genuine history has no room for the merely probable or the merely possible; all it permits the historian to assert is what the evidence before him obliges him to assert.

PART V
EPILEGOMENA

§ 1. *Human Nature and Human History*

(i) *The science of human nature*

MAN, who desires to know everything, desires to know himself.
Nor is he only one (even if, to himself, perhaps the most interesting) among the things he desires to know. Without some knowledge of himself, his knowledge of other things is imperfect: for to know something without knowing that one knows it is only a half-knowing, and to know that one knows is to know oneself. Self-knowledge is desirable and important to man, not only for its own sake, but as a condition without which no other knowledge can be critically justified and securely based.

Self-knowledge, here, means not knowledge of man's bodily nature, his anatomy and physiology; nor even a knowledge of his mind, so far as that consists of feeling, sensation, and emotion; but a knowledge of his knowing faculties, his thought or understanding or reason. How is such knowledge to be attained? It seems an easy matter until we think seriously about it; and then it seems so difficult that we are tempted to think it impossible. Some have even reinforced this temptation by argument, urging that the mind, whose business it is to know other things, has for that very reason no power of knowing itself. But this is open sophistry: first you say what the mind's nature is, and then you say that because it has this nature no one can know that it has it. Actually, the argument is a counsel of despair, based on recognizing that a certain attempted method of studying the mind has broken down, and on failure to envisage the possibility of any other.

It seems a fair enough proposal that, in setting out to understand the nature of our own mind, we should proceed in the same way as when we try to understand the world about us. In studying the world of nature, we begin by getting acquainted with the particular things and particular events that exist and go on there; then we proceed to understand them, by seeing how they fall into general types and how these general types are interrelated. These interrelations we call laws of nature;

and it is by ascertaining such laws that we understand the things and events to which they apply. The same method, it might seem, is applicable to the problem of understanding mind. Let us begin by observing, as carefully as possible, the ways in which our own minds and those of others behave under given circumstances; then, having become acquainted with these facts of the mental world, let us try to establish the laws which govern them.

Here is a proposal for a 'science of human nature' whose principles and methods are conceived on the analogy of those used in the natural sciences. It is an old proposal, put forward especially in the seventeenth and eighteenth centuries, when the principles and methods of natural science had been lately perfected and were being triumphantly applied to the investigation of the physical world. When Locke undertook his inquiry into that faculty of understanding which 'sets Man above the rest of sensible Beings, and gives him all the Advantage and Dominion which he has over them', the novelty of his project lay not in his desire for a knowledge of the human mind, but in his attempt to gain it by methods analogous to those of natural science: the collection of observed facts and their arrangement in classificatory schemes. His own description of his method as an 'historical, plain Method' is perhaps ambiguous; but his follower Hume was at pains to make it clear that the method to be followed by the science of human nature was identical with the method of physical science as he conceived it: its 'only solid foundation', he wrote, 'must be laid on experience and observation'. Reid, in his *Inquiry into the Human Mind*, was if possible even more explicit. 'All that we know of the body, is owing to anatomical dissection and observation, and it must be by an anatomy of the mind that we can discover its powers and principles.' And from these pioneers the whole English and Scottish tradition of a 'philosophy of the human mind' was derived.

Even Kant did not take an essentially different view. He certainly claimed that his own study of the understanding was something more than empirical; it was to be a demonstrative science; but then he held the same view concerning the science of nature; for that also, according to him, has in it an *a priori* or demonstrative element, and is not based merely on experience.

It is evident that such a science of human nature, if it could attain even a tolerable approximation to the truth, could hope for results of extreme importance. As applied to the problems of moral and political life, for example, its results would certainly be no less spectacular than were the results of seventeenth-century physics when applied to the mechanical arts in the eighteenth century. This was fully realized by its promoters. Locke thought that by its means he could 'prevail with the busy Mind of Man, to be more cautious in meddling with things exceeding its Comprehension; to stop, when it is at the utmost of its Tether; and to sit down in a quiet Ignorance of those Things, which, upon Examination, are found to be beyond the reach of our Capacities'. At the same time, he was convinced that the powers of our understanding are sufficient for our needs 'in this state', and can give us all the knowledge we require for 'the comfortable provision for this life, and the way that leads to a better'. 'If [he concludes] we can find out those Measures, whereby a Rational creature, put in the state which Man is in this World, may and ought to govern his Opinions and Actions depending thereon, we need not be troubled that some other things escape our knowledge.'

Hume is even bolder. ''Tis evident', he writes, 'that all the sciences have a relation, more or less, to human nature . . . since they lie under the cognizance of men, and are judged of by their powers and faculties. 'Tis impossible to tell what changes and improvements we might make in these sciences were we thoroughly acquainted with the extent and force of human understanding.' And in sciences directly concerned with human nature, like morals and politics, his hopes of a beneficent revolution are proportionately higher. 'In pretending, therefore, to explain the principles of human nature, we in effect propose a complete system of the sciences, built on a foundation almost entirely new, and the only one upon which they can stand with any security.' Kant, for all his habitual caution, claimed no less when he said that his new science would put an end to all the debates of the philosophical schools, and make it possible to solve all the problems of metaphysics at once and for ever.

It need not imply any underestimate of what these men actually achieved if we admit that these hopes were in the main unfulfilled, and that the science of human nature, from Locke to the present day, has failed to solve the problem of understanding what understanding is, and thus giving the human mind knowledge of itself. It was not through any lack of sympathy with its objects that so judicious a critic as John Grote found himself obliged to treat the 'philosophy of the human mind' as a blind alley out of which it was the duty of thought to escape.

What was the reason for this failure? Some might say that it was because the undertaking was in principle a mistake: mind cannot know itself. This objection we have already considered. Others, notably the representatives of psychology, would say that the science of these thinkers was not sufficiently scientific: psychology was still in its infancy. But if we ask these same men to produce here and now the practical results for which those early students hoped, they excuse themselves by saying that psychology is still in its infancy. Here I think they wrong themselves and their own science. Claiming for it a sphere which it cannot effectively occupy, they belittle the work it has done and is doing in its proper field. What that field is, I shall suggest in the sequel.

There remains a third explanation: that the 'science of human nature' broke down because its method was distorted by the analogy of the natural sciences. This I believe to be the right one.

It was no doubt inevitable that in the seventeenth and eighteenth centuries, dominated as they were by the new birth of physical science, the eternal problem of self-knowledge should take shape as the problem of constructing a science of human nature. To any one reviewing the field of human research, it was evident that physics stood out as a type of inquiry which had discovered the right method of investigating its proper object, and it was right that the experiment should be made of extending this method to every kind of problem. But since then a great change has come over the intellectual atmosphere of our civilization. The dominant factor in this change has not been the development of other natural sciences like chemistry and biology, or the transformation of physics itself since more began to be known about electricity, or the progressive application of all these new ideas to manufacture and industry, important though these have been; for in principle they have done nothing that might not have been foreseen as implicit in seventeenth-century physics itself. The really new element in the thought of to-day as compared with that of three centuries ago is the rise of history. It is true that the same Cartesian spirit which did so much for physics was already laying the foundations of critical method in history before the seventeenth century was out;[1] but the modern conception of history as a study at once critical and constructive, whose field is the human past in its entirety, and whose method is the reconstruction of that past from documents written and unwritten, critically analysed and interpreted, was not established until the nineteenth, and is even yet not fully worked out in all its implications. Thus history occupies in the world of to-day a position analogous to that occupied by physics in the time of Locke: it is recognized as a special and autonomous form of thought, lately established, whose possibilities have not yet been completely explored. And just as in the seventeenth and eighteenth centuries there were materialists, who argued from the success of physics in its own sphere that all reality was physical, so among ourselves the success of history has led some people to suggest that its methods are applicable to all the problems of knowledge, in other words, that all reality is historical.

This I believe to be an error. I think that those who assert it are making a mistake of the same kind which the materialists made in the seventeenth century. But I believe, and in this essay I shall try to show, that there is at least one important element of truth in what they say. The thesis which I shall maintain is that the science of human nature was a false attempt —falsified by the analogy of natural science—to understand the mind itself, and that, whereas the right way of investigating nature is by the methods called scientific, the right way of investigating mind is by the methods of history. I shall contend that the work which was to be done by the science of human nature is actually done, and can only be done, by history: that history is what the science of human nature professed to be, and that Locke was right when he said (however little he understood what he was saying) that the right method for such an inquiry is the historical, plain method.

[1] 'Historical criticism was born in the seventeenth century from the same intellectual movement as the philosophy of Descartes.' E. Bréhier, in *Philosophy and History: Essays presented to Ernst Cassirer* (Oxford, 1936), p. 160.

(ii) *The field of historical thought*[1]

I must begin by attempting to delimit the proper sphere of historical knowledge as against those who, maintaining the historicity of all things, would resolve all knowledge into historical knowledge. Their argument runs in some such way as this.

The methods of historical research have, no doubt, been developed in application to the history of human affairs: but is that the limit of their applicability? They have already before now undergone important extensions: for example, at one time historians had worked out their methods of critical interpretation only as applied to written sources containing narrative material, and it was a new thing when they learnt to apply them to the unwritten data provided by archaeology. Might not a similar but even more revolutionary extension sweep into the historian's net the entire world of nature? In other words, are not natural processes really historical processes, and is not the being of nature an historical being?

Since the time of Heraclitus and Plato, it has been a commonplace that things natural, no less than things human, are in constant change, and that the entire world of nature is a world of 'process' or 'becoming'. But this is not what is meant by the historicity of things; for change and history are not at all the same. According to this old-established conception, the specific forms of natural things constitute a changeless repertory of fixed types, and the process of nature is a process by which instances of these forms (or quasi-instances of them, things approximating to the embodiment of them) come into existence and pass out of it again. Now in human affairs, as historical research had clearly demonstrated by the eighteenth century, there is no such fixed repertory of specific forms. Here, the process of becoming was already by that time recognized as involving not only the instances or quasi-instances of the forms, but the forms themselves. The political philosophy of Plato and Aristotle teaches in effect that city-states come and go, but the

[1] In the argument of this section I owe much to Mr. Alexander's admirable essay on 'The Historicity of Things', in the volume on *Philosophy and History* already quoted. If I seem to be controverting his main thesis, that is not because I disagree with his argument or any part of it, but only because I mean more than he does by the word 'historicity'. For him, to say that the world is 'a world of events' is to say that 'the world and everything in it is historical'. For me, the two things are not at all the same.

idea of the city-state remains for ever as the one social and political form towards whose realization human intellect, so far as
it is really intelligent, strives. According to modern ideas, the
city-state itself is as transitory a thing as Miletus or Sybaris. It
is not an eternal ideal, it was merely the political ideal of the
ancient Greeks. Other civilizations have had before them other
political ideals, and human history shows a change not only in
the individual cases in which these ideals are realized or partially
realized, but in the ideals themselves. Specific types of human
organization, the city-state, the feudal system, representative
government, capitalistic industry, are characteristic of certain
historical ages.

At first, this transience of specific forms was imagined to be
a peculiarity of human life. When Hegel said that nature has
no history, he meant that whereas the specific forms of human
organization change as time goes on, the forms of natural
organization do not. There is, he grants, a distinction of higher
and lower in the specific forms of nature, and the higher forms
are a development out of the lower; but this development is
only a logical one, not a temporal, and in time all the 'strata'
of nature exist simultaneously.[1] But this view of nature has
been overthrown by the doctrine of evolution. Biology has
decided that living organisms are not divided into kinds each
permanently distinct from the rest, but have developed their
present specific forms through a process of evolution in time.
Nor is this conception limited to the field of biology. It appeared
simultaneously, the two applications being closely connected
through the study of fossils, in geology. To-day even the stars
are divided into kinds which can be described as older and
younger; and the specific forms of matter, no longer conceived
in the Daltonian manner, as elements eternally distinct like the
living species of pre-Darwinian biology, are regarded as subject
to a similar change, so that the chemical constitution of our
present world is only a phase in a process leading from a very
different past to a very different future.

This evolutionary conception of nature, whose implications
have been impressively worked out by philosophers like M. Bergson, Mr. Alexander, and Mr. Whitehead, might seem at first

---

[1] *Naturphilosophie: Einleitung. System der Philosophie*, § 249, *Zusatz (Werke*,
Glockner's edition, vol. ix, p. 59).

sight to have abolished the difference between natural process and historical process, and to have resolved nature into history. And if a further step in the same resolution were needed, it might seem to be provided by Mr. Whitehead's doctrine that the very possession of its attributes by a natural thing takes time. Just as Aristotle argued that a man cannot be happy at an instant, but that the possession of happiness takes a lifetime, so Mr. Whitehead argues that to be an atom of hydrogen takes time—the time necessary for establishing the peculiar rhythm of movements which distinguishes it from other atoms—so that there is no such thing as 'nature at an instant'.

These modern views of nature do, no doubt, 'take time seriously'. But just as history is not the same thing as change, so it is not the same thing as 'timefulness', whether that means evolution or an existence which takes time. Such views have certainly narrowed the gulf between nature and history of which early nineteenth-century thinkers were so conscious; they have made it impossible to state the distinction any longer in the way in which Hegel stated it ; but in order to decide whether the gulf has been really closed and the distinction annulled, we must turn to the conception of history and see whether it coincides in essentials with this modern conception of nature.

If we put this question to the ordinary historian, he will answer it in the negative. According to him, all history properly so called is the history of human affairs. His special technique, depending as it does on the interpretation of documents in which human beings of the past have expressed or betrayed their thoughts, cannot be applied just as it stands to the study of natural processes; and the more this technique is elaborated in its details, the farther it is from being so applicable. There is a certain analogy between the archaeologist's interpretation of a stratified site and the geologist's interpretation of rock-horizons with their associated fossils; but the difference is no less clear than the similarity. The archaeologist's use of his stratified relics depends on his conceiving them as artifacts serving human purposes and thus expressing a particular way in which men have thought about their own life ; and from his point of view the palaeontologist, arranging his fossils in a time-series, is not working as an historian, but only as a scientist thinking in a way which can at most be described as quasi-historical.

Upholders of the doctrine under examination would say that here the historian is making an arbitrary distinction between things that are really the same, and that his conception of history is an unphilosophically narrow one, restricted by the imperfect development of his technique; very much as some historians, because their equipment was inadequate to studying the history of art or science or economic life, have mistakenly restricted the field of historical thought to the history of politics. The question must therefore be raised, why do historians habitually identify history with the history of human affairs? In order to answer this question, it is not enough to consider the characteristics of historical method as it actually exists, for the question at issue is whether, as it actually exists, it covers the whole field which properly belongs to it. We must ask what is the general nature of the problems which this method is designed to solve. When we have done so, it will appear that the special problem of the historian is one which does not arise in the case of natural science.

The historian, investigating any event in the past, makes a distinction between what may be called the outside and the inside of an event. By the outside of the event I mean everything belonging to it which can be described in terms of bodies and their movements: the passage of Caesar, accompanied by certain men, across a river called the Rubicon at one date, or the spilling of his blood on the floor of the senate-house at another. By the inside of the event I mean that in it which can only be described in terms of thought: Caesar's defiance of Republican law, or the clash of constitutional policy between himself and his assassins. The historian is never concerned with either of these to the exclusion of the other. He is investigating not mere events (where by a mere event I mean one which has only an outside and no inside) but actions, and an action is the unity of the outside and inside of an event. He is interested in the crossing of the Rubicon only in its relation to Republican law, and in the spilling of Caesar's blood only in its relation to a constitutional conflict. His work may begin by discovering the outside of an event, but it can never end there; he must always remember that the event was an action, and that his main task is to think himself into this action, to discern the thought of its agent.

In the case of nature, this distinction between the outside and the inside of an event does not arise. The events of nature are mere events, not the acts of agents whose thought the scientist endeavours to trace. It is true that the scientist, like the historian, has to go beyond the mere discovery of events; but the direction in which he moves is very different. Instead of conceiving the event as an action and attempting to rediscover the thought of its agent, penetrating from the outside of the event to its inside, the scientist goes beyond the event, observes its relation to others, and thus brings it under a general formula or law of nature. To the scientist, nature is always and merely a 'phenomenon', not in the sense of being defective in reality, but in the sense of being a spectacle presented to his intelligent observation; whereas the events of history are never mere phenomena, never mere spectacles for contemplation, but things which the historian looks, not at, but through, to discern the thought within them.

In thus penetrating to the inside of events and detecting the thought which they express, the historian is doing something which the scientist need not and cannot do. In this way the task of the historian is more complex than that of the scientist. In another way it is simpler: the historian need not and cannot (without ceasing to be an historian) emulate the scientist in searching for the causes or laws of events. For science, the event is discovered by perceiving it, and the further search for its cause is conducted by assigning it to its class and determining the relation between that class and others. For history, the object to be discovered is not the mere event, but the thought expressed in it. To discover that thought is already to understand it. After the historian has ascertained the facts, there is no further process of inquiring into their causes. When he knows what happened, he already knows why it happened.

This does not mean that words like 'cause' are necessarily out of place in reference to history; it only means that they are used there in a special sense. When a scientist asks 'Why did that piece of litmus paper turn pink?' he means 'On what kinds of occasions do pieces of litmus paper turn pink?' When an historian asks 'Why did Brutus stab Caesar?' he means 'What did Brutus think, which made him decide to stab Caesar?' The cause of the event, for him, means the thought in the mind of the person by whose agency the event came about: and this is not something other than the event, it is the inside of the event itself.

The processes of nature can therefore be properly described as sequences of mere events, but those of history cannot. They are not processes of mere events but processes of actions, which have an inner side, consisting of processes of thought; and what the historian is looking for is these processes of thought. All history is the history of thought.

But how does the historian discern the thoughts which he is trying to discover? There is only one way in which it can be done: by re-thinking them in his own mind. The historian of philosophy, reading Plato, is trying to know what Plato thought when he expressed himself in certain words. The only way in which he can do this is by thinking it for himself. This, in fact, is what we mean when we speak of 'understanding' the words. So the historian of politics or warfare, presented with an account of certain actions done by Julius Caesar, tries to understand these actions, that is, to discover what thoughts in Caesar's mind determined him to do them. This implies envisaging for himself the situation in which Caesar stood, and thinking for himself what Caesar thought about the situation and the possible ways of dealing with it. The history of thought, and therefore all history, is the re-enactment of past thought in the historian's own mind.

This re-enactment is only accomplished, in the case of Plato and Caesar respectively, so far as the historian brings to bear on the problem all the powers of his own mind and all his knowledge of philosophy and politics. It is not a passive surrender to the spell of another's mind; it is a labour of active and therefore critical thinking. The historian not only re-enacts past thought, he re-enacts it in the context of his own knowledge and therefore, in re-enacting it, criticizes it, forms his own judgement of its value, corrects whatever errors he can discern in it. This criticism of the thought whose history he traces is not something secondary to tracing the history of it. It is an indispensable condition of the historical knowledge itself. Nothing could be a completer error concerning the history of thought than to suppose that the historian as such merely ascertains 'what so-and-so thought', leaving it to some one else to decide 'whether it was true'. All thinking is critical thinking; the thought which re-enacts past thoughts, therefore, criticizes them in re-enacting them.

It is now clear why historians habitually restrict the field of historical knowledge to human affairs. A natural process is a process of events, an historical process is a process of thoughts. Man is regarded as the only subject of historical process, because man is regarded as the only animal that thinks, or thinks enough, and clearly enough, to render his actions the expressions of his thoughts. The belief that man is the only animal that thinks at all is no doubt a superstition; but the belief that man thinks more, and more continuously and effectively, than any other animal, and is the only animal whose conduct is to any great extent determined by thought instead of by mere impulse and appetite, is probably well enough founded to justify the historian's rule of thumb.

It does not follow that all human actions are subject-matter for history; and indeed historians are agreed that they are not. But when they are asked how the distinction is to be made between historical and non-historical human actions, they are somewhat at a loss how to reply. From our present point of view we can offer an answer: so far as man's conduct is determined by what may be called his animal nature, his impulses and appetites, it is non-historical; the process of those activities is a natural process. Thus, the historian is not interested in the fact that men eat and sleep and make love and thus satisfy their natural appetites; but he is interested in the social customs which they create by their thought as a framework within which these appetites find satisfaction in ways sanctioned by convention and morality.

Consequently, although the conception of evolution has revolutionized our idea of nature by substituting for the old conception of natural process as a change within the limits of a fixed system of specific forms the new conception of that process as involving a change in these forms themselves, it has by no means identified the idea of natural process with that of historical process; and the fashion, current not long ago, of using the word 'evolution' in an historical context, and talking of the evolution of parliament or the like, though natural in an age when the science of nature was regarded as the only true form of knowledge, and when other forms of knowledge, in order to justify their existence, felt bound to assimilate themselves to that model, was the result of confused thinking and a source of further confusions.

There is only one hypothesis on which natural processes could be regarded as ultimately historical in character: namely, that these processes are in reality processes of action determined by a thought which is their own inner side. This would imply that natural events are expressions of thoughts, whether the thoughts of God, or of angelic or demonic finite intelligences, or of minds somewhat like our own inhabiting the organic and inorganic bodies of nature as our minds inhabit our bodies. Setting aside mere flights of metaphysical fancy, such an hypothesis could claim our serious attention only if it led to a better understanding of the natural world. In fact, however, the scientist can reasonably say of it 'je n'ai pas eu besoin de cette hypothèse', and the theologian will recoil from any suggestion that God's action in the natural world resembles the action of a finite human mind under the conditions of historical life. This at least is certain: that, so far as our scientific and historical knowledge goes, the processes of events which constitute the world of nature are altogether different in kind from the processes of thought which constitute the world of history.

(iii) *History as knowledge of mind*

History, then, is not, as it has so often been mis-described, a story of successive events or an account of change. Unlike the natural scientist, the historian is not concerned with events as such at all. He is only concerned with those events which are the outward expression of thoughts, and is only concerned with these in so far as they express thoughts. At bottom, he is concerned with thoughts alone; with their outward expression in events he is concerned only by the way, in so far as these reveal to him the thoughts of which he is in search.

In a sense, these thoughts are no doubt themselves events happening in time; but since the only way in which the historian can discern them is by re-thinking them for himself, there is another sense, and one very important to the historian, in which they are not in time at all. If the discovery of Pythagoras concerning the square on the hypotenuse is a thought which we to-day can think for ourselves, a thought that constitutes a permanent addition to mathematical knowledge, the discovery of Augustus, that a monarchy could be grafted upon the Republican constitution of Rome by developing the implications of *proconsulare imperium* and *tribunicia potestas*, is equally a thought which the student of Roman history can think for himself, a permanent addition to political ideas. If Mr. Whitehead is justified in calling the right-angled triangle an eternal object, the same phrase is applicable to the Roman constitution and the Augustan modification of it. This is an eternal object because it can be apprehended by historical thought at any time; time makes no difference to it in this respect, just as it makes no difference to the triangle. The peculiarity which makes it historical is not the fact of its happening in time, but the fact of its becoming known to us by our re-thinking the same thought which created the situation we are investigating, and thus coming to understand that situation.

Historical knowledge is the knowledge of what mind has done in the past, and at the same time it is the redoing of this, the perpetuation of past acts in the present. Its object is therefore not a mere object, something outside the mind which knows it; it is an activity of thought, which can be known only in so far as the knowing mind re-enacts it and knows itself as so doing. To the historian, the activities whose history he is studying are not spectacles to be watched, but experiences to be lived through in his own mind; they are objective, or known to him, only because they are also subjective, or activities of his own.

It may thus be said that historical inquiry reveals to the historian the powers of his own mind. Since all he can know historically is thoughts that he can re-think for himself, the fact of his coming to know them shows him that his mind is able (or by the very effort of studying them has become able) to think in these ways. And conversely, whenever he finds certain historical matters unintelligible, he has discovered a limitation of his own mind; he has discovered that there are certain ways in which he is not, or no longer, or not yet, able to think. Certain historians, sometimes whole generations of historians, find in certain periods of history nothing intelligible, and call them dark ages; but such phrases tell us nothing about those ages themselves, though they tell us a great deal about the persons who use them, namely that they are unable to re-think the thoughts which were fundamental to their life. It has been said that *die Weltgeschichte ist das Weltgericht*; and it is true, but in a sense not always recognized. It is the historian himself who stands at the bar of judgement, and there reveals his own mind in its strength and weakness, its virtues and its vices.

But historical knowledge is not concerned only with a remote past. If it is by historical thinking that we re-think and so rediscover the thought of Hammurabi or Solon, it is in the same way that we discover the thought of a friend who writes us a letter, or a stranger who crosses the street. Nor is it necessary that the historian should be one person and the subject of his inquiry another. It is only by historical thinking that I can discover what I thought ten years ago, by reading what I then wrote, or what I thought five minutes ago, by reflecting on an action that I then did, which surprised me when I realized what I had done. In this sense, all knowledge of mind is historical. The only way in which I can know my own mind is by performing some mental act or other and then considering what the act is that I have performed. If I want to know what I think about a certain subject, I try to put my ideas about it in order, on paper or otherwise; and then, having thus arranged and formulated them, I can study the result as an historical document and see what my ideas were when I did that piece of thinking: if I am dissatisfied with them, I can do it over again. If I want to know what powers my mind possesses as yet unexplored, for example, whether I can write poetry, I must try to write some, and see whether it strikes me and others as being the real thing. If I want to know whether I am as good a man as I hope, or as bad as I fear, I must examine acts that I have done, and understand what they really were: or else go and do some fresh acts and then examine those. All these inquiries are historical. They proceed by studying accomplished facts, ideas that I have thought out and expressed, acts that I have done. On what I have only begun and am still doing, no judgement can as yet be passed.

The same historical method is the only one by which I can know the mind of another, or the corporate mind (whatever exactly that phrase means) of a community or an age. To study the mind of the Victorian age or the English political spirit is simply to study the history of Victorian thought or English political activity. Here we come back to Locke and his 'historical, plain Method'. Mind not only declares, but also enjoys or possesses, its nature, both as mind in general and as this particular sort of mind with these particular dispositions and faculties, by thinking and acting, doing individual actions which express individual thoughts. If historical thinking is the way in which these thoughts are detected as expressed in these actions, it would seem that Locke's phrase hits the truth, and that historical knowledge is the only knowledge that the human mind can have of itself. The so-called science of human nature or of the human mind resolves itself into history.

It will certainly be thought (if those who think in this way have had patience to follow me thus far) that in saying this I am claiming more for history than it can ever give. The false view of history as a story of successive events or a spectacle of changes has been so often and so authoritatively taught in late years, especially in this country, that the very meaning of the word has become debauched through the assimilation of historical process to natural process. Against misunderstandings arising from this source I am bound to protest, even if I protest in vain. But there is one sense in which I should agree that the resolution of a science of mind into history means renouncing part of what a science of mind commonly claims, and, I think, claims falsely. The mental scientist, believing in the universal and therefore unalterable truth of his conclusions, thinks that the account he gives of mind holds good of all future stages in mind's history: he thinks that his science shows what mind will always be, not only what it has been in the past and is now. The historian has no gift of prophecy, and knows it; the historical study of mind, therefore, can neither foretell the future developments of human thought nor legislate for them, except so far as they must proceed—though in what direction we cannot tell—from the present as their starting-point. Not the least of the errors contained in the science of human nature is its claim to establish a framework to which all future history must conform, to close the gates of the future and bind posterity within limits due not to the nature of things (limits of that kind are real, and are easily accepted) but to the supposed laws of the mind itself.

Another type of objection deserves longer consideration. It may be granted that mind is the proper and only object of historical knowledge, but it may still be contended that historical knowledge is not the only way in which mind can be known. There might be a distinction between two ways of knowing mind. Historical thought studies mind as acting in certain determinate ways in certain determinate situations. Might there not be another way of studying mind, investigating its general characteristics in abstraction from any particular situation or particular action? If so, this would be a scientific, as opposed to an historical, knowledge of mind: not history, but mental science, psychology, or the philosophy of mind.

If such a science of mind is to be distinguished from history, how is the relation between the two to be conceived? It seems to me that two alternative views of this relation are possible.

One way of conceiving it would be to distinguish between what mind is and what it does: and to entrust the study of what it does, its particular actions, to history, and reserve the study of what it is for mental science. To use a familiar distinction, its functions depend on its structure, and behind its functions or particular activities as revealed in history there lies a structure which determines these functions, and must be studied not by history but by another kind of thought.

This conception, however, is very confused. In the case of a machine, we distinguish structure from function, and think of the latter as depending on the former. But we can do this only because the machine is equally perceptible to us in motion or at rest, and we can therefore study it in either state indifferently. But any study of mind is a study of its activities; if we try to think of a mind absolutely at rest, we are compelled to admit that if it existed at all (which is more than doubtful) at least we should be quite unable to study it. Psychologists speak of mental mechanisms; but they are speaking not of structures but of functions. They do not profess ability to observe these so-called mechanisms when they are not functioning. And if we look closer at the original distinction we shall see that it does not mean quite what it seems to mean. In the case of a machine, what we call function is really only that part of the machine's total functioning which serves the purpose of its maker or user. Bicycles are made not in order that there may be bicycles, but in order that people may travel in a certain way. Relatively to that purpose, a bicycle is functioning only when some one is riding it. But a bicycle at rest in a shed is not ceasing to function: its parts are not inactive, they are holding themselves together in a particular order; and what we call possession of its structure is nothing but this function of holding itself thus together. In this sense, whatever is called structure is in reality a way of functioning. In any other sense, mind has no function at all; it has no value, to itself or to any one else, except to be a mind, to perform those activities which constitute it a mind. Hume was therefore right to maintain that there is no such thing as 'spiritual substance', nothing that a mind is, distinct from and underlying what it does.

This idea of a mental science would be, to use Comte's famous distinction, 'metaphysical', depending on the conception of an occult substance underlying the facts of historical activity; the alternative idea would be 'positive', depending on the conception of similarities or uniformities among those facts themselves. According to this idea, the task of mental science would be to detect types or patterns of activity, repeated over and over again in history itself.

That such a science is possible is beyond question. But two observations must be made about it.

First, any estimate of the value of such a science, based on the analogy of natural science, is wholly misleading. The value of generalization in natural science depends on the fact that the data of physical science are given by perception, and perceiving is not understanding. The raw material of natural science is therefore 'mere particulars', observed but not understood, and, taken in their perceived particularity, unintelligible. It is therefore a genuine advance in knowledge to discover something intelligible in the relations between general types of them. What they are in themselves, as scientists are never tired of reminding us, remains unknown: but we can at least know something about the patterns of facts into which they enter.

A science which generalizes from historical facts is in a very different position. Here the facts, in order to serve as data, must first be historically known; and historical knowledge is not perception, it is the discerning of the thought which is the inner side of the event. The historian, when he is ready to hand

over such a fact to the mental scientist as a datum for generalization, has already understood it in this way from within. If he
has not done so, the fact is being used as a datum for generalization before it has been properly 'ascertained'. But if he has
done so, nothing of value is left for generalization to do. If, by
historical thinking, we already understand how and why Napoleon established his ascendancy in revolutionary France, nothing
is added to our understanding of that process by the statement
(however true) that similar things have happened elsewhere. It
is only when the particular fact cannot be understood by itself
that such statements are of value.

Hence the idea that such a science is valuable depends on a
tacit and false assumption that the 'historical data', 'phenomena of consciousness', or the like upon which it is based are
merely perceived and not historically known. To think that
they can be thus merely perceived is to think of them not as
mind but as nature; and consequently sciences of this type tend
systematically to dementalize mind and convert it into nature.
Modern examples are the pseudo-history of Spengler, where the
individual historical facts which he calls 'cultures' are frankly
conceived as natural products, growing and perishing 'with the
same superb aimlessness as the flowers of the field', and the
many psychological theories now fashionable, which conceive
virtues and vices, knowledge and illusion, in the same way.

Secondly, if we ask how far the generalizations of such a
science hold good, we shall see that its claim to transcend the
sphere of history is baseless. Types of behaviour do, no doubt,
recur, so long as minds of the same kind are placed in the same
kind of situations. The behaviour-patterns characteristic of a
feudal baron were no doubt fairly constant so long as there were
feudal barons living in a feudal society. But they will be sought
in vain (except by an inquirer content with the loosest and most
fanciful analogies) in a world whose social structure is of another
kind. In order that behaviour-patterns may be constant, there
must be in existence a social order which recurrently produces
situations of a certain kind. But social orders are historical facts,
and subject to inevitable changes, fast or slow. A positive
science of mind will, no doubt, be able to establish uniformities
and recurrences, but it can have no guarantee that the laws it
establishes will hold good beyond the historical period from

which its facts are drawn. Such a science (as we have lately been taught with regard to what is called classical economics) can do no more than describe in a general way certain characteristics of the historical age in which it is constructed. If it tries to overcome this limitation by drawing on a wider field, relying on ancient history, modern anthropology, and so on, for a larger basis of facts, it will still never be more than a generalized description of certain phases in human history. It will never be a non-historical science of mind.

To regard such a positive mental science as rising above the sphere of history, and establishing the permanent and unchanging laws of human nature, is therefore possible only to a person who mistakes the transient conditions of a certain historical age for the permanent conditions of human life. It was easy for men of the eighteenth century to make this mistake, because their historical perspective was so short, and their knowledge of cultures other than their own so limited, that they could cheerfully identify the intellectual habits of a western European in their own day with the intellectual faculties bestowed by God upon Adam and all his progeny. Hume, in his account of human nature, never attempted to go beyond observing that in point of fact 'we' think in certain ways, and left undiscussed the question what he meant by the word 'we'. Even Kant, in his attempt to go beyond the 'question of fact' and settle the 'question of right', only showed that we must think in these ways if we are to possess the kind of science which we actually possess. When he asks how experience is possible, he means by experience the kind of experience enjoyed by men of his own age and civilization. He was, of course, not aware of this. No one in his time had done enough work on the history of thought to know that both the science and the experience of an eighteenth-century European were highly peculiar historical facts, very different from those of other peoples and other times. Nor was it yet realized that, even apart from the evidence of history, men must have thought in very different ways when as yet they were hardly emerged from the ape. The idea of a science of human nature, as entertained in the eighteenth century, belonged to a time when it was still believed that the human species, like every other, was a special creation with unalterable characteristics.

The fallacy inherent in the very idea of a science of human

nature is not removed by pointing out that human nature, like every kind of nature, must according to the principles of modern thought be conceived as subject to evolution. Indeed, such a modification of the idea only leads to worse consequences. Evolution, after all, is a natural process, a process of change; and as such it abolishes one specific form in creating another. The trilobites of the Silurian age may be the ancestors of the mammals of to-day, including ourselves; but a human being is not a kind of wood-louse. The past, in a natural process, is a past superseded and dead. Now suppose the historical process of human thought were in this sense an evolutionary process. It would follow that the ways of thinking characteristic of any given historical period are ways in which people must think then, but in which others, cast at different times in a different mental mould, cannot think at all. If that were the case, there would be no such thing as truth: according to the inference correctly drawn by Herbert Spencer, what we take for knowledge is merely the fashion of present-day thought, not true but at the most useful in our struggle for existence. The same evolutionary view of the history of thought is implied by Mr. Santayana, when he denounces history as fostering 'the learned illusion of living again the life of the dead', a subject fit only for 'minds fundamentally without loyalties and incapable or fearful of knowing themselves'; persons interested not in 'the rediscovery of an essence formerly discovered or prized', but only in 'the fact that people once entertained some such idea'.[1]

The fallacy common to these views is the confusion between a natural process, in which the past dies in being replaced by the present, and an historical process, in which the past, so far as it is historically known, survives in the present. Oswald Spengler, vividly realizing the difference between modern mathematics and that of the Greeks, and knowing that each is a function of its own historical age, correctly argues from his false identification of historical with natural process that to us Greek mathematics must be not only strange but unintelligible. But in fact, not only do we understand Greek mathematics easily enough, it is actually the foundation of our own. It is not the dead past of a mathematical thought once entertained by persons whose names and dates we can give, it is the living past

[1] *The Realm of Essence*, p. 69.

of our own present mathematical inquiries, a past which, so far as we take any interest in mathematics, we still enjoy as an actual possession. Because the historical past, unlike the natural past, is a living past, kept alive by the act of historical thinking itself, the historical change from one way of thinking to another is not the death of the first, but its survival integrated in a new context involving the development and criticism of its own ideas. Mr. Santayana, like so many others, first wrongly identifies historical process with natural process, and then blames history for being what he falsely thinks it to be. Spencer's theory of the evolution of human ideas embodies the error in its crudest form.

Man has been defined as an animal capable of profiting by the experience of others. Of his bodily life this would be wholly untrue: he is not nourished because another has eaten, or refreshed because another has slept. But as regards his mental life it is true; and the way in which this profit is realized is by historical knowledge. The body of human thought or mental activity is a corporate possession, and almost all the operations which our minds perform are operations which we learned to perform from others who have performed them already. Since mind is what it does, and human nature, if it is a name for anything real, is only a name for human activities, this acquisition of ability to perform determinate operations is the acquisition of a determinate human nature. Thus the historical process is a process in which man creates for himself this or that kind of human nature by re-creating in his own thought the past to which he is heir.

This inheritance is not transmitted by any natural process. To be possessed, it must be grasped by the mind that possesses it, and historical knowledge is the way in which we enter upon the possession of it. There is not, first, a special kind of process, the historical process, and then a special way of knowing this, namely historical thought. The historical process is itself a process of thought, and it exists only in so far as the minds which are parts of it know themselves for parts of it. By historical thinking, the mind whose self-knowledge is history not only discovers within itself those powers of which historical thought reveals the possession, but actually develops those powers from a latent to an actual state, brings them into effective existence.

It would therefore be sophistical to argue that, since the historical process is a process of thought, there must be thought already present, as its presupposition, at the beginning of it, and that an account of what thought is, originally and in itself, must be a non-historical account. History does not presuppose mind; it is the life of mind itself, which is not mind except so far as it both lives in historical process and knows itself as so living.

The idea that man, apart from his self-conscious historical life, is different from the rest of creation in being a rational animal is a mere superstition. It is only by fits and starts, in a flickering and dubious manner, that human beings are rational at all. In quality, as well as in amount, their rationality is a matter of degree: some are oftener rational than others, some rational in a more intense way. But a flickering and dubious rationality can certainly not be denied to animals other than men. Their minds may be inferior in range and power to those of the lowest savages, but by the same standards the lowest savages are inferior to civilized men, and those whom we call civilized differ among themselves hardly less. There are even among non-human animals the beginnings of historical life: for example, among cats, which do not wash by instinct but are taught by their mothers. Such rudiments of education are something not essentially different from an historic culture.

Historicity, too, is a matter of degree. The historicity of very primitive societies is not easily distinguishable from the merely instinctive life of societies in which rationality is at vanishing-point. When the occasions on which thinking is done, and the kinds of things about which it is done, become more frequent and more essential to the life of society, the historic inheritance of thought, preserved by historical knowledge of what has been thought before, becomes more considerable, and with its development the development of a specifically rational life begins.

Thought is therefore not the presupposition of an historical process which is in turn the presupposition of historical knowledge. It is only in the historical process, the process of thoughts, that thought exists at all; and it is only in so far as this process is known for a process of thoughts that it is one. The self-knowledge of reason is not an accident; it belongs to its essence. This is why historical knowledge is no luxury, or mere amusement of a mind at leisure from more pressing occupations, but a prime duty, whose discharge is essential to the maintenance, not only of any particular form or type of reason, but of reason itself.

(iv) *Conclusions*

It remains to draw a few conclusions from the thesis I have tried to maintain.

First, as regards history itself. The methods of modern historical inquiry have grown up under the shadow of their elder sister, the method of natural science; in some ways helped by its example, in other ways hindered. Throughout this essay it has been necessary to engage in a running fight with what may be called a positivistic conception, or rather misconception, of history, as the study of successive events lying in a dead past, events to be understood as the scientist understands natural events, by classifying them and establishing relations between the classes thus defined. This misconception is not only an endemic error in modern philosophical thought about history, it is also a constant peril to historical thought itself. So far as historians yield to it, they neglect their proper task of penetrating to the thought of the agents whose acts they are studying, and content themselves with determining the externals of these acts, the kind of things about them which can be studied statistically. Statistical research is for the historian a good servant but a bad master. It profits him nothing to make statistical generalizations, unless he can thereby detect the thought behind the facts about which he is generalizing. At the present day, historical thought is almost everywhere disentangling itself from the toils of the positivistic fallacy, and recognizing that in itself history is nothing but the re-enactment of past thought in the historian's mind; but much still needs to be done if the full fruits of this recognition are to be reaped. All kinds of historical fallacies are still current, due to confusion between historical process and natural process: not only the cruder fallacies of mistaking historical facts of culture and tradition for functions of biological facts like race and pedigree, but subtler fallacies affecting methods of research and the organization of historical inquiry, which it would take too long to enumerate here. It is not until these have been eradicated that we can see how far historical thought, attaining at last its proper shape and stature, is able to make good the claims long ago put forward on behalf of the science of human nature.

Secondly, with regard to past attempts to construct such a science.

The positive function of so-called sciences of the human mind, whether total or partial (I refer to such studies as those on the theory of knowledge, of morals, of politics, of economics, and so forth), has always tended to be misconceived. Ideally, they are designed as accounts of one unchanging subject-matter, the mind of man as it always has been and always will be. Little acquaintance with them is demanded in order to see that they are nothing of the sort, but only inventories of the wealth achieved by the human mind at a certain stage in its history. The *Republic* of Plato is an account, not of the unchanging ideal of political life, but of the Greek ideal as Plato received it and re-interpreted it. The *Ethics* of Aristotle describes not an eternal morality but the morality of the Greek gentleman. Hobbes's *Leviathan* expounds the political ideas of seventeenth-century absolutism in their English form. Kant's ethical theory expresses the moral convictions of German pietism; his *Critique of Pure Reason* analyses the conceptions and principles of Newtonian science, in their relation to the philosophical problems of the day. These limitations are often taken for defects, as if a more powerful thinker than Plato would have lifted himself clean out of the atmosphere of Greek politics, or as if Aristotle ought to have anticipated the moral conceptions of Christianity or the modern world. So far from being a defect, they are a sign of merit; they are most clearly to be seen in those works whose quality is of the best. The reason is that in those works the authors are doing best the only thing that can be done when an attempt is made to construct a science of the human mind. They are expounding the position reached by the human mind in its historical development down to their own time.

When they try to justify that position, all they can do is to exhibit it as a logical one, a coherent whole of ideas. If, realizing that any such justification is circular, they try to make the whole depend on something outside itself, they fail, as indeed they must; for since the historical present includes in itself its own past, the real ground on which the whole rests, namely the past out of which it has grown, is not outside it but is included within it.

If these systems remain valuable to posterity, that is not in spite of their strictly historical character but because of it. To us, the ideas expressed in them are ideas belonging to the past; but it is not a dead past; by understanding it historically we incorporate it into our present thought, and enable ourselves by developing and criticizing it to use that heritage for our own advancement.

But a mere inventory of our intellectual possessions at the present time can never show by what right we enjoy them. To do this there is only one way: by analysing them instead of merely describing them, and showing how they have been built up in the historical development of thought. What Kant, for example, wanted to do when he set out to justify our use of a category like causation, can in a sense be done; but it cannot be done on Kant's method, which yields a merely circular argument, proving that such a category can be used, and must be used if we are to have Newtonian science; it can be done by research into the history of scientific thought. All Kant could show was that eighteenth-century scientists did think in terms of that category; the question why they so thought can be answered by investigating the history of the idea of causation. If more than this is required; if a proof is needed that the idea is true, that people are right to think in that way; then a demand is being made which in the nature of things can never be satisfied. How can we ever satisfy ourselves that the principles on which we think are true, except by going on thinking according to those principles, and seeing whether unanswerable criticisms of them emerge as we work? To criticize the conceptions of science is the work of science itself as it proceeds; to demand that such criticism should be anticipated by the theory of knowledge is to demand that such a theory should anticipate the history of thought.

Finally, there is the question what function can be assigned to the science of psychology. At first sight its position appears equivocal. On the one hand, it claims to be a science of mind; but if so, its apparatus of scientific method is merely the fruit of a false analogy, and it must pass over into history and, as such, disappear. And this is certainly what ought to happen so far as psychology claims to deal with the functions of reason itself. To speak of the psychology of reasoning, or the psychology of the moral self (to quote the titles of two well-known books), is to misuse words and confuse issues, ascribing to a quasi-naturalistic science a subject-matter whose being and development are not natural but historical. But if psychology avoids this danger and renounces interference with what is properly the subject-matter of history, it is likely to fall back into a pure science of nature and to become a mere branch of physiology, dealing with muscular and nervous movements.

But there is a third alternative. In realizing its own rationality, mind also realizes the presence in itself of elements that are not rational. They are not body; they are mind, but not rational mind or thought. To use an old distinction, they are psyche or soul as distinct from spirit. These irrational elements are the subject-matter of psychology. They are the blind forces and activities in us which are part of human life as it consciously experiences itself, but are not parts of the historical process: sensation as distinct from thought, feelings as distinct from conceptions, appetite as distinct from will. Their importance to us consists in the fact that they form the proximate environment in which our reason lives, as our physiological organism is the proximate environment in which they live. They are the basis of our rational life, though no part of it. Our reason discovers them, but in studying them it is not studying itself. By learning to know them, it finds out how it can help them to live in health, so that they can feed and support it while it pursues its own proper task, the self-conscious creation of its own historical life.

§ 2. *The Historical Imagination*

An inquiry into the nature of historical thinking is among the tasks which philosophy may legitimately undertake; and at the present time [1935] there are reasons, as it seems to me, for thinking such an inquiry not only legitimate but necessary. For there is a sense in which, at particular periods of history, particular philosophical problems are, as it were, in season, and claim the special attention of a philosopher anxious to be of service to his age. In part, the problems of philosophy are unchanging; in part, they vary from age to age, according to the special characteristics of human life and thought at the time; and in the best philosophers of every age these two parts are so interwoven that the permanent problems appear *sub specie saeculi*, and the special problems of the age *sub specie aeternitatis*. Whenever human thought has been dominated by some special interest, the most fruitful philosophy of the age has reflected that domination; not passively, by mere submission to its influence, but actively, by making a special attempt to understand it and placing it in the focus of philosophical inquiry.

In the Middle Ages theology was the interest that served in this way to focus philosophical speculation. In the seventeenth century it was physical science. To-day, when we conventionally date the beginnings of modern philosophy to the seventeenth century, we mean, I think, that the scientific interest which then began to dominate human life still dominates it. But if we compare the seventeenth-century mind, in its general orientation, with that of to-day, by comparing the subjects dealt with in their literature, we can hardly fail to be struck by one important difference. Since the time of Descartes, and even since the time of Kant, mankind has acquired a new habit of thinking historically. I do not mean that there were no historians worthy of the name until a century and a half ago; that would be untrue: I do not even mean that since then the bulk of historical knowledge and the output of historical books have enormously increased; that would be true but relatively unimportant. What I mean is that during this time historical thought has worked out a technique of its own, no less definite in its character and certain in its results than its elder sister, the technique of natural science; and that, in thus entering upon the *sichere Gang einer Wissenschaft*, it has taken a place in human life from which its influence has permeated and to some extent transformed every department of thought and action.

Among others, it has profoundly influenced philosophy; but on the whole the attitude of philosophy towards this influence has been more passive than active. Some philosophers are inclined to welcome it; others to resent it; comparatively few have thought philosophically about it. Attempts have been made, chiefly in Germany and Italy, to answer the questions: What is historical thinking? and What light does it throw on the traditional problems of philosophy? and by answering these questions to do for the historical consciousness of to-day what Kant's transcendental analytic did for the scientific consciousness of the eighteenth century. But for the most part, and especially in this country, it has been usual to ignore all such questions, and to discuss the problems of knowledge in seeming unawareness that there is such a thing as history. This custom can of course be defended. It may be argued that history is not knowledge at all, but only opinion, and unworthy of philosophical study. Or it may be argued that, so far as it is knowledge, its problems are those of knowledge in general, and call for no special treatment. For myself, I cannot accept either defence. If history is opinion, why should philosophy on that account ignore it ? If it is knowledge, why should philosophers not study its methods with the same attention that they give to the very different methods of science ? And when I read the works of even the greatest contemporary and recent English philosophers, admiring them deeply and learning from them more than I can hope to acknowledge, I find myself constantly haunted by the thought that their accounts of knowledge, based as they seem to be primarily on the study of perception and of scientific thinking, not only ignore historical thinking but are actually inconsistent with there being such a thing.

No doubt, historical thought is in one way like perception. Each has for its proper object something individual. What I perceive is this room, this table, this paper. What the historian thinks about is Elizabeth or Marlborough, the Peloponnesian War or the policy of Ferdinand and Isabella. But what we perceive is always the this, the here, the now. Even when we hear a distant explosion or see a stellar conflagration long after it has happened, there is still a moment at which it is here and now perceptible, when it is this explosion, this new star. Historical thought is of something which can never be a this, because it is never a here and now. Its objects are events which have finished happening, and conditions no longer in existence. Only when they are no longer perceptible do they become objects for historical thought. Hence all theories of knowledge that conceive it as a transaction or relation between a subject and an object both actually existing, and confronting or compresent to one another, theories that take acquaintance as the essence of knowledge, make history impossible.

In another way history resembles science: for in each of them knowledge is inferential or reasoned. But whereas science lives in a world of abstract universals, which are in one sense everywhere and in another nowhere, in one sense at all times and in another at no time, the things about which the historian reasons are not abstract but concrete, not universal but individual, not indifferent to space and time but having a where and a when of their own, though the where need not be here and the when cannot be now. History, therefore, cannot be made to square with theories according to which the object of knowledge is abstract and changeless, a logical entity towards which the mind may take up various attitudes.

Nor is it possible to give an account of knowledge by combining theories of these two types. Current philosophy is full of such combinations. Knowledge by acquaintance and knowledge by description; eternal objects and the transient situations into which they are ingredient; realm of essence and realm of matter; in these and other such dichotomies, as in the older dichotomies of matters of fact and relations between ideas, or truths of fact and truths of reason, provision is made for the peculiarities both of a perception which grasps the here and now, and of the abstract thought that apprehends the everywhere and always: the αἴσθησις and νόησις of philosophical tradition. But just as history is neither αἴσθησις nor νόησις, so it is not a combination of the two. It is a third thing, having some of the characteristics of each, but combining them in a way impossible to either. It is not partly acquaintance with transient situations and partly reasoned knowledge of abstract entities. It is wholly a reasoned knowledge of what is transient and concrete.

My purpose here is to offer a brief account of this third thing which is history; and I will begin by stating what may be called the common-sense theory of it, the theory which most people believe, or imagine themselves to believe, when first they reflect on the matter.

According to this theory, the essential things in history are memory and authority. If an event or a state of things is to be historically known, first of all some one must be acquainted with it; then he must remember it; then he must state his recollection of it in terms intelligible to another; and finally that other must accept the statement as true. History is thus the believing some one else when he says that he remembers something. The believer is the historian; the person believed is called his authority.

This doctrine implies that historical truth, so far as it is at all accessible to the historian, is accessible to him only because it exists ready made in the ready-made statements of his authorities. These statements are to him a sacred text, whose value depends wholly on the unbrokenness of the tradition they represent. He must therefore on no account tamper with them. He must not mutilate them; he must not add to them; and, above all, he must not contradict them. For if he takes it upon himself to pick and choose, to decide that some of his authority's statements are important and others not, he is going behind his authority's back and appealing to some other criterion; and this, on the theory, is exactly what he cannot do. If he adds to them, interpolating in them constructions of his own devising, and accepting these constructions as additions to his knowledge, he is believing something for a reason other than the fact that his authority has said it; and this again he has no right to do. Worst of all, if he contradicts them, presuming to decide that his authority has misrepresented the facts, and rejecting his statements as incredible, he is believing the opposite of what he has been told, and committing the worst possible offence against the rules of his craft. The authority may be garrulous, discursive, a gossip and a scandal-monger; he may have overlooked or forgotten or omitted facts; he may have ignorantly or wilfully mis-stated them; but against these defects the historian has no remedy. For him, on the theory, what his authorities tell him is the truth, the whole accessible truth, and nothing but the truth.

These consequences of the common-sense theory have only to be stated in order to be repudiated. Every historian is aware that on occasion he does tamper in all these three ways with what he finds in his authorities. He selects from them what he thinks important, and omits the rest; he interpolates in them things which they do not explicitly say; and he criticizes them by rejecting or amending what he regards as due to misinformation or mendacity. But I am not sure whether we historians always realize the consequences of what we are doing. In general, when we reflect on our own work, we seem to accept

what I have called the common-sense theory, while claiming
our own rights of selection, construction, and criticism. No
doubt these rights are inconsistent with the theory; but we
attempt to soften the contradiction by minimizing the extent
to which they are exercised, thinking of them as emergency
measures, a kind of revolt into which the historian may be driven
at times by the exceptional incompetence of his authorities, but
which does not fundamentally disturb the normal peaceful
régime in which he placidly believes what he is told because he
is told to believe it. Yet these things, however seldom they are
done, are either historical crimes or facts fatal to the theory:
for on the theory they ought to be done, not rarely, but never.
And in fact they are neither criminal nor exceptional. Throughout the course of his work the historian is selecting, constructing,
and criticizing; it is only by doing these things that he maintains
his thought upon the *sichere Gang einer Wissenschaft*. By
explicitly recognizing this fact it is possible to effect what, again
borrowing a Kantian phrase, one might call a Copernican revolution in the theory of history: the discovery that, so far from
relying on an authority other than himself, to whose statements
his thought must conform, the historian is his own authority
and his thought autonomous, self-authorizing, possessed of a
criterion to which his so-called authorities must conform and
by reference to which they are criticized.

The autonomy of historical thought is seen at its simplest in
the work of selection. The historian who tries to work on the
common-sense theory, and accurately reproduce what he finds
in his authorities, resembles a landscape-painter who tries to
work on that theory of art which bids the artist copy nature.
He may fancy that he is reproducing in his own medium the
actual shapes and colours of natural things; but however hard
he tries to do this he is always selecting, simplifying, schematiz-
ing, leaving out what he thinks unimportant and putting in what
he regards as essential. It is the artist, and not nature, that is
responsible for what goes into the picture. In the same way, no
historian, not even the worst, merely copies out his authorities;
even if he puts in nothing of his own (which is never really
possible), he is always leaving out things which, for one reason
or another, he decides that his own work does not need or
cannot use. It is he, therefore, and not his authority, that is

responsible for what goes in. On that question he is his own master: his thought is to that extent autonomous.

An even clearer exhibition of this autonomy is found in what I have called historical construction. The historian's authorities tell him of this or that phase in a process whose intermediate phases they leave undescribed; he then interpolates these phases for himself. His picture of his subject, though it may consist in part of statements directly drawn from his authorities, consists also, and increasingly with every increase in his competence as an historian, of statements reached inferentially from those according to his own criteria, his own rules of method, and his own canons of relevance. In this part of his work he is never depending on his authorities in the sense of repeating what they tell him; he is relying on his own powers and constituting himself his own authority; while his so-called authorities are now not authorities at all but only evidence.

The clearest demonstration of the historian's autonomy, however, is provided by historical criticism. As natural science finds its proper method when the scientist, in Bacon's metaphor, puts Nature to the question, tortures her by experiment in order to wring from her answers to his own questions, so history finds its proper method when the historian puts his authorities in the witness-box, and by cross-questioning extorts from them information which in their original statements they have withheld, either because they did not wish to give it or because they did not possess it. Thus, a commander's dispatches may claim a victory; the historian, reading them in a critical spirit, will ask: 'If it was a victory, why was it not followed up in this or that way?' and may thus convict the writer of concealing the truth. Or, by using the same method, he may convict of ignorance a less critical predecessor who has accepted the version of the battle given him by the same dispatches.

The historian's autonomy is here manifested in its extremest form, because it is here evident that somehow, in virtue of his activity as an historian, he has it in his power to reject something explicitly told him by his authorities and to substitute something else. If that is possible, the criterion of historical truth cannot be the fact that a statement is made by an authority. It is the truthfulness and the information of the so-called authority that are in question; and this question the historian has to answer for himself, on his own authority. Even if he accepts what his authorities tell him, therefore, he accepts it not on their authority but on his own; not because they say it, but because it satisfies his criterion of historical truth.

The common-sense theory which bases history upon memory and authority needs no further refutation. Its bankruptcy is evident. For the historian there can never be authorities, because the so-called authorities abide a verdict which only he can give. Yet the common-sense theory may claim a qualified and relative truth. The historian, generally speaking, works at a subject which others have studied before him. In proportion as he is more of a novice, either in this particular subject or in history as a whole, his forerunners are, relatively to his incompetence, authoritative; and in the limiting case where his incompetence and ignorance were absolute, they could be called authorities without qualification. As he becomes more and more master of his craft and his subject, they become less and less his authorities, more and more his fellow students, to be treated with respect or contempt according to their deserts.

And as history does not depend on authority, so it does not depend upon memory. The historian can rediscover what has been completely forgotten, in the sense that no statement of it has reached him by an unbroken tradition from eyewitnesses. He can even discover what, until he discovered it, no one ever knew to have happened at all. This he does partly by the critical treatment of statements contained in his sources, partly by the use of what are called unwritten sources, which are increasingly employed as history becomes increasingly sure of its own proper methods and its own proper criterion.

I have spoken of the criterion of historical truth. What is this criterion? According to the common-sense theory, it is the agreement of the statements made by the historian with those which he finds in his authorities. This answer we now know to be false, and we must seek another. We cannot renounce the search. Some answer to the question there must be, for without a criterion there can be no criticism. One answer to this question was offered by the greatest English philosopher of our time in his pamphlet on *The Presuppositions of Critical History*. Bradley's essay was an early work with which in his maturity he was dissatisfied; but, unsatisfactory though it certainly is, it bears the stamp of his genius. In it Bradley faces the question how it is possible for the historian, in defiance of the common-sense theory, to turn the tables on his so-called authorities and to say 'This is what our authorities record, but what really happened must have been not this but that'.

His answer to this question was that our experience of the world teaches us that some kinds of things happen and others do not ; this experience, then, is the criterion which the historian brings to bear on the statements of his authorities. If they tell him that things happened of a kind which, according to his experience, does not happen, he is obliged to disbelieve them ; if the things which they report are of a kind which according to his experience does happen, he is free to accept their statements.

There are many obvious objections to this idea, on which I shall not insist. It is deeply tinged with the empiricist philosophy against which Bradley was soon so effectively to rebel. But apart from this there are certain special points in which the argument appears to me defective.

First, the proposed criterion is a criterion not of what did happen but of what could happen. It is in fact nothing but Aristotle's criterion of what is admissible in poetry ; and hence it does not serve to discriminate history from fiction. It would no doubt be satisfied by the statements of an historian, but it would be satisfied no less adequately by those of an historical novelist. It cannot therefore be the criterion of critical history.

Secondly, because it can never tell us what did happen, we are left to rely for that on the sheer authority of our informant. We undertake, when we apply it, to believe everything our informant tells us so long as it satisfies the merely negative criterion of being possible. This is not to turn the tables on our authorities ; it is blindly to accept what they tell us. The critical attitude has not been achieved.

Thirdly, the historian's experience of the world in which he lives can only help him to check, even negatively, the statements of his authorities in so far as they are concerned not with history but with nature, which has no history. The laws of nature have always been the same, and what is against nature now was against nature two thousand years ago ; but the historical as distinct from the natural conditions of man's life differ so much at different times that no argument from analogy will hold.

That the Greeks and Romans exposed their new-born children in order to control the numbers of their population is no less true for being unlike anything that happens in the experience of contributors to the *Cambridge Ancient History*. In point of fact Bradley's treatment of the subject grew not out of the ordinary course of historical study but out of his interest in the credibility of the New Testament narratives, and in particular their miraculous element; but a criterion which only serves in the case of miracle is of sadly little use to the weekday historian.

Bradley's essay, inconclusive though it is, remains memorable for the fact that in it the Copernican revolution in the theory of historical knowledge has been in principle accomplished. For the common-sense theory, historical truth consists in the historian's beliefs conforming to the statements of his authorities; Bradley has seen that the historian brings with him to the study of his authorities a criterion of his own by reference to which the authorities themselves are judged. What it is, Bradley failed to discover. It remains to be seen whether, sixty years later, his problem, which in the meantime I believe no English-speaking philosopher has discussed in print, can be advanced beyond the point at which he left it.

I have already remarked that, in addition to selecting from among his authorities' statements those which he regards as important, the historian must in two ways go beyond what his authorities tell him. One is the critical way, and this is what Bradley has attempted to analyse. The other is the constructive way. Of this he has said nothing, and to this I now propose to return. I described constructive history as interpolating, between the statements borrowed from our authorities, other statements implied by them. Thus our authorities tell us that on one day Caesar was in Rome and on a later day in Gaul; they tell us nothing about his journey from one place to the other, but we interpolate this with a perfectly good conscience.

This act of interpolation has two significant characteristics. First, it is in no way arbitrary or merely fanciful: it is necessary or, in Kantian language, *a priori*. If we filled up the narrative of Caesar's doings with fanciful details such as the names of the persons he met on the way, and what he said to them, the construction would be arbitrary: it would be in fact the kind of construction which is done by an historical novelist. But if our construction involves nothing that is not necessitated by the evidence, it is a legitimate historical construction of a kind without which there can be no history at all.

Secondly, what is in this way inferred is essentially something imagined. If we look out over the sea and perceive a ship, and five minutes later look again and perceive it in a different place, we find ourselves obliged to imagine it as having occupied intermediate positions when we were not looking. That is already an example of historical thinking; and it is not otherwise that we find ourselves obliged to imagine Caesar as having travelled from Rome to Gaul when we are told that he was in these different places at these successive times.

This activity, with this double character, I shall call *a priori* imagination; and, though I shall have more to say of it hereafter, for the present I shall be content to remark that, however unconscious we may be of its operation, it is this activity which, bridging the gaps between what our authorities tell us, gives the historical narrative or description its continuity. That the historian must use his imagination is a commonplace; to quote Macaulay's *Essay on History*, 'a perfect historian must possess an imagination sufficiently powerful to make his narrative affecting and picturesque'; but this is to underestimate the part played by the historical imagination, which is properly not ornamental but structural. Without it the historian would have no narrative to adorn. The imagination, that 'blind but indispensable faculty' without which, as Kant has shown, we could never perceive the world around us, is indispensable in the same way to history: it is this which, operating not capriciously as fancy but in its *a priori* form, does the entire work of historical construction.

Two misunderstandings may here be forestalled. First, it may be thought that by imagining we can present to ourselves only what is imaginary in the sense of being fictitious or unreal. This prejudice need only be mentioned in order to be dispelled. If I imagine the friend who lately left my house now entering his own, the fact that I imagine this event gives me no reason to believe it unreal. The imaginary, simply as such, is neither unreal nor real.

Secondly, to speak of *a priori* imagination may seem a paradox, for it may be thought that imagination is essentially capricious, arbitrary, merely fanciful. But in addition to its historical function there are two other functions of *a priori* imagination which are, or ought to be, familiar to all. One is the pure or free, but by no means arbitrary, imagination of the artist. A man writing a novel composes a story where parts are played by various characters. Characters and incidents are all alike imaginary; yet the whole aim of the novelist is to show the characters acting and the incidents developing in a manner determined by a necessity internal to themselves. The story, if it is a good story, cannot develop otherwise than as it does; the novelist in imagining it cannot imagine it developing except as it does develop. Here, and equally in all other kinds of art, the *a priori* imagination is at work. Its other familiar function is what may be called the perceptual imagination, supplementing and consolidating the data of perception in the way so well analysed by Kant, by presenting to us objects of possible perception which are not actually perceived: the under side of this table, the inside of an unopened egg, the back of the moon. Here again the imagination is *a priori*: we cannot but imagine what cannot but be there. The historical imagination differs from these not in being *a priori*, but in having as its special task to imagine the past: not an object of possible perception, since it does not now exist, but able through this activity to become an object of our thought.

The historian's picture of his subject, whether that subject be a sequence of events or a past state of things, thus appears as a web of imaginative construction stretched between certain fixed points provided by the statements of his authorities; and if these points are frequent enough and the threads spun from each to the next are constructed with due care, always by the *a priori* imagination and never by merely arbitrary fancy, the whole picture is constantly verified by appeal to these data, and runs little risk of losing touch with the reality which it represents.

Actually, this is very much how we do think of historical work, when the common-sense theory has ceased to satisfy us, and we have become aware of the part played in it by the constructive imagination. But such a conception is in one way seriously at fault: it overlooks the no less important part played by criticism. We think of our web of construction as pegged down, so to speak, to the facts by the statements of authorities, which we regard as data or fixed points for the work of construction. But in so thinking we have slipped back into the theory, which we now know to be false, that truth is given us ready made in these statements. We know that truth is to be had, not by swallowing what our authorities tell us, but by criticizing it; and thus the supposedly fixed points between which the historical imagination spins its web are not given to us ready made, they must be achieved by critical thinking.

There is nothing other than historical thought itself, by appeal to which its conclusions may be verified. The hero of a detective novel is thinking exactly like an historian when, from indications of the most varied kinds, he constructs an imaginary picture of how a crime was committed, and by whom. At first, this is a mere theory, awaiting verification, which must come to it from without. Happily for the detective, the conventions of that literary form dictate that when his construction is complete it shall be neatly pegged down by a confession from the criminal, given in such circumstances that its genuineness is beyond question. The historian is less fortunate. If, after convincing himself by a study of the evidence already available that Bacon wrote the plays of Shakespeare or that Henry VII murdered the Princes in the Tower, he were to find an autograph document confessing the fact, he would by no means have verified his conclusions; the new document, so far from closing the inquiry, would only have complicated it by raising a new problem, the problem of its own authenticity.

I began by considering a theory according to which everything is given: according to which all truth, so far as any truth is accessible to the historian, is provided for him ready made in the ready-made statements of his authorities. I then saw that much of what he takes for true is not given in this way but constructed by his *a priori* imagination; but I still fancied that this imagination worked inferentially from fixed points given in the same sense. I am now driven to confess that there are for historical thought no fixed points thus given: in other words, that in history, just as there are properly speaking no authorities, so there are properly speaking no data.

Historians certainly think of themselves as working from data; where by data they mean historical facts possessed by them ready made at the beginning of a certain piece of historical research. Such a datum, if the research concerns the Peloponnesian War, would be, for example, a certain statement of Thucydides, accepted as substantially true. But when we ask what gives historical thought this datum, the answer is obvious: historical thought gives it to itself, and therefore in relation to historical thought at large it is not a datum but a result or achievement. It is only our historical knowledge which tells us that these curious marks on paper are Greek letters; that the words which they form have certain meanings in the Attic dialect; that the passage is authentic Thucydides, not an interpolation or corruption; and that on this occasion Thucydides knew what he was talking about and was trying to tell the truth. Apart from all this, the passage is merely a pattern of black marks on white paper: not any historical fact at all, but something existing here and now, and perceived by the historian. All that the historian means, when he describes certain historical facts as his data, is that for the purposes of a particular piece of work there are certain historical problems relevant to that work which for the present he proposes to treat as settled; though, if they are settled, it is only because historical thinking has settled them in the past, and they remain settled only until he or some one else decides to reopen them.

His web of imaginative construction, therefore, cannot derive its validity from being pegged down, as at first I described it, to certain given facts. That description represented an attempt to relieve him of the responsibility for the nodal points of his fabric, while admitting his responsibility for what he constructs between them. In point of fact, he is just as responsible for the one as for the other. Whether he accepts or rejects or modifies or reinterprets what his so-called authorities tell him, it is he that is responsible for the statement which, after duly criticizing them, he makes. The criterion that justifies him in making it can never be the fact that it has been given him by an authority.

This brings me back to the question what this criterion is. And at this point a partial and provisional answer can be given. The web of imaginative construction is something far more solid and powerful than we have hitherto realized. So far from relying for its validity upon the support of given facts, it actually serves as the touchstone by which we decide whether alleged facts are genuine. Suetonius tells me that Nero at one time intended to evacuate Britain. I reject his statement, not because any better authority flatly contradicts it, for of course none does; but because my reconstruction of Nero's policy based on Tacitus will not allow me to think that Suetonius is right. And if I am told that this is merely to say I prefer Tacitus to Suetonius, I confess that I do: but I do so just because I find myself able to incorporate what Tacitus tells me into a coherent and continuous picture of my own, and cannot do this for Suetonius.

It is thus the historian's picture of the past, the product of his own *a priori* imagination, that has to justify the sources used in its construction. These sources are sources, that is to say, credence is given to them, only because they are in this way justified. For any source may be tainted: this writer prejudiced, that misinformed; this inscription misread by a bad epigraphist, that blundered by a careless stonemason; this potsherd placed out of its context by an incompetent excavator, that by a blameless rabbit. The critical historian has to discover and correct all these and many other kinds of falsification. He does it, and can only do it, by considering whether the picture of the past to which the evidence leads him is a coherent and continuous picture, one which makes sense. The *a priori* imagination which does the work of historical construction supplies the means of historical criticism as well.

Freed from its dependence on fixed points supplied from without, the historian's picture of the past is thus in every detail an imaginary picture, and its necessity is at every point the necessity of the *a priori* imagination. Whatever goes into it, goes into it not because his imagination passively accepts it, but because it actively demands it.

The resemblance between the historian and the novelist, to which I have already referred, here reaches its culmination. Each of them makes it his business to construct a picture which is partly a narrative of events, partly a description of situations, exhibition of motives, analysis of characters. Each aims at making his picture a coherent whole, where every character and every situation is so bound up with the rest that this character in this situation cannot but act in this way, and we cannot imagine him as acting otherwise. The novel and the history must both of them make sense; nothing is admissible in either except what is necessary, and the judge of this necessity is in both cases the imagination. Both the novel and the history are self-explanatory, self-justifying, the product of an autonomous or self-authorizing activity; and in both cases this activity is the *a priori* imagination.

As works of imagination, the historian's work and the novelist's do not differ. Where they do differ is that the historian's picture is meant to be true. The novelist has a single task only: to construct a coherent picture, one that makes sense. The historian has a double task: he has both to do this, and to construct a picture of things as they really were and of events as they really happened. This further necessity imposes upon him obedience to three rules of method, from which the novelist or artist in general is free.

First, his picture must be localized in space and time. The artist's need not; essentially, the things that he imagines are imagined as happening at no place and at no date. Of *Wuthering Heights* it has been well said that the scene is laid in Hell, though the place-names are English; and it was a sure instinct that led another great novelist to replace Oxford by Christminster, Wantage by Alfredston, and Fawley by Marychurch, recoiling against the discord of topographical fact in what should be a purely imaginary world.

Secondly, all history must be consistent with itself. Purely imaginary worlds cannot clash and need not agree; each is a world to itself. But there is only one historical world, and everything in it must stand in some relation to everything else, even if that relation is only topographical and chronological.

Thirdly, and most important, the historian's picture stands in a peculiar relation to something called evidence. The only way in which the historian or any one else can judge, even tentatively, of its truth is by considering this relation; and, in practice, what we mean by asking whether an historical statement is true is whether it can be justified by an appeal to the evidence: for a truth unable to be so justified is to the historian a thing of no interest. What is this thing called evidence, and what is its relation to the finished historical work?

We already know what evidence is not. It is not ready-made historical knowledge, to be swallowed and regurgitated by the historian's mind. Everything is evidence which the historian can use as evidence. But what can he so use? It must be something here and now perceptible to him: this written page, this spoken utterance, this building, this finger-print. And of all the things perceptible to him there is not one which he might not conceivably use as evidence on some question, if he came to it with the right question in mind. The enlargement of historical knowledge comes about mainly through finding how to use as evidence this or that kind of perceived fact which historians have hitherto thought useless to them.

The whole perceptible world, then, is potentially and in principle evidence to the historian. It becomes actual evidence in so far as he can use it. And he cannot use it unless he comes to it with the right kind of historical knowledge. The more historical knowledge we have, the more we can learn from any given piece of evidence; if we had none, we could learn nothing. Evidence is evidence only when some one contemplates it historically. Otherwise it is merely perceived fact, historically dumb. It follows that historical knowledge can only grow out of historical knowledge; in other words, that historical thinking is an original and fundamental activity of the human mind, or, as Descartes might have said, that the idea of the past is an 'innate' idea.

Historical thinking is that activity of the imagination by which we endeavour to provide this innate idea with detailed content. And this we do by using the present as evidence for its own past. Every present has a past of its own, and any imaginative reconstruction of the past aims at reconstructing the past of this present, the present in which the act of imagination is going on, as here and now perceived. In principle the aim of any such act is to use the entire perceptible here-and-now as evidence for the entire past through whose process it has come into being. In practice, this aim can never be achieved. The perceptible here-and-now can never be perceived, still less interpreted, in its entirety; and the infinite process of past time can never be envisaged as a whole. But this separation between what is attempted in principle and what is achieved in practice is the lot of mankind, not a peculiarity of historical thinking. The fact that it is found there only shows that herein history is like art, science, philosophy, the pursuit of virtue, and the search for happiness.

It is for the same reason that in history, as in all serious matters, no achievement is final. The evidence available for solving any given problem changes with every change of historical method and with every variation in the competence of historians. The principles by which this evidence is interpreted change too; since the interpreting of evidence is a task to which a man must bring everything he knows: historical knowledge, knowledge of nature and man, mathematical knowledge, philosophical knowledge; and not knowledge only, but mental habits and possessions of every kind: and none of these is unchanging. Because of these changes, which never cease, however slow they may appear to observers who take a short view, every new generation must rewrite history in its own way; every new historian, not content with giving new answers to old questions, must revise the questions themselves; and—since historical thought is a river into which none can step twice—even a single historian, working at a single subject for a certain length of time, finds when he tries to reopen an old question that the question has changed.

This is not an argument for historical scepticism. It is only the discovery of a second dimension of historical thought, the history of history: the discovery that the historian himself, together with the here-and-now which forms the total body of evidence available to him, is a part of the process he is studying, has his own place in that process, and can see it only from the point of view which at this present moment he occupies within it.

But neither the raw material of historical knowledge, the detail of the here-and-now as given him in perception, nor the various endowments that serve him as aids to interpreting this evidence, can give the historian his criterion of historical truth. That criterion is the idea of history itself: the idea of an imaginary picture of the past. That idea is, in Cartesian language, innate; in Kantian language, *a priori*. It is not a chance product of psychological causes; it is an idea which every man possesses as part of the furniture of his mind, and discovers himself to possess in so far as he becomes conscious of what it is to have a mind. Like other ideas of the same sort, it is one to which no fact of experience exactly corresponds. The historian, however long and faithfully he works, can never say that his work, even in crudest outline or in this or that smallest detail, is done once for all. He can never say that his picture of the past is at any point adequate to his idea of what it ought to be. But, however fragmentary and faulty the results of his work may be, the idea which governed its course is clear, rational, and universal. It is the idea of the historical imagination as a self-dependent, self-determining, and self-justifying form of thought.

§ 3. *Historical Evidence*

Introduction

'History,' said Bury, 'is a science; no less, and no more.'

Perhaps it is no less: that depends on what you mean by a science. There is a slang usage, like that for which 'hall' means a music-hall or 'pictures' moving pictures, according to which 'science' means natural science. Whether history is a science in that sense of the word, however, need not be asked; for in the tradition of European speech, going back to the time when Latin speakers translated the Greek ἐπιστήμη by their own word *scientia*, and continuing unbroken down to the present day, the word 'science' means any organized body of knowledge. If that is what the word means Bury is so far incontestably right, that history is a science, nothing less.

But if it is no less, it is certainly more. For anything that is a science at all must be more than merely a science, it must be a science of some special kind. A body of knowledge is never merely organized, it is always organized in some particular way. Some bodies of knowledge, like meteorology, are organized by collecting observations concerned with events of a certain kind which the scientist can watch as they happen, though he cannot produce them at will. Others, like chemistry, are organized not only by observing events as they happen, but by making them happen under strictly controlled conditions. Others again are organized not by observing events at all, but by making certain assumptions and proceeding with the utmost exactitude to argue out their consequences.

History is organized in none of these ways. Wars and revolutions, and the other events with which it deals, are not deliberately produced by historians under laboratory conditions in order to be studied with scientific precision. Nor are they even observed by historians, in the sense in which events are observed by natural scientists. Meteorologists and astronomers will make arduous and expensive journeys in order to observe for themselves events of the kinds in which they are interested, because their standard of observation is such that they cannot be satisfied with descriptions by inexpert witnesses; but historians do not fit out expeditions to countries where wars and revolutions are going on. And this is not because historians are less energetic or courageous than natural scientists, or less able to obtain the money such expeditions would cost. It is because the facts which might be learned through such expeditions, like the facts which might be learned through the deliberate fomenting of a war or a revolution at home, would not teach historians anything they want to know.

The sciences of observation and experiment are alike in this, that their aim is to detect the constant or recurring features in all events of a certain kind. A meteorologist studies one cyclone in order to compare it with others; and by studying a number of them he hopes to find out what features in them are constant, that is, to find out what cyclones as such are like. But the historian has no such aim. If you find him on a certain occasion studying the Hundred Years War or the Revolution of 1688, you cannot infer that he is in the preliminary stages of an inquiry whose ultimate aim is to reach conclusions about wars or revolutions as such. If he is in the preliminary stages of any inquiry, it is more likely to be a general study of the Middle Ages or the seventeenth century. This is because the sciences of observation and experiment are organized in one way and history is organized in another. In the organization of meteorology, the ulterior value of what has been observed about one cyclone is conditioned by its relation to what has been observed about other cyclones. In the organization of history, the ulterior value of what is known about the Hundred Years War is conditioned, not by its relation to what is known about other wars, but by its relation to what is known about other things that people did in the Middle Ages.

Equally obvious is the difference between the organization of history and that of the 'exact' sciences. It is true that in history, as in exact science, the normal process of thought is inferential; that is to say, it begins by asserting this or that, and goes on to ask what it proves. But the starting-points are of very different kinds. In exact science they are assumptions, and the traditional way of expressing them is in sentences beginning with a word of command prescribing that a certain assumption be made: 'Let ABC be a triangle, and let AB = AC.' In history they are not assumptions, they are facts, and facts coming under the historian's observation, such as, that on the page open before him there is printed what purports to be a charter by which a certain king grants certain lands to a certain monastery. The conclusions, too, are of different kinds. In exact science, they are conclusions about things which have no special habitation in space or time: if they are anywhere, they are everywhere, and if they are at any time they are at all times. In history, they are conclusions about events, each having a place and date of its own. The exactitude with which place and date are known to the historian is variable; but he always knows that there were both a place and a date, and within limits he always knows what they were; this knowledge being part of the conclusion to which he is led by arguing from the facts before him.

These differences in starting-point and conclusion imply a difference in the entire organization of the respective sciences. When a mathematician has made up his mind what the problem is which he desires to solve, the next step before him is to make assumptions which will enable him to solve it; and this involves an appeal to his powers of invention. When an historian has similarly made up his mind, his next business is to place himself in a position where he can say: 'The facts which I am now observing are the facts from which I can infer the solution of my problem.' His business is not to invent anything, it is to discover something. And the finished products, too, are differently organized. The scheme upon which exact sciences have been traditionally arranged depends on relations of logical priority and posteriority: one proposition is placed before a second, if understanding of the first is needed in order that the second should be understood; the traditional scheme of arrangement in history is a chronological scheme, in which one event is placed before a second if it happened at an earlier time.

History, then, is a science, but a science of a special kind. It is a science whose business is to study events not accessible to our observation, and to study these events inferentially, arguing to them from something else which is accessible to our observation, and which the historian calls 'evidence' for the events in which he is interested.

(i) *History as inferential*

History has this in common with every other science: that the historian is not allowed to claim any single piece of knowledge, except where he can justify his claim by exhibiting to himself in the first place, and secondly to any one else who is both able and willing to follow his demonstration, the grounds upon which it is based. This is what was meant, above, by describing history as inferential. The knowledge in virtue of which a man is an historian is a knowledge of what the evidence at his disposal proves about certain events. If he or somebody else could have the very same knowledge of the very same events by way of memory, or second sight, or some Wellsian machine for looking backwards through time, this would not be historical knowledge; and the proof would be that he could not produce, either to himself or to any other critic of his claims, the evidence from which he had derived it. Critic, not sceptic; for a critic is a person able and willing to go over somebody else's thoughts for himself to see if they have been well done; whereas a sceptic is a person who will not do this; and because you cannot make a man think, any more than you can make a horse drink, there is no way of proving to a sceptic that a certain piece of thinking is sound, and no reason for taking his denials to heart. It is only by his peers that any claimant to knowledge is judged.

This necessity of justifying any claim to knowledge by exhibiting the grounds upon which it is based is a universal characteristic of science because it arises from the fact that a science is an organized body of knowledge. To say that knowledge is inferential is only another way of saying that it is organized. What memory is, and whether it is a kind of knowledge or not, are questions that need not be considered in a book about history: for this at least is clear, in spite of what Bacon and others have said, that memory is not history, because history is a certain kind of organized or inferential knowledge, and memory is not organized, not inferential, at all. If I say 'I remember writing a letter to So-and-so last week', that is a statement of memory, but it is not an historical statement. But if I can add 'and my memory is not deceiving me; because here is his reply', then I am basing a statement about the past on evidence; I am talking history. For the same reason, there is no need in an essay like this to consider the claims of people who say that when they are in a place where a certain event has recurred they can in some way see the event going on before their eyes. What actually happens on occasions like this, and whether the people to whom it happens thereby obtain knowledge of the past, are certainly interesting questions, but this is not the right place to discuss them; for even if these people do obtain knowledge of the past, it is not organized or inferential knowledge; not scientific knowledge; not history.

(ii) *Different kinds of inference*

Different kinds of science are organized in different ways; and it should follow (indeed, this would seem to be only the same thing in other words) that different kinds of science are characterized by different kinds of inference. The way in which knowledge is related to the grounds upon which it is based is in fact not one and the same for all kinds of knowledge. That this is so, and that therefore a person who has studied the nature of inference as such—let us call him a logician—can correctly judge the validity of an inference purely by attending to its form, although he has no special knowledge of its subject-matter, is a doctrine of Aristotle; but it is a delusion, although it is still believed by many very able persons who have been trained too exclusively in the Aristotelian logic and the logics that depend upon it for their chief doctrines.[1]

The main scientific achievement of the ancient Greeks lay in mathematics; their main work on the logic of inference was naturally, therefore, devoted to that form of inference which occurs in exact science. When at the end of the Middle Ages the modern natural sciences of observation and experiment began

[1] The reader will perhaps forgive me a personal reminiscence here. I was still a young man when a very distinguished visitor addressed an academic society on an archaeological subject that came within my special field of studies. The point he made was new and revolutionary, and it was easy for me to see that he had proved it up to the hilt. I imagined, foolishly enough, that so lucid and cogent a piece of reasoning must convince any hearer, even one who previously knew nothing about its subject-matter. I was at first much disconcerted, but in the long run greatly instructed, by finding that the demonstration had quite failed to convince the (very learned and acute) logicians in the audience.

to take shape, a revolt against Aristotelian logic was inevitable; in particular, a revolt against the Aristotelian theory of demonstration, which could by no manner of means be made to cover the technique actually used in the new sciences. Thus, by degrees, there came into existence a new logic of inference, based on analysis of the procedure used in the new natural sciences. The text-books of logic in use to-day still bear the marks of this revolt in the distinction they draw between two kinds of inference, 'deductive' and 'inductive'. It was not until late in the nineteenth century that historical thought reached a stage of development comparable with that reached by natural science about the beginning of the seventeenth; but this event has not yet begun to interest those philosophers who write text-books of logic.

The chief characteristic of inference in the exact sciences, the characteristic of which Greek logicians tried to give a theoretical account when they formulated the rules of the syllogism, is a kind of logical compulsion whereby a person who makes certain assumptions is forced, simply by so doing, to make others. He has freedom of choice in two ways: he is not compelled to make the initial assumption (a fact technically expressed by saying that 'the starting-points of demonstrative reasoning are not themselves demonstrable'), and when once he has done so he is still at liberty, whenever he likes, to stop thinking. What he cannot do is to make the initial assumption, to go on thinking, and to arrive at a conclusion different from that which is scientifically correct.

In what is called 'inductive' thinking there is no such compulsion. The essence of the process, here, is that having put certain observations together, and having found that they make a pattern, we extrapolate this pattern indefinitely, just as a man who has plotted a few points on squared paper and says to himself 'the points I have plotted suggest a parabola', proceeds to draw as much of the parabola as he likes in either direction. This is technically described as 'proceeding from the known to the unknown', or 'from the particular to the universal'. It is essential to 'inductive' thinking, though the logicians who have tried to construct a theory of such thinking have not always realized this, that the step so described is never taken under any kind of logical compulsion. The thinker who takes it is logically free to take it or not to take it, just as he pleases. There is nothing in the pattern formed by the observations he or some-one else has actually made which can oblige him to extrapolate in that particular way, or indeed to extrapolate at all. The reason why this very obvious truth has been so often overlooked is that people have been hypnotized by the prestige of Aristote-lian logic into thinking that they see a closer resemblance than actually exists between 'deductive' and 'inductive' thinking, that is, between exact science and the sciences of observation and experiment. In both cases there are, for any given piece of thinking, certain starting-points, traditionally called premisses, and a certain terminal point, traditionally called a conclusion; and in both cases the premisses 'prove' the conclusion. But whereas in exact science this means that they enforce the con-clusion, or make it logically obligatory, in the sciences of observation and experiment it means only that they justify it, that is, authorize anybody to think it who wishes to do so. What they provide, when they are said to 'prove' a certain conclusion, is not compulsion to embrace it, but only permission; a perfectly legitimate sense of the word 'prove' (*approuver*, *probare*), as there should be no need to show.

If in practice this permission, like so many permissions, amounts to virtual compulsion, that is only because the thinker who avails himself of it does not regard himself as free to extra-polate or not, just as he pleases. He regards himself as under an obligation to do so, and to do it in certain ways: obligations which, when we inquire into their history, we find to have their roots in certain religious beliefs about nature and its creator God. It would be out of place to develop this statement more fully here; but not, perhaps, to add that if to-day it seems to some readers paradoxical, that is only because the facts have been obscured by a smoke-screen of propagandist literature, beginning with the 'illuminist' movement of the eighteenth century and prolonged by the 'conflict between religion and science' in the nineteenth, whose purpose was to attack Christian theology in the supposed interests of a 'scientific view of the world' which in fact is based upon it and could not for a moment survive its destruction. Take away Christian theology, and the scientist has no longer any motive for doing what inductive thought gives him permission to do. If he goes on doing it at all, that is only because he is blindly following the conventions of the professional society to which he belongs.

(iii) *Testimony*

Before trying to describe the special characteristics of historical inference positively, we shall find it useful to describe them negatively: to describe something that is very often, but mistakenly, identified with it. Like every science, history is autonomous. The historian has the right, and is under an obligation, to make up his own mind by the methods proper to his own science as to the correct solution of every problem that arises for him in the pursuit of that science. He can never be under any obligation, or have any right, to let someone else make up his mind for him. If anyone else, no matter who, even a very learned historian, or an eyewitness, or a person in the confidence of the man who did the thing he is inquiring into, or even the man who did it himself, hands him on a plate a ready-made answer to his question, all he can do is to reject it: not because he thinks his informant is trying to deceive him, or is himself deceived, but because if he accepts it he is giving up his autonomy as an historian and allowing someone else to do for him what, if he is a scientific thinker, he can only do for himself. There is no need for me to offer the reader any proof of this statement. If he knows anything of historical work, he already knows of his own experience that it is true. If he does not already know that it is true, he does not know enough about history to read this essay with any profit, and the best thing he can do is to stop here and now.

When the historian accepts a ready-made answer to some question he has asked, given him by another person, this other person is called his 'authority', and the statement made by such an authority and accepted by the historian is called 'testimony'. In so far as an historian accepts the testimony of an authority and treats it as historical truth, he obviously forfeits the name of historian; but we have no other name by which to call him.

Now, I am not for a moment suggesting that testimony ought never to be accepted. In the practical life of every day, we constantly and rightly accept the information that other people offer us, believing them to be both well informed and truthful, and having, sometimes, grounds for this belief. I do not even deny, though I do not assert it, that there may be cases in which, as perhaps in some cases of memory, our acceptance of such testimony may go beyond mere belief and deserve the name of knowledge. What I assert is that it can never be historical knowledge, because it can never be scientific knowledge. It is not scientific knowledge because it cannot be vindicated by appeal to the grounds on which it is based. As soon as there are such grounds, the case is no longer one of testimony. When testimony is reinforced by evidence, our acceptance of it is no longer the acceptance of testimony as such; it is the affirmation of something based upon evidence, that is, historical knowledge.

(iv) *Scissors and paste*

There is a kind of history which depends altogether upon the testimony of authorities. As I have already said, it is not really history at all, but we have no other name for it. The method by which it proceeds is first to decide what we want to know about, and then to go in search of statements about it, oral or written, purporting to be made by actors in the events concerned, or by eyewitnesses of them, or by persons repeating what actors or eyewitnesses have told them, or have told their informants, or those who informed their informants, and so on. Having found in such a statement something relevant to his purpose, the historian excerpts it and incorporates it, translated if necessary and recast into what he considers a suitable style, in his own history. As a rule, where he has many statements to draw upon, he will find that one of them tells him what another does not; so both or all of them will be incorporated. Sometimes he will find that one of them contradicts another; then, unless he can find a way of reconciling them, he must decide to leave one out; and this, if he is conscientious, will involve him in a critical consideration of the contradictory authorities' relative degree of trustworthiness. And sometimes one of them, or possibly even all of them, will tell him a story which he simply cannot believe, a story characteristic, perhaps, of the superstitions or prejudices of the author's time or the circle in which he lived, but not credible to a more enlightened age, and therefore to be omitted.

History constructed by excerpting and combining the testimonies of different authorities I call scissors-and-paste history. I repeat that it is not really history at all, because it does not satisfy the necessary conditions of science; but until lately it was the only kind of history in existence, and a great deal of the history people are still reading to-day, and even a good deal of what people are still writing, belongs to this type. Consequently people who know little about history (some of whom, in spite of my recent farewell, may still be reading these pages) will say with some impatience: 'Why, this thing that you say is not history, is just history itself; scissors and paste, that is what history is; and that is why history is not a science, which is a fact that everybody knows, in spite of groundless claims by professional historians magnifying their office'. I shall therefore say a little more about the vicissitudes of scissors-and-paste history.

Scissors and paste was the only historical method known to the later Greco-Roman world or the Middle Ages. It existed in its simplest form. An historian collected testimony, spoken or written, using his own judgement as to its trustworthiness, and put it together for publication: the work which he did on it being partly literary—the presentation of his material as a connected, homogeneous, and convincing narrative—and partly rhetorical, if I may use that word to indicate the fact that most ancient and medieval historians aimed at proving a thesis, in particular some philosophical or political or theological thesis.

It was only in the seventeenth century, when the post-medieval reform of natural science had attained completion, that historians began to think their house also needed to be set in order. Two new movements in historical method now began. One was a systematic examination of authorities, in order to determine their relative credibility, and in particular to establish principles according to which this determination should be carried out. The other was a movement to broaden the basis of history by making use of non-literary sources, such as coins and inscriptions and suchlike relics of antiquity which hitherto had been of interest not to historians but only to collectors of curiosities.

The first of these movements did not overstep the limits of scissors-and-paste history, but it permanently altered its character. As soon as it became understood that a given statement, made by a given author, must never be accepted for historical truth until the credibility of the author in general and of this statement in particular had been systematically inquired into, the word 'authority' disappeared from the vocabulary of historical method, except as an archaistic survival; for the man who makes the statement came henceforth to be regarded not as someone whose word must be taken for the truth of what he says, which is what was meant by calling him an authority, but as someone who has voluntarily placed himself in the witness-box for cross-examination. The document hitherto called an authority now acquired a new status, properly described by calling it a 'source', a word indicating simply that it contains the statement, without any implications as to its value. That is *sub judice*; and it is the historian who judges.

This is 'critical history', as it was worked out from the seventeenth century onwards, and officially acclaimed in the nineteenth as the apotheosis of the historical consciousness. There are two things to observe about it: that it was still only a form of scissors and paste; and that it had already, in principle, been superseded by something very different.

(1) The problem of which historical criticism offers a solution is a problem interesting to nobody but the practitioner of scissors-and-paste history. The presupposition of the problem is that in a certain source we have found a certain statement which bears on our subject. The problem is: Shall we incorporate this statement in our own narrative or not? The methods of historical criticism are intended to solve this problem in one or other of two ways: affirmatively or negatively. In the first case, the excerpt is passed as fit for the scrap-book; in the second, it is consigned to the waste-paper basket.

(2) But many historians in the nineteenth century, and even in the eighteenth, were aware that this dilemma was fallacious. It was by now a commonplace that if in some source you found a statement which for some reason could not be accepted as literally true, you must not on that account reject it as worthless. It might be a way, perhaps a well-established way according to the custom of the time when it was written, of saying something which you, through ignorance of that custom, did not recognize as its meaning.

The first person to make this point was Vico, at the beginning of the eighteenth century. It is true that in Germany, the home of 'critical history' in the late eighteenth and early nineteenth centuries, the importance of Vico's work was not as widely recognized as it ought to have been; but he was not entirely unknown there; indeed, some very famous German scholars, like F. A. Wolf, actually borrowed some of his ideas. Now, any-one who had read Vico, or even a second-hand version of some of his ideas, must have known that the important question about any statement contained in a source is not whether it is true or false, but what it means. And to ask what it means is to step right outside the world of scissors-and-paste history into a world where history is not written by copying out the testimony of the best sources, but by coming to your own conclusions.

Critical history is of interest to the student of historical method to-day only as the final form taken by scissors-and-paste history on the eve of its dissolution. I will not venture to name any historian, or even any historical work, as one from which the last traces of it have disappeared. But I will venture to say that any historian (if there is any) who practises it consistently, or any historical work written entirely on this method, is at least a century out of date.

So much for one of the two movements which gave new life to history in the seventeenth century. The other, the archaeological movement, was totally hostile to the principles of scissors-and-paste history, and could have arisen only when those principles were moribund. No very profound knowledge of coins and inscriptions is needed in order to realize that the assertions they make are by no means uniformly trustworthy, and indeed are to be judged more as propaganda than as statements of fact. Yet this gives them an historical value of their own; for propaganda, too, has its history.

If any reader still thinks that history as practised to-day is a scissors-and-paste affair, and is willing to go to a little trouble in order to settle the question, let him take the history of Greece down to the end of the Peloponnesian War, which I mention as an example peculiarly favourable to himself because Herodotus and Thucydides have there maintained the position of 'authorities' to a quite peculiar degree, and compare in detail the account of it given by Grote with that given in the *Cambridge Ancient History*. Let him mark in each book every sentence of which he can find the original in Herodotus or Thucydides; and by the time he is through with the job he will have learnt something about how historical method has changed in the last hundred years.

(v) *Historical inference*

In (ii) it was pointed out that proof might be either compulsive, as in exact science, where the nature of inference is such that nobody can affirm the premisses without being obliged to affirm the conclusion also, or permissive, as in 'inductive' science, where all a proof can do is to justify the thinker in affirming its conclusion, granted that he wishes to do so. An inductive argument with a negative conclusion is compulsive, that is to say it absolutely forbids the thinker from affirming what he wishes to affirm; with a positive conclusion, it is never more than permissive.

If history means scissors-and-paste history, the only kind of proof known to the historian is of this latter kind. For the scissors-and-paste historian, there is only one kind of problem which is capable of being settled by any sort of argument. This is the problem whether to accept or reject a certain piece of testimony bearing upon the question in which he is interested. The sort of argument by which he settles a problem of this kind is, of course, historical criticism. If criticism leads him to a negative conclusion, viz. that the statement or its author is untrustworthy, this forbids him to accept it, just as a negative result in an 'inductive' argument (for example, a result showing that events of the kind in which he is interested happen in the absence of that kind of event which he hopes to identify as their cause) forbids the inductive scientist to affirm the view he hoped to affirm. If criticism leads him to a positive conclusion, the most it gives him is a *nihil obstat*. For the positive conclusion is in effect that the man who made the statement is not known to be either ignorant or mendacious, and that the statement itself bears upon it no recognizable marks of being untrue. But it may be untrue for all that: and the man who made it, though in general he bears a good name for being well informed and honest, may on this one occasion have fallen a victim to misinformation about his facts, misunderstanding of them, or a desire to suppress or distort what he knew or believed to be the truth.

To avert a possible misunderstanding, it may be added here

that one might think there was another kind of problem for the scissors-and-paste historian, beside the kind which consists in whether to accept or reject a given piece of testimony, which therefore has to be settled by methods other than those of historical criticism: the problem, namely, of what implications follow from a piece of testimony that he has accepted, or would follow if he did accept it. But this is not a problem specially belonging to scissors-and-paste history; it is a problem which arises in history or pseudo-history of any kind whatever, and indeed in any kind of science or pseudo-science. It is simply the general problem of implication. When it occurs in scissors-and-paste history, however, it presents one peculiar feature. If a certain statement coming to the historian by way of testimony has a certain implication, and if this implicational relation is a compulsive one, nevertheless if the inference which leads him to accept the testimony is only permissive the same permissive character attaches to his assertion of its implication. If he has only borrowed his neighbour's cow, and she has a calf in his field, he cannot claim the calf as his own property. Any answer to the question whether the scissors-and-paste historian is obliged or only permitted to accept certain testimony carries with it a corresponding answer to the question whether he is obliged or only permitted to accept the implications of that testimony.

One hears it said that history is 'not an exact science'. The meaning of this I take to be that no historical argument ever proves its conclusion with that compulsive force which is characteristic of exact science. Historical inference, the saying seems to mean, is never compulsive, it is at best permissive; or, as people sometimes rather ambiguously say, it never leads to certainty, only to probability. Many historians of the present writer's generation, brought up at a time when this proverb was accepted by the general opinion of intelligent persons (I say nothing of the few who were a generation ahead of their time), must be able to recollect their excitement on first discovering that it was wholly untrue, and that they were actually holding in their hands an historical argument which left nothing to caprice, and admitted of no alternative conclusion, but proved its point as conclusively as a demonstration in mathematics. Many of these, again, must be able to recollect the shock of discovering on reflection that the proverb was not, strictly speaking, an error about history, history as they were practising it, the science of history, but a truth about something else, namely scissors-and-paste history.

If any reader wishes to rise here on a point of order and protest that a philosophical question, which ought therefore to be settled by reasoning, is being illegitimately disposed of by reference to the authority of historians, and quote against me the good old story about the man who said 'I'm not arguing, I'm telling you', I can only admit that the cap fits. I am not arguing; I am telling him.

Is this wrong of me? The question I want settled is whether an inference of the kind used in scientific history, as distinct from scissors-and-paste history, yields compulsion or only permission to embrace its conclusion. Suppose the question had been not about history but about mathematics. Suppose somebody had wanted to know whether Euclid's proof of what is called Pythagoras' theorem compels or merely permits a man to adopt the view that the square on the hypotenuse is equal to the sum of the squares on the other two sides. I speak with submission; but for myself I can think of only one thing that a sensible man in that situation would do. He would try to find somebody whose mathematical education had got as far as Euclid I. 47, and ask him. And if he did not like his answer, he would look for other people similarly qualified to give one, and ask them. If all else failed to convince him, he would have to get down to it and study the elements of plane geometry for himself.

The one thing that he will not do, if he is a man of any intelligence, is to say 'This is a philosophical question, and the only answer I will be satisfied with is a philosophical answer'. He can call it anything he pleases; he cannot alter the fact that the only way of knowing whether a given type of argument is cogent or not is to learn how to argue that way, and find out. Meanwhile, the second best thing is to take the word of people who have done so for themselves.

(vi) *Pigeon-holing*

Scissors-and-paste historians who have become disgusted with the work of copying out other people's statements, and, conscious of having brains, feel a laudable desire to use them, are often found satisfying this desire by inventing a system of pigeon-holes in which to arrange their learning. This is the origin of all those schemes and patterns into which history has again and again, with surprising docility, allowed itself to be forced by such men as Vico, with his pattern of historical cycles based on Greco-Roman speculations; Kant, with his proposal for a 'universal history from a cosmopolitan point of view'; Hegel, who followed Kant in conceiving universal history as the progressive realization of human freedom; Comte and Marx, two very great men who followed Hegel's lead each in his own way; and so on down to Flinders Petrie, Oswald Spengler, and Arnold Toynbee in our own time, whose affinities are less with Hegel than with Vico.

Although we find it as late as the twentieth century and as early as the eighteenth, not to mention isolated occurrences even earlier, this impulse towards arranging the whole of history in a single scheme (not a chronological scheme merely, but a qualitative scheme, in which 'periods' each with its own pervasive character follow one another in time, according to a pattern which may be necessary *a priori* on logical grounds, or may be forced upon our minds by the fact of its frequent repetition, or may be a bit of both) is in the main a nineteenth-century phenomenon. It belongs to the period when scissors-and-paste history was on its last legs; when people were becoming dissatisfied with it but had not yet broken away from it. This is why the people who have indulged it have been, in general, men with a high degree of intelligence and a real talent for history, but a talent which has been to some extent thwarted and baffled by the limitations of scissors and paste.

It is typical of this condition that some of them described their pigeon-holing enterprise as 'raising history to the rank of a science'. History as they found it meant scissors-and-paste history; that, obviously, was no science, because there was nothing autonomous, nothing creative, about it; it was merely the transhipment of ready-made information from one mind into another. They were conscious that history might be something more than this. It might have, and it ought to have, the characteristics of a science. But how was this to be brought about? At this point the analogy of the natural sciences came, they thought, to their aid. It had been a commonplace ever since Bacon that a natural science began by collecting facts, and then went on to construct theories, that is, to extrapolate the patterns discernible in the facts already collected. Very well: let us put together all the facts that are known to historians, look for patterns in them, and then extrapolate these patterns into a theory of universal history.

It proved to be not at all a difficult task for anybody with an active mind and a taste for hard work. For there was no need to collect all the facts known to historians. Any large collection of facts, it was found, revealed patterns in plenty; and extrapolating such patterns into the remote past, about which there was very little information, and into the future, about which there was none, gave the 'scientific' historian just that sense of power which scissors-and-paste history denied him. After being taught to believe that he, as an historian, could never know anything except what his authorities told him, he found himself discovering, as he fancied, that this lesson had been a fraud; that by converting history into a science he could ascertain, entirely for himself, things that his authorities had concealed from him or did not know.

This was a delusion. The value of each and all of these pigeon-holing schemes, if that means their value as means for discovering historical truths not ascertainable by the interpretation of evidence, was exactly nil. And in fact none of them ever had any scientific value at all; for it is not enough that science should be autonomous or creative, it must also be cogent or objective; it must impress itself as inevitable on anyone who is able and willing to consider the grounds upon which it is based, and to think for himself what the conclusions are to which they point. That is what none of these schemes can do. They are the offspring of caprice. If any of them has ever been accepted by any considerable body of persons beside the one who invented it, that is not because it has struck them as scientifically cogent, but because it has become the orthodoxy of what is in fact, though not necessarily in name, a religious community. This was to some extent achieved by Comtism, and to a much greater extent by Marxism. In these cases, or at any rate in the case of Marxism, historical schemes of the kind in question proved to have an important magical value, as providing a focus for emotions and in consequence an incentive to action. In other cases they have had an amusement value, not without its function in the life of a jaded scissors-and-paste man.

And the delusion was not complete. The hope that scissors-and-paste history would one day be replaced by a new kind of history that should be genuinely scientific was a well-grounded hope, which has in fact been realized. The hope that this new kind of history would enable the historian to know things that his authorities could not or would not tell him was also well grounded, and has also been fulfilled. How these things have happened, we shall very soon see.

(vii) *Who killed John Doe?*

When John Doe was found, early one Sunday morning, lying across his desk with a dagger through his back, no one expected that the question who did it would be settled by means of testimony. It was not likely that anyone saw the murder being done. It was even less likely that someone in the murderer's confidence would give him away. It was least likely of all that the murderer would walk into the village police-station and denounce himself. In spite of this, the public demanded that he should be brought to justice, and the police had hopes of doing it; though the only clue was a little fresh green paint on the handle of the dagger, like the fresh green paint on the iron gate between John Doe's garden and the rector's.

This was not because they hoped that, in time, testimony would be forthcoming. On the contrary, when it did come, in the shape of a visit from an elderly neighbouring spinster asserting that she killed John Doe with her own hand because he had made a dastardly attempt upon her virtue, even the village constable (not an exceptionally bright lad, but kindly) advised her to go home and have some aspirin. Later in the day the village poacher came along and said that he had seen the squire's gamekeeper climbing in at John Doe's study window; testimony which was treated with even less deference. Finally the rector's daughter, in a state of great agitation, rushed in and said she had done it herself; the only effect of which was to make the village constable ring up the local Inspector and remind him that the girl's young man, Richard Roe, was a medical student, and presumably knew where to find a man's heart ; and that he had spent Saturday night at the rectory, within a stone's throw of the dead man's house.

There had been a thunderstorm that night, with heavy rain, between twelve and one ; and the Inspector, when he questioned the rectory parlour-maid (for the living was a good one), was told that Mr. Roe's shoes had been very wet in the morning. Questioned, Richard admitted having gone out in the middle of the night, but refused to say where or why.

John Doe was a blackmailer. For years he had been black-mailing the rector, threatening to publish the facts about a certain youthful escapade of his dead wife. Of this escapade the rector's supposed daughter, born six months after marriage, was the fruit ; and John Doe had letters in his possession that proved it. By now he had absorbed the whole of the rector's private fortune, and on the morning of the fatal Saturday he demanded an instalment of his wife's, which she had left to him in trust for her child. The rector made up his mind to end it. He knew that John Doe sat at his desk late into the night ; he knew that behind him, as he sat, there was a french window on the left and a trophy of Eastern weapons on the right ; and that on hot nights the window was left open until he went to bed. At midnight, wearing gloves, he slipped out ; but Richard, who had noticed his state of mind and was troubled about it, happened to be leaning out of his window and saw the rector cross the garden. He hurried into his clothes and followed ; but by the time he reached the garden the rector was gone. At this moment the thunderstorm broke. Meanwhile the rector's plan had succeeded perfectly. John Doe was asleep, his head fallen forward on a pile of old letters. Only after the dagger had reached his heart did the rector look at them, and see his wife's handwriting. The envelopes were addressed ' John Doe, Esq.' Until that moment, he had never known who his wife's seducer had been.

It was Detective-Inspector Jenkins of Scotland Yard, called in by the Chief Constable at the entreaty of his old friend's little girl, who found in the rectory dustbin a lot of ashes, mostly from writing paper, but including some from leather, probably a pair of gloves. The wet paint on John Doe's garden gate—he had painted it himself that day, after tea—explained why the gloves might have been destroyed; and among the ashes were metal buttons bearing the name of a famous glove-maker in Oxford Street whom the rector always patronized. More of John Doe's paint was found on the right cuff of a jacket, ruined as to shape by a recent wetting, which on Monday the rector bestowed on a deserving parishioner. The Detective-Inspector was severely blamed, later on, for allowing the rector to see in what direction his inquiries were tending, and thus giving him an opportunity to take cyanide and cheat the hangman.

The methods of criminal detection are not at every point identical with those of scientific history, because their ultimate purpose is not the same. A criminal court has in its hands the life and liberty of a citizen, and in a country where the citizen is regarded as having rights the court is therefore bound to do something and do it quickly. The time taken to arrive at a decision is a factor in the value (that is, the justice) of the decision itself. If any juror says: 'I feel certain that a year hence, when we have all reflected on the evidence at leisure, we shall be in a better position to see what it means,' the reply will be: 'There is something in what you say; but what you propose is impossible. Your business is not just to give a verdict; it is to give a verdict now; and here you stay until you do it.' This is why a jury has to content itself with something less than scientific (historical) proof, namely with that degree of assurance or belief which would satisfy it in any of the practical affairs of daily life.

The student of historical method will hardly find it worth his while, therefore, to go closely into the rules of evidence, as these are recognized in courts of law. For the historian is under no obligation to make up his mind within any stated time. Nothing matters to him except that his decision, when he reaches it, shall be right: which means, for him, that it shall follow inevitably from the evidence.

So long as this is borne in mind, however, the analogy between legal methods and historical methods is of some value for the understanding of history; of sufficient value, I think, to justify my having put before the reader in outline the above sample of a literary genre which in the absence of any such motive it would, of course, be beneath his dignity to notice.

(viii) *The question*

Francis Bacon, lawyer and philosopher, laid it down in one of his memorable phrases that the natural scientist must 'put Nature to the question'. What he was denying, when he wrote this, was that the scientist's attitude towards nature should be one of respectful attentiveness, waiting upon her utterances and building his theories on the basis of what she chose to vouchsafe him. What he was asserting was two things at once: first, that the scientist must take the initiative, deciding for himself what he wants to know and formulating this in his own mind in the shape of a question; and secondly, that he must find means of compelling nature to answer, devising tortures under which she can no longer hold her tongue. Here, in a single brief epigram, Bacon laid down once for all the true theory of experimental science.

It is also, though Bacon did not know this, the true theory of historical method. In scissors-and-paste history the historian takes up a pre-Baconian position. His attitude towards his authorities, as the very word shows, is one of respectful attentiveness. He waits to hear what they choose to tell him, and lets them tell it in their own way and at their own time. Even when he has invented historical criticism, and his authorities have become mere sources, this attitude is at bottom unchanged. There is a change, but it is only superficial. It consists merely in the adoption of a technique for dividing witnesses into sheep and goats. One class is disqualified from giving testimony; the other is treated exactly as authorities were treated under the old dispensation. But in scientific history, or history proper, the Baconian revolution has been accomplished. The scientific historian no doubt spends a great deal of time reading the same books that the scissors-and-paste historian used to read—Herodotus, Thucydides, Livy, Tacitus, and so forth—but he reads them in an entirely different spirit; in fact, a Baconian spirit. The scissors-and-paste historian reads them in a simply receptive spirit, to find out what they said. The scientific historian reads them with a question in his mind, having taken the initiative by deciding for himself what he wants to find out from them. Further, the scissors-and-paste historian reads them on the understanding that what they did not tell him in so many words he would never find out from them at all; the scientific historian puts them to the torture, twisting a passage ostensibly about something quite different into an answer to the question he has decided to ask. Where the scissors-and-paste historian said quite confidently 'There is nothing in such-and-such an author about such-and-such a subject', the scientific or Baconian historian will reply 'Oh, isn't there? Do you not see that in this passage about a totally different matter it is implied that the author took such-and-such a view of the subject about which you say his text contains nothing?'

To illustrate from my fable. The village constable does not arrest the rector's daughter and beat her periodically with a rubber truncheon until she tells him that she thinks Richard did the murder. What he tortures is not her body, but her statement that she killed John Doe. He begins by using the methods of critical history. He says to himself: 'The murder was done by somebody with a good deal of strength and some knowledge of anatomy. This girl certainly hasn't the first, and probably hasn't the second; at any rate, I know she has never attended ambulance classes. Further, if she had done it she wouldn't be in such a hurry to accuse herself. The story is a lie.'

At this point the critical historian would lose interest in the story and throw it in the waste-paper basket: the scientific historian begins to be interested in it, and tests it for chemical reactions. This he is able to do because, being a scientific thinker, he knows what questions to ask. 'Why is she telling a lie? Because she is shielding someone. Whom is she shielding? Either her father or her young man. Is it her father? No; fancy the rector! Therefore it is her young man. Are her suspicions of him well founded? They might be; he was here at the time; he is strong enough; and he knows enough anatomy.' The reader will recollect that in criminal detection probability is required, of a degree sufficient for the conduct of daily life, whereas in history we demand certainty. Apart from that, the parallel is complete. The village constable (not a clever lad, as I explained; but a scientific thinker does not have to be clever, he has to know his job, that is, know what questions to ask) has been trained in the elements of police work, and this training enables him to know what questions to ask and thus to interpret the untrue statement that she did it herself into evidence for the true conclusion that she suspects Richard Roe.

The constable's only mistake was that in the excitement of answering the question 'Whom does this girl suspect?' he lost sight of the question 'Who killed John Doe?' This is where Inspector Jenkins, not so much because he was a cleverer man as because he had learned the job more thoroughly, had the advantage of him. The way I see the Inspector going to work is like this.

'Why does the rector's daughter suspect Richard Roe? Probably because she knows that he was involved in something queer which happened at the rectory that night. We know that one queer thing happened at the rectory: Richard was out in the storm, and that was quite enough to make the girl suspicious. But what we want to know is, did he kill John Doe? If he did, when did he do it? After the thunderstorm broke, or before? Not before, because here are his tracks going both ways in the mud of the rectory garden path: you see them beginning a few yards from the garden door, going away from the house; so that is where he was, and that is the direction he was going in, when the downpour began. Well, did he carry mud into John Doe's study? No: none there. Did he take off his shoes before going in? Think a moment. What position was John Doe in when he was stabbed? Was he leaning back or sitting upright in his chair? No; because the chair would have protected his back. He must have been leaning right forward. Possibly, indeed probably, asleep in the position in which he still lies. How exactly did the murderer proceed? If Doe was asleep, nothing easier: step quietly inside, take the dagger and in it goes. If Doe was awake and merely leaning forward, the same might be done, but not so easily. Now, did the murderer pause outside to take off his shoes? Impossible. In either case, speed was the first thing necessary: the job had to be done before he leaned back, or woke up. So the absence of mud in the study lets Richard out.

'Then, once more, why did he go into the garden? For a walk? Not with that thunderstorm growling about. For a smoke? They smoke all over the house. To meet the girl? No signs that she was in the garden; and why should he? They had had the drawing-room to themselves ever since dinner, and the rector isn't one to shoo young people off to bed. Broad-minded sort of chap. Had trouble, I shouldn't wonder. Now, why did young Richard go into that garden? Something must have been

going on there. Something queer. A second queer thing that
night at the rectory, one we don't know about.

'What could it have been? If the murderer had come from
the rectory, which that paint suggests he did, and if Richard
saw him from his window, it might have been that; because the
murderer got to Doe's house before the rain began, and Richard
was caught in it ten yards from the garden door. Just time.
Let's see what would follow, if the murderer did come from the
rectory. Probably he went back there afterwards. No tracks in
the mud; why? Because he knew the garden well enough to
keep on the grass all the way, even in that pitch darkness. If so,
he knew the rectory very well and also spent the night there.
Was it the rector himself?

'Now why does Richard refuse to say what made him go into
the garden? It must be to keep somebody out of trouble;
almost certainly, trouble about the murder. Not himself,
because I've told him we know he didn't do it. Somebody else.
Who? Might be the rector. Can't think of anybody else it might
be. Suppose it was the rector; how would he have worked it?
Very easy. Go out about midnight, in tennis shoes and gloves.
Quite silent on the rectory paths—no gravel on them. Reach
that little iron gate into John Doe's garden. Does he know it's
wet paint? Probably not; it was only painted after tea. So he
grabs it. Paint on glove. Probably paint on jacket too. Walk
on the grass to Doe's study window. Doe is leaning forward in
his chair, or likelier asleep. Now for a bit of quick work, easy for
a good tennis-player. Left foot inside, right foot to the right,
grab that dagger thing, left foot forward, in it goes.

'But what had John Doe been doing at that desk? Nothing
on it, you know. Queer. Does a man spend the evening sitting
at an empty desk? There must have been something there.
What do we know about the chap at the Yard? Blackmailer,
that's it. Had he been blackmailing the rector? and gloating
over the letters, or what not, all evening? And did the rector,
if it was the rector, find him asleep on top of them? Well, that's
not our business. We'll pass it on to the defence, for what it's
worth. I'd rather not use a motive like that in prosecution.

'Now then, Jonathan, don't go ahead too fast. You've got
him in there, you've got to get him out again. What exactly
does he do? About now it begins to rain cats and dogs. Back he

goes through it. More paint at the gate. Walk on grass, no mud brought in. Back in the house. All soaked: gloves covered with paint, too. Wipe paint off door-knob. Lock up. Put letters (if it was letters), and anyhow gloves, in the hot-water furnace— the ashes may be in the dustbin now. Put all clothes in the bath-room cupboard; they will be dry by morning. And so they are; but the jacket will be hopelessly out of shape. Now what did he do with that jacket? First, he'd look for paint on it. If he found paint, he'd have to destroy the thing; and I pity the man who tries to destroy a jacket in a house overrun with women. If he didn't find any, he would certainly give it away on the quiet to a poor man.

'Well, well: there's a pretty story for you; but how can we tell whether it's true or not? There are two questions we've got to ask. First: can we find the ashes of those gloves? And the metal buttons, if they are like most of his gloves? If we can, the story is true. And if we can find a lot of writing-paper ash as well, the blackmail bit is true, too. Second: where is that jacket? Because if we can find the tiniest speck of John Doe's paint on it, there's our case.'

I have gone to some length in this analysis because I wish to bring home to the reader the following points about the questioning activity which is the dominant factor in history, as it is in all scientific work.

(1) Every step in the argument depends on asking a question. The question is the charge of gas, exploded in the cylinder-head, which is the motive force of every piston-stroke. But the metaphor is not adequate, because each new piston-stroke is produced not by exploding another charge of the same old mixture but by exploding a charge of a new kind. No one with any grasp of method will go on asking the same question all the time, 'Who killed John Doe?' He asks a new question every time. And it is not enough to cover the ground by having a catalogue of all the questions that have to be asked, and asking every one of them sooner or later: they must be asked in the right order. Descartes, one of the three great masters of the Logic of Questioning (the other two being Socrates and Bacon), insisted upon this as a cardinal point in scientific method, but so far as modern works on logic are concerned, Descartes might never have lived. Modern logicians are in a conspiracy to

pretend that a scientist's business is to 'make judgements', or 'assert propositions', or 'apprehend facts', and also to 'assert' or 'apprehend' the relations between them; suggesting that they have no experience whatever of scientific thinking, and wish to palm off, as an account of science, an account of their own haphazard, unsystematic, unscientific consciousness.

(2) These questions are not put by one man to another man, in the hope that the second man will enlighten the first man's ignorance by answering them. They are put, like all scientific questions, to the scientist by himself. This is the Socratic idea which Plato was to express by defining thought as 'the dialogue of the soul with itself', where Plato's own literary practice makes it clear that by dialogue he meant a process of question and answer. When Socrates taught his young pupils by asking them questions, he was teaching them how to ask questions of themselves, and showing them by examples how amazingly the obscurest subjects can be illuminated by asking oneself intelligent questions about them instead of simply gaping at them, according to the prescription of our modern anti-scientific epistemologists, in the hope that when we have made our minds a perfect blank we shall 'apprehend the facts'.

(ix) *Statement and evidence*

It is characteristic of scissors-and-paste history, from its least critical to its most critical form, that it has to do with ready-made statements, and that the historian's problem about any one of these statements is whether he shall accept it or not: where accepting it means reasserting it as a part of his own historical knowledge. Essentially, history for the scissors-and-paste historian means repeating statements that other people have made before him. Hence he can get to work only when he is supplied with ready-made statements on the subjects about which he wants to think, write, and so forth. It is the fact that these statements have to be found by him ready-made in his sources that makes it impossible for the scissors-and-paste historian to claim the title of a scientific thinker, for this fact makes it impossible to attribute to him that autonomy which is everywhere essential to scientific thought; where by autonomy I mean the condition of being one's own authority, making statements or taking action on one's own initiative and not because those statements or actions are authorized or pre-scribed by anyone else.

It follows that scientific history contains no ready-made state-ments at all. The act of incorporating a ready-made statement into the body of his own historical knowledge is an act which, for a scientific historian, is impossible. Confronted with a ready-made statement about the subject he is studying, the scientific historian never asks himself: 'Is this statement true or false?', in other words 'Shall I incorporate it in my history of that subject or not?' The question he asks himself is: 'What does this statement mean?' And this is not equivalent to the question 'What did the person who made it mean by it?', although that is doubtless a question that the historian must ask, and must be able to answer. It is equivalent, rather, to the question 'What light is thrown on the subject in which I am interested by the fact that this person made this statement, meaning by it what he did mean?' This might be expressed by saying that the scientific historian does not treat statements as statements but as evi-dence: not as true or false accounts of the facts of which they profess to be accounts, but as other facts which, if he knows the right questions to ask about them, may throw light on those facts. Thus in my fable the rector's daughter tells the constable that she killed John Doe. As a scientific historian, he begins attending seriously to this statement at the point where he stops treating it as a statement, that is, as a true or false account of her having done the murder, and begins treating the fact that she makes it as a fact which may be of service to him. It is of service to him because he knows what questions to ask about it, beginning with the question: 'Now why does she tell this story?' The scissors-and-paste historian is interested in the 'content', as it is called, of statements: he is interested in what they state. The scientific historian is interested in the fact that they are made.

A statement to which an historian listens, or one which he reads, is to him a ready-made statement. But the statement that such a statement is being made is not a ready-made state-ment. If he says to himself 'I am now reading or hearing a statement to such and such effect', he is himself making a state-ment; but it is not a second-hand statement, it is autonomous. He makes it on his own authority. And it is this autonomous statement that is the scientific historian's starting-point. The evidence from which the constable infers that the rector's daughter suspects Richard Roe is not her statement 'I killed John Doe', but his own statement 'the rector's daughter tells me that she killed John Doe'.

If the scientific historian gets his conclusions not from the statement that he finds ready-made, but from his own autonomous statement of the fact that such statements are made, he can get conclusions even when no statements are made to him. The premisses of his argument are his own autonomous statements: there is no need for these autonomous statements to be themselves statements about other statements. To illustrate once more from the story of John Doe. The premisses from which the Detective-Inspector argued to the innocence of Richard Roe were all premisses of the Detective-Inspector's own stating, autonomous statements resting on no authority but his own: and not one of them was a statement about statements made by anybody else. The essential points were that Richard Roe had got his shoes muddy while going away from the rectory, that no mud was to be seen in John Doe's study, and that the circumstances of the murder had been such that he would not have stopped to clean or remove his shoes. Each of these three points, in its turn, was the conclusion of an inference, and the statements upon which they severally rested were no more statements about other people's statements than were these three points themselves. Again: the ultimate case against the rector did not logically depend upon any statements made by the Detective-Inspector about statements made by other persons. It depended upon the presence of certain objects in a certain dustbin, and of certain paint-smears on the cuff of a jacket made in the conventional clerical style and shrunk by wetting; and these facts were vouched for by his own observation. I do not mean that the scientific historian can work better when no statements are made to him about the subjects on which he is working; it would be a pedantical way of avoiding scissors-and-paste history, to avoid occasions of this type which might be a trap for the weaker brethren; what I mean is that he is not dependent on such statements being made.

This is important because it settles by appeal to principle a controversy which, even if it is no longer so urgent as it was, has not yet ceased to echo in the minds of historians. This was the controversy between those who maintained that history was ultimately dependent on 'written sources', and those who maintained that it could also be constructed from 'unwritten sources'. The terms were unhappily chosen. 'Written sources' were not conceived as excluding oral sources, or as having any special connexion with handwriting as distinct from chiselling in stone or the like. 'Written sources', in fact, meant sources containing ready-made statements asserting or implying alleged facts belonging to the subject in which the historian was interested. 'Unwritten sources' meant archaeological material, potsherds, and so forth, connected with the same subject. Of course, the word 'source' was in no sense applicable to these, for a source means something from which water or the like is drawn ready made; in the case of history, something from which the historian's statements are drawn ready made, and the point of describing potsherds as 'unwritten sources' was to indicate that, not being texts, they contained no ready-made statements and were therefore not written sources. (Inscribed potsherds or 'ostraka' were, of course, 'written sources'.)

In effect, this was a controversy between people who believed that scissors-and-paste history was the only possible kind and people who, without impugning the validity of scissors-and-paste methods, claimed that there could be history without them. According to my own recollection the controversy was alive, though giving one an impression of obsolescence, in academic circles in this country thirty years ago; all statements of the issue, so far as I can recall them, were extremely confused, and the philosophers of the time, though it gave them an excellent opportunity for doing a useful job of work on a subject of high philosophical interest, cared for none of these things. My impression is that the controversy fizzled out in the feeblest of compromises, the partisans of scissors-and-paste history accepting the principle that 'unwritten sources' could give valid results, but insisting that this could happen only on a very small scale and when they were used as an auxiliary arm to 'written sources'; and only about low matters like industry and commerce, into which an historian with the instincts of a gentleman would not inquire. This amounted to saying that historians brought up to regard history as an affair of scissors and paste were beginning, very timidly, to recognize the possibility of something quite different; but that when they tried to convert this possibility into an actuality they were still too incompletely fledged for any but the shortest flights.

(x) *Question and evidence*

If history means scissors-and-paste history, where the historian depends on ready-made statements for all his knowledge about his subject, and where the texts in which he finds these statements are called his sources, it is easy to define a source in a way which has some practical utility. A source is a text containing a statement or statements about the subject; and this definition has some practical utility because it helps the historian to divide the whole of extant literature, once he has determined his subject, into texts which might serve him as sources, and must therefore be looked at, and those which cannot, and may therefore be ignored. What he has to do is to run over his library shelves, or his bibliography of the period, asking himself at every title: 'Could this contain anything about my subject?' And, in case he cannot give the answer out of his head, aids of several kinds have been provided: notably indexes and specialized or classified bibliographies. Even with all these aids, he may still miss an important piece of testimony, and thus provide sport for his friends; but on any given question the amount of testimony that exists is a finite quantity, and it is theoretically possible to exhaust it.

Theoretically, but not always practically: for the amount may be so large, and some parts of it so difficult of access, that no historian can hope to see it all. And one sometimes hears people complaining that nowadays so much raw material for history is being preserved that the task of using it is becoming impossible; and sighing for the good old days when books were few and libraries small, and an historian could hope to master his subject. What these complaints mean is that the scissors-and-paste historian is on the horns of a dilemma. If he possesses only a small amount of testimony about his subject, he wants more; because any new piece of testimony about it would, if really new, throw new light on it, and might make the view he is actually putting forward untenable. So, however much testimony he has, his zeal as an historian makes him want more.

But if he has a large amount of testimony, it becomes so difficult to manipulate and work up into a convincing narrative that, speaking as a mere weak mortal, he wishes he had less.

Consciousness of this dilemma has often driven men into scepticism about the very possibility of historical knowledge. And quite rightly, if knowledge means scientific knowledge and history means scissors-and-paste history. Scissors-and-paste historians who brush the dilemma aside with the blessed word 'hypercriticism' are only confessing that in their own professional practice they do not find that it troubles them, because they work to such a low standard of scientific cogency that their consciences become anaesthetized. Such cases in contemporary life are highly interesting, because in the history of science one often meets with them and wonders how such extraordinary blindness was possible. The answer is that the people who exhibit it have committed themselves to an impossible task, in this case the task of scissors-and-paste history, and since for practical reasons they cannot back out of it they have to blind themselves to its impossibility. The scissors-and-paste historian protects himself from seeing the truth about his own methods by carefully choosing subjects which he is able to 'get away' with, exactly as the nineteenth-century landscape-painter protected himself from seeing that his theory of landscape was all wrong by choosing what he called paintable subjects. The subjects must be those about which a certain amount of testimony is accessible, not too little and not too much; not so uniform as to give the historian nothing to do, not so divergent as to baffle his endeavours to do it. Practised on these principles, history was at worst a parlour game, and at best an elegant accomplishment. I have used the past tense; I leave it to the conscience of historians who are capable of self-criticism to decide how far I might justly have used the present.

If history means scientific history, for 'source' we must read 'evidence'. And when we try to define 'evidence' in the same spirit in which we defined 'sources', we find it very difficult. There is no short and easy test by which we can decide whether a given book is or is not capable of providing evidence about a given subject, and indeed no reason why we should limit our search to books. Indexes and bibliographies of sources are of no use at all to a scientific historian. This is not to say that he cannot use indexes and bibliographies; he can and does; but they are indexes and bibliographies not of sources but of monographs or the like: not of evidence, but of previous discussions which he can take as a starting-point for his own. Consequently, whereas the books mentioned in a bibliography for the use of a scissors-and-paste historian will be, roughly speaking, valuable in direct proportion to their antiquity, those mentioned in a bibliography for the use of a scientific historian will be, roughly speaking, valuable in direct proportion to their newness.

In my fable there is only one obvious characteristic common to all the pieces of evidence used by the Detective-Inspector in his argument: they are all things observed by himself. If we ask what kind of things, it is not easy to give an answer. They include such things as the existence of certain footprints in certain mud, their number, position, and direction, their resemblance to prints produced by a certain pair of shoes, and the absence of any others; the absence of mud on the floor of a certain room; the position of a dead body, the position of a dagger in its back, and the shape of the chair in which it is sitting; and so on, a most variegated collection. This, I think, we can safely say about it: that no one could possibly know what could or could not find a place in it until he had got all his questions not only formulated but answered. In scientific history anything is evidence which is used as evidence, and no one can know what is going to be useful as evidence until he has had occasion to use it.

Let us put this by saying that in scissors-and-paste history, if we allow ourselves to describe testimony—loosely, I admit—by the name of evidence, there is potential evidence and there is actual evidence. The potential evidence about a subject is all the extant statements about it. The actual evidence is that part of these statements which we decide to accept. But in scientific history the idea of potential evidence disappears; or, if we like to put the same fact in these other words, everything in the world is potential evidence for any subject whatever. This will be a distressing idea to anyone whose notions of historical method are fixed in a scissors-and-paste mould; for how, he will ask, are we to discover what facts are actually of service to us, unless we can first of all round up the facts that might be of service to us? To a person who understands the nature of scientific thinking, whether historical or any other, it will present no difficulty. He will realize that, every time the historian asks a question, he asks it because he thinks he can answer it: that is to say, he has already in his mind a preliminary and tentative idea of the evidence he will be able to use. Not a definite idea about potential evidence, but an indefinite idea about actual evidence. To ask questions which you see no prospect of answering is the fundamental sin in science, like giving orders which you do not think will be obeyed in politics, or praying for what you do not think God will give you in religion. Question and evidence, in history, are correlative. Anything is evidence which enables you to answer your question—the question you are asking now. A sensible question (the only kind of question that a scientifically competent man will ask) is a question which you think you have or are going to have evidence for answering. If you think you have it here and now, the question is an actual question, like the question 'What position was John Doe in when he was stabbed?' If you think you are going to have it the question is a deferred question, like the question 'Who killed John Doe?'

It was a correct understanding of this truth that underlay Lord Acton's great precept, 'Study problems, not periods'. Scissors-and-paste historians study periods; they collect all the extant testimony about a certain limited group of events, and hope in vain that something will come of it. Scientific historians study problems: they ask questions, and if they are good historians they ask questions which they see their way to answering. It was a correct understanding of the same truth that led Monsieur Hercule Poirot to pour scorn on the 'human bloodhound' who crawls about the floor trying to collect everything, no matter what, which might conceivably turn out to be a clue; and to insist that the secret of detection was to use what, with possibly wearisome iteration, he called 'the little grey cells'. You can't collect your evidence before you begin thinking, he meant: because thinking means asking questions (logicians, please note), and nothing is evidence except in relation to some definite question. The difference between Poirot and Holmes in this respect is deeply significant of the change that has taken place in the understanding of historical method in the last forty years. Lord Acton was preaching his doctrine in the heyday of Sherlock Holmes, in his inaugural lecture at Cambridge in 1895;

but it was caviare to the general. In Monsieur Poirot's time, to judge by his sales, the general cannot have too much of it. The revolution which dethroned the principles of scissors-and-paste history, and replaced them by those of scientific history, had become common property.

§ 4. *History as Re-enactment of Past Experience*

How, or on what conditions, can the historian know the past? In considering this question, the first point to notice is that the past is never a given fact which he can apprehend empirically by perception. *Ex hypothesi*, the historian is not an eyewitness of the facts he desires to know. Nor does the historian fancy that he is; he knows quite well that his only possible knowledge of the past is mediate or inferential or indirect, never empirical. The second point is that this mediation cannot be effected by testimony. The historian does not know the past by simply believing a witness who saw the events in question and has left his evidence on record. That kind of mediation would give at most not knowledge but belief, and very ill-founded and improbable belief. And the historian, once more, knows very well that this is not the way in which he proceeds; he is aware that what he does to his so-called authorities is not to believe them but to criticize them. If then the historian has no direct or empirical knowledge of his facts, and no transmitted or testimoniary knowledge of them, what kind of knowledge has he: in other words, what must the historian do in order that he may know them?

My historical review of the idea of history has resulted in the emergence of an answer to this question: namely, that the historian must re-enact the past in his own mind. What we must now do is to look more closely at this idea, and see what it means in itself and what further consequences it implies.

In a general way, the meaning of the conception is easily understood. When a man thinks historically, he has before him certain documents or relics of the past. His business is to discover what the past was which has left these relics behind it. For example, the relics are certain written words; and in that case he has to discover what the person who wrote those words meant by them. This means discovering the thought (in the widest sense of that word: we shall look into its preciser meaning in § 5) which he expressed by them. To discover what this thought was, the historian must think it again for himself.

Suppose, for example, he is reading the Theodosian Code, and has before him a certain edict of an emperor. Merely reading the words and being able to translate them does not amount to knowing their historical significance. In order to do that he must envisage the situation with which the emperor was trying to deal, and he must envisage it as that emperor envisaged it. Then he must see for himself, just as if the emperor's situation were his own, how such a situation might be dealt with; he must see the possible alternatives, and the reasons for choosing one rather than another; and thus he must go through the process which the emperor went through in deciding on this particular course. Thus he is re-enacting in his own mind the experience of the emperor; and only in so far as he does this has he any historical knowledge, as distinct from a merely philological knowledge, of the meaning of the edict.

Or again, suppose he is reading a passage of an ancient philosopher. Once more, he must know the language in a philological sense and be able to construe; but by doing that he has not yet understood the passage as an historian of philosophy must understand it. In order to do that, he must see what the philosophical problem was, of which his author is here stating his solution. He must think that problem out for himself, see what possible solutions of it might be offered, and see why this particular philosopher chose that solution instead of another. This means re-thinking for himself the thought of his author, and nothing short of that will make him the historian of that author's philosophy.

It cannot, I think, be denied by anybody that these descriptions, whatever their ambiguities and shortcomings, do actually call attention to the central feature of all historical thinking. As descriptions of that experience, their general accuracy is beyond question. But they still require a great deal of amplification and explanation; and perhaps the best way of beginning this is to expose them to the criticism of an imaginary objector.

Such an objector might begin by saying that the whole conception is ambiguous. It implies either too little or too much. To re-enact an experience or re-think a thought, he might argue, may mean either of two things. Either it means enacting an experience or performing an act of thought resembling the first, or it means enacting an experience or performing an act of thought literally identical with the first. But no one experience can be literally identical with another, therefore presumably the relation intended is one of resemblance only. But in that case the doctrine that we know the past by re-enacting it is only a version of the familiar and discredited copy-theory of knowledge, which vainly professes to explain how a thing (in this case an experience or act of thought) is known by saying that the knower has a copy of it in his mind. And in the second place, suppose it granted that an experience could be identically repeated, the result would only be an immediate identity between the historian and the person he was trying to understand, so far as that experience was concerned. The object (in this case the past) would be simply incorporated in the subject (in this case the present, the historian's own thought); and instead of answering the question how the past is known we should be maintaining that the past is not known, but only the present. And, it may be asked, has not Croce himself admitted this with his doctrine of the contemporaneity of history?

Here we have two objections, which we must consider in turn. I suppose the person who maintained the first would be implying some such view of experience as this. In every experience, at any rate so far as it is cognitive, there is an act and an object; and two different acts may have the same object. If I read Euclid and find there the statement that the angles at the base of an isosceles triangle are equal, and if I understand what is meant and recognize that it is true, the truth which I recognize, or the proposition which I assert, is the same truth which Euclid recognized, the same proposition which he asserted. But my act of asserting it is not the same act as his; that is sufficiently proved by either of the two facts that they are done by different persons and are done at different times. My act of apprehending the equality of the angles is therefore not a revival of his act, but the performance of another act of the same kind; and what I know by performing that act is not that Euclid knew the angles at the base of an isosceles triangle to be equal, but that they are equal. In order to know the historical fact that Euclid knew them to be equal I shall have not to copy his act (that is, to perform one like it) but to perform a quite different one, the act of thinking that Euclid knew them to be equal. And the question how I manage to achieve this act is not at all illuminated by saying that I repeat Euclid's act of knowing in my own mind; for if repeating his act means apprehending the same truth or asserting the same proposition which he apprehended or asserted, the statement is untrue, for Euclid's proposition 'the angles are equal' and mine 'Euclid knew the angles to be equal' are different; and if repeating his act means performing the same act over again, it is nonsense, for an act cannot be repeated.

On this view, the relation between my act of now thinking 'the angles are equal' and my act of thinking it five minutes ago is a relation of numerical difference and specific identity. The two acts are different acts but acts of the same kind. They thus resemble one another, and either of these acts resembles Euclid's act in the same way; hence the conclusion that the doctrine we are considering is a case of the copy-theory of knowledge.

But is this a true account of the relation between these two acts? Is it the case that when we speak of two persons performing the same act of thought or of one person as performing the same act at two different times, we mean that they are performing different acts of the same kind? It is, I think, clear that we mean nothing of the sort; and that the only reason why anyone should fancy that we do is because he has accepted a dogma that whenever we distinguish two things and yet say that they are the same (which, as everyone admits, we often do) we mean that they are different specimens of the same kind, different instances of the same universal, or different members of the same class. The dogma is not that there is no such thing as identity in difference (nobody believes that), but that there is only one kind of it, namely specific identity in numerical difference. Criticism of the dogma, therefore, turns not on proving that this kind of identity in difference does not exist, but on proving that other kinds exist, and that the case we are considering is one of them.

It is contended by our supposed objector that Euclid's act of thought and mine are not one but two: numerically two though specifically one. It is also contended that my act of now thinking 'the angles are equal' stands in the same relation to my act of thinking 'the angles are equal' five minutes ago. The reason why this seems quite certain to the objector is, I believe, that he conceives an act of thought as something that has its place in the flow of consciousness, whose being is simply its occurrence in that flow. Once it has happened, the flow carries it into the past, and nothing can recall it. Another of the same kind may happen, but not that again.

But what precisely do these phrases mean? Suppose that a person continues for an appreciable time, say five seconds together, to think 'the angles are equal'. Is he performing one act of thought sustained over those five seconds; or is he performing five, or ten, or twenty acts of thought numerically different but specifically identical? If the latter, how many go to five seconds? The objector is bound to answer this question, for the essence of his view is that acts of thought are numerically distinct and therefore numerable. Nor can he defer answering until he has appealed to further research, for example in the psychological laboratory: if he does not already know what constitutes the plurality of acts of thought, the psychological laboratory can never tell him. But any answer he gives must be both arbitrary and self-contradictory. There is no more reason to correlate the unity of a single act of thought with the time-lapse of one second, or a quarter of a second, than with any other. The only possible answer is that the act of thought is one act sustained through five seconds; and the objector, if he likes, may admit this by saying that such identity in a sustained act of thought is 'the identity of a continuant'.

But does a continuant, here, imply continuousness? Suppose that, after thinking 'the angles are equal' for five seconds, the thinker allows his attention to wander for three more; and then, returning to the same subject, again thinks 'the angles are equal'. Have we here two acts of thought and not one, because a time elapsed between them? Clearly not; there is one single act, this time not merely sustained, but revived after an interval. For there is no difference in this case that was not already present in the other. When an act is sustained over five seconds, the activity in the fifth second is just as much separated by a lapse of time from that in the first, as when the intervening seconds are occupied by an activity of a different kind or (if that be possible) by none.

The contention that an act cannot happen twice because the flow of consciousness carries it away is thus false. Its falsity arises from an *ignoratio elenchi*. So far as experience consists of mere consciousness, of sensations and feelings pure and simple, it is true. But an act of thought is not a mere sensation or feeling. It is knowledge, and knowledge is something more than immediate consciousness. The process of knowledge is therefore not a mere flow of consciousness. A person whose consciousness was a mere succession of states, by whatever name these states are called, could have no knowledge whatever. He could not remember his own past states, for (even granting that his states are connected together by certain psychological laws, *ex hypothesi* to him unknowable) he would not remember being burnt but would only fear the fire. Nor could he perceive the world around him; he would fear, but would not recognize that which he feared as the fire. Least of all would he, or anyone else, know that his consciousness was the mere succession of states that it is alleged to be.

If, then, mere consciousness is a succession of states, thought is an activity by which that succession is somehow arrested so as to be apprehended in its general structure: something for which the past is not dead and gone, but can be envisaged together with the present and compared with it. Thought itself is not involved in the flow of immediate consciousness; in some sense it stands outside that flow. Acts of thought certainly happen at definite times; Archimedes discovered the idea of specific gravity at a time when he was in the bath; but they are not related to time in the same way as mere feelings and sensations. It is not only the object of thought that somehow stands outside time; the act of thought does so too: in this sense at least, that one and the same act of thought may endure through a lapse of time and revive after a time when it has been in abeyance.

Take a third case, then, where the interval covers the whole lapse of time from Euclid to myself. If he thought 'the angles are equal' and I now think 'the angles are equal', granted that the time interval is no cause for denying that the two acts are one and the same, is the difference between Euclid and myself ground for denying it? There is no tenable theory of personal identity that would justify such a doctrine. Euclid and I are not (as it were) two different typewriters which, just because they are not the same typewriter, can never perform the same act but only acts of the same kind. A mind is not a machine with various functions, but a complex of activities; and to argue that an act of Euclid's cannot be the same as an act of my own because it forms part of a different complex of activities is merely to beg the question. Granted that the same act can happen twice in different contexts within the complex of my own activities, why should it not happen twice in two different complexes?

The objector, although explicitly denying that this can happen, is covertly assuming that it can and does. He maintains that although the object of two people's acts of thought may be the same, the acts themselves are different. But, in order that this should be said, it is necessary to know 'what someone else is thinking' not only in the sense of knowing the same object that he knows, but in the further sense of knowing the act by which he knows it: for the statement rests on a claim to know not only my own act of knowing but someone else's also, and compare them. But what makes such comparison possible? Anyone who can perform the comparison must be able to reflect 'my act of knowledge is *this*'—and then he repeats it: 'from the way he talks, I can see that his act is *this*'—and then he repeats it. Unless that can be done, the comparison can never be made. But to do this involves the repetition by one mind of another's act of thought: not one like it (that would be the copy-theory of knowledge with a vengeance) but the act itself.

Thought can never be mere object. To know someone else's activity of thinking is possible only on the assumption that this same activity can be re-enacted in one's own mind. In that sense, to know 'what someone is thinking' (or 'has thought') involves thinking it for oneself. To reject this conclusion means denying that we have any right to speak of acts of thought at all, except such as take place in our own minds, and embracing the doctrine that my mind is the only one that exists. Against anyone who accepts that form of solipsism I shall not stay to argue. I am considering how history, as the knowledge of past thoughts (acts of thought), is possible; and I am only concerned to show that it is impossible except on the view that to know another's act of thought involves repeating it for oneself. If a person who rejects that view is driven in consequence to this kind of solipsism, my point is proved.

We now pass to the second objection. It will be said: 'Has not this argument proved too much? It has shown that an act of thought can be not only performed at an instant but sustained over a lapse of time; not only sustained, but revived; not only revived in the experience of the same mind but (on pain of solipsism) re-enacted in another's. But this does not prove the possibility of history. For that, we must be able not only to re-enact another's thought but also to know that the thought we are re-enacting is his. But so far as we re-enact it, it becomes our own; it is merely as our own that we perform it and are aware of it in the performance; it has become subjective, but for that very reason it has ceased to be objective; become present, and therefore ceased to be past. This indeed is just what Oakeshott has explicitly maintained in his doctrine that the historian only arranges *sub specie praeteritorum* what is in reality his own present experience, and what Croce in effect admits when he says that all history is contemporary history.'

The objector is here saying two different things. First, he is saying that mere re-enactment of another's thought does not make historical knowledge; we must also know that we are re-enacting it. Secondly, he is arguing that this addition, the knowledge that we are re-enacting a past thought, is in the nature of the case impossible; since the thought as re-enacted is now our own, and our knowledge of it is limited to our own present awareness of it as an element in our own experience.

The first point is obviously right. The fact that someone performs an act of thought which another has performed before him does not make him an historian. It cannot, in such a case, be said that he is an historian without knowing it: unless he knows that he is thinking historically, he is not thinking historically. Historical thinking is an activity (and not the only one, unless the others are somehow parts of it) which is a function of self-consciousness, a form of thought possible only to a mind which knows itself to be thinking in that way.

The second point is that the *condicio sine qua non* demanded by the first can never be realized. The argument adduced to prove this point is important; but let us look first at the point proved. It is that although we can re-enact in our own minds another's act of thought, we can never know that we are re-enacting it. But this is an explicit self-contradiction. The objector confesses to a knowledge that something happens and at the same time denies that such knowledge is possible. He might try to remove the paradox by saying 'I did not mean that it does happen; I only meant that, for all I know, it may; what I maintain is that, if it did, we could not know that it was happening'. And he might cite, as a parallel case, the impossibility of knowing that any two persons experience indistinguishably similar colour-sensations on looking at the same blade of grass. But the parallel is not exact; what he was actually saying was something very different. He was saying not that, if it happened, some other circumstance would prevent us from knowing it: he was saying that if it did happen the very fact of its happening would make us unable to know that it was happening. And this makes it an event of a very peculiar kind.

There is only one kind of thing which may happen in a mind, of which it can be said that the very fact of its happening would render it impossible for us to know that it was happening: namely being under an illusion or error. What the objector is saying, therefore, is that the first of the two indispensable conditions of historical knowledge is an illusion or error on just that point of which knowledge is required. No doubt this in itself would not make historical knowledge impossible. For a condition of something's existing may be related to that thing in either of two ways: either as something that must exist first, but ceases to exist when that thing comes into existence, or as something that must exist so long as that thing exists. If the contention were that historical knowledge can only come into existence as replacing historical error, it would at any rate be worth considering. But the re-enactment of past thought is not a pre-condition of historical knowledge, but an integral element in it; the effect of the contention, therefore, is to make such knowledge impossible.

We must turn to the argument on which this contention rests. It was urged that an act of thought by becoming subjective ceases to be objective, and thus, by becoming present, ceases to be past; I can only be aware of it as the act I am here and now performing, not as the act which someone else has performed at another time.

Here again there are various points to be distinguished. Perhaps the first is the meaning of the phrase 'be aware of it.' The term 'awareness' is often used in an equivocal manner. To be aware of a pain is loosely used for simply feeling it, without knowing that it is a toothache or a headache or even a pain at all: the phrase refers simply to the immediate experience of having or undergoing the pain. Some philosophers would call this immediate experience by the name 'acquaintance': but that is a most misleading term for it, since acquaintance is a familiar English word denoting the kind of way in which we know individual persons or places or other things as permanent objects that recur, recognizably identical with themselves, in the course of our experience: something far removed from immediate feeling. But the term 'awareness' is also used in two other ways. It is used as a name for self-consciousness, as when a person is said to be aware of losing his temper; where what is meant is not only that he immediately experiences a feeling of anger which, as a matter of fact, is increasing, but that he knows this feeling to be his feeling, and an increasing one: as distinct from the case, for example, where he experiences the feeling but attributes it, as people often do, to his neighbours. And thirdly, it is used for perception, as when a person is said to be aware of a table, especially when the perception is somewhat dim and uncertain. It is well to clear up this ambiguity by settling how to use the word; and the best English usage would suggest its restriction to the second meaning, reserving feeling for the first and perception for the third.

This requires a reconsideration of the thesis. Does it mean that I merely feel the act going on, as an element in the flow of immediate experience; or that I recognize it as my act with a determinate place in my mental life? Clearly the second, though this does not exclude the first. I am aware of my act not only as an experience but as my experience, and an experience of a determinate kind: an act, and an act of thought which has arisen in a certain way, and has a certain cognitive character, and so forth.

If that is so, it can no longer be said that the act, because it is subjective, cannot be objective. Indeed, to say that would be to contradict oneself. To say that an act of thought cannot be objective is to say that it cannot be known; but anyone who said this would be claiming thereby to state his knowledge of such acts. He must therefore modify it, and will perhaps say that one act of thought may be an object to another act, but not to itself. But this again needs modification, for any object is properly the object not of an act but of an agent, the mind that performs that act. True, a mind is nothing except its own activities; but it is all these activities together, not any one separately. The question is, then, whether a person who performs an act of knowing can also know that he is performing or has performed that act. Admittedly he can, or no one would know that there were such acts, and so no one could have called them subjective; but to call them merely subjective, and not objective too, is to deny that admission while yet continuing to assume its truth.

The act of thinking, then, is not only subjective but objective as well. It is not only a thinking, it is something that can be thought about. But, because (as I have already tried to show) it is never merely objective, it requires to be thought about in a peculiar way, a way only appropriate to itself. It cannot be set before the thinking mind as a ready-made object, discovered as something independent of that mind and studied as it is in itself, in that independence. It can never be studied 'objectively', in the sense in which 'objectively' excludes 'subjectively'. It has to be studied as it actually exists, that is to say, as an act. And because this act is subjectivity (though not mere subjectivity) or experience, it can be studied only in its own subjective being, that is, by the thinker whose activity or experience it is. This study is not mere experience or consciousness, not even mere self-consciousness: it is self-knowledge. Thus the act of thought in becoming subjective does not cease to be objective; it is the object of a self-knowledge which differs from mere consciousness in being self-consciousness or awareness, and differs from being mere self-consciousness in being self-knowledge: the critical study of one's own thought, not the mere awareness of that thought as one's own.

Here it is possible to answer a tacit question which was left open when I said that a person who performs an act of knowing can also know that he 'is performing or has performed' that act. Which is it? Clearly, the first: for the act of thought has to be studied as it actually exists, that is, as an act. But this does not exclude the second. We have already seen that if mere experience is conceived as a flow of successive states, thought must be conceived as something that can apprehend the structure of this flow and the forms of succession which it exhibits: that is, thought is able to think the past as well as the present. Where thought studies the activity of thinking itself, therefore, it is equally able to study past acts of thinking and compare them with the present act. But there is a difference between the two cases. If I now think about a feeling which I had in the past, it may be true that thinking about it occasions, or else perhaps depends for its possibility on the independent occurrence of, an echo of that feeling in the present: that, for example, I could not think of the anger I once felt except so far as I now experience at least a faint vibration of anger in my mind. But whether this is true or not, the actual past anger of which I am thinking is past and gone; that does not reappear, the stream of immediate experience has carried it away for ever; at most there reappears something like it. The gap of time between my present thought and its past object is bridged not by the survival or revival of the object, but only by the power of thought to overleap such a gap; and the thought which does this is memory.

If, on the contrary, what I think about is a past activity of thought, for example a past philosophical inquiry of my own, the gap is bridged from both sides. To think at all about that past activity of thought, I must revive it in my own mind, for the act of thinking can be studied only as an act. But what is so revived is not a mere echo of the old activity, another of the same kind; it is that same activity taken up again and re-enacted, perhaps in order that, doing it over again under my own critical inspection, I may detect in it false steps of which critics have accused me. In thus re-thinking my past thought I am not merely remembering it. I am constructing the history of a certain phase of my life: and the difference between memory and history is that whereas in memory the past is a mere spectacle, in history it is re-enacted in present thought. So far as this thought is mere thought, the past is merely re-enacted; so far as it is thought about thought, the past is thought of as being re-enacted, and my knowledge of myself is historical knowledge.

The history of myself is thus not memory as such, but a peculiar case of memory. Certainly, a mind which could not remember could not have historical knowledge. But memory as such is only the present thought of past experience as such, be that experience what it may; historical knowledge is that special case of memory where the object of present thought is past thought, the gap between present and past being bridged not only by the power of present thought to think of the past, but also by the power of past thought to reawaken itself in the present.

To return to our supposed objector. Why did he think that the act of thought, by becoming subjective, ceased to be objective? The answer should by now be plain. It is because he understood by subjectivity not the act of thinking, but simply consciousness as a flow of immediate states. Subjectivity for him means not the subjectivity of thought but only the subjectivity of feeling or immediate experience. Even immediate experience has an object, for in every feeling there is something felt and in every sensation there is something sensed: but in seeing a colour what we see is the colour, not our act of seeing the colour, and in feeling cold we feel the cold (whatever exactly cold may be) but not the activity of feeling it. The subjectivity of immediate experience is thus a pure or mere subjectivity; it is never objective to itself: the experiencing never experiences itself as experiencing. If, then, there were an experience from which all thought were excluded (whether such an experience really exists or not, it is beside the point to inquire), the active or subjective element in that experience could never be an object to itself, and if all experience were of the same kind it could never be an object at all. What the objector was doing, therefore, was to assume that all experience is immediate, mere consciousness, devoid of thought. If he denies this, and says that he fully recognizes the presence of thought as an element in experience, we must reply that he may have recognized it in name but that he has not recognized it in fact. He has found a place for thought only by the expedient of selecting some items in the flow of consciousness and conferring upon them the title of thought, without asking what it implied; so that what he calls thought is in fact just one kind of immediate experience, whereas thought differs precisely from sensation or feeling in that it is never an immediate experience. In the immediate experience of sight, we see a colour; only by thinking can we know ourselves to be seeing it and also know that what we see is what we do not see it to be: an object at a distance from us, for example, which we have seen before. And even if he went so far as to recognize this, he failed to take the next step, and realize that by thinking we know ourselves to be thinking.

There is still one point in the objection that has not been cleared up. Granted that it is possible to reconstruct the history of one's own mind, by an extension of the general act of memory to the special case where what is remembered is an act of think-ing, does it follow that the past which can be thus knowingly re-enacted is any past but my own? Does it not rather seem that, since history has been described as a special case of memory, each of us can be the historian only of his own thought?

In order to answer this question we must inquire further into the relation between memory and what, as distinct from memory, I will call autobiography, using that name for a strictly historical account of my own past. If anyone of us were setting out to compose such an account, he would be con-fronted with two kinds of task of which one must come before the other. I do not mean that one must be completed before the other begins, but only that in every part of the work one side of it must be taken in hand before the other can be carried out. The first task is that of recollecting: he must search his memory for a vision of past experiences, and use various means of stimulating it, for example by reading letters and books that he once wrote, revisiting places associated in his mind with cer-tain events, and so forth. When this is done, he has before his mind a spectacle of the relevant parts of his own past life: he sees a young man undergoing such and such experiences, and knows that this young man was himself. But now begins the second task. He must not merely know that this young man was himself, he must try to rediscover that young man's thoughts. And here recollection is a treacherous guide. He remembers how he walked in the garden at night, wrestling with a thought; he remembers the scent of the flowers, and the breeze in his hair; but if he relies on these associations to tell him what the thought was, he is more than likely to be misled. He will probably fall into the mistake of substituting for it another which came to him later. Thus politicians, in writing their autobiographies, remember very well the impacts and emotions of a crisis, but are apt, in describing the policy they then advocated, to contaminate it with ideas that belonged in fact to a later stage in their career. And this is natural: because thought is not wholly entangled in the flow of experience, so that we constantly reinterpret our past thoughts and assimilate them to those we are thinking now.

There is only one way in which this tendency can be checked. If I want to be sure that twenty years ago a certain thought was really in my mind, I must have evidence of it. That evidence must be a book or letter or the like that I then wrote, or a picture I painted, or a recollection (my own or another's) of something I said, or of an action that I did, clearly revealing what was in my mind. Only by having some such evidence before me, and interpreting it fairly and squarely, can I prove to myself that I did think thus. Having done so, I rediscover my past self, and re-enact these thoughts as my thoughts; judging now better than I could then, it is to be hoped, their merits and defects.

Now it is certainly true that, unless a man could do this for himself, he could not do it for anybody else. But there is nothing which the autobiographer does, in this second part of his task, that the historian could not do for another. If the auto-biographer, although from the point of view of simple recollection his past thoughts are inextricably confused with his present ones, can disentangle them with the help of evidence, and decide that he must have thought in certain ways although at first he did not remember doing so, the historian, by using evidence of the same general kind, can recover the thoughts of others; coming to think them now even if he never thought them before, and knowing this activity as the re-enactment of what those men once thought. We shall never know how the flowers smelt in the garden of Epicurus, or how Nietzsche felt the wind in his hair as he walked on the mountains; we cannot relive the triumph of Archimedes or the bitterness of Marius; but the evidence of what these men thought is in our hands; and in re-creating these thoughts in our own minds by interpretation of that evidence we can know, so far as there is any knowledge, that the thoughts we create were theirs.

We put into the objector's mouth the statement that if experience could be repeated, the result would be an immediate identity between the historian and his object. This deserves further discussion. For if a mind is nothing but its own activities, and if to know the mind of a person in the past—say Thomas Becket—is to re-enact his thought, surely in so far as I, the historian, do this, I simply become Becket, which seems absurd.

Why is it absurd? It might be said, because to be Becket is one thing, to know Becket is another: and the historian aims at the latter. This objection, however, has already been answered. It depends on a false interpretation of the distinction between subjectivity and objectivity. For Becket, in so far as he was a thinking mind, being Becket was also knowing that he was Becket; and for myself, on the same showing, to be Becket is to know that I am Becket, that is, to know that I am my own present self re-enacting Becket's thought, myself being in that sense Becket. I do not 'simply' become Becket, for a thinking mind is never 'simply' anything: it is its own activities of thought, and it is not these 'simply' (which, if it means anything, means 'immediately'), for thought is not mere immediate experience but always reflection or self-knowledge, the knowledge of oneself as living in these activities.

It may be well to enlarge on this point. An act of thought is certainly a part of the thinker's experience. It occurs at a certain time, and in a certain context of other acts of thought, emotions, sensations, and so forth. Its presence in this context I call its immediacy; for although thought is not mere immediacy it is not devoid of immediacy. The peculiarity of thought is that, in addition to occurring here and now in this context, it can sustain itself through a change of context and revive in a different one. This power to sustain and revive itself is what makes an act of thought more than a mere 'event' or 'situation', to quote words that have been applied to it, for example, by Whitehead. It is because, and so far as, the act of thought is misconceived as a mere event that the idea of re-enacting it seems paradoxical and a perverse way of describing the occurrence of another, similar, event. The immediate, as such, cannot be re-enacted. Consequently, those elements in experience whose being is just their immediacy (sensations, feelings, &c. as such) cannot be re-enacted; not only that, but thought itself can never be re-enacted in its immediacy. The first discovery of a truth, for example, differs from any subsequent contemplation of it, not in that the truth contemplated is a different truth, nor in that the act of contemplating it is a different act; but in that the immediacy of the first occasion can never again be experienced: the shock of its novelty, the liberation from perplexing problems, the triumph of achieving a desired result, perhaps the sense of having vanquished opponents and achieved fame, and so forth.

But further: the immediacy of thought consists not only in its context of emotions (together, of course, with sensations, like the buoyancy of Archimedes' body in the bath) but in its context of other thoughts. The self-identity of the act of thinking that these two angles are equal is not only independent of such matters as that a person performing it is hungry and cold, and feels his chair hard beneath him, and is bored with his lesson: it is also independent of further thoughts, such as that the book says they are equal, or that the master believes them to be equal; or even thoughts more closely relevant to the subject in hand, as that their sum, plus the angle at the vertex, is 180 degrees.

This has sometimes been denied. It has been said that anything torn from its context is thereby mutilated and falsified; and that in consequence, to know any one thing, we must know its context, which implies knowing the whole universe. I do not propose to discuss this doctrine in its whole bearing, but only to remind the reader of its connexion with the view that reality is immediate experience, and its corollary that thought, which inevitably tears things out of their context, can never be true. On such a doctrine Euclid's act of thinking on a given occasion that these angles are equal would be what it was only in relation to the total context of his then experience, including such things as his being in a good temper and having a slave standing behind his right shoulder: without knowing all these we cannot know what he meant. If (which the doctrine in its strict form would not allow) we brush aside as irrelevant everything except the context of his geometrical thought, we do not even so escape absurdity; for in composing his proof of the theorem he may have thought 'this theorem enables me to prove that the angle in a semicircle is a right angle', and a hundred other things which it is just as impossible for us to know. Very likely he never thought of his fifth theorem without some such context; but to say that because the theorem, as an act of thought, exists only in its context we cannot know it except in the context in which he actually thought it, is to restrict the being of thought to its own immediacy, to reduce it to a case of merely immediate experience, and so to deny it as thought. Nor does anyone who attempts to maintain such a doctrine maintain it consistently. For example, he tries to show that a rival doctrine is untrue. But the doctrine he criticizes is a doctrine taught by some-body else (or even one accepted in unregenerate days by himself). On his own showing, this doctrine is what it is only in a total context that cannot be repeated and cannot be known. The context of thought in which his adversary's doctrine has its being cannot ever be the context which it has in the critic's experience; and if an act of thought is what it is only in relation to its context, the doctrine he criticizes can never be the doc-trine taught by his opponent. And this not owing to any defects in exposition or comprehension, but owing to the self-frustrating character of the attempt to understand another's thought, or indeed to think at all.

Others, who have taken warning by these consequences, have embraced the opposite doctrine that all acts of thought are atomically distinct from one another. This makes it both easy and legitimate to detach them from their context; for there is no context; there is only a juxtaposition of things standing to one another in merely external relations. On this view, the unity of a body of knowledge is only that kind of unity which belongs to a collection: and this is true both of a science, or system of things known, and of a mind, or system of acts of knowing. Once more I am not concerned with the whole bearing of such a doctrine, but only to point out that by substituting logical analysis for attention to experience (the constant appeal to which was the strength of the rival doctrine) it overlooks the immediacy of thought, and converts the act of thinking, from a subjective experience, into an objective spectacle. The fact that Euclid performed a certain operation of thought becomes just a fact, like the fact that this paper rests on this table; mind is merely a collective name for such facts.

History is no more possible on this view than on the other. That Euclid performed a certain operation of thought may be called a fact, but it is an unknowable fact. We cannot know it, we can only at most believe it on testimony. And this appears a satisfactory account of historical thought only to persons who embrace the fundamental error of mistaking for history that form of pseudo-history which Croce has called 'philological history': persons who think that history is nothing more than scholarship or learning, and would assign to the historian the self-contradictory task of discovering (for example) 'what Plato thought' without inquiring 'whether it is true'.

To disentangle ourselves from these two complementary errors, we must attack the false dilemma from which they both spring. That dilemma rests on the disjunction that thought is either pure immediacy, in which case it is inextricably involved in the flow of consciousness, or pure mediation, in which case it is utterly detached from that flow. Actually it is both immediacy and mediation. Every act of thought, as it actually happens, happens in a context out of which it arises and in which it lives, like any other experience, as an organic part of the thinker's life. Its relations with its context are not those of an item in a collection, but those of a special function in the total activity of an organism. So far, not only is the doctrine of the so-called idealists correct, but even that of the pragmatists who have developed that side of it to an extreme. But an act of thought, in addition to actually happening, is capable of sustaining itself and being revived or repeated without loss of its identity. So far, those who have opposed the 'idealists' are in the right, when they maintain that what we think is not altered by alterations of the context in which we think it. But it cannot repeat itself *in vacuo*, as the disembodied ghost of a past experience. However often it happens, it must always happen in some context, and the new context must be just as appropriate to it as the old. Thus, the mere fact that someone has expressed his thoughts in writing, and that we possess his works, does not enable us to understand his thoughts. In order that we may be able to do so, we must come to the reading of them prepared with an experience sufficiently like his own to make those thoughts organic to it.

This double character of thought provides the solution of a logical puzzle that has a close connexion with the theory of history. If I now re-think a thought of Plato's, is my act of thought identical with Plato's or different from it? Unless it is identical, my alleged knowledge of Plato's philosophy is sheer error. But unless it is different, my knowledge of Plato's philosophy implies oblivion of my own. What is required, if I am to know Plato's philosophy, is both to re-think it in my own mind and also to think other things in the light of which I can judge it. Some philosophers have attempted to solve this puzzle by a vague appeal to the 'principle of identity in difference', arguing that there is a development of thought from Plato to myself and that anything which develops remains identical with itself although it becomes different. Others have replied with justice that the question is how exactly the two things are the same, and how exactly they differ. The answer is that, in their immediacy, as actual experiences organically united with the body of experience out of which they arise, Plato's thought and mine are different. But in their mediation they are the same. This perhaps calls for further explanation. When I read Plato's argument in the *Theaetetus* against the view that knowledge is merely sensation, I do not know what philosophical doctrines he was attacking; I could not expound these doctrines and say in detail who maintained them and by what arguments. In its immediacy, as an actual experience of his own, Plato's argument must undoubtedly have grown up out of a discussion of some sort, though I do not know what it was, and been closely connected with such a discussion. Yet if I not only read his argument but understand it, follow it in my own mind by re-arguing it with and for myself, the process of argument which I go through is not a process resembling Plato's, it actually is Plato's, so far as I understand him rightly. The argument simply as itself, starting from these premises and leading through this process to this conclusion; the argument as it can be developed either in Plato's mind or mine or anyone else's, is what I call the thought in its mediation. In Plato's mind, this existed in a certain context of discussion and theory; in my mind, because I do not know that context, it exists in a different one, namely that of the discussions arising out of modern sensationalism. Because it is a thought and not a mere feeling or sensation, it can exist in both these contexts without losing its identity, although without some appropriate context it could never exist. Part of the context in which it exists in my mind might, if it was a fallacious argument, be other activities of thought consisting in knowing how to refute it; but even if I refuted it, it would still be the same argument and the act of following its logical structure would be the same act.

§ 5. *The Subject-matter of History*

If we raise the question, Of what can there be historical knowledge? the answer is, Of that which can be re-enacted in the historian's mind. In the first place, this must be experience. Of that which is not experience but the mere object of experience, there can be no history. Thus there is and can be no history of nature, whether as perceived or as thought by the scientist. No doubt nature contains, undergoes, or even consists of, processes; its changes in time are essential to it, they may even (as some think) be all that it has or is; and these changes may be genuinely creative, no mere repetitions of fixed cyclical phases but the development of new orders of natural being. But all this goes no way towards proving that the life of nature is an historical life or that our knowledge of it is historical knowledge. The only condition on which there could be a history of nature is that the events of nature are actions on the part of some thinking being or beings, and that by studying these actions we could discover what were the thoughts which they expressed and think these thoughts for ourselves. This is a condition which probably no one will claim is fulfilled. Consequently the processes of nature are not historical processes and our knowledge of nature, though it may resemble history in certain superficial ways, e.g. by being chronological, is not historical knowledge.

Secondly, even experience is not as such the object of historical knowledge. In so far as it is merely immediate experience, a mere flow of consciousness consisting of sensations, feelings, and the like, its process is not an historical process. That process can, no doubt, be not only directly experienced in its immediacy, but also known; its particular details and its general characteristics can be studied by thought; but the thought which studies it finds in it a mere object of study, which in order to be studied need not be, and indeed cannot be, re-enacted in the thinking about it. In so far as we think about its particular details, we are remembering experiences of our own or entering with sympathy and imagination into those of others; but in such cases we do not re-enact the experiences which we remember or with which we sympathize; we are merely contemplating them as objects external to our present selves, aided perhaps by the presence in ourselves of other experiences like them. In so far as we think about its general characteristics, we are engaging in the science of psychology. In neither case are we thinking historically.

Thirdly, even thought itself, in its immediacy as the unique act of thought with its unique context in the life of an individual thinker, is not the object of historical knowledge. It cannot be re-enacted; if it could, time itself would be cancelled and the historian would be the person about whom he thinks, living over again in all respects the same. The historian cannot apprehend the individual act of thought in its individuality, just as it actually happened. What he apprehends of that individual is only something that it might have shared with other acts of thought and actually has shared with his own. But this something is not an abstraction, in the sense of a common characteristic shared by different individuals and considered apart from the individuals that share it. It is the act of thought itself, in its survival and revival at different times and in different persons: once in the historian's own life, once in the life of the person whose history he is narrating.

Thus the vague phrase that history is knowledge of the individual claims for it a field at once too wide and too narrow: too wide, because the individuality of perceived objects and natural facts and immediate experiences falls outside its sphere, and most of all because even the individuality of historical events and personages, if that means their uniqueness, falls equally outside it; too narrow, because it would exclude universality, and it is just the universality of an event or character that makes it a proper and possible object of historical study, if by universality we mean something that oversteps the limits of merely local and temporal existence and possesses a significance valid for all men at all times. These too are no doubt vague phrases; but they are attempts to describe something real: namely the way in which thought, transcending its own immediacy, survives and revives in other contexts; and to express the truth that individual acts and persons appear in history not in virtue of their individuality as such, but because that individuality is the vehicle of a thought which, because it was actually theirs, is potentially everyone's.

Of everything other than thought, there can be no history. Thus a biography, for example, however much history it contains, is constructed on principles that are not only non-historical but anti-historical. Its limits are biological events, the birth and death of a human organism: its framework is thus a framework not of thought but of natural process. Through this framework—the bodily life of the man, with his childhood, maturity and senescence, his diseases and all the accidents of animal existence—the tides of thought, his own and others', flow crosswise, regardless of its structure, like sea-water through a stranded wreck. Many human emotions are bound up with the spectacle of such bodily life in its vicissitudes, and biography, as a form of literature, feeds these emotions and may give them wholesome food; but this is not history. Again, the record of immediate experience with its flow of sensations and feelings, faithfully preserved in a diary or recalled in a memoir, is not history. At its best, it is poetry; at its worst, an obtrusive egotism; but history it can never be.

But there is another condition without which a thing cannot become the object of historical knowledge. The gulf of time between the historian and his object must be bridged, as I have said, from both ends. The object must be of such a kind that it can revive itself in the historian's mind; the historian's mind must be such as to offer a home for that revival. This does not mean that his mind must be of a certain kind, possessed of an historical temperament; nor that he must be trained in special rules of historical technique. It means that he must be the right man to study that object. What he is studying is a certain thought: to study it involves re-enacting it in himself; and in order that it may take its place in the immediacy of his own thought, his thought must be, as it were, pre-adapted to become its host. This does not imply, in the technical sense of the phrase, a pre-established harmony between the historian's mind and its object; it is not, for example, an endorsement of Coleridge's saying that men are born Platonists or Aristotelians; for it has not prejudged the question whether a Platonist or an Aristotelian is born or made. A man who at one time of life finds certain historical studies unprofitable, because he cannot enter for himself into the thought of those about whom he is thinking, will find at another time that he has become able to do so, perhaps as a result of deliberate self-training. But at any given stage in his life the historian as he stands is certain to have, for whatever reason, a readier sympathy with some ways of thinking than with others. Partly this is because certain ways of thinking are altogether, or relatively, strange to him: partly it is because they are all too familiar, and he feels the need of getting away from them in the interests of his own mental and moral welfare.

If the historian, working against the grain of his own mind because it is demanded of him that he should study such uncongenial subjects, or because they are 'in the period' which his own misguided conscience fancies he ought to treat in all its aspects, tries to master the history of a thought into which he cannot personally enter, instead of writing its history he will merely repeat the statements that record the external facts of its development: names and dates, and ready-made descriptive phrases. Such repetitions may very well be useful, but not because they are history. They are dry bones, which may some day become history, when someone is able to clothe them with the flesh and blood of a thought which is both his own and theirs. This is only a way of saying that the historian's thought must spring from the organic unity of his total experience, and be a function of his entire personality with its practical as well as its theoretical interests. It need hardly be added that since the historian is a son of his time, there is a general likelihood that what interests him will interest his contemporaries. It is a familiar fact that every generation finds itself interested in, and therefore able to study historically, tracts and aspects of the past which to its fathers were dry bones, signifying nothing.

Historical knowledge, then, has for its proper object thought: not things thought about, but the act of thinking itself. This principle has served us to distinguish history from natural science on the one hand, as the study of a given or objective world distinct from the act of thinking it, and on the other from psychology as the study of immediate experience, sensation, and feeling, which, though the activity of a mind, is not the activity of thinking. But the positive meaning of the principle needs further determination. How much or how little is meant to be included under the term 'thought'?

The term 'thought', as hitherto used in this section and its predecessor, has stood for a certain form of experience or mental activity whose peculiarity may be negatively described by saying that it is not merely immediate, and therefore is not carried away by the flow of consciousness. The positive peculiarity which distinguishes thought from mere consciousness is its power of recognizing the activity of the self as a single activity persisting through the diversity of its own acts. If I feel cold, and later feel warm, there is for mere feeling no continuity between the two experiences. It is true, as Bergson points out, that the feeling cold 'interpenetrates' the subsequent feeling warm, and gives it a quality which it would not otherwise have had; but the feeling warm, though it owes that quality to the previous feeling cold, does not recognize the debt. The distinction between mere feeling and thought may thus be illustrated by the distinction between simply feeling cold and being able to say 'I feel cold'. To say that, I must be aware of myself as something more than the immediate experience of cold: aware of myself as an activity of feeling which has had other experiences previously, and remains the same throughout the difference of these experiences. I need not even remember what these experiences were; but I must know that they existed and were mine.

The peculiarity of thought, then, is that it is not mere consciousness but self-consciousness. The self, as merely conscious, is a flow of consciousness, a series of immediate sensations and feelings; but as merely conscious it is not aware of itself as such a flow; it is ignorant of its own continuity through the succession of experiences. The activity of becoming aware of this continuity is what is called thinking.

But this thought of myself as an activity of feeling, which remains the same activity through its various acts, is only the most rudimentary form of thought. It develops into other forms by working outwards from this starting-point in various directions. One thing which it may do is to become more clearly aware of the precise nature of the continuity: instead of only conceiving 'myself' as having previously had some experiences, indeterminate in their nature, considering what in particular these experiences were: remembering them and comparing them with the immediate present. Another is to analyse the present experience itself, to distinguish in it the act of feeling from what is felt, and to conceive what is felt as something whose reality (like the reality of myself as the feeler) is not exhausted by its immediate presence to my feeling. Working along these two lines, thought becomes memory, the thought of my own flow of experiences, and perception, the thought of what I experience as something real.

A third way in which it develops is by recognizing myself as not only a sentient being but as a thinking being. In remembering and perceiving, I am already doing more than enjoying a flow of immediate experience; I am also thinking; but I am not (simply in remembering or perceiving as such) aware of myself as thinking. I am only aware of myself as feeling. This awareness is already self-consciousness or thought, but it is an imperfect self-consciousness, because in possessing it I am performing a certain kind of mental activity, namely thinking, of which I am not conscious. Hence the thinking which we do in memory or perception as such may be called unconscious thinking, not because we can do it without being conscious, for in order to do it we must be not only conscious but self-conscious, but because we do it without being conscious that we are doing it. To be conscious that I am thinking is to think in a new way, which may be called reflecting.

Historical thinking is always reflection; for reflection is thinking about the act of thinking, and we have seen that all historical thinking is of that kind. But what kind of thinking can be its object? Is it possible to study the history of what was just now called unconscious thinking, or must the thinking which history studies be conscious or reflective thinking?

This amounts to asking whether there can be a history of memory or perception. And it is clear that there cannot. A person who should sit down to write the history of memory or the history of perception would find nothing to write about. It is conceivable that different races of mankind, and for that matter different human beings, have had different ways of remembering or perceiving; and it is possible that these differences were sometimes due, not to physiological differences (such as the undeveloped colour-sense which has been ascribed, on very dubious grounds, to the Greeks), but to different habits of thought. But if there are ways of perceiving which for such reasons have prevailed here and there in the past, and are not practised by ourselves, we cannot reconstruct the history of them because we cannot re-enact the appropriate experiences at will; and this is because the habits of thought to which they are due are 'unconscious', and therefore cannot be deliberately revived. For example, it may be true that civilizations other than our own have enjoyed as part of their normal equipment the faculty of second sight or the power of seeing ghosts. It may be that, among them, these things arose out of certain habitual ways of thinking, and were therefore a familiar and understood way of expressing genuine knowledge or well-founded belief. Certainly, when Burnt Njál in the saga used his second sight as a means of giving advice to his friends, they were profiting by the wisdom of a sound lawyer and a shrewd man of the world. But, supposing all this to be true, it is still impossible for us to write a history of second sight; all we can do is to collect instances in which it has been alleged, and to believe that the statements about it are statements of fact. But this would be, at most, belief in testimony; and we know that such belief stops where history begins.

In order, therefore, that any particular act of thought should become subject-matter for history, it must be an act not only of thought but of reflective thought, that is, one which is performed in the consciousness that it is being performed, and is constituted what it is by that consciousness. The effort to do it must be more than a merely conscious effort. It must not be the blind effort to do we know not what, like the effort to remember a forgotten name or to perceive a confused object; it must be a reflective effort, the effort to do something of which we have a conception before we do it. A reflective activity is one in which we know what it is that we are trying to do, so that when it is done we know that it is done by seeing that it has conformed to the standard or criterion which was our initial conception of it. It is therefore an act which we are enabled to perform by knowing in advance how to perform it.

Not all acts are of this kind. Samuel Butler was confusing the issue from one side when he said that an infant must know how to suck, or it could not do it; others have confused it from the opposite side by maintaining that we never know what we are going to do until we have done it. Butler was trying to make out that acts which are unreflective are really reflective, exaggerating the place of reason in life, in order to oppose a prevailing materialism; these others are contending that reflective acts are really unreflective, because they conceive all experience as immediate. In its immediacy, as a unique individual, complete with all details and in the full context in which alone it can immediately exist, our future act can certainly never be planned in advance; however carefully we have thought it out, it will always contain much that is unforeseen and surprising; but to infer that therefore it cannot be planned at all is to betray the assumption that its immediate being is the only being it has. An act is more than a mere unique individual; it is something having a universal character; and in the case of a reflective or deliberate act (an act which we not only do, but intend to do before doing it) this universal character is the plan or idea of the act which we conceive in our thought before doing the act itself, and the criterion by reference to which, when we have done it, we know that we have done what we meant to do.

There are certain kinds of act which cannot be done except on these terms: that is to say, cannot be done except reflectively, by a person who knows what he is trying to do and is therefore able, when he has done it, to judge his own action by reference to his intention. It is characteristic of these acts that they should be done, as we say, 'on purpose': that there should be a basis of purpose upon which the structure of the act should be erected, and to which it must conform. Reflective acts may be roughly described as the acts which we do on purpose, and these are the only acts which can become the subject-matter of history.

From this point of view, it can be seen why certain forms of activity are, and others are not, matter of historical knowledge. It would be generally admitted that politics is a thing that can be historically studied. The reason is that politics affords a plain instance of purposive action. The politician is a man with a policy; his policy is a plan of action conceived in advance of its performance; and his success as a politician is proportional to his success in carrying out his policy. No doubt, his policy is not prior to his action in the sense of being fixed once for all before his action begins; it develops as his action develops; but at every stage of his action policy precedes its own fulfilment. If it were possible to say of any man that he acted with no idea whatever what would come of it, but did the first thing that came into his head and merely waited to see the consequences, it would follow that such a man was no politician, and that his action was merely the intrusion into political life of a blind and irrational force. And if it has to be said of a certain man that he doubtless had a policy but that we cannot discover what it was (and one sometimes feels inclined to say this of, for example, certain early Roman emperors), this is as much as to say that one's attempts to reconstruct the political history of his action have failed.

For the same reason, there can be a history of warfare. In a general way, the intentions of a military commander are easy to understand. If he took an army into a certain country and engaged its forces, we can see that he meant to defeat it, and from the recorded account of his acts we can reconstruct in our own minds the plan of campaign which he tried to carry out. Once more, this depends on the assumption that his acts were done on purpose. If they were not, there can be no history of them; if they were done on a purpose that we cannot fathom, then we at least cannot reconstruct their history.

Economic activity, too, can have a history. A man who builds a factory or starts a bank is acting on a purpose which we can understand; so are the men who accept wages from him, buy his goods or his shares, or make deposits and withdrawals. If we are told that there was a strike at the factory or a run on the bank, we can reconstruct in our own minds the purposes of the people whose collective action took those forms.

Again, there can be a history of morals; for in moral action we are doing certain things on purpose, in order to bring our practical life into harmony with the ideal of what it ought to be. This ideal is at once our conception of our own life as it should be, or our intention of what we mean to make it and our criterion of whether what we have done has been done well or ill. Here too, as in the other cases, our purposes change as our activity develops, but the purpose is always in advance of the act. And it is impossible to act morally except when, and in so far as, one acts on purpose; duty cannot be done by accident or inadvertence; no one can do his duty except a person who means to do his duty.

In these cases we have examples of practical activities which are not merely as a matter of fact pursued on purpose, but could not be what they are unless they were so pursued. Now, it might be thought that all purposive action must be practical action, because there are two stages in it: first conceiving the purpose, which is a theoretical activity or act of pure thought, and then executing it, which is a practical activity supervening on the theoretical. On this analysis it would follow that acting, in the narrow or practical sense of the word, is the only thing that can be done on purpose. For, it might be argued, you cannot think on purpose, since if you conceived your own act of thought before executing it, you would have executed it already. The theoretical activities, it would follow, cannot be purposive: they must be, as it were, done in the dark, with no conception of what is to come from engaging in them.

This is an error, but it is an error of some interest for the theory of history, because it has actually influenced the theory and practice of historiography to the extent of making people think that the only possible subject-matter of history is the practical life of men. The idea that history concerns itself, and can concern itself, only with such matters as politics, warfare, economic life, and, in general, the world of practice, is still widespread and was once almost universal. We have seen how even Hegel, who showed so brilliantly how the history of philosophy should be written, committed himself in his lectures on the philosophy of history to the view that history's proper subject-matter is society and the state, the practical life, or (in his own technical language) objective mind, mind as expressing itself outwardly in actions and institutions.

To-day it is no longer necessary to argue that art, science, religion, philosophy, and so forth are proper subjects of historical study; the fact of their being studied historically is too familiar. But it is necessary to ask why this is so, in view of the argument to the contrary that has been stated above.

In the first place, it is not true that a person engaged in purely theoretical thinking is acting without a purpose. A man doing a certain piece of scientific work, such as inquiring into the cause of malaria, has a quite definite purpose in mind: to discover the cause of malaria. True, he does not know what this cause is; but he knows that when he finds it he will know that he has found it by applying to his discovery certain tests or criteria which he has before him from the start. The plan of his discovery, then, is the plan of a theory which will satisfy these criteria. Similarly for the historian or philosopher. He is never sailing an uncharted sea; his chart, however little detail it contains, is marked with the parallels of latitude and longitude, and his purpose is to discover what there is to put down on and between those lines. In other words: every actual inquiry starts from a certain problem, and the purpose of the inquiry is to solve that problem; the plan of the discovery, therefore, is already known and formulated by saying that, whatever the discovery may be, it must be such as to satisfy the terms of the problem. As in the case of practical activity, this plan of course changes as the activity of thought proceeds; some plans are abandoned as impracticable and replaced by others, some are carried out successfully and found to lead to new problems.

In the second place, the difference between conceiving and executing a purpose was not correctly described as the difference between a theoretical act and a practical one. To conceive a purpose or form an intention is already a practical activity. It is not thought forming an anteroom to action; it is action itself in its initial stage. If this is not at once recognized, it may be recognized by considering its implications. Thought, as theoretical activity, cannot be moral or immoral; it can only be true or false. That which is moral or immoral must be action. Now, if a man forms the intention of committing murder or adultery, and then decides not to carry out his intention, the intention itself already exposes him to condemnation on moral grounds. It is not said of him 'he accurately conceived the nature of murder or adultery, so his thought was true and therefore admirable'; it is said of him 'he is doubtless not so wicked as if he had carried his intention out to the end; but to intend such action at all was wicked'.

The scientist, the historian, and the philosopher are thus, no less than the practical man, proceeding in their activities according to plans, thinking on purpose, and thus arriving at results that can be judged according to criteria derived from the plans themselves. Consequently there can be histories of these things. All that is necessary is that there should be evidence of how such thinking has been done and that the historian should be able to interpret it, that is, should be able to re-enact in his own mind the thought he is studying, envisaging the problem from which it started and reconstructing the steps by which its solution was attempted. In practice, the common difficulty for the historian is to identify the problem, for whereas the thinker is generally careful to expound the steps of his own thought, he is talking as a rule to contemporaries who already know what the problem is, and he may never state it at all. And unless the historian knows what the problem was at which he was working, he has no criterion by which to judge the success of his work. It is the historian's endeavour to discover this problem that gives importance to the study of 'influences', which is so futile when influences are conceived as the decanting of ready-made thoughts out of one mind into another. An intelligent inquiry into the influence of Socrates on Plato, or Descartes on Newton, seeks to discover not the points of agreement, but the way in which the conclusions reached by one thinker give rise to problems for the next.

There might seem to be a special difficulty about the case of art. The artist, even if his work can be called reflective at all, seems a great deal less reflective than the scientist or philosopher. He does not appear to set out on a particular piece of work with a clearly formulated problem, and judge his result by reference to the terms of the problem. He seems to be working in a world of pure imagination, where his thought is absolutely creative, never in any sense knowing what he is going to do until he has done it. If thinking means reflection and judgement, it would seem that the genuine artist does not think at all; his mental labour seems to be a labour of pure intuition, where no concept either precedes or sustains or judges the intuition itself.

But the artist does not create his works out of nothing. He begins in every case with a problem before him. This problem, in so far as he is an artist, is not the problem of decorating a given room or designing a house to comply with given utilitarian requirements; these are the special problems of applied art, and in art as such they do not arise. Nor is it the problem of making something out of paint, or sounds, or marble; he only begins to be an artist when those problems cease to be problems at all, and the materials of his craft have become obedient servants of his imagination. The point at which he begins creating a work of art is the point at which that work is grafted on the body of his unreflective experience: his immediate sensitive and emotional life with its development, rational but unconscious, through memory and perception. The problem with which he is confronted is the problem of feeding this experience into a work of art. He has encountered some experience that stands out from the rest as significant or moving; its unexpressed significance lies on his mind as a burden, challenging him to find some way of uttering it; and his labour in creating a work of art is his response to that challenge. In this sense the artist knows very well what he is doing and what he is trying to do. The criterion of his having done it rightly is that, when it is done, it should be seen as expressing what he wanted to express. All that is peculiar to him is the fact that he cannot formulate his problem; if he could formulate it, he would have expressed it; and the work of art would have been achieved. But although he cannot in advance of the work itself say what the problem is, he knows that there is a problem, and he is aware of its peculiar nature; only not reflectively aware until the work has been done.

This indeed seems to be the special character of art and its peculiar importance in the life of thought. It is the phase of that life in which the conversion from unreflective to reflective thought actually comes about. There is therefore a history of art, but no history of artistic problems, as there is a history of scientific or philosophical problems. There is only the history of artistic achievements.

There is also a history of religion; for religion, no less than art or philosophy or politics, is a function of reflective thought. In religion man has a conception of himself as a thinking and active being, which he sets over against a conception of God in which his notion of thought and action, knowledge and power, are raised to the level of infinity. The task of religious thought and religious practice (for in religion the theoretical and practical activities are fused into one) is to find the relation between these two opposed conceptions of myself as finite and God as infinite. The absence of any definite relation, the mere difference of the two, is the problem and torment of the religious mind. The discovery of a relation is at once the discovery of my thought as reaching God and of God's thought as reaching me: and, indistinguishable from this, the performance of an act of mine by which I establish a relation with God and an act of God's by which he establishes a relation with me. To fancy that religion lives either below or above the limits of reflective thought is fatally to misconceive either the nature of religion or the nature of reflective thought. It would be nearer the truth to say that in religion the life of reflection is concentrated in its intensest form, and that the special problems of theoretical and practical life all take their special forms by segregation out of the body of the religious consciousness, and retain their vitality only so far as they preserve their connexion with it and with each other in it.

§ 6. *History and Freedom*

We study history, I have maintained, in order to attain self-knowledge. By way of illustrating this thesis, I shall try to show how our knowledge that human activity is free has been attained only through our discovery of history.

In my historical sketch of the idea of history I have tried to show how history has at last escaped from a state of pupilage to natural science. The disappearance of historical naturalism, however, entails the further conclusion that the activity by which man builds his own constantly changing historical world is a free activity. There are no forces other than this activity which control it or modify it or compel it to behave in this way or in that, to build one kind of world rather than another.

This does not mean that a man is always free to do what he pleases. All men, at some moments in their lives, are free to do what they want: to eat, being hungry, for example, or to sleep, being tired. But this has nothing to do with the problem to which I have referred. Eating and sleeping are animal activities, pursued under the compulsion of animal appetite. With animal appetites and their gratification or frustration history is not concerned. It makes no difference to the historian, as an historian, that there should be no food in a poor man's house; though it may and must make a difference to him as a man with feelings for his fellow creatures; and though as an historian he may be intensely concerned with the shifts by which other men have contrived to bring about this state of things in order that they should be rich and the men who take wages from them poor; and equally concerned with the action to which the poor man may be led not by the fact of his children's unsatisfied hunger, the fact, the physiological fact, of empty bellies and wizened limbs, but by his thought of that fact.

Nor does it mean that a man is free to do what he chooses; that in the realm of history proper, as distinct from that of animal appetite, people are free to plan their own actions as they think fit and execute their plans, each doing what he set out to do and each assuming full responsibility for the consequences, captain of his soul and all that. Nothing could be more false. Henley's rhyme does no more than utter the fantasy of a sick child who has discovered that he can stop himself crying for the moon by making believe that he has got it. A healthy man knows that the empty space in front of him, which he proposes to fill up with activities for which he accordingly now begins making plans, will be very far from empty by the time he steps into it. It will be crowded with other people all pursuing activities of their own. Even now it is not as empty as it looks. It is filled with a saturate solution of activity, on the point of beginning to crystallize out. There will be no room left for his own activity, unless he can so design this that it will fit into the interstices of the rest.

The rational activity which historians have to study is never free from compulsion: the compulsion to face the facts of its own situation. The more rational it is, the more completely it undergoes this compulsion. To be rational is to think; and for a man who proposes to act, the thing that it is important to think about is the situation in which he stands. With regard to this situation, he is not free at all. It is what it is, and neither he nor anyone else can ever change that. For though the situation consists altogether of thoughts, his own and other people's, it cannot be changed by a change of mind on the part of himself or anyone else. If minds change, as they do, this merely means that with the lapse of time a new situation has arisen. For a man about to act, the situation is his master, his oracle, his god. Whether his action is to prove successful or not depends on whether he grasps the situation rightly or not. If he is a wise man, it is not until he has consulted his oracle, done everything in his power to find out what the situation is, that he will make even the most trivial plan. And if he neglects the situation, the situation will not neglect him. It is not one of those gods that leave an insult unpunished.

The freedom that there is in history consists in the fact that this compulsion is imposed upon the activity of human reason not by anything else, but by itself. The situation, its master, oracle, and god, is a situation it has itself created. And when I say this I do not mean that the situation in which one man finds himself exists only because other men have created it by a rational activity not different in kind from that by which their successor finds himself to be in it and acts in it according to his lights; and that, because human reason is always human reason, whatever may be the name of the human being in whom it works, the historian can ignore these personal distinctions and say that human reason has created the situation in which it finds itself. I mean something rather different from that. All history is the history of thought; and when an historian says that a man is in a certain situation this is the same as saying that he thinks he is in this situation. The hard facts of the situation, which it is so important for him to face, are the hard facts of the way in which he conceives the situation.

If the reason why it is hard for a man to cross the mountains is because he is frightened of the devils in them, it is folly for the historian, preaching at him across a gulf of centuries, to say 'This is sheer superstition. There are no devils at all. Face facts, and realize that there are no dangers in the mountains except rocks and water and snow, wolves perhaps, and bad men perhaps, but no devils.' The historian says that these are the facts because that is the way in which he has been taught to think. But the devil-fearer says that the presence of devils is a fact, because that is the way in which he has been taught to think. The historian thinks it a wrong way; but wrong ways of thinking are just as much historical facts as right ones, and, no less than they, determine the situation (always a thought-situation) in which the man who shares them is placed. The hardness of the fact consists in the man's inability to think of his situation otherwise. The compulsion which the devil-haunted mountains exercise on the man who would cross them consists in the fact that he cannot help believing in the devils. Sheer superstition, no doubt: but this superstition is a fact, and the crucial fact in the situation we are considering. The man who suffers from it when he tries to cross the mountains is not suffering merely for the sins of his fathers who taught him to believe in devils, if that is a sin; he is suffering because he has accepted the belief, because he has shared the sin. If the modern historian believes that there are no devils in the mountains, that too is only a belief he has accepted in precisely the same way.

The discovery that the men whose actions he studies are in this sense free is a discovery which every historian makes as soon as he arrives at a scientific mastery of his own subject. When that happens, the historian discovers his own freedom: that is, he discovers the autonomous character of historical thought, its power to solve its own problems for itself by its own methods. He discovers how unnecessary it is, and how impossible it is, for him, as historian, to hand these problems over for solution to natural science; he discovers that in his capacity as historian he both can and must solve them for himself. It is simultaneously with this discovery of his own freedom as historian that he discovers the freedom of man as an historical agent. Historical thought, thought about rational activity, is free from the domination of natural science, and rational activity is free from the domination of nature.

The intimacy of the connexion between these two discoveries might be expressed by saying that they are the same thing in different words. It might be said that to describe the rational activity of an historical agent as free is only a roundabout and disguised way of saying that history is an autonomous science. Or it might be said that to describe history as an autonomous science is only a disguised way of saying that it is the science which studies free activity. For myself, I should welcome either of these two statements, as providing evidence that the person who made it had seen far enough into the nature of history to have discovered (a) that historical thought is free from the domination of natural science, and is an autonomous science, (b) that rational action is free from the domination of nature and builds its own world of human affairs, *Res Gestae*, at its own bidding and in its own way, (c) that there is an intimate connexion between these two propositions.

But at the same time I should find in either statement evidence that the person who made it was unable (or for some ulterior purpose had decided to profess himself unable) to distinguish between what a person says and what is implied in what he says: unable, that is, to distinguish the theory of language, or aesthetics, from the theory of thought, or logic; and was therefore committed, for the time being at least, to a verbalistic logic, in which the logical connexion between two thoughts which imply each other is confused with the linguistic connexion between two sets of words which 'stand for the same thing'.

I should see, too, that his attempt to burke the problems of logic by substituting for them problems in linguistics was not based on any very just appreciation of the nature of language, because I should see that, of two synonymous verbal expressions, he was assuming that one really and properly means the thing 'for which it stands', while the other means this only for the insufficient reason that the person who uses it means that by it. All of which is very disputable. Rather than approve such errors, I should prefer to leave the matter where I have left it; to say that these two statements (the statement that history is an autonomous science and the statement that rational activity is free in the sense described) are not synonymous forms of words, but express discoveries neither of which can be made without making the other. And arising out of this, I will observe that the 'free-will controversy' which was so prominent in the seventeenth century had a close connexion with the fact that the seventeenth century was the time when scissors-and-paste history in its simpler forms was beginning to dissatisfy people, and when historians were beginning to see that their own house needed setting in order or that historical studies ought to take example from the study of nature, and raise themselves to the level of a science. The desire to envisage human action as free was bound up with a desire to achieve autonomy for history as the study of human action.

But I do not leave the matter there; because I wish to point out that of the two statements I am considering, one is necessarily prior to the other. It is only by using historical methods that we can find out anything about the objects of historical study. No one will assert that he knows more than historians do about certain actions done in the past concerning which historians claim to have knowledge, and that he knows this in such a way that he can satisfy both himself and other people that that claim is groundless. It follows that we must first achieve a genuinely scientific and therefore autonomous method in historical study before we can grasp the fact that human activity is free.

This may seem contrary to facts; for surely, it will be said, many people were already aware that human activity is free, long before that revolution took place by which history raised itself to the level of a science. To this objection I will offer two answers, not mutually exclusive, but the one relatively superficial, the other, I hope, a little more profound.

(i) They were aware, perhaps, of human freedom; but did they grasp it? Was their awareness a knowledge that deserved the name of scientific? Surely not; for in that case they would not only have been convinced of it, they would have known it in a systematic way, and there would have been no room for controversy about it, because those who were convinced of it would have understood the grounds of their conviction and been able to state them convincingly.

(ii) Even if the revolution by which history has become a science is only about a half-century old, we must not be deceived by the word 'revolution'. Long before Bacon and Descartes revolutionized natural science by expounding publicly the principles on which its method was based, people here and there had been using these same methods, some more often, some more rarely. As Bacon and Descartes so justly pointed out, the effect of their own work was to put these same methods within the grasp of quite ordinary intellects. When it is said that the methods of history have been revolutionized in the last half-century, this is what is meant. It is not meant that examples of scientific history will be sought in vain before that date. It is meant that whereas, earlier, scientific history was a thing of rare occurrence, hardly to be found except in the work of outstanding men, and even in them marking moments of inspiration rather than the even tenor of study, it is now a thing within the compass of everyone; a thing which we demand of everybody who writes history at all, and which is widely enough understood, even among the unlearned, to procure a livelihood for writers of detective stories whose plot is based upon its methods. The sporadic and intermittent way in which the truth of human freedom was grasped in the seventeenth century might, to say the least of it, have been a consequence of this sporadic and intermittent grasp on the method of scientific history.

§ 7. *Progress as created by Historical Thinking*

The term 'progress', as used in the nineteenth century when the word was much in people's mouths, covers two things which it is well to distinguish: progress in history, and progress in nature. For progress in nature the word 'evolution' has been so widely used that this may be accepted as its established sense; and in order not to confuse the two things I shall restrict my use of the word 'evolution' to that meaning, and distinguish the other by the name 'historical progress'.

'Evolution' is a term applied to natural processes in so far as these are conceived as bringing into existence new specific forms in nature. This conception of nature as evolution must not be confused with the conception of nature as process. Granted the latter conception, two views of natural process are still possible: that events in nature repeat one another specifically, the specific forms remaining constant through the diversity of their individual instances, so that 'the course of nature is uniform' and 'the future will resemble the past', or that the specific forms themselves undergo change, new forms coming into existence by modification of the old. The second conception is what is meant by evolution.

In one sense, to call a natural process evolutionary is the same thing as calling it progressive. For if any given specific form can come into existence only as a modification of one already established, the establishment of any given form presupposes that of which it is a modification, and so on. If a form b is a modification of a, and c of b, and d of c, the forms a, b, c, d, can only come to exist in that order. The order is progressive in the sense that it is a series of terms which can come into existence only in that order. To say this, of course, implies nothing as to why the modifications arise, or whether they are large or small. In this sense of the word 'progress', progressive only means orderly, that is, exhibiting order.

But progress in nature, or evolution, has often been taken to mean more than this: namely the doctrine that each new form is not only a modification of the last but an improvement on it. To speak of improvement is to imply a standard of valuation. This, in the case of breeding new forms of domestic animals or plants, is intelligible enough: the value implied is the new form's utility for human purposes. But no one supposes that natural evolution is designed to produce such utilities; the standard implied, therefore, cannot be that. What is it?

Kant held that there was one form of value, and only one, that was independent of human purposes, namely the moral value of the good will. All other kinds of goodness, he argued, are merely goodness for some postulated purpose, but the goodness of morality does not depend on any postulated purpose, and thus moral goodness, as he put it, is an end in itself. On this view the evolutionary process has been truly progressive, because it has led through a determinate series of forms to the existence of man, a creature capable of moral goodness.

If this view is rejected, it is very doubtful whether any other standard of valuation can be found which would entitle us to call evolution progressive except merely in the sense of being orderly. Not because the idea of value finds no place in our view of nature, for it is difficult to think of any organism except as striving to maintain its own existence, and such effort implies that, at least for itself, its existence is not a mere matter of fact but something of value; but because all values seem merely relative. The archaeopteryx may in fact have been an ancestor of the bird, but what entitles us to call the bird an improvement on the archaeopteryx? A bird is not a better archaeopteryx, but something different that has grown out of it. Each is trying to be itself.

But the view of human nature as the noblest outcome of the evolutionary process did undoubtedly underlie the nineteenth-century conception of historical progress as guaranteed by a law of nature. That conception, in fact, depended on two assumptions or groups of assumptions. First, that man is or contains in himself something of absolute value, so that the process of nature in its evolution has been a progress in so far as it has been an orderly process leading to the existence of man. From this it followed that, since man obviously did not control the process leading to his own existence, there was in nature as such an inherent tendency towards the realization of this absolute value: in other words, 'progress is a law of nature'. Secondly, the assumption that man, as a child of nature, is subject to natural law, and that the laws of historical process are identical with the laws of evolution: that historical process is of the same kind as natural process. It followed that human history was subject to a necessary law of progress, in other words that of the new specific forms of social organization, art and science, and so forth, which it brings into existence each is necessarily an improvement on the last.

The idea of a 'law of progress' may be attacked by denying either of these two assumptions. It may be denied that man has in him anything of absolute value. His rationality, it may be said, only serves to make him the most maleficent and destructive of the animals, and is rather a blunder or a cruel joke of nature than her noblest work; his morality is only (as the modern jargon goes) a rationalization or ideology which he has devised to conceal from himself the crude fact of his bestiality. From this point of view, the natural process that has led to his existence can no longer be regarded as a progress. But further: if the conception of historical process as a mere extension of natural process is denied, as it must be by any sound theory of history, it follows that there is no natural and in that sense necessary law of progress in history. The question whether any particular historical change has been an improvement must consequently be a question to be answered on its merits in each particular case.

The conception of a 'law of progress', by which the course of history is so governed that successive forms of human activity exhibit each an improvement on the last, is thus a mere confusion of thought, bred of an unnatural union between man's belief in his own superiority to nature and his belief that he is nothing more than a part of nature. If either belief is true, the other is false: they cannot be combined to produce logical offspring.

Nor can the question, whether in a given case an historical change has or has not been progressive, be answered until we are sure that such questions have a meaning. Before they are raised, we must ask what is meant by historical progress, now that it has been distinguished from natural progress; and, if anything is meant, whether the meaning is one applicable to the given case we are considering. For it would be hasty to assume that, because the conception of historical progress as dictated by a law of nature is nonsensical, the conception of historical progress itself is therefore nonsensical.

Assuming, then, that the phrase 'historical progress' may still have a meaning, we must ask what it means. The fact that it has suffered confusion through contamination with the idea of evolution does not prove it meaningless; on the contrary, it suggests that it has a certain basis in historical experience.

As a first attempt to define its meaning, we might suggest that historical progress is only another name for human activity itself, as a succession of acts each of which arises out of the last. Every act whose history we may study, of whatever kind it is, has its place in a series of acts where one has created a situation with which the next has to deal. The accomplished act gives rise to a new problem; it is always this new problem, not the old problem over again, which the new act is obliged to solve. If a man has discovered how to get a meal, next time he is hungry he must find out how to get another, and the getting of this other is a new act arising out of the old. His situation is always changing, and the act of thought by which he solves the problems it presents is always changing too.

This is no doubt true, but it is not to our purpose. It is just as true of a dog as of a man, that every meal must be a different meal: just as true, that every time a bee gathering honey visits a flower, it must be a different flower; just as true, that every time a body moving in a straight line or an open curve comes to a part of space, it must be a different part. But these processes are not historical processes, and to quote them as throwing light on the historical process would betray the old fallacy of naturalism. Moreover, the novelty of the new situation and the new act is not a specific novelty, for the new act may be a new act of exactly the same kind (for example, setting the same snare again in the same place); so that we are not even discussing the evolutionary aspect of natural process, which is the point at which that process seems most akin to the historical. The search for a fresh meal takes place even in the most completely static or non-progressive society.

The idea of historical progress, then, if it refers to anything, refers to the coming into existence not merely of new actions or thoughts or situations belonging to the same specific type, but of new specific types. It therefore presupposes such specific novelties, and consists in the conception of these as improvements. Suppose, for example, a man or a community had lived on fish, and, the fish-supply failing, had sought food in a new way, by digging for roots: this would be a change in the specific type of situation and activity, but it would not be regarded as a progress, because the change does not imply that the new type is an improvement on the old. But if a community of fish-eaters had changed their method of catching fish from a less to a more efficient one, by which an average fisherman could catch ten fish on an average day instead of five, this would be called an example of progress.

But from whose point of view is it an improvement? The question must be asked, because what is an improvement from one point of view may be the reverse from another; and if there is a third from which an impartial judgement can be passed on this conflict, the qualifications of this impartial judge must be determined.

Let us first consider the change from the point of view of the persons concerned in it: the older generation still practising the old method while the younger has adopted the new. In such a case the older generation will see no need for the change, knowing as it does that life can be lived on the old method. And it will also think that the old method is better than the new; not out of irrational prejudice, but because the way of life which it knows and values is built round the old method, which is therefore certain to have social and religious associations that express the intimacy of its connexion with this way of life as a whole. A man of the older generation only wants his five fish a day, and he does not want half a day's leisure; what he wants is to live as he has lived. To him, therefore, the change is no progress, but a decadence.

It might seem obvious that by the opposite party, the younger generation, the change is conceived as a progress. It has given up the life of its fathers and chosen a new one for itself: it would not do this (one might suppose) without comparing the two and deciding that the new is better. But this is not necessarily the case. There is no choice except for a person who knows what both the things are between which he is choosing. To choose between two ways of life is impossible unless one knows what they are; and this means not merely looking on one as a spectacle, and practising the other, or practising one and conceiving the other as an unrealized possibility, but knowing both in the only way in which ways of life can be known: by actual experience, or by the sympathetic insight which may take its place for such a purpose. But experience shows that nothing is harder than for a given generation in a changing society, which is living in a new way of its own, to enter sympathetically into the life of the last. It sees that life as a mere incomprehensible spectacle, and seems driven to escape from sympathy with it by a kind of instinctive effort to free itself from parental influences and bring about the change on which it is blindly resolved. There is here no genuine comparison between the two ways of life, and therefore no judgement that one is better than the other, and therefore no conception of the change as a progress.

For this reason, the historical changes in a society's way of life are very rarely conceived as progressive even by the generation that makes them. It makes them in obedience to a blind impulse to destroy what it does not comprehend, as bad, and substitute something else as good. But progress is not the replacement of the bad by the good, but of the good by the better. In order to conceive a change as a progress, then, the person who has made it must think of what he has abolished as good, and good in certain definite ways. This he can only do on condition of his knowing what the old way of life was like, that is, having historical knowledge of his society's past while he is actually living in the present he is creating: for historical knowledge is simply the re-enactment of past experiences in the mind of the present thinker. Only thus can the two ways of life be held together in the same mind for a comparison of their merits, so that a person choosing one and rejecting the other can know what he has gained and what he has lost, and decide that he has chosen the better. In short: the revolutionary can only regard his revolution as a progress in so far as he is also an historian, genuinely re-enacting in his own historical thought the life he nevertheless rejects.

Let us now consider the change in question, no longer from the standpoint of those concerned in it, but from that of an historian placed outside it. We might hope that, from his detached and impartial point of view, he would be able to judge with some chance of fairness whether it was a progress or not. But this is a difficult matter. He is only deceived if he fastens on the fact that ten fish are caught where five were caught before, and uses this as a criterion of progress. He must take into account the conditions and consequences of that change. He must ask what was done with the additional fish or the additional leisure. He must ask what value attached to the social and religious institutions that were sacrificed for them. In short, he must judge the relative value of two different ways of life, taken as two wholes. Now, in order to do this, he must be able to enter with equal sympathy into the essential features and values of each way of life: he must re-experience them both in his own mind, as objects of historical knowledge. What makes him a qualified judge, therefore, is just the fact that he does not look at his object from a detached point of view, but re-lives it in himself.

We shall see, later, that the task of judging the value of a certain way of life taken in its entirety is an impossible task, because no such thing in its entirety is ever a possible object of historical knowledge. The attempt to know what we have no means of knowing is an infallible way to generate illusions; and this attempt to judge whether one period of history or phase of human life, taken as a whole, shows progress as compared with its predecessor, generates illusions of an easily recognizable type. Their characteristic feature is the labelling of certain historical periods as good periods, or ages of historical greatness, and of others as bad periods, ages of historical failure or poverty. The so-called good periods are the ones into whose spirit the historian has penetrated, owing either to the existence of abundant evidence or to his own capacity for re-living the experience they enjoyed; the so-called bad periods are either those for which evidence is relatively scanty, or those whose life he cannot, for reasons arising out of his own experience and that of his age, reconstruct within himself.

At the present day we are constantly presented with a view of history as consisting in this way of good and bad periods, the bad periods being divided into the primitive and the decadent, according as they come before or after the good ones. This distinction between periods of primitiveness, periods of greatness, and periods of decadence, is not and never can be historically true. It tells us much about the historians who study the facts, but nothing about the facts they study. It is characteristic of an age like our own, where history is studied widely and successfully, but eclectically. Every period of which we have competent knowledge (and by competent knowledge I mean insight into its thought, not mere acquaintance with its remains) appears in the perspective of time as an age of brilliance: the brilliance being the light of our own historical insight. The intervening periods are seen by contrast as, relatively speaking and in different degrees, 'dark ages': ages which we know to have existed, because there is a gap of time for them in our chronology, and we have possibly numerous relics of their work and thought, but in which we can find no real life because we cannot re-enact that thought in our own minds. That this pattern of light and darkness is an optical illusion proceeding from the distribution of the historian's knowledge and ignorance is obvious from the different ways in which it is drawn by different historians and by the historical thought of different generations.

The same optical illusion in a simpler form affected the historical thought of the eighteenth century, and laid the foundations for the dogma of progress, as that was accepted in the nineteenth. When Voltaire laid it down that 'all history is modern history',[1] and that nothing could be genuinely known before about the end of the fifteenth century, he was saying two things at once: that nothing earlier than the modern period could be known, and that nothing earlier deserved to be known. These two things came to the same thing. His inability to reconstruct genuine history from the documents of the ancient world and the Middle Ages was the source of his belief that those ages were dark and barbarous. The idea of history as a progress from primitive times to the present day was, to those who believed in it, a simple consequence of the fact that their historical outlook was limited to the recent past.

The old dogma of a single historical progress leading to the present, and the modern dogma of historical cycles, that is, of a multiple progress leading to 'great ages' and then to decadence, are thus mere projections of the historian's ignorance upon the screen of the past. But, setting dogmas aside, has the idea of progress no other basis than this? We have already seen that there is one condition on which that idea can represent a genuine thought, and not either a blind feeling or a mere state of ignorance. The condition is that the person who uses the word should

---

[1] *Dictionnaire philosophique*, art. 'Histoire'; *Œuvres* (1784), vol. xli, p. 45.

use it in comparing two historical periods or ways of life, both of which he can understand historically, that is, with enough sympathy and insight to reconstruct their experience for himself. He must satisfy himself and his readers that no blind spot in his own mind, and no defect in his equipment of learning, prevents him from entering into the experience of either less fully than into the other's. Then, having fulfilled that condition, he is entitled to ask whether the change from the first to the second was a progress.

But when he asks this, what exactly is he asking? Obviously, he is not asking whether the second comes nearer to the way of life which he accepts as his own. By re-enacting the experience of either in his own mind he has already accepted it as a thing to be judged by its own standards: a form of life having its own problems, to be judged by its success in solving those problems and no others. Nor is he assuming that the two different ways of life were attempts to do one and the same thing, and asking whether the second did it better than the first. Bach was not trying to write like Beethoven and failing; Athens was not a relatively unsuccessful attempt to produce Rome; Plato was himself, not a half-developed Aristotle.

There is only one genuine meaning for this question. If thought in its first phase, after solving the initial problems of that phase, is then, through solving these, brought up against others which defeat it; and if the second solves these further problems without losing its hold on the solution of the first, so that there is gain without any corresponding loss, then there is progress. And there can be progress on no other terms. If there is any loss, the problem of setting loss against gain is insoluble.

According to this definition, it would be idle to ask whether any one period of history taken as a whole showed a progress over its predecessor. For the historian can never take any period as a whole. There must be large tracts of its life for which he has either no data, or no data that he is in a position to interpret. We cannot, for example, know what the Greeks enjoyed in the way of musical experience, though we know that they greatly valued it; we have not enough material; and on the other hand, though we have no lack of data about Roman religion, our own religious experience is not of such a kind as to qualify us for reconstructing in our own minds what it meant to them. We must select certain aspects of experience and confine our search for progress to these.

Can we speak of progress in happiness or comfort or satisfaction? Obviously not. Different ways of life are differentiated by nothing more clearly than by differences between the things that people habitually enjoy, the conditions which they find comfortable, and the achievements they regard as satisfactory. The problem of being comfortable in a medieval cottage is so different from the problem of being comfortable in a modern slum that there is no comparing them; the happiness of a peasant is not contained in the happiness of a millionaire.

Nor does it mean anything to ask whether there is progress in art. The artist's problem, so far as he is an artist, is not the problem of doing what his predecessor has done and going on to do something further which his predecessor failed to do. There is development in art, but no progress: for though in the technical processes of art one man learns from another, Titian from Bellini, Beethoven from Mozart, and so on, the problem of art itself consists not in mastering these technical processes but in using them to express the artist's experience and give it reflective form, and consequently every fresh work of art is the solution of a fresh problem which arises not out of a previous work of art but out of the artist's unreflective experience. Artists do better or worse work in so far as they solve these problems well or ill; but the relation between good and bad art is not an historical relation, because the problems arise out of the flow of unreflective experience, and that flow is not an historical process.

In one sense, there is no progress in morality. The life of morality consists not in the development of moral codes, but in their application to individual problems of conduct, and to a great extent these problems, like those of art, arise out of unreflective experience. The course of our moral life is conditioned by the succession of our desires; and, though our desires change, they do not change historically. They arise out of our animal nature, and though this may change from youth to old age, or vary in different peoples and climates, its differences are part of the process of nature, not of history.

In another sense, however, there is or may be moral progress. Part of our moral life consists of coping with problems arising not out of our animal nature but out of our social institutions, and these are historical things, which create moral problems only in so far as they are already the expression of moral ideals. A man who asks himself whether he ought to take voluntary part in his country's war is not struggling with personal fear; he is involved in a conflict between the moral forces embodied in the institution of the State, and those embodied not merely in the ideal, but in the equally actual reality, of international peace and intercourse. Similarly the problem of divorce arises not out of the whims of sexual desire, but out of an unresolved conflict between the moral ideal of monogamy and the moral evils which that ideal, rigidly applied, brings in its train. To solve the problem of war or of divorce is only possible by devising new institutions which shall recognize in full the moral claims recognized by the State or by monogamy, and shall satisfy these claims without leaving unsatisfied the further claims to which, in historical fact, the old institutions have given rise.

The same double aspect appears in the economic life. So far as that consists in finding from moment to moment the means of satisfying demands which spring not from our historical environment but from our nature as animals with certain desires, there can be no progress in it; that would be a progress in happiness or comfort or satisfaction, which we have seen to be impossible. But not all our demands are for the satisfaction of animal desires. The demand for investments in which I can put my savings to support me in old age is not an animal desire; it arises out of an individualistic economic system in which the old are supported neither statutorily by the State nor customarily by their families, but by the fruits of their own labour, and in which capital commands a certain rate of interest. That system has solved a good many problems, and therein lies its economic value; but it gives rise to a good many others which as yet it has failed to solve. A better economic system, one whose substitution for this would be a progress, would continue to solve the same problems which are solved by individualist capitalism, and solve these others as well.

The same considerations apply to politics and law, and I need not work out the application in detail. In science, philosophy, and religion the conditions are rather different. Here, unless I am mistaken, the question of coping with our animal nature and satisfying its needs does not arise. The problem is a single one instead of a double.

Progress in science would consist in the supersession of one theory by another which served both to explain all that the first theory explained, and also to explain types or classes of events or 'phenomena' which the first ought to have explained but could not. I suppose that Darwin's theory of the origin of species was an example. The theory of fixed species explained the relative permanence of natural kinds within the recorded memory of man; but it ought to have held good for the longer stretch of geological time, and it broke down, too, for the case of selectively-bred animals and plants under domestication. Darwin propounded a theory whose claim to merit rested on its bringing these three classes under one conception. I need hardly quote the now more familiar relation between Newton's law of gravitation and that of Einstein, or that between the special and general theories of relativity. The interest of science, in relation to the conception of progress, seems to be that this is the simplest and most obvious case in which progress exists and is verifiable. For this reason, those who have believed most strongly in progress have been much in the habit of appealing to the progress of science as the plainest proof that there is such a thing, and often, too, have based their hope of progress in other fields on the hope of making science the absolute mistress of human life. But science is and can be mistress only in her own house, and forms of activity which cannot progress (such as art) cannot be made to do so by subjecting them, if that phrase meant anything, to the rule of science; whereas those which can must progress by finding out for themselves how to improve in doing their own work.

Philosophy progresses in so far as one stage of its development solves the problems which defeated it in the last, without losing its hold on the solutions already achieved. This, of course, is independent of whether the two stages are stages in the life of a single philosopher, or are represented by different men. Thus, suppose it true that Plato grasped the necessity for an eternal object, the world of Ideas or Idea of the Good, and also for an eternal subject, the soul in its double function of knower and mover, as solutions for the problems with which his predecessors' work had left him confronted: but was baffled to say how these two were related; and suppose Aristotle saw that the problem of the relation between them, as Plato had stated it, or rather as he himself saw it in his long apprenticeship to Plato's teaching, could be solved by thinking of them as one and the same, pure intellect being identical with its own object, and its knowledge of that object being its knowledge of itself; then, so far (though conceivably not in other respects) Aristotle's philosophy would mark a progress on Plato's, granted that by that new step Aristotle sacrificed nothing that Plato had achieved by his theory of Ideas and his theory of soul.

In religion, progress is possible on the same terms. If Christianity, bating no jot or tittle of what Judaism had won by its conception of God as one God, just and terrible, infinitely great over against man's infinite littleness and infinitely exacting in his demands on man, could bridge the gulf between God and man by the conception that God became man in order that we might become God, that was a progress, and a momentous one, in the history of the religious consciousness.

In such senses and in such cases as these, progress is possible. Whether it has actually occurred, and where and when and in what ways, are questions for historical thought to answer. But there is one other thing for historical thought to do: namely to create this progress itself. For progress is not a mere fact to be discovered by historical thinking: it is only through historical thinking that it comes about at all.

The reason for this is that progress, in those cases (common or rare) when it happens, happens only in one way: by the retention in the mind, at one phase, of what was achieved in the preceding phase. The two phases are related not merely by way of succession, but by way of continuity, and continuity of a peculiar kind. If Einstein makes an advance on Newton, he does it by knowing Newton's thought and retaining it within his own, in the sense that he knows what Newton's problems were, and how he solved them, and, disentangling the truth in those solutions from whatever errors prevented Newton from going further, embodying these solutions as thus disentangled in his own theory. He might have done this, no doubt, without having read Newton in the original for himself; but not without having received Newton's doctrine from someone. Thus Newton stands, in such a context, not for a man but for a theory, reigning during a certain period of scientific thought. It is only in so far as Einstein knows that theory, as a fact in the history of science, that he can make an advance upon it. Newton thus lives in Einstein in the way in which any past experience lives in the mind of the historian, as a past experience known as past—as the point from which the development with which he is concerned started—but re-enacted here and now together with a development of itself that is partly constructive or positive and partly critical or negative.

Similarly with any other progress. If we want to abolish capitalism or war, and in doing so not only to destroy them but to bring into existence something better, we must begin by understanding them: seeing what the problems are which our economic or international system succeeds in solving, and how the solution of these is related to the other problems which it fails to solve. This understanding of the system we set out to supersede is a thing which we must retain throughout the work of superseding it, as a knowledge of the past conditioning our creation of the future. It may be impossible to do this; our hatred of the thing we are destroying may prevent us from understanding it, and we may love it so much that we cannot destroy it unless we are blinded by such hatred. But if that is so, there will once more, as so often in the past, be change but no progress; we shall have lost our hold on one group of problems in our anxiety to solve the next. And we ought by now to realize that no kindly law of nature will save us from the fruits of our ignorance.

PRELIMINARY DISCUSSION
THE IDEA OF A PHILOSOPHY OF SOMETHING, AND, IN PARTICULAR, A PHILOSOPHY OF HISTORY (1927)[1]

WHEN we speak of the *philosophy of something* (e.g. of art, of religion, of history) we mean to designate a body of thoughts which arise in us when we think about that thing. These thoughts must be philosophical; that is, they must be universal and necessary. A fortuitous association of ideas—for instance, the association of framed canvasses with the thought of art—is not philosophy; no thoughts can claim to be the philosophy of a subject unless they arise universally and necessarily in the mind of everyone who thinks about that subject.

For this reason, we must exclude from the philosophy of a subject not only fortuitous associations, but thoughts of the peculiar kind which are called scientific, in the sense in which scientific thought is distinguished from philosophical. A scientific thought is universal only in the sense that it is universally applicable to a limited sphere; it is empirically universal, not absolutely universal; it applies to all the facts that make up the field of an inquiry, but not to all facts whatever, on the contrary, were it applicable to all facts, it would cease to be a scientific law and would become a philosophical; and this

---

The source document can be found in the Bodleian Library Collingwood Papers, dep. 14.

[1] After the title is written by Collingwood: 'added April 1927'. Collingwood wrote this essay while staying in Rome with his friend the Italian philosopher de Ruggiero. It was meant as an additional introduction to the Lectures on the Philosophy of History, written in 1926. A note subsequently added to the title-page reads: 'Written in Rome, by fits and starts, April 1927. I haven't read it since, but from my recollection of the frame or frames of mind in which it was composed I suspect it of being chaotic and practically valueless. Die, April 1928.'

Collingwood added the note while on vacation in the country-house Le Martouret, Die, France, during April 1928. It was there that he wrote his Outlines of a Philosophy of History (mentioned in *An Autobiography*, p. 107). Despite Collingwood's own negative assessment of this 'Preliminary Discussion' it is nevertheless valuable as an illustration of his thinking at that time on the nature of the philosophy of history.

is what has happened to mathematics in the opinion of the mathematical logicians, who wrongly think that mathematics is applicable to all facts whatever.

The philosophy of a subject must, therefore, include nothing arbitrary or hypothetical. It cannot consist of, or even include, classifications of its subject-matter; for every classification is so far arbitrary that, so long as it is merely a classification, it is capable of being set aside, or replaced by another. Thus the classification of arts into arts of sight and arts of hearing, or arts in space and arts in time, can have no place in the philosophy of ·art; the classification of documents into written and unwritten can have no place in the philosophy of history. Such classifications can only claim a position in the philosophy of a subject if they can be shown to be more than classifications: if they can be shown to be universal and necessary thoughts arising inevitably in the mind of everyone who thinks about art and history. As long as they are *mere* classifications, that is, convenient and useful ways of dividing the field of inquiry, they are non-philosophical.

Similarly, there cannot be anything hypothetical in a philosophical study. We cannot, in such studies, consider the hypothetical case of a perfect specimen of its kind—a perfectly beautiful painting or a perfectly true or exhaustive history. The reason for this is that the philosophy of art or history is concerned to investigate the idea of aesthetic or historical perfection; it consists of an attempt to elucidate and define this idea: and therefore it is illegitimate to proceed by assuming that we already know what such perfection is or would be. For example, Plato proceeds to philosophize about politics by constructing a hypothetical picture of a perfect state. This is an error in method. The idea of a perfect πόλις, considered in abstraction from the particular historical conditions under which alone political institutions exist, falsifies the realities of political life and leaves us with a political theory whose value—for it has very great value—is due to the fact that Plato has not strictly carried out his own programme, and is describing, not the abstract idea of the state, but the actual Greek state, modified by the introduction of a few bold, perhaps overbold, reforms. A genuine philosophical inquiry is an inquiry into actual facts, not into hypotheses; the political philosopher ought to describe not the best possible state but the actual life of the actual state, and if he does this faithfully he will find that the actual *is* the best possible—in the circumstances. This differentiates political philosophy from sociology, which is not philosophical but scientific, and is concerned with hypothetical entities very much as medicine is concerned with the hypothetical entity of an accurately typical case of typhoid, or geometry with the hypothetical entity of an exactly straight line.

The philosophy of history, then, will consist of thoughts arising universally and necessarily in the mind of everyone who thinks about history; and these thoughts will not be concerned with classifications or hypothetical entities, but with the actual concrete facts of which history is the collective name. These facts must exist, in order that the philosophy of history may arise; and at every step in our philosophical inquiry we must keep our eye on them, in the sure conviction that if we let our vision of them grow dim our philosophical inquiry will evaporate into nothing.

The facts whose collective name is history consist of a certain type of human activities which may be conveniently denominated as historical studies. In a specialized form these studies are pursued by specialized persons called historians; and in this form history constitutes a class of activity, whose distinction from others is effected by a classificatory logic like that which distinguishes mammals from reptiles. We have already seen that this classificatory kind of distinction is foreign to the nature of philosophical thinking. The logic of philosophy distinguishes, but it does not classify: the distinctions which it recognizes are not classificatory distinctions but distinctions of a different type. What is this type?

If we reflect on the distinction asserted by formal logic, between affirmative and negative judgements, we shall see that in the first instance it presents itself as a classificatory distinction: some judgements are affirmative, others are negative. But under closer scrutiny it appears in a wholly different light. We now find that every judgement, regarded as merely affirmative, is indefinite or ambiguous in significance: it only becomes precise when to its affirmative element we add a negative element. Thus, a man says 'I am a Liberal', and this statement only conveys a precise meaning—if indeed it does so at all—

because we understand it as expressing not only his acceptance of certain principles but his rejection of others; and if we did not know what he was rejecting, we should not really know what he meant by calling himself a Liberal. Similarly, if we are told that twice two is four, we do not understand this statement until we are able to say: 'I see, twice two couldn't make three or five or six or anything else except four'. The negation provides a background against which the affirmation stands out in relief; without this background, it is the mere outline of a possible judgement, not a judgement actually grasped and judged. And it is even easier to see that a mere negation has no real meaning unless in making it we also make an affirmation, not of course necessarily expressed in words, which finds in the negation a background.

Affirmation and negation are thus not classes of judgements but elements distinguishable within one and the same judgement. Every judgement must possess both elements; and therefore the conceptions of affirmation and negation are universal and necessary concepts arising within us whenever we think about judgement. They belong, that is to say, to the philosophy of judgement, or logic considered as a philosophical science. This gives us an example of the way in which the philosophy of a subject makes its distinctions. It does so by analysing the facts which it is studying into their universal and necessary elements, and every element so detected will of necessity appear in any and every instance of the subject studied.

But how are we to know that the elements found in this particular fact will reappear in others? How are we to know that the results of our analysis are of universal validity?

The answer may be discovered by considering the familiar solution of the same problem in the case of mathematics. We propound the theorem that the square on the hypotenuse is equal to the sum of the squares on the other two sides, and we prove this by taking a case, the case of a particular triangle having sides of (say) 3, 4, and 5 inches long and being drawn in pencil on white paper. Now granted that our proof works for this case, how do we know it will work for every other case? The answer is that in proving our theorem we appealed to those characteristics of our triangle, and only those, which made it a right-angled triangle: all other characteristics we ignored: and therefore our proof is unaffected by variations in these other characteristics. Similarly, then, our analysis of judgement will be universally valid if and so far as we confine ourselves to those characteristics in a judgement which make it a judgement: our analysis of history, if it is confined to those characteristics of history in virtue of which it is history, etc.

But how do we know what those characteristics are? May not the essential nature of judgement, history, etc. be entirely hidden from us? And is not the view I have expounded based on the ridiculous (or at any rate exceedingly bold) claim that we actually know what it is that makes any given thing what it is?

Certainly it is based on such a claim. Just as the mathematician, in order to take a single step in mathematics, must commit himself irrevocably to the assertion that he knows what makes a triangle triangular—namely, the possession of three straight sides—so the philosopher must commit himself to the assertion that he knows the essence of judgement, history, moral action, etc. Now we are in general ready to admit the reasonableness of the mathematician's claim; is there any ground for regarding that of the philosopher as any more daring?

There would be no such ground, if philosophy were as hypothetical as mathematics. The reason why we find no difficulty about the mathematician's claim to know the essence of a triangle is because we recognize that the mathematician is only claiming to tell us what a triangle would essentially be, if such a thing as a triangle existed; and the fact that the triangle is a merely hypothetical entity justifies him in laying down the law about it. He says, in effect, let us suppose triangles, and by that I mean, let us suppose three-sided rectilinear figures, and see what happens. Here the essence, as distinct from the consequent properties, of the triangle, is fixed by the initial act of supposition; and that act does not claim to be or to involve a profound insight into the nature of things.

But when the philosopher claims to know what it is that makes a judgement a judgement, he is assuming that judgements really exist, and that their real nature is such that what he calls their essence is the thing about them which it is most important for us to know. This, clearly, is a bold and paradoxical claim; so bold and paradoxical, that whole schools of thought have recoiled from it and attempted to construct a theory of philosophical method which should avoid the necessity of making it. These schools of thought are, broadly speaking, the empiricist schools, which attempt to treat philosophy as if it were science and to explain its logic as a hypothetical and classificatory logic. The failure of all such attempts is inevitable, and is due to the fact that their very existence is a standing refutation of their own doctrines. For they consist of judgements; whether these judgements are categorical or hypothetical, they are actually judged: and that being so, it cannot be an open question whether there are any judgements. Geometry studies the properties of triangles, and treats them as hypothetical entities; this it can reasonably do, because geometry is not itself a triangle. If geometry were a triangle, then so long as geometry existed it could not be doubted whether triangles existed. But logic studies the properties of judgements: and logic is itself a judgement or assemblage of judgements: therefore the existence of logic guarantees the actual reality of its own subject-matter, for it is a subject-matter to itself.

Let us recapitulate. Our difficulty is this: how can we claim such insight into the essential nature of actual things as is involved in saying that we know what constitutes the essence of a judgement? We cannot resolve the difficulty by copying the procedure of the mathematician, because his procedure is based on the unreality of his object, whereas our object becomes real because by thinking about it we are creating an instance of it. The fact that we create the instance is the source of the whole difficulty. Strangely enough, it is also the key to the solution of the difficulty. For though, if we merely found a certain kind of object such as an elephant existing in an external world, we could never know its real essence, a thing which we create must be a thing whose essence we understand at least so far as is necessary in order to decide whether or no what we have created is really the thing we take it for. Thus, if I say, I have made a theory, I am claiming in that assertion to know what a theory is; not only in the sense that I can recognize a theory (like an elephant) when I see one, but in the far profounder sense that while I am making the theory I know what it ought to be like, and am trying to make it more what it ought to be; that is, I claim to have insight into the real essence of a theory, to understand what it is that makes a theory a theory. Hence, while I recognize an elephant by marks which may be quite accidental and superficial, I recognize a theory by my insight into its essence: and that applies to everything which I create by a conscious and rational effort, by an activity working according to criteria.

Granted, then, that the historian's business may be described as constructing a narrative (and here the word narrative means not a fictitious narrative, but a true narrative; or rather, not a narrative intended to be fictitious but a narrative intended to be true), it follows that the essence of all historical narratives as such is an essence present to the historian's mind as a criterion or ideal during the whole time that he is carrying on his business. He knows what he is trying to do; he knows what desiderata his narrative ought to satisfy, and actually does satisfy so far as it succeeds in being history; and it is for him to judge whether or not it does succeed. Obviously, he must be competent to judge; for if the historian cannot tell the difference between good history and bad history, no one can; and if that were so, no one would be capable of judging whether the work of a particular historian is well done or ill done; that is, there could be no such thing as historical criticism. Because historical criticism actually exists, the people who pursue it must be possessed of standards enabling them to distinguish good history from bad; but this means distinguishing that which really is history—that which possesses the essential attributes of history—from that which possesses only its accidental attributes and is therefore in essence not history at all.

Now the question may be raised, whether the standards which the critic has been proved to possess may not be false standards. Surely it is common knowledge that critics often judge by wrong standards, calling that good history which satisfies some non-historical test, because for the moment, or habitually, they substitute this for the truly historical test. This is perfectly true. But anyone who says that this or that critic is judging by a wrong standard is in effect claiming to be himself possessed of the right, or at any rate a better, standard. This is sometimes denied. People sometimes point out that we can know a certain account of a matter to be false without knowing what account of it is true: for instance, I know that Lord Bacon did not write the Letters of Junius, but I do not know who did. Therefore, they argue, I may know that a certain critical standard is false and yet not be possessed of a standard which I regard as true.

This argument, though plausible, is a confused piece of thinking. It is my positive knowledge of the style and contents of the letters of Junius that prevents my ascribing them to Bacon; that is, it is because I know what they *are* that I know what they are *not*. Similarly, it can only be my knowledge of what history *is* that enables me to reject false accounts of its essence and say that it is *not* this or that. Further, there is a confusion between possessing a criterion, as the historical critic possesses it, and stating it in speculative terms, which is the business of the philosopher. The historical critic, as such, need not philosophize; the speculative statement of principles is not his business, and if asked to state them he may confess without shame that he cannot. But he absolutely must possess these principles, and use them in his actual work; they must control his work in the way in which our bones control the movements of our limbs; they must be immanent in his critical thinking, even if he never disentangles them from the concrete criticism, never treats them as independent and self-contained entities. If he can truthfully say that, even in this immanent sense, he possesses no positive standards, it only proves him incapable of doing that particular kind of critical work.

The essence of history, therefore, is an open secret in the sense that every historical critic believes himself, rightly or wrongly, to possess it, to grasp it as an immanent criterion in his everyday work. And the terms historical critic and historian are for this purpose synonymous; since the term historical critic only means a person able to distinguish between good and bad history, and this is a power which every historian possesses in so far as he refrains from propounding one version of a narrative and propounds another instead because he thinks it historically preferable.

But this still leaves us confronted with the question, how are we to know whether we are right or wrong in believing that our own standards are the right ones? Granted that some people join their faith to false standards, false criteria, by what criterion can the falseness of these criteria be demonstrated? It is an important question because, if it cannot be answered, my philosophy of history will become a mere account of the principles on which I personally work at what I personally call history; and thus all universality and necessity vanish. Nor can it be answered by appeal to the fact that people agree pretty widely as to what should be called history: for that fact is explicable on the hypothesis that such agreement, like the widespread agreement about the rules of Association football, is an acquiescence in something fundamentally arbitrary.

As stated, the problem is insoluble; for it presupposes the possibility that two people might work on genuinely different principles, according to criteria fundamentally incompatible, and yet think that they were trying to do the same thing. That is to say, it presupposes the *im*possibility of their communicating with one another or of studying one another's activities in such a way as to recognize the fundamental diversity of their criteria and therefore of their tasks. This is solipsism; and though it would be entirely false to say that solipsism is unanswerable, it is true enough that it cannot be answered until it is recognized for what it is, and the principles underlying it brought to light.

Here, in this special case, solipsism consists in the assertion of a necessary and irreducible misunderstanding between two persons, each thinking that because *he* is doing something therefore the other is doing it too, which he is not. Now if A misunderstands B's action, A is a bad historian of B's action; and if his historical principles compel him to misunderstand it, his historical principles are really anti-historical principles, principles not of historical truth but of historical error. Therefore in asserting our difficulty we were tacitly assuming that both A and B were in a condition, not only of error, but of invincible error; and certainly, if they *are* in invincible error, they *are* in invincible error; if we begin by assuming it, we must not be surprised if its results follow necessarily from the assumption.

Suppose, on the contrary, that their error was not invincible. It follows that when A uses a false (i.e. non-historical) standard in his study of B, and as a result condemns as false

the perhaps sound historical thought of B, he does not necessarily persist in using the term historical to describe his own
thinking; recognizing that there is a difference of kind between
his thought and B's, he may have the intelligence to agree with
B upon a difference of terminology and find a new name for
the principles which led to a result which, though bad history,
may be good art or psychology, or the like.

In saying this, we are assuming that a principle which leads
to bad history is not merely a non-historical principle, not
merely a principle of historical error, but has also a positive
value in relation to some other field of thought. And this
assumption is perfectly sound. Any principle must have some
positive or constructive side; it cannot be simply negative, it
must be somehow affirmative too. This may be illustrated by
an example from morals: the principle of always cheating
when you can is not a moral principle; it is an immoral principle; but to call it immoral is to say what it is *not*, not what it *is*;
and it has a positive or constructive character of its own, as a
principle of consistent self-enrichment, in addition to its negative or destructive character as a principle fatal to sound
morality. This is not a peculiarity of this principle or of any
special kind of principles: it is a matter of general logic that a
negation must have a positive side, and it is true of every negation. Hence standards which are bad and false in history must,
if they are standards at all and not sheer confusions of
thought, be good and true somewhere else; and the misunderstanding between two people who pin their faith to different
historical criteria is always capable of removal by the discovery that they have been at cross-purposes, each asserting what
the other was not in reality concerned to deny.

And clearly this must be the case if, as we began by saying,
the philosophy of history is composed of universal and necessary thoughts about history. For that statement implies that
nobody who thinks about the subject at all can wholly miss the
truth, and that therefore philosophical error consists not in
believing something purely and absolutely false but in the
application of principles with a legitimate sphere of their own
to spheres where they are illegitimate. And this is a true
account of error in all its forms; indeed, we can see that it *must*
be true, if we reflect that, just as there must be what is called a

'motive' for a crime, so there must be a 'reason' for an error. The 'motive' of a crime is a positive principle such as that of self-gratification, self-enrichment, the maintenance of one's own life or that of one's dependants; in the light of these principles the crime is seen not solely as a bad act but as a kind of good act and this goodness gives it a motive. The 'reason' for an error lies in the fact that the erring person is applying a positive principle, whose value he appreciates, to the case in hand; and it is important to recognize that what makes his error an error is not his application of this positive principle but his failure to apply also some further principle. It is not untrue that this crime will enrich me; it is perfectly true; but I ought not to be thinking only about that; I ought also to judge it by the standards of political or ethical conduct. Similarly it is not untrue that scientific methods can be applied to the subject-matter of philosophical problems; it is perfectly true; but the error of those who advocate this application consists in forgetting that, so far as the problem in hand is a *philosophical* problem, it cannot be solved except by appealing to principles and methods strictly philosophical.

It is at this point that the necessity of a philosophy of history becomes apparent. If two people A and B are using different and incompatible principles in their critical or constructive historical labours, then one of the two, to say the least, is producing bad history; he is being misled by false principles very much as an immoral man is misled by false principles when he sets out to gratify his desires instead of doing what is right. Now A cannot be convicted of a fundamental error of principle by appeal to the fact that his history comes out different from B's; on the contrary, he will regard this as a merit, and B will conversely regard it as a merit in *his* history that it should be unlike A's. Suppose for instance that A is a historical materialist of the school of Karl Marx, and believes that the forces which ultimately determine all historical events are economic forces. The result of this will be that historical narrative, as produced by A, will be a narrative of economic events, a materialistic narrative. But you cannot convert A from his principles by saying to him 'see how materialistic history becomes on your view'; he will reply 'that is what I want it to be'. And if B is attached to an opposite school of thought, B will regard it as a merit in his own history that it says little about economics, which is precisely what A considers to be B's defect as an historian.

What, in this state of things, is one to do? Only two courses are open. Either we may solve by an appeal to blind caprice a problem whose rational solution we have renounced, and say, some people like their history materialistic and others don't, or we may decide to think out a genuine solution of the problem by stating in a philosophical form the principles at stake, and subjecting them to a philosophical criticism. By stating them in a philosophical form I mean merely stating them as general principles, instead of being content to be guided by them in the actual work of historical thought. Thus the materialistic historian resolves all non-economic, or apparently non-economic, facts into results of economic forces; this habit of mind implies principles which, when stated, take the shape of a materialistic philosophy; and the question whether it is good history or bad history to resolve everything into terms of economics can only be settled by stating and criticizing this materialistic philosophy.

The philosophy of history, so understood, means bringing to light the principles used in historical thinking, and criticizing them; its function is to criticize and regulate these principles, with the object of making history truer and historically better. It thus arises by an absolute necessity out of the practice of historical thinking, and the historian can evade the necessity of engaging in the philosophy of history only so long as he can evade entangling himself in the problems of methodology; that is, the problems of how he ought to handle historical materials and what kind of result he ought to aim at attaining. (This conception of philosophical inquiry as having a utility beyond itself, of assisting towards the development of something which is not itself philosophy, is a scandal to various people who, trying to keep the various interests of human life in watertight compartments, insist that philosophy serves no purpose except that of supplying academic answers to academic questions; but human life is not really divided into watertight compartments, and it is a very foolish method of combating utilitarianism to say that the things in which utilitarianism sees *only* utility really possess *no* utility.)

The philosophy of history, so understood, is the methodology of history. Arising spontaneously in an unsystematic form out of actual historical work, it cannot ever be expressed in the form of a completed doctrine; it must consist of topics raised and discussed in the shape given them by the peculiar circumstances in which they arise, and the natural method of treating it is by isolated and self-contained discussions. As instances of themes to be discussed in this way, one might mention such questions as the following. Ought history to pay special attention to any one side of human life, such as (according to Marx) economics, or (according to the present Regius Professor) politics? Is it possible, or desirable, to write separate histories of art, of religion, of warfare, of constitutional law, and the like; or do these things, by being separated from their historical environment, become unintelligible in their development? Is the ideal of history a single universal history, a history of the world, or a number of separate histories, and if the latter, how ought they to be divided up? Is it possible to produce good history by portioning out different parts of the subject to different authors after the Cambridge fashion, and if not, why not? Ought history to aim at biographical form, at presenting the reader with individual portraits, or ought it to suppress the biographical element and describe movements whose magnitude transcends the individual? Ought it to admit an imaginary element, a conjecture as to what may have happened when evidence fails as to what did happen; or ought it to state nothing but what, on the available evidence, is certain? Ought the historian to write with an eye to his own times, and to see the past in the light of the present, as Grote saw Athenian democracy in the light of nineteenth-century radicalism, or ought he to leave behind as profane all interest in the present when he enters the temple of Clio? Ought the historian to pass moral judgements on his characters? Ought he to take sides in the conflicts whose history he narrates? Ought he to ascribe their issue to necessity, or to chance, or to the agency of human wills? Questions like these are concerned with the historian's duty in matters where, at least to all appearances, a choice is open to him; but there are others, no less urgent, which begin not with the word *ought* but with the word *can*. Thus, can history exist in the absence of written records? Can there be a history, in the proper sense of the word, concerning the Bronze Age, for example? Can the historian determine why things happened, or only what it was that happened? Can he appreciate the motives of his characters, or do their actions necessarily remain for him mere opaque facts? Within what limits, if at all, can the historian go behind his sources and criticize and correct them? and if at all, on what principles?

To enumerate such questions is to discover that their number is infinite; and as one turns them over in one's mind, one gradually perceives two facts standing out more and more clearly. The first is, that all these questions revolve round one central question, the question of the fundamental nature, meaning, purpose, and value of history: the question: what *is* history? is it a genuine form of knowledge, or is it an illusion? can it really make good its claim to be a mental discipline and an approach to reality, or is it a confused mass of heterogeneous and half-developed tendencies of thought? If it is a genuine form of knowledge, what place has it in knowledge as a whole, and how is it related to other forms? I say that this is one question, though it seems many; but it is one in the sense that any answer to any one of the many involves an answer to all the others, and any alteration in the answer given to one involves an alteration in the answers given to all the others. But, further, a properly thought-out answer to the central question 'what *is* history?' provides a point of view from which the various methodological questions to which I have referred can be approached and solved; for these infinite methodological questions have this in common, that they all involve the application of a concept of history to some particular case or type of case; and the possession of a properly thought-out concept of history is therefore an indispensable condition of their solution.

The second fact which emerges is that these various questions bring us face to face with problems from every department of philosophy. We cannot, for instance, decide whether the historian ought to ascribe historical events to necessity, chance, or human will, without raising, and settling as best we can, the problem of human freedom and necessity. We cannot say whether it is best to write a separate history of art or to include it in a general history of civilization, without discussing the question in what sense art is a separate thing, a self-contained part of human life. Thus the methodological problems of history lead us not simply to a specialized philosophy of history but to a perfectly general or universal philosophy, to philosophy as a whole.

There are thus three aspects of the philosophy of history. First, as a complex of particular methodological problems growing immediately out of historical thinking. Secondly, as the attempt to answer the question, what is history? Thirdly, as identical with philosophy in general. Now clearly, these three aspects are in no sense three distinct departments of the subject. They are bound up together in such a way that neither can exist without the others. The first is the *matter* of the philosophy of history; the second and third together make up its *form*. The matter is a mere plurality of particular philosophical problems, in themselves chaotic, shapeless, capable of enumeration to infinity; the form is a unity which brings unity into this matter by relating its parts to one another in the light of a whole which is the form itself. When I know what history is, then and then only I can see a rational necessity and a rational answer for the various questions of methodology which beset me when I try to write it; and on the other hand, it is only in this concrete experience of historical work and its difficulties that I can be said to know what history is at all. Take away the matter, and the form becomes an empty and worthless formula. The form makes the matter intelligible, the matter makes the form actual.

Now the form has two elements or aspects, corresponding to the two elements in the phrase philosophy of history. First, to take them in their logical order, the philosophy of history must be *philosophy*; and to call it philosophy means that it is universal and necessary and that it is not a part of philosophy, but the whole of it, a whole in which every part *is* the whole because every part is necessary to the whole and no part can be understood except in the light thrown upon it by every other. Secondly, it must be *of history*; which means that we are dealing not with pure philosophy—if that were conceivable—but with philosophy approached from a certain angle, seen under a particular aspect: philosophy with its problems focused at a particular point, namely the concept of history. Thus the concept of history forms the immediate object of our philosophical reflexion, and the other concepts which make up the whole body of philosophy are thought of as mediated through this; we think of them so far and in such a way as to elucidate the concept of history, and in no other way.

The philosophy of history thus means philosophy in general seen from the point of view of history; that is, philosophy in general with the conception of history in the foreground and the rest in the background. And it is worth noticing that whenever we think of any complex whole we always see it with a foreground and a background in this way. If I say $x = y$, I may appear to have before me a whole of two parts, x and y, with a reciprocal relation between them, standing (so to speak) equidistant from me and on a perfect equality; but this is never really the case; when I say $x = y$, I am always in actual fact bringing one term up to another with which I am comparing it, so that one figures as a comparatively stable background, a standard of comparison, while the other is superimposed upon this background to be compared with it. The reciprocity of x and y is only a potential reciprocity, arising out of the fact that we recognize, when we say $x = y$, that we might legitimately have said $y = x$. The propositions $x = y$ and $y = x$ are no more, though no less, synonymous than the propositions 'Dr. Grundy agrees with Thucydides' and 'Thucydides agrees with Dr. Grundy'. Similarly, the mass of interrelated conceptions which we call philosophy must be grasped somewhere; we cannot have every part of it before our minds with the same degree of immediacy or directness at one and the same time; and therefore we must necessarily individualize some one aspect of it, to be treated as the immediate problem in hand, while keeping its other aspects as a background or framework of reference, a body of concepts which we either have worked out or hope to work out, and to which we can therefore refer particular points in our present inquiry for actual or possible solution. Thus in discussing ethical problems we come up against metaphysical difficulties, and say either 'we know from our metaphysical inquiries that the answer to this question is so-and-so, and therefore we can put in this answer and go ahead', or else 'we have not yet solved this metaphysical difficulty, so we must postpone that point for the present'.

This conception of philosophy as an articulated whole, which is present to the mind as a whole or not at all, but must be presented in some particular position, with some part of itself in the foreground of thought and the rest in the background, is the only conception which can explain at once the unity of philosophy and the distinction within it of various philosophical disciplines or sciences such as logic, ethics, and so forth. But one must bear in mind that the idea of philosophy as a complete whole, to be turned this way and that in order to contemplate it from different angles, is so far misleading that it never is complete; we turn it this way and that not in order to contemplate the perfections of a finished article, but in order to continue the work of bringing it into existence. The side from which we are contemplating it is the side which we are actively engaged in constructing; and while we are constructing one side, the other sides are present to our minds only as principles exemplified in the object of our present thought, not as independent objects.

Subject to this qualification, then, we may continue to speak of philosophy as a whole of parts, each part being a concept, and each concept being capable of becoming the immediate centre or focus of philosophical thought, the rest serving as background and elucidating it. Now the question at once arises, whether every concept forms a part of the body of philosophy, or whether some do and others do not. If the former, there is a philosophy of teacups and of bald-headed stationmasters; these are concepts, and therefore they have an equal right to a philosophy of their own with any other concepts. If the latter, how do we know that history is not one of those concepts that must be banished from the body of philosophy, and on what principles are we to decide?

The answer to the question follows naturally from our original description of the philosophical as the universal and necessary. A philosophical concept is universal in the sense that it arises necessarily whenever anybody thinks about a subject, as we said; but the word subject here means concept, and therefore our phrase, if regarded as a definition, was a circular definition. To escape the circle, we must insist that the subject itself must be a philosophical, or universal, concept; and that can only mean a concept applicable to everything that exists.

It is a familiar idea in philosophy that there are such concepts; in scholastic terminology they are called transcendentals, and you will find, in Spinoza for instance, that *ens*, *res*, and *unum* are given as examples of transcendentals. It was this conception of a transcendental that set the problem and created the terminology of Kant's philosophy. The Transcendental Aesthetic is the theory of those transcendentals, *ubi* and *quando*, which apply to everything *qua* object of sense; the Transcendental Logic is the theory of those transcendentals, unity, reality and the like, which apply to everything *qua* object of thought; and Transcendental Idealism means the idealism of transcendentals, that is, the theory that transcendentals have no existence apart from the mind. The view which I am putting forward, then, is that the concepts which compose the body of philosophy are transcendentals. Philosophy has nothing to say about teacups, because there are things which are not teacups; the concept of teacup is an empirical or non-transcendental concept, a concept applicable only to a certain class of things but not to others. But philosophy has something to say about thought, because everything that can be talked about at all is, so far as we talk about it, an object of thought; it has something to say about action, because everything affords a field or opportunity for action; it has something to say about art, because everything is a legitimate object of aesthetic contemplation, about science, because everything is a legitimate object of scientific investigation, and about history, because everything that exists is an historical fact.

Now the discovery of Kant was that these transcendentals formed a single whole, such that, in spite of apparent antitheses between one of them and another, they were all necessary to each other. Thus unity and plurality seem to contradict one another; yet everything that exists is both one and manifold; and this is not the least irrational or unintelligible; on the contrary, we all understand perfectly well that nothing could be a unity unless it were also a manifold, nothing a manifold unless it were *a* manifold, *one* manifold, that is, a unity. Similarly, the artistic attitude towards things is not only different from the scientific, but opposed to it; and therefore if the world is so constituted as to be a legitimate object of aesthetic contemplation, one would suppose that it cannot also be a legitimate object of scientific inquiry. And we do frequently make this supposition in all good faith, and impale ourselves on the horns of a dilemma by arguing that *either* the artistic attitude towards reality is the right one and the scientific the wrong, *or* the scientific is right and the artistic wrong; where *right* or *wrong* means justified or unjustified by the unalterable character of reality itself. But the answer to the dilemma is that both are right, and that each is wrong if it claims to exclude or supersede the other; because the opposition between them is like the opposition of unity and plurality—an opposition in which each term is necessary to the other. As unity and plurality are categories or transcendentals of pure logic, which means that any object of logical thought must necessarily be thought of as both one and manifold, so art and science are categories or transcendentals of the mind, which means that any activity or operation of the mind must have the characteristics of art and also the characteristics of science.

This means that we are all of us artists and scientists, not in shifts or by turns, but during the whole of our life, so far as that life is a mental and not a merely physiological life. The professional artist is not the only artist; his professional life consists in a specialized performance of functions common to all mankind, and this is the reason why his work appeals to an audience of more than one. Here lies the explanation of a certain tendency to cross-purposes apparent in almost any discussion of art carried on between a philosopher and an artist. For the philosopher, art is a transcendental concept; what he is investigating under that name is something equally apparent in every operation of the mind. For the artist, art is an empirical concept; what he is investigating under that name is something present in, say, the design of Blenheim Palace and absent from, say, the design of the Randolph Hotel; because in trying to be an artist he is trying to produce good works of art and to avoid producing bad ones, and he sees that the phrases *work of art* and *good work of art* must be synonymous, and that a bad work of art, so far as it is bad, is to that extent *not* a work of art. The philosopher has to reply that the Randolph Hotel is at least *trying* to be a work of art, and that such an attempt cannot conceivably be an unmitigated failure; therefore the Randolph Hotel, paradoxical as this statement may appear, must be, within certain limits, both a work of art and a good work of art. At this point in the discussion the artist will probably leave the room, banging the door; and the moral of the discussion is that art must be regarded not merely as a concept indifferently exemplified in every operation or creation of the mind, as might appear from calling it a transcendental, nor merely as an empirical concept exemplified in some things and not in others; but as a concept exemplified indeed everywhere but only revealing itself in any given case to a mind capable of recognizing the peculiar and unique form under which it appears on this particular occasion. The universal is not indifferently and identically present in particulars whose distinction from one another is due to merely material or numerical difference: there are no merely material or numerical differences; what we call such are really differences whose qualitative character we choose to ignore. The universal itself is differentiated in the different particulars: different works of art represent not different embodiments of one and the same beauty but different beauties, different ways of being beautiful. It might almost be said, though I do not say it because it suggests a false antithesis, that there are as many different senses of the word beauty as there are beautiful things. But that would be untrue because it would suggest that the connexion between these various senses was merely verbal, whereas it is in fact real and necessary, and there is nothing capricious about it. The distinction between the various things which I am here calling senses of the word beauty is really the articulation of the artistic activity of the mind, a necessary articulation in the sense that the oneness of all art must be correlative to a certain manifoldness, so that if all art is one, every form of art must also be unique and different from every other.

From this it follows that, just as every operation of the mind must display the characteristics both of art and of science, so every work of art (that is, every operation of the mind *qua* work of art) must display a number of different characteristics which are the transcendentals or categories of art. I do not at the moment pause to enumerate any of these; I only wish to point out that the distinction between them lies at the root of those divergences of ideal which cause the quarrels between various schools of art—naturalistic and formal, classical and romantic, and so on; and that the individuality of a work of art, in the aesthetic sense of the word individuality, consists not in its purely material difference from any other work, but in its embodying an idea of its own, a form of beauty never before realized as a conscious and deliberately chosen end. This new form of beauty must have been present as an element in previous works of art, indeed in *all* previous works of art; but what makes the new work original is that which previously existed only as an implicit, partial, or subordinate element now comes into the foreground and determines the explicit character of the whole, as the central motive in the mind of the artist. This central motive is called the *subject* of the work of art; and the individual work of art may be defined as a particular subject raised to the level of beauty, or beauty—all the beauty in the universe—expressing itself in the form of a particular subject. Thus the relation between the particular work of art and art in general is parallel to that between a particular philosophy such as the philosophy of history and philosophy in general.

The question which we now have to consider is, therefore, whether history is a transcendental or an empirical concept; whether, that is, there can be a philosophy of history at all. We are now ready to ask this question, because we have considered the general nature of transcendental concepts.

History is a kind of inquiry, that is, a kind of mental activity; but the question is, whether it is a mere species of activity, like long division or reading a novel, or a necessary and universal form of activity which is present, explicitly or implicitly, wherever there is mental activity of any kind whatever.

Clearly, history is an empirical conception if it means that activity which distinguishes persons called historians from others called scientists, trombone-players, or ophthalmic surgeons. History in this sense, as an empirical concept, means the investigation of certain arbitrarily defined problems known as historical problems. Consider for instance what is involved in the fact that a book 350 pages long may be called 'History of England'. It implies either that everything which has ever happened in England can be discussed in 350 pages, which is absurd, or that everything known to the author about what has happened in England can be stated in 350 pages, which is equally absurd, or else that there are certain quite arbitrary conventions as to what ought and what ought not to be included under that title. That this is the case, everyone knows; and everyone knows that the conventions change, and that whereas once the names and dates of kings and battles were considered to form the main bulk of the History of England, that position is nowadays accorded to a description of social and economic conditions. Thus if you consult professional historians on the question what ought to be contained in books of history, you will find that they give various answers which, just because they are merely empirical, cannot be reduced to agreement, precisely as artists will differ about the proper subjects for artistic representation. They will all agree that the historian ought to select for narration that which is somehow important; but this idea of importance is necessarily indefinable, because they differ from one another precisely as to the qualities which constitute importance. And the idea of selection really gives away the empirical character of the whole doctrine; for selection implies that something is selected from a body of material; now that which is selected is *ex hypothesi* history, but the material from which it is selected is precisely history as a whole, and therefore the idea of selection implies that the historian must *first* know the whole of history and *then* select from it something to narrate. How then does he come to know the whole of history, or indeed any part of it? *Ex hypothesi* his work as an historian only begins when he already knows everything: therefore no place is left for the acquisition of knowledge, for historical investigation or inquiry.

If on the other hand history means the acquisition or possession of historical knowledge, and not merely the retailing of certain parts of it to others, it must be a transcendental conception. For the object of this knowledge is not the history of England or the history of this or that particular empirical thing, but history as such, whatever history there is, everything historically knowable; and this is a perfectly universal conception. Moreover it is a necessary conception, in the sense that it is implied as a condition in all mental activity. The scientist, in the course of his inquiries, makes use of observations and experiments which, at the moment of his using them for scientific purposes, are historical facts historically attested. The artist, in producing a work of art, is adding a new fact to the history of art, a fact which has a necessary relation with what in that history has preceded it. Thus history is a transcendental conception, like art and science, when regarded as a pure form of activity; though it becomes, like them, an empirical conception when it is arbitrarily restricted to certain specialized embodiments of that form. If anyone says 'that isn't history, because there isn't a book about it in the historical section of this library, or because a professor of history would not bother to lecture about it, or because it never occurred to the people concerned to call it history', he is using a perfectly legitimate criterion to exclude it from history in the empirical sense, but he is not even attempting to deny that it is history in the transcendental sense: that is to say, that it contains those characteristics which, in a more conspicuous degree or form, confer the name of history upon the things generally so designated. For the empirical concept is nothing but the *prima facie* application of the transcendental concept. Any fool can see that what we call history-books are examples of history, but it takes rather more analysis to see that the scientist's use of statistics is also history: and this degree of obviousness is the one and only ground for giving the name in the former case and withholding it in the latter.

The philosophy of history, then, is the exposition of the transcendental concept of history, the study of history as a universal and necessary form of mental activity. A person who did not understand the idea of a transcendental conception might think it reasonable to ask that this study should begin with a definition of history; but to do that would be to betray a confusion between transcendental and empirical concepts. An empirical concept must be defined, because it is neither universal nor necessary: therefore we must be shown how to frame it before we can go on to discuss it. But a transcendental concept *need* not be defined, because we are all possessed of it so far as we think at all; nor *can* it be defined, because, being necessary to all thought, it is necessarily presupposed in its own definition and the definition thus becomes circular. Let anyone try to define the transcendentals I quoted from Spinoza (*ens, res, unum*) and he will see not only that it cannot be done but that the reason why it cannot be done is not that he is ignorant of their meaning but that he recognizes their meaning to be of a kind which makes definition impossible. Definition, in short, is an operation peculiar to empirical conceptions. Hence if anyone objects to my procedure because I do not, either now or later, offer any definition of history, I shall not apologize; and if the omission genuinely puzzles him, I shall reply that there can only be two reasons for his puzzlement: either he has not enough experience of historical studies to connect my remarks with his personal experiences, and therefore has got hold of the wrong end of the stick and thinks I am discussing an empirical concept instead of a transcendental; or else he is ignorant of the English language and confronted with merely verbal difficulties.

LECTURES ON THE PHILOSOPHY OF HISTORY (1926)[1]

THE purpose of these lectures is to raise and, as far as I can do so, to answer certain questions relating to the study of history and to the object, called history, which in that study we investigate. The fundamental question is, what are we doing when we study history? and this raises three allied questions: (1) What are we doing it *for*? in other words, how does this study fit into our general view of the aims and purposes of human life? (2) What is the best way of doing it? in other words, what are the principles of method by which historical study is or ought to be guided? (3) What are we doing it *to*? in other words, what is the true nature of the thing which we call the past, which historical thought takes as its object?

I propose to begin by raising the last question. This will help us to form a general idea of what history is trying to do. I shall then go on to ask how it does it; this will mean discussing the data of historical thought and the methods by which it interprets these data. I shall then, lastly, take history as a finished product, when it has done the work of interpreting its data, and ask what the value of this finished product is.

Our tradition, in Oxford, is to combine historical with philosophical studies. In my own case, this combination has led to a constant and obstinate self-questioning as to the right methods and the ultimate value of historical studies; and my only object in thinking out the notions which I shall lay before you has been to settle accounts with myself as to why I study history and how I can do it more intelligently. To some extent I have achieved this settlement of accounts: and I am giving these lectures in the hope that some of you who may have been afflicted by the same difficulties as myself, may derive help of some kind from the flickering light of my own thoughts. Whether you regard that light as marking the entrance to harbour or the presence of rocks, I leave you to determine.

The source document can be found in the Bodleian Library Collingwood Papers, dep. 14.
[1] Collingwood adds to the title: 'written January, 9–13, 1926, for delivery in Hilary Term, 1926.'

Contents

a. *Introductory: General Idea of History*

1. History in the ordinary or current sense of the word is knowledge of the past; and in order to understand its peculiarities and its special problems, we must ask what the past is. This means inquiring into the nature of time.

2. Time is generally figured or imagined to ourselves in a metaphor, as a stream or something in continuous and uniform motion. These metaphors, when we try to think them out, are very perplexing. The metaphor of a stream means nothing unless it means that the stream has banks, relatively to which it is in motion; but when we apply this to time it is impossible to say that the lapse or process of time is relative to something else which does not proceed or move: for this other thing could *ex hypothesi* only be another time, a time which remained stationary instead of moving. Nor can we strictly say that time moves, or lapses, or proceeds; for all motion presupposes time, and whereas a moving body moves in time, time itself cannot move in time, unless there are (as aforesaid) two times, and it certainly cannot move *except* in time.

3. It is so difficult to think of time itself as moving, that we are naturally tempted to give up this conception and say that it is not time that moves or changes, but events or processes that change or move *in* time. Time is, on this view, regarded as stationary while events move or change past it, as the hands of a clock move past the figures on its face. But this view is no advance: for just as nothing can move except in time, so nothing can stand still except in time, and if we say that time is stationary while events move past it we are assuming another time relatively to which what we called time stands still. Nor is this the only difficulty. For the figures on a clockface stand still in the sense that they are all there together; but clearly, one o'clock and two o'clock and three o'clock and so on are *not* all there together.

4. But we are not really better off if we drop the clock metaphor as well as the stream metaphor and concentrate on the image of a straight line. If we think of time as a line, we think of the present as one point in it, with the past on one side and the future on the other; the present, I suppose, is imagined as travelling into the future so that what was future becomes by degrees first present and then past, and then more and more remote in the past. But this figure only seems appropriate so long as we forget that the line is really regarded as consisting of events arranged in a temporal series, and that therefore we are thinking of all events, not as *happening*, but as *existing* from eternity to eternity and merely waiting to be revealed by a kind of searchlight or pinhole called the present, when it reaches them. Unless we think of them thus, the figure of a line has no applicability whatever; for the events of the future do not really await their turn to appear, like the people in a queue at a theatre awaiting their turn at the box office: they do not yet exist at all, and they therefore cannot be grouped in any order whatever. Similarly about the events of the past; which, because they have happened, and therefore are not now happening, do not exist and therefore cannot be arranged along a line. The temporal series regarded as a line, therefore, is in reality a line consisting of one point only, the present.

5. The present alone is actual: the past and the future are ideal and nothing but ideal. It is necessary to insist upon this because our habit of 'spatializing' time, or figuring it to ourselves in terms of space, leads us to imagine that the past and future exist in some way analogous to the way in which, when we are walking up the High past Queens, Magdalen and All Souls exist.[2] This is simply an illusion, though a tenacious one; and it is necessary to eradicate it with great care before one begins to realize the true problem of history. For we commonly suppose, in our more illogical and slipshod moments, that the past still exists and lies somewhere concealed behind us, and that by using appropriate instruments and methods we can discover it and investigate its nature; and this idea is conformed by the dogmas of certain philosophies now current, which argue as follows:

That which is known must have a real existence:
The past is known in historical thought and in memory:
Therefore the past must really exist.

_____

[2] The High refers to High Street in Oxford. Queens, Magdalen, and All Souls are colleges along this street.

Of this syllogism, I suppose the major to be true; the minor, is, however, false; not absolutely false, but false unless qualified in such a way as to make the conclusion no longer true. The past as such is not known, either in historical thought or in memory, in any kind of sense in which knowledge could guarantee real existence. The conclusion therefore falls to the ground.

6. Another attempt to bolster up the belief in the survival of the past comes from physiological or psychological theories of memory, which argue that past events are remembered by us in virtue of the permanent, or at any rate the lasting, effects which they leave on our psycho-physical organism. Now it is very likely true that an event which left no trace at all on our organism would not be remembered; but the effect and the remembering are not the same thing. Indeed psycho-analysis shows that in many cases the lack of memory is simply due to the magnitude of the effect, as when a person is driven half-mad by terror and, for that very reason, cannot remember the thing that frightened him. It is necessary to distinguish very clearly between the past event, which we remember from the present residue of that event in our organism. It is also necessary (in order to guard against another false theory of memory) to distinguish the event which we remember from other events which may accompany the remembrance. Thus: a person is annoyed by the barking of a dog. This annoyance may produce a permanent effect, namely a chronic tendency to be annoyed by dogs, a dislike of dogs. But the dislike of dogs is quite distinct from the recollection of the event which originated that dislike. Further: when he remembers that first event, he may, and very likely will, experience a certain revival of the original annoyance: he may think 'what a beastly dog that was!' But this revival of annoyance is not identical with the memory of the original incident; indeed the incident must be remembered in order that the annoyance may be, in this particular way, revived. The fallacious theories which identify memory with residual traces or revivifications of past experiences are valuable so far as they bring into prominence certain things that undoubtedly do happen when we remember: but they are wrong so far as they try to make memory consist of something that is in reality not even its inseparable concomitant, since

residual traces and revivifications of past experiences can and
do occur without any memory of the original experiences. The
source of these errors is the prejudice that the object of memory must be something now existing. This prejudice, which is
a deduction, no doubt unconscious in the main, from the epistemological dogma that all states of consciousness must have a
real object independent of themselves, prevents its victims
from realizing that what we remember is the past, not the present; and that while it exists we cannot conceivably remember
it. It must first cease to exist, and then for the first time it is in
a position to be remembered.

7. History and memory are wholly different things, but they
have this in common, that the object is in each case the past.
The difference between them is that memory is subjective and
immediate, history objective and mediate. By calling memory
subjective I mean that its object is always something that has
happened to ourselves or in our own circle of experience. I do
not remember the Crimean War, but I do remember the Boer
War; I do not remember Santa Sophia, but I do remember St
Mark's. As soon as the object falls outside my personal experience, I can no longer remember it. Yet, it is important to
notice, I may imagine it just as vividly and just as accurately as
if I did remember it. A child who has often heard of something that happened in his family before he was born may
come to imagine it quite as clearly and as veraciously as he
imagines the incidents which he remembers, and this may lead
him to think that he remembers what in fact he does not
remember at all. For instance, I can recollect things that happened to me when I was less than two, but so dimly and
vaguely that they are actually less vivid than my imagination
of things which older members of my family described to me
as a child and which happened before I was born. And I have
no doubt that this accounts for many things that appear at first
sight to be pre-natal memories. By calling memory *immediate*,
I mean that we neither have, nor can have, nor can even want,
any guarantee or ground for it except itself. The question
'why do you remember this?', meaning, 'what reason have you
for remembering it?' is a question that can never be answered
except with an irrelevant or nugatory answer, like, 'oh, I have
a very good memory', or, 'it made a great impression on me',

or the like. I can certainly come to realize that what I took for memory cannot be memory, as when I say that I remember posting a letter which I afterwards find in my pocket, when it becomes clear that I really imagined or dreamed that I posted it. But though I may have grounds for thinking this to be a case of memory or not a case of memory, I cannot have grounds for remembering. I simply remember, and there is an end of it.

8. History on the other hand is *objective*, by which I mean that its concern is not with my own personal past but with the past in general, the past depersonalized, the past simply as fact. And although I may be in firmer and completer possession of my own history than of anyone else's, this is not by any means necessarily the case. I may know more about the Crimean War, which I do not remember, than about the Boer War, which I do; and I may know more about the early history of my children, which I have studied with the intelligence of an adult human being, than about my own, which happened when I was too young to realize what was happening. And it is conceivable, though not very likely, that a student of retiring habits might be able to give a better and truer historical account of society and politics in ancient Athens than of the same things in his own country during his own lifetime. And when I call history *mediate* I mean that the statements which it makes are always made on grounds which the historian can state when challenged. 'Why do you believe this?', meaning 'what reasons have you for making this historical statement?', is an essentially answerable question, and in proportion as the historian knows his job he can give a reasonable and acceptable answer.

9. This answer will always take the same general form: namely, 'I find in my sources certain information which leads me to the belief'. And this answer is characteristic of history. Other kinds of thinking are mediate and can, when challenged, state their grounds; but in no other field of thought are the grounds called sources, evidences, or the like. We must therefore examine this conception and see what it implies.

b. *The Sources of History*

10. A source, authority, or document is the raw material out of which history is made. It may be itself a statement of past fact, that is to say it may be homogeneous with the finished product into which the historian tries to convert it; but it need not be. It may be a document such as a charter or deed or proclamation, which takes the form of a command; and in this case nothing is easier than to convert it into narrative by saying 'in the year x, king y gave such and such lands to such and such an abbey'; but one must bear in mind the possibilities that the command was not obeyed and that the person who gave it did not even intend it to be obeyed. For that matter, when one's documents take the form of narrative, one must bear in mind the possibility that the narrator was ignorantly, or intentionally, circulating falsehoods. The case becomes more complicated when the source is not even a command, but a mere relic of action, such as a dropped coin, or the remains of buildings and utensils. Here it becomes evident, even to the least reflective mind, that the document tells one nothing unless, by the application of principles, one can succeed in interpreting it, arguing that buildings of this kind must necessarily have been intended for a certain purpose, built at a certain time, and so forth. But what is true of these non-verbal sources is in fact true of all sources whatever. All are dumb except to a mind that can interpret them; and even a source consisting of simple narrative—a Thucydides or a Froissart—yields no historical results whatever, good or bad, till some kind of method of interpreting it has been worked out.

11. The interpretation of sources, then, is the formal element of history, counterbalancing the material element which is the source itself. Without these two elements, there is no history. And whereas the sources themselves have to be found, collected, assembled by the historian as data which limit the field of his activity, the work of interpreting them proceeds according to principles which he creates out of nothing for himself; he does not find them ready-made but has to decide upon them by an act of something like legislation. The 'receptivity' of the historian towards his sources is counterbalanced by his

'spontaneity' in respect of the principles by which he interprets them.

12. Sources, then, must be found, given to the historian ready-made. His work is to collect them, and this implies searching for them. But he cannot search for them until he has agreed with himself upon some principles of interpretation; for till that is done, he does not know what to look for. He must know what kind of document will yield results under the methods at his command; for different methods demand wholly different types of document. Hence a complete collection of sources is an impossibility, even with respect to a limited period or a particular problem within that period. For every advance in the study of the problem brings to light a new type of source. Thus, a hundred years ago, the sources for the history of the Roman Empire consisted not exclusively but almost exclusively of ancient historical writers. During the nineteenth century the importance of inscriptions, never wholly overlooked, was for the first time fully recognized, and the Corpus of Latin Inscriptions was set on foot—it is not yet complete, and it never will be—in order to collect this newly-realized source of knowledge into a form in which historians could handle it. At the end of the nineteenth century a quite new type of source was tapped, namely pottery; and others will certainly emerge as the intensive study of the period goes forward. But all we can do with sources is to recognize and interpret them; we cannot add a single fragment where it is lacking; where we draw a blank in our search for documents, we can do nothing to help ourselves. When, as a result of Lord Birkenhead's Real Property Act of 1923, title-deeds became unnecessary for the tenure of land, a systematic destruction of them, all over the country, was set on foot among the solicitors and agents in whose keeping they lay; and this destruction of unexamined and uninterpreted potential sources of medieval history has been the gravest blow that knowledge has received since the French Revolution; because such a loss of material is absolutely irreparable: there can be no possible means of recovering the information which this holocaust has put beyond our reach.

13. Where one type of source is lacking, however, the historian devises new methods of interpretation and reveals

another. Thus, medieval history is rich in written documents and in datable architecture. Anyone can learn to interpret Gothic mouldings and medieval script in a very short time, and there is any amount of them; and therefore the historian who wants to reconstruct the story of an abbey never troubles to go beyond these sources. But in the Roman Empire we find no written documents to speak of, except inscriptions, which tell one very little except personal details, and practically no datable architecture; so we are driven back on other sources, and have devised a complicated science of archaeology whose aim is to interpret chronologically the superimposed strata of an inhabited site and the objects contained in them. Archaeology in this sense does not exist for the medieval period; no living soul knows a fiftieth part about medieval pottery, for instance, that any beginner knows about Greek or Roman pottery.

14. The supply of sources is thus infinite, in the sense that no one working at any historical problem can ever have reached the end of them, and the point at which we think we have exhausted the sources is only the point at which our own principles of interpretation have exhausted the peculiar type of material to which they can be applied. But the sources actually tapped at any given point by any given student are always finite. Hence it is possible to give a list of the sources that have been used in the solution of a particular problem, but not to give a list of the sources that might be used in the solution of a problem not yet solved.

15. A student who knows the sources is called a scholar; and scholarship, or erudition, is that element—a necessary element—in history which consists in possessing the materials of history. A learned man is not necessarily an historian; but an historian must be a learned man. Yet there is a natural tendency to confuse the two conceptions and to identify history with erudition. This is a very common type of mistake. Where a distinction exists between a factor in experience which is given and one which is supplied by the experiencing mind, the very constancy of the mind's activity leads to its escaping notice, so that the whole experience is ascribed to the given factor. Thus artists who paint landscapes and other natural objects tend to think that they find their works of art ready-

made in the external world, and overlook the fact that in painting a landscape they are always performing acts of selection, adaptation, conventionalization, and idealization, without which the picture would simply not be a picture. Similarly, people often discuss the influence of environment on physique and character as if the idiosyncrasy of the person on whom the environment is supposed to act had nothing to do with its action. It is often the most active and spontaneous people who most overlook the existence of their own spontaneous activity: and it is the very ease and success with which the historian interprets his sources that lead him to fancy that he is not interpreting them at all—that they are interpreting themselves, have their meaning written large on their faces, require, to be understood, nothing but bare inspection. Hence the sources become falsely identified with the history which can be written from them; and when so misconceived, history is regarded as the simple transcription of sources. From this point of view the sources become authorities, or collections of statements which the historian accepts and transplants into his own narrative; whereas the historian's finished product is nothing but a patchwork of quotations from his authorities, more or less welded together by external literary means. Most histories that are built on a large scale and cover a considerable extent of ground show traces of this defect; the narrative seems to change its key in a curious way when one authority takes the place of another; thus every history of Greece undergoes a change of tone when Herodotus gives way to Thucydides, and it is very difficult to study the history of the early Roman Empire without falling a victim to Tacitean melodrama. The defect may even be defended, by the plea that the historian cannot go behind his sources and has no option but to accept them and believe what they tell him. But this is altogether false. The historian, even at the most rudimentary level of thought, is responsible for accepting his authorities as authorities; he believes what they say not because they say it but because he has made it a principle to believe them; he always has an option, though the alternative to accepting what he is told may be, and often is, the decision that trustworthy information on this particular question is at present unattainable. It is always a mark of stupidity to plead that one is bound by what one's authorities say; yet it is true of the material side of historical thought, however untrue of the formal.

16. A consequence of the error which regards history as contained ready-made in its sources is the distinction between history and prehistory. From the point of view of this distinction, history is coterminous with written sources, and prehistory with the lack of such sources. It is thought that a reasonably complete and accurate narrative can only be constructed where we possess written documents out of which to construct it, and that where we have none we can only put together a loosely constructed assemblage of vague and ill-founded guesses. This is wholly untrue: written sources have no such monopoly of trustworthiness or of informativeness as is here implied, and there are very few types of problem which cannot be solved on the strength of unwritten evidence. For instance, it is often said that chronological problems absolutely require written sources for their solution; but even written chronology is often very hard to interpret, referring as it does to eras which we cannot certainly correlate with our own (e.g. the Egyptian Sothic cycle, which is a period of 1,460 years, and exposes us to the uncertainty, for all early Egyptian history, whether an event happened at one or the other of two dates 1,460 years apart), and on the other hand unwritten chronological data, like the yearly mud-deposits of the retreating glaciers at the end of the Ice Age, may at times give extraordinarily accurate results. Strictly speaking, all history is prehistory, since all historical sources are mere matter, and none are ready-made history; all require to be converted into history by the thought of the historian. And on the other hand, no history is mere prehistory, because no source or group of sources is so recalcitrant to interpretation as the sources of prehistory are thought to be.[3]

17. But at a certain level of thought the distinction between history and prehistory is of value. If we take the historian at an arrested point in his development, instead of considering him in his idea or as what he ought to be; if we take the case of the beginner in historical work, we shall find that for him, and for

---

[3] On the opposite page the following addition appears: 'N.B. Prehistory *may* mean history not yet formed. Cf. p. 67.' (The passage referred to is to be found on pp. 417–18 of the present volume.)

him alone, a distinction exists between crude historical material—deeds and charters, ruined buildings, coins and potsherds—and predigested historical material—ready-made narrative. The difference is that the predigested material has been already worked up into something homogeneous with that into which he is trying to convert it, whereas the crude material makes demands upon him which he is quite unable to fulfil. He does not know how to interpret deeds and potsherds: they are to him mere curiosities, things at which he stares unintelligently in museum cases; but he does know, in a sense, how to read a history-book, and it conveys something to his mind when the crude material would convey nothing. Hence the beginner in history is introduced to ready-made history-books, out of which he gets something; though his later studies show him that most of what he got was false. Still, this falsehood was a necessary stage towards the truth. And this must be borne in mind in connexion with the historical teaching of the very young. Stories of Noah, of Romulus and Remus, of King Alfred and the cakes, may be wholly untrue, but a child who has not been nourished on these, or equally fabulous, stories, has little chance of ever acquiring that healthy appetite for history which alone can supersede these stories by truer ones. The textbooks that we use in school are one or two degrees truer than Alfred and the cakes; but they too are infected with the same taint of legend, and it is a pretty safe generalization that by the time a statement has found its way into a school textbook it has been either disproved or at least gravely shaken by the advance of knowledge.

18. The relation between two types of source, the crude material and the predigested material or ready-made narrative, is parallel to the distinction between the beauty of nature and the beauty of art. When a child is learning to draw, it finds it much easier to copy a picture of something than to draw direct from the thing itself, because the picture is a predigested version of the thing; someone has already tackled the problem of how to draw the thing, and the child profits by his predecessor's experience. This is why it is easy to draw things in a conventionalized version and hard to draw them naturalistically. Similarly, it is much easier to see the beauty of a thing as interpreted and idealized in a work of art than it is when the

thing is presented to us in its natural crudity: the artist points out to other people beauties which without his help they would have failed to see. Hence it would be an absurd pedantry to insist that no one shall ever copy drawings, but always draw from nature, and equally absurd to demand that people should ignore works of art and lean always, for their aesthetic experience, on nature and their own imaginative powers. In the language of religion, this is to neglect the means of grace that are given us for the advancement of our own spiritual life, and this is to blaspheme against the spirit that provides these means in order to lead us into all truth.

19. The historian as learner, then, takes narrative as he finds it, on trust, and is as yet incompetent either to go behind it and criticize it, or (which is the same thing) construct his own narrative for himself out of crude materials. But in this stage he is only an historian *in fieri*, not an historian *in esse*. He is accepting ready-made narrative on trust, and he has not yet attained to the conception of historical truth, a truth that emerges out of criticism and can withstand criticism. He is not in a position to call the narrative which he accepts a true narrative; all he can say is that this is what he finds in his authorities. And at this stage, when as yet he has not learnt to construct narrative for himself, he is wholly dependent on ready-made narrative, and history is therefore, for him, coterminous with the totality of ready-made narratives. Where these fail him, he finds not history but prehistory, materials which he cannot with any precision and confidence interpret.

20. But even at this elementary stage in historical thought, the historian is not so passive as he thinks. He does, after all, accept his authorities, and this implies a certain principle of preference, however little recognized as such; and he does interpret them, in the sense that he reads their narratives and finds in them only what his knowledge of the language in which they are written permits him to find there. And at a very early stage he becomes aware that in reading this or that book he must make allowances for this or that idiosyncrasy or bias on the part of the writer, and must remember that the writer in his turn was limited by *his* authorities and cannot in any case have been a self-sufficient eyewitness of all that he relates. These conceptions begin to modify the uncritical

reproduction of the ready-made narrative; and they become more and more prominent as the attempt to reproduce the ready-made narrative becomes more and more consistent. As soon as the learner begins to supplement his study of one book by studying others, he finds perforce that their points of view differ and that their versions of the same narrative never entirely agree: and hence he becomes aware that his own history, the narrative which he is trying to build up in his own mind, cannot follow one authority without diverging from another. And hence he is forced to take the responsibility of choosing whom to believe.

21. This power of choosing one's authorities from a number of competing claimants is the first and most rudimentary form in which the historian becomes aware of his own freedom. But because it is a primitive stage in the development of historical freedom, it does not follow that the difficulties which it presents are easy to solve. They are not; they are in fact, at the level of thought which we have now reached, insoluble. For *ex hypothesi* any authority, however bad an authority, knows a great deal more about the events in question than the student: how then can the student decide to reject any of them? It would appear that any choice between authorities must be capricious; that we merely decide to follow A and ignore B for no reason except that we decide to do so. Or, if a reason must be given, it will be an irrelevant reason: as, that A is a better writer than B and states his version more attractively; or, that A is a source with which we have long been familiar and B's version is a newly-discovered and therefore surprising statement; or, that A's version harmonizes with our personal prejudices, political, psychological, or the like. And when we reflect on the badness of the reasons that lead us to prefer A to B, we may easily conclude that our faith in A is groundless; and this may lead to a general scepticism with regard to historical beliefs, and the conviction that all historical narrative is (as Voltaire said) a *fable convenue*,[4] and that historical inquiry is

---

[4] In a letter to Horace Walpole, dated 15 July 1768, Voltaire said: 'J'ai toujours pensé comme vous, monsieur, qu'il faut se défier de toutes les histoires anciennes. Fontenelle, le seul homme du siècle de Louis XIV qui fût à la fois poète philosophe et savant, disait qu'elles étaient *des fables convenues*'

(as Rousseau called it) *l'art de choisir, entre plusieurs mensonges, celui qui ressemble le plus à la vérité.*[5] This scepticism is indeed a necessary consequence of regarding history as a transcription of ready-made narratives, and people who do not sooner or later fall into it escape it only because they are too lacking in logical consistency, or too frivolous in their attitude to their own historical inquiries, ever to get so far. But historical thought does not simply end here in disaster. It is not weakness, but strength, that has brought it to this pass; if it had been feebler, it would have remained content with merely reproducing ready-made narratives; but it has become dissatisfied with that because it has recognized that even in reproducing ready-made narrative it has been exercising a free choice of authorities, and the problem now before it is to understand what is implied in this free choice. When this problem is solved, the conception of history as the transcription of authorities will disappear, and the historian will have emerged from the stage of apprenticeship into the stage of independent and self-reliant inquiry. This transition may be described as the transition from dogmatic history to critical history: dogmatic history being history as it appears to the beginner, critical history being history as it appears to the competent student. Similar transitions are found in the development of art, religion, philosophy, and indeed in every discipline: for it is always the rule that we learn to master an activity by at first accepting unquestioningly the commands of others who have mastered it before us. The place of dogmatism in human life is a necessary and permanent place, and those who would banish it wholesale only betray, by this desire, the fact that they do not yet understand human life and therefore have not yet transcended the stage of requiring dogmatism for their souls' good; but the place of dogmatism is in the school. The learner's first business is to learn what he is

(*Oeuvres complètes de Voltaire*, Nouvelle édition, Correspondance générale, ix (Paris, 1822), p. 271).

Likewise in *Jeannot et Colin* Voltaire wrote: 'Toutes les histoires anciennes, comme le disait un de nos beaux esprits, ne sont que des fables convenues' (*Oeuvres complètes de Voltaire*, Nouvelle édition, Romans, ii (Paris, 1821), p. 123).

[5] J.-J. Rousseau, *Émile ou de l'éducation* (Paris, 1957), p. 283. The last words should be 'le mieux à la vérité'.

taught, and to do what he is told to do; if he were able by now to think for himself and to choose for himself what to do, he would not be a learner. Hence all teaching is necessarily dogmatic, and history as taught must be dogmatic history, ready-made narrative simply handed out to the pupil for him to learn and reproduce.

c. The Interpretation of Sources

22. The point in the development of historical thought which we are now considering is the point at which the historian has ceased to be contented with ready-made narrative, and asks for reasons why he should accept one version rather than another. Within the circle of dogmatic history, the answer is easy: the teacher tells him what narrative he must accept, and the acceptance therefore is a matter not of reasoning but of school discipline. But when the disciplinary motive is no longer applied, and the learner leaves school, he becomes himself responsible for his choice of an authority to follow, and, as we have seen, he cannot help discovering that any reason against following any one authority applies *mutatis mutandis* to any other, with the result that he is landed in scepticism.

23. The way out of this scepticism is found when it is realized that sources are not authorities but only sources: that the historian's attitude towards them must consist neither in acceptance nor in rejection, but in interpretation. We have seen that in some sense the acceptance of an authority always implies interpretation; but if this only means that the reader must know the language he is reading and translate it into his own, the interpretation applies only to the words of the authority and not to his thought. The point which we have now reached requires us to ask not only 'what did this writer intend to convey when he used these words?' which is a question of merely linguistic interpretation, but 'what is the historical truth that lies behind the meaning he intended to convey?' which is a question of historical interpretation in the proper sense, and assumes that the truth of which we are in search was not possessed, ready-made, by the writer whom we are studying, or at any rate not intended by him to be conveyed to us in the words he is using. In short, we are now trying to get behind our authorities, which is exactly what, in the dogmatic stage of historical thought, we said could never be done; we are devising means of protecting ourselves against authorities who are ignorant of the facts which we are trying to learn from them, or actually intend to conceal these facts from us.

24. This is not really quite so difficult as it sounds. The only difficulty of any importance is the psychological difficulty of persuading ourselves to treat critically sources which hitherto we have been treating dogmatically. It is puzzling and rather shocking to face the fact that the writers whom one has regarded as authoritative and incorruptible channels of truth are completely misapprehending the events which they describe, or deliberately telling lies about them; and when experienced historians assure us that all sources are tainted with ignorance and mendacity, we are apt to ascribe the opinion merely to cynicism. Yet this opinion is really the most precious possession of historical thought. It is a working hypothesis without which no historian can move a single step. It is absolutely necessary, when one comes across any piece of narrative which one is trying to use as historical material, to put the narrator in the witness box and to exert all one's ingenuity in order to shake his testimony. And no one will resent this treatment who realizes the extreme difficulty of narrating facts correctly. But we are now concerned with a more advanced stage than the mere discrediting of a witness; we are by now agreed that all witnesses are discredited, in the sense that we are never justified in merely transcribing their narrative into our own without modification, and we are dealing with the question how to extract the truth from a witness who does not know it or is trying to conceal it. This is the positive or constructive stage of criticism.

25. The problem, as I have already suggested, resembles that of cross-examining a witness in court; but it differs because in this case the witness, not being present before us, cannot be made to answer questions, and therefore we cannot test the coherence of his narrative in the most convincing of all possible ways. But we can do something similar. We can study our witness's character, situation, and attitude, and this enables us to establish a kind of personal coefficient which gives at least a partial result when applied to his statements.

We find, for instance, that such and such a writer is an admirer of democracy, and will always say everything he can to its advantage and to the disadvantage of other political systems; that another writer wishes to support a contemporary political programme by the indirect method of historical narrative—for instance, to support Socialism by describing the sufferings of working men employed by capitalists; that another is powerfully affected by admiration or hatred for a central figure in his narrative, such a person perhaps as Julius Caesar or Napoleon, whose extraordinary genius makes it almost impossible to contemplate him without some kind of emotion. I am not at present raising the question whether the historian can, or ought to, hold himself aloof from these disturbing influences; I am only pointing out that they are disturbing influences, and that we cannot safely use narratives as sources without making allowance for them.

26. Now this means that we must postpone the task of determining the truth about a given event till we have determined the truth about the historian who has written about it. We have to deal not only with history itself, but with what I shall call history of the second degree, or history of history. One might be tempted to think of history of the second degree as a kind of supererogatory historical exercise, interesting to historians as being the history of their own craft, rather as the history of one's own college is interesting, but on the whole irrelevant to the pursuit of history of the first degree, an excrescence upon it, and, on the whole, a useless and trivial excrescence. But the truth is the very opposite of this. History of the second degree is an absolutely necessary element in history of the first degree; no historical problem about any past event can be settled until we have settled the problem of the history of its history. For instance, no one would dream of claiming to have solved the problems that surround the battle of Marathon until he had studied the literature of the subject and arranged it in such a way as to build up in his own mind a narrative of the history of Marathonian theory and inquiry. For a person who had solved the problem of Marathon, a history of the inquiries into that problem would no doubt be supererogatory and pointless; but that is only because a person who had solved the problem would *ex hypothesi* have passed through all these earlier stages of inquiry in his own person, except those which were too silly to attract his attention for a moment; and to retail them in a fresh historical narrative would be merely going over old ground. A person who has solved a problem and retains the solution vividly and fully in his mind is still conscious of the articulations of thought which the problem and its solution involve: that is, he still bears in mind the various elements of apprehended truth that are enshrined in the solution, and the various possible errors between which he has succeeded in steering his course. Now the past (and *ex hypothesi* unsuccessful) inquirers into the same problem have no doubt apprehended some of these truths and avoided some of the corresponding errors; if they have not, there is no reason for mentioning them in a history of the inquiry. They have also, so far as they were in the long run unsuccessful, made ultimate shipwreck on some one error. The successful inquirer, therefore, is in a superior position to any of them and has nothing to learn from studying them; the narrative of their thought is for him, therefore, a narrative without interest. But it has great interest in either of two contingencies: first, for the hitherto unsuccessful inquirer, who wishes to solve the problem for himself: and secondly, for the successful inquirer who has ceased to be fully conscious of the import and articulations of his own discovery, and can in no way recall these better than by recalling the struggles of earlier inquirers to solve the same problem. And these two functions are the permanent justification of history of the second degree. In the first place, no problem of the first degree can be solved without a preliminary review of the history of thought on the subject, which enables the inquirer consciously to insert himself in his proper place in the succession of inquirers; in the second place, it fertilizes and revivifies the achieved solution of every problem to look back at past attempts to solve it, and without such revivification the solution hardens into a mere formula repeated, parrot-like, without intelligence.

27. But it may seem a contradiction in terms to say that every problem of the first degree demands for its solution the previous solution of a problem of the second degree. If, for instance, we cannot justly appreciate the character of Julius Caesar without first appreciating the character of Mommsen

(and that is what I have been saying), it is easy to point out that Mommsen is just as much an historical personage as Julius Caesar, and that therefore the problem of studying his character is a problem of exactly the same kind as the problem of studying Julius Caesar's, namely an historical problem of the first degree. All we have said, therefore, is that before we have solved one problem we must solve another of the same kind, which therefore, presumably, presents the same kind of difficulty and must be solved in the same kind of way—in this case, by studying the biographies and literary remains of Mommsen, and, as a preliminary to this, studying his biographers' idiosyncrasies, and so *ad infinitum*. If therefore we are to avoid the absurdity of an infinite regress, which will prevent us from ever solving any problem whatever by always presenting us with another to be solved first, we must surely reject the view I have been putting forward, and argue that history of history is not a logical antecedent, but a logical consequent, of history itself.

28. Against the contention that history of the second degree is a logical consequent of history of the first degree I have already argued that the opposite is proved by the uniform and indispensable practice of all historians. And because an ounce of practice is worth a ton of theory, a fact like this may be safely left to justify itself against difficulties of the kind just stated. But our business here is theory, and we are therefore bound to meet the difficulty by argument. This can only be done by pointing out that all history works backwards from the present. That which is prior in time is, as Aristotle would say, posterior to us. We start from ourselves, from the world in which we live; and only so far as we have a certain grasp of that can we hope to grasp the truth of anything in the past. The history of history is an easier study than history, in so far as the historians who are there the objects of our study stand closer to ourselves and are more open to our inspection than the persons about whom they write. We know Mr A personally, and this enables us to predict with some confidence the kind of prejudice that will betray itself in his books about medieval history; we know Mr B by hearsay and Mr C by a fresh and consistent tradition, and the same is true of them. The psychology of Mommsen is easier to grasp than the psychology of Julius Caesar because, though he was not a personal acquaintance of ours, he was a modern European, a nineteenth-century German, and we know incalculably more about the kind of person he was likely to be, to judge from his environment and training, than we ever can do about Julius Caesar. But the same principle applies even to historians of the remote past. Because Thucydides and Velleius Paterculus have left us their own writings, we have far better evidence concerning the character and attitude of Thucydides and Velleius Paterculus than we can ever have concerning those of Cleon and Tiberius. Hence the history of history always presents us with easier problems than those of history of the first degree, problems for which the evidence is more voluminous and more reliable. But the difference is not exhausted by this distinction of degree. It is not merely that history of the second degree is better documented; it has a kind of directness or immediacy, by contrast with which history of the first degree is always indirect and inferential. The historian has placed himself directly before us by writing for us to read; there is only a difference of degree between our acquaintance with him and our acquaintance with people whom we meet and with whom we converse; whereas we can never have this direct acquaintance, in however slight a degree, with Alexander the Great or William the Conqueror. This makes the problems of history of the second degree not merely easier than those of history pure and simple, but actually simpler in their structure and therefore capable of solution by methods too crude for the successful treatment of the latter.

29. The critical attitude, then, recognizes that whereas our acquaintance with our sources is direct, or mediated only by linguistic interpretation, our acquaintance with the events which we are studying is always indirect, mediated through a critical interpretation of our sources. We no longer think that in reading Livy or Gibbon we are face to face with the early or late history of Rome; we realize that what we are reading is not history but only material out of which, by thinking for ourselves, we may hope to construct history. From this point of view, Livy and Gibbon are no longer authorities, but sources merely: they are not to be followed, but to be interpreted. They are now seen to be only one element in the finished

product; the other element being, not *other* sources, but our own principles of interpretation, which we have to mix with them in the same sense in which Michelangelo said that he mixed his colours with brains.

30. The interpretation of sources must proceed according to principles. It is not enough to interpret them according to the dictates of intuition, to deal with individual cases as if each was unique and unlike any other. People sometimes advocate this happy-go-lucky or intuitive method of dealing with the problems presented by moral conduct, art, science, or even philosophy under the name of dealing with every case on its merits, and support their contention by a polemic against casuistry and the tyranny of abstract rules. And certainly abstract rules are bad masters. It does not follow that they are not good servants. And it is sometimes forgotten that to deal with a case on its merits is impossible unless is has merits, that is to say unless it has recognizable points of contact with other cases whose merits are of the same general kind. It is doubtless true that every case is unique; but uniqueness does not exclude points of identity with other unique cases; and a denial of the genuineness of universals is at least no less disastrous than a denial of the uniqueness of their particulars. In point of fact, no one would dream of trying to interpret an historical document except in the light of general principles, e.g. that this kind of script is characteristic of English thirteenth-century writing, or that silver coinage suddenly becomes very rare in the early fifth century A.D., or that official documents tend to exaggerate successes and to minimize failures; and the only real question is whether we shall merely assume our principles and remain, so far as possible, unconscious of them, or bring them out into the light of full discussion. That they must exist, is undeniable.

31. Various views are, however, held as to their derivation and basis. It is sometimes held, and widely at the present time, that principles of interpretation are derived inductively from the inspection and comparison of historical sources; and that having been thus derived they are then applied to the interpretation of more difficult cases. We find by experience, it is thought, that official documents are what is called 'optimistic', by comparing them with other sources; and this enables us to guard against being misled by their generic tendency in cases where we have no other sources with which to compare them. The strong and weak points of this view are the strong and weak points of inductive logic in general. In a psychological sense it is no doubt true that we recognize the principles by examining instances of them, and we very likely first vividly realize the optimistic tendency of official reports by coming across a case in which two combatants both officially claim decisive victories in the same battle, or the like. But from a less psychological point of view, which means a point of view less easily satisfied with the first superficial appearance of the facts, it becomes obvious that we accept the principle not because we have seen an example of it but because the principle itself proves acceptable; and that it possesses a certainty far more complete than the certainty that attaches to the fact which, we fancied, guaranteed it. The function of the instance now seems to be, rather, to reveal to us the principles which we implicitly accept, not to introduce to us principles to which till now we were strangers. And this must be the case; because what we have really done is not to find the principle of official mendacity written large upon the face of the facts, but to appeal to that principle in order to make the facts intelligible, and only afterwards to assume that the facts must have been inherently an instance of the principle, because we assume that facts must be inherently intelligible and we do not see how they could have been intelligible otherwise. Hence a little further reflexion inevitably convinces us that our principles of interpretation have their origin, not in the facts as we observe them, but in the thought which we bring to bear upon them.

32. But this discovery, true as it is, exposes us to a new confusion. If our canons of interpretation originate not in the facts but in our thought, they are merely subjective, and this appears to imply not only that they are creatures of mind but that they are creatures of caprice. On this view the individual thinker is free to select any principles that appeal to him, and construct historical narrative by their help without any attempt to show that these principles, and no others, are justifiable. If he has a bad conscience about this, he may placate it after the event by showing that the principles he has arbitrarily chosen have, after all, 'worked', or yielded a more or less coherent narrative; but that is no proof that they are valid, for the question remains whether the narrative so constructed is true. For instance, suppose a writer were constructing a history of the Anglo-Saxon settlement. He might work on the assumption that contemporary writers were the best informed, and consequently accept everything said by Gildas as true; he might further assume that Anglo-Saxon popular tradition retained for several centuries an accurate account of the facts, and consequently accept the Anglo-Saxon Chronicle; he might also accept Nennius as trustworthy because Nennius enshrines traditions going back to the 5th century, and these, like those contained in the Chronicle, may be accurate. Having made these assumptions, he may then recognize that modern archaeological study has produced results quite incompatible with these assumptions, and this may lead him to embrace the further principle that archaeological inquiry is in the main powerless to produce historical results. Applying these principles to the problem in hand, he will get a fairly definite narrative of the main events of his period; but the question is, will his narrative be true? And that question now resolves itself into the question, are his principles satisfactory? Clearly, if his principles are the right principles, his narrative will be true, or as true as it is possible, with the evidence we possess, to make it. And we have no way of deciding whether the narrative is true except by asking whether it is legitimately derived from the evidence: it is not as if we had some independent method of establishing the truth of the narrative and so proving the validity of the principles *a posteriori*. There is no alternative except either to regard principles as a matter for capricious personal choice, in which case the resulting narrative no longer has any claim to be considered anything more than a work of imagination, or to insist that principles shall be justified *a priori*, that is, made into objects of critical study and discussion by a scientific methodology of history.

33. This methodology will be concerned with abstract or general problems connected with the various concepts used in historical thought. Because these concepts are treated abstractly, the science that deals with them will be highly fissiparous, and will issue in an indefinite number of historical sciences each concerned with the methods of handling and interpreting one kind of evidence. For it is to be observed that the transition from dogmatic to critical history involves an immense widening of the field of evidence. Whereas dogmatic history recognizes no sources but only authorities, which must consist of ready-made narrative, critical history treats these narratives not as authorities, or history ready-made, but as sources, or evidence to be made into history by interpreting it: and this means ignoring the fact that they are narratives and treating them in a way in which they might equally have been treated had they not been narratives. The methods of critical history are therefore applicable to an indefinite variety of objects all of which become historical sources so far as historians can find ways of employing them as such. There is now no *a priori* distinction between facts that can and facts that cannot be used as the materials of history; everything depends on the ability of the historian to discover materials that he can use, and these will be of the most widely divergent kinds and the principles of their employment infinitely various. This is the *raison d'être* of such sciences as palaeography and diplomatics, epigraphy, numismatics, historical architecture, and all the ramifications of archaeology in its application to various kinds of implements and relics. All these sciences combine a theoretical side, consisting of general propositions concerning such things as the period of history at which this or that moulding or piece of ornament was used, and a practical side, consisting of general recommendations as to the search for the special kind of evidence in question. In part, these sciences can be discovered set forth in textbooks; but only in a very small part. The student who is anxious to learn them must get himself apprenticed to the trade by working in company with skilled exponents; he will find them in museums, in libraries, on the staffs of excavations, and even in universities. These bodies of skilled historical investigators, handing down by personal instruction and word of mouth a vast amount of knowledge that never finds its way into books, form one of the most interesting features of our civilization on its intellectual side. It reminds one of the medieval gild system, and it has the same strong points: it ensures, as nothing else can, a high and fairly consistent level of work, and makes it difficult for a totally incompetent or untrained person to undertake a delicate piece of research and impose his valueless results on the public. For the fact is that sound technical training can only be provided by some such system of personal and prolonged intercourse as is given in apprenticeship: and just as a man must apprentice himself to the technique of handicraft if he is to become a sound craftsman, so he must apprentice himself to the technique of historical research if he is to become a competent historian. It is, however, worth pointing out that our habit of printing and publishing technical details is apt to mislead aspirants to historical knowledge. So much is to be found in print e.g. about numismatics by anyone who chooses to read it, that people are often tempted to imagine that they can become numismatists or even form a general impression of the extent, cogency, and historical value of numismatics by simply reading books. This is a complete mistake. The books which such a person reads are positively misleading, except to a person who has constantly handled coins in the company of people able to call his attention to their salient features; and no amount of book-learning can make up for this personal instruction and personal experience in the handling of actual objects. The fisherman who found his way home in a fog by smelling the lead, after sounding with it, was hardly more independent of book-learning than the archaeologist who rubs his thumb along the edge of a potsherd and says 'they never feel like that much after the reign of Domitian'.

34. To scientific treatment of this kind, narrative is no less amenable than any other kind of historical material. The peculiar treatment which narrative demands is generally called by such names as higher criticism, *Quellenkritik*, and so forth. A very remarkable and almost unique example is to be found in the present state of New Testament criticism, which has been undertaken with the deliberate intention of testing with the utmost possible rigour the trustworthiness of those narratives on whose truth Christianity stakes its hope of human happiness and salvation. The fact that this critical study of the New Testament has been taken in hand entirely by persons anxious to believe as much of the Christian faith as possible is an extraordinary and almost incredible testimony to the moral dignity and intellectual sincerity of our age; and the fact that, to find a perfect example of modern historical method, it is necessary to turn to this particular field, shows that the theologians have by no means adopted a weapon which others had prepared, but have gone ahead of historians in the sphere of historical technique. It is safe to say that nowadays the average professional historian is far less critical in his attitude to Herodotus than the average professional theologian in his attitude to St Mark.

35. So far, however, we have been considering only that part of historical methodology which is empirical, or concerned with the peculiarities of different kinds of evidence. But there is another and much more important part of historical methodology, namely general or pure methodology. This is concerned with problems of method which are never absent from any piece of historical thinking. An example of such a problem is that of the argument from silence. The problem is this: can we say that a certain event did not happen because we are not told that it did? On the one side, it may be argued that we cannot, because our sources do not exhaust the whole of the events in their period, and any number of things may have happened about which they say nothing. But on the other side, it may be argued that all historians always do rely on the argument from silence when they accept a narrative based on a certain source because they have no other sources and therefore cannot check the one which they possess; thus our account of any event for which we have only one authority would certainly have to be modified if we discovered a second authority (e.g. the account of the Athenian revolution of 411, and its modification after the discovery of Aristotle's Ἀθηναίων πολιτεία). Hence there is always an implicit argument from silence in every historical inference. And this becomes explicit when we find such arguments as this: No objects found on this site can be dated earlier than the year x or later than the year y, and therefore it was only occupied during the period xy. Here we argue directly from the fact that we have not found certain types of object. Yet no archaeologist would hesitate to use arguments of this kind. Thus on principle the argument from silence seems obviously indefensible, but in practice every historian uses it and uses it incessantly. But every now and then someone starts up in the course of a controversy and says to his opponent: 'this won't do: you are resting your case

on the argument from silence'. It is the business of pure historical methodology to settle this problem and others like it, which are concerned with the perfectly general question of the principles on which evidence must be interpreted.

36. Methodology in this general or pure part is in point of fact almost wholly neglected by historians. They live in this respect from hand to mouth, and on the rare occasions when they start thinking about the subject they are apt to conclude that all historical thought is logically indefensible, though they sometimes add a saving clause to the effect that they personally can interpret evidence pretty well because they have a mysterious intuitive *flair* for the truth, a kind of δαιμόνιον σήμειον which informs them when their authorities are telling lies. Now this attitude is intelligible enough, because it is the attitude which most people always take up towards any philosophical problem. They are helpless when asked to think it out, and they fall back on dogmatic and almost instinctive convictions which under critical inspection are seen to shift and waver with every breath of wind. If you take for instance the attitude of an unphilosophical person towards the general problems of ethics, you will find that he can never present a coherent statement or defence of any one attitude, but that his actual position is a chaotic mixture of all the ethical theories you ever heard of, all presented as intuitively certain and guaranteed by all the sanctity of instinctive conviction. And the upshot is that they know well enough what to do, but can't explain why they do it or how they know they ought to do it. Similarly the ordinary historian can give no account of the processes by which he extracts narrative from sources; all he can say is that he succeeds in doing it somehow, that something, which he may call instinct in order to mark the fact that he does not know its real name, guides him in deciding what evidence is sound and in what direction it points.

37. But we cannot accept this account of the matter. To accept it means falling back on a merely obscurantist, because psychological and subjective, theory of interpretative principles, and the weaknesses of this theory have been already considered. No one would for a moment tolerate the suggestion that instinctive convictions may teach us the right dating of

Corinthian pottery, because, as we have seen, that suggestion reduces history to the level of fable. But exactly the same result follows if the same suggestion is applied to general or pure interpretative principles. If it is merely a *flair* that leads us to select and interpret this evidence in this way, how do we know that the resulting narrative is true? A narrative of some kind will doubtless result from any kind of interpretation; but the historian is not satisfied with any kind of narrative; he wants a true narrative; and unless he will condescend to the ignominy of seriously claiming that he has a direct intuitive perception of the difference between a true and a false narrative, like the magical cups in fairy-tales that broke when poison was poured into them, he must admit in this case what we have argued in the case of empirical principles, that the principles must be independently established *a priori* in order that the narrative constructed by their means may be known to be true.

38. There must, therefore, be a general logic of historical thought, and this must be a philosophical as opposed to an empirical science, and must establish *a priori* the pure principles on which all historical thinking is to proceed. Without the explicit and definite construction of such a philosophical methodology, the results of our historical inquiries may be true, but we cannot know them to be true: we can only hope that, this time, we have not fallen into the trap of an illicit use of the argument from silence or the like, but we cannot be sure of it. Croce, than whom no living philosopher is better qualified to discuss the problems of historical thought, even goes so far as to say that the entire task of philosophy consists in nothing but this construction of a methodology for history. I am not sure that I could follow him quite so far, but I am at any rate equally convinced of the necessity for a philosophical methodology of history, if history is to be more than an arbitrary construction of fantastic narratives out of evidence interpreted at haphazard.

d. *Narrative*

39. When we have found and interpreted our evidence, the result is history as a finished product, or narrative. I say as a finished product, but it must be remembered that the product is never actually finished. The work of collecting sources is as endless as is the work of interpreting them, and therefore every narrative that we can at any given moment put forward is only an interim report on the progress of our historical inquiries. Finality in such a matter is absolutely impossible. We can never say 'this is how it happened', but only and always 'this is how, as at present advised, I suppose it to have happened'.

40. Because final and complete truth, with regard even to quite a small historical problem, is unattainable, it does not follow that there can be no solid advance in historical knowledge. We shall certainly never know all that we want to know about, say, the battle of Marathon; but it would be hasty to infer that all possible accounts of it are therefore equally far from the truth. It may seem paradoxical to say that one account is nearer to the truth than another while yet confessing that we do not know what the truth is; but we must face this paradox, and try to clear it up later, clinging for the moment to the obvious fact that we can and do substitute one narrative for another, not on grounds of personal preference but on wholly objective grounds, grounds whose cogency anyone would have to admit if he looked into them, while yet fully aware that our own narrative is not the whole truth and is certainly in some particulars untrue. One account of an event like the battle of Marathon is demonstrably preferable to another, although neither is wholly true.

41. If this is called scepticism, it is a very different scepticism from that which we analysed at an earlier stage of our inquiry, the scepticism which, assuming that history was to be found ready-made in our authorities, had made the discovery that no authority deserves to be taken at face value. This is a more advanced and less helpless scepticism; for it is a scepticism which only affects the absolute truth of our historical thinking, and does not touch its relative truth, that is to say, the truth of the judgement that *this* historical narrative is preferable to *that*. And if it is argued that without absolute truth this relative truth cannot exist, we shall reply, on the contrary, unless this relative truth were certain, the argument against absolute truth would fall to the ground. [For it is only

the experience of refuting this or that historical theory that
leads us to believe in the ultimate refutability of all such theories; and if we are wrong in thinking that this or that theory
has been genuinely refuted, there is no reason to think that all
must be capable of refutation. But to refute a particular historical theory means to supersede it; for the only way in which
it]⁶ can be refuted is by reinterpreting the evidence on which it
rests, and showing that the evidence really points in a different
direction. The only certainty that we can ever have in historical thinking is the certainty of having made a definite advance
on previous theories. If we want more than that, we cannot
have it. If we hope that by pursuing our inquiries we can come
to know the past exactly as it happened, our hope is vain. This
is perhaps generally recognized, but I may be pardoned for
reminding you of the grounds on which we recognize it.

42. We depend, in history, on sources. We do not depend on
authorities: that is, we are not at the mercy of our informants'
knowledge and veracity; for we can to some extent detect and
allow for their failings, and supplement their information by
evidence of other kinds. But whatever kind of evidence we use,
there is at any given stage in our inquiry a certain amount of it
at our disposal and no more. Now we do not, as if we were
inductive logicians, commit the imbecility of assuming that
the unknown will resemble the known. We do not for a
moment imagine that the sources which we do not possess
would tell the same tale as those which we do. On the contrary, we know that they might tell a different tale, and that is
why we lament their absence and do all we can to find them.
But, as we have already seen, the kind of evidence that the historian can use depends on himself, not on the evidence. And
therefore the totality of evidence on any given subject can
never be exhausted: we always know that if we were more
painstaking we could discover more evidence, and that if we

⁶ Written on the opposite page is the following: 'Not right. I should have
said:—For this argument depends on the principle that historical theories
admit of refutation; that is to say, on the principle that criticism may be
effective. But if criticism is effective, it results in the replacement of the
refuted view by a less inadequate view, that is, one relatively true. For the
only way in which an historical theory'. The brackets in the text are Collingwood's.

were more ingenious we could squeeze more information out of the evidence we possess. For instance, Greek history in the fifth century B.C. is a valuable study for the beginner in historical work because there are so few sources for it that the beginner can grasp them as a whole, and proceed to the work of interpreting them for himself with a remarkably small equipment of scholarship. Hence, within a few months of beginning the study of the period, he is able to form a tolerably good judgement of the merits of any theory that may be put forward. When, on the other hand, he deals with Roman history of the early Empire, he is embarrassed by the immense mass of the available sources, especially those derived from epigraphy; here, therefore, he is confronted with the opposite problem, the problem of acquiring a sound scholarship or acquaintance with the sources, and the work of interpreting them falls comparatively into the background. The student of ancient history as it is taught in this university has therefore two different problems successively before him: in his Greek history he has to exercise himself in squeezing the last drop, by subtle interpretation, out of a given body of sources, and in his Roman history he has to exercise himself in mastering a body of sources whose extent is, within the limits of time allowed him, practically inexhaustible. But this distinction between Greek and Roman history is only a *prima facie* distinction, and disappears on closer acquaintance. For one soon begins to realize that hope of real progress in Greek history is bound up with the hope of enlarging the body of available evidence by calling into play the resources of archaeology, anthropology, and so forth; and on the other hand it is possible, given more time, to master pretty completely the sources for the history of the early Empire, and then comes the task of interpreting them.

43. Both these tasks are endless, and therefore, when the historian says 'ich will nur sagen wie es eigentlich geschehen ist'[7]—I will only state what actually happened (to quote Ranke's famous programme)—he is merely making a promise that he can never redeem: unless indeed the word *will* implies

---

[7] Collingwood has misremembered the quotation. It should be: 'Er will bloss sagen, wie es eigentlich gewesen' (L. Ranke, *Geschichten der romanischen und germanischen Völker von 1494 bis 1535* (Leipzig, 1824), p. vi).

not a promise but a desire—not 'I will' but 'I want to', in which case the phrase is a statement of an ideal, but an unattainable ideal. For it is clear that however long the historian goes on working he will never arrive at the point at which he can say 'I have now collected all the evidence that can ever be collected, and have interpreted it as exhaustively as it can ever be interpreted.' History, regarded as knowledge of past fact, is unattainable.

44. This brings us face to face with a new problem. What is it that we are trying to do in our historical researches? We have hitherto assumed that what we are trying to do is to narrate facts as they actually happened. This, we now see, cannot be done. Now it is possible to explain this by saying that there is a discrepancy between what we are trying to do and what we succeed in doing; what we are trying to do is to know past events, what we succeed in doing is to improve on previous attempts to know them. Hence it is an illusion to think that we can ever know what really happened: but it is a necessary and beneficent illusion, in so far as it is the necessary condition of the real advance which we actually make. Similarly, we are always trying to be good in the sense of morally perfect; that we never shall be; but by trying to do the impossible we actually succeed in doing something which, without this, would itself be impossible—namely, becoming better. All true progress, it may be argued, is rendered possible only by setting before itself a goal which is unattainable.

45. There is no doubt a certain plausibility, and even a certain truth, in this. It is certainly the case that many people misunderstand the actions which they nevertheless do; and it is certain that in some cases, if we understood what we were doing, we should cease to do it. There are historical students who believe that by their researches they can discover the past *wie es eigentlich geschehen ist*;[8] indeed, that is a perfectly natural belief to hold, before one has thought carefully about the matter. And there may be some of these who, if and when they learnt the falsity of this belief, would drop their historical studies. But I am in a position to state confidently that not all would do so; for I myself have learnt the falsity of this naïve

[8] As mentioned in the previous note this quotation from Ranke is not correct.

realism, and have never for a moment been tempted to give up historical research in consequence; precisely as a modern scientist, who has learnt that the world of physics is an abstraction and not a metaphysical reality, does not therefore cease to study physics. And in general, it cannot be argued[9] that ignorance of what we are doing, even to the extent of positive misunderstanding of it, is necessary to the doing of it. We generally believe that our most successful actions are those which we most clearly think out and most completely understand. No doubt there are many things which we often call actions, such as digesting our dinner, that can be done quite unconsciously; but these cases do not really throw light on the difficulty. For although we do not operate our digestive organs in the deliberate design of digesting our dinner, we certainly do not operate them in any other deliberate purpose; we operate them, if we can be said to operate them, without any purpose at all. The action is an unconscious action, involving no purpose: and therefore it does not help to explain the peculiar relation of a purposive action, like thinking historically or acting morally, to a purpose which it sets before itself and does not achieve. In cases in which we are aiming at the achievement of some end, it seems hardly disputable that we aim most efficiently when we think most clearly of the end; and to say that a certain action is only rendered possible by our cherishing a misconception of the end seems a contradiction in terms.

46. Can we, then, give a new and improved account of historical thinking by saying that what we are really trying to do is not to know the past but to improve upon previous attempts to know it? Can we define history in terms not of the unattainable ideal but of the actually achieved progress?

We cannot. For in actual historical work the desire to go one better than other people or our own past selves is in no sense a central motive. The historian is not trying to discredit his predecessors, but to get at the facts; that is the account of the

---

[9] In the manuscript the passage from 'It is certainly the case' (second sentence of paragraph 45) until 'it cannot be argued' is added at a later date and written on the opposite page. In the original text at the beginning of the second sentence of paragraph 45 'But it involves the curious doctrine' is crossed out.

matter which he would always give. And further, if you say that the ideal, because it is unattainable, cannot be actually operative as an ideal, you take away the criterion by which alone the advance is known to be an advance. We can say '*this* historical work is nearer than *that* to my conception of what history ought to be', only so far as we have a conception of what history ought to be. I do not say that the separation between what is and what ought to be is in the long run metaphysically satisfactory; but I do say that it is a lesser evil than the arbitrary reduction of the dualism by denying one of its terms and trying to conceive a progress without any ideal at all except the ideal of progress itself, which is not an ideal but a term correlative to an ideal other than itself.

47. We are, therefore, left in some perplexity as to the purpose of history. We have seen that history cannot be the mere satisfaction of a detached curiosity respecting the past, because this curiosity cannot be satisfied. Nor can it be the mere expression of the pugnacious instincts of historians, for though of course historians have pugnacious instincts, they are also historians, and they want to express their pugnacious instincts through historical controversy, whose peculiar features are left unexplained if we call it a mere example of pugnacity.

48. At this point it may be suggested that the purpose of history is pragmatic: that is to say, its value consists in the moral which we can derive from it for our guidance in present action. Now I do not want to deny that history has morals of this kind. People sometimes say that it has not, because it never repeats itself, and, since the same situation never recurs, an action appropriate for one situation is not appropriate for another. But we need not suppose that it is. Surely one may be allowed to say that we learn by experience how to handle cases of influenza, without being held to the doctrine that all cases of influenza exactly resemble each other. Nobody thinks they do; but everybody thinks that they resemble each other quite enough to justify us in applying to them all certain general rules, such as keeping a feverish patient in bed in a warm room and being very careful about after-effects. These rules we have undoubtedly learnt from historical cases of influenza in our own and other people's experience, and it would be sheer folly to pretend that the same principle does not hold good in strategy and legislation as well as in medicine. Indeed, a soldier or statesman who knew nothing of the history of war or politics would be quite unfit for his work. But this is not to say that its pragmatic value is the essence of history, the value in virtue of which it is history. On the contrary: history pragmatically conceived is conceived first as having completed its proper task of determining past facts, and then as proceeding on the strength of this to give advice concerning the present. When, therefore, it is pointed out that the past facts can never be completely determined, pragmatic history is nipped in the bud. We are raising the question 'what good is history if it can't determine past facts?' and it is no answer to reply, as the pragmatic conception does, 'the good of history is that, having determined past facts, it can tell you what to do in the present'.

49. But the pragmatic theory of history is out of date. No one preaches it now, for people generally recognize that it assumes a finality about the results of historical research which they do not possess. Its place has been taken by a new form of the same general tendency. When you realize that it is impossible first to establish the facts and then to deduce their moral, you can get over the difficulty by allowing the moral to determine the facts. For instance: you want to warn people against intoxication. You say 'Noah got drunk, and that is why negroes are black. Take warning by that awful calamity'. That is pragmatic history. But if you realize that the inebriation of Noah is a matter of serious debate among the learned, and if you are still obsessed by the moral value of history, you say: 'some people say Noah got drunk: others say he didn't, but only had a glass or two. *I* shall say he got drunk, because I am a total abstainer and I want to inculcate a horror of alcohol.' This is tendentious, as opposed to pragmatic, history: the difference being that in tendentious history the moral has got inside the process of historical thought and has played a decisive part in determining its conclusion.

50. Tendentious history, so understood, is commoner than might appear at first sight. It is normal where the historian is personally and immediately attached to one of the parties in the events he is describing; in this case he may allow his attachment quite unconsciously to modify his view of the facts, and reject evidence that tells against his friends because he cannot believe that his friends would have done anything so discreditable; or he may deliberately, in the spirit of an advocate, state his friends' case (or, of course, his own) in a one-sided way because he knows that others have stated the opposite case. And this cannot be condemned without condemning almost all biography, and certainly all autobiography, as historically worthless; and the same applies to histories of England in which the writer obviously rejoices at her victories and laments her defeats, takes pride in her glories and feels shame at her disgraces; or to political histories written by a member of one party who wishes to explain and justify the programme for which his party stands; or to a history of the Reformation written, as we say, from a Protestant or a Catholic point of view; or the like. But further: where the historian is not personally attached to one of the actors on his own stage, he may still have an ideal attachment. Thus a modern democrat may, like Grote, write a history of Greece with the more or less deliberate purpose of vindicating ancient democracy and thus, indirectly, glorifying modern democracy; or a Mommsen may make Julius Caesar his hero because of his own political predilection for autocratic government. And we must remember that a Grote without Grote's political ideals would never have written a history of Greece at all, still less the history which we are all thankful to possess. In a sense, that is true of all historians. All history is tendentious, and if it were not tendentious nobody would write it. At least, nobody except bloodless pedants, who mistake the materials of history for history itself, and think they are historians when they are only scholars.

51. On the other hand, the ineradicable tendentiousness of history is, wherever it appears, a vice. To succumb to it means ceasing to be an historian and becoming a barrister; a good and useful member of society, in his right place, but guilty of an indictable fraud if he calls himself an historian. And therefore, though we all approach history infected with tendentiousness, our actual historical labour must consist largely in overcoming it and purifying ourselves of it, endeavouring to bring ourselves to a frame of mind which takes no sides and

rejoices in nothing but the truth. We shall not ever bring ourselves wholly to this frame of mind, and of that we can be sure
when we see that people like Tacitus and Livy and Gibbon
and Mommsen have never quite done so; but we must go on
trying, and above all never argue, 'because Mommsen, in the
long run, wrote tendentiously, I will write tendentiously: I
will let myself go and write history as I want it to have been'.
It is necessary to emphasize that, because at the present time
there are people who argue thus. It is said, and widely
believed, that history has hitherto been written by capitalists,
and from a capitalist point of view. It is time, therefore, to
take it out of their hands and write it deliberately from a prole-
tarian point of view, to construct a history of the world in
order to show the proletariat as the permanently oppressed
hero and the capitalist as the permanent villain and tyrant of
the human drama. This proposal, however strange it may
seem in an Oxford lecture-room, is today a matter of practical
politics; numerous people are acting on it, and are manufac-
turing the literature which it demands. The result is a type of
history somewhat recalling the anti-religious histories of the
eighteenth century—a history inspired by hatred and endeavouring to justify itself by, most anachronistically, projecting
the object of that hatred, by an obsession that partakes of the
nature of madness, into the whole course of human development. Similarly, there are anti-Semite histories, representing
all history as a melodrama with the Jew for villain; the late war
produced something like a crop of anti-Teuton histories, and
for a combination of anti-Teutonism and anti-Semitism we
may go to Mr Hilaire Belloc. Of such things I will here say no
more than that anyone with the very faintest spark of historical consciousness in him will regard them as scientists would
regard a man who, wishing to generate life in the laboratory,
had deliberately refrained from sterilizing his apparatus. Such
persons are the vulgar criminals of history, and with such it is
useless to argue. But it is encouraging to remember that the
anti-religious history of the eighteenth century did after all
produce a Gibbon, warped by the prevailing vices of his generation, but an historian of the first rank. And I rather suspect
that the next really great history will be an anti-capitalist history inspired by the mythology of socialism.

52. Great history, however, is never merely tendentious; Gibbon was no mere anti-religious pamphleteer, and though certainly his anti-religious passion was one of the forces that moved him to write, the force that sustained him in his work was sheer devotion to history. Now when the tendentiousness which, as I have said, is universal among true historians, has been conquered by the love of truth and impartiality, a new moral atmosphere is created in the historian's mind: he now takes sides not with any one party but with history itself, with the process of events that has generated all parties alike out of itself and has reabsorbed them into itself. History, from this point of view, ceases to be a melodrama and becomes a theodicy, the only possibly theodicy. The historical process is seen as an absolute, all-embracing whole within which all conflicts arise without disintegrating its unity, for its unity alone holds the conflicting parties face to face in their death-struggle, and these conflicting parties are nothing but embodiments of the time-spirit, created by it in order that it may through them achieve its own concrete, objective existence. The world-spirit is in history striving to objectify itself perfectly, and to this end passes through a succession of phases in each of which its true nature is partly revealed; but in each phase the conflict between the partial revelation and the unrealized ideal tears asunder the objective world that has been realized, destroys it in the creation of something new that shall supersede it and approach more closely to the ideal. Hence the conflict between Athens and Sparta is not a conflict between right on one side and wrong on the other; it is properly conceived not as a conflict *between* two forces, but as a conflict *within* one organism, namely the Hellenic world. It is a symptom of something wrong with that organism as a whole, some endemic malady which, because no cure for it has been found, breaks out in a self-destructive rage, the suicide of the civilization on which it feeds. And the new Hellenistic civilization that arises on the ruins of the Hellenic survives it because it deserves to survive, because it has diagnosed the essential malady of its predecessor and has devised a cure for it. Hellenism, in fact, succeeded because it overcame the political atomism that broke up the Hellenic world into a plurality of hostile units, and achieved political coherence, at whatever cost. Rome conquered Hellenism because Rome, the pupil of Alexander, learnt the lesson of Hellenism but added to it something more, a toughness of moral fibre, a force of character, that was lacking in the vague cosmopolitan culture of the Hellenistic period. Rome thus combines the city-state of the Hellenic world, its vivid and inspiring self-consciousness, with the political breadth and inclusiveness of the Hellenistic; and therefore Augustus succeeded where Alexander and Pericles had failed. He succeeded because he deserved to succeed, because he had solved the problem which they had failed to solve.

53. That is an example of history conceived as theodicy, Weltgeschichte als Weltgericht. Its fundamental thesis is that in every struggle—and it conceives all history as a history of struggles—the winner is he who deserves to win, because he has broken through the bounds of thought that limit his contemporaries and called into play the more potent forces of a new and superior phase in the world's history. The fittest survives; for no one survives except by solving the problems with which life presents him, and his solution of these problems is the accurate measure of his powers. God, said Napoleon, is on the side of the big battalions; and that is a true expression of this view of history, so long as we remember that it means no more than this: in a world where fighting is the rule, the better man or the better nation shows superiority and therefore fitness to survive either by fighting better than anybody else, or by finding means to abolish war and set his powers free for another occupation.

54. This conception of history has found its classical advocate in Hegel; and it is certainly true that no one has done more than Hegel to lay down the general lines on which modern thought in the last hundred years has moved. So much is that true in this particular case, that I cannot think of any considerable historian or philosopher of modern times who would not to some extent identify himself with the view I have outlined. Even Croce, who is no friend to Hegel's philosophy of history, uncompromisingly accepts this essential part of it in the doctrine which he calls the positivity of history. In history, says he, there is no such thing as a bad fact, a bad period: the historical process is not a transition from bad to good (still less from good to bad) but from good to better; what we call bad

being nothing but good itself seen in the light of the better. Hence it is not the function of the historian to pass judgement, but to explain; and to explain is always to justify, to show the rationality of that which is explained; for (he goes on) whereas the practical consciousness always looks to the future and tries to bring into existence something better than what now exists, and therefore always regards the present as bad, whereas it can regard the past as good simply because it is not real and therefore has not to be opposed and improved, the theoretical or historical consciousness, concerned simply with what is, must regard the present with an impartial eye and must therefore see in it the outcome of all the past's endeavour, and therefore better than the past. And Croce, equally with Hegel, condemns as sentimentality the conception of history as (to use Hegel's words) the shambles in which the happiness of peoples, the wisdom of states, and the virtue of individuals have been mercilessly sacrificed, and sacrificed for nothing. The terms in which Hegel describes this pessimistic view of history make it impossible to charge his own view with a shallow optimism; and indeed, if history is to be regarded as a theodicy, the world-spirit whose ways it justifies is a god no less terrible than just.

55. Such a god hardly requires our attempts to justify him. And with this reflection we may take our leave both of historical optimism and of historical pessimism. To say that the whole course of history has been a continual passage from the good to the better is true and valuable, if it means that we must look at history not with a view to criticizing it but with a view to accepting it and reconciling ourselves to it, not it to ourselves. But it is false if it means that we are called upon to pass moral judgements on its course and at the same time restricted from passing any but a favourable judgement. We are not called upon to pass moral judgements at all. Our business is simply to face the facts. To say that the Greek victory at Marathon was a good thing or the Renaissance papacy a bad thing is simply to indulge in fantasies that impede, instead of advancing, the course of historical study. The real holocaust of history is the historian's holocaust of his emotional and practical reactions towards the facts that it presents to his gaze. True history must be absolutely passionless, absolutely devoid of all judgements of value, of whatever kind.

56. This may seem a hard saying, but I appeal to everyone who has any experience of historical studies for confirmation of it. And if we find it difficult to accept, we do so, I think, because we forget what it is that in historical thought we are studying. We are studying the past. You will remember that Huckleberry Finn, when the Widow and Miss Watson undertook his belated religious education, began by being all in a sweat about Moses, till Miss Watson let out one day that Moses had been dead a considerable time: whereupon he lost interest, because, as he said, he took no stock in dead men. Now the true historian, like Huckleberry Finn, takes no stock in dead men. He does not get in a sweat about them, just because they are dead; he does not do what I suppose Huckleberry Finn to have done at first, namely pass moral judgements and take up practical or volitional attitudes towards the objects of his study. But it is easy to forget that what we are studying is the past, and to deceive ourselves into thinking that Athens and Sparta are as real as France and Germany. When we do this, we feel about them as we feel about France and Germany, that it is up to us to *do* something about it, to decide upon a course of action, or at least to make up our minds how we should act if opportunity arose to act. It will not arise; and for that very reason we may take the same kind of self-deceptive pleasure in making up our minds how we *should* act that we take in framing pungent repartees to an adversary whom we know we shall not meet. We are amusing ourselves by transplanting ourselves in imagination into a scene whose very essence, as object of historical thought, is that we are not in it and never can be in it: and this not only confuses our historical thinking but squanders in fantasies a moral energy which it is our duty to devote to the actual problems of life.

57. At the beginning of these lectures I insisted that the past, which is the object of historical thought, was not a mass of stuff existing somewhere though removed from our immediate vision by the passage of time, but consisted of events which because they have happened are not now happening and do not in any sense exist at all. The past is in no sense whatever actual. It is wholly ideal. And that is why our attitude towards it is wholly different from our attitude towards the present, which, because it is actual, is the scene of our practical activity and the proper subject of our moral judgements. To pass moral judgements on the past is to fall into the fallacy of imagining that somewhere, behind a veil, the past is still happening; and when we so imagine it we fall into a kind of rage of thwarted activity as if the massacre of Corcyra was now being enacted in the next room and we ought to break open the door and stop it. To rescue ourselves from this state of mind we need only realize clearly that these things have been; they are over; there is nothing to be done about them; the dead must be left to bury their dead and to praise their virtues and lament their loss.

58. History, so conceived, may be called a very cold-blooded business, and I may be accused of withdrawing from it all that makes it attractive. I am not afraid of the accusation; I do not think that anyone who can so accuse me is really more interested in history or more devoted to its study than I am myself. But I may certainly be asked to explain why it is attractive, if the past can never be known as it actually happened and if we may not even use it as a catharsis for our emotions and our moral judgements. The answer is, that history is ideal; and the ideal is an abstraction from the actual and exists for the sake of the actual.

59. There is, properly speaking, only one knowable object, namely the actual—that which now exists: and every intellectual problem that can possibly be raised properly concerns our knowledge of this one object or complex of objects. And our knowledge of the actual is inseparable from our own volitional activity and emotional reaction towards it. The actual, the present, is the only possible object of our knowledge, field for our activity, and stimulus to our feelings. We cannot know the future, because it is not there to be known; we cannot know the past, because it is not there to be known. And this explains at once why it is impossible to know the past as it actually happened, and why it is impossible to take up practical or emotional attitudes towards it. Does this, then, prove that history is an illusion and that to pursue it is folly? No: because though the past has no actual existence, it is an ideal element in the present, and can therefore be studied in the same general way and to the same extent to which any abstraction may be

studied. The present is the past transformed. In knowing the present, we are knowing that into which the past has changed. The past has become the present, and therefore if we ask where the past is to be found in living and concrete actuality, the answer is, in the present. But whereas the past exists actually as the present, it exists ideally as the past—as what it was before it turned into the present. Now all knowledge proceeds by analysis and synthesis—taking a given whole to pieces, studying the pieces separately, and putting them together again. But this process is altogether an ideal process: we do not really take the whole apart, for it won't come apart; what we do is to make ideal distinctions within it and study what we have so distinguished. And the elements that we have distinguished are not real: they are only ideal. It is the object as a whole that is real; and the real whole is composed of ideal parts. If this seems difficult, if anyone thinks that a real whole must be composed of real parts, let him reflect that the qualities into which we analyse any perceptible object—its blueness, its squareness, and so forth—are not real things that can be picked up and stuck together; they are abstractions, but abstractions which together do really make up the object.[10]

60. The present is composed in this way of two ideal elements, past and future. The present *is* the future of the past, and the past of the future; it is thus both future and past in a synthesis that is actual. (Of course, any future time will, when it comes, have what is now the present as its past and a further future as its future: so any moment of time is a synthesis of past and future; but until it arrives this synthesis is not actual but only ideal.) The present is generally imagined as a mathematical point between the past and the future; but that is a false metaphor: for really it is not a point but a world, a complex of events actually going on, and instead of *its* being a mere abstraction, a mathematical point between two real extensions, *they* are mere abstractions and *it*, as actuality, contains both past and future as ideal elements within itself.

[10] The opposite page contains the following statement: 'or think of Newton's analysis of the moon's elliptical orbit into (a) a rectilinear falling movement towards the earth (b) a second rectilinear tangential movement—both wholly ideal.'

61. Our knowledge, so called, of the past, is therefore not knowledge of the past as of an actual object, and therefore not true knowledge; it is only the reconstruction of an ideal object in the interests of knowing the present. The purpose of history is to enable us to know (and therefore to act relatively to) the present: that is the truth contained in the pragmatic view of history. But the knowledge of the past must not be misconceived as knowledge of one object, the past, which when achieved serves as means to the knowledge of another object, the present. That is the error of the pragmatic view. The past and the present are not two objects: the past is an element in the present, and in studying the past we are actually coming to know the present, not coming to know something else which will lead us on to know or to manipulate the present.

62. This principle, the ideality of the past, explains both why we cannot and why we need not know the past as it actually happened. We cannot, because there is nothing to know; nothing exists to be studied: there are no past facts except so far as we reconstruct them in historical thought. And we need not, because the purpose of history is to grasp the present, and therefore any past fact which has left no visible traces on the present is not, need not be, and cannot be a real problem to historical thought. From a purely abstract point of view it would seem possible to raise the question what was the favourite wine of the maternal grandfather of the standard-bearer who jumped ashore from Caesar's ships on the coast of Kent, and it might be made a reproach to the historian that he neither knows nor cares. But the fact is that the historian does not raise problems at haphazard in this way: they raise themselves, and what he has to do is to settle them when they have done so. And an actual historian when confronted with a problem of this kind will say, if he troubles to explain his attitude towards it, 'that problem hasn't arisen in my inquiries, and I shan't attend to it till it does'. Now this attitude would be culpably subjective if the whole world of past fact were a world actually existing which it was the historian's business to discover and explore in its entirety; for in that case every fact in it, being as actual as every other, has an equal right to his attention, and to attend to one and not to others is indefensible. But all historical problems arise within present experience, and a problem that does not in any way fit into present experience and alter our attitude to that is not a genuine problem but a nonsense problem, as truly a nonsense problem as the childish puzzle of the irresistible force and the immovable post, which belongs to the realm of nonsense physics.

63. The ways in which historical problems arise are of various kinds whose differences are not altogether without interest. They all have this in common, that they are problems arising in the attempt to understand what I am and what my world is. When I ask what I am, I begin recollecting, and thinking what in my actions and experiences I have shown myself to be: and in trying to criticize and verify my recollections I build up a more or less coherent account of what, at this given moment, I find myself being. This account of myself is the necessary basis for any action which demands self-consciousness as part of its conditions. When I ask what the objective world is, recollection does not help me much; I must study the world as I now find it and reconstruct its past not immediately, as I can do in memory in the case of myself, but inferentially. And in so far as this activity of reconstructing the past becomes habitual, a new kind of present comes into being which is related to the past not merely as its consequence or the present metamorphosis of itself but as the deliberate and systematic record of it. I refer to such present realities as conversations about the past, history-books, and so forth. Now these are part of the present, but they have the curious double function of being both consequences of the past (as is everything in the present) and also expressions of thought concerning the past. They are products of the *historical* consciousness and not merely of consciousness in general, still less of the world-process in general. And this reveals the curious fact that the attempt to reconstruct the past ideally, because it is an activity going on in the present, contributes to the present a series of objective realities which give rise not only to a fresh problem of knowledge, but to a problem of a peculiar kind. History in the primary sense, history of the first degree, is the ideal reconstruction of the past as such; history of the second degree is the reconstruction of this reconstruction. Thus, the primary historical problem arises in the attempt to answer questions like, What is that ruined building? What are these curious goings-on that happen at a coronation? Why are we wearing gowns? The secondary historical problem arises in the attempt to answer questions like, Why have people expressed such divergent views about the battle of Marathon? Why does Macaulay say what he does about the state of the currency in the late seventeenth century? and so forth. In the former case the historical problem arises out of the attempt to understand the world as it stands irrespectively of the existence of any historians: and if all historians were guillotined in a revolution and all their books burnt, it would be these problems that would ensure a speedy revival of historical studies. In the latter case historians themselves and their special products are among the elements of the problem which interests us; and in this case the problems of history may be called academic or artificial problems, which need not be discussed at all if it was not the fact that they are discussed. Hence, if I ask myself what it is in my present experience that I hope to elucidate by my historical inquiries, there are two kinds of answer: first, that it is something I find in the world of nature or of human institutions; secondly, that it is something I have read or heard in my historical studies. This distinction is of importance because if we say that the purpose of history is to make the actual world more intelligible and then have to admit that some historical investigations help only to render intelligible the statements of certain historians (which we clearly must admit), we seem involved in a circle. The way out of the circle would seem to lie in distinguishing history from the history of history.

64. Hitherto we have assumed that the only function of the history of history was to serve the methodological purpose of clearing the ground for history of the first degree. But once historical thinking is recognized as a necessary activity of the human mind—and that recognition is achieved when we recognize that the analysis of the present into past and future is a necessary stage in its comprehension—it follows that the organization and perpetuation of historical thought is a necessary part of the institutions which go to make up civilized life, and therefore the history of history is as necessary to civilized man as the history of war or the history of science. When history itself is objectified into libraries and schools of historical learning, to study in these libraries and schools automatically becomes an exercise in the history of history, and henceforth it becomes impossible to say that the problems of history are of vital interest while those of the history of history are of merely academic interest. On the contrary, as it becomes clearer that past fact as such and in its entirety cannot be known, as people progressively recognize that the only past we can know or need know is the past that has preserved recognizable traces in the present, so people must come to see more and more that all history is really history of history, that in stating what we take to be past facts we are really only and always recounting and summarizing our own and other people's investigations concerning the past. This does not mean that for the statement 'it was so' is substituted the statement 'A thinks it was thus, B thinks it was thus, C thinks it was thus; I leave the reader to take his choice'; for that is not resolving history into the history of history but merely shirking the whole problem. The real formula will run: 'A thinks it was thus; B thinks it was thus; C thinks it was thus; *and I*, having diligently studied their views and all other evidence, *think it was thus*'. Here the history of history culminates where it ought to culminate, in the present. For a history that stops short of the present is a truncated history, a fragment of circumference without a centre.

65. History of the first degree and history of the second degree are thus the two sides of history itself, the immediate or objective side in which the mind is turned towards the past event, and the reflective or subjective side in which it is turned towards its own attempts to grasp that event: and these two converge and unite in a present act of thought which is at once history, 'it was so', and history of history 'I think it was so'. When we say 'it was so', we are in reality talking not about the past but about the present, because we cannot ever say what the past in itself truly was, but only what the evidence now at our disposal enables us to say that it was; and, as we have seen, it is quite certain that this evidence is always fragmentary and inadequate. The past which we reconstruct in historical thought is not the real past (if there were a real past, which there is not); it is the past that can be disentangled from the present objective world by the present act of thinking. Hence the subjective present tense in '*I think* it was so' ought to be balanced by an objective present tense, turning 'it was so' into 'the evidence now to hand indicates that it was so'. And these two judgements are synonymous. History and the history of history turn out to be identical. The present or actual reality, as we find it in and for the historical consciousness, is not a mere world or a mere mind, but a mind knowing its world or a world being known by a mind; and it is impossible for the mind to know its world without at the same time knowing itself. This is intended not as a generic statement about all kinds of cognition, but as a specific statement about historical thought. No one, for instance, would wish to maintain that perception involved as a necessary part of itself the perception of perception; but we have shown that history does so involve the history of history.

66. The present, I said, is a concrete reality analysable into two elements, past and future. I recur to that statement in order to guard against a possible misconception. It might be argued that if one of these ideal elements, the past, can be made the object of historical thought, the future also ought to be the object of a kind of anticipatory historical thought. Now clearly this is not the case. Yet *ought* it not to be the case, on our view? For we are not in a position to refute it as some people would refute it, by pleading that the past is real and the future unreal. On that view, the present is essentially a moment of creation, in which things are brought into being out of nothing: having been created, they stay created, and so the universe is constantly becoming fuller and fuller of facts. It never gets positively clogged with facts because it goes on somehow expanding to make room for them. Now we have dismissed this idea of the past as a kind of silt or sediment of facts, on the ground that the past really consists of events that are not happening, that is to say of unrealities. But we may in passing point out that the whole idea of a perpetual creative process which creates without destroying is a sheer confusion of thought. If the present is conceived as creative, then what it creates must either be conserved, which means continuing to be a present reality, or not be conserved, which means passing by, becoming past and therefore becoming non-existent. But the conception has at least this merit, that it makes a distinction of principle between past and future, and does not conceive them as the same kind of thing. And our own contention that the past and future are both ideal, or abstractions, does not compel us to hold that they are abstractions of the same kind. To take a case which we took before: the shape and the colour of a triangle are abstractions; but it does not follow that because the science of geometry gives us an *a priori* account of its shape, therefore geometry or indeed any other science can give us an *a priori* account of its colour.

67. Past and future, then, are heterogeneous; they are not the same kind of thing, even though they are both ideal. Mr Bertrand Russell, failing to recognize this and deceived by the idea of time as a continuous line whose segments are necessarily homogeneous with each other, says that 'it is a mere accident that we have no memory of the future; for future events are just as determined as past, in the sense that they will be what they will be', and goes on to say that there is no philosophical reason for scepticism with regard to the claim, which some people make, to a power of foretelling the future (*Our Knowledge of the External World*; quoted from memory).[11] The answer to this is easy. To call the absence of 'forward memory' a mere accident is to admit that it is a fact and to add that one's own philosophy is impotent to give any account of it; to admit that some people can perhaps foretell the future is to retract the first admission and to assert that memory of the future does exist, though rarely; and to leave it an open question whether their claims are justified is to confess that they are not justified, because no one can regard it as an open question whether or not we remember the past. Further: because we remember the past and thus have an immediate awareness of it, we can build up on this foundation the entire structure of critical history, which starts from memory but goes far beyond it. If even a few people really possessed a forward memory or immediate vision of the future it would be possible to construct on that basis a critical history of the future, having

[11] The passage referred to by Collingwood runs as follows: 'It is a mere accident that we have no memory of the future. We might—as in the pretended visions of seers—see future events immediately, in the way in which we see past events. They certainly will be what they will be, and are in this sense just as determined as the past' (Bertrand Russell, *Our Knowledge of the External World* (London, 1914), p. 238).

methods and results similar in principle to that of the past. But this cannot be done, and nobody really thinks it can. No one can possibly forecast the course of European history, even in the next ten years, with anything approaching the certainty and precision with which even the least competent historian can reconstruct its course in the last ten or even in the last ten thousand. We can certainly anticipate the future, but all our anticipations are guesses, or mere statements of what so far as we can see may happen, whereas our reconstructions of the past are never guesses, but always statements of what, so far as we can see, must have happened. And this applies even to the most systematic and satisfactory of our predictions, namely the astronomical anticipations which are elaborately set forth in the Nautical Almanack. These are not cases of forward-looking history. They are one and all hypothetical: they are statements of what will happen if no disturbing element arises, as it always may arise, to upset our calculations. But, it may be said, our statements about the past are hypothetical too: they state what happened subject to the hypothesis that the evidence we possess is reliable. This is, however, not a true parallel. We reconstruct the past, it is true, only so far as the present state of things permits us to do so; and we also forecast the future as far as the present permits us to do so. But the shortage of evidence and our liability to misinterpret it, which affect both kinds of thinking, are a drawback different in kind from the possibility of disturbing influences, which is a quite fresh difficulty affecting our forecast of the future and not our reconstruction of the past. It may be said that an ideally perfect astronomy would be able to eradicate this difficulty. But we are discussing not what we might be able to do under ideal (that is, impossible) conditions, but what we actually do; and however far astronomy progresses it will always operate under actual conditions, never under ideal conditions.

68. The difference, then, between the past and the future is that the past can be, within the limits imposed by present circumstances, critically reconstructed as it must have been; the future, still within the same limits, can only be guessed at or described in hypothetical propositions. Stating this difference in logical terms, we get this result: the present is the actual:

the past is the necessary: the future is the possible. Necessity and possibility are the two abstract elements which together make up actuality. The present both may be and must be what it is; the past must, but cannot, be what it is; the future may, but need not, be what it is. Hence the past, in spite of its unreality, can be the object of critical and rigorous inferential thinking, for everything that it contains it contains necessarily, and there is in the study of it no room for imagination or caprice or any kind of assertion which cannot justify itself by the production of valid reasons. The future, on the other hand, is the contingent, the indeterminate, that which can only be described by saying 'if A happens, then x will follow; if B happens, then y will follow; but though it may be wise to assume that A will happen and B will not, we cannot give valid reasons for the assumption.' Of course, the future will be what it will be; but that only means that when it happens it will be the present, and will have all the actuality of the present. It is not lying somewhere ready formed, waiting to happen, which is what Mr Russell evidently thinks is meant by the phrase it will be what it will be.

69. The conception of the ideality of the past has further consequences. When we think of the past as a limitless reservoir of facts all existing side by side in a closely-packed mass and awaiting our inspection, we are bound to distinguish the actual characteristics which these facts possess in themselves from the adventitious and subjective characteristics which we bestow upon them for our own purposes in the course of our historical labours. Thus, for example, we distinguish ancient history from modern history, and this distinction obviously inheres not in the facts themselves but in our own point of view towards them; we regard as modern those facts which we recognize as continuous with those of the world in which we live, and as ancient those which belong to an order of things that has by now disappeared. If, then, the past is an actual object or complex of objects, and if our study of it is an attempt to apprehend it in its actuality, the distinction between ancient and modern history must be banished from our minds as an illusion incidental to our point of view. But if, as we have seen to be the case, the past is ideal and has being only as an object of historical thought, its relation to our point of view is its very essence, and whatever is necessarily implied in our point of view is a real and legitimate element in its own nature. Now the distinction between ancient and modern history *is* necessarily implied in our point of view towards history. For the past is that which has turned into the present; but every past time was a present when it existed, and is now thought of by the historian as an ideal present, having its own past; and therefore all historical thought necessarily generates a distinction between the past and the past of the past. But the past, or recent past, must have a different character from the past of the past, or remote past; for the recent past is that which has turned into the present, and the remote past, if it had resembled the recent past, would have turned into the present too, and not, as it actually did, into the recent past. Hence it follows from the purely logical structure of the time-series as an ideal construction that there must be a broad general difference of character between two parts of history, modern history, regarded as that which has immediately produced the present, and ancient history, regarded as that which produced the recent or modern past and therefore produced the present mediately. But the subdivision of the past cannot end here. Within the recent past and the remote past similar distinctions will reappear, so that these two main periods will reveal an internal structure reduplicating in principle their relation to each other. If this search for distinctions were pushed *ad infinitum*, the result would be a homogeneous flow of time-units, each following the one before it and preceding the one after it; and the events happening at these times would lose all their special character of ancient, modern and so forth and would be reduced to a dead-level of pastness. But we cannot in fact ever push it *ad infinitum*; we have no time to do so, and there would be no point in doing so. We are concerned with history as actually studied by actual historians, not with the ideal of history as it would be studied by a calculating-machine. For a calculating-machine, there would be no necessity to bring the past into relation with the present; and therefore a calculating-machine would not need to divide up the past according as its relation to the present was immediate or mediate. But then, the past is only ideal; it is only generated by historical thought in order to bring it into relation with the present; and therefore, where this need has vanished, the past has vanished too.[12]

70. So long, therefore, as we think of the past at all, we must think of it as possessing that kind of determinate structure which consists in a sequence of more or less clearly-defined periods having characteristics of their own and each possessing precisely those characteristics which would necessitate their turning into the next, and so on. We must, that is to say, find in history a pattern or scheme which makes it a self-contained and logically-articulated whole. And we can determine this structure *a priori*. The actuality of history is the present; its ideality is the past; and the past is either recent or remote according as we conceive it as turning directly or indirectly into the present. Now that which turns into something else is by definition *not* that something; hence the recent past is always conceived as different from the present, a contrast with it, but a contrast of such a kind as to necessitate a change into that with which it is a contrast. The recent past, therefore, is necessarily conceived as a state of things in unstable equilibrium, containing within itself the seeds of change into its own opposite. And every period, as the recent past of that which is to follow it, must be conceived in this general way. But when it is said that every period changes into its own opposite, this does not mean that history is an alternation of A, not-A, A, not-A, and so on *ad infinitum*. If that were so, the present would have happened already an infinite number of times; and this is absurd, because the present is what is happening now, and it cannot also have happened in the past. Ancient and modern are

---

[12] On the opposite page Collingwood later wrote the following notes: 'Problem of Historical Phases and Cycles. Theological, Metaphysical, Positive (Comte), Organic and Critical (recurring) St Simon. Platonic Cycle— 36,000 solar years. Aristotle agrees. "This doctrine of recurrence is not popular today: but whether we like it or not, no other view of the macrocosm is even tenable." Inge, Outspoken Essays II 160. (he means, *physically* speaking.) Goethe quoted as a believer in cycles, but he is vague.

Cycle versus progress—theme of Inge's superficial lecture. He holds with cycles and denies progress.

Cycle theory cannot be taken literally. The present is now only: it must be somehow distinct from all its opposite numbers in the past, even if in some ways indistinguishable. Otherwise we would not be able to use a plural of the word cycle.'

opposites which together make up the past, and past and present are opposites; thus when the recent or modern past
changes into the present what happens is not that the modern
has changed into its own opposite, which would be the
ancient, but that modern and ancient together, the past as a
whole, has changed into its opposite. Hence the formula for
the structure of history is that A changes into its opposite not-
A, and the complex period composed of A and not-A together
changes into a new period B, which is its opposite. Every
period is thus the opposite of all that has gone before, not
merely of its last phase; which is self-evident, for the present is
the opposite not of the immediate past but of the past.[13]

This formula gives the necessary structure of all historical
narrative. So far as the narrative shows this formula, so far it is
well-written, well-thought out, intelligible as history. And
where this pattern is not visible we have not history at all, but

---

[13] Page 65 ends here in the manuscript. Inserted—between p. 65 and p.
66—at a later date is a separate page with the heading 'insert after 65 [sum-
mary of what I said on this in 1927]', which reads as follows: 'All history is
divided into ancient and modern in this way. It is not a distinction expressible in years; the idea of stating a date at which ancient history ends and
modern history begins is absurd. It is a distinction inherent in the historian's
point of view. However wide or however narrow his chronological range,
whether he embraces a period of 10 or 100 or 100,000 years in his backward
view, he necessarily discriminates within this view a *past* (modern history)
and a *past of the past* (ancient history). And the past will always be his own
opposite, the past of the past the opposite of his own opposite and therefore
at bottom akin to or somehow felt as identical with himself. A culture which
feels the Victorian Age as its own immediate past, and therefore repulsive,
feels the previctorian age (perhaps the 18th century) as akin to itself: its cultural history only goes back as far as that; if it went further, the distinction
between ancient and modern would fall in a different place. *Nostalgia for the
ancient* has here its logical basis and is inevitable,—Golden Ages, sense of the
heroic character of origins (felt as heroic *because* they are felt as origins i.e.
ancient), returns to paganism, etc., are all based on the fact that history is a
cycle; not a series of cycles, but *one* cycle, therefore the past, however much
or little of it we know, necessarily appearing to us as *one* vast cycle with a single rhythm of ancient–modern–present. Yet within this cycle, the primary
cycle, we can find an infinity of epicycles at any point on its circumference,
because any point we take becomes an ideal present and therefore acquires an
ideal history—modern history and ancient history—of its own. But these
epicycles shift and change as we move our microscope over the field of history: they are all ἀγωνίσματα ἐς τὸ παραχρῆμα—the great cycle of all
known history is a κτῆμα ἐς ἀεί.'

at best a mass of chronological detail or other material out of which history is to be constructed.

71. But having deduced the formula, we must make a few observations on it. Just as you cannot think scientifically by taking any kind of stuff that passes itself off as thought and forcing it into the shape of a syllogism, so you cannot think historically by playing games with any formulae, however good they are. The formula which we have laid down is to be found growing wild in all historical narrative; where it does not grow of itself, it cannot be introduced; and in stating it we are not (God forbid) suggesting to historians that they should import it forcibly into their work, or bang it out with one finger as a bad pianist bangs out the theme of a fugue. Further: this formula will not help anyone to determine any historical fact. Historical facts cannot be deduced from formulae like the fourth term in a rule-of-three sum; that is just the difference between history and mathematics. Unless you have evidence in your hand and the skill to interpret it, you cannot move a step in historical thought; and if you know anything about history, you will not try. It is idle to protest that a formula like this involves an attempt to construct history *a priori* instead of by legitimate historical methods. You might as well argue that any statement of the principles of logic involves an attempt to construct science *a priori* instead of by observation and experiment. Anyone who feels that a formula of this kind is an offence to his sensitive historical conscience is merely confessing his inability to understand its meaning.

72. It is well known that Hegel discovered the presence of this structure in all history, and that his exposition of it has been generally rejected as unsatisfactory. The reasons for this rejection are, I think, wholly bound up with the positivistic view of history as a crude lump or magma of existing fact, a real and therefore structureless past whose elements can be studied by the historian but not, without a dangerous concession to subjectivity, arranged in any kind of pattern. This theory of the real past underlies, so far as I can see, all the objections to Hegel's main idea. Thus, it is pointed out that Hegel succeeded in arranging the past quite neatly according to his formula although his historical knowledge was, compared to ours, very small; and because his facts were so incomplete his pattern ought to have showed gaps, which it did not do. But to argue thus is to forget that Hegel was talking not about the past as known to us but about the past as known to him; and that because the past is altogether ideal, Hegel had a perfect right to treat his knowledge of the past as exhausting what there was to know. Again, it is pointed out that Hegel deliberately left outside his pattern the history of the Far East and indeed all history except that of Europe and the near East; and this is held to show that, in order to make his pattern work, he had to restrict it to a quite small portion of history at large. But this is to forget that the pattern is a telescope-pattern, and goes on in any direction as far as you choose to take it; Hegel was devoting one course of lectures to the subject, and bit off as much of history as he thought he could, in the time, profitably chew. I do not deny that Hegel does rather thump out the theme of his fugue; and I wish he had spent more time on explaining what it was that he was doing, and less on doing it; but to wish that is only to wish that he had written for our generation instead of his own.

73. To speak of the past as presenting a definite pattern implies not only that it has a necessary structure, but that this structure culminates in or centres round the present; and this means that the past is conceived as existing for the purpose of leading up to the present, to be the means of which the present is the end. It is certainly the case that when we think of the past we do all of us tend so to think of it; we think, even while we blame ourselves for our ridiculous egotism in thinking it, that the whole past has been so ordered by some providence as to create for us a world in which to live. If the past is real, this is obviously an illusion, for it exists not for our sake but for its own. But if the past is ideal, we are right to think of it as informed by a providential purpose: for this purpose is precisely our own purpose; it is we who create the past in order that we may understand the present, and therefore it is true, though not in the sense in which we naïvely believe it, that the present is the goal of all past history. Similarly the future, if we could tell what it would be, would be necessarily regarded as the goal of the present; but it cannot be so regarded because we cannot tell what it will be.

74. Another question that is answered by the conception of

the ideality of the past is the question of the possibility of universal history in the sense of a history of the world. With regard to this question the theory of the past as real lands us in an unpleasant dilemma. The business of the historian is to ascertain past fact; his business is not done until he has ascertained the whole of it. But past fact is infinite in amount and in complexity; and however much of it the historian discovers, the infinite quantity that remains to be discovered is undiminished. And this becomes even worse when, as every historian must do, he recognizes that no historical fact can be truly ascertained until we have ascertained its relations with its context. The so-called theory of external relations, which lays down that the relations subsisting between A and B are irrelevant to the essential nature both of A and of B, is a true account of the relations that are found in mathematics, but a wholly false account of those that are found in history. It is absolutely impossible to say anything at all about any historical event, even its date, which is the most abstract thing you can say about it, except in relation to other events; and all history consists of nothing whatever but narrative, which is not an enumeration of distinct events but a statement of their relations or articulations. Hence the presence of an uninvestigated context infects with uncertainty and misconception that part of history that has been investigated: a truth which is familiar to every historical student who has got beyond the schoolroom stage. Now if all past facts are real, and exist in a solid block for us to study, the number that can be ascertained is infinitely outweighed by those on which we can get no evidence whatever, and therefore our historical knowledge, however far we push it, remains not only infinitely short of completion but, even within its narrow compass, infinitely short of certainty. Hence the dilemma, that either the historian must know the whole past, which he can never do because to know it consists in enumerating an infinity of facts, or he must only know a part of it, which he can never do because his knowledge of the part is vitiated by his ignorance of the whole. If he aspires to write the history of the world, the result will be a merely ludicrous assemblage of facts chosen at haphazard, getting scantier and scantier as the history becomes more and more remote till at last it fails entirely and is bolstered up by vague speculations concerning the origins of man, of life, of the earth: no more a history of the world than the *Golden Treasury* is English literature. But if he aspires to write a monograph on the Peasants' Revolt he is no better off, for not only is there an infinity of facts concerning the Peasants' Revolt that simply cannot now be discovered, but even if they could, the Peasants' Revolt would remain unintelligible when torn from its context in the history of the world.

What, then, ought we to aim at doing—to widen our historical knowledge or to deepen it? Both, if the past is real, are futile. But if the past is ideal, both are possible, and possible together.

75. All history is an attempt to understand the present by reconstructing its determining conditions. It is clear that this is an endless task, not because its conditions are a regress of efficient causes which, however far back we trace them, still hang in the air at the further extremity, but because the present is a concrete reality and therefore inexhaustible by analysis. When we have analysed it as far as we can, the residue is not outside our grasp; it is here and now, it is immediately present to us as actual fact; unanalysed and uncomprehended, but not unperceived. Hence, when we have traced the course of history back into the remotest past which our plummet can sound, and find ourselves compelled to call that the beginning of history; and when the question is raised, 'how did this beginning happen, and what right have you to assume at the very start of your history, as you must do, the world as a going concern?' the answer is 'what I am assuming as the presupposition of my history is precisely that part of the world, as I now find it, of whose historical origin I can give no account'. Thus, the saying that nature has no history means that nature is our name for that whose origin we have not hitherto been able to trace, and therefore it is a presupposition of history in the sense in which a hitherto unsolved problem is the presupposition of any attempt to solve it. The present world, as we apprehend it in perception, is the starting-point of history: history attempts to explain this present world by tracing its origins; that part of it whose origins we cannot trace remains unexplained, is left on our hands at the end of the inquiry, and is therefore posited at the opening of our narrative. All history

is therefore universal history in the sense that it is an attempt
to give an account, as complete as possible, of the present
world; but because the present world is inexhaustible in its
content, the account can never be complete and all history has
to begin somewhere, to take something for granted, to special-
ize on some particular problem to the exclusion of others.
Every history is in fact an historical monograph, a discussion
of a limited historical problem: and this is true even of so-
called histories of the world, which are always written from
some particular point of view and deal with some particular
subject or group of subjects to the exclusion of others; but
because the writer of a history of the world is apt to deceive
himself into thinking that there is such a thing as history as a
whole, and that he is simply relating the whole of it, his subject and purpose are apt to be insufficiently or mistakenly
defined in his own thought, and the result is apt to be a disjointed series of amateurish monographs, each an object of
ridicule to a person who has patiently inquired into the problems it presents. But a genuine and competent historical
monograph is really a universal history or history of the world,
in the sense that its writer has been driven to write it by the
way in which the world now presents itself to him. Among the
mass of things which present themselves to his gaze and com-
pete for his attention there is one thing which stands out as
especially demanding that he, and very likely nobody else,
should try to understand it: partly because it is a matter of
general importance to the world that it should be understood,
partly because his special temperament and training make him
the right man to investigate it. If the first motive alone is operative, his work will be valuable on account of its popularity,
but deficient in skill; if the second, it will be a good piece of
work in itself but of mainly academic interest. But in either
case, he is tackling the problem of understanding the present
world at the point where, for him, its centre of intelligibility
lies. And therefore his work will be a real history of the world
as being the history of that part of the world whose history is
for him, here and now, capable of being written. There is
therefore no real conflict between the idea of a history of the
world and that of a discussion of some special historical problem. Because the past is ideal, the history which we, to the best

of our ability, investigate, is all the history there is. And this does not mean that when we have written our monograph we have exhausted all the history there is; for, unless we are very bad historians, the monograph itself will create for us a whole crop of new historical problems.

76. I have spoken of historical books and monographs as if such things were the chief outcome of historical thought; and this may suggest that history is mainly the concern of professional persons called historians. That is the last suggestion that I should wish to make. History is nothing but the attempt to understand the present by analysing it into its logical components of necessity, or the past, and possibility, or the future; and this is an attempt that is made by everybody and at all times. Nobody ever attempts to do a job of plumbing or to ride a motor bicycle without historically reconstructing the preconditions of the situation with which he is faced, and there is no difference in principle, only a difference in degree, between the historical thinking done by a bricklayer in the exercise of his craft and that done by a Gibbon or a Grote. The problem is the same, the categories of thought involved are the same, and the solution is the same. History is one of the necessary and transcendental modes of mind's activity, and the common property of all minds.

77. In conclusion, I may be expected to say something of the relation between history and philosophy. In a very real sense they are and must be the same. For their problem is the same. There is and can be only one problem for any conceivable kind of thought—the problem of understanding reality, of discovering what the world is. And there is only one world, namely that which actually exists. This world is present in the immediacy of sensation to every mind, and in that immediacy it presents itself as that which is not yet understood, the problem, the eternal Sphinx which in its visible bodily presence confronts the eternal Oedipus of mind, bidding it solve the riddle or perish. And this riddle is not only presented to the civilized and educated man; it presents itself with at least equal urgency to the child, the savage, and the lunatic. Nor is its solution a matter of disinterested intellectual satisfaction; it is a wholly practical matter, and failure means suffering, disease, misery, and death. For it is certainly true that if we could

fully understand the world we should be as gods, enjoying an immortal blessedness. As men, we understand it by various expedients to this extent, that we can tame the Sphinx for a time, make it fetch and carry for us, call it by its name and compel it to obey us. But sooner or later our understanding of it breaks down, and it frees itself from our grasp and stands over against us once more with the menace of its immediate sensible externality, and that is death. This is the law under which every man lives.

Now our struggle to understand the world is carried on by various devices of our own invention, worked out by us in our struggle for existence. Of these devices we can distinguish a few which are so universal, so inevitable, that we can hardly help ascribing them to causes that are permanently operative. Those which, for my own part, I find to be thus universal are what we call art, religion, and thought. By art I understand the creation of an imaginary world within ourselves, intelligible just because we create it and find it in the act of creating it transparent to our own eyes. This world is the world of beauty, and its function is to practise our mental powers, as it were in a self-imposed athletic exercise, for grappling with the real world that lies beyond it. And this it truly does; but it only brings us to the threshold of the real problem. By religion I understand the realization that what we have imagined in art is a symbol or shadow of the real, and that therefore the real world is at bottom akin to the world of art—a world that has a creative spirit at its core and is peopled by beings that exist only in and for that spirit's consciousness. And here, too, we have made progress and advanced towards the solution of our problem; but we have not achieved it: for our conception of this creative spirit is only a dim and oblique vision, distorted by the mists of the imaginative symbols that express it. By thought I understand the direct approach to reality as it really is, a setting aside of the imaginary and symbolic and a grappling with the substance instead of the shadow. But here again I find permanent and necessary distinctions. The first, simplest, and least adequate form of thought is that in which we truly grasp real properties of the real, but try to understand these by taking them singly, in abstraction from the rest, hoping that each, just because it is a fair sample of the real world, will reveal the secret of the real world. And so, in a sense, it does; but the secret has now been broken up into small change, and we are offered instead an endless plurality of secrets, all genuine, all valuable, but all leaving untouched the central secret, which is the bond that holds them together. This way of thought I call science. The second way is to analyse the real into elements, but to recognize that these elements are ideal, and not to think that they contain the secret of the world in themselves, but that they show the *why* of things in abstraction from their actual existence. This is history. History understands, as science does not, that the abstract is merely ideal and not real: for while science thinks that its substances and attributes are real and knowable, history understands that its past events are past, are ideal, and that the present, the actual, is analysable not into real parts but only into ideal parts. But history tries to understand the real by analysing it into ideals, and the concrete cannot be exhausted by analysing it into abstractions; hence, however far history goes, it always leaves a residue of immediacy, of unanalysed and uncomprehended actuality. Philosophy is that form of thought which makes it its business to overcome all abstractions, whether the real abstraction of science or the ideal abstraction of history, and to see the abstract only in its place in the concrete. It is thus the only form of thought which even attempts to apprehend reality as it really is, in its entirety, instead of confining itself to the apprehension of something else, something which it has itself created and substituted for reality as an object of study. Hence philosophy goes a step further than history towards answering the riddle of knowledge. But of all other forms of thought, history is that which stands nearest to philosophy and most shares its spirit. Most of the difficulties which people find in studying philosophy are due to the fact that they have been accustomed to practise themselves in science and in no other form of thought; and these difficulties would be almost wholly overcome if they approached philosophy after a thorough training in history. But philosophy is nothing at all without a constant fertilization from all the forms of consciousness that I have enumerated. It has its own problems and its own methods, and demands a very rigorous and conscientious training—more so, in fact, than any other form of mental labour; but without a supply of material from the immediate world of experience philosophy collapses into a mere bag of tricks. This material, originally supplied from crude sensation, reaches philosophy as progressively transformed by the work of art, religion, science, and history. And therefore history is the immediate and direct source of all philosophical problems. Destroy history, and you destroy the nourishment on which philosophy feeds; foster and develop a sound historical consciousness, and you have under your hand all, except its own methods, that philosophy needs. All philosophy is the philosophy of history.

OUTLINES OF A PHILOSOPHY OF HISTORY
(1928)[1]

PREFACE

THIS essay deals with what appear to the writer the most important questions in the theory of history. They are arranged under four heads, which, out of compliment to the Kantian critiques, are called Quality, Quantity, Relation, and Modality. Under Quality, the question is raised whether history is real, and if so in what sense; and the answer to this question is the conception hereinafter called the ideality of history. This comes first because it is fundamental: all the other questions raised are solved by reference to it or deduced from it. Under Quantity, the question raised is that of universality *versus* particularity: the question whether history is properly conceived as a single universal world-history, or a plurality of particular histories. The answer is that, from the point of view of the ideality of history, the distinction disappears: and we are left with the conception of historical thought as the attempt to solve an historical problem, which is particular because it is always a fresh and different problem, but universal because, being the only problem in the historian's mind, it is for him, at the moment, the only historical problem there is. Under Relation, the question raised is that of the inner structure of historical fact. Granted the conception of the monograph in its universality and particularity, already arrived at under Quantity, we now find that the first condition of such a monograph is unity of subject; the second is orderly sequence of events; and the third is the completeness with which the events expound the subject, so as to form a complete whole of reciprocally explanatory parts. From this point of view it is possible to explain the precise meaning of progress. Under Modality, the question of the certainty or logical status of history is dealt with. Granted the ideality of history, the scepticism which denies the scientific value of

The source document can be found in the Bodleian Library Collingwood Papers, dep. 12.

[1] On the title-page is written 'April 1928'.

history can be conclusively answered: and we can show how, by the empirical methodology of archaeological science and the pure methodology of philosophy, the historian is enabled, not indeed to 'know' the past as it actually happened, which he neither can do nor wants to do, but to solve with accuracy and certainty the particular historical problems which present themselves to his mind, in terms of the evidence at his disposal.

The whole essay is, as it stands, a skeleton or sketch of what might be more easily written at greater length, with illustrations, criticisms, and alternative statements inserted. In its present form it is certain to mislead a reader, because its argument appears to rest on a single point—the ideality of history—and to be developed deductively from that. The reader who wants to destroy the argument will therefore naturally concentrate his attention on the ideality of history and try to undermine that proposition, thinking that when it falls the whole argument will fall with it. But he will be mistaken. The various points made in the course of the argument are in point of fact observations made in the course of historical studies pursued with a special eye to problems of method. Not one of them has been reached deductively from the conception of the ideality of history. On the contrary, the idea of considering them in the light of that conception only occurred to the writer very late in the day, after most of them had been long familiar to him as the fruits of experience in historical research. Therefore, when they are set out as they are here, in the form of a single chain of argument, the reader is asked to remember that the position of each link in the chain is guaranteed not simply by its relation to the first link but by cross-bearings from experience of historical inquiry. The principle of the ideality of history is not the ground of the objections brought, in the second section, against the conceptions of merely universal and merely particular history; those are objections whose force is obvious to anyone who will think them over, and is already familiar to all thoughtful historians; all that the principle of the ideality of history can do in this case, is to provide a point of view from which these objections may be answered and the ordinary procedure of historians vindicated.

In adopting the four Kantian headings, the writer no doubt courts hostility by seeming to endorse the architectonic pedantries of a bygone day. It is thought nowadays that any system is worse than no system, and that the attempt to arrange a series of problems in their natural order, instead of merely putting them down in the order in which they occurred to the writer's mind, is a mark not only of pedantry but of a barren mind. But perhaps current fashion goes a little too far in its reaction against systems. Certainly no system is more than a temporary resting-place for thought, the momentary crystallization of something that will dissolve again very soon; and certainly, no system can wholly satisfy any two minds, any more than it can wholly satisfy the same mind at different times. But if anyone takes this for an argument against systematic thinking, he ought to be reminded of the servant who refused to clean his master's boots because they would be dirty again next day. To think systematically means to think in a clear and tidy manner, to cast up one's accounts in the business of thinking so as to show where one stands and how one's trade is going. A statement of accounts is not intended to describe the state of one's business for ever; still less to act as a substitute for the daily work of the shop; but a person who refrains from casting up his accounts because of these facts is merely showing that he does not understand business, and incidentally providing his neighbours with an excellent reason for not giving him credit. In the same way a philosopher who, out of deference to the rapid advance of his own thought, refrains from the attempt to express what he now thinks in a systematic form, gives his neighbours reason to believe that what is going on in his mind is not an advance—which must be an advance from somewhere definite to somewhere else— but a confusion. Some system, then, is necessary wherever a statement is made: and for the present purpose, the old four-fold distinction of Quality, Quantity, Relation, and Modality has proved a convenient form for the materials demanding expression.

One problem which the reader might expect to be formally discussed at the outset has been left wholly on one side: that of the relation between history *a parte subjecti*, historical thought, and history *a parte objecti*, historical fact. Implicitly, this problem is discussed and solved by the doctrine of the ideality of history: for that doctrine lays it down that historical fact, as known to the historian, is essentially relative to the thought that knows it. But it may be proper in this preface to consider a certain aspect of this problem: namely the question whether the philosophy of history is a theory of historical thinking or a theory of historical fact; in other words, whether it is methodological or metaphysical in its purpose.

The philosophy of history, in the eighteenth-century sense of the phrase, was a metaphysical philosophy. It attempted to construct a theory of the nature and structure of historical fact, and to show that this, regarded as a special kind of reality, had special characteristics, contained in itself special kinds of sequence, recurrence, or progress, and the like. Even in the hands of Hegel, the last great exponent—and by far the most profound—of the old conception, the metaphysical aspect of the philosophy of history remained uppermost, and in his successors, such as Comte and Marx and Spencer, the idea of a metaphysical philosophy of history reigned unopposed.

It was not until the turn of the century that this idea was destroyed. Before that, the conception of a philosophical theory of historical thought, as a special branch of logic or theory of knowledge, had already made considerable progress; but it was not until Croce's work on the subject that the metaphysical philosophy of history was systematically replaced by the methodological. This was the first really decisive step forward that the philosophy of history had made since Hegel.

But when the methodological view of the philosophy of history is combined with the doctrine of the ideality of history, all objection to a metaphysical philosophy of history vanishes. For the necessary forms and conditions of historical thought are now seen to determine the necessary forms and conditions of its object. Everything that is said about history *a parte subjecti* can therefore be repeated, *mutatis mutandis*, about history *a parte objecti*.

This is the point of view adopted in the present essay. The gulf which, on an empiricist or positivistic philosophy, separates historical thought from historical fact, has disappeared. Historical thought and its object are seen to be inseparable, the latter having only an ideal existence in and for the former;

and therefore a methodological theory of the necessary forms of historical thought is also a metaphysical theory of the necessary forms of historical fact.[2]

[2] The preface ends with: 'April 1928. Le Martouret, Die, Drôme'. Le Martouret is the name of a country-house, near the little town of Die, in the department Drôme, in south-east France. It is referred to by Collingwood in his *Autobiography*, p. 107.

INTRODUCTORY LECTURE[3]

1. The phrase *Philosophy of History*, in the title of these lectures, is used in a sense analogous to that of the phrases philosophy of art, philosophy of religion. In these cases the expression means that art or religion is a specific form of human activity, a specific form of knowledge or conduct or both, which for some reason deserves or demands special study by philosophers.

For *what* reason? The answer is, that art or religion is a universal and necessary form of human activity: not an accidental or optional form, which may in certain circumstances be dispensed with, but a form which is and must be present throughout the range of human experience. If one thinks that art (e.g.) is in this sense universal and necessary; if one thinks that every human being at every moment of his conscious life is an artist, and that the artistic activity is among the essential constituents of our experience, then one thinks that there is or ought to be a philosophy of art, that is, a philosophical science dealing with human experience as a whole considered in this aesthetic aspect.

On the other hand, if one thinks that art is not in this sense universal and necessary: if one thinks that some people are artists and others not, and that those who are artists are artists at certain times and not at others, then one thinks that there is and can be no philosophy of art but only an empirical or psychological science of art as a particular contingent type of experience.

Now there is one sense in which art really is a universal and necessary element in all experience, a sense in which we are all and always artists. This is the most profound and true meaning of the word art. And in this sense the science of art is a philosophical science. But there is also a sense—a relatively shallow and unimportant sense—in which some people are artists and others not: and in this sense there is room for an empirical or psychological science of art side by side with the philosophy of art. Similarly, there is a sense of the word religion in which religion is coextensive with human experience,

---

[3] In the manuscript is added: 'May 1–1928'.

of which it forms a universal and necessary element: a sense in which everyone has a religion. In that sense, the science of religion is a philosophical science. But there is also a sense in which we speak of a person as abandoning all religion, being irreligious, having no religious feelings, and so forth: this is the empirical sense of the word religion, and in this sense the science of religion is an empirical science, a psychological study of the varieties and idiosyncrasies of religious experience.

The philosophy of religion or art, then, means the theory of religion or art regarded as universal and necessary forms, aspects, or constituents of human experience. Similarly, in these lectures, the philosophy of history means the theory of history as a necessary form of human experience: a thing not peculiar to certain persons called historians, but common to all thinking beings at all times.

2. It is necessary to make this clear at the outset because the phrase has long been used in a different sense. It came into use in the eighteenth century, and was first used by Voltaire; after him it was taken up by numerous writers of the late eighteenth and early nineteenth centuries, and in the mouths of all these writers it had a meaning quite other than that which I have defined.

Voltaire was anxious to give a new direction to historical studies. Before his time they had devoted their attention in part to the uncritical and credulous repetition of improbable stories concerning remote antiquity, in part to the narration of military affairs and the biographies of kings and queens. He wished to jettison the greater part of ancient history, on the ground that it consisted of old wives' tales which no enlightened and critical mind could believe: and to concentrate the attention of historians upon the history of arts and crafts, manners and customs, and what we should call social and economic questions. To this reformed history he gave the name of the philosophy of history: where philosophy only meant systematic and critical thinking. By using the word in this sense he meant that history, so treated, would become in the wide sense of the word a science: a subject worthy of the attention and credence of minds trained in accurate and methodical thought.

Voltaire's lead was followed. Ancient history was not indeed abolished but it was drastically revised by a succession of writers who brought to it a new standard of criticism and a new insistence on the scientific study of evidence; and modern history was at the same time decisively turned towards social and economic questions. Thus history did undergo the change which Voltaire demanded, and all modern historical study is what he called the philosophy of history. But to call it by that name would involve retaining a long obsolete sense of the term philosophy, and moreover laying an exaggerated stress on the resemblances between the methods of critical history and those of natural science, or philosophy in Newton's sense of the word.

Subsequent writers, adopting Voltaire's phrase, gave it a slightly new sense. Kant did not use the phrase, but he wrote a remarkable essay called 'An idea of a universal history from a cosmopolitan point of view', in which he maintained that human history as a whole could be seen as a gradual development and realization of the conception of citizenship: that is, as a progressive development of political institutions and organization. Here we have Voltaire's idea of history as the history of social life, applied to the whole extent of human history. Kant's successors, notably Schlegel, applied to this idea the name philosophy of history. Thus in post-Kantian Germany the phrase philosophy of history became the regular name for universal history regarded as the history of human progress. The most famous attempt at such a reading of universal history is Hegel's lectures on the philosophy of history.

Kant had pointed out that any such attempt—which he himself modestly refused to make—demanded two qualifications: a philosophical head, and a great store of historical learning. Obviously, the task of writing a history of the world demands the latter qualification; and the task of envisaging this history as one of progress demands a philosophical head because it cannot be carried out except by a person who is willing to think out very clearly what progress means and what relation there is between various values which are realized in various phases of historical development. Both qualifications were possessed in an eminent degree by the great German philosophers of history, notably Hegel himself; and though their works meet with little favour nowadays, they did an immense service to the advancement of historical studies. The reason why they are out of favour today is partly because historical knowledge has advanced enormously in the last hundred years and their facts are out of date: partly because we realize that history is too complicated a thing to be expressible in the form of a single chain of continuous progress. But the attempt so to express it proceeded from a sound and thoroughly historical motive, namely the recognition of history as a continuous whole, in which everything is significant and everything worthy of study: and this is why the influence of these philosophers of history on historical thought was, on the whole, highly beneficial.

3. This leaves the phrase vacant and unoccupied by any idea; and at the same time a new idea has arisen, namely the idea of a philosophical science of historical thought. In this sense, therefore, the phrase is here used.

A philosophy of history in this sense will have two aspects which are so closely intertwined that we need not try to keep them separate. History means both a special kind of knowledge, and a special kind of object, the proper object of that knowledge. History *a parte subjecti* means the thinking that goes on in the historian's mind and is reported upon in his writings; history *a parte objecti* means the facts or events about which he thinks, and whose nature, so far as he discovers it, he expounds. Now the philosophy of history in the old Voltairean and Hegelian sense is concerned only with history *a parte objecti*. It does not study the processes or activities of the historian's mind: its object is historical fact or the sequence of historical events. But the philosophy of history in our sense is concerned with history *a parte subjecti*. Its primary business is to study the thinking that goes on in the historian's mind; it is primarily a logic of historical method.

On the other hand, if historical method is adequate to the study of its proper object, as it must be if it is really historical method, then it follows that in studying the necessary and universal features of historical method we are studying the necessary and universal features of historical fact, its proper object. Logic and metaphysics are the same, in the sense that a law which really is a logical law—a law, that is, of thought *qua* valid, not a merely psychological law—must be a metaphysical law too: for a law of thought *qua* valid must be a law binding on the reality known by that thought. Our business, then, may be defined as that of discovering how historians always and necessarily think; but this must be understood as identical with the business of discovering how historical fact is always and necessarily constituted.

For this reason, it would be misleading to call the philosophy of history simply the science of historical method, the methodology of history. It is at once a methodology of historical thought and a metaphysic of historical reality, and it will only be a satisfactory science so long as these two aspects, the subjective and the objective, are kept together.

4. History *a parte subjecti* is the knowledge of the past; and history *a parte objecti* is the past itself. This double statement is not, I think, controversial: it will be generally admitted as true: but certain remarks must be made upon it at once.

(a) History and *memory* are not the same thing, though they are akin. The historian may remember the events he narrates, but he need not. And so far as he narrates them merely because he remembers them, he is hardly a real historian. To deserve that title, he ought to check his memories by getting into touch with other sources of information: he ought to leave out some things that he remembers, as irrelevant to his subject, and put in some that he does not. History and memory are akin in that their object is the past: but whereas the object of history is the past as inferentially 'reconstructed' from evidence, the object of memory is the past as immediately 'apprehended' by an act in which inference plays no part.

(b) So far as memory is immediate and devoid of explicit ground, it is doubtful whether it deserves the title of knowledge. The fallibility of memory depends on the fact that, in remembering, we have before us no evidence of that which we are trying to remember: therefore there is no way of checking our memory. The historian who has made a mistake may correct it by asking himself whether the evidence before him proves his view or not, and recognizing that it does not; but in remembering we cannot do this. Therefore history is more like real knowledge than memory is: for it has an element of self-criticism about it which memory lacks.

(c) For this reason it might almost be doubted whether the distinction between true and false was applicable to memory, any more than it is applicable to sensation. Memory is fallible, but (it may be reasonably said) not false: it may lead us into error, but it cannot itself be erroneous. History, on the other hand, consisting as it does of reasoned judgements about the past, is true or false.[4]

---

[4] At the end of the page Collingwood writes: 'Begin here the Martouret essay'.

Contents[5]

[5] Following the table of contents under the heading 'Topics dealt with in Martouret Ms.', a list of 'Topics to be worked in' is added, which reads as follows:

1. History as understanding of *process* (but history not a mere series of events) leads on to:

2. History as understanding of the *present* (but not the whole present)— leads on to:

3. *Contingency* of history.

4. Historical imagination (i.e. closer study of nature of historical *inference*).

5. Bradley's theory.

6. *A priori* element in history (i.e. the historian's point of view as starting point) (cf. history of history).

7. Bias, subjectivity, judgement of value (connected with 6).

8. Historical process and natural process.

Since in this list Bradley's theory is mentioned, it must have been added at a later date. For it is only in 1932 that Collingwood read Bradley's *Presuppositions of Critical History*, published in 1874, a copy being sent to him by the philosopher Joseph. In a letter to Joseph, dated 15 July 1932, Collingwood writes: 'It is very good of you to have lent me this rarity, which I have long wanted to see and have never seen before' (Bodleian Library, MS Eng. lett., c 453, nr. 202). In 'The Historical Imagination' (1935) and 'Human Nature and Human History' (1936) some of the topics mentioned were indeed dealt with by Collingwood. That Collingwood has read the Martouret manuscript again in 1935 is made clear by the addition he made in that year (see p. 470). The list of 'topics to be worked in' therefore probably dates from the same time.

I. *Quality*

History *a parte objecti*, the object of historical thought, is of course in some sense real, for if it were not, there would be no sense in which historical judgements could be true, or indeed false. But in what sense are historical facts (using that term to denote the objects of historical thought) real?

Realistic philosophies seem generally to equate reality with existence and subsistence. Existence is the reality of a thing which is actual, which has a determinate position in space and time and determinate characters actualised in it. Subsistence is the reality of actualised characters: or possibly (according to some theories) of any character whatever, actualised or not [that, at least, would be true of the quasi-Platonic essences of Santayana].

But the reality of historical facts falls under neither of these heads. An historical fact is rather a thing than an essence. It *has* characters, it *is* not character. Therefore it does not subsist; it ought to exist. But an historical fact does not exist. An historical fact is an event. The actuality of an event, that in it which is parallel or analogous to existence, is called occurrence. An actual thing is one which is existing: an actual event is one which is occurring. But no historical event is ever occurring at any moment when historical thought takes it as an object. Certainly a writer may compose the history of a war as the war proceeds. But in such a case the particular battles and campaigns whose history he narrates year by year are always, when he describes them, events in the past; and until the war as a whole is an event in the past, he can never be said to have written the history of the war as a whole. He has only written the history of its earlier stages—those, namely, which are now events in the past.

The object of historical thought is thus *the past*: that is, past events. How much of the infinite whole of past events is a legitimate or necessary object of historical thought, and what meaning can attach to the words 'infinite whole of past events', are questions belonging to a further stage in this inquiry and will be dealt with under the head of Quantity.

Now an event that is happening is actual: an event that has happened is not happening and is not actual. All events that are objects of historical thought are events which are not happening because they have ceased to happen: they are therefore not actual.

This proposition I shall call *the Ideality of History*. By the word ideality I intend to signify the quality of being an object of thought without having actuality: thus an ideal thing would be an object of thought without actually existing, an ideal quality would be an object of thought without being anywhere actually exemplified in any existing thing, an ideal event would be an event which was the object of thought without actually occurring. In all these cases the word 'actually' implies simultaneity with the thought in question. It may be fancied that an object may be both ideal and actual, in this sense, that an object present to thought only as ideal may be actual without being known as such—e.g. an archaeologist may put together an historical account of a primitive civilization without knowing that this type of civilization still subsists and may be studied as an actual state of things in a part of the earth unvisited by him. But in a case like this the object of the historian's thought is not the Bronze Age as such, irrespective of time and place, but (for instance) the Bronze Age of north-western Europe, which began and ended at dates that are within certain limits determinable: and it is only a non-historical and abstractive or generalizing type of thought that will forget the differences (differences not only of time and place but of character also) that lie between the ancient Bronze Age of north-western Europe and the Bronze civilization today subsisting elsewhere on the earth. The object of history, then, because it is not a thing or a character, but an event, cannot be both ideal and actual: it must be wholly and only ideal. A thing (e.g. the Matterhorn) may be both ideal and actual: the Matterhorn as I remember it ten years ago is ideal, the Matterhorn as I see it now is actual: but the mountain as it was then and the mountain as it is now are the same mountain. But an object of historical thought cannot have this double reality. I may write a history of music, and it may be said that the relation between music in the present and music in the past is much like the relation between the Matterhorn in the present and the Matterhorn in the past: and so it is; but music in the present never enters into my purview as historian of music. If I close with a chapter on 'Present-Day Tendencies', either I am writing the history of the most recent past, which is still wholly past and in no sense present, or else I am illegitimately (for an historian) taking upon myself to prophesy as to the future or to engage in polemics concerning the present. For the historian as historian the present as present has no interest. The present of music belongs not to historians of music but to musical composers and musical critics. If therefore anyone says that music is both ideal (as past music) and actual (as present music) it must be replied that the term music is here ambiguous: in one case it means past events in musical history, which are always purely past, purely ideal: in the other it means present events which are always purely actual or present. And no event in musical history can fall in both these categories at once.

But this example of musical history illustrates another and an important point. No historian of music deserves the name unless he has studied for himself the old music whose growth and development he is trying to describe. He must have listened to Bach and Mozart, Palestrina and Lasso, and possess personal acquaintance with their works. This means that he must have been present at actual performances of these works either physically or in imagination; and in the latter case the imaginative power is acquired only by actually hearing similar things performed—e.g. a man who had never heard an orchestra of the Beethoven period could not read a symphony of Beethoven in score with any chance of obtaining a good imaginative hearing of it. We may therefore boldly say that the *sine qua non* of writing the history of past music is to have this past music *re-enacted in the present*. Just the same thing is true of other arts: e.g. we must read old poetry for ourselves, see old pictures for ourselves with the dirt of age actually or in imagination removed and the colours restored to their old values. Similarly, to write the history of a battle, we must re-think the thoughts which determined its various tactical phases: we must see the ground of the battlefield as the opposing commanders saw it, and draw from the topography the conclusions that they drew: and so forth.[6] The past event, ideal though it is, must be actual *in the historian's re-enactment* of it.

---

[6] This sentence was a later addition to the manuscript.

In this sense, and this sense only, the ideality of the object of history is compatible with actuality and indeed inseparable from actuality. The historian of music will certainly not be able to write the history of any musical work which he has not heard—which has not been actually enacted within his own musical experience. In what, then, does the Ninth Symphony differ from the Matterhorn? Is the former any more ideal than the latter?[7]

We are not concerned here to ask whether there is any field of thought in which a realistic philosophy is a plausible or even adequate account of the facts. We are only concerned to show that in the case of history, at any rate, it is neither. Perhaps the Matterhorn is as ideal as the battle of Marathon; but short of embarking on inquiries which might or might not lead to that conclusion, we[8] must reply that for the moment we are

---

[7] After this sentence Collingwood added the encircled words 'Distinction between present and past'.

[8] Here a sheet of paper with a new text is stuck over the original. The original text runs as follows: 'must here reply that the ideality of the Ninth Symphony consists in the fact that whereas for the mere musical critic the Ninth Symphony is a contemporary musical experience, in connexion with which the questions to be asked are: is it well written? Is it well performed? For the musical historian the contemporary musical experience is as it were a medium through which he sees to the original experience of the composer and his first performers and first audiences. Instead of saying, "how sublime, or, how naïvely sentimental, is this hymn to joy", the historian says: "how interesting an example of Romanticism!" Now Romanticism is not the historian's own frame of mind: it's a frame of mind whose history he is writing. Therefore he must both experience it and not experience it: he must enter into it, reconstitute it with his own mind, and at the same time objectify this very reconstitution, so as to prevent it from mastering his mind and running away with him.

The historical event is this actual and ideal at once: but not at all in the same way in which the Matterhorn is actual and ideal at once. The Matterhorn, because it is a physical thing, not an event, persists in time and may therefore be at once perceived and remembered. But the object of historical thought is an event, and does not persist. Its very permanence, so far as it has permanence, consists in its complete non-existence: death once dead, there's no more dying then; the event, once over and done with, can be re-enacted in the historian's mind anywhere and any time because it nowhere and at no time can actually recur. Its actuality is only another name for its ideality: regarded as itself, it is purely and only ideal: regarded as the object of *this* act of historical thought it is actual in so far as the act of thought is actual.

The re-enacting of history in the historian's mind is the opposite or

discussing a far simpler question than this. We are pointing out a distinction, which becomes obvious as soon as our attention is called to it, between the way in which a man looking at the Matterhorn finds the actual object present to his gaze, and the way in which a man thinking historically about the battle of Hastings has to reconstruct the battle in his head. And we are pointing out that this distinction is not done away with by saying that the past is re-enacted in the present. As so re-enacted, it remains merely ideal. The historian does not, by thinking out the battle of Hastings, cause a real battle to be fought there once more, neither does he fall into the error of believing that the battle he has reconstructed in thought is actually going on merely because he has reconstructed it. This applies equally to the historian of music. Ancient art does not become modern art simply by being performed over again. It is both interesting and delightful to sing madrigals and masses of the sixteenth century; but the historian is well aware, when he sings them and hears others sing them, that their place is in the sixteenth century and not in the twentieth. He listens to them not simply as music—not simply as the expression of feeling in musical language—but as sixteenth-century music, music belonging to a bygone world whose mind and civilization he is trying to understand. All we are concerned with at the moment is to call attention to the fact that these two attitudes to music are possible: the attitude of the contemporary critic, who hears music as an expression of the actual life of his own age, and the attitude of the historian, who hears it as an expression of the life of the past which he is trying to reconstruct. We are all familiar with the distinction between these

complementary aspect of the ideality of history. Because the historical fact is ideal it has an actuality of its own, an actuality of a peculiar kind: it is *actualised* by the activity of the thought for which it has its ideal being. The object of history, then, while having no existence at all apart from thought, and being so far ideal, is actualised by the thought that thinks it.

Nevertheless this conception is a somewhat difficult one. How can the historian genuinely re-enact history in his mind? How can he call the dead to live again and repeat events that have happened once for all and are irrevocably past? And does not the idea of a literal revival of the past in the historian's mind savour of a crude magical necromancy rather than of a serious theory of knowledge?' The original text ends here. Then follow the words 'It is easy to answer', which are crossed out.

two attitudes, and at present I only want to emphasize its existence: later we shall ask how it is possible and what it implies.

The historian, then, re-enacts the past in his mind: but in this re-enactment it does not become a present or an actuality. The actuality is the actual thought of the historian that re-enacts it. The only sense in which the object of historical thought is actual, is that it is actually thought about. But this does not confer any kind of actuality upon *it*, taken in itself. It remains wholly ideal.

But how *can* the historian re-enact the past? What has happened has happened: it cannot be made to happen again by thinking about it. How can the historian call the dead to life by scientific research? Does not such a theory savour of crude magic, necromancy, rather than of serious philosophical inquiry? The answer is[9] that, without any necromancy, the historian may re-enact a past event if that event is itself a thought. When Archimedes discovered the idea of specific gravity he performed an act of thought which we can without difficulty repeat: he was drawing certain conclusions from certain data, and we can draw the same conclusions from the same data. Not only *can* we do this but if we are to write the history of Hellenistic science we *must* do it, and must do it knowing that we are repeating Archimedes's thought in our own mind. Similarly, if we are to narrate the history of a battle, we must see for ourselves the tactical problem that the victorious commander saw, and see the solution as he saw it. If we are to narrate the history of a constitutional reform, we must see what the facts were that the reformer had before him, and how his way of dealing with the facts seemed to meet the necessities as he felt them to exist. In all these cases, that is, in all cases where the history in question is the history of thought,[10] a literal re-enactment of the past is possible and is an essential element in all history.

Not only is the history of thought possible, but, if thought is understood in its widest sense, it is the only thing of which there can be history. Nothing but thought can be treated by the historian with that intimacy without which history is not history; for nothing but thought can be re-enacted in this way

---

[9] The new text which was stuck on the original ends here.

[10] 'history of thought' is encircled in the manuscript.

in the historian's mind. The birth of solar systems, the origins of life on our planet, the early course of geological history—all these are not strictly historical studies because the historian can never really get inside them, actualise them in his mind: they are science, not history, because, however much they may take the form of narrative, they are generalized narratives, accounts of how things must have happened in any world, not accounts of how things actually happened in this world. They are hypotheses, which, however probable, do not even approximate to the status of documented history.

All history, then, is the history of thought, where thought is used in the widest sense and includes all the conscious activities of the human spirit.[11] These activities, as events in time, pass away and cease to be. The historian re-creates them in his own mind: he does not merely repeat them, as a later scientist may re-invent the inventions of an earlier: he re-enacts them consciously, knowing that this is what he is doing and thus conferring upon this re-enactment the quality of a specific activity of the mind. This activity is a free activity. It differs *toto caelo* from the imitativeness which may induce a man or a beast to do what others do because these others are observed to be doing it. For the historian does not observe others to be doing the things which he does over again. Until he has done them over again he does not know what they are. It is only after I have grasped the idea of specific gravity that I can see what it was that Archimedes had done when he shouted ηὕρηκα: I am therefore in no sense imitating Archimedes.

A philosophical or pseudo-philosophical objection to the conception of the historian as re-enacting the past must here be met. It may be said that no such re-enactment is possible because nothing can happen twice. Archimedes discovered the idea of specific gravity: I can know that he did so, but I cannot re-discover the idea, for discovery implies priority. The second person who thinks of the idea is not discovering it. Nor is this, it may be said, a merely logical distinction: for there is a peculiar quality in the experience of discovery or invention, a peculiar feeling of being the first human being to penetrate

[11] The words 'All history, then, is the history of thought' is underlined in the manuscript.

into the presence of this particular truth, which the historian can never recapture just because it attaches to discovery as such. Clearly, then, if the historian knows the past by re-enacting it, he cannot re-enact this element of discovery or originality and therefore cannot know it historically: hence, from the view here maintained, the *reductio ad absurdum* follows that no discovery, no thought that is really original or unique (and what genuine thought is not?) can be historically known.

We shall answer this objection by admitting it. Surely everybody knows that the peculiar thrill with which the victorious commander watches the collapse of an enemy's defence is a thrill which the historian cannot recapture. No one thinks that the historian of Hellenistic science ought to leap out of his bath and run about the town naked when he comes to Archimedes in writing his history. It is obvious that the historian's duty of re-enacting the discovery or the battle does not extend to the impossible feat of actually discovering the law or defeating the enemy over again, but only to such re-enactment of the past as is possible.

For a certain kind of re-enactment *is* possible, as we have shown; and if the objector says that *no* kind of re-enactment is possible, merely because nothing can happen twice, we shall treat his objection with less courtesy: pointing out that he would himself not hesitate to speak of dining twice in the same inn, or bathing twice in the same river, or reading twice out of the same book, or hearing the same symphony twice. Is the binomial theorem as known to him, we should ask, the same theorem that Newton invented, or not? If he says yes, he has admitted all we want. If he says no, we can easily convict him of self-contradiction: for he is assuming that in our mutual discourse we have ideas in common, and this is inconsistent with his thesis.

But we must turn to a more serious difficulty. It is all very well to appeal to a 'peculiar thrill' as differentiating the act itself from the historian's re-enactment of it: but such a distinction is really no more than Hume's distinction between impressions and ideas on the ground that impressions are livelier and more vivid. We may, and must, recognize that the historian is unable to share the emotional heat with which the characters in his narrative did the things narrated of them; and that *his* emotional heat attaches only to feats of historical research, historical discoveries made and historical perplexities removed; but we must go on to ask the question, why, if the historian really re-enacts the past, is this re-enactment unaccompanied by the emotional heat, the vividness and liveliness of impression, which accompanied its original enactment: and conversely, how, if this re-enactment is devoid of so important an element of the original enactment, can it be called the same thing over again and not a mere pale copy of it or something radically different?

The answer is that to re-enact the past in the present is to re-enact it in a context which gives it a new quality. This context is the negation of the past itself. Thus, the historian of poetry, reading Dante, re-enacts the medieval experience which that poem expresses: but while doing this he remains himself: he remains a modern man, not a medieval: and this means that the medievalism of Dante, while genuinely revived and re-experienced within his mind, is accompanied by a whole world of fundamentally non-medieval habits and ideas, which balance it and hold it in check and prevent it from ever occupying the whole field of vision. For Dante, the *Commedia* was his whole world. For me, the *Commedia* is at most half my world, the other half being all those things in me which prevent me from literally becoming Dante. These things include, for instance, Shakespeare and Newton and Kant, who also have gone to form my personality. In reading Dante I do not lose this personality; on the contrary, it is only by using my powers to the full that I succeed in reading Dante at all, and these powers are what they are, for better or worse, because of my going to school with Shakespeare and Newton and Kant. If I cease to be what these have made me, I cease to be able to do anything so recondite as reading Dante; but if I continue to be what they have made me, I approach Dante and his medievalism through a medium of my own modernity, and I must keep this modernity unimpaired by my contact with Dante's medievalism.

I thus genuinely re-enact Dante's medievalism—if I do not, I simply fail to understand or appreciate his poetry—but I re-enact it in a context (namely the rest of my mental outfit and equipment) which gives it a new quality, the quality of being *one element* within a whole of thought that goes beyond it, instead of being a whole of thought outside which there is nothing. This quality of being an element within my experience, an element checked and balanced by others and so contributing to the equilibrium of the whole, is the ideality of history. The whole is actual and only actual; when William the Conqueror was fighting the battle of Hastings, his tactical plan was actual for him because in this plan was summed up everything he knew about fighting battles, and therefore it was for him a complete whole. For the historian of the art of war, the tactics of Hastings form a thought, a plan, which he can re-think in his own mind: but this plan is for him never a whole, it is only a part which goes along with others to form that whole which he calls the history of war—that is, his entire actual historical knowledge, which is the whole of his present thought just as the tactical plan of Hastings was the whole of William's thought.

The conception here expounded may perhaps be made clearer, or at least certain of its implications may be brought to light, by contrasting it with two familiar theories of knowledge: the realistic theory and the copy-theory.

According to the realistic theory, the object of knowledge is always something actual, whose actuality is independent of all cognitive activity on the part of the mind that knows it. The mind and the object are generally, in such theories, conceived as two independent actually existing things, which come together in such a way that the mind 'knows' the object. It is assumed that 'to know' is properly a transitive verb, and the grammatical object of that verb is a thing towards which the mind takes up a cognitive attitude or with which it enters into a relation called knowledge. The realist is in the habit of insisting that this event makes no difference to the object, which was just as real before the event as after it: a statement which is sometimes supported by arguing that if the act of knowing an object produced alterations in it, the act would precisely not be one of knowing, since knowing *implies* that what we know is not altered by our knowing it.

It is at once clear that from the point of view of an ordinary realistic theory of knowledge, history is impossible. A theory which regards knowledge as 'apprehension' of an independent object is reasonable if perception is taken as the only legitimate example of knowledge; it is plausible if knowledge is conceived Platonically as the knowledge of abstract ideas; it has no shadow of plausibility in the case of history. The historian who writes a monograph on the battle of Marathon is not 'apprehending' a thing, namely the battle of Marathon, that exists independently of the apprehending and, as it were, stands there to be apprehended. The battle of Marathon was an event which ceased happening some 2,400 years ago; there is nothing there to apprehend; in the realistic sense of the term object, there is no object whatever for the historian to know. And therefore, since without object there can be no knowledge, history as a form of knowledge is, realistically speaking, an absurdity.

Perhaps some ingenious realist will evade this difficulty by appeal to the four-dimensional space-time of modern physical theory. If time is only one of the four dimensions, and if any dimension may at will be taken as the temporal, the 2,400 years which separate us from the battle of Marathon may be at pleasure reduced to nothing by being taken, not as time, but as space; and a person actually at Marathon might at will interpret his spatial situation on the battle-field as temporal simultaneity with the battle. He will then, presumably, see it going on, and his task as historian will be greatly simplified. But until a realistic philosopher has actually witnessed the battle of Marathon by this method, we may forbear to contemplate the possibility of such an argument's being seriously put forward.

In opposition to all realism, then, any philosophy of history must assert the ideality, as opposed to the reality, of historical fact. It asserts that the past as past has no existence whatever, consisting as it does of occurrences no longer occurring, events that have finished happening: and it holds that these events can be historically known not by anything in the least analogous to perception, observation, or any process or act intelligibly describable as 'apprehension', but by their re-enactment in the mind of the historian.

This may seem to assimilate the present theory to the 'copy-theory' of knowledge, which pretends to explain how we know things by the hypothesis of images 'inside' our minds, mental images, copying the appearance of objects 'outside' our mind. The past, as no longer present, is necessarily outside our mind, unknown, and unknowable: but we make a replica of it inside our mind, and know *that*, and so, mediately, come to know the past.

This is a wholly false comparison, and entails an unrecognizable travesty of the theory here maintained. The past is, for us, not outside the mind (whatever that means), it is wholly and utterly non-existent. The re-enactment of it in our mind is therefore not a copy of it in any sense whatever. How could anyone make a copy of something that does not exist? The re-enactment of the past in the present *is the past itself* so far as that is knowable to the historian. We understand what Newton thought by thinking—not *copies* of his thoughts—a silly and meaningless phrase—but his thoughts themselves over again. When we have done that, we know what Newton thought, not mediately, but immediately.

The historian's thought, then, neither is nor contains nor involves any copy of its object. The historian's thought is, or rather contains as one of its elements, that object itself, namely the act of thought which the historian is trying to understand, re-thought in the present by himself. A person who failed to realize that thoughts are not private property might say that it is not Newton's thought that I understand, but only my own. That would be silly because, whatever subjective idealism may pretend, thought is always and everywhere *de jure* common property, and is *de facto* common property wherever people at large have the intelligence to think in common.[12]

II. *Quantity*

The question here to be considered is, what is the scope of historical thought? Practically, this is equivalent to the question, what is the right or best form of historical composition? Theoretically, it amounts to this:—what are the limits of historical knowledge?

The simplest, and in that sense the best, form of historical composition is the memoir or contemporary history: the form

[12] Here Collingwood added a separate encircled note saying 'Dilthey's Nachbild'.

whose outstanding example is the History of Thucydides. The extraordinary merit of Thucydides's work is closely connected with the limitation of its scope. Apart from the introductory matter contained in the first book, it is concerned with events falling in the writer's lifetime, and under his own observation or that of persons with whom he could speak face to face. The problems of collecting sources and interpreting them—the two cardinal problems of historical research—were, not indeed eliminated, but reduced to a state of extreme simplicity, and this simplicity relieved Thucydides of all the more technical and elaborate part of the historian's work and put him automatically in the position of a man who has completed the collection and interpretation of his sources: a position in which he was able to use his enormous literary powers without hesitation or embarrassment.

Many histories of the same kind have been written since then; but no one, since the work done by the Hellenistic and Roman historians, would describe this as the ideal type of history. It is a form which, technically, can only be called rudimentary. It is applicable only [to] the simplest possible type of historical problem, and this is a type of problem that ceases to interest people when their field of vision widens beyond their own immediate concerns and embraces the life of other peoples and the past of their own. With this widening of interest the magic circle of a simple egotism is broken, and henceforth the problem of determining the proper scope and limits of historical inquiry becomes urgent. Thucydides represents the straightforward egotism of the Greek, for whom everything not Greek is barbarian and therefore unworthy of serious study. But the Roman can say 'humani nihil a me alienum puto', and this commits him in theory to studying, so far as he can, the history of the whole world.

This widening of interest leads to complications not because it introduces into history any genuinely new factors, for it does not: all the technical problems of the most advanced and complex historical thought are already present in what we have called the most rudimentary type of history: but because it introduces into history new interests, the interest in things foreign and remote and unfamiliar, in dealing with which the historian is compelled to find a new answer to the question 'why am I dealing with this particular subject rather than any other?' So long as his subject is the events of his own lifetime, he can plead that the subject has been forced upon him by the mere fact that these interesting things have been going on before his eyes; failing that, the responsibility of choosing his subject lies with him. On what principles is he to choose it?

We are here confronted by the conception of *choice*, which seems to imply that the historian has access to a vast expanse of facts, out of which he must choose something to study. History in its completeness, the sum total of historical fact, stretches out before him: an object, clearly, too large to be taken in at a simple glance: he must select some manageable part of it and ignore the rest, at any rate for the time being, while he acquires a competent knowledge of this part.

Thus arises the idea of the historical monograph or essay on a single circumscribed historical subject. It may be only a page long, or it may be as large as the *Decline and Fall of the Roman Empire*; but it is still a monograph, if it presents itself as a particular, not a universal, history: the statement of a part, not the whole, of historical truth.

But the monograph is always open to theoretical objections and beset by practical difficulties. Every historian who has tried to write one knows that the exclusion of certain subjects, as alien to the monograph, leads to the presence, within the monograph itself, of loose ends, errors in perspective and emphasis, misleading expressions and downright blunders. How far the body of the treatise may be infected by these failings is a question which never admits of accurate determination. Historical facts are certainly never intelligible and never truly discoverable except in relation to their context; if you do not know what the La Tène civilization of Gaul was like, you do not know what the problem was which Caesar had before him when he undertook the conquest of that country, and therefore you do not understand the chief task of Caesar's life, and therefore you do not understand the chief figure in the closing phases of the Roman republic. It may be said that this is hypercriticism, because the amount of misunderstanding concerning Roman history as a whole which can arise from ignorance of La Tène civilization is very small. But how small it is, cannot be discovered until it has been corrected. The whole reputation of a general may turn on the question whether he was right in thinking that a certain operation conducted against a certain enemy would be successful; and points that seem small to an ignorant person may have been the determining factors in his forming that opinion.

Practically, then, the monograph is always in difficulties because it impinges at every point on questions whose answers it is compelled to take for granted but into whose rights and wrongs it cannot enter. And theoretically, it is always open to the objection that since historical facts are what they are only in relation to other facts, the mere severance of certain facts from their context, in order to make them up into a monograph, is an act of false abstraction and a voluntary embracing of error.

Considerations like these led writers of the eighteenth century to attempt the composition of universal histories. The attempt, or something like it, had been made before, more than once; but for our purpose little interest attaches to these earlier endeavours, and we may confine our attention to the idea of universal history as that was formulated by eighteenth-century philosophy. The idea was that history should be looked at as a whole, and would, from that point of view, be found to possess a definite organic unity either as exemplifying constant general laws or as developing a single plan. This idea met with very wide acceptance in all civilized countries, and served as a powerful stimulus to historical research. It fostered, in especial, the tendency towards research into obscure and little-known periods, whose history was required for insertion into the scheme in order to make that complete; and it did more than anything else could have done to teach historians that other things beside their own immediate present were worthy of serious study. It broke down parochialism in history much as the Newtonian theory of universal gravitation finally broke down parochialism in astronomy.

Now that these results have been achieved, the idea of universal history has sunk into obscurity, like a town house in a quarter that was once fashionable and is now barely respectable. It is fully recognized by all serious historians that, if the monograph is open to objection, universal history is far more so, in proportion as its pretensions are far greater. It can never be written, because the whole of history is too large a matter for anyone to bring together into a single literary work; and therefore every so-called universal history is a mere selection of the facts which the writer happens to think important or interesting or in some way capable of grinding his particular axe. In the time of the Venerable Bede it was possible to conflate all known history into a treatise; that only marked the poverty of the time; nowadays, a universal history is never even an honest attempt at real universality, it is only a veiled attempt to impose on the reader the prejudices and superstitions of the writer. No one with any pretensions to historical learning would attempt such a work today, unless it were as a mere textbook for examination purposes, containing frankly, not the history of the world, but those selected facts which candidates for certain examinations would do well to remember. And thus the writing of universal history has fallen into the hands of two classes of persons: the dishonest and the ignorant: the dishonest telling a garbled tale in order to spread their own opinions by specious falsehood, the ignorant naïvely writing down everything they know about history and not suspecting that they know it all wrong.

So complete is the discredit into which universal history has fallen, that we find it hard to look with tolerance or sympathy at the eighteenth and early nineteenth-century writers who brought it into favour. We tend to look on their works as attempts to close the doors of historical research and to institute a canon of historical fact outside which there shall be no salvation, and therefore we ridicule them for not knowing a great deal that every historian knows today. But if we wish to understand them we must invert this attitude. We must look on them not as closing, but as opening, the doors of historical research. We must regard their systems not as summaries of work done but as programmes of work to be put in hand. The truth about these systems is that they are forecasts, and in the main fairly accurate forecasts, of the lines which historical inquiry was to follow in the next few generations.

Outside the circle of professional historians, this extreme reaction against universal history has never been felt. The general public has always been eager for it; never more so than today, when brief abstracts of all knowledge are a staple food of the intelligent public and a staple source of income to many publishing firms. Universal histories of the two classes mentioned above are being produced and bought and read all over the world in quantities that would have brought tears to the eyes of Voltaire, and may well produce misgivings in the monograph-writing historians of our own time. Indeed, it evidently does produce some misgivings; enough to induce some of them to make remunerative if rather shamefaced contribution to journalistic outlines of history and popular collections of cheap little books, and others to invent and execute ingenious compromises, in the shape of works in many volumes, described on their covers as universal histories, but inwardly consisting of excellent monographs, each numbered as a chapter.

While, however, the professional historian tries in vain to reach the universal by adding particular to particular—a vain attempt, because the universality of a universal history consists not in the number of separate monographs out of which it is built up, but in the unity of the point of view from which it is envisaged—the general public, representing common sense as opposed to technical ideals, complains that the wood cannot be seen for the trees, and looks forward to a time when this passion for detail is tempered by a broader and humaner outlook on the problems of history as a whole. It suspects, not without reason, that the absorption of historians in points of detail is not merely distracting their attention from these larger problems, but is depriving them of the power to deal with such problems at all; that it is producing an intellectual myopia which, becoming endemic among trained historians, compels the reader who is interested in these problems to turn away from their works in despair and to look for what he wants in the writings of journalists and novelists and clergymen, who, just because they are only novices in history, have never taken a vow to refrain from dealing with interesting questions.

The professional historian may argue that this taste on the part of the public is a vicious and morbid taste, or at any rate a taste for something that is not history: a taste for sermons, for fiction, and for journalism; and he may contend that historians are right to refuse to satisfy this taste, and show a proper understanding of their own task when they leave these so-called larger problems severely alone and confine themselves to problems that are genuinely historical; which, he may say, is what they are now doing. For, he may argue, history consists in finding out facts: and until one has sifted every scrap of evidence bearing on the facts, one is simply running away from one's duty as an historian if one allows oneself to wander from the point and indulge in edifying generalizations. 'Let the journalist and the parson', he may say, 'draw moral and political lessons from the decline of the Roman Empire; my business is to discover what exactly that decline was: what changes it involved in finance and administration and so forth; here is my work waiting for me, and unless I do it, people will go on using the old traditional language about the decline of the Roman Empire in the old traditional state of complete ignorance as to the nature of the thing they are talking about.' And he will settle down again to his study of the monetary history of the reign of Honorius.

But this extreme particularism (so to call it), like the extreme universalism against which it reacts, is based on a false view of historical fact. The universalism of a hundred years ago was based on the idea that there was such a thing as the sum total of historical fact, and that this whole could be narrated with some kind of completeness. Shallow thinkers fancied that this whole had been more or less discovered and was already stated more or less completely, though piecemeal, in historical works: and supposed that the task of the philosophical historian was only to put it together and thus bring its significance to light. Profounder minds regarded this whole as something not yet known, but awaiting discovery and capable of being discovered: even if some past facts could not be discovered, those that mattered for the completeness of the scheme, they thought, could. The essence of the error was the thinking of history as a kind of pattern, a complete body of fact, with articulations of its own and a structure of its own, which the historian had simply to discover. This involved denying the ideality of history: for if history is ideal, it cannot be a single self-contained body of fact awaiting discovery, it must be a growing and changing body of thoughts, decomposed and recomposed by every new generation of historical workers, and the exhaustibility of historical fact, which is implied in the idea of universal history, is an illusion.

The same illusion lies at the root of historical particularism. The devotee of the historical monograph aims at collecting all the evidence there is, and interpreting it completely, so as to give a final account of some point of detail. Here again, we meet with the notion of exhaustibility. 'All the evidence there is' implies that upon any point there is a finite quantity of evidence which is capable of being exhaustively handled in a monograph. But this is simply untrue. A given writer, or a given generation, possesses only a finite quantity of evidence on a given subject; but another writer, or a later generation, succeeds in tapping new sources of information; and where is the process to end? It cannot ever be ended until historical research is ended. Therefore the reasons which our historian gave for confining himself to minute details are bad reasons. They amounted to this: that such details admit of rigorous and scientific handling, which the 'larger' questions do not. But we now see that, precisely as the ignorant man thinks that the larger questions can be definitively settled, and is thereby merely showing his own ignorance, so, when the professional historian thinks that minuter questions can be definitively settled, he too is betraying, not ignorance of what has been done, but ignorance concerning the possibilities of future discovery. The idea of the evidence concerning this or that point as a given finite whole is just as false as the idea of history at large as a given finite whole. In both cases the ideality of history is denied. For to assert the ideality of history implies asserting that the evidence concerning a particular problem consists of everything which historical research has found, or shall find, to be relevant to it.

However wide the universal historian casts his net, there are left as good fish in the sea as ever he gets out of it, not to mention the million species that slip through the mesh. However large the magnification which the monograph-writer uses for his microscope, there are left, ultra-microscopic, as many pieces of evidence as he discovers, not to mention those which the magnification itself removes from his field of vision. Does this point to the futility of all historical research?

Far from it, if we assert the ideality of history. For on that view, the infinite things that are left undiscovered do not vitiate what we have discovered; they are only a name for the infinite possibilities of future discovery. Whereas if historical fact were an actually existing reality, the universal historian would have failed altogether if anything had fallen outside his scheme and the monograph-writer would have failed with equal completeness if any evidence on his subject had escaped his scrutiny. To explain this, let us take an example. A and B are two historians of forty years ago, both specialists in the Athenian constitution, and holding divergent views on a certain point. After the controversy between them has developed and served to sharpen their views, the learned world is shaken by the discovery of Aristotle's *Constitution of the Athenians*. The new evidence thus discovered proves, to the satisfaction of all concerned, that A and B were both wrong. What follows? If historical fact is an actually existing reality, and if the truth of historical thought lies in its correspondence with historical fact, and if the value of historical thought lies in its truth, the value of both views, A's and B's, is zero: and both A and B were therefore fools, and equally fools, to hold their respective views.

But no one will accept this result. Everybody will agree that views held before the discovery of the *Constitution* must be judged in the light of the evidence available when they were held, and the arguments by which that evidence was made to support them. So judged, most people will agree that A's view was better than B's, and that neither was wholly valueless. Are we then to argue that the value of an historical view is something other than its truth? Impossible. Neither A nor B nor anyone else will acquiesce in that. We are forced to say that what A and B were both alike aiming at was 'a verdict in accordance with the evidence', a theory of the Athenian Constitution strictly consistent with the evidence available to them at that time. And, since the discovery of the Aristotelian treatise has not rendered us omniscient on the subject, the same thing must be said about ourselves. A view which is right for us to hold will be wrong when the next important new find of evidence has been made.

One of two consequences follows. Either the attainment of truth, even on points of small detail, is deferred until *all* new finds of evidence have been made—that is, deferred for ever, because in the nature of things further evidence might always turn up—in which case every historical view is exactly as false as every other, that is, absolutely false: or else *the truth* about any point means the truth relatively to the evidence possessed by the person who raises the point. The principle of the ideality of history makes it perfectly clear that the second answer is the right one. The first answer implies the denial of that principle, for it implies that historical fact is an unknown and unknowable thing in itself: the second answer implies its assertion, for it implies that the object of historical thought is always present, and always grasped, wherever historical thought exists.

This leads to results of some importance. It shows that the monograph-writer, however wrong he may be to suppose that he is deciding anything once for all, and closing the doors of historical research, is perfectly right to review with all the care and skill at his command, all the available evidence on the question, however small, which he is studying. But the reason why he is right is because there is no such thing as a large or small question; any question that any historian actually and effectively studies is just large enough to fill his mind, and no larger. The monograph-writer is thus justified by the fact that, because historical fact is ideal and not actual, there are no historical problems except those which historical thought raises; and if I devote my life to the monetary policy of Honorius, the monetary policy of Honorius is for me the whole of history.

But by the same principle the writer of a universal history is equally justified. He is justified by his very failings. What proves him right is what we thought had proved him wrong— namely the fact that, after all, his universal history is not universal, not complete, but a mere selection of facts arranged to illustrate or prove some particular point. For this makes him a monograph-writer, and removes the sting from that appellation. All that is wrong with his book is, now, its title: it was called 'A History of the World'; it ought to have been called 'The Oppression of the Proletariat in the last Twenty-five Centuries', or 'The Growth of the Modern Conception of Liberty', or the like. And even to call it 'A History of the World' is not wholly wrong, for, as we have seen, the subject of the monograph that I am writing is, for me, the whole of history, and every monograph is in a sense a history of the world—the best solution I can offer, at the moment, of the only historical problem which, at the moment, I feel to be a real problem. But because every history is equally a history of the world in that sense, and cannot be a history of the world at all in any other, nothing is gained by ever using the title.

The popular demand for histories dealing with 'larger' questions is also, from this point of view, justified. But this is not because these questions really are larger than those with which historians generally deal. It is because they are questions more interesting to ordinary unacademic people. A question does not cease to· be scientifically answerable merely because it happens to interest unscientific people; and this applies as much to history as to any other branch of knowledge. The reason why modern historical thought has moved away from the problems most interesting to ordinary people is partly that it has been influenced by a false theory and a false ideal of historical method. The notion of historical fact as an actual and exhaustible whole has led it to seek that wholeness in smaller and smaller parcels of material; and this has led to the ruling-out of any question that any ordinary man would wish to ask, as being too complicated for the present state of knowledge. But no question is ever too complicated for an inquirer who will ask it resolutely and set about answering it to the best of his ability. The search for questions that are inherently simple and therefore capable of exhaustive treatment is a false atomism of knowledge, and can only lead to disappointment. To pursue that search, to the exclusion of questions which genuinely interest one, is to incur and to justify the ridicule which has always been directed at the pedantic scholar.

On the other hand, it would be wrong entirely to condemn the present specialization of historical studies. It would be wrong to imagine that this specialization is altogether based on a fallacious theory of history. Often a fallacious theory is only invented to justify a practice which is sound enough in itself and needs no justification. The specialism of modern historical research is a necessary and a fine thing. It is a school of disinterested accuracy, of cool and logical thinking, and of careful observation, which is in no way inferior to that specialism of scientific research whose praises have been so often and eloquently sung. Modern historical research is a younger thing than modern scientific research, and its achievements are less known and its virtues less valued by the public; but they are equally real, and equally important elements in the life of the modern world. And further, the results which are being built up by this specialized research are very far from being lost to knowledge by an excess of specialism. They are, on the whole, easily accessible to students and provide an enormous and ever-increasing field for the activity of historians sufficiently wide in their interests to use them effectively. The phase of specialization through which historical studies have been passing is certainly the prelude to a phase when the narrowness of the specialist, which the public today finds repellent, will give way before a return to those 'larger' questions which, as if by an act of self-denial, historians of the present refuse to raise. When that happens, it will perhaps be realized that every new synthesis and every broadening of view has been made possible by the detailed and laborious specialism of a generation of scholars whose work, while they lived, was regarded as the mere indulgence of an eccentric antiquarianism.[13]

At this point it will be well to introduce a conception of great importance for the theory of historical method: namely the conception of history of the second degree, or the history of history.

The history of history arises when the historian, in trying to solve a particular problem, proceeds by collecting and criticizing the solutions which have already been offered. This collection and criticism of previous solutions may be done in two ways: either by treating the various solutions in a disconnected manner, dealing with each separately and discussing them in a haphazard order, or else by treating them historically, showing how each expressed a certain attitude which was itself an historical phenomenon, and established itself by criticizing its predecessors. For historical thought itself has a history, and there is no more sense in criticizing a particular historical theory without considering the conditions in which it arose, than there is in criticizing a political or military system without

[13] Following this Collingwood writes: '[addition, May 1928]'. This addition deals with the subject of the history of history, which is also discussed in the lectures of 1926. It runs until the last paragraph of p. 469.

such consideration. We have already seen that the value of historical work done in the past can only be assessed by putting ourselves in the position of the people who did it, thinking over the problem as it confronted them, and making use of the evidence which they possessed. This is only a way of saying that historical thought itself, when it is past historical thought, may be and must be an object for present historical thought.

Now it is plain enough that historical thought is one of the things that historians may think about; and that among the infinite possible subjects for historical research, some may legitimately be drawn from the past development of historical research itself. But to say that would be to misrepresent the real nature and importance of the history of history. For the fact is, that the history of history holds a quite peculiar position in historical studies: a position which may be defined by saying that all history is, or at least involves and presupposes, the history of history.

By saying this, I mean that anyone who is anxious to solve a particular historical problem must find out where he stands, and what his problem exactly is, by looking into the history of the problem itself: that is, into the history of research concerning the subject. Suppose the subject is the Peasants' Revolt, and suppose this becomes a problem for you because for some reason you have made up your mind to write an essay on it or, in general, to form an opinion as to what exactly it was. Now the first thing you do is to read it up in a standard and up-to-date history; and if you are not going deeply into the matter, you will simply swallow what you find there, and go no further. But if you get interested, or if you are sceptical about something in your history-book, you will go to other accounts of the Peasants' Revolt in other books; and you will find that these differ from the first and from each other. If you are determined to get at the truth, you must begin by trying to reduce these differences to order, and this can only be done by discovering how the various accounts grew out of each other. You now find that A's account, modified by removing certain inconsistencies, became B's; B's account, with additions from certain newly-discovered sources, gave rise to C's; C's account was so obviously one-sided that it provoked a controversial reply from D; C and D together resulted in the eclectic compromise advocated by E; and so on. Now the point is that, where all this work has already been done on the subject, no one is justified in putting forward a new view of his own without taking it into account. To do so, is to neglect not only possible assistance but certain dangers. A theory framed without reference to previous theories denies itself the help that may be got from seeing the points that have been already emphasized, and it runs the risk—which in practice is more than a mere risk, it is a practical certainty—of advocating views which have already been conclusively disproved. For these reasons all historians regard it as a *sine qua non* of research that one should begin by getting up the literature of the subject, and every historian regards it as peculiarly disgraceful to be found ill-read in the writings of other historians who have handled his theme. The historian has to study two kinds of material: 'original sources' and 'modern works', as they are called in bibliographies. To study the original sources is history: to study the modern works, and to trace in them the development of thought, is the history of history.

All history concerning a given subject, then, involves as a necessary part of itself the history of history concerning the same subject. And it must further be observed that the history of history precedes history of the first degree. I cannot compose my monograph on the Peasants' Revolt until after I have completed my bibliography of it and studied the works therein contained. The reason for this is easy to understand. The problem which I am trying to solve is a problem which has been left on my hands by some previous research on the same subject. I am not merely asking in a quite vague and general way 'what was the Peasants' Revolt?', I am asking for answers to certain definite and specific questions about it; and these are the questions which have been raised by previous inquiry. Now, unless I am careful to go over this previous inquiry in my mind—to re-enact it, or narrate its history—I shall not clearly see what the problem before me is and how it arose. And in that case I am not likely to be successful in trying to answer it. The presupposition of answering a question is that one should know what the question is that is being asked; and this means finding out how it came to be asked.

Examples are easy to find. If a student is told by his tutor to write an essay on the battle of Salamis, he must certainly master all the original authorities for that battle; but everyone knows that he must also look up what has been written about the battle by modern scholars. And it is obvious enough that the value of his essay will largely depend on the clearness with which he has grasped the problems with which these modern scholars have been dealing, and the reasons for which they have differed from one another. Again, if a scholar is asked to write a popular life of Napoleon, the value of this, considered simply as a popular book, will depend upon the way in which the writer realizes how much the half-educated reader knows already, and what he wants to know next. The popular life of Napoleon must link itself on to the process of historical thought that has been already going forward in the minds of its readers; and this means that the writer must know the history of his reader's historical education. And lastly, if a student has led so lonely and so highly-specialized a life that his subject is one that has no literature, because no one but himself studies it and he does not publish his researches; even then, his progress in this field will still depend on his study of history of the second degree. For his progress at any given moment will depend on his solving the problem that has now been raised in his mind by the progress of his own thought; and in order to grasp this problem he must know how his own thought has been moving and how this new problem has arisen. In this case, the history of history will be the intellectual autobiography of the historian.

The history of history, then, is not an external addition or accretion tacked on to history, still less is it a mere special kind of history, like the history of art or the history of warfare. It is a permanent and indispensable element in history itself. It is the historian's consciousness of how he has arrived at the particular problem which confronts him. Everyone who is given to thinking knows that at times one loses the thread of one's thought; one pursues a question until one forgets how it arose and where it was leading; and at these times the question suddenly becomes meaningless and ceases to be a real problem. From this condition one emerges by turning round upon oneself and asking 'what was I going to say? what was I thinking about? how did I get myself into this position?' or the like.

These questions are concerned with the history of one's own thought; and their function is to preserve that thought's self-conscious continuity. Where the thought is historical thought, its self-conscious continuity is preserved by history of the second degree.

The conception of the history of history as an element in history itself is open to an obvious objection, which is intensified by the doctrine that the history of history is a presupposition of history itself. If history involves or presupposes the history of history, then (so the objection will run) the history of history will involve or presuppose the history of the history of history, and this, the history of the history of the history of history, and so *ad infinitum*. We are involved in an infinite regress, with the absurd result that we must begin by studying history to the *n*th, where *n* is an infinite number, and work back from that by degrees, before we can answer the simple question 'when was the battle of Hastings fought?'

This objection certainly contains an element of truth; but the truth is so overlaid by falsehood as to be, at first sight, barely visible. The truth is this: that if A's view led to B's, and B's to C's, and C's to D's, and my view is based on D's, then in narrating the history of research leading through A, B, C, and D to myself I am narrating a history each term of which already sums the whole series. The summation does not wait for me. B's view already involved the consciousness of his own relation to A; C's view involved the consciousness of C's relation to B; therefore C's history of the problem was already not only a history of history but a history of the history of history, because it involved explaining not only how B had conceived the Peasants' Revolt, but also how B had conceived the relation between his own account of it and A's. If therefore I narrate the history of thought from A to D, this involves at least the following terms: A's theory, B's alterations, B's view of the relation between them and the original theory, C's alterations, C's view of the relation between them and B's theory, C's view of B's view of the relation between B's view and A's, and so on. And this enumeration of terms, tedious as it would be, is illicitly abbreviated by the false assumption that B's theory was a single unitary theory instead of being, as it really must have been, a constant process of self-criticism in which attempts at theories were advanced and corrected and left behind. In short, since each phase in the process of advancing research sums up the process as a whole and constitutes an interim report on the advance made, each phase is not only a review of the facts but a review of the past reviews of the facts and therefore a review of the reviews of the reviews of the facts and so, if you like, *ad infinitum*.

So much for the element of truth. What then is the error? It is simply the old error of Achilles and the tortoise. You begin by cutting up the distance between Achilles and the tortoise into an infinite number of distinct distances, each to be traversed in a separate movement; you then infer that in order to make an infinite number of separate movements Achilles will require an infinite amount of time and will never overtake the tortoise. The reason why Achilles in practice manages to overtake the tortoise is that his movement is not cut up into an infinite number of separate movements; it is a single continuous movement. Similarly, if you cut up the single continuous process of historical thought into distinct events, each called a theory or view or position, the result will be that you can distinguish as many of these positions as you please, and therefore since their number is infinite you cannot ever traverse the totality of them. The error here lies in the attempt to reduce a process, the process of historical thinking, into a series of static positions. No position, in this sense, ever exists. Any historical view or theory is a complex of thoughts which already contains movement within itself. It is not a cross-section of the stream of thought, it is a short length of that stream. The views of the historian do not remain absolutely fixed throughout his exposition of his subject; as he reaches a more interesting part his thought rises in temperature and he becomes more penetrating; as he returns to a duller or less carefully studied part he relapses into an uncritical acceptance of ideas which elsewhere he has left behind. This is not mere human weakness; it is a necessary condition of all knowledge, for in all knowledge we are fighting against errors and prejudices, and the battle never reaches a phase of complete stability. Even when we stop thinking in order to avoid going on changing our minds, as some people do, our object is not achieved, for our errors and prejudices then begin to solidify by degrees round our thought and our mind undergoes a kind of progressive paralysis and decay.

Our thought, then, is advancing all the time; it does not advance by jerks from point to point, its advance is continuous; and therefore when we say that at each phase it must sum up its whole previous course, this sum must not be taken for an arithmetical sum of single static positions. Just as history is not a succession of distinct, isolated, atomic events, so the history of history is not a succession of distinct, isolated, atomic historical thoughts. When that is realized, the force of the objection we are considering disappears. There is no infinite regress, because there is no series of separate terms, but only a continuous process of thinking.

From the point of view of the history of history we can see a new aspect of the universality of history. We have already seen that any particular historical study, however particular it may be in the sense that its subject is a single historical problem, is universal in the sense that this problem is the only problem actually raised at the moment, the only thing that occupies the historian's mind and therefore, for him, all the history there is. But regarded as a study in the history of history, his study of this problem is universal in a further sense. It is universal in the sense of being a review and summary of all the historical work that has ever been done on this problem. *Qua* history, my study deals only with the monetary policy of Honorius; *qua* history of history, it deals with everything that has ever been written or said about the monetary policy of Honorius, down to the present day. Thus every historical work comes down to the present and traverses a process of which it is itself the last phase. As history of the first degree, it need not do this; a history of Rome has a perfect right to stop at the battle of Actium or the reign of Romulus Augustulus, and need not come down to Mussolini; but as history of history, it cannot stop short of the present day; it must take into account the latest discoveries and the latest theories, and put itself forward as continuing these discoveries and theories.

The doctrine that all history comes down to the present day is a doctrine of great importance in connexion with the question why people study history and what they hope to gain by the study. It is clear that in some cases history is an attempt to understand the present: for instance, if we ask why we live under the peculiar laws and customs which we find existing around us, we are asking a question which can be answered, in a sense, by history. We understand our laws and customs better than we did, if we come to see them as the result of a historical process which has shaped them into the form they now present. And therefore it might seem reasonable to define the value and purpose of history by saying that history is the explanation of how the actual world in which we live has come to be what it is.

The objection to this is obvious. It is, that historians often concern themselves with questions that have no bearing on the actual world. If the historian spends time on inventing a new theory of Sumerian chronology, he is not doing anything to explain the social or political or economic conditions of the world in which he lives. And therefore we shall have to infer either that this account of the value of history is false, or that all history is valueless except that of the recent past.

But this objection can be answered from the point of view of the history of history. The historian of Sumerian dynasties is not merely concerned with Sumerian dynasties, he is also, and even more intimately, concerned with modern historical theories about them. He is indeed trying to reconstruct very ancient history; but he is also trying to reconstruct the very modern history of this history. Hence, though he is not bringing down the history of the Sumerians to the present day, he is bringing down the history of Assyriology to the present day. And Assyriology is just as much a real element of the modern world as coal-mining.[14] Hence the Assyriologist has a twofold purpose: both to describe the Sumerian dynasties, and also to summarize and criticize and comment upon a certain feature of modern life, namely Assyriological study. The popular view of the historian as a visionary whose mental gaze is turned wholly away from the present upon a distant and long-vanished past is therefore a false view. The distant past is as it were the stalking-horse from behind which the historian observes and criticizes the present. If this seems a fanciful and exaggerated view, a glance at the facts will suffice to convince

[14] In the manuscript is added: 'and the forms of thought which Assyriologists reveal are the characteristic forms of the modern world'.

any clear-sighted observer of its truth. The great historians—Macaulay, Hume, Grote, Gibbon, Mommsen, Maitland—are men keenly interested in their own present day; and every page of their history betrays the fact that in writing it they are concerned not simply to discover the truth about the distant past, but to combat historical errors which spring from faults in contemporary civilization and in turn flatter and foster those faults. The rationalistic history of Hume and Gibbon is an attack on what the eighteenth century called enthusiasm, i.e. superstition; the materialistic history of nineteenth-century economists is an attack on nineteenth-century romanticism; the prehistoric studies of today are an attack on our modern tendency to over-emphasize the value of material civilization and to regard the savage as a slave to exploit and a brute to despise. The great historians are sharply conscious of these motives; their academic and imitative followers may or may not have a dim consciousness of them.

Thus it may be said that while all history is particular in that it has a particular problem or ostensible subject, it is universal in that it must review the entire history of research concerning that subject. And therefore, while in one sense it always deals with the past, which may be a very distant past, in another sense it always deals with the present by setting itself up as a model of how the present ought to think of the past and of its own relation to the past. In this way the quantitative aspect of history—the question of its universality or particularity—is defined by the conception of history as particular in its content, as dealing with a special problem in historical research, and universal in its form, as linking that problem up with the whole extent of actual present-day life.

Attention may here be called to a special form, prominent today, of the attempt to combine particular history with universal history. Every particular history, or monograph, has certain characteristics derived from the fact of its being a monograph, and these it therefore has in common with all other monographs. Just as a tragedy, according to Aristotle, must have a certain size and must have a beginning, a middle, and an end, so an historical monograph must begin somewhere, proceed through a definite course, and end somewhere. Before its beginning and after its end there is darkness, that is

to say, a context not studied by this monograph and not illuminated, on this occasion, by the light of historical thought.
The point of greatest illumination will probably fall in some
approximately central position, and on either side of this point
there will be a diminution of light due to the encroachment of
the surrounding darkness. In the early phases of the period,
we shall have only a very incomplete understanding of the
events owing to our ignorance of that out of which they are
developing: in the latest phases, we shall again partially fail to
understand them owing to our ignorance of that into which
they are turning. And this relative unintelligibility of the two
ends of the period under review will appear emotionally as a
relative uninterestingness or low degree of value:[15] the beginning will appear as a kind of dull, stupid, barbaric phase,
interesting only for its visible promise of what is to come out
of it; the end will appear as equally dull, stupid and barbaric,
but, this time, the barbarism will be not the primitive barbarism of youth but the sophisticated barbarism of decadence.[16]

In so far as certain monographic points of view become conventionalized and fixed, this triple phase of primitive, mature,
and decaying civilization becomes, in certain cases, an
accepted dogma. Today, there are various historical periods

[15] This sentence is underlined in the manuscript.

[16] On the opposite page, dated 1935, the following statement was added:
'Emotionally is wrong. The point is, I think, that history (in spite of the contrary opinion of the "pure scholarship" school) is never composed simply of
judgements of fact (such and such a thing happened): there is always
involved a judgement of value. I think that the judgement of value tends to
become positive in proportion as the events studied are more and more
clearly understood: from which proposition the consequences in the text will
follow.

If it is asked, why should there be *any* judgement of value? The answer is
not merely psychological (i.e. that in fact we simply shouldn't, and couldn't,
seriously study anything that did not arouse our sympathy and earn our
approval: this is the question what we think *worth* studying or *historically
important*). It is also, that if we re-enact the past in our own thought, the past
thought which we re-enact is seen in re-thinking it as valid. (This is Croce's
doctrine of the positivity of history, which wants careful stating.) The more
adequately we re-enact the past, the more valid we see it to be: hence the *dif-
ferential* result. What we judge negatively as error or evil in history is what
we fail to understand.'

which are thus fixed into organized unities by a monographic point of view: thus, we are in the habit of regarding the Greek world as arising out of primitiveness in the eighth to the sixth centuries, culminating in a classical phase in the fifth, and lapsing into decay in the fourth, with the collapse of the city-state and the growth of Hellenism. Again, we are in the habit of recognizing a classical phase of medieval culture, represented in especial by the plastic art of the Gothic cathedral, which arises out of the primitive barbarism of the dark ages and passes into the sophisticated barbarism of decaying medievalism.

When a number of such periods are recognized, they may be collected into a single scheme by the conception of historical cycles. The theory is invented that history moves through a regular succession of waves, in which culture periodically culminates in classical phases of perfection, reached by primitive phases in which it is emerging from barbarism and succeeded by decadent phases in which the classical energy and purity are giving way to mechanical apathy and confusion. And remarkable feats of ingenuity may be performed in the attempt to work out a system of cycles, tracing the parallels between one and another and the peculiarities which distinguish each from the rest.

Such attempts are vain. Essentially, they are based on the fallacy of tacking one monograph externally to another and so hoping to arrive at universal history. If two monographs—for instance, one on Greek culture and one on 'Magian'—to use a conception familiarized by Spengler—instead of being merely tacked together, were thought out into a single whole, the transition from one period to the other being carefully traced and the relations between them adequately studied, we should no longer have a pair of waves, we should have a single wave. And conversely, if instead of being content with the conventional adulation of the fifth century at the expense of everything before it and after it, we devoted a little specialized study to the Hellenistic period, we should find in this period a character and an excellence of its own, and should be forced to regard it in certain respects as a culmination of tendencies which in the fifth century had not yet outgrown the stage of primitiveness.

It is certainly true that everything which is realized in the historical process comes into being and passes away through certain phases of growth and decay. In that sense, the idea of all history as made up of cycles each exhibiting a triple phase is correct. And it is also true that the various aspects or elements of a single culture change together: so that the characteristic qualities of the poetry of a period are also visible in its architecture and politics and science. But every historical change is a change in both directions at once. It is the growth of what comes after, and the decay of what comes before; and it is also the perfection of itself. It is only when we are unable to free ourselves from the accidents of historical specialization as practised conventionally in our own time, that we see one of these aspects and are blind to the rest.

III. *Relation*

Every historical work, as we have now seen, deals with a particular and limited problem, and is thus, as we have called it, a monograph. But such a treatise has a universal as well as a particular aspect: for the particular and limited problem is, to the person whose mind is concentrated upon it, the only genuine problem in existence. Into this problem he pours all his technical resources, and he illuminates it with the light of all the history he knows. Thus the whole of history is concentrated into this one monograph and it becomes a history of the world from a special point of view.

The monograph has both a unity and a plurality in its composition. As a unity, it is a single narrative, artistically and logically bound up into a whole; subjectively, it is one treatise; objectively, it is about one thing. As a plurality, it consists of a number of statements attaching predicates to that one thing. The one thing is an event: for instance, the French Revolution, or the Wars of the Roses, or the Evolution of the Pointed Arch. This is called the subject of the monograph, because it is the logical subject of all the statements contained in it—they are all statements about the French Revolution or whatever it may be. But this event is a complex thing, consisting of many aspects, each aspect being itself an event: and to write the history of the single event is to enumerate the various events that composed it. A history of the Wars of the Roses will therefore consist of an enumeration of the various campaigns, battles, and so forth which went to constitute these wars: each battle being sufficiently described to individualize its contribution to the whole narrative.

From this point of view, the monograph as a whole is a sum of parts, each part being so designed as to make its proper contribution to the whole, and the whole being simply the organized system of parts. For instance, we should describe the battle of Trafalgar in different ways according as we were composing a treatise on naval tactics, on the Napoleonic Wars, on the life of Nelson, or on the influence of sea-power on history. Or we might be simply composing a monograph on the battle of Trafalgar, which would demand a different treatment again. Thus the whole must precede the part, in this sense, that the part must be thought out in relation to the whole. The converse is not true. The whole is not thought out in relation to the part. The whole simply is the mutual organization of the parts. For instance, an history of the Napoleonic Wars contains nothing except accounts of the various operations which collectively go by that name. The whole, then, is a regulative scheme dictating the details of the work:[17] apart from the details, it is a mere abstraction, or, at most, a name for someone's intention of writing an historical work, or the bare fact that someone has done so.

The practical consequence of this is that, in composing an historical work, the first thing to do is to decide upon a subject. This may seem a truism; but people sometimes fall into the error of allowing history to compose itself by adding essay to essay, hoping that if the essays more or less 'cover the ground' of a certain period the resulting book will be an history of that period. This is the fault, already mentioned, of tacking monographs together externally; to avoid it, the historian must begin with the idea of his work as a whole, and develop every part in relation to this whole. If a fragment composed without reference to the whole is incorporated in the structure, it will destroy the unity of the fabric unless it is so modified as to be brought into focus with the rest of the

---

[17] This sentence is underlined in the manuscript.

work. That this is the case with a work of art is notorious; and it is therefore obvious that it must apply to an historical work in so far as that is literature. But it applies no less to history as history. It would be absurd to suggest that any account of the battle of Trafalgar, so long as it was accurate, would do as well as any other to fill a place in a history of the Napoleonic Wars; every historian will recognize that the significance of this battle from the standpoint of the Napoleonic Wars is not the same thing as its significance from the standpoint of the biography of Nelson, and that a perfectly accurate account of it from the latter standpoint would be valueless, or indeed misleading and therefore inaccurate, from the former.

Granted the ideality of history, this is intelligible enough: for on that theory, the truth about an event is relative to the point of view from which one approaches it, and an account of an event written from a wrong point of view is therefore not merely irrelevant but false, for the giving of it amounts to claiming that it is relevant, and this misleads the reader and makes him seem to see connexions where there are none.

The various parts of a treatise, however, are not only related to the whole: they are related to each other. Primarily, they are related chronologically: they state a temporal sequence and therefore constitute a narrative. But the relation between them is very far from being merely chronological. They constitute not merely a sequence but a process. Each part leads to the one which follows and rests on the one which precedes.

In a sense it may be said that this process is a chain of causes and effects, each event being the cause of the one after and the effect of the one before it. And certainly it is true that each is in some sense the condition of the one after, and conditioned by the one before. Had it been legitimate to speak of the nebular hypothesis or the theory of geological epochs as history, we should have had examples of historical processes which were strictly causal. But we have seen that all history is the history of thought. A thought can never be either an effect or a cause; but thoughts may form a sequence of conditioned and conditioning elements. For instance, in a game of chess, it is because White has moved in a particular way that Black replies with a particular move: and this again determines the next move of White. But this determination is not causal.

What happens is that White's move places Black in a certain situation, and in this situation there is only one move by which Black can avoid defeat: in order to avoid defeat, he therefore chooses to make that move, and this again creates a new situation for White. It is only because each is a free and intelligent agent that he acts as he does; what is said to determine his act only creates a situation in which he exercises his freedom and intelligence.

This is the nature of historical sequence. Every event, so far as that event is an expression of human thought, is a conscious reaction to a situation, not the effect of a cause. This reaction in turn originates a new situation, and a new reaction follows. But the only reason why a given situation leads to a given action is that the agent is guided by certain principles: in the case of chess, the rules of the game. Apart from these rules, his reaction to his opponent's move would have no meaning and would be unintelligible: but if you know the rules of the game and know that he wants to win, you can see why he moved as he did; unless indeed his move was due to an oversight, in which case the best you can do is to understand what he meant, but failed, to achieve.

The principles here referred to are different from the causal laws of natural science in that they do not operate except consciously. It is only because the player knows the rules of the game that the rules of the game explain his moves. Consequently these principles cease to operate when people cease to think of them; and therefore they are themselves historical phenomena. It is the task of the historian to discover what principles guided the persons whose actions he is studying, and not to assume that these have always been the same.

To forget this is to fall into the error of naturalistic or materialistic history: a history which replaces principles by causal laws, and assumes that these laws, like the laws of nature, are constant. The result is that historical sequences are converted falsely into causal sequences, and the historian loses his grasp both on the free and intelligent character of the acts which he is narrating, the parts of his subject, and also on the individuality of this subject as a whole, as a particular historical fact with a character and physiognomy of its own. If the determining forces in history were unchangeable natural laws, every period of history would be just like every other except in merely external and irrelevant details: it would be nature, and nature has no history. What individualizes historical periods is the diversity of the principles on which men act; but the historical materialist is obliged to deny this diversity and impose upon all men alike a single uniform set of motives and springs of action.

The excuse for falling into this error lies in the fact that in one sense all rational beings do, and must, act on the same principles: the principles which define what rationality is. It is necessary therefore to distinguish between two kinds of principles: these universal and necessary principles, apart from obedience to which there is no such thing as action at all, and others, which may be called empirical principles, which can be changed without such consequence. To take an example: different political organizations may differ very widely in their positive laws; one community may make it compulsory to drive on the right of the road, another on the left; and the historian ought to keep count of such differences. But all political organizations must agree in making laws and enforcing them, however inefficiently they do these things. It may be optional what laws, in detail, we have; but it is not optional that we must have some laws, and, having them, insist on their being obeyed.

Two complementary errors are therefore possible: the error of regarding as necessary what is really optional, and the error of regarding as optional what is really necessary. The first we have already mentioned. The second is the error advocated by those who, anxious to distinguish sharply between the workings of the civilized and the uncivilized mind, assert that the savage does not think logically as we do, but has other laws which take the place, in his mind, which the fundamental laws of logic take in ours. These so-called laws are in fact not laws at all; they are empirical descriptions of certain types of error to which all men are prone, whether civilized or uncivilized; and a very little clear thinking is sufficient to show that person who falls into errors of this type is just as loyal to the laws of identity, contradiction, and excluded middle as the most highly trained scientist.

The chronological sequence of events, which, as we have

seen, is also a logical sequence of reactions to situations, might seem capable of stretching out infinitely in both directions and so producing a universal history in (so to speak) one dimension. Obviously this is a false idea. Granted a single thread of this kind, it will cross and re-cross other threads, and there will also be threads which, so far as one can see, will never come into contact with it at all. Plainly, history as a whole cannot consist of a single narrative, recounting a single one-dimensional series of events. But it is equally plain that it cannot consist of any number, however large, of such one-dimensional narratives. This is because a sequence of this kind is discoverable only within a period whose limits have already been laid down. When we have determined the subject of our historical study, we can arrange its parts chronologically; but to suppose that the chronological sequence thus established is a selection from an infinite chronological sequence existing ready-made, like a road along one part of which we elect to make a journey, is to repeat the error of conceiving historical fact as something having actual existence. Because historical fact is ideal, those parts or aspects of it which we are not studying do not exist; what exists is the abstract possibility that we might have been studying them. This abstract possibility is the only kind of reality that attaches to chronological schemes and abstracts of history in general. These things are enumerations—very incomplete enumerations—of the various ways in which we might employ ourselves in historical thought. They resemble guide-books regarded as lists of possible excursions; but they do not resemble them regarded as descriptions of actual places.

An actually thought-out chronological scheme, then, exists only as the organization of detail within an historical monograph. Thus there is a certain resemblance between the chronological structure of an historical monograph, and the rhythmical structure of a symphony. The time-beats of a symphony do not go on *ad infinitum* before the music begins and after it ends; they form an organization which exists only in the symphony itself. They serve to articulate the symphony as a whole; and it is only when we have the symphony as a whole before us (as the composer must have it, and every really intelligent hearer does have it), with its successive parts so interpenetrating one another that each colours the rest and gives them their peculiar significance, that the rhythmical structure becomes intelligible and visibly necessary. Thus the parts of a symphony, though they are certainly played at different times, are seen as parts of the same symphony only when the listener overcomes this difference of time by being conscious of all the parts at once. This may seem recondite, but it is a very simple and very familiar fact. It is because the rhythm and key of the first subject continue to ring in one's head that the contrasting rhythm and key of the second subject are felt to be significant; and to a person who knows the symphony well, it is in part because he knows how the second subject is going to contrast with it that he appreciates the meaning of the first subject—a fact which, under the name of Sophoclean irony, is a commonplace of dramatic theory. The downfall of Oedipus, though it has not yet happened, is felt by every instructed spectator to overshadow his greatness. In that sense, the parts of the play are simultaneously experienced, though successively performed.

The substance of an historical monograph must be simultaneously experienced in the same way. What appears chronologically as a sequence must appear as a simultaneous whole in the historian's thought. He is recounting the history of Gothic architecture: he must see in each phase of that history the fruit of what has gone before and the seed of what is to come. He must feel the earlier phases as preparing the way for the later, and the later as explaining the true meaning of the earlier. He must, in a word, see the inner structure of his subject as a development.

This conception of development, or progress, defines a necessary character of every historical period, where period means a particular subject of historical study—the subject-matter of a monograph. Development is only possible where there is unity: there must be one thing that develops, and when it changes into something that is not recognizably the same, it cannot any longer be said to be developing. Development also implies a plurality of phases within the process; and it further implies that the process brings out by degrees some characteristic of the one thing which at first was not clear. Development is an ideal process, not an actual process: it consists in something's becoming more and more intelligible. Similarly, progress is an ideal process. Crudely and falsely conceived, it consists of something's getting absolutely better and better; an idea which is obviously false, because to get better from one point of view means to get worse from another. But progress relatively to a certain conception of that which is progressing is intelligible enough. If I have a certain conception of what science is, then I may be able to say that science progressed in the nineteenth century; that is to say, my history of nineteenth-century science may show it as becoming more and more scientific. If I had a different conception of what science is, I might have been obliged to say that it was becoming less and less scientific. Now, if I take my conception of science from the nineteenth century itself, I must necessarily say that science in the nineteenth century progressed: for that merely amounts to saying that nineteenth-century science had an ideal of its own and progressively realized that ideal in its development.

Progress is universal because ideals are always progressively realized. A people which fails to realize a certain ideal is a people which does not regard that as an ideal. Ideals are the principles which persons and communities set before themselves to guide their actions; if they really set these before themselves, their actions are really guided by them. If their actions are not guided by them, they are guided by some other principles, and these are their ideals. This is obscured by the hypocrisy which leads men to conceal their real ideals and do lip-service to others; but when that is seen through, the truth is clear enough.

Now when we isolate a period of history for study, we do so in virtue of a unity or homogeneity which we see it to possess. Since all history is the history of thought, this unity is a unity of thought—a unity in the thought of the persons whose actions form our period. That is to say, it is a unity of principles or ideals. Our history of the period is at bottom the history of these ideals. From the point of view of these ideals, the narration of the history reveals it as a development: that is, the actions which make up the period progressively show what the ideals in question are, just as the actions of a tragedy progressively show what the plot (or ideal unity) of the tragedy is.

And this development is a progress because, as the period advances, it becomes clearer and clearer to the historian what these ideals were, and therefore the actions of the characters more and more strikingly conform to them.

A special case, and one which has excited most discussion, is that of the recent past—the past immediately leading up to the present. In this case, as in every other, the history of the period shows a progressive realization of the ideals of that period. But in this case the ideals are our own; for we stand in, or on the edge of, the period itself. It is therefore exceptionally easy to see that there is progress. A person who glances over the history of Roman politics from the Gracchi to the Antonines does not see that it exhibits progress, unless he is able to grasp and sympathize with the Roman political ideals of the period; and this requires some study and some breadth of mind. But everybody, by being born and bred in a certain period, learns to accept the great majority of that period's ideals, however much he may rebel against it in detail. Therefore everybody who glances over the history of the immediate past must see in it the development of his own ideals, and therefore must regard it as a period of progress. People who deny that they can detect progress in the recent past are people who exaggerate the extent of their own rebellion against the ideals of the present; and since every man of thoughtful and independent mind has in him an element of this rebellion, no thoughtful and independent man can describe the immediate past as a period of progress without certain reservations; because he sees it as, in part, the growth of the things against which he has to fight. The fact is, that the ideals of the immediate past are never quite our own, but only very like our own; and therefore, to see this period as one of progress, we must take pains to distinguish between its ideals and ours, and to judge it by its own standards.

Progress, then, is universal in the sense that a narrative of any particular historical period as it proceeds, reveals more and more clearly the nature of that period's ideals; and it is by these ideals that it ought to be judged. It does not follow that the next period will be still better according to the same standards. On the contrary, it will certainly be worse; and at the same time, according to its own standards, better. But to hold two periods together in this way side by side for comparison is bad history. If two periods are thought of together, they must be fused into one period and their common characteristics brought to light. If they have no common characteristics, it is idle even to compare them. No one would wish to compare any two things, unless he thought he detected something in common between them. But by bringing to light these common characteristics one is treating the two periods in question as articulations of one single period, and their ideals as modifications of a common ideal. And if anyone can really manage to treat all history from, say, 3000 B.C. to A.D. 1900 as a single period, grasped in a single act of thought and expounded in a monograph (instead of grasping various of its parts as periods, and expounding it in a series of disjointed monographic essays), he will certainly see it, in the same way, as a progressive development of a single ideal. It is certain that no living historian can do this; perhaps no one ever will; but it is by no means certain that some historian might not select from this vast period one single limited aspect and treat the whole period as a genuine unity from that limited point of view. One may recall the fact that Kant's idea of universal history was conceived exclusively 'from a cosmopolitan (*weltbürgerlich*) point of view'; that is to say, he threw out the suggestion that the idea of cosmopolitan citizenship could be treated (by a very learned and very philosophical historian—not by himself) as the subject-matter of an essay covering the whole of recorded history. And if it were so treated, he saw, and saw rightly, that the narrative would be a narrative of progress, of the gradual consolidation of an ideal whose presence in one form or another could be traced throughout that period.

In any other sense than this, progress is an illusion. To suppose that the world will go on getting better according to our own peculiar ideas of goodness, is to be beyond the reach of reason. Of one thing we may be certain: our posterity will live in a world which corresponds to their ideals quite as well as this, in which we live, corresponds to ours.

IV. *Modality*

The fourth question to be dealt with concerns the certainty of history, the nature of the grounds on which it rests, and its status as genuine knowledge. This question, from the point of view of the realism and empiricism which go to make up the theories of knowledge now fashionable, has been already answered: for, according to those theories, knowledge as such is knowledge of an object which is actual independently of the knowing; and, since the whole of our discussion hitherto has turned on the conception of the ideality of history, we stand irrevocably committed to the view that, on a realistic or empiricist theory, the historian has nothing to know and therefore his thought is not knowledge.

The ideality of history is so obvious and undeniable a truth, that realist and empiricist philosophers habitually treat history with coolness or even positive hostility. They find themselves most at home in dealing with the theory of perception, where it seems clear that the object is actual and in some sense independent of the percipient; and it is easy for them to make out a case for applying their views to natural science, where there is always a perceptible object being observed and experimented with, or even to pure mathematics, where they can hypostatize numbers and so forth and claim an intellectual intuition of these entities. In the case of history, this method breaks down, and the realist finds himself on the horns of a dilemma. Either he has to set his face against all historical thought as a form of illusion, which is easy to do by way of *obiter dicta*, but impossible to do in a consistent and reasoned manner, owing to the impossibility of explaining how the illusion reaches such an extraordinary level of consistency and apparent scientific perfection; or else he has to assert that the object of historical thought is not the past at all, but a trace or residue of the past in the present. The latter is at present the orthodox empiricist view of memory, and would no doubt be applied to history if empiricists and realists thought history a thing worth theorizing about. But it is obvious that any such view is bankrupt from the beginning. The whole of the present consists of traces or residues of the past, for the present is that into which the past has turned, and the past was that which has turned into the present. To speak, therefore, of traces of the past in the present is to speak of the present and nothing but the present. The psychologists who would 'explain' memory by referring to such traces of the past, are putting forward a theory which, at best, would account for certain hallucinations like the apparent swaying of the land after a rough sea-voyage; but it could never explain why there is a difference between thinking that the land sways and remembering that the ship swayed.

The view which will here be maintained has something in common with both horns of this dilemma. We shall see that, if the purpose of history is to know the past, to become acquainted with things as they actually happened, which is what the realist necessarily supposes to be its purpose, then history is certainly an illusion. We shall then see that actual historical thought is intimately bound up with traces of the past in the present.

If anyone thinks that he can, by historical research, discover what the past was like in its actuality and completeness, a very little reflexion on the conditions of historical research will undeceive him. All he can do is to interpret the evidence at his command. He will, if he is a very uncritical soul, assume that the evidence which happens to have reached him is a fair sample of what has been lost; and that the past which he reconstructs from these fragments is the past as it really was. But it must be difficult for anyone to be so uncritical as this. Most historians realize very plainly that, the more fragmentary their evidence is, the more fragmentary must be their knowledge of the past; that the gaps between these fragments of knowledge cannot be filled by legitimate inference, and must not be filled by imagination; and that an overwhelming majority of past events must remain permanently unknown and unknowable. But most historians also realize that the past is not a plurality of atomic incidents, any one of which may be 'known' in an adequate way without the rest, but a whole in which parts are so related as to explain one another and render one another intelligible. It follows that, the more extensive our ignorance concerning the past is, the more infected with misunderstanding and error will be our knowledge of those fragments which we claim to know. But when one thinks how vast is the extent of our ignorance even concerning the last general election, or the life of Gladstone, or the reign on which one has just written a successful prize essay, one cannot shut one's eyes to the fact that, even in the most favourable cases, one's ignorance is infinite, and one's historical knowledge consists only of a few atoms lost in the void of endless space. It is necessary to reflect carefully on this point, because we are apt to think that we know 'all about' something, that is to say, possess a complete knowledge of it, when we know all *that is known* about it; we mistake the coincidence between our information and the extant information for a coincidence between our information and the object. Once this confusion is cleared up, no historian would hesitate to say that, even in the period he knows best, there are infinities of things he does not know for every one that he does.

Certainly, then, history is an illusion, if it means knowledge of the past in its actuality and completeness. But does it really mean that? It is easy to answer the question by experiment. Take an historian who has made a special study of the battle of Waterloo: and ask him the name of the hundredth man to be put out of action by musketry fire. He will not be able to answer; but the question is, will he be disconcerted by his inability, or not? He will not; he will think it a silly question, and will be rather annoyed at your asking it instead of taking the opportunity to discuss all the interesting problems concerning the battle on which he has something to say. This proves that he does not want to obtain a complete knowledge of the battle of Waterloo in all its details; he knows, and accepts the fact, that his knowledge of it is and must always be a partial knowledge; he confesses, or rather he contends, that it is not the purpose of history to know the past in its actuality and completeness. He thereby implies that its purpose is something else.

Suppose you pressed him to explain why he was not interested in the name of the hundredth man. He would reply that there is nothing about it in the records of the battle, and that his business as an historian is to study and interpret these records. Now these records, which may be of various kinds— despatches, correspondence, descriptions by eye-witnesses or from hearsay, even tombstones and objects found on the battlefield—are traces left by the past in the present. Any aspect or incident of the battle which has left no trace of itself must remain permanently unknown; for the historian's business can go no further than reconstituting those elements of the past whose traces in the present he can perceive and decipher.

In this sense history is the study of the present and not of the past at all. The documents, books, letters, buildings, potsherds, and flints from which the historian extracts all he knows, all he can ever know, about the past, are things existing in the present. And if they in turn perish—as, for instance, the writings of an historian may perish—they in turn become things of the past, which must leave their traces in the present if he is to have any knowledge of them. These traces must be something more than mere effects. They must be recognizable effects; recognizable, that is, to the historian. It is conceivable that nothing in the past fails to leave an effect somewhere in the present; that the last thought that flitted through the mind of a dying man left some trace in his brain-cells, which left some trace in his cremated ashes; but until we learn how to read these traces they are not historical evidence, because they cannot be recognized and interpreted; and therefore, relatively to our present knowledge, we must say that this thought left no trace whatever.

The historian is bound by his evidence. His business is to interpret it, and not to reconstitute any past to which it does not point him. In the abstract, the whole present world consists of traces of the past, and of the whole past; theoretically therefore (in the common and false sense of the word) any part of the present can be used as evidence, complete and sufficient evidence, for a universal history. Practically, which means truly, evidence is only evidence when it is interpreted; and this means that someone must interpret it. But first of all he must look for it; and this means that he must have in his mind a question which he is trying to answer. The question must be what we have called the subject of an historical monograph. Only when such a subject has been envisaged, as an historical problem, can there be such a thing as evidence; for evidence means facts relevant to a question, pointing towards an answer. It is therefore an inversion of the truth to describe the world as a solid block of evidence on every conceivable historical question; until a question has been asked, there is no evidence for it; and since any question is a particular question, a question selected from among possible questions, the evidence bearing on it consists of particular facts, the rest being irrelevant to it. Hence it is necessary to select or discover the evidence, as well as to interpret it.[18]

This is familiar ground. Every historian knows that evidence, even the most complete and striking evidence, is convincing and indeed significant only to one who approaches it with the right question in his mind. In following a difficult piece of reasoning, expounded to one by a person who has made an historical discovery, it happens over and over again that one's success in apprehending the drift of the argument depends on one's being able to ask the right questions at the crucial points; and conversely, it is easy to see that people who are unconvinced by such an exposition fail to be convinced because they do not see what the questions at issue are. They hope to be convinced if they merely come with an open mind; forgetting that an open mind means a mind which is not bent on getting a definite answer to a definite question, and that, to such a mind, the clearest evidence is meaningless.

This shows the difference between the principles of the theory of memory criticized above and those of the present theory of history. The empiricist theory of memory is content to observe that certain elements in the present are effects of the past: and it jumps to the conclusion that in being conscious of these elements the mind is *ipso facto* remembering or apprehending the past. But the traces of the past in the present are revelations of the past only to a mind which approaches them with a resolve to treat them as evidence of the past. Mere observation of the present, however much the present may be the effect of the past, would never arouse in the mind the idea of the past. The idea of the past must be possessed *a priori* by

---

[18] A later addition on the opposite page reads: 'The question which the historian asks is a question which only *he* can ask: it is a function of his individuality, and therefore of his generation. It expresses, in its own special way, the attitude of mind, both theoretical and practical, that is characteristic of his own age. This is why no generation can ever take over, ready-made, the historical conclusions of an earlier generation—It rejects them not because they are false but because they do not tell it what it wants to know.'

the mind: only so, approaching the present, can it ask the question 'what does this tell me about the past?' and, until that is asked, nothing is told.

From this point of view the question as to the certainty of history appears in a new light. The historian cannot have certain knowledge of what the past was in its actuality and completeness; but neither has he uncertain knowledge of this, or even conjecture or imagination of it. The past in its actuality and completeness is nothing to him; and, as it has finished happening, it is nothing in itself; so his ignorance of it is no loss. The only knowledge that the historian claims is knowledge of the answer which the evidence in his possession gives to the question he is asking. And the question itself is relative to the evidence, as the evidence is to the question: for, just as nothing is evidence unless it gives an answer to a question which somebody asks, so nothing is a genuine question unless it is asked in the belief that evidence for its answer will be forthcoming. A question which we have no materials for answering is not a genuine question; such a question is never asked by the historian, unless inadvertently; and his inability to answer it, if anyone asks it of him, is a sign, not of his incompetence, but precisely of his competence: it is a sign that he knows his business.

The certainty of history, then, is the certainty that the evidence in our possession points to one particular answer to the question we ask of it. This truth is partly expressed by the opinion—a false opinion, but with an element of truth in it—that the business of the historian is to hand on a tradition of information that has come down to him from the past: that he learns a story from his informants, and repeats that story, combined no doubt at his discretion with others, in his historical works.

To say that would be to ignore the element of spontaneous, critical, independent thought which is contained more or less in all history, and most in that which most deserves the name. Ignoring that, history is regarded as the repeating of stories, handed down from generation to generation, laid up in the memory of man or compiled by him into written volumes, out of which they may be copied and translated and re-combined by other men indefinitely. The historian's sources are, from this point of view, 'authorities', that is to say, places where he finds his statements ready-made; his equipment consists simply of a retentive memory, and his methods of work are comprised in scissors and paste.

Many people, even some historians, believe that this is a fair description of history. They think that historical writing means copying out selected passages from trustworthy authorities, and that to be a good historian means remembering a great many things that you have read in such books. And there is a good deal in this; at any rate, it describes one feature without which neither history nor any other form of thought can arise—namely, blind reliance on authority and the passive acceptance of ideas which one lacks the ability or the inclination to criticize. But it is just as true of science as of history. Scientists often copy each other's ideas, borrow each other's formulae, and describe each other's experiments; small blame to them; if they did not, they would waste a great deal of time that might be better spent. But this passive acceptance of second-hand results is not science; it is, at most, the means of laying down a solid foundation in the mind, on which a structure of genuine, that is original and critical, scientific thought can be built. Similarly historians passively accept a great deal of what they find other historians saying; but this acceptance is not history, it is only an elementary or nursery stage of historical education.

The real business of history begins when this dogmatic stage is left behind and historical thought becomes critical. At this stage, authorities vanish and we are left with sources instead.[19] The difference is that whereas an authority makes statements which we accept and repeat, a source is something which enables us to make a statement of our own. In using authorities we are passive, in using sources we are active. In authorities we find history ready-made, in sources we find the materials out of which we have to make it for ourselves. An authority must, because it gives us ready-made history, consist of statements: that is, it must be couched in words, it must be a book or a discourse or an inscription or the like. And its

---

[19] On the opposite page of the manuscript, added at a later date, are the words: 'we must *cross-question* the evidence (cf. Bacon)—not merely *listen* to it—This destroys the conception of *authorities* and leads to that of *sources*.'

essence, as authoritative, consists in the fact that we take its statements as true and incorporate them into the body of our own historical beliefs. If we cease to take its statements as true, and criticize them; consider whether they really are true, try to read between the lines, ask ourselves what the speaker is concealing and by what motives he is induced to say what he does; then the written or spoken word ceases to be an authority and becomes a source. But when we have learnt to do this, we can use other things as sources, beside written and spoken words. The tone of voice, the involuntary gestures, of a witness giving evidence; the grammar and vocabulary, the script, the paper of a document; even the gestures of a person not giving evidence and the materials and form of something not meant for a document; all these can now be used with equally valuable results as historical sources.

There is no distinction of principle between written and unwritten sources. The distinction which is really meant, when people draw this distinction, is between authorities and sources. It is thought to be easier to use written sources than unwritten; and it is gravely doubted whether history can exist at all where written sources are altogether lacking; on their presence or absence is based the distinction between history, with its certainty and explicitness, and the twilight of prehistory. But in all these cases the question at issue is whether critical history is possible, or whether the historian must remain for ever in his nursery stage. It is easier to use written sources than unwritten, simply and solely because written sources can be used as authorities, copied out instead of being criticized, swallowed whole instead of being thought over. If written sources are used as sources, criticized instead of being dogmatically accepted, they are not a bit easier to use than unwritten. To say that written sources are easier to use than unwritten is like saying that it is easier to swim in your depth than out of it; because you can swim with one foot on the ground, if you call that swimming. Again, the doubt whether history can dispense with written sources at all, merely means that perhaps history cannot dispense with authorities, whose statements can be copied out uncritically, to act as an uncriticized foundation for a critical superstructure. And here again we detect the theory that no one can swim out of his depth—

now modified, so as to assert only that the swimmer must be allowed to touch bottom every few strokes. The advocates of such a theory ought to agree as to the maximum number of strokes permissible between touch and touch: in other words, how far exactly can one go without falling back on authority? Finally, the alleged uncertainty of prehistory consists merely in the fact that prehistory knows no authorities, only sources. Here the historian is frankly thrown in out of his depth; and the orthodox opinion among our professional historians seems in favour of giving him up for lost. *E pur si muove*; prehistory has achieved enormous triumphs in the last fifty years; its position is now so secure that it can face without serious perturbation even the situation of a wholesale forgery of objects whose genuineness is sworn to by several eminent men learned in other branches of scholarship than prehistory. The Glozel affair is the happiest possible augury for the future of prehistoric studies; the quiet, almost taciturn, certainty with which every prehistorian saw through the fraud proves that we are here standing on ground which will not shift beneath our feet, and vindicates the claim of historical thought to have got clear of the nursery.

This claim rests on the possession of means to criticize sources and extract history from them; and this implies, on the part of the historian, a technical equipment of the kind that is generally called scientific. No such equipment is required to enable people to swallow whole or copy out what others have said; and it is therefore the presence or absence of this technical equipment that marks most clearly the distinction between an active and critical history, using sources, and a passive or dogmatic history accepted from authorities. Critical history classifies its sources into groups, and then subdivides these groups, framing rules for the manipulation of the various subdivisions. Taken as a whole, this technique is an abstract or classificatory science, which has no general name, unless that of archaeology is used for it, and is subdivided into numerous departmental sciences such as palaeography, numismatics, epigraphy, and so forth. These archaeological sciences are a *sine qua non* of critical history. They are not themselves history; they are only methods of dealing with the sources of history; but without them history cannot pass beyond the dogmatic or nursery stage. They form, as it were, the bones of all historical thinking. History itself must be flexible, but it must have rigid bones, unless it is to lose all power of independent locomotion and become a parasite. Classificatory and abstract thought is the negation of history, which is individual and concrete through and through; but the concreteness of history can only be reached through the abstractness of the archaeological sciences.

Every advance in critical history rests on an advance in the interpretation of evidence, that is, an advance in archaeological science. Every advance in archaeological science consists in the discovery that some class of facts can be made to yield historical knowledge, which has hitherto yielded none. The archaeologist feeling his way towards new advances is constantly asking himself whether this or that detail of script or moulding or pottery can be proved characteristic of a certain date or a certain origin; he collects instances, perhaps thousands of instances, to test the suggestion, and may end by committing himself to the generalization that this feature has a definite significance. His fellow-archaeologists learn the new idea very much as medical men learn a new method of diagnosis: partly by reading his papers, far more by personal contact with the material and re-discovering the trick from his indications. That is what makes archaeology so tedious to people who are not archaeologists. It seems to be contained in books and reports, which, when one reads them, prove either unintelligible or flagrantly illogical. But these books and reports are only indications, addressed to the trained man, how to handle his material in order to get certain results; they are no more truly archaeology than a surveyor's field-book is a map.

Archaeology is the methodology of history. An historian innocent of all archaeology is an historian with no power of genuine historical thought, able only to accept what he finds his authorities saying. As soon as he begins to criticize his authorities, he begins to develop methods of archaeological work: bibliography, textual criticism, and so forth. But archaeology, even in its widest possible acceptation, provides only one side of the methodology required for historical work that shall be fully critical. Archaeology is empirical methodology; the methods of any archaeological science are applicable only to a limited sphere, where materials of a certain type are found. There is another methodology which is pure methodology: the science which lays down universal canons of method for dealing with all kinds of sources and constructing any kind of narrative about any subject. This pure methodology is the philosophy of history; a science dealing with the universal and necessary characteristics of all historical thinking whatever, and differentiating history from other forms of thought.

This science is practical, or methodological in the sense of providing guidance in the pursuit of historical knowledge, in that it studies what history everywhere and always is, and therefore what history everywhere and always ought to be. It is easy to object that, on this showing, history always is what it ought to be, and therefore the philosophy of history can have no practical value. This would be true, were it not that people who refrain from pursuing philosophical inquiries are generally more or less at the mercy of philosophical fallacies. Often they are affected by a number of opposing fallacies, which in the long run cancel out and do little to disturb their practical life; but often, and especially in the case of people who pride themselves on being logical thinkers and clear-headed men, a single fallacy will impose itself and become an obsession, uncompensated by any opposing forces, until irreparable damage has been done.

Thus obsessed, logical thinkers have distorted history in various directions. They have advocated historical materialism; they have destroyed the continuity of history by asserting fantastic distinctions between the savage and civilized minds; they have tried to reduce history to a science by suppressing all that makes it history; they have invented the doctrine of historical cycles; they have asserted a mechanical law of progress; they have denied progress altogether; they have committed a hundred fallacies of the same kind, each involving an error in the philosophy of history and each in consequence falsifying the whole structure of their historical thought.[20] Most grievous error of all, they have been pre-

---

[20] On the opposite page, added at a later date, Collingwood wrote: 'To avoid these consequences of bad philosophy there is no way except by finding a better philosophy: in this sense the philosophy of history, as we have tried to

vented from seeing the value, the logical solidity and intellectual respectability, of historical studies, and have taken upon themselves to denounce as vicious and philosophically sinful an activity which is one of the universally necessary and universally pleasant occupations of the human mind. Philosophers are not exempt from the general danger that besets specialists, the danger of priggishness and pedantry; and among philosophers these vices take the form of a tendency to set themselves up as judges of the various practical and theoretical pursuits of mankind and to declare in sweeping terms that art or religion or, in this case, history is a delusion and an error. When pedantry runs wild in this sort of philosophical crusade, it gives ground for more than a suspicion that the fault is in the pedant's own philosophy. For the pedant's accusations against the thing he is attacking are based on the assumption that, at bottom, the thing in question is irrational and therefore unworthy of attention on the part of rational beings. But if it is really irrational, why does it exist? It is easy to say that the people who pursue it are labouring under a delusion; but this is mere idle recrimination unless [it] is accompanied by some explanation of the sources and true nature of the alleged error. Unless this explanation is given, no one can object to the crude retort 'you're another'. If the philosopher dogmatically pronounces history to be rooted in error, he may be told that the error is precisely in his own theory of what history is.

If, as Burke said in a famous passage, you cannot draw up an indictment against a nation, *a fortiori* you cannot draw up an indictment against an entire department of human experience. Those who profess themselves enemies of philosophy are those who cherish a philosophy of their own which is so unphilosophical that they instinctively hide it under a bushel and protect it from the cold light of explicit thought. Those who, being themselves philosophers, profess themselves enemies of art or science or what not, and make this profession in proper philosophical form by pronouncing what they dislike to be irrational, are those who cherish a faulty philosophical

expound it here, acts as a practical guide to the logical problems of historical thought.'

theory of the thing they are attacking. It is quite easy to fall into a philosophical error of a kind which involves, as a necessary consequence, a faulty theory of this or that department of human experience. For instance, a person whose theory of knowledge reduced knowledge to terms of an irrational intuition, might be a lover of art, but he would almost certainly hold science in contempt. A person whose theory of knowledge reduced knowledge to the apprehension of universal essences might speak respectfully of science, but he would have no use for history. But these hatreds show, not that something is wrong with science or history, but that something is wrong with the person who hates it.

A thing like art or science or history does not ask for justification at the hands of philosophy. It is capable of justifying itself. The fact that numbers of people have worked at it for a long time, building up between them a coherent system of thoughts by means of methods devised and elaborated for the special purposes of their pursuit, is itself the proof of its rationality. If anyone thinks otherwise, I do not know how to help him except by inviting him to overhaul the fundamental ideas on which his philosophy is based; and invitations to do anything so arduous as this are generally refused. But nothing short of this will bring conviction: just as nothing short of this would convince an astronomer that he was wrong if he said that the orbits of the planets are rational things and a credit to the law of universal gravitation, but that the orbits of comets are a crying scandal and ought to be prevented by a cosmic police force. Astronomers realize that, so long as comets actually move in parabolic orbits, their business is to accept the facts and reduce them to some kind of formula. But perhaps this is only because astronomers are forced to recognize that it is useless for them to preach at comets, whereas philosophers are not always clear how far it is of use to preach at human beings. And if they are too conceited to take seriously the advice of Oliver Cromwell—'I beseech you, brethren, think it *possible* that ye may be mistaken'—they will make every one of their own errors an excuse for preaching at the person or institution or practice about which they are in error.

The philosopher who sets out to theorize about human life must accept human life, in the spirit in which Margaret Fuller 'accepted the universe'. This does not mean that he must swallow it whole. He must understand it; and, in order to do that, he must analyse and dissect it, and refuse to accept anything unanalysed. But he must not fall into the error of thinking that it is his analysis that makes it rational. He can only find in it the reason which is in it already.

In this way, it is not open to the philosopher to find that the object of his analysis is irrational. To bring in such a verdict as that is to condemn himself for failing to find what he set out to find. But there is another side to this question. If philosophy simply studies historical thought as an object, something quite other than itself and independent of itself, as the astronomer studies the movements of the stars, it is bound indeed to find it rational, but only in the sense in which the movements of the stars are rational—that is, determined by laws of which it is unconscious. The philosopher who studies history from the outside thus finds history to be a rational and necessary form of thought, but he does not find in it the same necessities or logical connexions which the historian finds. Therefore he thinks of the historian as, at best, somewhat illogically logical and irrationally rational. This difficulty is only removed when the philosopher studies history from the inside: that is, when the philosopher and the historian are the same person and when this person's philosophical and historical work react on one another. In this case the philosopher is sure that the historian's historical thought is rational, because he is himself the historian, and he is merely assuring himself of the rationality of his own thought. It is no mere act of faith, but an examination of conscience, that makes him accept historical thought as a reasonable pursuit for a sane man. But conversely, the historian is able to depend for some things upon the philosopher. The philosopher is concerned, in his theory of historical knowledge, to think out certain questions concerning the limits, validity, and purpose of history: and the historian is able to bring his historical research into conformity with the results of this enquiry.

Thus a double result will follow. The philosopher's philosophy will become more trustworthy because of his personal and intimate experience of the subject about which he is theorizing; and the historian's history will become more rational because it is being brought into increasing conformity with the philosophical idea of itself. History supplies philosophy with data, and philosophy supplies history with methods.

Archaeology has been described as the methodology of history. But there are two methodologies: an empirical methodology, concerned with particular varieties of historical material and the varieties of ways in which they should be handled, and a general or universal methodology, which deals with the universal problems of method which affect every piece of historical work just as much as every other. This universal methodology is the philosophy of history regarded as a study undertaken by the historian himself in the endeavour to clear up his own ideas about the nature and aims of historical research.

In this union of history with philosophy, as studied by a single person and reacting on one another, history for the first time becomes really rational, and philosophy for the first time apprehends this rationality not by a mere act of faith, but by virtue of the fact that history must be as rational as philosophy wants it to be, since philosophy itself has made it so.

INDEX

OXFORD

MORE OXFORD PAPERBACKS

This book is just one of nearly 1000 Oxford Paperbacks currently in print. If you would like details of other Oxford Paperbacks, including titles in the World's Classics, Oxford Reference, Oxford Books, OPUS, Past Masters, Oxford Authors, and Oxford Shakespeare series, please write to:

UK and Europe: Oxford Paperbacks Publicity Manager, Arts and Reference Publicity Department, Oxford University Press, Walton Street, Oxford OX2 6DP.

Customers in UK and Europe will find Oxford Paperbacks available in all good bookshops. But in case of difficulty please send orders to the Cash-with-Order Department, Oxford University Press Distribution Services, Saxon Way West, Corby, Northants NN18 9ES. Tel: 01536 741519; Fax: 01536 746337. Please send a cheque for the total cost of the books, plus £1.75 postage and packing for orders under £20; £2.75 for orders over £20. Customers outside the UK should add 10% of the cost of the books for postage and packing.

USA: Oxford Paperbacks Marketing Manager, Oxford University Press, Inc., 200 Madison Avenue, New York, N.Y. 10016.

Canada: Trade Department, Oxford University Press, 70 Wynford Drive, Don Mills, Ontario M3C 1J9.

Australia: Trade Marketing Manager, Oxford University Press, G.P.O. Box 2784Y, Melbourne 3001, Victoria.

South Africa: Oxford University Press, P.O. Box 1141, Cape Town 8000.

KEYNES

Robert Skidelsky

John Maynard Keynes is a central thinker of the twentieth century. This is the only available short introduction to his life and work.

Keynes's doctrines continue to inspire strong feelings in admirers and detractors alike. This short, engaging study of his life and thought explores the many positive and negative stereotypes and also examines the quality of Keynes's mind, his cultural and social milieu, his ethical and practical philosophy, and his monetary thought. Recent scholarship has significantly altered the treatment and assessment of Keynes's contribution to twentieth-century economic thinking, and the current state of the debate initiated by the Keynesian revolution is discussed in a final chapter on its legacy.

RUSSELL

A. C. Grayling

Bertrand Russell (1872–1970) is one of the most famous and important philosophers of the twentieth century. In this account of his life and work A. C. Grayling introduces both his technical contributions to logic and philosophy, and his wide-ranging views on education, politics, war, and sexual morality. Russell is credited with being one of the prime movers of Analytic Philosophy, and with having played a part in the revolution in social attitudes witnessed throughout the twentieth-century world. This introduction gives a clear survey of Russell's achievements across their whole range.

OPUS

A HISTORICAL INTRODUCTION TO THE PHILOSOPHY OF SCIENCE

John Losee

This challenging introduction, designed for readers without an extensive knowledge of formal logic or of the history of science, looks at the long-argued questions raised by philosophers and scientists about the proper evaluation of scientific interpretations. It offers an historical exposition of differing views on issues such as the merits of competing theories; the interdependence of observation and theory; and the nature of scientific progress. The author looks at explanations given by Plato, Aristotle, and Pythagoras, and through to Bacon and Descartes, to Nagel, Kuhn, and Laudan.

This edition incorporates an extended discussion of contemporary developments and changes within the history of science, and examines recent controversies and the search for a non-prescriptive philosophy of science.

'a challenging interdisciplinary work'
New Scientist

RETHINKING LIFE AND DEATH
THE COLLAPSE OF OUR TRADITIONAL ETHICS

Peter Singer

A victim of the Hillsborough Disaster in 1989, Anthony Bland lay in hospital in a coma being fed liquid food by a pump, via a tube passing through his nose and into his stomach. On 4 February 1993 Britain's highest court ruled that doctors attending him could lawfully act to end his life.

Our traditional ways of thinking about life and death are collapsing. In a world of respirators and embryos stored for years in liquid nitrogen, we can no longer take the sanctity of human life as the cornerstone of our ethical outlook.

In this controversial book Peter Singer argues that we cannot deal with the crucial issues of death, abortion, euthanasia and the rights of nonhuman animals unless we sweep away the old ethic and build something new in its place.

Singer outlines a new set of commandments, based on compassion and commonsense, for the decisions everyone must make about life and death.

OXFORD

FOUR ESSAYS ON LIBERTY

Isaiah Berlin

'those who value liberty for its own sake believe that
to be free to choose, and not to be chosen for, is an
inalienable ingredient in what makes human beings
human'
Introduction to *Four Essays On Liberty*

Political Ideas in the Twentieth Century
Historical Inevitability
Two Concepts of Liberty
John Stuart Mill and the Ends of Life

These four essays deal with the various aspects of
individual liberty, including the distinction between
positive and negative liberty and the necessity of
rejecting determinism if we wish to keep hold of the
notions of human responsibility and freedom.

'practically every paragraph introduces us to half a
dozen new ideas and as many thinkers—the landscape flashes past, peopled with familiar and unfamiliar people, all arguing incessantly'
New Society

OPUS

TWENTIETH-CENTURY FRENCH PHILOSOPHY

Eric Matthews

This book gives a chronological survey of the works of the major French philosophers of the twentieth century.

Eric Matthews offers various explanations for the enduring importance of philosophy in French intellectual life and traces the developments which French philosophy has taken in the twentieth century from its roots in the thought of Descartes, with examinations of key figures such as Bergson, Sartre, Marcel, Merleau-Ponty, Foucault, and Derrida, and the recent French Feminists.

'*Twentieth-Century French Philosophy* is a clear, yet critical introduction to contemporary French Philosophy. . . . The undergraduate or other reader who comes to the area for the first time will gain a definite sense of an intellectual movement with its own questions and answers and its own rigour . . . not least of the book's virtues is its clarity.'
Garrett Barden
Author of *After Principles*

WORLD'S ⚙ CLASSICS

PRINCIPLES OF HUMAN KNOWLEDGE AND THREE DIALOGUES

GEORGE BERKELEY

Edited by Howard Robinson

Berkeley's idealism started a revolution in philosophy. As one of the great empiricist thinkers he not only influenced British philosophers from Hume to Russell and the logical positivists in the twentieth century, he also set the scene for the continental idealism of Hegel and even the philosophy of Marx.

There has never been such a radical critique of common sense and perception as that given in Berkeley's *Principles of Human Knowledge* (1710). His views were met with disfavour, and his response to his critics was the *Three Dialogues* between Hylas and Philonous.

This edition of Berkeley's two key works has an introduction which examines and in part defends his arguments for idealism, as well as offering a detailed analytical contents list, extensive philosophical notes and an index.

POLITICS IN OXFORD PAPERBACKS
GOD SAVE ULSTER!

The Religion and Politics of Paisleyism

Steve Bruce

Ian Paisley is the only modern Western leader to have founded his own Church and political party, and his enduring popularity and success mirror the complicated issues which continue to plague Northern Ireland. This book is the first serious analysis of his religious and political careers and a unique insight into Unionist politics and religion in Northern Ireland today.

Since it was founded in 1951, the Free Presbyterian Church of Ulster has grown steadily; it now comprises some 14,000 members in fifty congregations in Ulster and ten branches overseas. The Democratic Unionist Party, formed in 1971, now speaks for about half of the Unionist voters in Northern Ireland, and the personal standing of the man who leads both these movements was confirmed in 1979 when Ian R. K. Paisley received more votes than any other member of the European Parliament. While not neglecting Paisley's 'charismatic' qualities, Steve Bruce argues that the key to his success has been his ability to embody and represent traditional evangelical Protestantism and traditional Ulster Unionism.

'original and profound . . . I cannot praise this book too highly.' Bernard Crick, *New Society*

HISTORY IN OXFORD PAPERBACKS
TUDOR ENGLAND
John Guy

Tudor England is a compelling account of political and religious developments from the advent of the Tudors in the 1460s to the death of Elizabeth I in 1603.

Following Henry VII's capture of the Crown at Bosworth in 1485, Tudor England witnessed far-reaching changes in government and the Reformation of the Church under Henry VIII, Edward VI, Mary, and Elizabeth; that story is enriched here with character studies of the monarchs and politicians that bring to life their personalities as well as their policies.

Authoritative, clearly argued, and crisply written, this comprehensive book will be indispensable to anyone interested in the Tudor Age.

'lucid, scholarly, remarkably accomplished . . . an excellent overview' *Sunday Times*

'the first comprehensive history of Tudor England for more than thirty years' Patrick Collinson, *Observer*

HISTORY IN OXFORD PAPERBACKS

THE STRUGGLE FOR
THE MASTERY OF EUROPE 1848–1918

A. J. P. Taylor

The fall of Metternich in the revolutions of 1848 heralded an era of unprecedented nationalism in Europe, culminating in the collapse of the Hapsburg, Romanov, and Hohenzollern dynasties at the end of the First World War. In the intervening seventy years the boundaries of Europe changed dramatically from those established at Vienna in 1815. Cavour championed the cause of *Risorgimento* in Italy; Bismarck's three wars brought about the unification of Germany; Serbia and Bulgaria gained their independence courtesy of the decline of Turkey—'the sick man of Europe'; while the great powers scrambled for places in the sun in Africa. However, with America's entry into the war and President Wilson's adherence to idealistic internationalist principles, Europe ceased to be the centre of the world, although its problems, still primarily revolving around nationalist aspirations, were to smash the Treaty of Versailles and plunge the world into war once more.

A. J. P. Taylor has drawn the material for his account of this turbulent period from the many volumes of diplomatic documents which have been published in the five major European languages. By using vivid language and forceful characterization, he has produced a book that is as much a work of literature as a contribution to scientific history.

'One of the glories of twentieth-century writing.'
Observer